THE ROYAL HORTICULTURAL GARDENERS HANDBOOK 1999

EDITORS
CHARLES QUEST-RITSON & CHISTOPHER BLAIR

DORLING KINDERSLEY
LONDON • NEW YORK • SYDNEY • MOSCOW
www.dk.com

A DORLING KINDERSLEY BOOK
www.dk.com

First published in 1994
This edition published 1998 by Dorling Kindersley
9 Henrietta Street, Covent Garden, London WC2E 8PS

ISBN 0-7513-0560-X

Copyright © 1998 Dorling Kindersley Limited, London
Text copyright © Charles Quest-Ritson and Christopher Blair,
1994, 1995, 1996, 1997, 1998

The right of Charles Quest-Ritson and Christopher Blair to be identified as the authors of this work has been asserted by them in accordance with Copyright, Designs and Patents Acts of 1998.

Project Editors *Sharon Lucas, Lesley Malkin*
Line Illustrations *Sarah Young*

All rights reserved. No part of this publication may be reproduced, stored in a retrieval system, or transmitted in any form or by any means, electronic, mechanical, photocopying, recording or otherwise, without the prior written permission of the copyright owner.

1 3 5 7 9 8 6 4 2

Note: Whilst every care has been taken to ensure that the information contained in this directory is both accurate and up-to-date, neither the editors, the RHS nor the publisher accept any liability to any party for loss or damage occurred by reliance placed on the information contained in this book or through omission or errors, howsoever caused.

A CIP catalogue record for this book is available from the British Library.

ISBN 0 7513 06525

The opinions expressed in this work are the opinions of the authors and not of the publishers or the Royal Horticultural Society.

Data management and typesetting by
Hodgson Williams Associates, Tunbridge Wells and Cambridge

Printed and bound in Italy by Lego

Contents

INTRODUCTION 6

PART ONE
REVIEW OF 1998

GARDENING NEWS HIGHLIGHTS 8
WEATHER REVIEW 12
WEATHER DATA 15
SHOW REVIEWS 18
NEW PLANTS 25
NEW BOOKS 30
GARDENING ON THE INTERNET 34

PART TWO
CALENDAR FOR 1999

SHOW VENUES 40
DIARY DATES 43

PART THREE
OUT AND ABOUT

GARDENS TO VISIT 134
AWARDS TO GARDENS 259
HOLIDAYS FOR GARDENERS 260
IMPORTING & EXPORTING PLANTS 268
EUROPEAN NURSERIES 270
COURSES FOR AMATEURS 289

PART FOUR
USEFUL ADDRESSES

SOCIETIES 298
SPECIALIST BOOKSHOPS 320
SEED MERCHANTS 324
ORGANISATIONS 329

INDEX 342

Step into a world of

Membership of the RHS is all about beautiful gardens. From a free monthly gardening magazine, *The Garden*, to discounted tickets to the world's most famous flower shows, RHS Membership gives you the inspiration to realise your gardening dreams.

Membership normally costs £34 for 12 months, which includes a one-off £7 joining fee. But if you join today, you can take advantage of a special introductory saving of £5 – meaning you pay just £29.

Outstanding benefits for gardeners

To see if you would enjoy being a Member, simply take a look at the special Membership benefits listed opposite and tick all those which appeal to you.

If you have ticked more than two boxes, then we think that you would enjoy Membership of Britain's top gardening club.

Joining couldn't be easier

Simply call us today on ☎ 0171-821 3000 (quoting code 1266) or complete and return the application form opposite.

THE ROYAL HORTICULTURAL SOCIETY

beautiful gardens

Membership brings you all this:

- FREE monthly copy of *The Garden* magazine (worth £33).
- FREE entry for you and a guest to RHS Gardens Wisley, Rosemoor and Hyde Hall.
- FREE entry to a further 24 beautiful gardens.
- Privileged tickets and Members' only days to the Chelsea and Hampton Court Palace Flower Shows.
- FREE gardening advice from RHS experts.
- Privileged admission to the new RHS Flower Show at Tatton Park, BBC Gardeners' World Live, Scotland's National Gardening Show, and the Malvern Spring and Autumn Flower Shows.
- Discounted admission to hundreds of demonstrations, workshops, talks and garden tours.
- FREE entry to the monthly RHS Westminster Flower Shows.
- FREE seeds from RHS Garden Wisley.
- Access to the famous Lindley Library.

Join today ☎ 0171-821 3000
(Please quote code 1266)

The credit card hotline is open from 9.00am to 5.30pm Monday to Friday.

RHS Membership Offer – Save £5

Title   Surname   Initials

Address

Postcode   Daytime Tel. No.

☐ I enclose a cheque for £29 made payable to The Royal Horticultural Society

☐ Please debit my RHS Mastercard / Mastercard / Visa / Diners / AmEx

Card No.

Expiry   /   Signature   Code 1266

Please return this form to The Royal Horticultural Society, Membership Department, PO Box 313, London SW1P 2PE
This offer is valid until 31 October 1999.

INTRODUCTION

WELCOME TO THIS fully updated edition of *The RHS Gardener's Handbook*. As always, we aim to include as much information as possible about every aspect of the British horticultural scene for the year ahead. There are details of gardening events for the whole of 1999; concise descriptions of nurseries and gardens in the British Isles; lists of specialist societies both regional, national and international; reviews of books and shows; information on courses for both amateur and professional and much more besides. Recent legislation has made the riches of European nurseries easier to obtain than ever: we list some of the best and explain the rules on importing plants. This year we also give details of as many websites as possible: the Internet has already made a big impact on the world of horticulture and will shortly affect us all, even the least computer-wise.

The contents page at the front will point you towards the broad subject categories we use, such as Specialist Bookshops or Show Venues. To find information about a specific garden, organisation, or subject, turn to the index at the back: it should take you straight to the page you need. In the listings of gardens and nurseries, the entries appear by the county. This makes the book easy to use when you are travelling or planning a visit, but a little care is needed. We try to give the county where the garden or nursery is physically located rather than just the postal address. Despite the creeping abolition of counties in England (Scotland's regions and Wales's counties have already gone) few people are familiar with all these developments, so we have stuck to the 1974 counties of England and Wales and to the Scottish regional divisions with three exceptions. The counties of Avon, Cleveland and Humberside were deeply unpopular: we have redistributed their entries to Gloucestershire and Somerset, North Yorkshire and Lincolnshire. This may not be ideal, but if you get into difficulty the index should put you straight.

A large degree of selection has been necessary to keep the book within its bounds but we hope that there are few serious omissions. We rely to a great extent on information which has been submitted to us by third parties. Not everyone who was approached has replied – or replied in time – and this explains some gaps. Inclusion or exclusion should not be construed as a recommendation or condemnation. And, though we are delighted to carry the Royal Horticultural Society's endorsement, the views and opinions expressed in this book are ours, and ours alone.

A number of common abbreviations are used freely throughout the text, including AGS – the Alpine Garden Society; MAFF – Ministry of Agriculture, Fisheries and Food; NCCPG – National Council for the Conservation of Plants and Gardens; NGS – National Gardens Scheme; RHS – Royal Horticultural Society; RNRS – Royal National Rose Society; and SGS – Scotland's Garden Scheme.

The editors are very grateful to the many people who have helped in the compilation of this work. First and foremost we want to thank all the garden owners, nurseries, horticulturists, colleges, societies and everyone else who has kindly responded to our requests for information. We are greatly indebted to them, and regret that it is not always possible to give each the personal attention which is their due. Particular thanks go the staff of the Alpine Garden Society; English Heritage; the National Trust; Rodger Bain at the NCCPG; the Northern Horticultural Society; Tony Lord of the *RHS Plant Finder* and especially Ruth Anders, Wendy Crammond, Alan Leslie, Susanne Mitchell, Gordon Rae, Bob Sweet and Karen Wilson and others at the Royal Horticultural Society.

We must also acknowledge the considerable input of others who have worked with us on this project: John Hodgson; David Lamb; Barbara Levy; and all our editors at Dorling Kindersley. Finally thanks are due for their patience and endeavours to Madeline Quest-Ritson, Katharine Blair and Camilla Blair; and above all to Brigid Quest-Ritson, whose labours are represented throughout these pages.

Part One

Review of 1998

Gardening News Highlights
Weather Reports
Show Reviews
New Plants
New Books
Gardening on the Internet

Gardening News Highlights of 1998

At the annual RHS press conference last January, the Director-General Gordon Rae confirmed that increasing its membership numbers is a priority for the Society. Already over 250,000 at the beginning of last year, the Society's membership has grown steadily in recent years at around 7%. The Society is anxious to ensure that this increasing growth is matched by increased service to its members. It has therefore embarked upon a vigorous policy of regionalisation to make itself even more accessible to members in every part of the UK. We noticed how the programme of local lectures, demonstrations and events began to expand considerably last year, but it has increased again substantially this year: our Calendar section is bursting with events that are organised by or in conjunction with the RHS. These events take place at colleges, gardens and nurseries up and down the country. The Society's aim is to ensure that, so far as possible, its members enjoy parity of access to its services across the whole UK.

Leyland Cypress

A scientific report in *The Times* last January argued that Leyland cypresses, × *Cupressocyparis leylandii*, were the most efficient widely planted tree for filtering particle pollution from the air. Indeed, the researchers suggested that planting these fast-growing evergreens along city centre roads and motorways would help to protect vulnerable people from traffic fumes. Few trees have caused so much bad feeling in recent years as Leyland cypress, and precisely because of its greatest virtue, which is that it grows very rapidly to create a tall evergreen barrier. Later in the year, another case of neighbours falling out with each other about Leyland cypress came to court and received considerable publicity. Michael and Maureen Jones of Birmingham objected to the × *Cupressocyparis leylandii* trees bordering their garden and therefore trimmed them back, which resulted in a fifteen-year battle with their neighbour, Bernard Stanton. One outcome to this long and expensive legal case (which in a sense no-one actually won) was a government statement which was widely interpreted as a move towards legislation to help people blighted by overgrown hedges. Although this is still a long way from the statute book (and may never reach it), the government's announcement provoked a spate of panic buying in advance from garden centres up and down the country. The truth, as one wise commentator pointed out, is that it is not the trees that are the problem: it is the people who use them.

Another dispute between neighbours that was reported last year involved a 62-year-old from Hove in East Sussex who took objection to the rose petals which fell on his garden path, the culmination of a 30-year dislike of his neighbour's passion for gardening. The garden-hater decided to nip the roses in the bud, which he did literally, by pulling them off and throwing them back onto his neighbour's path. Unbeknownst to him, his garden-loving neighbour had set up a secret video-camera which filmed the attacker's assault upon his bushes. The offender duly ended up in court, where he denied causing £21-worth of criminal damage to the roses, but did agree to be bound over to keep the peace. He was quoted as saying 'It is unfair. My neighbour is not just a gardening enthusiast. He is a foliage fanatic.'

Peat and the Environment

Early last year the Royal Society for the Protection of Birds suggested that every 80-litre bag of peat should pay a special tax of 40p to compensate for the environmental losses which peat harvesting has wrought upon important wildlife habitats. The RSPB pointed out to the Treasury that the annual proceeds of such a tax, estimated at £12m, could be used to fund the revocation of council planning permission for the extraction of peat on sites of Special Scientific Interest and fund the development of peat-free alternatives. The long-term aim of the RSPB and its fellow members of the Peatland Campaign Consortium, an alliance of 13 environmental organisations including Friends of the Earth, is to bring an end to the extraction of peat on the 4,500 hectares currently farmed in the UK. It is perhaps worth pointing out that the RHS has for a long time taken a lead in promoting awareness of the need to conserve our natural assets and to develop horticultural alternatives to peat.

BENEFITS OF ST JOHN'S WORT

Early last spring a scientific report suggested that *Hypericum* species might successfully be used to relieve human depression. St John's wort contains a red pigment called hypericin which is thought to account for its anti-depressant powers. Clinical trials showed that 80% of depressed patients improved when taking hypericin and that it was particularly effective against Seasonal Affective Disorder (SAD), the gloom that descends on sufferers once the evenings draw in (and which is characterised by

> "... the RHS has for a long time taken a lead in promoting awareness of the need to conserve our national assets"

lethargy and a tendency to overeat during the winter months!). So it looks as if hypericums are set to follow yew trees, foxgloves and poppies as a source of useful natural drugs for the alleviation of human ills. St John's wort has in fact been used a herbal remedy for centuries, particularly for relief of menstrual problems, but presumably the ascetic St John the Baptist knew more of its tranquillising properties than its gynaecological powers.

MEMORIAL GARDEN PROPOSAL

The Diana, Princess of Wales, Memorial Committee was set up early last year to advise the government how best to commemorate the life of Diana, Princess of Wales. One of the projects commended to the government in the committee's preliminary advice was the creation of a memorial garden in Kensington Gardens. This proposal was however, made subject to public consultation which, together with an early environmental impact study, made it clear that such a garden, so far from solving the problem of how best to commemorate the Princess, would create considerable logistic and maintenance problems of

its own. Nevertheless, the idea has considerable public support.

Ken Livingstone let it be known last summer that he was contemplating an alternative career development path in the event of his failing to become London's new directly elected Mayor: he wants to become the Prime Minister's gardener at 10 Downing Street. In his opinion, the gardens at 10 Downing Street are 'boring' and suffer from Mr Blair's 'clear lack of interest in horticulture'. Mr Livingstone believes that No 10's garden should be developed to show off the natural flora of the British Isles in a garden that is a microcosm of the British landscape: a Scots pine, an oak tree, and perhaps even an arbutus or a patch of meadow where wild flowers like the scarlet field poppy could grow in natural profusion. Ken Livingstone's starting point? 'Tony Blair should give more attention to decent and popular pastimes like gardening.'

IMPORTANCE OF BIODIVERSITY

Another independently minded MP used his opportunity to initiate a private members' debate in the House of Commons on 17 June to promote the importance of biodiversity. Tam Dalyell, whose motion has not received the publicity it deserves in the gardening press, persuaded the government to initiate fresh action to protect rare British endemics which are on the red lists of rare and endangered species. Nineteen red-list plants are found in the UK, including the Lundy cabbage and the English sandwort. The government announced that individual 'Species Action Plans' were currently under preparation for 14 of these species, with the aim of ensuring that this precious part of our natural heritage continues to exist and flourish in the UK.

SEED MERCHANT CHANGES

The world of professional horticulture was shocked in August to learn that Johnson's Seeds, one of the country's oldest seed firms, had gone into liquidation after two years of heavy trading losses. The holding company W W Johnson Ltd of Boston in Lincolnshire blamed its collapse on a policy of diversification into selling bulbs and mail order, instead of concentrating on its traditional business of selling seeds. Nevertheless, when we spoke to them in October, the company was trading once again, though not in the traditional flower seed business for which the company has been famous since 1820. Instead, it was concentrating upon its domestic pre-pack grass seed sales of which it has some 85% of the home market. Johnsons Seeds were sold by the receivers to Perryfields to create the largest ornamental seed company in the UK, with a combined turnover of about £36m. That company will now concentrate upon wild flower, amenity grass and forage crop seeds for the agricultural market, which the Johnson part of the combined business will continue to offer from Lincoln. The retail packet seed operation was, however, bought by Mr Fothergill's Seeds Ltd, one of the UK's biggest retail brands, who transferred the business to the Fothergill base in Suffolk, while keeping Johnson's packet seeds as a stand-alone brand.

Giant and Native Wasps

One result of the series of hot dry summers we have enjoyed in recent years is that there has been a significant increase in the numbers of giant continental wasps nesting in south-east England. There were many stories circulating towards the end of last summer about the explosion in numbers of 'giant continental wasps'. Unlike our native wasps,

> "... it is now confidently expected that last year's wet summer will have restored the ecological balance"

which tend to nest in buildings or holes in the ground, Dolichovespula media chooses the branches of trees and shrubs to make their nests. Not only are the wasps said to be much larger than the native English species, but they are also reputed to be more aggressive, though our own experience suggests that there is little to choose between them either for temperament or for their ability to cause discomfort. However it is now confidently expected that last year's wet summer will have restored the ecological balance in favour of our smaller native wasps again – small comfort indeed to humans and greenfly alike, who each suffer in their different ways from the attentions of both types of wasp.

Popularity of Plants

There was a sad story last summer about the National Collection of Dahlias held by David Brown in Cornwall. Mr Brown spent ten years building up the collection until he had nearly 2,000 different species and cultivars. He reckoned that this unique work of conservation had, during that time, cost him about £50,000, and indeed run him into debt. He concluded that, as a consequence of this debt and of his own increasing age, his only remaining option was to offer the entire collection for sale. When we met him at the Hampton Court Show, where he had a major exhibition of unusual cultivars, he had not yet been successful in finding a buyer. People just did not seem to be as interested in dahlias as he is.

The popularity of plants has always been subject to fashion. It is sometimes difficult to understand why a particular genus is widely eulogised by the gardening *cognoscenti*, while another is almost universally execrated. Prejudice and snobbery have much to answer for. A genus which is definitely growing in popularity is *Pulmonaria* and a recent expert assessment of plant value was made by the *Pulmonaria* group of the Hardy Plant Society, when it inspected the trials at Wisley and asked their members which cultivars they considered to be garden-worthy'. The top four performers, in order of merit, were: *P.* 'Blue Ensign', *P.* saccharata 'British Sterling', *P. rubra* 'David Ward', and *P.* 'Opal'.

Malmaison carnations too are making a comeback. This strain of carnation vanished completely from the market place when perpetual-flowering carnations were introduced at the beginning of this century. Malmaison carnations have larger flowers, rather more incurved petals, and stronger scent than most modern cultivars. The National Collection is held by Jim Marshall, for many years the National Trust Gardens Adviser. He supplied propagating material to Seale Hayne College in Devon who micro-propagated the stock. It was then raised by a Norfolk grower – the horticultural industry has many layers – and later offered for sale by a Spalding wholesaler, until eventually Malmaison carnations found their way last year into Marks & Spencer's stores as part of that company's policy of reintroducing historic, forgotten flowers, especially highly scented ones.

The RNRS runs extensive trials every year of new rose cultivars, but there are not many occasions on which the roses are re-assessed after several years in the trade. This was one of the purposes of the International British Rose Awards Day which was held at the Gardens of the Rose in July in conjunction with the British Association Representing Breeders. The event was attended by leading breeders from the UK, America, Holland, Germany and Denmark and tested some 70 roses released during the last 10 years. The following varieties were winners in their sections: best Hybrid Tea 'Poetry in Motion'; best floribunda 'Gordon's College'; best shrub rose 'Blenheim'; best climbing rose 'Good as Gold'; best miniature/patio rose 'Festival'; best ground cover rose 'Kent'; best scented rose 'L'Aimant'; the overall champion rose was 'Kent', a small white ground cover rose introduced by Poulsen of Denmark in 1988. There is one small irony about this result: 'Kent' is practically scentless, while almost all the other new roses which were put to the test are strongly scented.

PESTICIDE DEVELOPMENTS

The well-known garden pesticide Roseclear was banned in 1997 following tests which showed that it could cause eye irritation in certain circumstances in a small number of people. It was however relaunched as a retail pesticide in a new formulation under the name Roseclear2 in July last year. Roseclear was (and Roseclear2 is) a combined insecticide/fungicide. The two fungicides are called bupirimate and triforine and are chosen to control powdery mildew, black spot and rust. The insecticide is pirimicarb, a systemic killer of aphids which is unique in the way it does not affect bees, ladybirds and other beneficial insects. We asked the manufacturers how the new formulation differed the old. Their answer was that the concentrations of bupirimate and triforine have been lowered from 6.25% each to 2.78%, while the concentration of pirimicarb has similarly been lowered from 5% to 2.2%. It has therefore been said that Roseclear2 is simply a less concentrated solution of the original Roseclear, one which is sufficiently dilute not to cause medical problems. There is, however, rather more to it than this, because the results of using the new formulation have proved that it is actually more effective than the original. The reason is that Roseclear2 has a different combination of wetting agents which makes its application measurably more effective than the original product.

The Agricultural Minister Jeff Rooker announced in May a review of certain organo-phosphate chemicals, including nine pesticides commonly used in ornamental horticulture. It seems likely that, in due course, the licence for some chemicals will be revoked. Although this reflects an increasing public concern about the use of artificial pesticides in general (and of organo-phosphates in particular), the truth is that many have in fact been overtaken by other, better, chemicals. Our own belief is that in the near future the horticultural industry will join the organo-phosphate-free world.

OBJECTIONS TO TERMINAL 5

When it was announced last summer that the British Airports Authority had applied for permission to build a fifth terminal at Heathrow airport, one of the principal objectors to the application was the Royal Botanic Gardens at Kew. Readers will know all too well that a visit to the famous gardens is often spoilt by the noise of aircraft flying in and out of Europe's busiest airport. A spokesman for BAA gave evidence to the Terminal 5 inquiry that planes are getting quieter and that the authority is proposing to introduce a 'noise-cap' to guarantee that there is no increase in the present levels of disturbance. Nevertheless, noise pollution appears to be only one of the grounds on which the Royal Botanic Gardens objects to the fifth terminal. The Director of Kew, Professor Sir Ghillean Prance, wrote to the inquiry that 'accidents or large objects falling from an aircraft might cause serious damage to the irreplaceable and internationally vital collections held in our herbarium.'

Weather Review of 1998

EVERYONE AGREES that 1998 was a 'bad' year for weather: cool, windy, overcast and, above all, wet. But this should be seen against the background of two exceptionally hot dry summers in 1996 and 1997. The rainfall figures for the period April 1995 to September 1997 were the lowest on record while, taken as a whole, 1997 was the third warmest year in England since records began in 1659.

It is difficult to believe that, at the beginning of 1998, there were several portentous warnings from such bodies as the Environment Agency that we were facing a summer of hose-pipe bans, reduced water levels and severe shortages. Garden watering accounts for no more than 5% of total domestic water consumption, but in a hot summer it can peak at more than 50%.

An Early Spring

1998 began with severe gales and heavy rain in all parts of the British Isles: mild south-westerly winds meant that temperatures were generally above average for the beginning of January. A tornado hit Selsey in West Sussex in the evening of 7th January. The minimum temperature in London on 9th January was 13°C and the daytime temperature at Prestatyn on 10th January reached a record 17.3°C, higher than Athens. The mild weather ushered in an early spring. Anglesey Abbey in Cambridgeshire opened for its annual snowdrop viewing at the end of January. At Mount Edgcumbe in Cornwall, the National Collection of camellias was in full flower a month earlier than usual. Figures for rainfall, temperature and sunshine were all above normal for the month though, just for the record, January 1998 was the dullest since records began.

Above-Average Temperatures

The arrival of anticyclonic weather on 18th January ushered in a period of dry, frosty weather which lasted into February. The temperature on the night of 3rd/4th February at balmy Bournemouth dropped to −7°C, but then first westerlies and then southerlies immediately brought milder conditions again. Temperatures soared during the second week of February, reaching records of 17.4°C in Leeds, 18.4°C in Bristol and 19.1°C in London on 13th February. At Barbourne near Worcester the temperature reached 19.6°C, which made it the warmest February day this century for anywhere in England. Meanwhile, exceptionally heavy rainfall caused flooding in the western Highlands. Above-average temperatures continued until the end of the month: it was the second warmest February in Britain since 1869. An early season meant early trading for the garden centres. Trade sales were reckoned to be 40% up on February 1997, and boosted their owners' seasonal cashflow. Open-ground nurserymen, by contrast, found that their season for lifting and selling came to an abrupt and early end. Some warned of the damaging effect which late frosts would have on plants that had broken into leaf early.

Warm and Mild

Warm weather meant that the grass grew early, lawns needed cutting, and the annual mower market got off to a good start. In fact, more than twice the number of new lawnmowers were sold in the first two months of the year than normal. The mild weather continued into March and had a disastrous effect on the bulb growers in Cornwall. Normally, they enjoy at least a two- or three-week advantage over the rest of the country, so that their daffodils have a ready market in late February and early March. But the warm weather in all parts of Britain eroded that advantage, and some Cornish growers threw away their entire crop. A large anticyclone established itself to the west of Ireland in the middle of March, bringing a prolonged spell of settled, dry weather to much of the British Isles. At the RHS Westminster show on 17th and 18th March, the camellia competition was particularly well supported in response to the warm winter, and the flowers of specimens grown outside were particularly large. Mild weather continued to the end of the month: the minimum overnight temperature at Rhyl in North Wales on the night of 29th/30th March reached a new British record of 15°C. The month as a whole was reckoned to be one of the mildest on record: the average daily temperature for Britain was as much as 2.3°C above the average. It was also one of the wettest. Nevertheless, there were parts of England, including East Anglia and the south-east, where a dry end to 1997 had meant that the overall rainfall in winter and early spring remained below average. Groundwater reserves would be dangerously low if a hot, dry summer were to follow.

COOL WEATHER AND INTENSE RAINFALL

April changed all that. It turned out to be the wettest in much of England and Wales since 1818, and the coolest for ten years. Cool weather and intense rainfall characterised the start of April and lasted over the Easter weekend, 10th–14th April: 76mm of rain fell in a 24-hour period on 9th/10th April at Pershore. The newspapers carried photographs of deer swimming to safety from the deer park at Charlecote in Warwickshire. Garden centres were badly hit: the Easter weekend is traditionally one of their busiest of the year. Nottcutts Garden Centre in Peterborough was submerged under floodwater and the whole area was put on a Red Alert Flood Warning by the Environment Agency. One garden centre in Huntingdon said that its best selling line on Easter Monday was Wellington boots. The rain and cool temperatures did not however hold back growth in the garden, and many orchard trees flowered as much as two weeks earlier than normal. Cherries were in flower by Easter time, and the bluebells were fully out in the woods of southern England by the end of the month.

PERFECT CONDITIONS AT CHELSEA

Warm, humid weather during the second week of May brought a rush of summer flowers: roses bloomed against house walls throughout the country and on the 13th the temperature in Aviemore, high in the Grampians, reached a May record of 28°C. May as a whole was the warmest since 1992 and the driest since 1991. Many visitors said that the Chelsea Flower Show was held in the most perfect weather conditions they could remember. Garden centres enjoyed record sales over the following Bank Holiday weekend.

GLASSHOUSES AND HAILSTONES

Their joy was short-lived: June proved to be exceptionally wet and unsettled. In fact it was the wettest-ever June – at least, since 1997. That was the wettest since records began, while June 1998 was reckoned to be the fourth wettest of the century. Temperatures were near to average, but the rain brought overcast skies and 20% less sunshine than normal. Thunderstorms were also a feature, though they did not do as much damage in Britain as in the nurseries of The Netherlands, where growers' glasshouses were destroyed by hailstones the size of golf balls. Fears of an explosion of aphid numbers – confidently predicted in the wake of the warm spring – were checked by the cool weather and in fact the summer as a whole was not widely regarded as a 'bad' summer for garden pests. On the other hand, owners who open their gardens to the public were badly hit by reduced visitor numbers at their peak period. Almost every garden open to the public reported fewer visitors than in 1997.

July saw no improvement. In most of England and Wales, it was the dullest since 1988 and the coolest since 1993. In Scotland it was also the wettest for ten years. Many garden centres assessed their sales and found that the weather had left them with piles of unsold stock. One large wholesaler was forced to dump 500,000 unsold perennial plant plugs. A large supplier of consumer irrigation products issued a stock market profits warning. Weather forecasters put on a brave face. One went so far as to claim that the month should be regarded as a warm one because the temperatures fell so little at night – a sure sign of low pressure and bad weather. Lord [Roy] Jenkins of Hillhead wrote a letter to *The Times* suggesting a new measurement of the quality of British summers: the number of days with (i) a maximum temperature of at least 70°F (21°C), (ii) nil rainfall, (iii) at least six hours of sunshine, and (iv) no more than a light breeze.

A MEDITERRANEAN CLIMATE?

Most climatologists believe that UK summers are getting hotter and dryer, while our winters are becoming warmer and wetter. In short, our climate is becoming more 'Mediterranean'. This has implications for all of us: we may, for example, encounter new problems with pests. Indeed, ADAS is concerned that pests like the greenhouse whitefly, which already overwinters outside in the Channel Islands, may be able to establish itself in parts of southern England. But there was little evidence last year of anything Mediterranean about the summer in England. August, however, was a month of contrasts.

Rainfall was less than average for the whole of the British Isles, and it was hot and sunny at times in the south of England. But, taken as a whole, it proved to be the coolest and dullest August for four years and the driest for three. Holidaymakers who stayed in England despite the strong pound and the wet start to the year were rewarded with weather that was quite acceptable, if not spectacular.

Hurricanes and Indian Summers

September brought the changes. The month began very wet and disturbed all over the British Isles, as the remnants of Hurricane Danielle raced across the Atlantic, slowed down and dominated most of the country for several days. Aberdeen enjoyed no more than 1½ hours sunshine during the entire first week of the month. Then much of the country enjoyed a brief Indian summer during the third week, before strong winds and heavy rains fell throughout the last week of the month. 59mm fell in High Wycombe over a 24-hour period on 26th/27th September. All in all, it was also an unsettled and wet month. But there was a surprise in the final statistics: September was the warmest in many places since 1961.

Small Fruit in Large Quantities

Last autumn was generally thought a good one for hedgerow fruits like hawthorns and sloes. This reflected the hot summer of 1997 and mild conditions when such species were flowering in the spring of 1998. The fruit-set on orchard trees was likewise good. In some parts of southern England, badly affected by spring frosts in 1997, the fruit on organically grown trees was remarkably free from pests and diseases because insect populations had been wiped out during the previous year of famine. In 1998, however, trees did not experience a 'June drop' so, unless they were artificially thinned, many produced very large quantities of rather small fruit. Small boys even complained that the conkers, though plentiful, were undersized.

All in all, the weather last summer and autumn made for excellent growth. A large number of gardeners said they could not remember a better year for plants. The weeds liked the rain too. Many garden-owners believe that, if they can get their gardens weed-free by the end of May, there is seldom any need to weed them again until the autumn, apart from pulling out the occasional rogue seedling. Last year was quite different. The soggy June and a soaking September meant that weeds continued to plague us right through the summer and early autumn. Rain also made for a year of disappointing autumn colour.

This was aggravated by high winds in October. The month was warm and wet, so that severe flooding affected Wales and the Peak District by the middle of the month and worsened towards the end. But it also meant that parts of southern England were still awaiting their first frost as we went to press at the end of October.

WEATHER DATA 15

ROYAL BOTANIC GARDEN, EDINBURGH

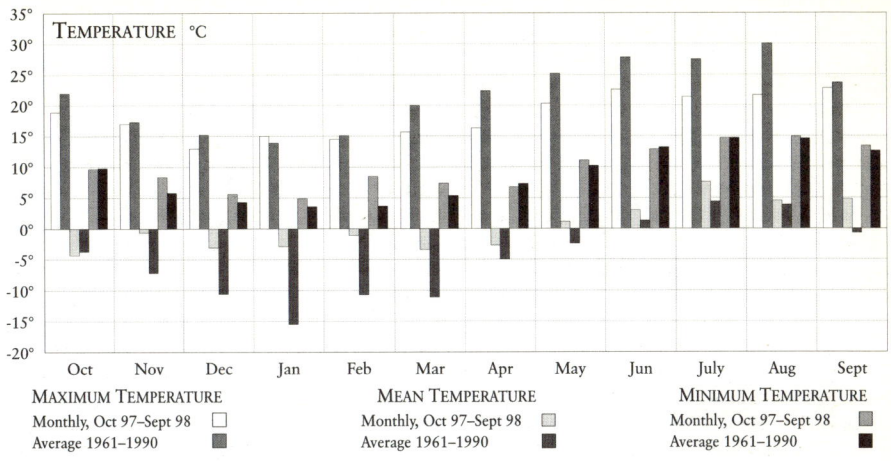

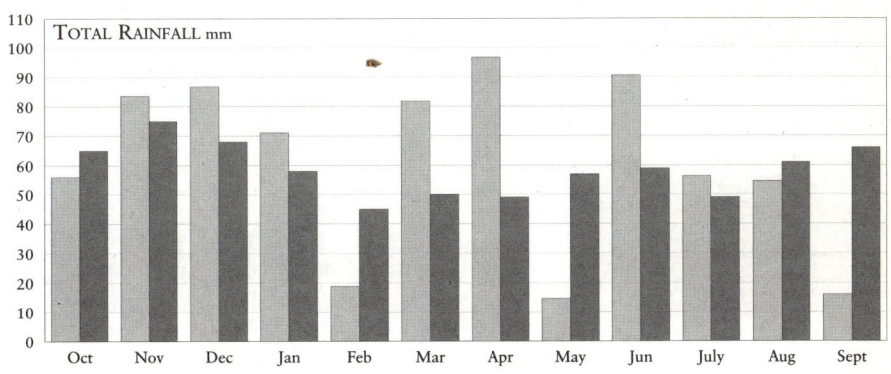

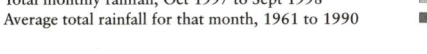

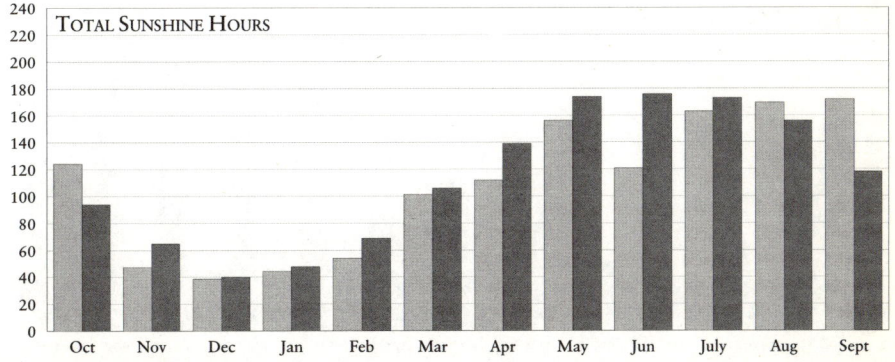

WEATHER DATA

RHS Garden Wisley, Surrey

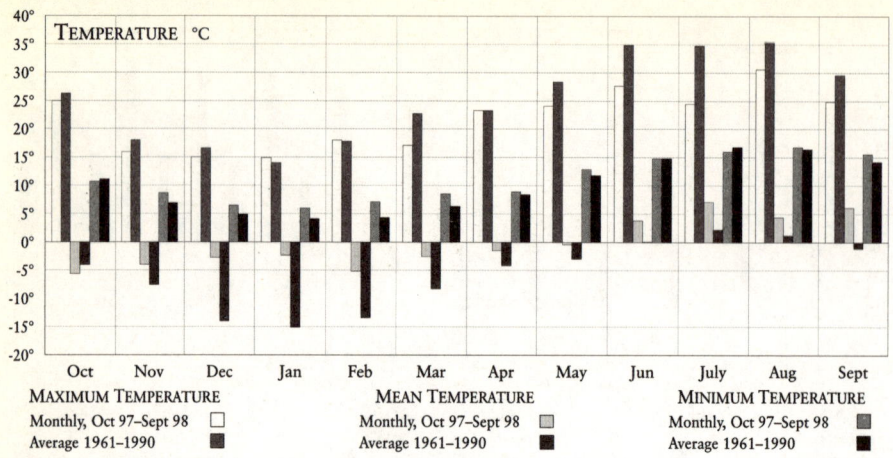

Total Rainfall mm

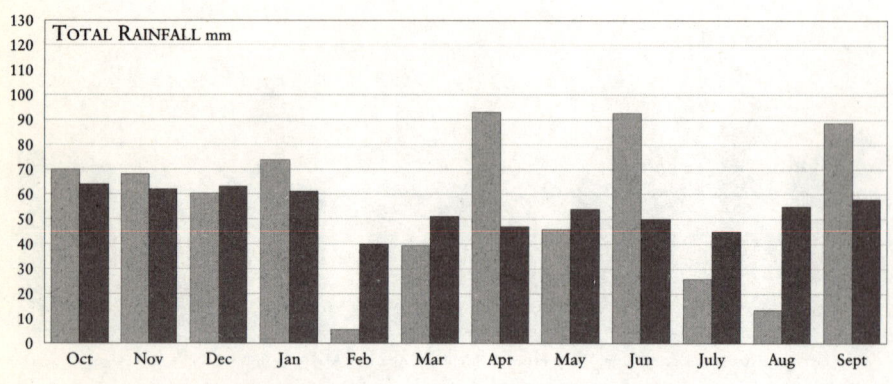

Total Sunshine Hours

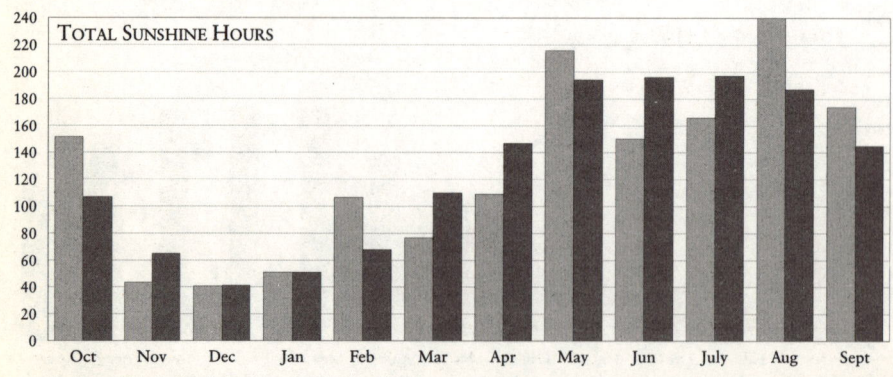

NESS BOTANIC GARDEN, CHESHIRE

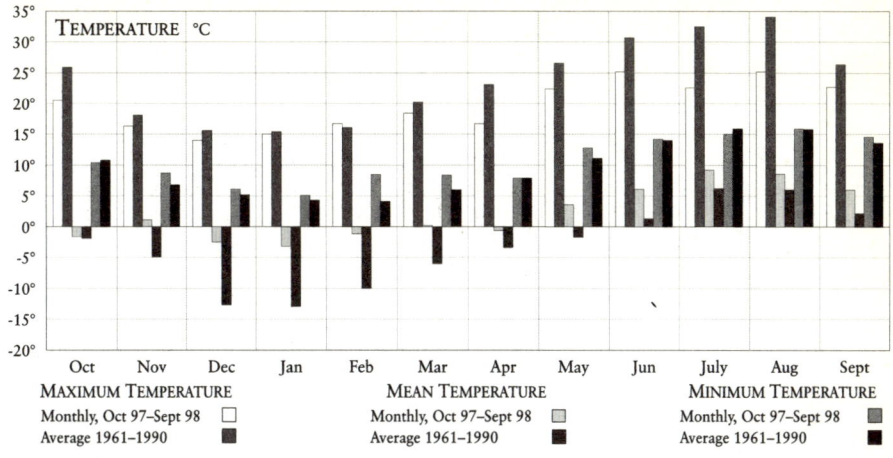

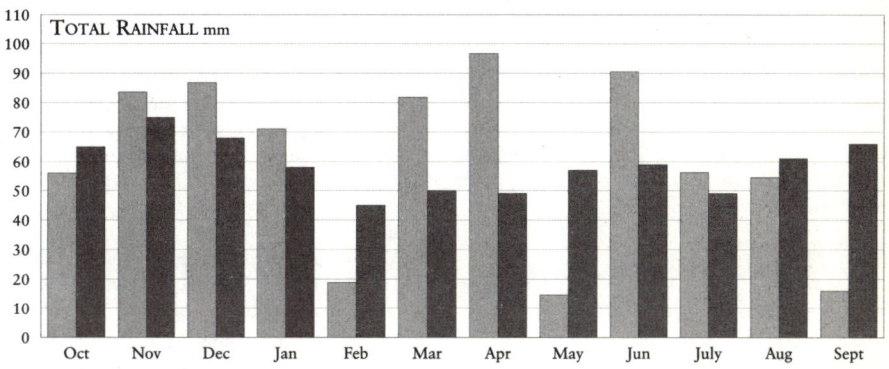

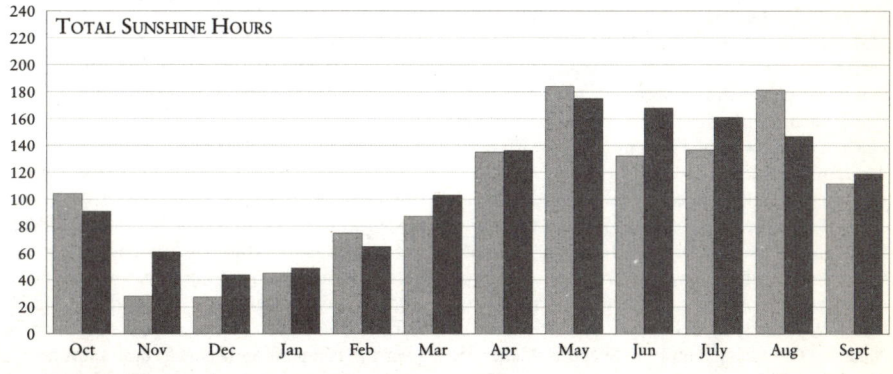

Show Reviews

THE RHS WAS FORMED in 1804 for 'the encouragement and improvement of the science, art and practice of horticulture'. Today gardening is the largest leisure industry in Britain and the RHS is riding a surging wave of interest in gardens and plants. Horticultural shows are a crucial part of that interest. We can give two instances of how the increased demand for gardening has affected RHS shows. First, there is such competition to exhibit at Chelsea that the RHS has a panel whose job is to select the nurseries, sundriesmen and garden-designers which are to be accepted. Second, there are many more photo-calls on Chelsea press day than there used to be. In fact, it is hard to imagine a greater assembly of fashionable faces. Last year you could have seen everyone from Rolf Harris, Harry Secombe, Germaine Greer, Brian Rix, Gloria Hunniford, Karl Lagerfeld, Tony Banks and Susan Hampshire to the Duchess of Kent, Trevor MacDonald and Sinead Cusack.

"Today gardening is the largest leisure industry in Britain"

Show attendances are still affected by the weather, but sunshine and warm weather alone do not explain the record attendance of almost 76,000 at the Malvern Spring Gardening Show. The Malvern Spring Show in May now has a massive 1.5 acre marquee and can accommodate nearly 100 nurserymen: it measures 115m. x 50m. and covers much of the showground's main arena. The Malvern Autumn Show, too, is definitely on the rise. Launched in 1995, it continues to attract more visitors and more nurseries every year. Last year saw an exhibit of perry pear trees from the National Collection of which some 65 'lost' cultivars have since been assembled, identified and conserved. Another promising new show is the National Amateur Gardening Show at Shepton Mallet in September. Now in its third year, it has an excellent large floral marquee and the only national giant vegetables championship. BBC Gardeners' World too was bigger and better than ever. Not only was the total floor space increased by over 13% in 1998, but the plant mall, already the longest in the world, was nearly a fifth bigger than in 1997. Nearly 100 nurserymen displayed their plants and were rewarded by a total of 19 RHS gold medals.

Scotland's National Gardening Show is already becoming known as 'the Chelsea of the North' but, as RHS director of shows Stephen Bennett says, 'I am determined that each should show a clear horticultural identity'. In 1998, Scotland's National Gardening Show had six floral marquees, instead of the four it had during its first year in 1997. Visitor numbers at the show were down some 4,000 from last year's 47,000, but this was attributed to the atrocious weather and everyone agreed that the show had managed to improve on its strong performance during its first year in 1997. Nurserymen felt that they did well, and that the members of the public who came were mostly keen and serious gardeners. There were some interesting and unusual exhibits at the show. Colgrave Seeds, for instance, launched the idea of selling strips of seeds in the colours representing teams from the Premier Division of Scottish football. A garden called

---

"'Fire and Ice' incorporated nearly 70,000 chrysanthemums for the carpet bedding"

'Taming the Wilderness' which showed the transition from a rugged highland landscape to a cultivated garden won the award for the best show garden: it was created by the Glorious Gardens of Argyll and Bute, the marketing group which represents 19 gardens on the west coast of Scotland. Another feature of Scotland's National Gardening Show has been the competition between local authorities to produce the most creative and colourful displays for the Thistle Trophy. Once again the trophy was won by South Lanarkshire Council, with an exhibit called 'Fire and Ice' which incorporated nearly 70,000 chrysanthemums for the carpet bedding. The Ice Age side of it featured a life-size woolly mammoth whose shaggy body was composed entirely of Spanish moss, Tillandsia usneoides. The 'fire' sides were reached across a glacier and represented by an erupting volcano with lava streaming down to a bubbling pool. It was clearly a mammoth success. There is no doubt that the Scots gardeners are avid plantsmen. David Knuckey of Burncoose and Southdown Nurseries said that he sold more than 1,500 Salix 'Fuiri-koriyanagi' and that on the last day of the show it was selling at three a minute. The quality of the exhibits was underlined by the award of 15 gold medals.

A couple of years ago, there was some concern that the number of people attending the Westminster Shows was declining, and that these were an old tradition which had not been recently evaluated. Not only were visitor numbers down: it was sometimes difficult to find enough exhibitors of sufficient quality. So the RHS set up a working party last year

"... attendances at every single Westminster Show in 1998 were up on 1997"

to consider the future of these shows, and to look (among other things) at the number of shows, the suitability of Westminster and whether all parties felt that the shows were worthwhile – exhibitors, members of the public and indeed the Society itself. One interesting suggestion was that some shows might be devolved to the regions, and become a regular feature of the Society's commitment to creating a presence for itself in every part of the UK. An unexpected development, however, was that attendances at every single Westminster show in 1998 were up on 1997, in some cases by more 20%. This may be attributed in part to better coverage in newspapers and such garden magazines as The Garden, but also to a growing realisation of the sheer excellence of the shows themselves. There are opportunities to see plants at their best, season by season; to talk to nurserymen and other experts about plants and problems; to make the acquaintance of new plants; to buy plants for your own garden (we are always impressed by how many people leave the Westminster Shows with a RHS bag filled with plants); and to meet friends and join in social activities like the RHS's lectures on show days.

IMPROVING QUALITY AT SHOWS

The RHS hopes to provide at least one special feature at every Westminster show this year. It will be an exhibit that brings together and shows us a range of unusual plants, such as the display of Vireya rhododendrons which came from the Royal Botanic Garden at Edinburgh last year. One remarkable exhibit that we would like to see repeated was the collection of 422 different potatoes shown at the Malvern Autumn Show. Many of the cultivars were tracked down and brought back from the edge of extinction by dedicated amateurs, including the four individuals from all over Britain who brought this exhibit to the show. One of these enthusiasts is Welshman David Chappell, who enjoys the nickname of 'Taffy Tattie'. Asked at the show which were his own favourites, Chappell listed the following ten potatoes: 'Alex', 'Catriona', 'Claret', 'Fanfare', 'Maori Chief', 'Red Duke of York', 'Winston', 'Heather', 'Rapida' and 'Pink Fir Apple'.

The RHS is keen to attract better exhibitors and younger nurserymen with a fresh approach to presentation. It now offers a limited number of discretionary grants to assist exhibitors, mainly amateurs or non-commercial organisations, to stage an exhibit of a particular genus. Nevertheless it is the nurseries that have a constantly changing stock, a range of novelties to interest visitors to every show, and a loyalty to the RHS itself, that are the backbone of the Westminster shows: the Society is fortunate that there are so many of them.

"... standards are improving and there is greater variety than ever before"

Competition among nurserymen for a place at Chelsea remains strong and, because of the high standard demanded of Chelsea, the Society advises would-be exhibitors to gain experience first at the fortnightly Westminster shows and at Hampton Court before setting their sights on Chelsea. Our own impression is that standards are improving and that there is greater variety than ever before. As one perceptive observer wrote immediately after the Chelsea Flower Show, 'the unremitting annual pursuit of ever-higher standards of quality is the force that makes Chelsea worthwhile, ensuring that the show continues to receive international acclaim. Similar, beneficial effects which force up standards of quality will be the greatest asset the RHS can graft into its newer shows'.

But there is more to shows than plants, and standards do vary between floral exhibitors and the rest. Nowhere was this more vividly seen last year than at BBC Gardener's World show, where no less than 19 gold medals were awarded to floral exhibits, but none to any of the show gardens or designs for small gardens. It is a pity that the same standards did not apply to the exhibits within the Rose Tent at Hampton Court, which were qualitatively quite different from those in the rest of the show. With the honourable exception of Peter Beales (Roses) Ltd of Norfolk, little effort was made to build and grade exhibits according to colour or to contrast them with other plants. The traditional form of display is to stuff large quantities of a single cultivar – as many as 50 or 100 – into a single vase on a stand. There must be a better way of displaying the beauties of the rose for the benefit of the public and the rose trade alike.

Provincial shows are a good opportunity for small nurseries and local designers to show off their capabilities. For many of these the time and expense of attending a major show like Hampton Court would be prohibitive. One of the best is the National Amateur Gardening Show which has much of the charm of the Royal Bath & West Show, whose showground site near Shepton Mallet it occupies. It also gives local garden centres a chance to design and plant substantial exhibits. Cadbury Garden Centre, south of Bristol, is one of the most successful garden centres in the UK, but little known outside the West Country. The National Amateur Gardening Show pulled off a coup last year by staging the giant vegetable championships. The wet summer was a good year for record-breaking growth, though size seldom does much for beauty.

Spring & Autumn Contrasts

The late winter and early spring shows at Westminster are particularly popular. Perhaps the RHS should run some out of London: there is nothing so uplifting on a cold dark day than the sight of the RHS New Hall filled with the colours and scents of flowers. The February show in 1998 was no exception. One of its stars was Ashwood Nurseries which, in addition to the other fashionable plants that it is developing, showed many cultivars of *Hepatica nobilis*. The colours ranged from darkest blue to purest white with crimson anthers. The floral shapes were equally remarkable and included full doubles, camellia forms and daisy shapes.

At the same show on 17 & 18 February, there were two fine exhibits of snowdrops, one from Foxgrove Plants and the other from the Snowdrop Company of Silton in Oxfordshire. Among many desirable cultivars were *Galanthus* 'Cassava Daglingworth' with broad glaucous leaves and broad segments, the large flowers of *G*. 'Bill Bishop', and *G*. 'Merlin' whose inner segments are entirely green.

By the time of the mid-April show, on 14 & 15 April last year, it is the alpine enthusiasts who have the best and brightest exhibits. Last year saw a particularly good show of daphnes, including *Daphne* 'Bramdean' (*D. collina* × *cneorum*), *D.* 'Tichbourne' (*D. collina* × *arbuscula*) and *Daphne arbuscula* itself, which won a Certificate of Merit and the prize for the best plant in the Show. In addition there were little-known hybrids from Italy and Austria, including Fritz Kummert's cross between *D. caucasica* and *D. petraea*, called *D.* × *maurbachii* 'Perfume of Spring'. In the class for rock plants which are distinct, new or rare in cultivation, there was a fine potful of *Fritillaria verticillata*, which was white rather than creamy-yellow, accompanied by a note that most fritillaries grown under this name are actually *F. thunbergii*. This was the true species from the Altai mountains.

> *"the rarest cultivars included 'Blue Pearmain', a crimson dual-purpose apple with very marked waxy bloom, almost like a plum"*

Despite the profusion of colour, scent and variety, Jack Elliott of the AGS told us that the quantity was perhaps a little down, and the quality somewhat disappointing. There were, for example, no hardy orchids on show this year. But these things fluctuate, and many regional shows run by the Alpine Garden Society itself last year had very large exhibits of the highest quality.

Contrast the joys of spring with the rewards of autumn. At the Great Autumn Show, Gerald Edwards of Pinner in north London, showed well-grown apples and quinces, including the seldom-seen 'Pinner Seedling' a good late-season dessert apple raised by James Camel in 1810. His remarkable amateur exhibit was however outshone by an exhibit of apples from the RHS gardens at Wisley: the rarest cultivars included 'Blue Pearmain', a crimson dual-purpose apple with very marked waxy bloom, almost like a plum. Other rare, unlisted cultivars were 'Fraise de Hofinger' (mid-late-season dessert apple with high colour – only fair quality) and 'Reinette d'Osnabruck', a late dessert apple dating from the late 18th-century.

But the greatest contrast of seasons we saw last year was brought to the Hampton Court show by Warmenhoven of Holland, who showed spring bulbs in high summer, including crocuses and *Narcissus bulbocodium*. The exhibit won only a bronze medal, but was a great feat of cultivation.

ANNIVERSARIES

Nurserymen and societies often mount a special exhibit to mark an important anniversary. The Daffodil Society celebrated its centenary last year. At the RHS April show at Westminster, the RHS staged an exhibit of over 60 AGM daffodil cultivars from its gardens at Wisley. Broadleigh Gardens, the small bulb specialists in Somerset run by RHS Council Member Christine Skelmersdale, offered a display of over 70 miniature daffodils. They ranged from tiny species like *Narcissus canaliculatus* to the early-flowering form of pheasant's-eye *Narcissus poeticus* 'Praecox'. Likewise, for the Hampton Court show, Hopleys of Much Hadham showed a series of plants that they had introduced since they were founded thirty years ago. These included *Salvia patens* 'White Trophy', *Tradescantia* 'Chedglow' and *Abelia × grandiflora* 'Hopleys', a bud mutation from 'Francis Mason' with yellow-variegated foliage that may on occasion turn to pink.

NEW PLANTS

Orchid Answers of West Sussex staged one of the best exhibits at the BBC Gardener's World show and used the opportunity to display for the first time a new range of *Phalaenopsis* called 'Brother Lancer'. Developed in Taiwan, these orchids are creamy yellow with distinct stripes and a salmon-coloured lip. Also seen for the first time in public in the UK at the BBC Gardener's World show was the 'Saxonia' range of ground-cover pelargoniums. These have been bred in Dresden in the former East Germany and are noticeable for their fast growth and free-branching trailing habit. So far, they come in shades of crimson, orange, purple and white.

Hampton Court is also a good show at which to launch a new plant. We particularly noticed *Salvia × jamensis* 'Pleasant Pink' last year, a new hybrid which is slightly salmon pink. The gold medal exhibit mounted by Tony Clement's African Violet Centre included a new *Saintpaulia* cultivar called 'Mandy' which has white petals with a bright purple stripe down the middle creating a stellar effect.

Webbs of Wychbold used the Malvern Spring Gardening Show to launch their new *Coreopsis grandiflora* 'Calypso'. This has distinctive variegated foliage as well as handsome maroon centres to the bright yellow flowers. We predict a good future for this plant which is ideal for the expanding market for patio plantings. Lilliesleaf Nursery used the occasion of Scotland's National Gardening Show to launch a new *Epimedium* with shiny dark purple winter foliage called 'Black Sea'.

But Chelsea is the traditional place to introduce new plant varieties, especially roses. David Austin's new cultivars last year included: 'Dr Herbert Gray', rather a lax grower bred from 'Bonica 82'; 'William Morris', a classic English rose shape with double musk-like flowers in a mixture of buff and pink like 'Penelope'; 'Tess of the d'Urbervilles', whose cerise-crimson represents a colour break for David Austin; 'Mary Magdalene', which opens mother-of-pearl pink, but whose outer petals change to quite a deep pink; and 'Buttercup', also in the hybrid musk tradition, with semi-double flowers and long twisted sepals which give the buds a very dainty air.

TRENDS

The journalists view of Chelsea was almost unanimous: this was one of the best ever. They were as quick as ever to spot the trends. Romantic gardens are in the ascendant. So are formal gardens and sculpture gardens: these often have an extra appeal because they are essays in low maintenance and because they extend the rule of good decoration from the house out into the garden. Even stronger

> *"There was also a noticeable trend ... towards promoting gardening as an extended form of interior decoration"*

colours were in evidence: instead of the subtle mauves and pinks that were so popular five years ago, we have ever bolder and more experimental combinations, such as a mixture of oranges and blues. There was also a noticeable trend, perhaps to attract a younger market, towards promoting gardening as an extended form of interior decoration which makes statements about an individual's lifestyle aspirations. And it seems that people have more to spend on ornamental features within their gardens: pavilions, summerhouses, tents, gazebos and leisure buildings to relax and enjoy the garden.

Conservation and environmental issues remain important. The RHS is keen to ensure that all exhibitors, whether garden designers, nurserymen or sundriesmen, are sensitive to such issues as the overuse of tropical hardwoods and the dangers inherent in large-scale peat-farming. We noticed last year that some of the formal gardens featured a wild area or conservation corner. Water preservation is another big issue. The water authorities are beginning to mount stands at Chelsea, while the Water Services Association sponsored the Press tent last year again. Actually, we wonder whether the public's sensitivity to such issues as water conservation is directly related to their recent experiences: after the wet summer last year will we see less water-conscious show gardens this year than we did following the hot dry summers of 1996 and 1997?

> *"Every basket and container at last year's shows seemed to burgeon with Surfinia petunias"*

There are fashions in plants, too: at present they are often architectural, sculptural, trained or shaped. And certain plants are very much in evidence at the moment. Every basket and container at last year's shows seemed to burgeon with Surfinia petunias, while the lifestyle garden designs and nursery exhibits were full of tree ferns: in fact, one or two observers within the RHS itself dubbed 1998 'The Year of the Dicksonia'. We were impressed by the size of the Chelsea stand of Rickards Hardy Ferns, laid out as a glade of tree ferns, dicksonias and cyatheas.

At Hampton Court we also detected a twinge of nostalgia. Lincluden, for example, showed an old garden shed with a wooden ladder, clay pots, rusty old tools and an ancient bicycle. The Forsham Cottage 'Blitz garden' was evidence of a barely credible nostalgia for the 1940s, while a good example of the retreat into naturalism was shown by the HMP Leyhill garden, with a stream and cowslips and cordon apples in the kitchen garden. Once again, there was more spending on accessories – statuary, seats, trelliswork, arbours, conservatories, pyramids, dovecotes, topiary frames – while the fashion in plants was summed up by Brian & Heather Hiley's gold medal exhibit of grasses and ferns. These included such ferns as: *Dicksonia antarctica*, *Cyathea cooperi*, *Todea barbara* and *Blechnum nudum*; magnificent pots of *Hakonechloa macra* 'Alboaurea', *Arthropodium candidum purpureum*, and *Cordyline australis* 'Red Star'.

PUBLICITY

Publicity is often the driving force behind a stand at Chelsea or Hampton Court. The Lost Gardens of Heligan came from Cornwall to Hampton Court to draw attention to the way they had been restored after years of neglect. The exhibit had two sides, a 'before' and an 'after'. Publicity of a different kind was sought by an interesting newcomer to Chelsea, a Sardinian consortium of native plant nurseries in the Mediterranean called Gemme & Fiori, whose aim is to make Mediterranean plants more widely grown. Although the RHS has no immediate plans to increase the numbers of European nurseries at Chelsea, there is clearly a great interest among European nurserymen in the possibility of exhibiting at Chelsea and, as will be seen from our European nurseries section, there is no limit to the talent available on the continent.

GARDENS AT CHELSEA

An exercise in fantasy and imagination earned a gold medal at Chelsea last year. Based on Karl Lagerfeld's idea of the sort of garden Coco Chanel might have made had such things interested her, Tom Stuart Smith of Elizabeth Banks Associates created a pastiche of an 18th-century French formal garden in green and white. This was highly artificial in its use of out-of season plants which would not have featured in originals of the time: self-conscious, but quite fun, if not as classic as Coco Chanel's clothes.

It is the gardens which get most publicity at the Chelsea Flower Show. Big prestigious gardens at Chelsea are the result of cooperation and commitment to a common end by a large number of separate individuals or organisations, each of which has different aspirations. Take, for instance, one of the gardens at last year's Chelsea called 'Impressions of Highgrove'. It was a stylish garden which was awarded a silver-gilt medal: indeed, many visitors thought that it deserved a place among the gold medallists. It was designed by Mike Miller as an evocation of the Prince of Wales's garden in Gloucestershire, a series of motifs taken from that garden and spun together in a miniature pastiche of the whole, rather as the overture to an opera gathers up the best tunes from the arias and blends them into a coherent stand-alone piece of music. As well as Mike Miller, the following people and organisations were involved: Clifton Nurseries, for many of the plants; Robert Mattock for the climbing and shrub roses on the stand; HDRA for the potager and for supplying the heritage seeds which filled it; Mr Fothergill's Seeds, for growing some of the vegetables; Jacques Amand for the bulbs; Blooms of Bressingham for some of the perennial plants; Charles Morris for designing the two arbours;

> *"there is nowhere to match Chelsea for sheer prestige"*

Europlants (as agents for Vanucci in Italy) for supplying some of the outsize trees; Marney Hall for growing the hedgerow; Isabel and Julian Bannerman for designing the rustic bench; the Dutch nursery called De Limieten for supplying some of the yews and hedging plants; Manor Farm Herbs of Oxford for growing and supplying the plants of Thyme; Lloyd Christie Garden Architecture for designing and making the gates; Pots & Pithoi for the Cretan pots that were used in the design; Northend Reclamation for the walling and paving; Alex Moir for the hazel hurdle surrounds; Home Composters for the working compost units. And, last but certainly not least, the distinguished jewellers Cartier and the smart magazine Harpers & Queen, who sponsored the exhibit, underwrote its costs, gave their names to it, and stood to gain most from the resultant publicity. Was it worth it? Any exhibitor would undoubtedly say Yes: there is nowhere to match Chelsea for sheer prestige. And the actual cost is piffling in comparison with the publicity it brings to the sponsor.

For many visitors the most impressive part of the Hampton Court Show was the Daily Mail Seaside Pavilion. A vast area like a 3D-stage set was given over to re-creating a West Country beach scene with a big blue and white boat and a reconstruction of a 'dream cottage'. The real cottage was the first prize in the Daily Mail's national garden competition: its replica, together with the reconstructed cliff-side, required 400 tonnes of Dorset stone. As a feat of sheer design it was remarkable, but from the horticultural perspective it was also extremely effective because the design made it possible to show a very wide spectrum of garden plants which will grow in seaside conditions and in inland coastal areas. Bamboos, gunneras and tree ferns were some of the exotic forms in this garden. The cliff-top area had plants which were suitable for exposed positions – gorse, broom and *Rosa rugosa* – while inland, so to speak, a more formal planting included yuccas, palms and cordylines.

RARE PLANT EXHIBITS

Plants that were once thought of as rare and unobtainable suddenly turn up in the stands of several exhibitors at an RHS show. This happened at the January show last year when *Helleborus thibetanus*, hitherto considered rare beyond belief, was included in a large display of hellebores from Ashwood Nurseries, West Midlands, and as a bold drift in the centre of the bulbs and other plants from Jacques Amand.

Perhaps the best single exhibit of the whole year was the collection of Vireya rhododendrons from south-east Asia which the Royal Botanic Garden in Edinburgh brought to the show on 17 & 18 March. The species which attracted most attention were those with large flowers. Among them were: white *R. jasminiflorum*; *R. rousei*, described in 1989 and collected by George Argent in the Philippines; and *R. sarcodes*, a dark coral also collected by Argent in the Philippines, this time in 1992. Some were very rare:

> *"Perhaps the best single exhibit of the whole year was the collection of Vireya rhododendrons from south-east Asia"*

the specimen of R. ericoides is probably the only one in the British Isles. Also remarkable was R. saxifragoides which is prostrate and grows above the tree-fern line in New Guinea. Its red campanulate flowers stick straight up from long petioles, which hang down over the foliage: it has been widely used by nurserymen in New Zealand for hybridisation. Another unusual species was R. taxifolium, with leaves like the needles of a yew-tree and small white campanulate flowers. The underplanting on the exhibit was also of New Guinea plants: cyatheas, dicksonias, Vaccinium species, Nertera granadensis, Arisaema polyphyllum and even an orchid, Pterostylis acuminata.

At the RHS Westminster Show on 23 & 24 June, the exhibit of *Lycaste* and *Anguloa* from the National Collection incorporated five cultivars new to science which were shown for the first time. These included the green-flowered *L. × silvae*, a natural hybrid found in Peru and thought to be a cross between *L. mathisae* and *L. locusta*, flowering for the first time in cultivation and *L. macrophylla* 'Alba', a white form of this dwarf species flowering for the first time. A separate stand had a number of hybrids from the French nurseries of Marcel Vacherot, a popular exhibitor at RHS shows, who is an active breeder of lycastes with a particular interest in developing small forms. Among his hybrids were 'Rosamond', a highly coloured dwarf cultivar which flowers for up to seven months, bred from a variant of *L. skinneri* crossed with *L. dowiana*, as well as such older hybrids as the free-flowering 'Imschootiana' which derives from a *L. skinner* × *cruenta* cross and was first registered in 1893.

At the same show on 23 & 24 June, John Ainsworth showed sarracenias from his National Collection at Bamber Bridge. Of particular interest were a new hybrid called 'Jenny Helen', not yet available in commerce which will be introduced by South West Carnivorous Plants when it has been bulked up, and a hybrid called S. × gilpinii 'Heterophylla', very much a collector's plant, which is entirely green with no other colouring in its parts. At the same show, four sarracenias were recommended for awards. Two from the National Collection were submitted as candidates for AGMs: a form of *S. flava* with a narrow tube and a veined lid, and a cross between *S. purpurea* ssp. *venosa* and *S. oreophila*. A certificate of cultivation was awarded to a potful of *S. psittacina* from Hampshire Carnivorous plants and a PC to a form of *S. flava* from the National Collection with a heavily veined, copper-coloured lid.

The NCCPG is a regular exhibitor at RHS shows, and the consistently high standard of its exhibits is all the more remarkable when one remembers that most are mounted by enthusiastic amateurs. The NCCPG Plant Heritage tent is a regular feature of Hampton Court now and displays plants from some 15 to 20 collections. It combines botanical and horticultural interest with a lesson in conservation, and is always among the most instructive parts of the show. Last year's design was very striking last year, particularly the story of clematis cultivation and development over the last four centuries which formed the extensive central exhibit. It was based on Raymond Evison's NCCPG National Collection in Guernsey, which now comprises over 600 cultivars. Another worthy exhibit at Hampton Court last year was of old *Dahlia* cultivars from Rosewarne. It included two German cultivars 'Stolle von Berlin' (1914) and a dark cerise-magenta collarette called 'La Cierva',

(1939), neither of which had previously been seen in the UK, perhaps because of their dates of introduction. A good example of the value of these old cultivars was 'Union Jack', dating from 1911 and rediscovered in a garden two years ago. The whole exhibit opened many visitors' eyes to the sheer diversity of this genus.

RELIABLE NURSERYMEN

All RHS shows depend upon the energy and goodwill of a number of regular and reliable exhibitors. The Bluebell Nursery have established themselves at Westminster as one of the leading introducers of new plants – in Bluebell's case, forms of trees and shrubs. At the show on 14 &15 April, they offered an old ivy cultivar, seldom seen, the striking bright orange-yellow-fruited *Hedera helix* ssp. *poetarum*. At the RHS Westminster Show on the 23 & 24 June, they showed *Zelkova serrata* 'Variegata', a bright-white variegation which turns to pink at the leaf-tips, a new beech cultivar called *Fagus sylvatica* 'Greenwood' and an unusual plant *Desmodium callianthum* which is unusual because it has pale patches in the centre of the leaflets. At the Great Autumn Show on 15 & 16 September Bluebell showed *Quercus dentata* 'Pinnatifida', a very beautiful large-leaved indented form of oak, and at the October show they showed the bright yellow-leaved *Ilex attenuata* 'Sunny Foster' and an unusual *Sorbus* called *S. fruticosa* with white berries and rich red leaves in autumn.

No less consistent and reliable as exhibitors of often tender exotic trees and shrubs are Burncoose & Southdown Nurseries of Cornwall. At the show on 17 & 18 February, Burncoose exhibited a particularly fine new form of *Acacia dealbata* called 'Gaulois Astier' with large buttercup-yellow flowers. The star of their exhibit on 17 & 18 March was a big plant of *Sophora tetraptera* with particularly large flowers and the evergreen *Viburnum tinus* 'French White' grown as a standard. At the show on 14 &15 April, Burncoose showed the first rose of the year, the yellow-flowered shrub *Rosa* 'Canary Bird', and a fine specimen of *Acacia retinoides*. Their well-balanced exhibit at Hampton Court centred on three small but unusually narrow specimens of the Italian cypress *Cupressus sempervirens* 'Stricta' but burgeoned with late-summer flowers – nerines, hydrangeas, sidalceas, agapanthus, astilbes and some of the tender shrubs for which Cornwall is famous, including *Polygala myrtifolia* and *Lophomyrtus* × *ralphii* 'Kathryn'.

New Plants

MANY HORTICULTURAL INSTITUTES, private and public, carry out tests and assessments on new and established varieties of plant. These include the Royal Horticultural Society, which runs both temporary and permanent trials of a very wide selection of annuals, perennials, shrubs, bulbs, fruit and vegetables; the Northern Horticultural Society, which tests the same range as the RHS, but limits its assessments to fewer varieties; *Fleuroselect*, which is mainly concerned with annuals grown from seed for summer bedding; and the Royal National Rose Society, which conducts three-year tests on over 200 new rose varieties every year. *Gardening from Which?* also undertakes useful trials of many types of plant, from annuals to trees, and publishes the results month-by-month in *Gardening from Which?* The results of all these trials is a good test of what is on the market and what may be expected when the introducers have been able to bulk up their stocks to a commercial volume.

The Royal Horticultural Society

Every gardener needs to know just which plants are good and easy and reliable. By far the most important and wide-reaching hallmark is the Award of Garden Merit (AGM) which the RHS gives to plants that offer the best all-round value. Over 6,000 plants carry this award, and you will often see the letters AGM and a trophy-shaped kite-mark, ❦, in gardening magazines and on plant tags at nurseries and garden centres.

In order to qualify as an AGM plant, it should: be of outstanding excellence for garden decoration or use; be available in the trade; be of good constitution; and require neither highly specialist growing conditions or care. AGMs are only awarded after a period of assessment by the relevant committee of the RHS. That assessment may take the form of: a trial at one of the RHS gardens or similar venue; visits to specialist collections; round table discussions which draw on the expertise and experience of committee members.

The AGM is subject to periodic review. Plants that no longer measure up to the stringent standards, cultivars that have been surpassed, or plants that have dropped out of circulation can be removed, keeping the award lists as relevant and up-to-date as possible. The first complete review of AGM plants will take place in 2002.

Permanent trials are conducted at Wisley with border carnations, chrysanthemums, daffodils, dahlias, day-lilies, delphiniums, garden pinks, irises and sweet peas. Permanent trials of camellias are situated on nearby Battleston Hill. These trials continue from year to year with periodic replanting, at which time additions and removals are made. The results of the trials are published in the horticultural press and in publications of the RHS available to members on request from the trials office at Wisley.

At present there are 13 committees conducting 63 different trials. These trials are not only the vehicle for the Award of Garden Merit, but also allow for plants to be described, photographed, mounted in the herbarium and correctly named – in effect, an archive for the future.

The trials for 1999 include the following flowers grown from seed: *Cosmos*, *Petunia* (Grandiflora cultivars, single only), *Viola* (overwintering cultivars sown in 1998), and *Bellis* (also sown in 1998). The flowers trialled from plants include: *Ajuga*, *Bellis*, *Eryngium*, *Miscanthus* and *Heuchera*, all of them planted last year except the eryngiums which were set out in 1997. In addition, the society will be trialling zonal, single-flowered pelargoniums and abutilons under glass this year.

The vegetable trials for 1999 include: asparagus (planted in 1997), borecole (curly kale), spring-sown broad beans, runner beans (climbing types), Brussels sprouts (hybrids only, to mature from November 1999 onwards), calabrese (early types sown in a plastic tunnel in October and judged April), carrots (early ones, sown in February for June cropping), Cos and semi-Cos lettuces planted in March under fleece, winter lettuces sown in 1999 in a plastic tunnel, melons in a plastic tunnel, and pumpkins (for demonstration only). The woody plant trials for 1999 will cover hardy fuchsias and *Prunus laurocerasus*. Meanwhile, of course, preparations are being made for next year's flower trials which have been billed as a 'golden spectacular for the millennium' and include annual *Coreopsis, Helianthus, Rudbeckia* and *Tagetes* (F1 African marigolds) all grown from seed, and perennial *Coreopsis, Helenium, Helianthella Helianthus, Heliopsis, Inula, Rudbeckia* and *Solidago* grown from plants.

Plants from Seed

Seed-raised bedding plants are a major industry. The market is driven by the introduction of new varieties. Breeders need to generate and maintain a healthy demand at the consumer level. This means persuading wholesalers, garden centres, public authorities and individuals to buy their latest novelties. The typical private customer is younger than many gardeners – someone who has just discovered the joys of gardening and is developing an enthusiasm for plants. Commercial bedding plants must be successful in a wide spectrum of growing conditions, from temperate to subtropical. Breeders innovate constantly, using a relatively narrow germplasm base and operating on a remorselessly increasing scale. The big seedhouses raise over 100,000 experimental new crosses every year as part of their development programmes and some will admit that their costs are rising faster than the market potential.

Nevertheless, there are clear trends and detectable growth areas. Plants for hanging baskets, containers, patios and conservatories have all enjoyed a substantial growth in demand over the last few years – witness the success of the trailing Surfinia petunias, which is also evidence of a general shift away from seed to vegetative propagation. Other industry trends include a move from open-pollinated strains to F1 hybrids, the greater use of plugs, and an ever-increasing emphasis on compactness and early flowering. We may expect these trends to continue over the next few years, but with certain changes and improvements. As well as developing new colours, combinations of colour, flower patterns and forms, the breeders predict a wider choice of flower habits, more interspecific hybrids, substantial developments within hitherto 'minor' genera, and a trend towards the annualising of perennials. *Digitalis, Fuchsia, Verbascum* and *Veronica* will be bred to flower within weeks of sowing.

The Fleuroselect Awards

Fleuroselect is an international marketing and sales organisation, based in The Netherlands, whose principal aim is to stimulate the breeding of new and better annual seed varieties. *Fleuroselect* has more than 90 members worldwide: together they are responsible for 90% of global flower seed production. Some 70 new varieties are trialled anonymously every year for germination, growth, performance and flowering period at 27 trial grounds from Scandinavia to Southern Italy. These include Colegraves Seeds, Floranova, Moles Seeds, Unwins Seeds and Thompson & Morgan in the UK. All are grown under code numbers so that no-one can guess the name or origin of the varieties on trial. Those which receive the most points are awarded the *Fleuroselect* Gold Medal: others receive the *Fleuroselect* Medal or Quality Mark. Variables like the weather will however have an effect on their performance both during their trials and in subsequent years. Plants like *Gazania splendens* 'Daybreak Bright Orange' will perform better in a summer like 1996 or 1997 than they did last year. Please note that *Fleuroselect* does not always give its winning varieties their correct botanical names: however we use *Fleuroselect*'s namings below to help readers to identify them in seed catalogues. Last year's winners and this year's are:

1998

Campanula medium 'Champion Pink'
Campanula medium 'Champion Blue'
Celosia cristata 'Bombay Yellow Gold'
Gazania splendens 'Daybreak Red Stripe'
Impatiens walleriana 'Victorian Rose'
Petunia grandiflora 'Prism Surprise'

1999

Nemesia strumosa 'Sundrops'
Verbena hybrida 'Quartz Burgundy'

'Sundrops' is the first truly compact *Nemesia*. The plants are uniformly sized and come in a wide range of colours. This is the first time that a Gold Medal has been awarded to a nemesia since Fleuroselect began its trials in 1973: 'Sundrops' brings a genus that has long been popular with amateur gardeners into the front line of bedding plants available for big public displays. It has already been chosen by the British Bedding & Pot Plant Association as Plant of the Year in 1999. No doubt we shall see new strains of *Nemesia* developed in future as the breeders learn to stabilise the individual colours. *Verbena hybrida* 'Quartz Burgundy' is a new colour-break for the genus – a deep, rich purple – and has good resistance to powdery mildew. Germination has often been a problem with verbenas in the past, but *Fleuroselect* has achieved a magnificent 85% germination rate for 'Quartz Burgundy'. *Zinnia* 'Profusion Cherry' is a breakthrough because it is a zinnia which flowers well in temperate climates like Britain's. It is a compact, well-branched grower which flowers within 60 days of sowing. The flowers are bright scarlet, with a central boss of yellow stamens.

Gardens where Fleuroselect plants may be seen growing in the annual border displays include: Capel Manor, London; Harlow Carr Botanical Gardens, North Yorkshire; RHS Garden Rosemoor, Devon; RHS Garden Wisley, Surrey; Scottish Agricultural College, Ayr; Sir Thomas & Lady Dixon Park, Belfast; Springfields Show Gardens, Lincolnshire; The Botanic Gardens, Swansea.

New Plants Last Year

New plants which hit the garden centre market last year include *Phygelius* 'Sunshine', whose orange-pink flowers are complemented by pale yellow leaves; the double pink clematis 'Josephine' a large flowered cultivar introduced by Raymond Evison at Chelsea; and the Marco Polo petunias (blue, pink and white) which are fully double but have the trailing habit of surfinias and are thus bound to be popular for baskets and containers. But for us the most interesting in garden centres last year was the large flowered form of *Sophora microphylla* called 'Sun King' which is claimed to be hardier than any other in the UK climate. If this proves to be the case, then we predict a great future for this tall evergreen shrub whose stunning yellow flowers appear from March to May.

To see new annuals and bedding plants, it is usually possible to visit the leading seedsmen on one of their open days towards the end of summer. Among the companies offering the public a chance to see their trial grounds and the flowers that we shall all be growing in years to come are: Moles Seeds, Turkey Cock Lane, Stanway, Colchester, Essex (01206 213213); Colegrave Seeds, Milton Road, West Adderbury, Banbury, Oxfordshire (01295 810632); Suttons Seeds, Totnes Road, Ipplepen, Newton Abbot, Devon (01803 612011); Thompson & Morgan, Poplar Lane, Ipswich, Suffolk (01473 688588).

Two mixed seed series from Unwins of Cambridge this year, which we greatly admired in their trial grounds last year, are *Dianthus* Champion Mixed with a wide colour range as well as striped and picotee flowers and *Helichrysum* Unwins Summer Spectrum which also has a wide range of colours as well as being good at the back of a border and useful for drying. The seed industry has come in for quite a lot of criticism in recent years for its tendency to reduce naturally tall growing plants to compact growing strains. So Unwins should be congratulated on reintroducing a tall growing petunia called 'Mirage Velvet', which is particularly floriferous and is good in mixed borders. Unwins also confirm that one of the current trends in ornamental plantings is towards hotter colours. Unwins themselves have long been famous for their sweet peas and so it is appropriate that one of their new introductions last autumn was the only sweet pea to be recommended for the RHS AGM and the Award of Merit for Exhibition following last year's Wisley Trials. 'Gwendolen' is a large-flowered soft lilac pink with long strong stems. It is also the top Spencer variety for fragrance.

Last autumn, Thomson and Morgan of Ipswich introduced a seed selection of hardy border geraniums which included *Geranium* 'Splish-splash', the striking blue and white bicolor which was their top selling variety. This spring they will bring out the first ever greenfly-resistant lettuce called 'Dynamite'. It is a medium-sized lettuce, bred in Holland and raised without genetic engineering: we have had no comments, as yet, on its taste. Another introduction from Thomson and Morgan, available for the first time this year, is a rhubarb called 'Livingstone', whose stems are best picked, not in the spring but in the autumn. This increases the season for enjoying fresh rhubarb at home enormously.

The boom in patio and conservatory gardening has also led to a much larger demand for scented plants. Many of the traditional pelargoniums with strongly scented leaves have somewhat ungainly habits – 'Citronella' and 'Greenlime' come to mind. New breedings and selections tend to concentrate on cultivars which are more compact, and the demand for scent is spreading out to such house plants as cyclamens and bedding plants like antirrhinums. Nevertheless, for cut flowers, scent will probably never be as important as vase life.

New Roses

So far as roses are concerned, there are three schemes which help to establish the best new cultivars for our gardens: the Rose of the Year Award, the Royal National Rose Society trials and the Roses of Special Merit Scheme. Last April the RNRS added thirty new cultivars to the Roses of Special Merit Scheme. The purpose of the scheme is to help gardeners to choose suitable roses for five typical garden situations: small containers, pillars and arches, mixed beds and borders, hedges, and ground cover. All must be well-established in cultivation and readily available. The additions include: 'Little White Pet' and 'Sweet Magic' for containers, 'Laura Ford' and 'Lavinia' for climbing purposes, 'Gertrude Jekyll' and 'L'Aimant' for mixed borders, 'Berkshire' and 'Suffolk' for ground cover, 'Golden Wings' and 'L. D. Braithwaite' for hedging.

Fryers Roses introduced no less than eight new roses at last year's Chelsea Flower Show. Their names are 'Flower Power' (a peachy pink patio), 'Westminster Pink' (a pink HT), 'Lions International' (a yellow HT), 'Scent-sation' (a pink HT named for its fragrance), 'Bob Greaves' (a salmon orange floribunda), 'Phab Gold' (a yellow floribunda), 'Bubbles' (a pink dwarf ground cover) and 'Britannia', a particularly fine pale orange HT which many suspect may last longer in cultivation than some of the others. More roses were launched at the BBC Gardener's World show shortly after Chelsea. Alain Meilland launched nine new 'traditional English' roses which combine the shape and scent of old roses with the free-flowering habit of new ones. All their names begin with the word 'Romantic', e.g. 'Romantic Serenade' (an apricot orange flower) or 'Romantic Fragrance' (a good pink with an apple scent). The Meilland family is perhaps best known for the introduction of the 'Peace' rose: the family company is now one of the largest in Europe. Other roses launched at BBC Gardener's World included two additions to Mattocks Roses' series of County Roses – Yorkshire and Lancashire. Each was appropriately coloured: these Oxfordshire nurserymen do not take sides in the wars of the roses.

Bill Le Grice Roses launched their pale creamy apricot rose at the Hampton Court Flower Show and called it 'Jilly Cooper'. It is a colour sport from 'Debs Delight', a prize winner at the RNRS trials and, at 18 inches high, is something between a low floribunda and a patio rose. Dicksons Nurseries Limited of Newtonards introduced three roses at Hampton Court including 'Greetings' which won the President's International Trophy at the RNRS trials and 'Brandysnap' which won the Harry Edland Memorial Medal for fragrance in the same trials. 'Greetings' was raised by an American, Keith Zary, and was the first American-raised cultivar to win the President's Trophy for more than 40 years.

One reason why roses remain very popular garden plants is that recent years have seen a marked trend towards disease resistance. Last year the HDRA went to the lengths of introducing a rose itself, because it was so highly disease-resistant. The pink and apricot HT called 'Natural Beauty' was raised by an amateur breeder and was successfully trialled for four years without receiving any pesticide sprays.

SPORTS FOR ALL

But roses are not the only flowers. We noticed that many of the new cultivars of other plants last year were actually foliage sports. A sport of *Buddleja* 'Royal Red', originating from a nursery in Knaresborough, North Yorkshire, was introduced last summer and was finding its way into garden centres towards the end of last year under the name of *Buddleja* 'Santana'. The leaves have a rich golden variegation combined with the purple-red flowers of its parent and it is thought to have a more compact habit than other *Buddleja davidii* cultivars. A very handsome variegated fuchsia also made its appearance last year: its public debut was at the Hampton Court Palace Flower Show, but we also saw 'Firecracker' playing its part in the famous bedding displays at Kew Gardens later in the year. It has the big bunches of orange-scarlet flowers typical of *Fuchsia triphylla*, but set off by creamy edges to the leaves. It should be widely available from garden centres this spring. Another colour-leaved sport which hit the markets last year was *Weigela* 'Jean's Gold'. This is a sport of 'Bristol Ruby' and has the glorious dark red flowers of that famous old cultivar which contrast with the bright yellow foliage. It is claimed that 'Jean's Gold' does not scorch in the sun (unlike the pink flowered 'Looymansii Aurea') and does not revert to the green type. Look out for another new *Weigela* this year called 'Pink Poppet'.

A PLUG FOR PLANTS

Undoubtedly the best source of information about the new plants coming into cultivation in the UK is the quarterly magazine *Plants*. Its editor, Dirk van der Werff, may sometimes be a little outspoken, but there is no doubting his enthusiasm for tracking down new plants and his ability to introduce them to his readership. Among the new introductions at Chelsea Flower Show which he held in greatest esteem are: the pink flowered form of *Gaura* called 'Siskiyou Pink', which we have noticed already in a number of smart gardens last summer; *Aquilegia* 'Swan Colorado', with long spurs and extremely large flowers which are white in the centre and backed by dark purple sepals; *Penstemon* 'Caroline Orr', a new and vigorous cultivar which van der Werff noted on the Hardy Plant Society stand, but was apparently not spotted by other commentators; and a new series of hydrangeas known as the

'Japanese Lady' series introduced from Japan by Burncoose and Southdown Nurseries – six of them in shades of blues, red, pink and purple. All were bred by Hiroshi Ebihara from the hydrangea cultivars that he imported into Japan from England in 1970. It is hard to imagine that these dainty new cultivars, all with a distinctive white picotee edge, are descended from the older hybrids that were, for the most part, bred in France in the 19th century.

PHYSIOLOGICAL BREAK-THROUGHS

An important break towards the end of last year came with the introduction into cultivation of *Verbena* 'Edith Eddelman'. The important new quality which this verbena possesses is hardiness: it is said to be hardy to -10°C. This means that, for the first time, we have a verbena that can be treated as a hardy perennial, not as a frost-tender bedding plant. The flowers are said to be particularly good, even for a verbena: large, sweetly scented bright red fading to pink with age. *Ficus* 'Violetta' is a new hardy fig that we can expect in British garden centres next year.

Introduced from Germany, it has the remarkable capacity for being hardy down to -20°C. Ornamental elders, too, have been very popular plants over the last ten years. A new purple-leaved cultivar will be introduced later this year which is a distinct improvement on *Sambucus nigra* 'Guincho Purple'. The new cultivar, to be called 'Black Beauty', has dark purple leaves at all times ('Guincho Purple' opens green) and deep pink flowers.

Finally, there is news of a breakthrough which may revolutionise the possibilities for growing rhododendrons in much of Britain. One of the troubles with rhododendrons is that they cannot be grown on limy soils and this means that they are a failure not only in such soils as the chalk downlands of southern England, but also in many small modern gardens where the soil has been contaminated by limy builders cement. However, a very promising rootstock has been trialled in Germany and is now to be introduced in the UK later this year as the graft stock for some 32 rhododendron cultivars. We predict a great future for it.

New Books

The Pan Plant Chooser Series
Roger Phillips and Martyn Rix (Pan)
£4.99 each

These splendid books, each for just less than a fiver, are excellent value: attractive, useful and well written. When you think that many of the plants would set you back as much or more than one of these books, they are clearly a good investment before you head off for a nursery or garden centre. The series shares the same design as its big brother, the hugely successful *Garden Plants Series*, which is also characterised by the authors' winning combination of studio portraits, garden shots and pictures of the plants growing in the wild. The writing has much to commend it too. For these almost pocket-sized books, the text is more discursive than before. Rix and Phillips' approach is consistently informative and intelligent, never bland or banal. For that reason, they are a pleasure to read and dip into, but that is not their primary purpose.

The series includes the following titles: *Salad plants for your garden*, *The best scented plants*, *Plants for shade*, *Climbers for walls and arbours*, *Herbs for cooking*, *Traditional old roses* and *Plants for pots and patios*. The aim is to help you choose a plant for a particular place or purpose, when you know what sort of thing you want but are not sure exactly what to get. So if you need to fill a shady border, for instance, *Plants for shade* presents about 250 choices, arranged by flowering season, and further divided into shrubs, bulbs and perennials. The choice is fairly mainstream, which means that you should not have difficulty obtaining specimens, and there are a few more challenging suggestions included. The volumes are easy to use (no symbols or shorthand to decipher), and offer all they promise and more. Good for giving, too.

What Houseplant Where
Roy Lancaster and Matthew Biggs
(Dorling Kindersley) £14.99

Almost everyone has houseplants, whether they garden or not. Bought or given, chosen or inherited, they often cause as much heartache as pleasure. Some people will tell you how plants always die for them. Others will tenderly nurse a stunted stem with one healthy leaf year after year with no reward. But, while plants can be wayward and uncooperative, it is more usually the owners who are at fault. The solution: put the plant in a type of room to which it is suited and give it what it likes. The idea is obvious really: in the wild plants choose to grow where they like; in cultivation, why not adopt the same principles and make things easy for yourself? This beautifully laid-out book, by two gardeners familiar from the page and the TV screen, is simplicity itself. It is equally suited to beginners and as a crib for the more experienced. You can choose the plants by what you want them to look like, by what you want them to do, and – best of all – by where you want to put them. There are clear pictures of each plant, and a concise description of its needs. The authors do not dwell on pests and diseases specific to each (there's a brief but useful section on houseplant problems), but, if you follow their advice on cultivation and positioning, you should not need to either. Plants which fit in more than one of the chosen categories may crop up more than once, but that means the information you need is usually where you seek it. If that is still too complicated, there is even a selection of 'plants tolerant of neglect'. A section on plants for the 'Home office' briefly conjured up pictures of Jack Straw with a spider plant, but is really devoted to plants which are both decorative and which improve the working atmosphere, soaking up computer emissions and improving air quality. The authors tell us that NASA research has established that plants, including the humble *Chlorophytum comosum*, significantly improve the indoor environment. Tough on grime, and tough on the causes of grime?

Conservatory and Indoor Plants
Roger Phillips and Martyn Rix (Pan)
2 vols., £14.99 each

First published in 1997 in hardback, both these volumes are now available in softcovers. Each is a breathtakingly seductive tour of distant and beautiful horizons. While the plants described originate from the warmer parts of the planet, gardeners in the UK can grow them in their greenhouses and conservatories, or perhaps outdoors in the mildest of areas. For a wider audience in southern Europe, the United States and the southern hemisphere, these are garden plants, and UK readers will encounter them in gardens abroad or in the wild on holiday. Gardening has always fostered the exotic in exile, not merely for novelty and the challenge of growing the difficult, but because of the dazzling beauty and excitement of other floras. There could be no better argument for extending one's range and interests than these volumes. The photographs – taken all over the world – are quite stunning. Such sequences as the vivid members of the convolvulus family, leading into purple echiums and then the *Solanum*, *Cestrum*, and *Datura* species and cultivars (to take a random example) set the horticultural pulse racing with desire and envy. For those without a conservatory, the books are still a delight. They are also a useful companion to gardens in the warmer climates, showing you what others can and do grow.

Rejuvenating a Garden
Stephen Anderton (Kyle Cathie) £19.99

Turn to this book when you buy a new house – whether there is a garden there or not; when you wake up and realise that your garden is as old as you feel and needs a fresh start; and when you decide finally to tackle that overgrown corner which was always a little bit too daunting. It is a thoroughly good book. Good sense shines through everything Anderton writes, and with charm and humour he tells it how it is. You are guided into what decisions to take and when, and if a plant is better cut out than restored he'll tell you. Again, if you will do better to look first and leap later, the advice is sensible and clear. Among the best bits is an invaluable section at the end which describes the reaction of a wide range of trees and shrubs to the pruner's saw. There are also many passages which all gardeners might commit to heart. How about, for example, 'the credo of labour-saving for its own sake can lead to some dreadfully boring gardening'.

Gardening with Grasses
Michael King and Piet Oudolf (Frances Lincoln) £20

Grasses are tough and adaptable – species and cultivars exist to suit a wide range of garden conditions. This has recently been recognised and, as a result, grasses are enjoying a period of fashionable popularity. The authors of this beautiful book are undoubtedly passionate about using grasses in every type of garden, but they have the sense not to make a plea for borders or gardens containing nothing else. As with many forms of gardening, monoculture easily becomes visual monotony. King and Oudolf realise that grasses show to greatest advantage when combined with other kinds of plants and, in this book, suggest how to achieve the best contrasts. Chapters describe the range of ornamental grasses and ways to plant them. There is a good section on plant combinations and convenient lists which summarise the authors' recommendations – grasses to use in particular situations, plants that look good with them. Unlike in many gardening books which incorporate a directory of plants which appears to be little more than a way of filling space at the end, this is an important and useful section which links to the lists in the earlier chapters and cross-refers to the suggestions for using grasses in particular situations or styles of plantings. The tone of the book is, however, rather earnest. Grasses are serious stuff. The traditional lawn – 'a colonial anachronism' – does get a section to itself, but the authors clearly prefer a different style of covering an open space. Nonetheless, for striking ideas on using grasses the book has much to offer the gardener.

Scots Roses
Mary McMurtrie (Garden Art Press) £19.95

Scots roses offer us delicacy and grace, as well as that hardy constitution which renders them in sympathy with the modern trend to wilder styles of planting which simulate nature. They are typical country-garden plants, and great survivors. Their tendency to sucker – which does not endear them to gardeners in more formal settings – has its uses here. This is fortunate for us, since Scots Roses have declined from a period of great popularity at the start of the 19th century to a mere handful of cultivars commercially available today. In recent years enthusiasts in Scotland have begun to collect other cultivars from around the country. Naming them is difficult: not only have the old names been lost or forgotten, but the roses themselves are often raised from seed. There are the usual problems of duplicate and synonymous names. And, of course, many cultivars are very similar. Mrs McMurtrie has produced a collection of portraits of those now in cultivation. She includes named varieties, pretty foundlings, species and hybrids. They are depicted in prose and soft watercolours with delicacy and great charm. She obviously has great affection for her subjects, rather as if she were introducing her readers to a group of old friends. This affinity makes the book a delight to handle and read.

Colour by Design
Nori and Sandra Pope (Conran Octopus) £25

'Colour by design' is an apt title. Although the style of planting favoured by the Popes is informal, the colour scheming this demands is actually highly designed. The book is written round a series of colour-themed essays, nine in all, which reflect the plantings at Hadspen Garden. It is a conscious exercise in colour combination. Although the Popes claim to have been influenced by Gertrude Jekyll, the way they work is quite different. She took a long border and ran it through a scale of different colours for effect. The Popes take a single colour at a time and play within its gamut on tone and hue throughout the seasons. Plants are grouped informally, and allowed to merge with their neighbours. It is a style suited to gentle movement, best appreciated by walking by slowly. Gardeners will find the book a fertile source of ideas, whether they are planning a small grouping, a border or an entire single-colour garden. The Popes' ideals are handsomely illustrated with photographs of Hadspen Garden by Clive Nichols, but less well served by the self-conscious design of the book.

The Garden Tree
Alan Mitchell and Allen Coombes (Weidenfeld & Nicolson) £30

Our first impressions of this book were very favourable. It has a welcoming cover photograph, handsome endpapers, lots of illustrations and a design which means that you can open it at any page and find something which looks as if it might be a good read. It is a guide to choosing and planting garden trees. The first part of the book is excellent. It explains the place that trees should have, both in the garden and in the wider landscape. It articulates the criteria to apply when you choose what to plant in your own garden. The authors encourage us to look at other people's trees, to understand what is growing in hedgerows, parks and private gardens. Then they give us lists of trees for special purposes: rapid growth; autumn colour; small gardens; specimen plantings; difficult soils; town gardens; winter effect; ornamental bark. All extremely useful, and a good read. But these bits occupy no more than one fifth of the book. It is the rest which is so disappointing: a boring crawl through tree after tree, listed alphabetically according to their Latin names. Then you realise that many of the photographs are too dark, so that it is difficult to pick out the leaves or flowers against the sky. You notice that some photographs have been used more than once, both in the introduction and in the plant lists, when a different one would have enhanced your appreciation of the tree in question. And you may come to the conclusion that we did, which is that this is rather a pedestrian book, despite its excellent introduction, and certainly no match for such established favourites as Hugh Johnson's *International Book of Trees*. Which is a pity, because both authors are among this century's greatest dendrologists.

Take Two Plants
Nicola Ferguson (David & Charles) £20

Why have we had to wait 15 years for Nicola Ferguson's second book? Her first was a mould-buster – *Right Plant, Right Place* – which, as its title made clear, told us how to pick the perfect plant for whatever place in the garden needed colour and form. It was the first to treat the subject in such a direct and practical manner, and it spawned a shoal of imitations. *Take Two Plants* is just as direct a title, and deals with a garden problem in just such a simple but original manner. Nicola Ferguson has hit on the idea of teaching people, from photographs, how to put two plants together in the garden to create a pleasing harmony or contrast of colour, shape, texture or form. There have of course been many books on the subject of 'felicitous juxtapositions' in the garden, but none has hitherto adopted such a simple and direct way of showing what works, and explaining just why. The format is straightforward. Each half-page carries a photograph of a good plant combination which, in a visual way, tells its own story. The text then describes the two plants (or, very occasionally, three) and analyses why they go so well together. It also explains how each plant will develop at other seasons of the year and how both should be cultivated for optimum effect. Then there are chapter introductions, analytical and allusive at the same time, and cross-references to other pairs of plants. Seldom does an author put so much thought into a book or go so far in trying to make it helpful to readers. We look forward to many more books from such an original and clear-headed writer, but hope we will not have to wait another 15 years for the next.

Natural Style for Gardens
Francesca Greenoak (Mitchell Beazley) £22.50

This is an important book, written by a distinguished author who has long made natural style a central tenet of her gardening credo but has never written about it at length. We can be grateful that she has found a publisher who is prepared to spend time and money on good design and excellent photographs, even if the illustrations seem to have been chosen more for their instant appeal during the ten seconds we browse through a book and decide whether or not to buy it than for their relevance to Francesca Greenoak's text. Our only complaint is that it is not long enough: but the publishers have clearly done their marketing and pitched it in at a reasonable price. Greenoak is best on the principles of natural gardening which she expounds clearly and stylishly. The secret is to work with nature, not against it.

Climate, soil and landscape are important factors. So are harmony, repetition and sound garden management: even if we suspect that, in the end, the beauty of a garden really is proportionate to the time, money and labour we put into it. The first part of Francesca Greenoak's book is particularly inspiring: it expounds the principles that should govern our approach to natural gardening. The problems start when she moves on to the practicalities – how to design the garden, choose the right plants and create different effects and yet have a garden which allows us our artistic expression, encourages wildlife, and fits with our family's often conflicting expectations of what a garden should look like. At this point it becomes possible to pick holes not in her arguments but in their implementation. Why plant blowsy, gawky Compassion on a rose arch, when you can have such supple, graceful and natural-looking ramblers as 'Phyllis Bide' or 'Madame Alice Garnier'? Why tell people how to make a nesting-box out of a single plank of timber when endless middle-brow how-to-garden books have already told you and me and everyone how to fill the world with nesting-boxes (which are easily bought from a garden centre anyway)? But *Natural Style for Gardens* is inevitably a compromise between Greenoak's ideas and her publisher's vision of a Good Book (meaning one that will sell), and the compromise is well worth the sheer joy of her inspired and inspiring exposition.

Gardening on the Internet

When we first worked on *The Gardener's Yearbook* in 1992, the world of gardening knew nothing of the Internet. Now the *RHS Gardener's Handbook* would be almost impossible to compile without recourse to the Internet, which provides links from a suitably equipped computer to horticultural sites all over the world. The best tend to be connected to academic or public institutions, but this is changing and, although an American bias remains, the Internet is nothing if not cosmopolitan.

Users of the Internet will be aware that the quality, quantity and currency of information accessible through the Net is variable. Sites tend to change their address or disappear for no apparent reason. A small selection of sites is listed below. Many have connections to other horticultural sites, so that an astonishingly diverse range of information is at your fingertips, starting from these pages. Readers can type the site addresses below directly into their Internet browser, but they may find it more convenient to access the electronic version of this page instead, at *www.rhs.org.uk/Around/links.asp*

The sites listed here are divided by subject into Organisations, Books and Bookshops, Colleges, Gardens, Individual Plants & Genera, Nurseries & Seed suppliers, Societies, and Magazine (general interest) sites. Details of how to access many of these bodies by more conventional means can be found in the Useful Addresses section. Two sites appear first: the RHS's own site and the site which we think has the best collection of horticultural resources:

www.rhs.org.uk.
Royal Horticultural Society. Describes a range of publications, events and services organised by the RHS. A good search engine gives instant in-depth access to a wide range of topics.

www.rhs.org.uk/rhs_sites/mirror/Botmenu.html
Internet directory for Botany. A UK location for the outstanding collection of links to botany and horticulture.

General

www.adas.co.uk
ADAS. Newly-privatised horticultural and agricultural consultancy

dialspace.dial.pipex.com/town/avenue/yi61
Arboricultural Association. This useful site includes full lists of all the Arboricultural Association's approved contractors and consultants

www.environment.gov.au/life/species/species_flora.html
Australian Environment Online. A link to the flora section of this mine of information

www.rbgkew.org.uk/BGCI
Botanic Gardens Conservation International. International conservation organisation based at RBG, Kew

www.visitbritain.com
British Tourist Authority. A wealth of information on Britain for visitors

www.btcv.org.uk
British Trust for Conservation Volunteers. Includes details of the BTCV's working holidays

www.cla.org.uk
Country Landowners Association

www.countryside.gov.uk
Countryside Commission. Public agency dedicated to protecting the English countryside

www.english-heritage.org.uk
English Heritage. Public organisation which protects the historic environment: some important gardens are under its care

www.english-nature.org.uk
English Nature

www.flowers.org.uk
Flowers and Plants Association. Association representing the UK cut-flower and pot plant trade

www.forestry.gov.uk
Forestry Commission. Information on the UK's forestry department

www.gardening-uk.com
A UK-only site for nurseries to advertise their wares

http://ourworld.compuserve.com/homepages/hort_therapy
Horticultural Therapy. Charitable organisation which uses horticulture for therapeutic purposes

www.martex.co.uk/hta
The Horticultural Trades Association (a UK trade body) has an excellent site

www.hri.ac.uk
Horticulture Research International. UK research institute

www.fertilizer.org
International Fertiliser Industry Association. Not fully set up as we went to press

www.horticulture.demon.co.uk
Institute of Horticulture. Association of professional horticulturists in the UK

www.maff.gov.uk
MAFF. Ministry of Agriculture, Fisheries and Food site

www.meto.gov.uk
The Met Office. Weather and meteorolgical information from the UK, with links further afield. Essential reading for all weather buffs around the world

www.compulink.co.uk/~museumgh
Museum of Garden History. The site needs updating, but has a few useful links

www.niab.com
National Institute of Agricultural Botany

www.nationaltrust/org.uk
National Trust. Information county by county on the Trust's many properties and full visitor information

www.nts.org.uk
National Trust for Scotland. Excellent site with full descriptions and pictures of Scottish gardens

www.nhm.ac.uk
Natural History Museum. Some useful links to botanical sites and gardens

www.ngs.org.uk
The National Gardens Scheme. Not fully set up as we went to press

www.NCCPG.org.uk
NCCPG. Brief information and contact details for the National Council for the Conservation of Plants and Gardens

www.plantamerica.org
Good US site with access to thousands of photographs of plants

www.riba.org
Royal Association of British Architects

www.wildlifetrust.org.uk
Wildlife Trusts. The homepage for the extensive network of local wildlife trusts and urban wildlife trusts, with thousands of nature reserves under their care

BOOKS AND BOOKSHOPS

www.abebooks.com
Advanced Book Exchange. The world's largest source of second-hand and out-of-print books

www.amazon.com
Amazon.com. Huge Internet bookseller

bookshop.blackwell.co.uk
Blackwells Online Bookshop. The Oxford-based bookseller's web shop

www.dk.com
Dorling Kindersley. Publisher of the *RHS Gardener's Handbook*, the *RHS Plant Finder* and many illustrated RHS gardening titles

www.heffers.co.uk
Heffers. Cambridge-based bookshop

www.plantfinder.co.uk/index.htm
The Plant Finder. *The RHS Plant Finder* and related taxonomic resources

www.timberpress.com
Timber Press are the leading American publishers of top-of-the-market gardening books, with a growing presence in UK

www.waterstones.co.uk
Waterstones. Searchable book database

Colleges

www.writtle.ac.uk
Writtle College. Chelmsford-based college, which holds some events for the nearby RHS Garden Hyde Hall

www.wye.ac.uk
Wye College, University of London

Gardens: United Kingdom

www.bordehill.co.uk
Borde Hill Garden. The garden in Sussex has its own page with useful information and photographs from the garden. Expect to see more sites like this in the future

www.reading.ac.uk/AcaDepts/sb/Research_Services /Ha-Ga/hg.html
The Harris Garden. New botanic garden at the University of Reading

www.swan.ac.uk/midlton
National Botanic Garden of Wales. Keep in touch with this new project on the Internet

www.merseyworld.com/nessgardens
Ness Botanic Gardens. Informative and attractive guide to these gardens, founded by A.K. Bulley

www.paigntonzoo.demon.co.uk/gardens.htm
Paignton Zoo & Botanical Gardens. Information about the gardens, with rather more on the zoo

Ourworld.compuserve.com/homepages/andy_ward /pinehome.htm
Pine Lodge Gardens. Modern Cornish garden with the National Grevillea collection

www.rbge.org.uk
Royal Botanic Garden, Edinburgh. Includes a searchable version of the Flora Europaea database

www.rbgkew.org.uk
Royal Botanic Gardens, Kew. Searchable databases of plant names; information about the gardens and a useful page of links to other botanical sites

www.gardenweb.com/gotw/standrew.html
St Andrews Botanic Garden. Former university botanic garden in Fife, now run by the local authority

www.dur.ac.uk/~deb0www/dubg/bghomep.html
University of Durham Botanic Garden

www.rbgkew.org.uk/wakehurst/index/html
Wakehurst Place. Kew Gardens' sister garden, in West Sussex

Gardens: Rest of the World

www.mobot.org/AABGA
The American Association of Botanic Gardens and Arboreta. Useful links to its member gardens throughout the USA

www.engref.fr/barres.html
Arboretum National des Barres: Quite a short site, with a link to ENGREF Ecole Nationale du Genie Rural des Eaux et des Forets)

arboretum.harvard.edu
Arnold Arboretum, Harvard University. Includes an inventory of the Arboretum's living collection

155.187.10.12/anbg.html
Australian National Botanic Gardens. A wealth of information about Australian plants and botany, with links to other botanic gardens in Australia

www.stadt-frankfurt.de/palmengarten
Palmengarten, Frankfurt

www.nybg.org
New York Botanical Garden

Individual Plant Families and Genera

www.theazaleaworks.com
The Azalea Works. Introductory azalea site, with links to other pages of interest

www.demon.co.uk/mace/cacmall.htm
The Cactus and Succulent Plant Mall. Jumping off point for cacti and succulent nurseries and societies

Probe.nalusda.gov:8000/otherdocs/cgc/tcn
The Cucurbit Network Description

www.dicom.se/fuchsias/menueng.html
Fuchsia Page. Extensive fuchsia resources, based in Stockholm but mostly in English

www.vol.it/mirror/rhododendron/rhodo05.html
The Rhododendron Page. Series of pages devoted to rhododendrons

www.rhododendron.org
American Rhododendron Society

Nurseries and Seeds Suppliers

www.gardening-uk.com/apuldram/frameset.html
Apuldram Roses

www.gardening-uk.com/architectural_plants/frameset.html
Architectural Plants

www.bruns.de
Bruns Pflanzen. One of the largest German wholesale nurseries

www.cfg.net
Cotswold Garden Flowers

www.crug-farm.demon.co.uk
Crug Farm Plants. Online catalogue of the Welsh nursery, which specialises in climbers and shade-loving plants

www.demon.co.uk/mace/tobees/tobees.html
Toobees Exotics. Specialists in succulents, palms and other exotica

rareplants.co.uk
Paul Christian Rare Plants. UK bulb specialists

www.roses.co.uk/harkness
Harkness Roses

www.demon.co.uk/mace/peten
Pete & Ken Cactus Nursery

www.seedman.com
SBE Seeds. US seed merchants with a substantial site which includes online ordering facilities

www.gardenweb.com/seedgd/about.html
Seed Guild. Scottish seed list and club, with material sourced from around the world

www.seeds-by-size.co.uk
Seeds-by-Size

members.aol.com/wescacti/pag1.htm
Westfield Cacti

Societies

www.avsa.org
African Violet Society of America

www.eskimo.com/~mcalpin/soc.html
List of Alpine Garden societies. List of alpine-related garden societies around the world, with links where available to contact mailboxes or Internet sites

www.pacificrim.net/~bydesign/acs.html
American Conifer Society. Suitably green homepage has some links to other conifer sites and general information about growing and choosing conifers

www.mc.edu/~adswww
American Daffodil Society

www2.trop-hibiscus.com/trop-hibiscus
American Hibiscus Society

www.eMall.com/ahs/ahs.html
American Horticultural Society

www.isomedia.com/homes/AIS
American Iris Society

pathfinder.com/vg/Gardens/AOS
American Orchid Society. The OrchidWeb site is a model of its type: well worth visiting

www.eskimo.com/~mcalpin/aps.html
American Primrose Society

www.ars.org
American Rose Society. Includes lists of rose societies all over the USA

www.i-55.com/plantweb/azaleasociety
Azalea Society of America. The Louisiana chapter of the ASA, which provides general information about the main society too

members.aol.com/bsbihgs
Botanical Society of the British Isles

www.rbge.org.uk/bss
Botanical Society of Scotland

www.demon.co.uk/mace/bcsshtml
British Cactus and Succulent Society

www.alfresco.demon.co.uk/cgs
Cottage Garden Society

www.rls.ox.ac/users/djh/ebs/ebsindex.htm
European Bamboo Society. Includes link to the bigger site of the American Bamboo Society

www.mirror.org/groups/crs
Canadian Rose Society

www.denney.demon.co.uk/cyclamen.html
The Cyclamen Society. Well-stocked new site including information on and illustrations of cyclamen species

www.gwynfryn.demon.co.uk/hebesoc/index.htm
Hebe Society

www.hdra.org.uk
HDRA. Henry Doubleday Research Association

www.med-rz.uni-sb.de/med_fak/physiol2/cammellia/home.htm#topics
International Camellia Society

www.eclipse.co.uk/jns
International Tree Foundation. New site with information about the ITF's projects and links to international sites planned for the future

www.h2olily.rain.com
International Water Lily Society

www.cragview.demon.co.uk
The Lakeland Horticultural Society

www.sarracenia.com
Carnivorous Plant Society: good links

www.linnean.org.uk
Linnean Society of London

www.tallahassee.net/~magnolia
The Magnolia Society. Home page of the American-based Magnolia Society

www.mobot.org/NARGS
North American Rock Garden Society

www.rnrs.org.uk
Royal National Rose Society. Information about the society and its Rose 2000 appeal is hosted on the Harkness rose nursery site

Ourworld.compuserve.com/homepages/marcdilasser.sbr.htm
Societe Bretonne du Rhododendron.

www.ozemail.com.au:80/~sgap
Society for Growing Australian Plants. Vibrantly coloured and useful site hosted by the Association of Societies for Growing Australian Plants

www.worldrose.org
World Federation of Rose Societies. Carries a short list of other rosy sites

Magazine Sites

www.oxalis.co.uk/index.html
British Gardening On-Line. Many useful links to British gardening firms

www.digmagazine.com
Dig magazine. On-line gardening magazine

www.aquil.demon.co.uk
Plant of the Week site of Plants magazine, edited by Dirk van der Werff. Excellent links to nurseries, especially in UK & USA

www.prairienet.org/garden-gate
Garden Gate

www.gardennet.com
GardenNet. "The Garden Center on the Net". It's American, and its good. Societies, gardens, catalogues – you name it

www.pix.za/garden
Garden South. A jumping off page for information on South African gardening

www.gardenweb.comGardenWeb
GardenWeb. Magazine-style site including information about gardens and societies; an on-line magazine; and the GardenWeb forums which gardeners use to swap and seek advice in a range of plant and topic based discussion sites

www.internetgarden.co.uk
The Internet Garden. Online gardening magazine

www.global-garden.com.au
Online Global Garden. Australian magazine site

vg.com
Virtual Garden. Useful and very substantial US site

Whilst every care has been taken to ensure that the information contained in these 'Gardening on the Internet' pages is both accurate and up-to-date, neither the editors nor the RHS accept any liability to any party for loss or damage incurred by reliance placed on the information contained in these 'Gardening on the Internet' pages or through omission or errors, howsoever caused.

Part Two

Calendar For 1999

Shows   Walks   Talks
Open Days   Plant Fairs
Demonstrations
Charity events
Plant Sales and Auctions
Lectures   Workshops

Show Venues

Ayr Flower Show
Burns House, Burns Statue Square, Ayr KA7 1UT
☎ 01292 616695
Contact Mrs J Turner, Strategic Services Department
Dates 26–28 August
Location Ayr Racecourse
Open 1 pm – 9 pm on 26th; 9.30 am – 9 pm on 27th; 9.30 am – 6 pm on 28th
Tickets Adults £6.50; Concessions £5.50; Children free
Parking and Travel On site

This continues to be a popular event (22,000 people last year) in south-west Scotland, attracting many exhibitors from both sides of the border.

BBC Gardeners' World Live
Royal Horticultural Society, PO Box 313, 80 Vincent Square, London SW1P 2PE
☎ 0171 834 4333
Dates 16–20 June
Location National Exhibition Centre, Birmingham
Open 9 am – 6 pm
Tickets Hotlines: 0121 767 4505 (Members); 0121 767 4111 (public); 0800 378985 (groups). RHS Members £11.50 (pre-booked)
Parking and Travel Parking extra

Now run by the RHS, this show has improved steadily and the horticultural part is excellent. The NEC location, though slightly lacking in atmosphere, has easy access and parking and there is a distinct buzz. Attractions include a large horticultural marquee (last year's was the longest in the world), feature gardens, and the presence every day of such personalities as Alan Titchmarsh, Nigel Colborn and Pippa Greenwood. Members' and group rate tickets must be booked in advance.

Chelsea Flower Show
Royal Horticultural Society, PO Box 313, 80 Vincent Square, London SW1P 2PE
☎ 0171 834 4333
Contact See the January edition of *The Garden*
Dates 25–28 May
Location Royal Hospital, Chelsea, London
Open 8 am – 8 pm, (but 5 pm on 28 May)
Tickets 25 & 26 May (Members only): £19 (£10 from 3.30 pm; £6 from 5.30 pm); 27 May: Members £15; Public £26 (£15 from 3.30 pm; £10 from 5.30 pm); 28 May: Members £13; Public £24
Groups No discounts for groups
Parking and Travel Battersea Park, with free shuttle bus. Public transport recommended (Sloane Square underground)

The world-famous annual flower show remains the most prestigious event in the horticultural calendar. Nurseries, societies and charities create display stands and gardens in the huge marquee, and outside in the grounds of the Royal Hospital. An exceptional range of garden furniture, machinery and other products is displayed outside, and items can be bought or ordered. Press attention usually centres on the display gardens: months of work goes into these beautifully staged displays which only last a week. There is a large flower-arranging marquee and a pavilion devoted to garden designers. Numbers are restricted, but even so the show is often very crowded. RHS Members have two days set aside exclusively for them, and can buy tickets at preferential rates: see the January copy of *The Garden*. Early morning and late evening are the best times to visit; on the first three days cheaper, timed tickets are available in the afternoon and evening. There is a hotline for members of the public to buy tickets: 0171 344 4343.

The Great Garden & Countryside Festival
Holker Hall, Cark in Cartmel, Grange over Sands LA11 7PL
☎ 01539 558838
Contact Show director
Dates 4 to 6 June
Location Holker Hall, Cumbria: west of Grange over Sands on B5277 and B5278.
Open 10 am – 6 pm (5.30 pm on last day)
Tickets Adults £7; OAPs £5.50; Children £3. Less if you pre-book
Parking and Travel Free parking on site
Facilities for the Disabled Disabled car & loos

The show covers horticulture, the countryside and the environment. In addition to displays by specialist nurseries, there are modern as well as traditional crafts, advice centres, floral art demonstrations and product displays.

Grow '99
Protech Promotions, Grenfell House, Grenfell Avenue, Hornchurch RM12 4DN
☎ 01708 455907
Dates 17 & 18 April
Location Sandown Exhibition Centre, Esher
Open 9 am – 6 pm (5 pm on second day)
Tickets Adults £5; OAPs £4
Parking and Travel On site

A new show devoted mainly to products, aimed at the general gardening public. In addition there

SHOW VENUES

are displays by nurseries, seminars and demonstrations.

HAMPTON COURT PALACE FLOWER SHOW
Royal Horticultural Society,
PO Box 313, 80 Vincent Square,
London SW1P 2PE
☎ 0171 834 4333
Contact Shows Department
Dates 8–11 July; Preview days 6 & 7 July
Location Hampton Court Palace, East Molesey, Surrey
Open 10 am – 7.30 pm (5.30 pm on last day)
Tickets 6th, £22 Members only; 7th, £17 (after 3 pm £11) Members only; 8th – 11th, Members £13 (after 3 pm £8), Public £18 (after 3 pm £10)
Groups Reduced rates for affiliated societies, senior citizens and groups
Parking and Travel £8 all day; £5 after 3 pm
Facilities for the Disabled One escort admitted free

This is now the biggest gardening show of its kind in the world. Unlike Chelsea the exhibitors can sell direct from their stands on all days. The show is also recommended for those who now find Chelsea too crowded. The Royal National Rose Society's British Rose Festival is held at the show. A Gala Evening is held on 6th July with music and fireworks.

HARROGATE GREAT AUTUMN FLOWER SHOW
North of England Horticultural Society, 4a South Park Road, Harrogate HG1 5QU
☎ 01423 561049
Contact Show organiser
Dates 17–19 September
Location Great Yorkshire Showground, Hookstone Oval, Harrogate
Open (Probably) 9.30 am – 6 pm (5.30 pm on last day)
Tickets £6
Parking and Travel Free on-site parking

As well as displays from nurseries and other trade stands, this show is particularly recommended for the society competitions (including dahlias and chrysanthemums), and for the Onion Weigh-in which will probably take place at 12 noon on the first day. There is a flower-arrangement section too.

HARROGATE SPRING FLOWER SHOW
North of England Horticultural Society, 4a South Park Road, Harrogate HG1 5QU
☎ 01423 561049
Contact Show secretary
Dates 22–25 April
Location Great Yorkshire Showground, Harrogate
Open 9.30 am – 5.30 pm (4.30 pm on last day)
Tickets Day tickets: 22nd, £10; 23rd & 24th, £9; 26th, £8.
Groups Discounts for party bookings
Parking and Travel Free parking

Run by the North of England Horticultural Society, the Spring Show has trade stands from nurseries as well as the Alpine Garden Society's North of England Show. A shuttle bus service runs from Harrogate to the Showground every 20 minutes.

JOURNÉES DES PLANTES DE COURSON
Domaine de Courson, 91680 Courson Monteloup
☎ 00 33 164 58 90 12
Dates 14–16 May; 15–17 October
Location 20 miles south of Paris
Parking and Travel On site

Prestigious French show with a unique atmosphere, held twice yearly in a country-house setting near Paris and once described as a cross between a French Chelsea Flower Show and an English village fête. The show has strong British connections, including a number of regular exhibitors.

MALVERN AUTUMN SHOW
Three Counties Agricultural Society, The Showground, Malvern WR13 6NW
☎ 01684 584900
Dates 25 & 26 September

Location Three Counties Showground, Malvern
Open 9 am – 6 pm (5 pm on last day)
Tickets RHS and Three Counties Agricultural Society Members: £6.50 (£5.50 in advance); Public: £7.50 (£6.50 in advance); Family ticket (2 + 3): £15 (£13 in advance)
Groups £5.50 for groups of 10 or more
Parking and Travel Free parking

Charming newish horticultural show which we highly recommend: last year saw the largest-ever exhibit of potatoes – over 400 different ones. Nursery displays and an RHS show. Includes identification clinics for fruit and fungi and rural crafts displays.

MALVERN SPRING GARDENING SHOW
Three Counties Agricultural Society, The Showground, Malvern WR13 6NW
☎ 01684 584900
Contact Show secretary
Dates 7–9 May
Location Three Counties Showground, Malvern
Open 9 am – 6 pm (5 pm on last day)
Tickets £11 (£9 if booked in advance); £8 for RHS and Three Counties Agricultural Society Members (in advance)
Groups £8.50 Affiliated Society Groups of 10 or more
Parking and Travel Free car parking

The Malvern Spring Gardening Show is organised by the Three Counties Agricultural Society and the Royal Horticultural Society together. The dramatic setting and rural location give this show its own unique character. The exhibitors include a wide range of nurseries, both national and local, and numerous products and sundries stands. The RHS advisory team is present. There is also a large floral art section.

RHS FLOWER SHOW AT TATTON PARK
Royal Horticultural Society,
PO Box 313, 80 Vincent Square,
London SW1P 2PE

☎ 0171 834 4333
Dates 22–25 July
Location Tatton Park, nr Knutsford, Cheshire
Open 22nd, 11 am – 6pm; 23rd and 24th, 10am – 6pm; 25th, 10am – 5pm
Tickets £14 (Members £10, Public £12 in advance: ☎ 0870 607 7447)
Groups £11 for groups of 10 or more booked in advance: ☎ 0171 416 6076)
Parking and Travel Cars £3, coaches free

A new show for 1999 staged by the RHS. With an emphasis on the history and horticultural heritage of the North West, it features floral marquees, show gardens, water gardens, specialist plant displays, the RHS advisory desk and practical demonstrations. Plant and gardening products will be on sale.

SCOTLAND'S NATIONAL GARDENING SHOW

Royal Horticultural Society, PO Box 313, 80 Vincent Square, London SW1P 2PE
☎ 0171 630 7422
Dates 4–6 June
Location Strathclyde Country Park
Open 4th, 11 am – 7 pm; 5th, 10 am – 6 pm; 6th, 10 am – 5 pm
Tickets £12 (Members £7, Public £10 in advance: Phone: 0990 900 123)
Groups £9 for groups of 10 or more. Phone: 0171 413 3306
Parking and Travel Free

The third year of this excellent show, staged by the RHS in Strathclyde Country Park, which is fast establishing itself as a major event in Scotland. As well as displays from nurseries from all over Great Britain, the show includes practical demonstrations.

SHREWSBURY FLOWER SHOW

Quarry Lodge, Shrewsbury SY1 1RN
☎ 01743 364051
Contact Show secretary
Dates 13 to 14 August
Location The Quarry, Shrewsbury
Open 13th, 10.30 am – 10 pm; 14th, 10 am – 10 pm
Tickets £8.50 (probably)
Groups Sale or return terms available
Parking and Travel Parking extra
Facilities for the Disabled Disabled loos. Disabled parking by prior arrangement

A large, traditional flower show. The show closes with a fireworks display on both nights.

SOUTHPORT FLOWER SHOW

42 Hoghton Street, Southport PR9 0PQ
☎ 01704 547147
Contact Show administrator
Dates 19–21 August
Location Victoria Park, Southport
Open 19th, 9 am – 7 pm; 20th, 9 am – 10 pm; 21st, 9 am – 5 pm
Tickets £8 (adult, pre-booked)
Parking and Travel Not on site

This prestigious annual flower show, which hopes to draw 100,000 visitors, has reverted to three days again. Nice northern flavour with lots of local nurseries that do not attend the numerous southern shows and some southerners who come to be beside the sea.

SPRING PLANT FAIR DAY

The National Trust, Spring Plant Fairs, Heywood House, Westbury BA13 4NA
☎ 01373 8268261
Dates 16 May
Location At around 50 National Trust properties nationwide
Open Contact individual properties for details

This new initiative was such a success in 1997 and 1998 that the National Trust has decided to run a repeat performance this year. Around 50 properties will host fund-raising plant fairs on the same day. The properties include: Anglesey Abbey; Batemans; Beningbrough Hall; Berrington Hall; Blickling Hall; Canons Ashby; Castle Drogo; Castle Ward; Charlecote; Claremont Landscape Garden; Cliveden; Clumber Park; Dunster Castle; Dyrham Park; Erddig; Florence Court; Greys Court; Ham House; Hanbury Hall; Hatchlands Park; Hinton Ampner Garden; Hughenden Manor; Kingston Lacy; Knightshayes; Knole; Nunnington Hall; Overbecks; Oxburgh Hall; Packwood House; Petworth House; Plas Newydd; Sizergh Castle; Sudbury Hall; The Vyne; Wallington Hall; Wimpole Hall. Some of these sales feature only specialist nurseries, but most will rely in large measure upon volunteers to supply plants and help man the stalls. Last year they raised over £100,000 for the Trust. For further information – and offers of help – please ring 0181 315 1111.

WISLEY FLOWER SHOW

RHS Garden Wisley, Woking GU23 6QB
☎ 01483 224234
Dates 24–26 August
Location RHS Garden Wisley
Open 10 am – 5.30 pm (5 pm on last day)
Tickets Normal garden admission rates (£5); RHS Members free
Parking and Travel Free parking

The setting in the garden at Wisley is a major attraction of this smallish show. The nurseries attending will be selling plants.

CALENDAR

THE CALENDAR, with two pages a week for most of the year, lists hundreds of gardening events up and down the country, and some international happenings too. They include lectures and talks, shows, workshops and demonstrations, garden walks, and plant sales. In order to cram in as much as possible, the details are deliberately concise. Most entries end with a contact number. For the rest, further information can frequently be found in other sections of the book – for example by looking up a society or a garden. Turn to the index at the back first. A few abbreviations are used: these are identified in the Introduction. A very substantial proportion of the events listed in this section relates to events organised by the RHS as part of its commitment to making itself accessible in every part of the UK. RHS members receive notice of all such events within their regions: we carry a near-complete list of RHS events throughout the country.

Many events, especially those organised by societies or the National Trust, must be booked in advance: if in doubt, check. Although we take care to be as accurate as possible, our information has to be obtained well in advance. Arrangements can change at short notice (and indeed a number of alterations had to be made while we were at the proof stage of this book), so do check with the organisers or in the press nearer the time, especially if you intend to travel any distance. Comprehensive and up-to-date information about forthcoming events is always printed in *The Garden*.

The attitude of societies towards admitting non-members to their lectures and events can vary considerably. In general, though, clubs and societies exist for their members so, if you find that you are interested in their events, you really should think about becoming a member. National societies who have local groups should be able to put you in touch with one near you. Most societies also hold open shows and plant sales (the AGS and NCCPG among them): the general public is invariably more than welcome at these events.

FRI 1

New Year's Day Walk. 11 am. Hillier Arboretum, Hants. ☎ 01794 368787.
Treasure Trail. Leeds Castle, Kent. ☎ 01622 765400.

NOTES

SAT 2

Orchid Auction. 2 pm. Orchid Society of Great Britain. Napier Hall, Hide Place, London. ☎ 01483 421423.

SUN 3

On This Day
Gales in the Midlands and Northern England on 3 January 1976 were responsible for the deaths of 28 people.

JANUARY

NOTES

MON 4
Lecture. 7 pm. Rosecarpe. 'The gardens of Cragside' by Andrew Sawyer. Civic Centre, Gateshead. ☎ 0191 252 7052.

'I WENT BY THE FIELD OF THE SLOTHFUL, AND BY THE VINEYARD OF THE MAN VOID OF UNDERSTANDING; AND LO, IT WAS ALL GROWN OVER BY THORNS, AND NETTLES COVERED THE FACE THEREOF, AND THE STONE WALL THEREOF WAS BROKEN DOWN. THEN I SAW, AND CONSIDERED IT WELL; I LOOKED UPON IT AND RECEIVED INSTRUCTION'.
PROVERBS, CH. 24, VV. 30-32.

TUE 5
Lecture. 7 pm. London Historic Parks & Gardens Trust at the Linnean Society. 'Women Career Gardeners from Jane Loudon to Sylvia Crowe' by Jane Brown. £5. ☎ 0171 839 3969.
Lecture. 7.30 pm. East Yorks AGS. Norwood High School, Beverley. 'Bulbs' by Ron Nurse. ☎ 01723 582684.

WED 6
Workshop. 10 am – 4 pm. RHS Garden Wisley, Surrey. 'Working with living willow' with Clare Wilks. ☎ 01483 224234.
Lecture. 1.30 pm. Reaseheath College, Cheshire. 'Winter interest in the garden' by Stephen Davies. RHS Members £6.95. Non-Members £7.95. ☎ 01270 625131.

THU 7
Lecture. 7.30 pm. Dorset AGS. Lytchett Matravers Village Hall. 'Irises for alpine gardeners' by Peter Maynard.

On This Day
A tornado hit Selsey in West Sussex on 7 January 1998.

JANUARY

NOTES

FRI 8

Lecture. 7.30 pm. Chilterns AGS. Great Kingshill Village Hall. 'The Burren' by Clive Daws & Stephen Waters.
☎ 01628 486709.

SAT 9

Lecture. 2.30 pm. South Lancashire AGS. Lord Street, Southport. 'The Chilean Flora' by Francis Ferns. ☎ 01744 609045.

SUN 10

Garden Walk. RHS Garden Wisley, Surrey. 'Winter colour in the garden' with Jim Gardiner. RHS Members £5. Non-Members £10. ☎ 01483 224234.
Lecture. 2 pm. 'Travels in South-East Tibet' by Dr Hugh McAllister. Friends of Ness Gardens, Cheshire. Visitor Centre, Ness. Free to RHS Members.
Workshop. Westonbirt Arboretum, Glos. 'An Introduction to conifer identification'. £10. ☎ 01666 880220.

On This Day
The daytime temperature at Prestatyn on 10 January 1998 reached a record 17.3°C.

January

NOTES

'THE MOST IMPORTANT PART OF THE GARDENER'S BODY IS NOT THE MUSCLES OR EVEN THE BRAIN: IT IS THE EYES WHICH MAKE OR BREAK A GARDENER'.
SIR PETER SMITHERS, *ADVENTURES OF A GARDENER*, 1995.

MON 11
Lecture. 7 pm. Askham Bryan College, York. 'Propagating plants from your garden' by Chris Rose. RHS Members £4. Non-Members £5. ☎ 01904 772277.
Lecture. 7 pm. Pencoed College, Bridgend. Mid Glamorgan. 'Vegetable growing for the amateur gardener' by Ivor Mace. RHS Members £5. Non-Members £6.50. ☎ 01656 860202.

TUE 12
Demonstration. 2 pm. Pershore & Hindlip College, Worcester. 'Your garden in January' by Bob Hares. RHS Members £5. Non-Members £10. ☎ 01386 554609.

WED 13
Lecture. 1.30 pm. Houghall College, Durham. 'Pruning your fruit trees for best results.' RHS Members £4. Non-Members £5. ☎ 0191 386 1351.
Lecture. 1.30 pm. Welsh College of Horticulture, Northop, Flintshire. 'Plant collecting' by Bleddyn Wynn Jones. RHS Members £8. Non-Members £10. ☎ 01352 841000.
Demonstration. 2 pm. Hadlow College, Tonbridge, Kent. 'Your garden in January' by Nick Egan. RHS Members £9.50. Non-Members £11. ☎ 01732 850551.
Lecture. 2 pm. Writtle College, Chelmsford, Essex. 'Garden conifers' by Cath Hayward. RHS Members £8. Non-Members £10. ☎ 01245 424200.
Demonstration. RHS Garden Rosemoor, Devon. 'Garden supports & hurdles' by Peter Earl. RHS Members £5. Non-Members £10. ☎ 01805 624067.
RHS Regional Lecture. 7.30 pm. Scottish Agricultural College, Auchincruive, Ayr. ☎ 01292 525393.
Lecture. Rose Society of Northern Ireland. 7.30 pm. 'Herbs & Healing' by Sally Taylor. Malone House, Barnet Demesne.
AGM. Royal Caledonian Horticultural Society. 7.30 pm. Lecture Hall, RBG Edinburgh.
Talk-In. 8 pm. National Pot Leek Society. Town End Farm Social Club, Sunderland. ☎ 0191 549 4274.

THU 14
Workshop. 10 am – 4 pm. RHS Garden Wisley, Surrey. 'Hurdle Making' with Carl Sadler. ☎ 01483 224234.
Demonstration. 2 pm. Pershore & Hindlip College, Worcester. 'Developing garden structure through trees & shrubs' by Frank Hardy. RHS Members £5. Non-Members £10. ☎ 01386 554609.
Lecture. 3 pm. Botanical Society of Scotland. 'Scotland's Rich Moss Flora' by David Long. RBG Lecture Theatre, Edinburgh. Admission free. ☎ 0131 552 7171.
Lecture. 8 pm. Garden Quadrangle Auditorium, St John's College, Oxford. 'Plants for all Seasons'. Dr James Compton. £7.50. ☎ 01865 276920.

JANUARY

FRI 15

Lecture. 7.45 pm. East Kent AGS. Godmersham Village Hall. 'The flowers of the Atacama' by Peter Abery. ☎ 01227 732348.

SAT 16

Orchids for All. RHS Garden Wisley, Surrey. Until 24 January.
Study Day. 10 am – 4 pm. Oxford Botanic Garden. '20th-century gardens & garden design'. Lecturers include Penelope Hobhouse & Richard Bisgrove. £30. ☎ 01865 276920.
Demonstration. 10 am. Pershore & Hindlip College, Worcester. 'Your garden in January' by Bob Hares. RHS Members £5. Non-Members £10. ☎ 01386 554609.
Lecture. 2 pm. Otley College, Ipswich, Suffolk. 'Plants of winter interest in your garden' by Christine Sheehan. RHS Members £5. Non-Members £6. ☎ 01473 785543.

SUN 17

Lecture. 2 pm. 'John Bartram's legacy in 18th-century botanical art' by Dr J Edmondson. Friends of Ness Gardens, Cheshire. Visitor Centre, Ness. Free to RHS Members.

NOTES

'*KITCHEN GARDEN:* DUNG SHOULD BE WHEELED IN FROSTY WEATHER WHEN OTHER WORK CANNOT BE DONE. *GREENHOUSE:* WINDOWS IN FROSTY WEATHER KEEP VERY CLOSE, AND PASTE STRIPS OF PAPER WHERE THE WIND BLOWS IN, FOR THAT INTRODUCES THE FROST.' RICHARD WESTON ESQ., *THE GARDENER'S POCKET CALENDAR,* 1783

JANUARY

NOTES

MON
18

TUE
19

RHS Flower Show. 2 days 19–20 Jan. 11 am – 7 pm. (10 am – 5 pm 2nd day.) RHS New Hall, Westminster. Ornamental Plant Competition. Botanical Paintings. 2 days 19–20 January.
RHS London Lecture. 2.15 pm. RHS Halls, Westminster. 'John Lindley's legacy 100 years on' by Dr Brent Elliott & Philip Cribb.
Lecture. 2 pm. Pershore & Hindlip College, Worcester. 'Gardens of China' by Duncan Coombs. RHS Members £5. Non-Members £10. ☎ 01386 554609.
Lecture. Royal Caledonian Horticultural Society. 'The Work of the RBG in China' by David Patterson. 7.30 pm. Lecture Hall, RBG Edinburgh. ☎ 0131 331 1011.

WED
20

Lecture. 2 pm. Cannington College, Somerset. 'Garden design: producing a plan' by John Addison. RHS Members £7.95. Non-Members £8.95. ☎ 01278 655000.
Lecture. 2 pm. Hadlow College, Tonbridge, Kent. 'Fertilisers for the garden' by David Carey. RHS Members £9.50. Non-Members £11. ☎ 01732 850551.
Lecture. 7.30 pm in the Library, Wentworth Castle (Northern College). 'Camellias around the world' by Jenny Trehane.
Lecture. RHS Garden Rosemoor, Devon. 'Trebah Garden Trust' by Major Tony Hibbert. ☎ 01805 624067.

THU
21

RHS Regional Lecture. Bristol. 'The world of poppies' by Chris Grey Wilson. ☎ 0171 821 3049.
Lecture. 1 pm. Welsh College of Horticulture, Northop, Flintshire. 'Creating garden styles' by Julia White. RHS Members £8. Non-Members £10. ☎ 01352 841000.
Lecture. 2 pm. Pershore & Hindlip College, Worcester. 'The wonder of witch-hazels' by Pat Edwards. RHS Members £5. Non-Members £10. ☎ 01386 554609.

JANUARY   49

FRI
22

NOTES

'HAD I NO GARDEN TO DIG IN I SHOULD BE IN DESPAIR WITH LACK OF OCCUPATION'. *THE DIARIES OF EVELYN WAUGH*, SUNDAY 17 SEPTEMBER 1939.

SAT
23

Study Day. 10 am – 5 pm. Rewley House, Wellington Square, Oxford. 'Botanical illustration from herbarium specimens'. £35. ☎ 01865 276920.
Lecture. 9.30 am. Welsh College of Horticulture, Northop, Flintshire. 'Creating garden styles' by Julia White. RHS Members £8. Non-Members £10. ☎ 01352 841000.
Orchid Weekend. Plant centre, RHS Garden Wisley, Surrey. 2 days 23–24 January.

SUN
24

Garden Open. Swallow Hayes, Shropshire. 11 am – 4 pm.
Lecture. 2 pm. 'Wonders of the American National Parks' by Ray Groome. Friends of Ness Gardens, Cheshire. Visitor Centre, Ness. Free to RHS Members.
Garden Walk. 2 pm. Hillier Arboretum, Hants. Witch-hazels. ☎ 01794 368787.

JANUARY

NOTES

MON 25
Lecture. 10.30 am. 'Plants & people & the Kew Collections' by Hew Prendergast. Friends of Wakehurst Place, West Sussex. £2. ☎ 01444 894035.
Lecture. 7 pm. Pencoed College, Bridgend. Mid Glamorgan. 'Garden plants for spring & summer colour' by Gareth Davies. RHS Members £5. Non-Members £6.50. ☎ 01656 860202.

TUE 26
Lecture. 2 pm. Pershore & Hindlip College, Worcester. 'Tough plants for tough places' by Michael Jefferson-Brown. RHS Members £5. Non-Members £10. ☎ 01386 554609.
Lecture. 7.30 pm. South Humberside AGS. New Waltham Village Hall. 'Saxifrages' by Adrian Young. ☎ 01652 678422.

WED 27
Winter Bird Walk. 10 am. Friends of Wakehurst Place, West Sussex. £2. ☎ 01444 894035.
Lecture. 2 pm. Cannington College, Somerset. 'Garden design: landscape principles' by John Addison. RHS Members £7.95. Non-Members £8.95. ☎ 01278 655000.
Workshop. 10 am – 4 pm. RHS Garden Wisley, Surrey. 'Working with living willow' with Clare Wilks. ☎ 01483 224234.
Lecture. 2 pm. Writtle College, Chelmsford, Essex. 'An introduction to plant science' by Anya Perera. RHS Members £8. Non-Members £10. ☎ 01245 424200.
Lecture. 7 pm. Hadlow College, Tonbridge, Kent. 'Wonderful witch-hazels' by Chris Lane. RHS Members £9.50. Non-Members £11. ☎ 01732 850551.

THU 28
Lecture. 2 pm. Pershore & Hindlip College, Worcester. 'A touch of history in your garden' by Lynn Stevens. RHS Members £5. Non-Members £10. ☎ 01386 554609.
Lecture. 8 pm. Garden Quadrangle Auditorium, St John's College, Oxford. 'The cutting garden'. Sarah Raven. £7.50. ☎ 01865 276920.

January

FRI 29

Demonstration. RHS Garden Rosemoor, Devon. 'Winter Pruning'. RHS Members £5. Non-Members £10. ☎ 01805 624067.

SAT 30

Lecture. 9.30 am. Welsh College of Horticulture, Northop, Flintshire. 'Fruit Pruning' by Richard Lewis. RHS Members £8. Non-Members £10. ☎ 01352 841000.

SUN 31

Workshop. 10 am – 5 pm. RHS Garden Wisley, Surrey. Black & white photography. ☎ 01483 224234.
Garden Walk. RHS Garden Wisley, Surrey. 'The changing face of Wisley' with John Battye. RHS Members £5. Non-Members £10. ☎ 01483 224234.
Lecture. 2 pm. 'Planting for walls & pergolas' by Ken Hulme. Friends of Ness Gardens, Cheshire. Visitor Centre, Ness. Free to RHS Members.
Garden Walk. 10 am. Friends of Oxford Botanic Garden. £2. ☎ 01865 276920.

NOTES

'A FEW YEARS AGO IT WAS CONSIDERED BAD TASTE TO ADMIRE A FUCHSIA; BUT I ALWAYS ADMIRED THEM AS VERY BRIGHT OBJECTS IN THE AUTUMN GARDEN, AND I AM TOLD THAT THEY ARE AGAIN BECOMING FASHIONABLE'. CANON HENRY ELLACOMBE, *IN A GLOUCESTERSHIRE GARDEN*, 1895.

FEBRUARY

NOTES

MON 1
Lecture. RHS Garden Wisley, Surrey. 'Encouraging wildlife in your garden' with Andrew Halstead. ☎ 01483 224234.
Lecture. 7 pm. Askham Bryan College, York. 'Fruit tree pruning' by Bob Scott. RHS Members £4. Non-Members £5.
☎ 01904 772277.
Lecture. 7.30 pm. Avon Wildlife Trust. 'The Somerset Levels' by Robin Williams. The Old Grammar School, Chipping Sodbury.
☎ 0117 926 8018.

TUE 2
Demonstration. 2 pm. Pershore & Hindlip College, Worcester. 'Your garden in February' by Bob Hares. RHS Members £5. Non-Members £10. ☎ 01386 554609.

On This Day
Candlemas Day. `If Candlemas day be cold and bright/ Winter will have another fight; If Candlemas day be cloudy with rain/ Winter is gone and comes not again'.

WED 3
Lecture. 1.30 pm. Myerscough College, Preston, Lancs. 'Bench-grafting wisteria' by Jeff Hodson. RHS Members £6. Non-Members £7.50. ☎ 01995 640611.
Lecture. 2 pm. Writtle College, Chelmsford, Essex. 'Plants of the Himalayas' by Lin Mason. RHS Members £8. Non-Members £10. ☎ 01245 424200.
Lecture. 2 pm. Cannington College, Somerset. 'Pruning Wall Shrubs & Climbers' by Peter Elliman. RHS Members £7.95. Non-Members £8.95. ☎ 01278 655000.
Demonstration. 2 pm. Hadlow College, Tonbridge, Kent. 'Your garden in February' by Nick Egan. RHS Members £9.50. Non-Members £11. ☎ 01732 850551.
Garden Walk. RHS Garden Wisley, Surrey. 'The changing face of Wisley' with John Battye. RHS Members £5. Non-Members £10. ☎ 01483 224234.
Lecture. 7 pm. Reaseheath College, Cheshire. 'Planting design for structure & style' by Alison Evans. RHS Members £6.95. Non-Members £7.95. ☎ 01270 625131.

THU 4
Flower Show. Springfields '99. Spalding, Lincs. 11 am – 9 pm. 4 days 4–7 Feb. £2.50. ☎ 01775 724843.
Workshop. 10 am – 4 pm. RHS Garden Wisley, Surrey. 'Making trugs' with Craftsmen from the Trug Store. ☎ 01483 224234.
Workshop. 2 pm. Pershore & Hindlip College, Worcester. 'The magic of root-cuttings' by Bob Hares. RHS Members £5. Non-Members £10. ☎ 01386 554609.
Talk-In. 8 pm. National Pot Leek Society. Iris Allotments Association, Heaton. ☎ 0191 549 4274.
Day Course. 10 am – 4 pm. Northern Horticultural Society, Harlow Carr. 'The Garden in Winter' by Rita Lait. NHS Members £19. Non-Members £22. ☎ 01423 565418.

FEBRUARY 53

FRI 5

Lecture. 8 pm. Kent Medway AGS. Bluebell Hill Village Hall. 'The Grossglockner in August' by T Colmer. ☎ 01622 746941.

SAT 6

Potato Day. A Celebration of the Humble Spud. Ryton Organic Gardens, Coventry. 2 days. ☎ 01203 303517.
Workshop. 10 am. Pershore & Hindlip College, Worcester. 'Introduction to fruit tree pruning' by John Edgeley. ☎ 01386 554609.
Garden Open. Brandy House Mount, Hants. 11 am – 4 pm.
Lecture. 2 pm. Orchid Society of Great Britain. 'The 15th World Orchid Congress' by Dick Payne. Napier Hall, Hide Place, London. ☎ 01483 421423.

SUN 7

Garden Open for snowdrops. Chelsea Physic Garden, London. 11 am – 3 pm.
Garden Walk. 2 pm. Hillier Arboretum, Hants. Witch-hazels. ☎ 01794 368787.
Garden Open. Brandy House Mount, Hants. 11 am – 4 pm.
Potato Day. Ryton Organic Gardens, Coventry. Last day.
Lecture. 2 pm. 'Woodland conservation & restoration' by Dr M Le Duc. Friends of Ness Gardens, Cheshire. Visitor Centre, Ness. Free to RHS Members.
Winter Lecture. Garden History Society. 6 pm. Scientific Societies Lecture Theatre, London. 'Tsarskoye Selo' by Dimitri Shvidkovsky. £7. ☎ 0171 608 2409.

NOTES

- February. Have you bought your tickets for the Chelsea Flower Show yet? Tel: 0171 344 4343.

February

NOTES

'THE ENGLISH CLIMATE IS SUPERB FOR PLANTS, BUT TERRIBLE FOR HUMAN BEINGS. NEVERTHELESS IT IS BECAUSE OF THEIR HABITS, RATHER THAN THEIR PLANTS, THAT ENGLISH PEOPLE SO OFTEN DIE OF CHILLS. THEIR FAVOURITE RECREATION IS WALKING ON WET GRASS'. PRINCE HERMANN PÜCKLER-MUSKAU, SEPTEMBER 1827.

MON 8

Workshop. 10 am – 4 pm. RHS Garden Wisley, Surrey. 2 days 8–9 Feb. 'Garden sculpture'. ☎ 01483 224234.
Garden Open. Brandy House Mount, Hants. 11 am – 4 pm.
Lecture. 7 pm. Pencoed College, Bridgend. Mid Glamorgan. 'The evolution of modern hybrid fuchsias' by Arthur Tickner. RHS Members £5. Non-Members £6.50. ☎ 01656 860202.

TUE 9

Lecture. 1 pm. Welsh College of Horticulture, Northop, Flintshire. 'Early vegetable crops' by Anne Lewis. RHS Members £8. Non-Members £10. ☎ 01352 841000.
Demonstration. 2 pm. Pershore & Hindlip College, Worcester. 'Success with seeds in spring' by Bob Hares. RHS Members £5. Non-Members £10. ☎ 01386 554609.
Lecture. 7 pm. London Historic Parks & Gardens Trust at the Linnean Society. 'Loudon's London' by Dr Brent Elliott. £5. ☎ 0171 839 3969.

WED 10

Lecture. 1.30 pm. Houghall College, Durham. 'Making more plants: propagation techniques.' RHS Members £4. Non-Members £5. ☎ 0191 386 1351.
Lecture. 2 pm. Scottish Agricultural College, Auchincruive, Ayr. 'Success with sowing seeds' by Michael Hitchon. RHS Members £4.95. Non-Members £5.95. ☎ 01292 525393.
Lecture. 2 pm. Writtle College, Chelmsford, Essex. 'Gardens of the world' by Andy Boorman. RHS Members £8. Non-Members £10. ☎ 01245 424200.
Lecture. 2 pm. Hadlow College, Tonbridge, Kent. 'Propagating plants by grafting' by Phil Thursby. RHS Members £9.50. Non-Members £11. ☎ 01732 850551.
Lecture. 2 pm. Cannington College, Somerset. 'Bench grafting' by John Bates. RHS Members £7.95. Non-Members £8.95. ☎ 01278 655000.
Winter Lecture. Garden History Society. 6 pm. Scientific Societies Lecture Theatre, London. 'Versailles' by Dr Christopher Thacker. £7. ☎ 0171 608 2409.
Lecture. Rose Society of Northern Ireland. 7.30 pm. 'Wild flowers of the countryside' by John Wilde. Malone House, Barnet Demesne.

February

THU 11

6th International Show. World Association of Flower Arrangers. Durban, South Africa. 4 days 11–14 Feb. ☎ 01603 672043.
RHS Regional Lecture. 7.30 pm. Writtle College, Chelmsford, Essex. 'Courageous planting' by Stephen Anderton. ☎ 0171 821 3049.
Lecture. 2 pm. Pershore & Hindlip College, Worcester. 'A potager for your garden' by David Everitt. RHS Members £5. Non-Members £10. ☎ 01386 554609.
Lecture. 3 pm. Botanical Society of Scotland. 'A fungal foray' by Stephan Helfer. RBG Lecture Theatre, Edinburgh. Admission free. ☎ 0131 552 7171.

On This Day
On 11 February 1895, a minimum temperature of -27°C, the lowest ever known in the United Kingdom, was recorded at Braemar in Aberdeenshire. It was equalled by a similar minimum temperature, also at Braemar, on 10 January 1982.

FRI 12

Lecture. 7.30 pm. Conway Valley Wildlife Trust. 'Orchids of Britain & Northern Europe' by Geoff Battershall. St David's Church Hall, Penrhyn Bay. ☎ 01492 581420.

SAT 13

Lecture. 9.30 am. Welsh College of Horticulture, Northop, Flintshire. 'Early vegetable crops' by Anne Lewis. RHS Members £8. Non-Members £10. ☎ 01352 841000.
Demonstration. 10 am. Pershore & Hindlip College, Worcester. 'Your garden in February' by Bob Hares. RHS Members £5. Non-Members £10. ☎ 01386 554609.
AGS Show. 10 am – 4 pm. Non-competitive display. Caerleon, Gwent. ☎ 01267 275205.
Summer Colour Weekend. Seeds & bulbs. Plant centre, RHS Garden Wisley, Surrey. 2 days 13–14 Feb.

SUN 14

Day Course. 10 am – 4 pm. Northern Horticultural Society, Harlow Carr. 'Raising plants from seed' by Nigel Hutchinson. NHS Members £18. Non-Members £21. ☎ 01423 565418.
Garden Open for snowdrops. Chelsea Physic Garden, London. 11 am – 3 pm.
Workshop. 10 am – 5 pm. RHS Garden Wisley, Surrey. Beginners' digital photography. ☎ 01483 224234.
Kew Orchid Festival 1999 open daily at Royal Botanic Gardens, Kew, for 6 weeks. ☎ 0181 332 5622.
Lecture. 2 pm. 'Yunnan in springtime' by P L Cunnington. Friends of Ness Gardens, Cheshire. Visitor Centre, Ness. Free to RHS Members.

NOTES

'A GARDEN CONSTITUTES AN UNWRITTEN AUTOBIOGRAPHY: SHOW ME YOUR GARDEN, AND I WILL TELL YOU WHAT YOU ARE LIKE'. ALFRED AUSTIN, *THE GARDEN THAT I LOVE*, 1894

FEBRUARY

NOTES

'I THINK THAT FEBRUARY IS ALMOST THE MOST INTERESTING MONTH OF THE YEAR TO THE GARDENER: IN NO OTHER MONTH ARE THERE SO MANY CHANGES'. CANON HENRY ELLACOMBE, *IN A GLOUCESTERSHIRE GARDEN*, 1895.

MON 15

Botanical Art Exhibition. RHS Garden Wisley, Surrey. Until 19 February. ☎ 01483 224234.

TUE 16

RHS Flower Show. 11 am – 7 pm. (10 am – 5 pm 2nd day.) RHS New Hall, Westminster. Ornamental Plant Competition. Botanical Paintings. 2 days 16–17 Feb.
RHS London Lecture. 2.15 pm. RHS Halls, Westminster. 'The cutting garden' by Sarah Raven.
Garden Study Day. West Dean, West Sussex. 'Towards an organic garden' by Joe Reardon-Smith. £45. ☎ 01243 811205.
Lecture. 2 pm. Pershore & Hindlip College, Worcester. 'What is natural gardening?' by Noël Kingsbury. RHS Members £5. Non-Members £10. ☎ 01386 554609.
Lecture. 7.30 pm. Royal Caledonian Horticultural Society. 'Plants for the rock & peat garden' by Ron McBeath. Lecture Hall, RBG Edinburgh. ☎ 0131 331 1011.
Workshop. Silk painting. RHS Garden Wisley, Surrey. 2 days 16–17 Feb. ☎ 01483 224234.

WED 17

Lecture & Walk. RHS Garden Rosemoor, Devon. 'The winter garden' by Helen Johnson & others. ☎ 01805 624067.
Lecture. 2 pm. Cannington College, Somerset. 'Propagating Herbaceous Plants & Alpines' by Geoff Hester. RHS Members £7.95. Non-Members £8.95. ☎ 01278 655000.
Workshop. 10 am – 4 pm. 'RHS Garden Wisley, Surrey. Working with living willow' with Clare Wilks. ☎ 01483 224234.
Lecture. 2 pm. Hadlow College, Tonbridge, Kent. 'Trees & shrubs with ornamental bark' by Chris Lane. RHS Members £9.50. Non-Members £11. ☎ 01732 850551.
Winter Lecture. Garden History Society. 6 pm. Scientific Societies Lecture Theatre, London. 'Stowe' by George Clark. £7. ☎ 0171 608 2409.
Lecture. 6.30 pm. Reaseheath College, Cheshire. 'Bedding plants from seed' by Frank Forrest. RHS Members £6.95. Non-Members £7.95. ☎ 01270 625131.

THU 18

Lecture. 2 pm. Pershore & Hindlip College, Worcester. 'Ferns for your garden' by Martin Rickard. RHS Members £5. Non-Members £10. ☎ 01386 554609.
Lecture. 8 pm. Garden Quadrangle Auditorium, St John's College, Oxford. '21st-century gardens'. Carol Klein. £7.50. ☎ 01865 276920.

February

NOTES

FRI 19

SAT 20

Orchid Show. North Bucks Orchid Society. Woburn Village Hall.
☎ 01908 373880.
AGM. British & European Geranium Society. St John's, Hindley, Leicester. ☎ 01772 453383.
Orchid Show. North Hampshire Orchid Society. Church Cottage, St Michael's Church, Basingstoke. ☎ 01256 320804.
Workshop. 10 am. Pershore & Hindlip College, Worcester. 'A further step to fruit tree pruning' by John Edgeley.
☎ 01386 554609.
Early Bulb Show. Scottish Rock Garden Club. Dunblane, Central. 10 am – 4 pm. ☎ 01224 314533.
Lecture. 1.30 pm. Myerscough College, Preston, Lancs. 'Pond construction' by Brian Burrows. RHS Members £6. Non-Members £7.50. ☎ 01995 640611.
Garden Open. Foxgrove, Berks. 2 pm – 6 pm.
Demonstration. 2 pm. Otley College, Ipswich, Suffolk. 'Practical pruning skills' by Mick Lavelle. RHS Members £5. Non-Members £6. ☎ 01473 785543.
Cyclamen Society Spring Show. RHS Garden Wisley, Surrey.
☎ 01483 224234.

SUN 21

Day Course. 10 am – 4 pm. Northern Horticultural Society, Harlow Carr. 'Raising plants from cuttings' by Nigel Hutchinson. NHS Members £18. Non-Members £21. ☎ 01423 565418.
Garden Open. Cambo Gardens, Fife, for snowdrops 10 am – 5 pm; Great Barfield, Bucks. 2 – 5 pm.
Workshop. Westonbirt Arboretum, Glos. 'The Role of evergreen trees & shrubs'. £10. ☎ 01666 880220.
Lecture. 2 pm. 'Plant hunting with a camera' by Phil Phillips. Friends of Ness Gardens, Cheshire. Visitor Centre, Ness. Free to RHS Members.

February

NOTES

MON 22

Half-Day Course. 1.30 – 4 pm. Northern Horticultural Society, Harlow Carr. 'An introduction to pruning' by Roger Brook. NHS Members £10. Non-Members £13. ☎ 01423 565418.
Lecture. 7 pm. Pencoed College, Bridgend. Mid Glamorgan. 'Cottage gardening into the millennium'. RHS Members £5. Non-Members £6.50. ☎ 01656 860202.

TUE 23

Lecture. 2 pm. Pershore & Hindlip College, Worcester. 'Plants & places of the Holy Land'. by Bob Hares. RHS Members £5. Non-Members £10. ☎ 01386 554609.
Lecture. 7.30 pm. Friends of the University of Dundee Botanic Garden. Room T9, Tower Building. 'Plant hunting in south-east Tibet' by Fred Hunt. ☎ 01382 566939.

WED 24

Workshop. Flower Arranging. 10 am – 3.30 pm. RHS Garden Wisley, Surrey. 'One month is past, another is begun' with Michael Bowyer. ☎ 01483 224234.
Day Course. 10 am – 4 pm. Northern Horticultural Society, Harlow Carr. 'An introduction to propagation' by Roger Brook. NHS Members £18. Non-Members £21. ☎ 01423 565418.
Workshop. 1.30 pm. Houghall College, Durham. 'Plant portraits.' RHS Members £4. Non-Members £5. ☎ 0191 386 1351.
Lecture. 2 pm. Cannington College, Somerset. 'Cannington in early spring' by John Addison. RHS Members £7.95. Non-Members £8.95. ☎ 01278 655000.
Lecture. 2 pm. Hadlow College, Tonbridge, Kent. 'Graft incompatibility' by Dr Gesa Reiss. RHS Members £9.50. Non-Members £11. ☎ 01732 850551.
Winter Lecture. Garden History Society. 6 pm. Scientific Societies Lecture Theatre, London. 'Scotland's National Botanic Gardens' by Alan Bennett. £7. ☎ 0171 608 2409.

THU 25

Garden History Day. 10 am – 2.30 pm. Northern Horticultural Society, Harlow Carr. 'Flowers, roses & conservatories in the 20th century' by Marilyn Elm. NHS Members £13. Non-Members £16. ☎ 01423 565418.
Lecture. 1 pm. Welsh College of Horticulture, Northop, Flintshire. 'Hellebores' by David Toyne. RHS Members £8. Non-Members £10. ☎ 01352 841000.
Half-Day Course. 1.30 pm – 4 pm. Northern Horticultural Society, Harlow Carr. 'Pruning roses' by Roger Brook. NHS Members £10. Non-Members £13. ☎ 01423 565418.
Lecture. 2 pm. Pershore & Hindlip College, Worcester. 'Harbingers of spring' by Daphne Chappell. RHS Members £5. Non-Members £10. ☎ 01386 554609.
Lecture. 7.30 pm. Zoology Dept., University of Aberdeen. Friends of the Cruickshank Botanic Garden. 'The plant history of Aberdeen' by Alison Cameron.

'A GARDEN IS NOT MADE IN A YEAR; INDEED IT IS NEVER MADE IN THE SENSE OF FINALITY. IT GROWS, AND WITH THE LABOUR OF LOVE SHOULD GO ON GROWING'. FREDERICK EDEN, *A GARDEN IN VENICE*, 1903.

FEBRUARY

26 FRI

Hopetoun House Homes & Gardens Show. Queensferry, Edinburgh. 3 days 26–28 Feb. ☎ 01565 723999.

27 SAT

Orchid Show. Bournemouth Orchid Society, Dorset. Beaufort Community Centre. ☎ 01703 558571.
Lecture. 9.30 am. Welsh College of Horticulture, Northop, Flintshire. 'Hellebores' by David Toyne. RHS Members £8. Non-Members £10. ☎ 01352 841000.
Lecture. 1.30 pm. Myerscough College, Preston, Lancs. 'Walls & fences in the garden' by John Smyth. RHS Members £6. Non-Members £7.50. ☎ 01995 640611.
Hellebore Weekend. Plant centre, RHS Garden Wisley, Surrey. 2 days 27–28 Feb. ☎ 01483 224234.
Bonsai Weekend. RHS Garden Wisley, Surrey. With members of RHS staff. 2 days 27–28 Feb. ☎ 01483 224234.
Conference. AGS, Birmingham Group. Himalayan plants & mountains. ☎ 01564 702765.

28 SUN

Orchid Show. Harrogate Orchid Society, North Yorkshire. The Mansion House, Roundhay Park, Leeds. ☎ 0113 294 2958.
Lecture. 2 pm. 'Aspects of Kentucky' by D Wakeham. Friends of Ness Gardens, Cheshire. Visitor Centre, Ness. Free to RHS Members.
Garden Open. Lime Close, Oxon. 2 – 6 pm.

NOTES

THE RAINFALL IN LONDON IN FEBRUARY 1891 WAS ONLY $1/10$ IN. (2.5MM.)

MARCH

NOTES

MON 1
Lecture. 7 pm. Askham Bryan College, York. 'Use of trees in your garden' by Nigel Harrison. RHS Members £4. Non-Members £5. ☎ 01904 772277.
Lecture. 7.30 pm. Bedfordshire AGS. Wilstead Village Hall. 'The Rocky Mountains of Colorado' by Ann Borrill. ☎ 01462 711295.

TUE 2
Demonstration. 2 pm. Pershore & Hindlip College, Worcester. 'Your garden in March' by Bob Hares. RHS Members £5. Non-Members £10. ☎ 01386 554609.
Lecture. Royal Caledonian Horticultural Society. 'Floral art: variations on a theme' by Lilias Hoskins. 7.30 pm. Lecture Hall, RBG Edinburgh. ☎ 0131 331 1011.

WED 3
Plantsman's Day. RHS Garden Rosemoor, Devon. 'Camellias' by Jennifer Trehane. ☎ 01805 624067.
Lecture. 1.30 pm. Myerscough College, Preston, Lancs. 'Hardy herbaceous perennials' by Jeff Hodson. RHS Members £6. Non-Members £7.50. ☎ 01995 640611.
Lecture. 1.30 pm. Reaseheath College, Cheshire. 'Planning the vegetable plot' by Derek Jones. RHS Members £6.95. Non-Members £7.95. ☎ 01270 625131.
Lecture. 2 pm. Cannington College, Somerset. 'Early spring pruning' by Peter Elliman. RHS Members £7.95. Non-Members £8.95. ☎ 01278 655000.
Lecture. 2 pm. Hadlow College, Tonbridge, Kent. 'Hellebores at Hadlow' by Keith Mexter. RHS Members £9.50. Non-Members £11. ☎ 01732 850551.
RHS Regional Lecture. 6.45 pm. Pershore & Hindlip College, Worcester. 'Brilliant borders' by Christopher Bailes.
☎ 0171 821 3049.
Demonstration. RHS Garden Wisley, Surrey. 'Rose Pruning' with Dean Peckett. RHS Members £5. Non-Members £10.
☎ 01483 224234.
Winter Lecture. Garden History Society. 6 pm. Scientific Societies Lecture Theatre, London. 'Belvedere, Co. Westmeath' by Belinda Jupp. £7. ☎ 0171 608 2409.

THU 4
RHS Regional Lecture. Pencoed College, Bridgend. Mid Glamorgan. 'Plant diseases & disorders' by Audrey Brooks.
☎ 0171 821 3049.
Half-Day Course. 1.30 – 4 pm. Northern Horticultural Society, Harlow Carr. 'An introduction to pruning' by Roger Brook. NHS Members £10. Non-Members £13. ☎ 01423 565418.
Lecture. 2 pm. Pershore & Hindlip College, Worcester.
'Sloping gardens and how to deal with them' by David Everitt. RHS Members £5. Non-Members £10. ☎ 01386 554609.
Lecture. 7.30 pm. Welsh College of Horticulture, Northop, Flintshire. 'Alpines for all seasons' by Keith Lever. RHS Members £8. Non-Members £10. ☎ 01352 841000.

MARCH

FRI 5
Lecture. 8 pm. Kent Medway AGS. Bluebell Hill Village Hall. 'Running an alpine nursery' by G Nicholls. ☎ 01622 746941.

SAT 6
Orchid Show. Cheltenham & District Orchid Society, Gloucestershire. St John's Church Hall, Churchdown. ☎ 01684 294485.
Study Day. 10 am – 4 pm. Oxford Botanic Garden. 'Glasshouses'. £30. ☎ 01865 276920.
Lecture. 1.30 pm. Myerscough College, Preston, Lancs. 'Successful tree-planting' by Mick Cottam. RHS Members £6. Non-Members £7.50. ☎ 01995 640611.
Lecture. 2 pm. Orchid Society of Great Britain. 'Travels in Peru' by Roy Barrow. Napier Hall, Hide Place, London. ☎ 01483 421423.
Garden Crafts. RHS Garden Wisley, Surrey. Until 14 March. ☎ 01483 224234.
Grafting Day. Brogdale, Kent. Grafting fruit trees while you wait. ☎ 01795 535286.
AGS Early Spring Show. 12 noon – 4.30 pm. Harlow, Essex. ☎ 01245 473982.

SUN 7
AGM & Leek Sale. 10 am. National Pot Leek Society. Pelaw & District Social Club, Heworth. ☎ 0191 549 4274.
Half-Day Course. 1.30 pm – 4 pm. Northern Horticultural Society, Harlow Carr. 'Alpine sinks & troughs' by Nigel Hutchinson. NHS Members £10. Non-Members £13. ☎ 01423 565418.
Lecture. 2 pm. 'Round the year with clematis' by R Kirkman. Friends of Ness Gardens, Cheshire. Visitor Centre, Ness. Free to RHS Members.
Garden Walk. 2 pm. Hillier Arboretum, Hants. 'Bursting Buds & Bulbs'. ☎ 01794 368787.
Garden Walk. RHS Garden Wisley, Surrey. 'Winter-flowering heathers' with Andy Collins. RHS Members £5. Non-Members £10. ☎ 01483 224234.

NOTES

'*KITCHEN GARDEN*: NASTURTIUMS, FOR PICKLING, SOW NOW. *FLOWER GARDEN*: AURICULAS SHOULD BE REMOVED INTO THE STAND, AND IF SOME FLAT OYSTER-SHELLS BE LAID ON THE EARTH, IT WILL SAVE TROUBLE IN WATERING THEM; GRAVEL WALKS WILL WANT TURNING AND ROLLING, AFTER BEING WEEDED AND CLEANED FROM MOSS WITH A BIRCH BROOM'. RICHARD WESTON ESQ. *THE GARDENER'S POCKET CALENDAR*, 1783

MARCH

NOTES

MON 8

TUE 9

Lecture. 1 pm. Welsh College of Horticulture, Northop, Flintshire. 'Your garden in spring' by Anne Lewis. RHS Members £8. Non-Members £10. ☎ 01352 841000.
Lecture. 2 pm. Pershore & Hindlip College, Worcester. 'The versatility of roses' by Michael Marriott. RHS Members £5. Non-Members £10. ☎ 01386 554609.
Lecture. 7 pm. London Historic Parks & Gardens Trust at the Linnean Society. 'Carshalton House Landscape' by Andrew Skelton. £5. ☎ 0171 839 3969.

WED 10

RHS Regional Lecture. 7.30 pm. Reaseheath College, Cheshire. 'Flowers of the Alps & Dolomites' by John Main. ☎ 0171 821 3049.
Lecture. 1.30 pm. Myerscough College, Preston, Lancs. 'Rock garden construction' by Brian Burrows. RHS Members £6. Non-Members £7.50. ☎ 01995 640611.
Demonstration. RHS Garden Wisley, Surrey. 'Practical gardening skills' with Bernard Boardman. RHS Members £5. Non-Members £10. ☎ 01483 224234.
Specialist Day. RHS Garden Wisley, Surrey. 'Getting started in the greenhouse' with Nick Morgan. ☎ 01483 224234.
Workshop. 1.30 pm. Houghall College, Durham. 'Spring pruning.' RHS Members £4. Non-Members £5. ☎ 0191 386 1351.
Lecture. 2 pm. Cannington College, Somerset. 'Grafting fruit trees, ornamental trees & shrubs' by John Bates. RHS Members £7.95. Non-Members £8.95. ☎ 01278 655000.
Lecture & Walk. RHS Garden Rosemoor, Devon. 'Small gardens'. ☎ 01805 624067.
Annual General Meeting. Rose Society of Northern Ireland. 7.30 pm. Malone House, Barnet Demesne.

'ONE OF THE FIRST FLOWERS TO GREET THE SPRING IS *PULMONARIA OFFICINALIS*. AND HOW WELCOME ARE THOSE JAUNTY SPRAYS OF INNOCENT FLOWERS IN BLUE AND PINK, OFTEN RISING ABOVE THE SNOW, AND FLUTTERING UNCONCERNEDLY IN THE BITTER WINDS OF MARCH'. MARGERY FISH, *COTTAGE GARDEN FLOWERS*, 1961

THU 11

Garden History Day. 10 am – 2.30 pm. Northern Horticultural Society, Harlow Carr. 'Ornaments, features and water in the 20th century' by Marilyn Elm. NHS Members £13. Non-Members £16. ☎ 01423 565418.
Course. 'Groundwork for gardeners' with Anne Jennings. Museum of Garden History, London. ☎ 0171 240 0863. 2 days 11–12 March.
Lecture. 2 pm. Pershore & Hindlip College, Worcester. 'Planting for the millennium' by Bob Hares. RHS Members £5. Non-Members £7. ☎ 01386 554609.
Lecture. 8 pm. Garden Quadrangle Auditorium, St John's College, Oxford. 'The Laskett: the creation of our garden' by Sir Roy Strong. £7.50. ☎ 01865 276920.
Spring Meeting & AGM. Hebe Society. RHS Garden Rosemoor, Devon. 2 days 11–12 March.

March

FRI 12

RHS Regional Lecture. Otley College, Suffolk. 'Gardens by design' by Prof. David Stevens. ☎ 0171 821 3049.
Day Course. 10 am – 4 pm. Northern Horticultural Society, Harlow Carr. 'Hedges in the garden & landscape' by Jane Cordingley & Peter Hemsley. NHS Members £19. Non-Members £22. ☎ 01423 565418.

SAT 13

Orchid Show. Southern Counties Orchid Society. Community Centre, Durrington, Worthing, West Sussex. ☎ 01273 728884.
AGM. National Sweet Pea Society. Soham Motel, Newmarket. ☎ 01353 720324.
Lecture. 9.30 am. Welsh College of Horticulture, Northop, Flintshire. 'Your garden in spring' by Anne Lewis. RHS Members £8. Non-Members £10. ☎ 01352 841000.
AGM. Royal National Rose Society. London. ☎ 01727 850461.
Demonstration. 10 am. Pershore & Hindlip College, Worcester. 'Your garden in March' by Bob Hares. RHS Members £5. Non-Members £10. ☎ 01386 554609.
Symposium. East Surrey Group of AGS. Bourne Hall, Ewell. 'All about alpine seed from collection'. ☎ 01386 554790.
Orchid Show. Wessex Orchid Society. Waltham Chase Village Hall, near Winchester. ☎ 01329 233048.
Early Primula Show. National Primula & Auricula Society (Southern Section). RHS Gardens Wisley.
Open Day. Ratcliffe Orchids Ltd. Pitcot Lane, Owlesbury, Winchester. 10 am – 4 pm.
Demonstration. 10 am. Reaseheath College, Cheshire. 'Spring in the fruit garden' by Bert Davies. RHS Members £6.95. Non-Members £7.95. ☎ 01270 625131.
AGS Show. 12 noon – 4.30 pm. Loughborough. ☎ 01509 261626.
Lecture. 2.30 pm. Wiltshire Gardens Trust. Devizes Town Hall. 'Sir Geoffrey Jellicoe' by Jane Balfour. ☎ 01225 722267.

SUN 14

Gardeners' Day at Sulgrave Manor, Northants. Demonstrations, plant sales, exhibitions & displays.
Open Day. Ratcliffe Orchids Ltd. Pitcot Lane, Owlesbury, Winchester. 10 am – 4 pm.
Demonstration. RHS Garden Wisley, Surrey. 'Practical gardening skills' with Bernard Boardman. RHS Members £5. Non-Members £10. ☎ 01483 224234.
Garden Open. Brandy House Mount, Hants. 2 – 5 pm.
Mother's Day Celebration. Noon. Hillier Arboretum, Hants. ☎ 01794 368787.
AGS Fritillaria Group Show. RHS Garden Wisley, Surrey. ☎ 01483 224234.

NOTES

'MAN WHO MAKES A GARDEN SHOULD HAVE A HEART FOR PLANTS THAT HAVE THE GIFT OF SWEETNESS AS WELL AS BEAUTY OF FORM OR COLOUR'. WILLIAM ROBINSON, *THE ENGLISH FLOWER GARDEN*.

MARCH

NOTES

MON 15

TUE 16
RHS Flower Show. 10.30 am – 7 pm. (10 am – 5 pm 2nd day.) RHS New Hall, Westminster. Early Camellia Competition. Early Rhododendron Competition. Ornamental Plant Competition. Early Daffodil Competition. 2 days 16–17 March.
Masters Memorial Lecture. 2 pm. RHS Halls, Westminster. 'Horticulture & genetic modification: fact, fiction & the future' by Prof David James.
Course. 'The Georgian garden' with Caroline Holmes. Museum of Garden History, London. ☎ 0171 240 0863.
Lecture. 2 pm. Pershore & Hindlip College, Worcester. 'Arisaemas' by Bleddyn Wynn Jones. RHS Members £5. Non-Members £10. ☎ 01386 554609.
Lecture. Royal Caledonian Horticultural Society. 'Bonsai' by Mary & Stuart Redfearn. 7.30 pm. Lecture Hall, RBG Edinburgh. ☎ 0131 331 1011.

WED 17
Lecture. 10 am. Cannington College, Somerset. 'Conservatory plants & plants for the cool greenhouse' by John Addison. RHS Members £7.95. Non-Members £8.95. ☎ 01278 655000.
Half-Day Course. 1.30 – 4 pm. Northern Horticultural Society, Harlow Carr. 'Making spring hanging baskets' by Simon Midgley. NHS Members £25. Non-Members £22.50. ☎ 01423 565418.
Lecture & Walk. RHS Garden Rosemoor, Devon. 'Small gardens'. ☎ 01805 624067.
Winter Lecture. Garden History Society. 6 pm. Scientific Societies Lecture Theatre, London. 'Castle Howard' by Dr Christopher Ridgway. £7. ☎ 0171 608 2409.
Lecture. 7 pm. Reaseheath College, Cheshire. 'Perennials for pleasure – modern planting styles' by Alison Evans. RHS Members £6.95. Non-Members £7.95. ☎ 01270 625131.
Lecture. 7.30 pm in the Library, Wentworth Castle (Northern College). 'Year-round interest in small gardens' by Chris Margrave.
Lecture. 7.30 pm. Friends of the University of Dundee Botanic Garden. Room T9, Tower Building. 'Plant of the Atlas Mountains' by David Tattersfield. ☎ 01382 566939.

THU 18
Garden Study Day. West Dean, West Sussex. 'Spring jobs in the garden' by Joe Reardon-Smith. £45. ☎ 01243 811205.
RHS Regional Lecture. Beverley, Yorks. ☎ 0171 821 3049.
Lecture. 2 pm. Pershore & Hindlip College, Worcester. 'Alpines in your garden' by Howard Drury. RHS Members £5. Non-Members £10. ☎ 01386 554609.
Half-Day Course. 1.30 – 4 pm. Northern Horticultural Society, Harlow Carr. 'Making spring hanging baskets' by Simon Midgley. NHS Members £25. Non-Members £22.50. ☎ 01423 565418.

MARCH

FRI 19
Lecture. 2 pm. 'My first expedition to Nepal' by Mike Sinnott. Friends of Wakehurst Place, West Sussex. £2. ☎ 01444 894035.

SAT 20
London Orchid Show. 10 am – 5 pm. RHS New Hall, Westminster. 2 days 20–21 March. ☎ 0171 316 4707.
RHS London Lecture. 2.15 pm. RHS Halls, Westminster. 'Judging Vanda flowers' by Dr Martin Motes.
Weekend Painting Course. 10 am – 5 pm. Oxford Botanic Garden. £70. 2 days 20–21 March. ☎ 01865 276920.
Weekend Garden Design Course. Pershore & Hindlip College, Worcester. 2 days 20–21 March. ☎ 01386 554609.
Lecture. 2 pm. Otley College, Ipswich, Suffolk. 'Zimbabwe: paradise lost or found' by Mick Lavelle. RHS Members £5. Non-Members £6. ☎ 01473 785543.
Joint Show. Scottish Rock Garden Club & Alpine Garden Society. Morecambe, Lancs. 12 noon – 4.40 pm. ☎ 01224 314533 or ☎ 01253 394993.
AGS Show. 12 noon – 4.30 pm. Gillingham, Kent. ☎ 01474 703822.
AGM. British & European Geranium Society. St John's, Hinckley, Leics. ☎ 01772 453383.
Workshop. 10.30 am – 3.30 pm. Brogdale, Kent. Grafting established trees. Friends of Brogdale £20. Others £30. ☎ 01795 535286.

SUN 21
Lecture. 2 pm. 'The gardens at Arley' by P Cook. Friends of Ness Gardens, Cheshire. Visitor Centre, Ness. Free to RHS Members.
Hanami. Admire the cherry blossom. Brogdale, Kent. ☎ 01795 535286.
Garden Walk. RHS Garden Wisley, Surrey. 'Spring flowers at Wisley' with David Hutchins. RHS Members £5. Non-Members £10. ☎ 01483 224234.
Demonstration. RHS Garden Wisley, Surrey. 'Rose pruning' with Dean Peckett. RHS Members £5. Non-Members £10. ☎ 01483 224234.
Garden Open. Crowe Hall, Somerset. 2 – 6 pm.
Garden Walk. Westonbirt Arboretum, Glos. Asiatic magnolias. £5.50. ☎ 01666 880220.

NOTES

- Have you bought your tickets for Scotland's National Gardening Show yet? Tel: 0171 344 4343.

MARCH

NOTES

MON 22

Day Course. 10 am – 4 pm. Northern Horticultural Society, Harlow Carr. 'Creating quality gardens' by Roger Brook. NHS Members £18. Non-Members £21. ☎ 01423 565418.
Lecture. 7 pm. Pencoed College, Bridgend. Mid Glamorgan. 'Rose breeding for the 21st century' by Lionel Poole. RHS Members £5. Non-Members £6.50. ☎ 01656 860202.

TUE 23

RHS Regional Lecture. Southampton. ☎ 0171 821 3049.
Course. 9.30 am – 12 noon. 'Filling your garden with year-round colour'. Friends of Ness Gardens, Cheshire. Visitor Centre, Ness. £6.50. ☎ 0151 353 0123.
Lecture. 1 pm. Welsh College of Horticulture, Northop, Flintshire. 'Pruning ornamental shrubs' by Anne Lewis. RHS Members £8. Non-Members £10. ☎ 01352 841000.
Lecture. 2 pm. Pershore & Hindlip College, Worcester. 'The exotic & the eccentric' by Brian Hiley. RHS Members £5. Non-Members £10. ☎ 01386 554609.

WED 24

RHS Regional Lecture. Hadlow, Essex. 'Plants with impact' by Jim Gardiner. ☎ 0171 821 3049.
Lecture. 1.30 pm. Myerscough College, Preston, Lancs. 'Open-ground grafting' by Peter Wiseman. RHS Members £6. Non-Members £7.50. ☎ 01995 640611.
Lecture. 2 pm. Hadlow College, Tonbridge, Kent. 'Cold hardiness & frost resistance' by Dr Gesa Reiss. RHS Members £9.50. Non-Members £11. ☎ 01732 850551.
Lecture & Walk. RHS Garden Rosemoor, Devon. 'Small gardens'. ☎ 01805 624067.
Evening Lecture. Museum of Garden History, London. 'The flora of the Falkland Islands' with Geoffrey Moir. ☎ 0171 240 0863.
Lecture. 6.30 pm. Reaseheath College, Cheshire. 'Flower arranging: ideas for Easter' by Mark Entwistle. RHS Members £6.95. Non-Members £7.95. ☎ 01270 625131.

- Reminder: all Chelsea tickets MUST be booked in advance.
Tel: 0171 344 4343.

THU 25

Course. 'Knot Gardens: Design and Maintenance' with Anne Jennings. Museum of Garden History, London. 2 days 25–26 March. ☎ 0171 240 0863.
Garden History Day. 10 am – 2.30 pm. Northern Horticultural Society, Harlow Carr. 'Lawns, leaves & Conservation in the 20th Century' by Marilyn Elm. NHS Members £13. Non-Members £16. ☎ 01423 565418.
Rare Plant Sale. 11 am – 4 pm. Battersea Town Hall, London. £3. ☎ 0117 969 1570.
Demonstration. 2 pm. Pershore & Hindlip College, Worcester. 'The potager in spring' by Bob Hares. RHS Members £5. Non-Members £10. ☎ 01386 554609.
Garden Design Course. RHS Garden Wisley, Surrey. Led by Robin Williams and Robin Templer Williams. 4 days 25–28 March. ☎ 01483 224234.

MARCH

FRI 26

Workshop. 11.30 am. RHS Garden Hyde Hall, Essex. 'Late winter colour' with Jo Cobb. RHS Members £5. Non-Members £10. ☎ 01245 400256.
Garden Walk. Westonbirt Arboretum, Glos. Millennium trees. £5.50. ☎ 01666 880220.
Welsh Beautiful Homes & Gardens Show. Swansea. 3 days 26–28 March. ☎ 01292 604306.

SAT 27

Lecture. 9.30 am. Welsh College of Horticulture, Northop, Flintshire. 'Pruning ornamental shrubs' by Anne Lewis. RHS Members £8. Non-Members £10. ☎ 01352 841000.
Workshop. 10 am. Pershore & Hindlip College, Worcester. 'Watercolour painting for Easter' by Audrey Robards. ☎ 01386 554609.
Orchid Show. Wiltshire Orchid Society. The Corn Exchange, Devizes. ☎ 01380 830801.
Rare Plant Sale. 11 am – 4 pm. The Pavilion, North Parade Road, Bath. £2. ☎ 0117 969 1570.
Show. Scottish Rock Garden Club. Edinburgh. 11.30 am – 4.30 pm. ☎ 01224 314533.
Lecture. 1.30 pm. Myerscough College, Preston, Lancs. 'Creating the perfect lawn' by Brian King. RHS Members £6. Non-Members £7.50. ☎ 01995 640611.
Primula Show. 2 – 4.30 pm. National Primula & Auricula Society (Midlands & West Section). Arden School, Knowle, West Midlands. 50p. ☎ 01225 872893.
Half-Day Course. 1.30 pm – 4 pm. Northern Horticultural Society, Harlow Carr. 'Basic bonsai' by James Holmes. NHS Members £10. Non-Members £13. ☎ 01423 565418.
AGS Show. 11.30 am – 4.30 pm. Bolton, Lancs. ☎ 0161 761 7891.

SUN 28

Orchid Show. South East Orchid Society. Beaver Road Ashford. ☎ 01303 256637.
Orchid Show. South West Orchid Society. St John's Garden Centre, Tone Way, Taunton. ☎ 01823 662001.
Bonsai Boot Sale. Birmingham Botanical Gardens. ☎ 0121 454 1860.
Orchid Show. North of England Orchid Society. Houghall College, Durham. ☎ 0191 489 6643.
Garden Open. Foxgrove, Berks. 2 – 6 pm.
Kew Orchid Festival 1999 ends.

NOTES

March • April

NOTES

- Have you bought your tickets for BBC Gardeners' World Live yet? Tel: 0171 344 4343.

MON 29
Spring Plant Sale. 10 am. Friends of Ness Gardens, Cheshire. Visitor Centre, Ness. Free to RHS Members.
NAFAS National Show. Bournemouth International Centre. 4 days 29 March–1 April. ☎ 0171 828 5145.
Lecture. Blackfordby Village Hall, Leics. 'A plantsman in Chile' by Roy Lancaster. Sponsored by Bluebell Nursery. £8.
☎ 01530 413700.

TUE 30
Demonstration. 2 pm. Pershore & Hindlip College, Worcester. 'Propagating hardy perennials' by Bob Hares. RHS Members £5. Non-Members £10. ☎ 01386 554609.

WED 31
Lecture. 1 pm. Writtle College, Chelmsford, Essex. 'Four seasons in the garden – spring' by Marion Polley. ☎ 01245 424200.

THU 1
Lecture. 8 pm. Garden Quadrangle Auditorium, St John's College, Oxford. 'Hidcote & the Edwardian garden' by Anna Pavord. £7.50. ☎ 01865 276920.
Lecture. 7.30 pm. Dorset AGS. Lytchett Matravers Village Hall. 'Mountain flowers of the Drakensberg' by Peter Erskine.

APRIL

FRI 2

Easter Craft Festival. Duncombe Park, North Yorkshire. 4 days 2–5 April. ☎ 01439 770213.
Lecture. 8 pm. Kent Medway AGS. Bluebell Hill Village Hall. 'The Atacama Desert' by Peter Abery. ☎ 01622 746941.

SAT 3

Conference. AGS. Dartington, Devon. 2 days 3–4 April.
☎ 01386 554790.
Orchid Show. Solihull & District Orchid Society.
☎ 01564 822897.
Dundee Spring Flower Show. Dick McTaggart Sports Centre. 2 days 3–4 April. ☎ 01382 434000.
Primula Show. National Primula & Auricula Society (Southern Section). Datchet Village Hall, Berks.
AGS Show. 12.30 pm – 4.30 pm. Stockton-on-Tees.
☎ 01429 231791.
Rare Plant Sale. 11 am – 4 pm. Pittville Pump Room, Cheltenham. £2. ☎ 0117 969 1570.

SUN 4

Gardeners' Weekend at **Elton Hall**, near Peterborough. 2 days 4–5 April. ☎ 0121 682 0860.
Easter Egg Hunt. Burton Constable Gardens, Yorkshire.
☎ 01964 562400.
Gardens Open. Great Barfield, Bucks. 2 – 5.30 pm; Fairfield House, Hants. 2 – 6 pm.
Easter Family Trail. 2 pm. Hillier Arboretum, Hants.
☎ 01794 368787.

NOTES

'*KITCHEN GARDEN:* APRIL BEING THE LATEST TIME FOR SOWING THE PRINCIPAL CROP OF THE KITCHEN-GARDEN, IF ANY THING DIRECTED LAST MONTH WERE OMITTED, PERFORM IT EARLY IN THIS. *FLOWER GARDEN:* WEEDS IN EVERY PART OF THE GARDEN SHOULD BE DESTROYED WHILE YOUNG, TO PREVENT THEIR INCREASING BY FEED. *GREENHOUSE:* WINDOWS MAY BE OPENED FROM ABOUT NINE TILL FOUR, ON ALL FINE DAYS, EXCEPT WHEN IT HAILS'.
RICHARD WESTON ESQ., *THE GARDENER'S POCKET CALENDAR,* 1783

APRIL

NOTES

- Have you bought your tickets for the RHS Summer Flower Show at Hampton Court Palace yet? Tel: 0171 344 4343.

MON 5

Daffodil Time & Plants for Sale 10.30 am – 5 pm. High Beeches, West Sussex. ☎ 01444 400589.
Lecture. 7 pm. Askham Bryan College, York. 'Lawn care' by Steve Prinn. RHS Members £4. Non-Members £5. ☎ 01904 772277.
Garden Open. Ammerdown Park, Somerset 11 am – 5 pm.

TUE 6

Garden Tour. 2 pm. 'Meet the gardener'. Mottisfont Abbey, Hants.
Lecture. 7 pm. London Historic Parks & Gardens Trust at the Linnean Society. 'The garden at Hurlingham House' by May Woods. £5. ☎ 0171 839 3969.
Lecture. 7.30 pm. Royal Caledonian Horticultural Society. 'Scaling up organic horticultural production' by Dr C Leifert. Lecture Hall, RBG Edinburgh. ☎ 0131 331 1011.
Easter Egg Hunt. Westonbirt Arboretum, Glos. £1. ☎ 01666 880220.

WED 7

THU 8

Specialist Day. RHS Garden Wisley, Surrey. 'Water gardens' with members of RHS staff. ☎ 01483 224234.
Children's Workshop. 1.30 – 3.30 pm. Northern Horticultural Society, Harlow Carr. 'Growing plants' by Deidre Walton. £6. ☎ 01423 565418.
Lecture. 2 pm. Pershore & Hindlip College, Worcester. 'Determining levels in your garden for design' by David Everitt. RHS Members £5. Non-Members £10. ☎ 01386 554609.
Lecture. 3 pm. Botanical Society of Scotland. 'Flowers of Scotland' by Colin Will. RBG Lecture Theatre, Edinburgh. Admission free. ☎ 0131 552 7171.

NOTES

FRI 9

Spring Gardening Show at Capel Manor, Enfield. 3 days 9–11 April. ☎ 01922 716128.
Lecture. 7.30 pm. Chilterns AGS. Great Kingshill Village Hall. 'The world of alpines' by Ann Borrill.

SAT 10

Orchid Show. Hinckley & District Orchid Society. St John's Hall, Brunell Road, Hinckley. ☎ 01455 845703.
Spring Flower Show. Royal Caledonian Horticultural Society. Meadowbank Stadium, Edinburgh. 2 days 10–11 April.
☎ 0131 331 1011.
Demonstration. 10 am. Pershore & Hindlip College, Worcester. 'Your garden in April' by Bob Hares. RHS Members £5. Non-Members £10. ☎ 01386 554609.
Workshop Weekend. Beginners Level Photography. 10 am – 5 pm. RHS Garden Wisley, Surrey. 2 days 10–11 April.
☎ 01483 224234.
Show. Scottish Rock Garden Club. Stirling. 10 am – 4 pm.
☎ 01224 314533.
AGS Shows 11.30 am – 4.30 pm. Chesterfield. ☎ 01509 261626. And 1.30 – 4 pm. Dublin. ☎ 00 353 1 2862616.
Open Day. Ratcliffe Orchids Ltd. Pitcot Lane, Owlesbury, Winchester. 10 am – 4 pm.

SUN 11

Spring Orchid Show. 2 pm. Orchid Society of Great Britain. Gatton Park, Reigate, Surrey. ☎ 01483 421423.
Orchid Show. Birmingham & Midland Orchid Society. Botanical Gardens, Birmingham. ☎ 0121 422 0904.
Open Day. Ratcliffe Orchids Ltd. Pitcot Lane, Owlesbury, Winchester. 10 am – 4 pm.
Gardens Open. Brandy House Mount, Hants. 2 – 5 pm; Stonehurst, West Sussex 11 am – 5 pm; Folly Farm, Berks 2 – 6 pm.
Garden Walk. RHS Garden Wisley, Surrey. 'The rock garden, alpine meadow & alpine house' with Allan Robinson. RHS Members £5. Non-Members £10. ☎ 01483 224234.
Garden Walk. Sheringham Park. Norfolk Wildlife Trust.
☎ 01603 625540.
AGM. British Hosta & Hemerocallis Society. Bridgemere, Cheshire.

APRIL

NOTES

• Book today for Scotland's National Gardening Show: Members' price tickets are only available in advance. Tel: 0171 344 4343.

MON 12
Lecture. 7 pm. Rosecarpe. 'The growing world of miniature roses' by Tom Foster. Civic Centre, Gateshead. ☎ 0191 252 7052.

TUE 13
Lecture. 9.30 am. Welsh College of Horticulture, Northop, Flintshire. 'Propagating herbaceous perennials' by Anne Lewis. RHS Members £8. Non-Members £10. ☎ 01352 841000.
RHS Flower Show. 10.30 am – 7 pm. (10 am – 5 pm 2nd day.) RHS New & Old Halls, Westminster. Daffodil Show. Main Camellia Competition. Ornamental Plant Competition. AGS Competition. 2 days 13–14 April.
RHS London Lecture. 2.15 pm. RHS Halls, Westminster. 'The gardens of modern China' by Duncan Coombs.
Specialist Day. RHS Garden Wisley, Surrey. 'Plantsman's Day'. ☎ 01483 224234.
Demonstration. 2 pm. Pershore & Hindlip College, Worcester. 'Your garden in April' by Bob Hares. RHS Members £5. Non-Members £10. ☎ 01386 554609.

WED 14
Plantsman's Day. RHS Garden Rosemoor, Devon. 'Orchids for everyone' by Christopher Bailes. ☎ 01805 624067.
Lecture. 1.30 pm. Houghall College, Durham. 'Starting from scratch: basic garden design.' RHS Members £4. Non-Members £5. ☎ 0191 386 1351.
Lecture. 2 pm. Scottish Agricultural College, Auchincruive, Ayr. 'Success in controlling those plant diseases' by Dr Mark McQuilken. RHS Members £4.95. Non-Members £5.95. ☎ 01292 525393.
Garden Walk. 2 pm. Claremont Landscape Garden, Surrey.
Lecture. 2 pm. Cannington College, Somerset. 'Plants for the instant garden' by John Addison. RHS Members £7.95. Non-Members £8.95. ☎ 01278 655000.
Garden Walk. RHS Garden Wisley, Surrey. 'The rock garden, alpine meadow & alpine house' with Allan Robinson. RHS Members £5. Non-Members £10. ☎ 01483 224234.
Workshop. Writtle College, Chelmsford, Essex. 'An introduction to garden design' with Bill Burford. ☎ 01245 424200.
AGM & Lecture. 7 pm. Wiltshire Gardens Trust. Bradford on Avon. 'Plant hunting in China' by Dr James Compton. ☎ 01225 722267.

THU 15
5th Australian Wildflower Conference. Melbourne, Victoria. 3 days 15–17 April. ☎ 0061 3 9419 6199.
Day Course. 10 am – 4 pm. Northern Horticultural Society, Harlow Carr. 'The garden in spring' by Rita Lait. NHS Members £19. Non-Members £22. ☎ 01423 565418.
Specialist Day. RHS Garden Wisley, Surrey. 'Container gardening' with members of RHS staff. ☎ 01483 224234.
Lecture. 2 pm. Pershore & Hindlip College, Worcester. 'Practical ways with wild flowers in the garden' by Lynn Stevens. RHS Members £5. Non-Members £10. ☎ 01386 554609.

APRIL

FRI 16

Day Course. 10 am – 4 pm. Northern Horticultural Society, Harlow Carr. 'Conifers in the garden & landscape' by Jane Cordingley & Peter Hemsley. NHS Members £19. Non-Members £22. ☎ 01423 565418.

SAT 17

Spring Gardeners' Weekend at Ragley Hall, Warwickshire. 2 days 17–18 April. ☎ 0121 682 0860.
Orchid Fair. Kibble Palace, Botanic Gardens, Glasgow. 10 am – 5 pm. 2 days 17–18 April. ☎ 0141 334 2422.
Study Day with Heather Angel. Plant Photography. 10 am – 5 pm. Oxford Botanic Garden. £50. ☎ 01865 276920.
Garden Festival. Borde Hill, West Sussex. £4. 2 days 17–18 April. ☎ 01444 450326.
Joint Show. Scottish Rock Garden Club & Alpine Garden Society. Hexham, Northumberland. 12 noon – 4.30 pm. ☎ 01224 314533 or ☎ 01661 871974.
Workshop. Silk painting. RHS Garden Wisley, Surrey. 2 days 17–18 April. ☎ 01483 224234.
Welsh Open Spring Show. 1 pm – 7 pm. Picton Castle, Dyfed. £3. 2 days 17–18 April. ☎ 01834 861287.
Rare Plant Sale. 11 am – 4 pm. Court Gardens, Marlow, Bucks. £2. ☎ 0117 969 1570.
AGS Show. 11.30 am – 4.30 pm. Solihull. ☎ 01384 396331.
West of England Primula & Auricula Show. 2 – 4 pm. National Primula & Auricula Society (Midlands & West Section). Saltford Hall, Saltford, Bath. 50p. ☎ 01225 872893.
Garden Walk. 2.15 pm. Hinton Ampner, Hants. 'Meet the Gardener'. Numbers limited. £1. ☎ 01962 771305.
Workshop. 2 pm. Otley College, Ipswich, Suffolk. 'Virtual gardens: planning with modern techniques' by Lara Hurley. RHS Members £5. Non-Members £6. ☎ 01473 785543.
Grow '99. Nurseries & garden sundries. Sandown, Esher, Surrey. 9 am – 6 pm. 2 days 17–18 April. Adults £5. OAPs £4. ☎ 01277 356635.
Greenhouse Weekend. Meet the experts. Leeds Castle, Kent. 2 days 17–18 April. ☎ 01622 765400.

SUN 18

Dawn bird-watch. 5.30 am. Hillier Arboretum, Hants. ☎ 01794 368787.
Spring Plant Fair. Pashley Manor Gardens, East Sussex. ☎ 01580 200692.
NCCPG Plant Sales. RHS Garden Rosemoor, Devon. ☎ 01805 624067. Capel Manor, London. ☎ 0181 366 4442.
Demonstration. 2 pm – 3.30 pm. Brogdale, Kent. Pruning stone fruits. Friends of Brogdale £6. Others £10. ☎ 01795 535286.
Garden Walk. 2 pm. Cragside, Northumberland. ☎ 01669 620150.
Gardens Open. The Old Rectory, Farnborough, Oxon. 2 – 6 pm; Crowe Hall, Somerset. 2 – 6 pm; Stillingfleet Lodge, York 1.30 – 5 pm (*Pulmonaria* Day).

NOTES

APRIL

NOTES

MON 19
Lecture. 7 pm. Pencoed College, Bridgend. Mid Glamorgan. 'Shrubs for all-year-round interest' by Dilys Ayling. RHS Members £5. Non-Members £6.50. ☎ 01656 860202.

TUE 20
Cincinnati Flower & Garden Show, USA, in association with the RHS. Gala Evening. ☎ 001 513 872 9555.

WED 21
RHS Regional Lecture. Taunton. 'From the mountains to your garden' by Michael Upward. ☎ 0171 821 3049.
Demonstration. Flower Arranging. 10 am – 12.30 pm. RHS Garden Wisley, Surrey. 'It's a good life' with Anna Sparks. ☎ 01483 224234.
Spring Walk. Bedgebury National Arboretum, Kent. Led by John Simmons. ☎ 01580 211044.
Garden Walk. RHS Garden Wisley, Surrey. 'Spring flowers at Wisley' with David Hutchins. RHS Members £5. Non-Members £10. ☎ 01483 224234.
Lecture. 1.30 pm. Reaseheath College, Cheshire. 'Plant diseases & disorders: recognition & prevention' by Harry Delaney. RHS Members £6.95. Non-Members £7.95. ☎ 01270 625131.
Lecture. 7 pm. Hadlow College, Tonbridge, Kent. 'Gardens in France' by Keith Backhouse. RHS Members £9.50. Non-Members £11. ☎ 01732 850551.
Workshop. Writtle College, Chelmsford, Essex. 'An introduction to garden design' with Bill Burford. ☎ 01245 424200.
Lecture & AGM. Friends of Wentworth Castle Gardens. 7.30 pm in the Library, Wentworth Castle (Northern College). 'China off the beaten track' by David Farnes.
Cincinnati Flower & Garden Show, USA, in association with the RHS. 5 days 21–25 April. ☎ 001 513 872 9555.

On This Day
'Snowed very hard for sixteen hours: the greatest snow that has fallen this year; and must have been a foot deep had it not for the greatest part melted as it fell. Went away without any frost, and seems to have done no damage'. Gilbert White, 1757.

THU 22
Harrogate Spring Flower Show. 4 days 22–25 April. ☎ 01423 561049.
16th World Orchid Conference, Vancouver, B.C. Daily until 3 May. ☎ 001 604 681 5226.
Lecture. 1 pm. Welsh College of Horticulture, Northop, Flintshire. 'Flower arranging from your garden'. RHS Members £8. Non-Members £10. ☎ 01352 841000.
Demonstration. 2 pm. Pershore & Hindlip College, Worcester. 'Ten ways to use brick walls' by David Everitt. RHS Members £5. Non-Members £7. ☎ 01386 554609.
Botanical Art Course. RHS Garden Wisley, Surrey. Beginners' level. 4 days 22–25 April. ☎ 01483 224234.

APRIL

FRI 23
Workshop. 11.30 am. RHS Garden Hyde Hall, Essex. 'Spring walk' with Jo Cobb. RHS Members £5. Non-Members £10. ☎ 01245 400256.
Primavera alla Landriana. Italian garden show near Rome. 3 days 23–25 April. ☎ 00 39 06 6876333.

SAT 24
Lecture. 9.30 am. Welsh College of Horticulture, Northop, Flintshire. 'Flower arranging from your garden'. RHS Members £8. Non-Members £10. ☎ 01352 841000.
Demonstration. 10 am. Reaseheath College, Cheshire. 'Getting started with vegetables: sowing the seeds' by Derek Jones. RHS Members £6.95. Non-Members £7.95. ☎ 01270 625131.
Workshop. 10 am. Pershore & Hindlip College, Worcester. 'Ideas for re-vamping your garden' by Ruth Chivers. ☎ 01386 554609.
Day Course. 10 am – 4 pm. Northern Horticultural Society, Harlow Carr. 'European flower design' by Faith Dawson. NHS Members £18. Non-Members £21. ☎ 01423 565418.
Midlands Auricula Show. 2 pm – 4.30 pm. National Primula & Auricula Society (Midlands & West Section). Arden School, Knowle, West Midlands. 50p. ☎ 01225 872893.
Study Day. 10 am – 4 pm. Oxford Botanic Garden. 'Propagation by cuttings'. £30. ☎ 01865 276920.
Show. Scottish Rock Garden Club. Perth. 12 noon – 4.30 pm. ☎ 01224 314533.
Auricula Show. National Primula & Auricula Society (Southern Section). Datchet Village Hall, Berks.
AGS Shows. 1 pm – 4 pm. Muckamore, Co Antrim. ☎ 012657 41288. And at Harrogate Spring Flower Show. ☎ 01909 566837.
Garden Open. Dam House Farm, Derbys. 11 am – 4 pm.
Cactus Sale. British Cactus & Succulent Society. Tropical World, Canal Gardens, Leeds. 2 days 24–25 April. ☎ 0113 266 1850.

SUN 25
Special Plant Fair. Spetchley Park, Worcester. ☎ 01905 345224.
Garden Open & Plant Sale. 16 Witton Lane, Little Plumpstead. Norfolk Wildlife Trust. £1.50. ☎ 01603 625540.
Garden Walk. RHS Garden Wisley, Surrey. 'Wisley's birds' with David Elliott. RHS Members £5. Non-Members £10. ☎ 01483 224234.
Gardens Open. Olivers, Essex 10 am – 6 pm; Goldney Hall, Glos. 2 – 6 pm; Oare House, Wilts. 2 – 6 pm; Munstead Wood, Surrey. 2 – 6 pm.
Garden Walk. Westonbirt Arboretum, Glos. Wild flowers. £5.50. ☎ 01666 880220.

NOTES

- Chelsea is just around the corner: have you bought your tickets yet? Tel: 0171 344 4343.

APRIL

NOTES

MON 26

TUE 27
RHS Flower Show. 11 am – 7 pm. (10 am – 5 pm 2nd day.) RHS New Hall, Westminster. Late Daffodil Competition. Ornamental Plant Competition. Tulip Competition. Main Rhododendron Competition. 2 days 27–28 April.
RHS London Lecture. 2.15 pm. RHS Halls, Westminster. 'Hardy ferns for every garden' by Martin Rickard.
Symposium. International Rhododendron Species. Bellevue, Washington, USA. 2 days 27–28 April. ☎ 001 707 725 3043.
Demonstrations & Talks. RHS Garden Wisley, Surrey. Alpine Specialist Day, with RHS staff members. ☎ 01483 224234.
Lecture. 2 pm. Pershore & Hindlip College, Worcester. 'Giving a tropical look to your garden' by Frank Hardy. RHS Members £5. Non-Members £10. ☎ 01386 554609.
RHS London Lecture. Jointly with RNRS. 6 pm. RHS Halls, Westminster.
Schools Workshop. 'Pumpkins'. RHS Garden Rosemoor, Devon. ☎ 01805 624067.

WED 28
Lecture. 10 am. Cannington College, Somerset. 'The drought-tolerant garden' by John Addison & Geoff Hester. RHS Members £7.95. Non-Members £8.95. ☎ 01278 655000.
Lecture. 1.30 pm. Myerscough College, Preston, Lancs. 'Hanging baskets' by P Rhodes. RHS Members £6. Non-Members £7.50. ☎ 01995 640611.
Workshop. 1.30 pm. Houghall College, Durham. 'Making more plants: propagation techniques.' RHS Members £4. Non-Members £5. ☎ 0191 386 1351.
Workshop. Writtle College, Chelmsford, Essex. 'An introduction to garden design' with Bill Burford. ☎ 01245 424200.
Demonstration. RHS Garden Wisley, Surrey. 'The mixed border' with David Jewell. RHS Members £5. Non-Members £10. ☎ 01483 224234.
Garden Walk. RHS Garden Wisley, Surrey. 'Trees, shrubs & herbaceous perennials' with Colin Crosbie. RHS Members £5. Non-Members £10. ☎ 01483 224234.
Lecture. 2 pm. Hadlow College, Tonbridge, Kent. 'Growing soft fruit in the garden' by Dave Ridgeway. RHS Members £9.50. Non-Members £11. ☎ 01732 850551.

● Book today for BBC Gardeners' World Live: Members' price tickets are only available in advance. Tel: 0171 344 4343.

THU 29
Tulip Festival. Pashley Manor Gardens, East Sussex. 5 days 29 April–3 May. ☎ 01580 200692.
Lecture. 2 pm. Pershore & Hindlip College, Worcester. 'Garden favourites for the connoisseur' by Bob Hares. RHS Members £5. Non-Members £10. ☎ 01386 554609.
Garden Walk. Westonbirt Arboretum, Glos. Badgers. £4. ☎ 01666 880220.

APRIL • MAY

FRI
30

SAT
1

Demonstration. RHS Garden Rosemoor, Devon. 'Working rural skills' with the Devon Rural Skills Trust. 2 days 1–2 May.
☎ 01805 624067.
Dawn Chorus Walk. Westonbirt Arboretum, Glos. £13.50.
☎ 01666 880220.
Spalding Flower Parade. 2 pm, but please arrive before 12 noon. Springfields, Spalding. £5. Plus Country Fair for 3 days.
☎ 01775 724843.
Plant Sale. Lakeland Horticultural Society, Windermere.
☎ 01539 446008..
Plant Sale. Suffolk Wildlife Trust. Parkers Mill, Mildenhall.
☎ 01473 890089.
Spring Gardeners' Weekend at **Audley End,** Essex. 3 days 1–3 May. ☎ 0121 682 0862.
AGS Shows 12.30 pm – 4.30 pm. Sudbury, Suffolk.
☎ 01787 247627. And 11.30 am – 4.30 pm. Macclesfield, Cheshire. ☎ 01625 423894.
Bath Spring Flower Show. 3 days 1–3 May. ☎ 01225 396021.
Bonsai Weekend. Leonardslee, West Sussex. 3 days 1–3 May.
☎ 01403 891212.
Bluebell Weekend. Kew Gardens. 3 days 1–3 May.
☎ 0181 332 5000.
Show. Scottish Rock Garden Club. Glasgow. 12 noon – 4.30 pm.
☎ 01224 314533.
Oxfordshire Craft Fair. Blenheim Palace. 3 days 1–3 May.
☎ 01993 811091.

SUN
2

Rare Plant Fair. 2 pm – 5 pm. Castle Bromwich Hall Gardens.
☎ 0117 969 1570.
Middlesex Garden Show. Uxbridge Showground. 2 days 2–3 May.
☎ 01795 474660.
Carlisle & Borders Spring Flower Show. Bitts Park. 2 days 2–3 May. ☎ 01228 625444.
Gardens Open. Preen Manor, Shropshire. 2 – 6 pm; Lower House Farm, Gwent for NGS; Carclew Gardens, Cornwall 2 – 5 pm; Glendoick Gardens, Tayside 2 – 5 pm; The Manor House, Bledlow, Bucks. 2 – 6 pm; Foxgrove, Berks. 2 – 6 pm.
Leicestershire County Show. Dishley Grange Farm. 2 days 2–3 May. ☎ 01509 646786.
South of England Spring Show. Ardingly, West Sussex. 2 days 2–3 May. ☎ 01444 892700.
Rare Plant Sale. Castle Bromwich Hall, West Midlands.
☎ 0121 749 4100.
Nursery Plant Sale. 11 am – 4 pm. Walled Gardens, Pigeonsford, Llangranog, Dyfed. £1.50 for admission: plant sale free.
☎ 01267 237275

NOTES

MAY

NOTES

MON 3

Flower Fair & NCCPG Auction. Hergest Croft Gardens, Hereford. £5.
Lecture. 7 pm. Askham Bryan College, York. 'Designing your own garden' by Paul Green. RHS Members £4. Non-Members £5. ☎ 01904 772277.
Lecture. 7 pm. Pencoed College, Bridgend. Mid Glamorgan. 'Hanging baskets & patio tubs' by Chris Neale. RHS Members £5. Non-Members £6.50. ☎ 01656 860202.
Gardens Open. Home Covert, Wilts. 2 pm – 6 pm; Stonehurst, West Sussex 11 am – 5 pm; Lower House Farm, Gwent for NGS.
Bluebell Time & Specialist Plant Sale 10.30 am – 5 pm. High Beeches, West Sussex. ☎ 01444 400589.

TUE 4

Lecture. 1 pm. Welsh College of Horticulture, Northop, Flintshire. 'Container gardening' by Anne Lewis. RHS Members £8. Non-Members £10. ☎ 01352 841000.
Garden Tour. 2 pm. 'Meet the gardener'. Mottisfont Abbey, Hants.
Demonstration. 2 pm. Pershore & Hindlip College, Worcester. 'Your garden in May' by Bob Hares. RHS Members £5. Non-Members £10. ☎ 01386 554609.

WED 5

Lecture. 1.30 pm. Myerscough College, Preston, Lancs. 'The wonderful world of the plant' by David Huntley. RHS Members £6. Non-Members £7.50. ☎ 01995 640611.
Lecture. 2 pm. Writtle College, Chelmsford, Essex and Shuttleworth College, Biggleswade, Bedfordshire. 'Create your own hanging baskets' by Thady Barrett & Ann Waring. RHS Members £7. Non-Members £10. ☎ 01245 424200.
Demonstration. 2 pm. Hadlow College, Tonbridge, Kent. 'Your garden in May' by Nick Egan. RHS Members £9.50. Non-Members £11. ☎ 01732 850551.
Lecture. Cannington College, Somerset. 'Cannington in May' by Peter Elliman. RHS Members £7.95. Non-Members £8.95. ☎ 01278 655000.
Lecture. 6.30 pm. Reaseheath College, Cheshire. 'Containers & hanging baskets' by Tony Saxon. RHS Members £6.95. Non-Members £7.95. ☎ 01270 625131.

THU 6

Demonstrations. RHS Garden Rosemoor, Devon. 'Colourful containers' by Jack Gingell. ☎ 01805 624067.
Lakeside Walk. 2 pm. Harewood House, W Yorks. Meet in gift shop. ☎ 0113 288 6331.

MAY

FRI 7

Malvern Spring Gardening Show. 9 am – 6 pm. The Showground, Malvern. 3 days 7–9 May. ☎ 01684 584900.
Specialist Day. RHS Garden Wisley, Surrey. 'Plantsman's day'. ☎ 01483 224234.
Scottish Rhododendron Society. Annual Show. Corran Halls, Oban. 2 days 7–8 May.
Castello di Masino. Tre giorni per i Giardini, Piemonte. Italian garden fair. 3 days 7–9 May. ☎ 00 39 011 660 4339.
Nottinghamshire County Show. Newark. 2 days 7–8 May. ☎ 01636 702627.

NOTES

KITCHEN GARDEN: NASTURTIUMS THIN TO A FOOT ASUNDER. SLUGS AND SNAILS MAY EASILY BE FOUND AND DESTROYED AFTER RAIN, OR IN THE MORNING. *FLOWER GARDEN:* GRASS WALKS WEED, ROLL, AND MOW, FREQUENTLY. ' RICHARD WESTON ESQ., *THE GARDENER'S POCKET CALENDAR*, 1783

SAT 8

Dawn Chorus Walk. Westonbirt Arboretum, Glos. £13.50. ☎ 01666 880220.
Plant Fair. Savill Gardens, Windsor Great Park. ☎ 01753 847518.
Lecture. 9.30 am. Welsh College of Horticulture, Northop, Flintshire. 'Container gardening' by Anne Lewis. RHS Members £8. Non-Members £10. ☎ 01352 841000.
Lecture. 10 am. Reaseheath College, Cheshire. 'Containers & hanging baskets' by Frank Forrest. RHS Members £6.95. Non-Members £7.95. ☎ 01270 625131.
Workshop. Writtle College, Chelmsford, Essex. 'An introduction to botanical illustration' with Gillian Dermer. 4 days 8–9 May, 29–30 May. ☎ 01245 424200.
Malvern Spring Gardening Show. 9 am – 6 pm. 2nd day. Includes AGS Show.

SUN 9

Spring Plant Fair. Newby Hall, North Yorks. ☎ 01423 322583.
Malvern Spring Gardening Show. 9 am – 5 pm. Last day.
Garden Open. Riseholme Hall, Lincs. 10 am – 5 pm; Brandy House Mount, Hants. 2 – 5 pm; Carclew Gardens, Cornwall 2 – 5 pm; Walpole House, London 2 – 6 pm; Crowe Hall, Somerset. 2 – 6 pm; Goldney Hall, Glos. 2 – 6 pm.
Garden Walk. 2 pm. Hillier Arboretum, Hants. ☎ 01794 368787.
Workshop. Westonbirt Arboretum, Glos. 'Green woodworking'. £25. ☎ 01666 880220.
Spring Meeting. Hardy Orchid Society. 9 am – 4 pm. Pershore & Hindlip College, Worcester.

MAY

NOTES

'AN ENGLISH GENTLEMAN HAS TWO SUITS IN HIS WARDROBE; ONE FOR SUCH CEREMONIES AS FUNERALS, CHRISTENINGS AND WEDDINGS, AND THE OTHER FOR GOING TO LONDON. WHEN THEY FALL TO PIECES, HE GIVES THEM TO THE GARDENER'.
ENZO BIAGI, *INGHILTERRA*, 1986

MON
10

TUE
11

Lecture. 1 pm. Welsh College of Horticulture, Northop, Flintshire. 'Hanging baskets' by Anne Lewis. RHS Members £8. Non-Members £10. ☎ 01352 841000.
Demonstration. 2 pm. Pershore & Hindlip College, Worcester. 'Soft fruit planting & training' by John Edgeley. RHS Members £5. Non-Members £10. ☎ 01386 554609.

WED
12

Demonstration. Flower Arranging. 10 am – 12.30 pm. RHS Garden Wisley, Surrey. 'Spare times, past times' with Eleanor Brown. ☎ 01483 224234.
Garden Walk. 2 pm. Claremont Landscape Garden, Surrey.
Lecture. 2 pm. Scottish Agricultural College, Auchincruive, Ayr. 'Plant up your hanging baskets' by Michael Hitchon. RHS Members £4.95. Non-Members £5.95. ☎ 01292 525393.
Lecture. 2 pm. Hadlow College, Tonbridge, Kent. 'Constructing a rock garden' by Keith Mexter. RHS Members £9.50. Non-Members £11. ☎ 01732 850551.
Lecture. 2 pm. Writtle College, Chelmsford, Essex. 'Houseplant propagation & cultivation' by Andy Boorman. ☎ 01245 424200.
Lecture. 2 pm. Cannington College, Somerset. 'Stocking the pond with water & bog plants' by John Addison. RHS Members £7.95. Non-Members £8.95. ☎ 01278 655000.
Lecture. 7.30 pm. St Alban's Hall, Norwich. 'Plant migration' by Gillian Beckett. Norfolk Wildlife Trust. ☎ 01603 625540.

THU
13

Day Course. 10 am – 4 pm. Northern Horticultural Society, Harlow Carr. 'Introduction to botanical painting' by Colin Swinton. NHS Members £21. Non-Members £25. ☎ 01423 565418.
Lecture. 1.30 pm. Houghall College, Durham. 'Garden photography: getting started.' RHS Members £4. Non-Members £5. ☎ 0191 386 1351.
Demonstration. 2 pm. Pershore & Hindlip College, Worcester. 'Hanging gardens & containers for summer display' by David Feaver. RHS Members £5. Non-Members £10. ☎ 01386 554609.
Garden Walk. Westonbirt Arboretum, Glos. Badgers. £4. ☎ 01666 880220.

MAY

FRI 14

Journées des Plantes de Courson. Garden show 35 km south of Paris. 3 days 14–16 May. ☎ 00 33 164 58 90 12.
Half-Day Course. 1.30 pm – 4 pm. Northern Horticultural Society, Harlow Carr. 'Making spring hanging baskets' by Simon Midgley. NHS Members £25. Non-Members £22.50.
☎ 01423 565418.
Lecture. 7.30 pm. Chilterns AGS. Great Kingshill Village Hall. 'Late summer in the High Savoy' by Tony Colmer.

SAT 15

Dawn Chorus Walk. Westonbirt Arboretum, Glos. £13.50.
☎ 01666 880220.
Wiltshire County Show. Warminster. 2 days. ☎ 01985 216644.
Study Day. 10 am – 4 pm. Oxford Botanic Garden. 'Plant naming'. £30. ☎ 01865 276920.
Hertfordshire Garden Show. Knebworth House. 2 days 15–16 May. ☎ 01438 812661.
Plant Sale & Open Weekend. Houghall College, Durham. 10 am – 5 pm. 2 days 15–16 May.
Lecture. 1.30 pm. Myerscough College, Preston, Lancs. 'Softwood cuttings' by Jeff Hodson. RHS Members £6. Non-Members £7.50. ☎ 01995 640611.
AGS Show. 11.30 am – 4.30 pm. Southport, Lancs.
☎ 01204 61233.
Spring Plant Sale. Royal Caledonian Horticultural Society. Saughton Winter Gardens, Edinburgh. ☎ 0131 331 1011.
Show. Scottish Rock Garden Club. Aberdeen. 11.30 am – 4 pm.
☎ 01224 314533.
Container Gardening Weekend. Plant centre, RHS Garden Wisley, Surrey. 2 days 15–16 May.

SUN 16

Open Day. Swiss Garden Beds. (Wine included!).
☎ 01767 627666.
Garden Open. Caythorpe Court (De Montfort University), Grantham, Lincs. 10 am – 5 pm. £3. Plant sales.
Garden Walk. 2 pm. Cragside, Northumberland.
☎ 01669 620150.
Workshop. Westonbirt Arboretum, Glos. 'Green woodworking'. £25. ☎ 01666 880220.
Gardens Open. Carclew Gardens, Cornwall 2 – 5 pm; Hill House, Herts. 2 – 5 pm; Stowell Park, Glos. 2 – 5 pm; Glendoick Gardens, Tayside 2 – 5 pm; Tirley Garth Trust, Cheshire. 2 – 6 pm; Cowdray Park, West Sussex 2 – 6 pm; Greenways, Oxford 2 – 6 pm; The Old Rectory, Farnborough, Oxon. 2 – 6 pm; Lime Close, Oxon. 2 – 6 pm; Stillingfleet Lodge, York. 1.30 – 5 pm; Fairfield House, Hants. 2 – 6 pm.
Garden Walk. RHS Garden Wisley, Surrey. 'Wisley's birds' with David Elliott. RHS Members £5. Non-Members £10.
☎ 01483 224234.
Rare Plant Sale. 11 am – 5 pm. Slimbridge, Glos. £2.
☎ 0117 969 1570.

NOTES

• Remember: Members' price tickets for the RHS Summer Flower Show at Hampton Court Palace must be bought in advance.
Tel: 0171 344 4343.

MAY

NOTES

MON 17
Garden Visit. Pencoed College, Bridgend, Mid Glamorgan. Pencoed Organic Growers, led by John Roberts. RHS Members £5. Non-Members £6.50. ☎ 01656 860202.

TUE 18
Workshop. 2 pm. Pershore & Hindlip College, Worcester. 'Taking cuttings' by Bob Hares. RHS Members £5. Non-Members £10. ☎ 01386 554609.
Garden Walk with John Anderson. Mount Usher, Co Wicklow. 7.30 pm. 'The world of flowers'. £5 Pre-book.
☎ 00 353 0 404 40116.

WED 19
Garden Visit. 9.30 am. Bodnant, Reaseheath College, Cheshire led by Stephen Davies. RHS Members £6.95. Non-Members £7.95. ☎ 01270 625131.
Lecture. 2 pm. Writtle College, Chelmsford, Essex. 'Growing exotic vegetables' by Suzanne Higgins. RHS Members £8. Non-Members £10. ☎ 01245 424200.
Lecture. 2 pm. Hadlow College, Tonbridge, Kent. 'Alleopathy: plant chemical warfare' by David Carey. RHS Members £9.50. Non-Members £11. ☎ 01732 850551.

THU 20
Devon County Show. Exeter. 3 days 20–22 May.
☎ 01392 444777.
Course. 10 am – 4 pm. 'Plant Photography: Getting in close'. Friends of Ness Gardens, Cheshire. Visitor Centre, Ness. £19.
☎ 0151 353 0123.
Demonstration. 2 pm. Pershore & Hindlip College, Worcester. 'Colour co-ordination in your garden' by Lynn Stevens. RHS Members £5. Non-Members £10. ☎ 01386 554609.
Evening Walk. Kingston Lacy, Dorset. See the rhodos. 6.30 pm. Meet in car park. £2.50. No dogs.

MAY

FRI 21

Shropshire & West Midlands Show. Shrewsbury. 2 days 21–22 May. ☎ 01743 362824.
Day Course. 10 am – 4 pm. Northern Horticultural Society, Harlow Carr. 'Close-up SLR flower & garden photography' by Peter Cordall. NHS Members £18. Non-Members £21.
☎ 01423 565418.
Garden Walk. Westonbirt Arboretum, Glos. 'Shrub & grub'. £8.
☎ 01666 880220.

NOTES

• Remember: Scotland's National Gardening Show is just around the corner: have you booked your tickets yet? Tel: 0171 344 4343.

SAT 22

Open Day. 10 am – 5 pm. Pershore & Hindlip College, Worcester. ☎ 01386 554609.
Hertfordshire Garden Show. Knebworth House. 2 days 22–23 May. ☎ 01795 474660.
Les Jardingues. Garden festival & nurserymen's plant sale. Espace Lac, Gérardmer, France. 2 days 22–23 May.
☎ 00 33 03 29 51 47 19.
Open Weekend. 12.30 pm – 5.30 pm. Reaseheath College, Cheshire. 2 days 22–23 May. ☎ 01270 625131.
Garden Walk. 2.15 pm. Hinton Ampner, Hants. 'Meet the gardener'. Numbers limited. £1. ☎ 01962 771305.
Spring Plant Sale. Royal Caledonian Horticultural Society. Saughton Winter Gardens, Edinburgh. ☎ 0131 331 1011.

SUN 23

Garden Tour. 10.30 am Belsay Hall, Northumberland, with Head Gardener Paul Harrigan. £6. Pre-book. ☎ 01661 881636.
Garden Walk. 2 pm. Hillier Arboretum, Hants.
☎ 01794 368787.
Gardens Open. Dam House Farm, Derbys. 2 – 4.30 pm; Carclew Gardens, Cornwall 2 – 5 pm; Crowe Hall, Somerset. 2 – 6 pm; Harwicke House, Cambs. 2 – 5.30 pm; Folly Farm, Berks 2 – 6 pm; Conock Manor, Wilts. 2 – 6 pm.
Workshop. 10 am – 5 pm. RHS Garden Wisley, Surrey. Advanced digital photography. ☎ 01483 224234.
Nursery Plant Sale. 11 am – 4 pm. Bryn Garw Country Park, Bridgend. £1.50 for parking. ☎ 01267 237275.

MAY

NOTES

MON 24
Chelsea Flower Show. Press day & Gala.

TUE 25
Chelsea Flower Show. RHS Members only. 8 am – 8 pm. Chelsea Hospital Grounds. 4 days 25–28 May.
Lecture. 7.15 pm. Hampshire AGS. Chilworth Hall, Southampton. 'Plant hunting near Lake Garda' by Peter Watt.
☎ 01703 252149.

WED 26
Chelsea Flower Show. RHS Members only. 8 am – 8 pm. 2nd day.
Lecture. 1.30 pm. Houghall College, Durham. 'Designing & planting hanging baskets & containers'. RHS Members £4. Non-Members £5. ☎ 0191 386 1351.
Lecture. 2 pm. Writtle College, Chelmsford, Essex. 'Organic growing & companion planting' by Suzanne Higgins. RHS Members £8. Non-Members £10. ☎ 01245 424200.
Lecture. 2 pm. Cannington College, Somerset. 'Softwood cuttings in summer' by John Bates. RHS Members £7.95. Non-Members £8.95. ☎ 01278 655000.
Lecture. 2 pm. Hadlow College, Tonbridge, Kent. 'Softwood cuttings of shrubs' by Phil Thursby. RHS Members £9.50. Non-Members £11. ☎ 01732 850551.
Garden Tour. 6 pm. Reaseheath College, Cheshire. Led by Anne Harrison. RHS Members £6.95. Non-Members £7.95.
☎ 01270 625131.

THU 27
Chelsea Flower Show. 8 am – 8 pm. 3rd day. Public tickets
☎ 0171 344 4343.
Lakeside Walk. 2 pm. Harewood House, W Yorks. Meet in gift shop. ☎ 0113 288 6331.
Garden Walk. Westonbirt Arboretum, Glos. Badgers. £4.
☎ 01666 880220.

MAY

FRI 28

Chelsea Flower Show. 8 am – 5.30 pm. Last day. Public tickets
☎ 0171 344 4343.
Exbury Gardens Event. Exbury Gardens, Hampshire. Crafts, Art, Food, Wine & Gardening. 4 days 28–31 May. ☎ 01703 891203.

SAT 29

Herts County Show. St Albans. 2 days 29–30 May.
☎ 01582 792626.
Spring Plant Sale. Royal Caledonian Horticultural Society. Saughton Winter Gardens, Edinburgh. ☎ 0131 331 1011.
Scottish Beer Festival. 12 noon – 5 pm & 7 – 11 pm. Traquair House, Borders. £3.50. ☎ 01896 830323.

SUN 30

Orchid Show. Sheffield & District Orchid Society. Edensor Institute, Chatsworth Park, Baslow. 2 days 30–31 May.
☎ 0114 230 4568.
Plant Sale. 2 pm. North Court, Isle of Wight. ☎ 01983 740415.
Berkshire County Fayre. Wokingham. ☎ 01635 868646.
City & County of Swansea Show. 2 days 30–31 May.
☎ 01792 635429.
Gloucestershire Country Show. Elmbridge Court. 2 days 30–31 May. ☎ 01242 692202.
Countryside Day. Mannington Gardens, Norfolk.
☎ 01263 584175.
Flower Show. Athelhampton House, Dorset. 5 days 30 May–3 June. ☎ 01305 848363.
Kent Garden Show. Detling. 2 days 30–31 May.
☎ 01795 474600.
Summer Cactus & Succulent Show. Birmingham Botanical Gardens. ☎ 0121 454 1860.
Nursery Plant Sale. 11 am – 4 pm. Gnoll Estate, Neath, West Glamorgan. Free. ☎ 01267 237275.
Gardens Open. Tirley Garth Trust, Cheshire. 2 – 6 pm; Munstead Wood, Surrey. 2 – 6 pm.
Garden Walk. Westonbirt Arboretum, Glos. Japanese cherries.
£5.50. ☎ 01666 880220.
Rare Plant Sale. 11 am – 5 pm. Fonmon Castle, Barry. £2.
☎ 0117 969 1570.

NOTES

- Remember: BBC Gardener's World Live is just around the corner: have you booked your tickets yet? Tel: 0171 344 4343.

MAY • JUNE

NOTES

MON 31

Azalea Time & Plants for Sale 10.30 am – 5 pm. High Beeches, West Sussex. ☎ 01444 400589.
Northumberland County Fair. Tynedale Park, Corbridge.
☎ 01434 344443.
Gardens Open. Ammerdown Park, Somerset 11 am – 5 pm; Tirley Garth Trust, Cheshire. 2 – 6 pm; Westwell Manor, Oxon. 2 – 6.30 pm.
Sherborne Castle Country Fair. Sherborne, Dorset.
☎ 01747 811216.
Surrey County Show. Stoke Park, Guildford. ☎ 01483 414651.
Country Fair. Duncombe Park, North Yorkshire.
☎ 01439 770213.
Valley Gardens Arts Fair, Harrogate. ☎ 01423 500600.

TUE 1

'COLOUR, FORM AND TEXTURE ALL PLAY AN IMPORTANT ROLE IN GARDEN DESIGN, AND PERENNIALS OFFER THE WIDEST CHOICE OF THOSE INGREDIENTS'.
ROY LANCASTER, *WHAT PLANT WHERE*, 1997.

WED 2

Staffordshire County Show. Stafford. 2 days 2–3 June.
☎ 01785 258060.
Specialist Day. RHS Garden Wisley, Surrey. 'Culinary herbs' with members of RHS staff. ☎ 01483 224234.
Suffolk County Show. Ipswich. 2 days 2–3 June.
☎ 01473 726847.
Wild Flowers Field Trip. 1.30 pm. Myerscough College, Preston, Lancs. Led by Brian Burrows. RHS Members £6. Non-Members £7.50. ☎ 01995 640611.
Lecture. 2 pm. Cannington College, Somerset. 'Encouraging wildlife into the garden' by Bob Skittrell & Derek Fawcett. RHS Members £7.95. Non-Members £8.95. ☎ 01278 655000.
Demonstration. 2 pm. Hadlow College, Tonbridge, Kent. 'Your garden in June' by Nick Egan. RHS Members £9.50. Non-Members £11. ☎ 01732 850551.

THU 3

NAFAS Flower Festival. Leeds Castle, Kent. 4 days 3–6 June.
☎ 01622 765400.
Guernsey Floral Show. Cambridge Park, St Peter Port. 3 days 3–5 June. ☎ 01481 723552.
Children's Workshop. 1.30 – 3.30 pm. Northern Horticultural Society, Harlow Carr. 'Growing plants' by Deidre Walton. £6.
☎ 01423 565418.
Lecture. 2 pm. Pershore & Hindlip College, Worcester. 'Lavenders'. RHS Members £5. Non-Members £10.
☎ 01386 554609.

JUNE

FRI 4

Scotland's National Gardening Show. Strathclyde Country Park. 11 am – 7 pm. 3 days 4–6 June. ☎ 0990 900123.
Holker Garden Festival. Holker Hall, Cumbria. 3 days 4–6 June. ☎ 01539 558328.
Demonstration & Workshop. (Demonstration 11.30 am, Workshop 2pm.) RHS Garden Hyde Hall, Essex. 'Planting containers' with Andrew Lodge & Ian LeGros. RHS Members £10. Non-Members £20. ☎ 01245 400256.
Garden Walk. Meet the Gardener. 1.30 pm. Hutton-in-the-Forest, Cumbria. ☎ 017684 84449.

SAT 5

Scotland's National Gardening Show. Strathclyde Country Park. 10 am – 6 pm. 2nd day.
British Iris Society Show. RHS Garden Wisley, Surrey. 2 days 5–6 June ☎ 01483 224234.
Gardeners' Weekend at Eastnor Castle, Herefordshire. 2 days 5–6 June. ☎ 0121 682 0860.
Gardeners' Weekend at Castle Bromwich Hall Gardens, West Midlands. 2 days 5–6 June. ☎ 0121 749 4100.
Pensthorpe's Plant & Gardener's Fair. Pensthorpe Wildfowl Park, Fakenham, Norfolk. 2 days 5–6 June. ☎ 01328 851465.
Specialist Plant Sale. Hardy Plant Society at Forde Abbey, Dorset. ☎ 01460 220231.
Leicestershire Gardening & Flower Festival. Stanford Hall, Lutterworth. 2 days 5–6 June. ☎ 01332 553429.
Woburn Garden Show. Woburn Abbey, Beds. 2 days 5–6 June. ☎ 01525 290666.
AGS Summer South Show. 12 noon – 4.30 pm. Merrist Wood, Guildford. ☎ 01932 346390.
Rhododendron Tour. 10.30 am Belsay Hall, Northumberland, with Head Gardener Paul Harrigan. £6. ☎ 01661 881636.
NCCPG Plant Fair. 12 noon – 4 pm. Felley Priory, Notts. ☎ 01773 810230.
Garden Walk. Meet the gardener. Coughton Court, Warwicks. ☎ 01789 400777.
Guided Walks. Brogdale, Kent. 2 days. ☎ 01795 535286.

SUN 6

Scotland's National Gardening Show. Strathclyde Country Park. 10 am – 5 pm. Last day.
Tatton Park Orchid Fayre. Tenants Hall, Tatton Park, Cheshire.
Viola & Pansy Display. Florists' & garden cultivars. Dudmaston Hall (National Trust), Bridgnorth. ☎ 01746 766909.
Gardens Open. Hill House, Herts. 2 – 5 pm; Tirley Garth Trust, Cheshire. 2 – 6 pm; Whitfield, Hereford & Worcester. 2 – 6 pm.
Rare Plant Sale. 11 am – 5 pm. Ashley Manor, Tetbury, Glos. £2. ☎ 0117 969 1570.
Garden Walk. RHS Garden Wisley, Surrey. 'A summer stroll in the garden' with Colin Crosbie. RHS Members £5. Non-Members £10. ☎ 01483 224234.

NOTES

'DO YOU EVER WONDER IF THE BBC GIVES GARDENING AND ITS POSSIBILITIES FOR BROADCASTING ANY THOUGHT AT ALL?'
HUGH JOHNSON, *RHSJ*, MAY 1980.

JUNE

NOTES

MON 7

Day Course. 10 am – 4 pm. Northern Horticultural Society, Harlow Carr. 'Naturalistic garden maintenance' by Roger Brook. NHS Members £18. Non-Members £21. ☎ 01423 565418.
Lecture. 7 pm. Askham Bryan College, York. 'Constructing basic garden features' by Andrew Mahy. RHS Members £4. Non-Members £5. ☎ 01904 772277.
Lecture. 7 pm. Pencoed College, Bridgend, Mid Glamorgan. 'Focus on flower photography' by Arthur Tickner. RHS Members £5. Non-Members £6.50. ☎ 01656 860202.

TUE 8

Demonstration. 2 pm. Pershore & Hindlip College, Worcester. 'Your garden in June' by Bob Hares. RHS Members £5. Non-Members £10. ☎ 01386 554609.

'KITCHEN GARDEN: AROMATIC HERBS, FOR DRYING AND DISTILLING, GATHER. *FLOWER GARDEN:* WEEDS IN THIS MONTH ARE OF THE UTMOST CONSEQUENCE TO BE DESTROYED. *GREENHOUSE:* ALOES, FRESH EARTH, AND PLACE NEAR THE WINDOWS, BUT TAKE OUT THE AMERICANS'. RICHARD WESTON ESQ., *THE GARDENER'S POCKET CALENDAR,* 1783.

WED 9

Specialist Day. RHS Garden Wisley, Surrey. 'Growing vegetables' with Jim England. ☎ 01483 224234.
Garden Walk. 2 pm. Scottish Agricultural College, Auchincruive, Ayr. Allan Coutts, Head Gardener. RHS Members £4.95. Non-Members £5.95. ☎ 01292 525393.
Demonstration. RHS Garden Wisley, Surrey. 'Summer treatment of grapes: indoors & out' with Jim Arbury & Ron Gilkerson. RHS Members £5. Non-Members £10. ☎ 01483 224234.
Jersey Early Summer Show. Howard Davis Park, Jersey. 2 days 9–10 June. ☎ 01534 866555.
Garden Walk. RHS Garden Wisley, Surrey. 'A summer stroll in the garden' with David Jewell. RHS Members £5. Non-Members £10. ☎ 01483 224234.
The Taming of the Shrew. Painswick Rococo Garden, Glos. 2 days 9–10 June. ☎ 01452 813204.
Lecture. 2 pm. Hadlow College, Tonbridge, Kent. 'Flowering' by Dr Gesa Reiss. RHS Members £9.50. Non-Members £11. ☎ 01732 850551.
Lecture. 6.30 pm. Reaseheath College, Cheshire. 'Flower arranging: summer' by Mark Entwistle. RHS Members £6.95. Non-Members £7.95. ☎ 01270 625131.

THU 10

Royal Cornwall Show. Wadebridge. 3 days 10–12 June. ☎ 01208 812183.
South of England Show. Ardingly, West Sussex. 3 days 10–12 June. ☎ 01444 892700.
Lecture. 2 pm. Pershore & Hindlip College, Worcester. 'Lupins' by Maurice Woodford. RHS Members £5. Non-Members £10. ☎ 01386 554609.
Garden Open. Preen Manor, Shropshire. 2 – 6 pm.
Grand Summer Sale (Homes & Gardens). 10 am – 6 pm. Ripley Castle, North Yorkshire. 4 days 10–13 June. ☎ 01423 770152.
Garden Walk. 7 pm. Cragside, Northumberland. ☎ 01669 620150.

FRI 11

Lecture. RHS Garden Rosemoor, Devon. 'Unusual plants' by David Squire. ☎ 01805 624067.

SAT 12

Flower Festival. Castle Howard. Plus **Plant Fair** in grounds (2 days). ☎ 01653 648444.
Garden Festival. Friends of Ness Gardens, Cheshire. Visitor Centre, Ness. 2 days 12–13 June. £3 to RHS Members.
Dulwich Country Fayre. 11 am – 6 pm. Dulwich Park, London. 2 days 12–13 June. ☎ 0171 525 1080.
Cactus Sale. British Cactus & Succulent Society. Tropical World, Canal Gardens, Leeds. 2 days 12–13 June. ☎ 0113 266 1850.
Study Day. 10 am – 4 pm. Oxford Botanic Garden. 'Basic garden skills for absolute beginners'. £30. ☎ 01865 276920.
Demonstration. 10 am. Pershore & Hindlip College, Worcester. 'Your garden in June' by Bob Hares. RHS Members £5. Non-Members £10. ☎ 01386 554609.
Workshop. 1.30 pm. Myerscough College, Preston, Lancs. Identifying pests & diseases. Led by Jeff Hodson & Peter Wiseman. RHS Members £6. Non-Members £7.50.
☎ 01995 640611.

SUN 13

National Pelargonium Show. Capel Manor, Enfield. Details from British Pelargonium & Geranium Society. Secretary Brian Archibald. ☎ 0181 467 5760.
Country Fair. Burton Constable Gardens, Yorkshire.
☎ 01964 562400.
Clonakilty Agricultural Show. Cork. ☎ 00 353 023 47390.
NCCPG Plant Sale. 10 am. Belsay Hall, Northumberland. £2.70.
☎ 01661 881636.
Gardens Open. Brook Lodge Farm Cottage, Surrey 2 – 5 pm; Hill House, Herts. 2 – 5 pm; The Old Vicarage, Edington, Wilts. 2 – 6 pm; Clinton Lodge, East Sussex 2 – 6 pm; Crowe Hall, Somerset. 2 – 6 pm.
Music in the Garden. Lea Gardens, Derbyshire. 2 pm.
☎ 01629 534380.
Nursery Plant Sale. 11 am – 4 pm. Colby Woodland Garden, Dyfed. £2.80 for admission: plant sale free. ☎ 01267 237275.

NOTES

JUNE

NOTES

MON 14
Garden Open. Clinton Lodge, East Sussex 2 – 6 pm.

TUE 15
Three Counties Show. Malvern. 3 days 15–17 June. ☎ 01684 584900.
Lecture. 2 pm. Pershore & Hindlip College, Worcester. 'Finding new plants' by Bob Brown. RHS Members £5. Non-Members £10. ☎ 01386 554609.
Rose Clinic. 6.45 – 8.30 pm. Mottisfont Abbey, Hants. Help with identifying old roses.

> 'EACH SEASON HAS ITS PARTICULAR CHARACTER AND BRINGS NEW FEATURES TO THE GARDEN LANDSCAPE. PERENNIALS MIRROR THIS SEASONAL PASSAGE BY OFFERING CONTINUAL CHANGES IN GROWTH, FOLIAGE AND FLOWERS'.
> ROY LANCASTER, *WHAT PLANT WHERE*, 1997.

WED 16
BBC Gardeners' World Live Show. 9 am – 6 pm. NEC, Birmingham. 5 days 16–20 June. Tickets: ☎ 0121 767 4505.
Lecture. 10 am. Cannington College, Somerset. 'Creating a cottage garden' by Brian Thames. RHS Members £7.95. Non-Members £8.95. ☎ 01278 655000.
Lecture. 2 pm. Writtle College, Chelmsford, Essex. 'Four seasons in the garden – summer' by Marion Polley. RHS Members £8. Non-Members £10. ☎ 01245 424200.
Garden Open. Brook Lodge Farm Cottage, Surrey 2 – 5 pm.
Lecture. 2 pm. Hadlow College, Tonbridge, Kent. 'Designing a herbaceous border' by Keith Mexter. RHS Members £9.50. Non-Members £11. ☎ 01732 850551.
Garden Walk. 2.30 pm. Sizergh Castle, Cumbria. With Head Gardener.

THU 17
BBC Gardeners' World Live Show. 9 am – 6 pm. NEC, Birmingham. 2nd day.
Lecture. 1 pm. Welsh College of Horticulture, Northop, Flintshire. 'Your garden in summer' by Anne Lewis. RHS Members £8. Non-Members £10. ☎ 01352 841000.
Summer Flower Festival. Pashley Manor Gardens, East Sussex. 4 days 17–20 June. ☎ 01580 200692.
Lecture. 2 pm. Pershore & Hindlip College, Worcester. 'Minimum effort for maximum effect' by Mary Payne. RHS Members £5. Non-Members £10. ☎ 01386 554609.
Day Course. 10 am – 4 pm. Northern Horticultural Society, Harlow Carr. 'The garden in summer' by Rita Lait. NHS Members £19. Non-Members £22. ☎ 01423 565418.
Botanical Art Course. RHS Garden Wisley, Surrey. Advanced level. 4 days 17–20 June. ☎ 01483 224234.

FRI 18

Flower & Garden Festival. Stapehill Abbey, Dorset. 4 days 18–21 June. ☎ 01202 861686.
Rose Clinic. 6.45 pm – 8.30 pm. Mottisfont Abbey, Hants. Help with identifying old roses.
East of England Show. Peterborough. 2 days 18–19 June. ☎ 01733 234451.
Essex County Show. Great Leighs, Chelmsford. 2 days 18–19 June. ☎ 01245 362412.
BBC Gardeners' World Live Show. 9 am – 6 pm. NEC, Birmingham. 3rd day.

SAT 19

Lecture. 9.30 am. Welsh College of Horticulture, Northop, Flintshire. 'Your garden in summer' by Anne Lewis. RHS Members £8. Non-Members £10. ☎ 01352 841000.
Garden Festival. 10 am – 6 pm. Abbotsbury gardens, Dorset. 2 days 19–20 June. ☎ 01305 871130.
Festival of Gardening. 10 am – 6 pm. Hatfield House, Herts. £6.50. 2 days 19–20 June.
National Forest Festival. Catton Park, Derbyshire. 2 days 19–20 June. ☎ 0115 937 4147.
Rose Weekend. Borde Hill, West Sussex. £4. 2 days 19–20 June. ☎ 01444 450326.
Delphinium Society Show. RHS Garden Wisley, Surrey. 2 days 19–20 June. ☎ 01483 224234.
Annual Show. British & European Geranium Society. Princess Royal Theatre, Port Talbot. ☎ 01772 453383.
Organic Gardening Weekend. HDRA, Ryton, Warks. 2 days 19–20 June. ☎ 01203 303517.
Lecture. 10 am. Reaseheath College, Cheshire. 'Botanical drawing: getting started' by Anne Harrison. RHS Members £6.95. Non-Members £7.95. ☎ 01270 625131.
Enfield Rose & Horticultural Show. Capel Manor, London. 2 days 19–20 June. ☎ 0181 366 4442.
AGS Summer North Show. 11.30 am – 4.15 pm. Pudsey, W Yorks. ☎ 01423 886302.
BBC Gardeners' World Live Show. 9 am – 6 pm. NEC, Birmingham. 4th day.
Rose Weekend. Mattocks Roses, Oxford. 9 am – 5.30 pm. 2 days 19–20 June. ☎ 01865 343454.

SUN 20

Covent Garden Flower Festival. London. 8 days 20–27 June. ☎ 0171 379 7020.
Rare Plant Fair. 11 am – 5 pm. The Old Rectory, Burghfield, Berks. £2. ☎ 0117 969 1570.
BBC Gardeners' World Live Show. 9 am – 6 pm. NEC, Birmingham. Last day.
Gardens Open. Hillbarn House, Wilts. 2 – 6 pm; Long Barn, Kent 2 – 5 pm; The Manor House, Bledlow, Bucks. 2 – 6 pm; Folly Farm, Berks 2 – 6 pm.

NOTES

JUNE 1998 WAS THE SECOND WETTEST JUNE THIS CENTURY IN MUCH OF ENGLAND. THERE WAS MORE RAIN LAST JUNE THAN IN ANY JUNE SINCE 1997. BOTH THESE STATEMENTS ARE TRUE.

JUNE

NOTES

MON 21
NAFAS National Assembly. 40th anniversary. Sheffield. 4 days 21–24 June. ☎ 0171 828 5145.
Day Course. 10 am – 4 pm. Northern Horticultural Society, Harlow Carr. 'Drawing flowers & plants' by Victoria Street. RHS Members £18. Non-Members £21. ☎ 01423 565418.
Lecture. 7 pm. Pencoed College, Bridgend. Mid Glamorgan. 'Pruning shrubs: how & when' by Philip Thomas. RHS Members £5. Non-Members £6.50. ☎ 01656 860202.

TUE 22
RHS Flower Show. 11 am – 7 pm. (10 am – 5 pm 2nd day.) RHS New Hall, Westminster. Ornamental Plant Competition. 2 days 22–23 June.
RHS Annual General Meeting. RHS Old Hall, Westminster.
Cheshire County Show. Tabley. 2 days 22–23 June.
☎ 01829 760020.
Lecture. 2 pm. Pershore & Hindlip College, Worcester. 'Plants for vertical gardening' by Michael Jefferson-Brown. RHS Members £5. Non-Members £10. ☎ 01386 554609.

WED 23
RHS London Flower Arrangement Demonstration. 2.15 pm. RHS Halls, Westminster. 'Flowers for the millennium' by Betty Jones & Angela Turner.
Day Course. 10 am – 4 pm. Northern Horticultural Society, Harlow Carr. 'Flower water-colour painting' by Victoria Street. NHS Members £18. Non-Members £21. ☎ 01423 565418.
Artists' Workshop. 1.30 pm. Houghall College, Durham. 'Plant portraits.' RHS Members £4. Non-Members £5. ☎ 0191 386 1351.
Demonstration. RHS Garden Wisley, Surrey. 'Pruning shrubs' with Bernard Boardman. RHS Members £5. Non-Members £10. ☎ 01483 224234.
Lecture. 2 pm. Hadlow College, Tonbridge, Kent. 'Growing vegetables in the garden' by Dave Ridgeway. RHS Members £9.50. Non-Members £11. ☎ 01732 850551.
Lecture. 2 pm. Cannington College, Somerset. 'Osteospermums & argyranthemums' by Peter Elliman. RHS Members £7.95. Non-Members £8.95. ☎ 01278 655000.
Garden Open. Clinton Lodge, East Sussex 2 – 6 pm.

THU 24
Day Course. 10 am – 4 pm. Northern Horticultural Society, Harlow Carr. 'Advanced water-colour painting of flowers' by Victoria Street. NHS Members £18. Non-Members £21. ☎ 01423 565418.
Specialist Day. RHS Garden Wisley, Surrey. 'Gardening for wheelchair users' with members of RHS staff. ☎ 01483 224234.
Royal Highland Show. Edinburgh. 4 days 24–27 June.
☎ 0131 335 6200.
Garden Open. Preen Manor, Shropshire. 2 – 6 pm.
Daily Telegraph House & Garden Fair. Olympia, London. 4 days 24–27 June. ☎ 0171 453 5326.

JUNE

FRI 25

Garden Walks. 11.30 am. RHS Garden Hyde Hall, Essex. 'Midsummer' with Andrew Lodge & Ian LeGros. RHS Members £5. Non-Members £10. ☎ 01245 400256.

SAT 26

Floral Festival at Benington Lordship, Herts. 12 noon – 6 pm. 2 days 26–27 June. ☎ 01438 869228.
Country Show. Sandringham, Norfolk. 2 days 26–27 June. ☎ 01553 772675.
Newbury Summer Show, including **International Orchid Show.** Newbury Show Ground, Berkshire. 2 days 26–27 June. ☎ 01529 421521.
National Southern Show. Royal National Rose Society. Shepperton, London. 2 days 26–27 June. ☎ 01727 850461.
Rose Weekend. RHS & RNRS. RHS Garden Rosemoor, Devon. 2 days 26–27 June. ☎ 01805 624067.
Garden Festival. Arley Hall, Cheshire. 2 days 26–27 June. ☎ 01565 777353.
Gardeners' Weekend. Hever Castle, Kent. 2 days 26–27 June. ☎ 01732 865224.
Garden Show. Groombridge Place, Kent. 10 am – 6 pm. Nurseries, crafts & garden equipment. 2 days 26–27 June.
Garden Event. West Dean, West Sussex. 2 days 26–27 June. ☎ 01243 811205.
Flower & Garden Show. Chatsworth, Derbys. 2 days 26–27 June. ☎ 01246 582204.
Birds, Bees & Butterflies Weekend. Plant centre, RHS Garden Wisley, Surrey. 2 days 26–27 June.
Lecture. 10 am. Reaseheath College, Cheshire. 'Botanical drawing: painting the plants' by Anne Harrison. RHS Members £6.95. Non-Members £7.95. ☎ 01270 625131.
Garden Open. Brandy House Mount, Hants. 2 – 5 pm.
Jersey Festival Rose Show. Samares Manor. 11 am – 7 pm. 2 days 26–27 June. ☎ 01534 852439.

SUN 27

Garden Open & Nurserymen's Plant Sale. 11 am – 4 pm. Wartnaby, Leicestershire. ☎ 01664 822549.
Rare Plant Fair. 11 am – 5 pm. The Manor House, Birlingham, Worcestershire. 25 Specialist Nurseries. ☎ 01386 750005.
Demonstration. RHS Garden Wisley, Surrey. 'Pruning shrubs' with Bernard Boardman. RHS Members £5. Non-Members £10. ☎ 01483 224234.
Gardens Open. Vale End, Surrey 10 am – 5 pm; Stillingfleet Lodge, York 1.30 – 5 pm; Stowell Park, Glos. 2 – 5 pm; Wartnaby Gardens, Leics. 11 am – 4 pm; Preen Manor, Shropshire. 2 – 6 pm; The Old Rectory, Farnborough, Oxon. 2 – 6 pm; Fairfield House, Hants. 2 – 6 pm.
Plant Sale. Wiltshire Gardens Trust. Chisenbury Priory, nr Enford. ☎ 01225 722267.
Open Day. Friends of the Botanic Garden. University of Leicester. 11 am – 4 pm.

NOTES

'ENGLAND IS A LITTLE GARDEN, FULL OF SOUR WEEDS'. (ATTRIBUTED TO KING LOUIS XIV OF FRANCE IN 1706.)

JUNE • JULY

NOTES

MON 28
Specialist Day. RHS Garden Wisley, Surrey. 'Cultivating herbs' with members of RHS staff. ☎ 01483 224234.

TUE 29
Provincial Show. National Sweet Pea Society. Cambridge Botanic Gardens. 2 days 29–30 June. ☎ 01794 301490.
Workshop. 10 am. Pershore & Hindlip College, Worcester. 'Flower arranging from your garden' by Sallie Campbell. ☎ 01386 554609.

'FEW COUNTRIES ARE BEFORE US (THE ENGLISH), EITHER IN THE ELEGANCE OF OUR GARDENS OR IN THE NUMBERS OF OUR PLANTS. AND NONE EQUALS US IN THE VARIETY OF FRUITS WHICH MAY JUSTLY BE CALLED GOOD'. SIR WILLIAM TEMPLE, *THE GARDENS OF EPICURUS*, 1692.

WED 30
Royal Norfolk Show. Norwich. 2 days. ☎ 01603 748931.
Demonstration. Flower Arranging. 10 am – 12.30 pm. RHS Garden Wisley, Surrey. 'Summer splendour' with Fred Wilkinson. ☎ 01483 224234.
Lecture. 2 pm. Cannington College, Somerset. 'Chip budding' by John Bates. RHS Members £7.95. Non-Members £8.95. ☎ 01278 655000.
Lecture. 2 pm. Hadlow College, Tonbridge, Kent. 'Trees for the small garden' by Keith Mexter. RHS Members £9.50. Non-Members £11. ☎ 01732 850551.
Garden Open. Clinton Lodge, East Sussex 2 – 6 pm.

THU 1
Day Course. 10 am – 4 pm. Northern Horticultural Society, Harlow Carr. 'Further steps in flower & garden photography' by Peter Cordall. NHS Members £18. Non-Members £21. ☎ 01423 565418.
Demonstration. 2 pm. Pershore & Hindlip College, Worcester. 'Garden designing with steps' by David Everitt. RHS Members £5. Non-Members £10. ☎ 01386 554609.

JULY

FRI 2

Demonstration & Workshop. 11.30 am. RHS Garden Hyde Hall, Essex. 'Pruning shrubs' with Andrew Lodge & Ian LeGros. RHS Members £5. Non-Members £10. ☎ 01245 400256.
Garden Walk. Meet the gardener. 1.30 pm. Hutton-in-the-Forest, Cumbria. ☎ 017684 84449.
Specialist Day. RHS Garden Wisley, Surrey. 'Plantsman's day'.
☎ 01483 224234.
Concert & Fireworks. Leighton Hall, Lancs. ☎ 01524 734474.

SAT 3

Gardeners' Weekend. 10 am – 6 pm. Shugborough Hall, Staffs. 2 days 3–4 July. ☎ 01889 881388.
Delphinium Society Show. RHS Garden Wisley, Surrey. 2 days 3–4 July. ☎ 01483 224234.
British Paphiopedilum Society. Summer Meeting. Hilton Hotel, Castle Donington. ☎ 01962 777372.
Steam Fair. Duncombe Park, North Yorkshire. 2 days 3–4 July.
☎ 01439 770213.
The Taming of the Shrew. Westonbirt Arboretum, Glos. £10.
☎ 01666 880220.
Garden Walk. Meet the gardener. Coughton Court, Warwicks.
☎ 01789 400777.
Balloon & Flower Festival. Southampton Common. Flowers 10 am – 7 pm. 2 days 3–4 July. Balloons 6 am & 6 pm. Tethered flights throughout the day. ☎ 01703 464466.

SUN 4

Nursery Plant Sale. 11 am – 4 pm. Walled Gardens, Pigeonsford, Llangranog, Dyfed. £1.50 for admission: plant sale free.
☎ 01267 237275.
Garden Open. Great Barfield, Bucks. 2 – 6 pm.
Garden Walk. 2 pm. Hillier Arboretum, Hants.
☎ 01794 368787.

NOTES

JULY

NOTES

MON 5

Royal Show. Stoneleigh, Warks. 4 days 5–8 July.
☎ 01203 696969.
Lecture. 7 pm. Pencoed College, Bridgend. Mid Glamorgan. 'Hard landscape in the garden' by Bryan Jones. RHS Members £5. Non-Members £6.50. ☎ 01656 860202.
Lecture. 7 pm. Rosecarpe. 'Cottage gardening' by Dianne Nichol-Brown. Civic Centre, Gateshead. ☎ 0191 252 7052.
Hampton Court Palace Flower Show Gala Preview. 7 pm. Tickets £200 (dinner) or £48 (garden party). ☎ 0171 630 5999.

'FLOWERS IN MASSES ARE MIGHTY STRONG COLOUR, AND IF NOT USED WITH A GREAT DEAL OF CAUTION ARE VERY DESTRUCTIVE TO PLEASURE IN GARDENING. ON THE WHOLE, I THINK THE BEST AND SAFEST PLAN IS TO MIX UP YOUR FLOWERS'. WILLIAM MORRIS, *ART & SOCIAL REFORM*, 1882

TUE 6

Hampton Court Palace Flower Show. 10 am – 7.30 pm. 6 days 6–11 July. RHS Members only day.
Demonstration. 2 pm. Pershore & Hindlip College, Worcester. 'Your garden in July' by Bob Hares. RHS Members £5. Non-Members £10. ☎ 01386 554609.
Entertainment at Parnham House, Dorset. 'Shakespeare on the lawn'. 7.30 pm; bring picnic & rug.

WED 7

Hampton Court Palace Flower Show. 10 am – 7.30 pm. 2nd day, for RHS Members only.
Lecture. 10 am. Cannington College, Somerset. 'The Flower arranger's garden' by John Addison & Sylvia Hanks. RHS Members £7.95. Non-Members £8.95. ☎ 01278 655000.
Lecture. 2 pm. Writtle College, Chelmsford, Essex. 'Plant ecology' by Cath Hayward. RHS Members £8. Non-Members £10. ☎ 01245 424200.
Demonstration. 2 pm. Hadlow College, Tonbridge, Kent. 'Your garden in July' by Nick Egan. RHS Members £9.50. Non-Members £11. ☎ 01732 850551.
Lecture. 6.30 pm. Reaseheath College, Cheshire. 'Pruning fruit trees & bushes' by Bert Davis. RHS Members £6.95. Non-Members £7.95. ☎ 01270 625131.

THU 8

Hampton Court Palace Flower Show. 10 am – 7.30 pm. 3rd day. Public tickets: ☎ 0171 344 9966.
Lecture. 1 pm. Welsh College of Horticulture, Northop, Flintshire. 'Friends & foes in the garden' by David Toyne. RHS Members £8. Non-Members £10. ☎ 01352 841000.

July

9 FRI
Hampton Court Palace Flower Show. 10 am – 7.30 pm. 4th day.
Public tickets: ☎ 0171 344 9966.

10 SAT
Hampton Court Palace Flower Show. 10 am – 7.30 pm. 5th day.
Public tickets: ☎ 0171 344 9966.
Lecture. 9.30 am. Welsh College of Horticulture, Northop, Flintshire. 'Friends & foes in the garden' by David Toyne. RHS Members £8. Non-Members £10. ☎ 01352 841000.
Demonstration. 10 am. Pershore & Hindlip College, Worcester. 'Your garden in July' by Bob Hares. RHS Members £5. Non-Members £10. ☎ 01386 554609.
Biennial Conference. Association of Societies for Growing Australian Plants. Brisbane, Queensland. 7 days. 10–16 July lg.murray@mailbox.uq.edu.au
Summer Fruit Festival. Brogdale, Kent. 2 days 10–11 July.
☎ 01795 535286.

11 SUN
Hampton Court Palace Flower Show. 10 am – 5.30 pm. Last day.
Public tickets: ☎ 0171 344 9966.
Falconry Demonstrations. Penshurst Place, Kent.
Country Fair & Plant Sale. Squerryes Court, Kent.
☎ 01959 562345.
Show. British National Carnation Society. Birmingham.
☎ 01327 351594.
Gardens Open. Crowe Hall, Somerset. 2 – 6 pm; Whitfield, Hereford & Worcester. 2 – 6 pm.
Nursery Plant Sale. 11 am – 4 pm. Gnoll Estate, Neath, West Glamorgan. Free. ☎ 01267 237275.

NOTES

> '*FLOWER GARDEN:* ANNUALS, TO FLOWER IN AUTUMN, STILL SOW. *FRUIT GARDEN:* ANTS, CATERPILLARS, FLIES AND WASPS, CONSTANTLY SEARCH FOR AND DESTROY.'
> RICHARD WESTON ESQ., *THE GARDENER'S POCKET CALENDAR,* 1783

July

NOTES

MON 12
Talk & Walk. RHS Garden Wisley, Surrey. 'Heathland & heathers' with Andy Collins. RHS Members £5. Non-Members £10. ☎ 01483 224234.

TUE 13
Great Yorkshire Show. Harrogate. 3 days 13–15 July. ☎ 01423 541000.
Garden Tour. 2 pm. Visiting the special plant unit. Pershore & Hindlip College, Worcester. Led by Margaret Sheward. RHS Members £5. Non-Members £10. ☎ 01386 554609.

WED 14
National Show. National Sweet Pea Society. Althorp Park, Northants. ☎ 01794 301490.
Summer Fruit & Vegetable Competition. RHS Garden Wisley, Surrey. ☎ 01483 224234.
Lecture. 2 pm. Scottish Agricultural College, Auchincruive, Ayr. 'Success with summer cuttings' by Peter MacDonald. RHS Members £4.95. Non-Members £5.95. ☎ 01292 525393.
Lecture. 2 pm. Writtle College, Chelmsford, Essex. 'Grasses'. RHS Members £8. Non-Members £10. ☎ 01245 424200.
Lecture. 2 pm. Cannington College, Somerset. 'Abutilons' by Peter Elliman. RHS Members £7.95. Non-Members £8.95. ☎ 01278 655000.
Garden Walk. 2 pm. Claremont Landscape Garden, Surrey.
Lecture. 2 pm. Hadlow College, Tonbridge, Kent. 'Climbing Plants' by Keith Mexter. RHS Members £9.50. Non-Members £11. ☎ 01732 850551.
Demonstration. RHS Garden Wisley, Surrey. 'Pruning fruit trees & bushes' with Jim Arbury & Charlie Day. RHS Members £5. Non-Members £10. ☎ 01483 224234.

THU 15
International Rose Trials Judging. Rose Society of Northern Ireland. Sir Thomas & Lady Dixon Park, Belfast. ☎ 01574 272658.
Kent Show. Detling, Maidstone. 3 days 15–17 July. ☎ 01622 630975.
Demonstration. 2 pm. Pershore & Hindlip College, Worcester. 'Success with budding' by Bob Hares. RHS Members £5. Non-Members £10. ☎ 01386 554609.
Specialist Day. RHS Garden Wisley, Surrey. 'Hedges & screens' with David Sewell. ☎ 01483 224234.

On This Day
St Swithin's Day. Tradition maintains that if there is rain on St Swithin's Day, it will continue for the next forty days.

JULY

FRI 16
Lecture. 6 pm. RHS Garden Rosemoor, Devon. 'History of Rosemoor' by David Squire. ☎ 01805 624067.
Concert & Fireworks. Kingston Lacy, Dorset. 8 pm (admission from 5.30 pm). Bournemouth Symphonietta. £12. ☎ 01985 843601.
Specialist Day. RHS Garden Wisley, Surrey. 'Garden pests & diseases' with Chris Prior & Andrew Halstead. ☎ 01483 224234.

On This Day
Four inches (102mm.) of rain fell in 1¼ hours at Wisley in Surrey on 16 July 1947.

SAT 17
Summer Rose Show. Rose Society of Northern Ireland. Wilmont House, Sir Thomas & Lady Dixon Park, Belfast. 2 days 17–18 July. ☎ 01574 272658.
Garden WeekeNd. Parham Park, West Sussex. Specialist nurseries, floral art & flower festival. 11 am – 6 pm. Adults £5; Children £1. 2 days 17–18 July. ☎ 01903 744888.
Lecture. 2 pm. Otley College, Ipswich, Suffolk. 'Summer colour in your garden' by Matt Tanton-Brown. RHS Members £5. Non-Members £6. ☎ 01473 785543.
Garden Walk. 2.15 pm. Hinton Ampner, Hants. 'Meet the gardener'. Numbers limited. £1. ☎ 01962 771305.
Derbyshire Gardening & Flower Festival. 10 am – 6 pm. Locko Park, Derby. 2 days 17–18 July. ☎ 01332 553429.
Jazz in the Park. 7.30 pm. Lanhydrock, Cornwall. ☎ 01208 74281.
Wildlife Fair & Plant Sale. 11 am – 5 pm. Dorset Wildlife Trust. Melbury House, Melbury Sampford. ☎ 01305 264620.
Country Fair. Holkham Hall, Norfolk. 2 days 17–18 July. ☎ 01328 710227.
Garden Theatre. Rockingham Castle, Leics. 'Twelfth Night'.

SUN 18
Workshop. Macro photography. 10 am – 5 pm. RHS Garden Wisley, Surrey. ☎ 01483 224234.
Garden Tour. 2 pm. 'Meet the gardener'. Mottisfont Abbey, Hants.
Gardens Open. Dam House Farm, Derbys. 2 – 4.30 pm; Brook Lodge Farm Cottage, Surrey 2 – 5 pm; Long Barn, Kent 2 – 5 pm; Greenways, Oxford 2 – 6 pm; Munstead Wood, Surrey. 2 – 6 pm.
Plant Sale. 2 pm. Cragside, Northumberland. ☎ 01669 620150.
Garden Walk. RHS Garden Wisley, Surrey. 'Summer borders' with David Hoodless. RHS Members £5. Non-Members £10. ☎ 01483 224234.
Nursery Plant Sale. 11 am – 4 pm. Bryn Garw Country Park, Bridgend. £1.50 for parking. ☎ 01267 237275.
Demonstration. RHS Garden Wisley, Surrey. 'Pruning fruit trees & bushes' with Jim Arbury & Charlie Day. RHS Members £5. Non-Members £10. ☎ 01483 224234.

NOTES

'GARDEN-LOVERS ARE GREEDY FOLK, AND ALWAYS WANT TO HAVE MORE AND MORE AND MORE! I WANT A ROSE-GARDEN, AND A TULIP-GARDEN, AND A CARNATION-GARDEN, AND A COLUMBINE-GARDEN, AND A FERN-GARDEN BUT, IF I WERE ABLE, THE FIRST I SHOULD MAKE WOULD BE A WALL-FLOWER GARDEN'. GERTRUDE JEKYLL, *HOME & GARDEN*, 1900.

July

NOTES

MON 19
Royal Welsh Show. Builth Wells, Powys. 4 days 19–22 July.
☎ 01982 553683.
Annual Show. National Viola & Pansy Society. St John's Church, Harborne, Birmingham. ☎ 01746 766909.

TUE 20
Demonstration. 2 pm. Pershore & Hindlip College, Worcester. 'The potager in the summer' by Bob Hares. RHS Members £5. Non-Members £7. ☎ 01386 554609.
Guided Tour of Terraces. 2 pm. Harewood House, W Yorks. Meet in gift shop. ☎ 0113 288 6331.
Specialist Day. RHS Garden Wisley, Surrey. 'Plant propagation' with David Hide. ☎ 01483 224234.

WED 21
Demonstration. Flower Arranging. 10 am – 12.30 pm. RHS Garden Wisley, Surrey. 'Flowers to charm & delight' with Keren Dean Taylor. ☎ 01483 224234.
Garden Tour. 1 pm. Wollerton Old Hall. Reaseheath College, Cheshire. Led by Alison Evans. RHS Members £6.95. Non-Members £7.95. ☎ 01270 625131.
Lecture. 2 pm. Cannington College, Somerset. 'Lawn maintenance' by John Addison. RHS Members £7.95. Non-Members £8.95. ☎ 01278 655000.
Garden Open. Brook Lodge Farm Cottage, Surrey 2 – 5 pm.
Lecture. 2 pm. Hadlow College, Tonbridge, Kent. 'Composts for containers' by David Carey. RHS Members £9.50. Non-Members £11. ☎ 01732 850551.
Garden Walk. RHS Garden Wisley, Surrey. 'Summer borders' with David Hoodless. RHS Members £5. Non-Members £10. ☎ 01483 224234.

On This Day
An intense tornado hit Wisley Garden on 21 July 1965, wreaking extensive damage over a period of 10 minutes.

THU 22
RHS Flower Show at Tatton Park. Knutsford, Cheshire. 10 am – 6 pm. 4 days 22–25 July. Recorded info ☎ 0171 649 1885.
A Midsummer Night's Dream. Painswick Rococo Garden, Glos. 3 days 22–24 July. ☎ 01452 813204.
Garden Open. Preen Manor, Shropshire. 2 – 6 pm.
Fête Champêtre. Stourhead, Wilts. Admission from 5.30 pm. 3 days 22–24 July. ☎ 01747 841152.

JULY   101

FRI 23

RHS Flower Show at Tatton Park. Knutsford, Cheshire. 10 am – 6 pm. 2nd day.

NOTES

'GOD *ALMIGHTIE* FIRST PLANTED A *GARDEN*. AND INDEED, IT IS THE PUREST OF HUMANE PLEASURES. IT IS THE GREATEST REFRESHMENT TO THE SPIRITS OF MAN'.
FRANCIS BACON, 1625.

SAT 24

RHS Flower Show at Tatton Park. 10 am – 6 pm. 3rd day.
Salisbury Country & Garden Show, Wiltshire. 2 days 24–25 July.
☎ 01635 867904.
Isle of Wight County Show. Newport, IOW. 2 days 24–25 July.
☎ 01983 826275.
Workshop. 10 am. Pershore & Hindlip College, Worcester. 'Watercolour painting for summer' by Audrey Robards.
☎ 01386 554609.
Provincial Show. National Sweet Pea Society. Wem, Shropshire. 2 days 24–25 July. ☎ 01794 301490.
Fireworks Concert. Coughton Court, Warwicks.
☎ 01789 400777.

SUN 25

RHS Flower Show at Tatton Park. Knutsford, Cheshire. 10 am – 6 pm. Last day.
Plant & Garden Fair. 10 am – 5 pm. Chenies Manor, Rickmansworth. ☎ 01494 762888.
Valley Gardens Fiesta. Harrogate. ☎ 01423 5'00600.
Demonstration. 2 – 3.30 pm. Brogdale, Kent. Summer pruning apples & pears'. Friends of Brogdale £6. Others £10. ☎ 01795 535286.
Garden Open. Oare House, Wilts. 2 – 6 pm.
Nursery Plant Sale. 11 am – 4 pm. Colby Woodland Garden, Dyfed. £2.80 for admission: plant sale free. ☎ 01267 237275.

JULY

NOTES

MON 26

TUE 27

Lecture. 11 am. 'British orchids & their conservation' by Steve Waite. Friends of Wakehurst Place, West Sussex. £3.
☎ 01444 894035.
New Forest Show. Brockenhurst, Hants. 3 days 27–29 July.
☎ 01590 622400.
Lecture. 2 pm. Pershore & Hindlip College, Worcester. 'How to start a plant collection'. RHS Members £5. Non-Members £10.
☎ 01386 554609.

'I AM CONSTANTLY STRUCK BY THE BEHAVIOUR OF VISITORS WHO STAND AND STARE AT SOME LONG-KNOWN, LONG-LOVED PLANT AS IF IT WERE SOME NEWLY DISCOVERED TREASURE ONLY RECENTLY DISCOVERED FROM THE EXCLUSIVE SLOPES OF SOME HORTICULTURAL PARNASSUS'. H E BATES, *A LOVE OF FLOWERS*, 1971.

WED 28

Sandringham Flower Show, Norfolk. ☎ 01553 772675.
Demonstration. 'Summer propagation' by Ros Cook. RHS Garden Rosemoor, Devon. RHS Members £5. Non-Members £10. ☎ 01805 624067.
Lecture. 2 pm. Hadlow College, Tonbridge, Kent. 'Plants for coastal areas' by Keith Mexter. RHS Members £9.50. Non-Members £11. ☎ 01732 850551.
Garden Walk. RHS Garden Rosemoor, Devon. 'The Perennials' with David Squire & Helen Round. RHS Members £5. Non-Members £10. ☎ 01805 624067.

THU 29

Lecture. 2 pm. Pershore & Hindlip College, Worcester. 'The true geraniums' by Julie Ritchie. RHS Members £5. Non-Members £10. ☎ 01386 554609.
Lakeside Walk. 2 pm. Harewood House, W Yorks. Meet in gift shop. ☎ 0113 288 6331.
Garden Open. Preen Manor, Shropshire. 2 – 6 pm.

July • August

FRI 30

Summer Craft Show. Broadlands, Romsey, Hampshire. 3 days 30 July–1 August. ☎ 01794 505056.

SAT 31

South-East Garden Festival. Chatham Dockyard, Kent. 2 days 31 July–1 August. ☎ 01634 823800.
Royal Lancashire Show. Astley Park, Chorley. 2 days 31 July–1 August. ☎ 01254 813769.
National Miniature Rose Show. RNRS Gardens of the Rose, St Albans. 2 days 31 July–1 August. ☎ 01727 850461.
Concert & Fireworks. Westonbirt Arboretum, Glos. £16. ☎ 01666 880220.
Family Fortnight at Wisley. Until 15 August. ☎ 01483 224234.

SUN 1

Falconry Demonstrations. Penshurst Place, Kent.
Garden Open. Vale End, Surrey 10 am – 5 pm.
Garden Walk. 2 pm. Hillier Arboretum, Hants.
☎ 01794 368787.

NOTES

'I CALL A PLANT EXCELLENT WHEN IT HAS THE FOLLOWING VIRTUES: THAT OF BEING ABLE TO STAND ON ITS OWN LEGS WITHOUT STAKES, OF PRODUCING FLOWER OF GREAT BEAUTY FOR WEEKS ON END AND OF SHOWING INCONTESTABLE GRACE OF FORM'. H E BATES, *A LOVE OF FLOWERS*, 1971.

AUGUST

NOTES

MON 2
Classic Car Rally. Mount Edgcumbe Gardens, Cornwall.
Lecture. 7.30 pm. Bedfordshire AGS. Wilstead Village Hall. 'Alpine flowers of Norway' by Keith Moorhouse. ☎ 01462 711295.

TUE 3
Demonstration. 2 pm. Pershore & Hindlip College, Worcester. 'Your garden in August' by Bob Hares. RHS Members £5. Non-Members £10. ☎ 01386 554609.
Guided Tour of Terraces. 2 pm. Harewood House, W Yorks. Meet in gift shop. ☎ 0113 288 6331.

On This Day
On 3 August 1990 the highest temperature ever recorded in the United Kingdom was 37.1°C (98.8°F) at Cheltenham, Gloucestershire.

WED 4
Guernsey South Show. Saumarez Manor. 2 days 4–5 August. ☎ 01481 716363.
Taunton Flower Show. Vivary Park, Taunton. 2 days 4–5 August. ☎ 01823 271597.
Garden Tour. 1.30 pm. Reaseheath College, Cheshire. Covering garden screens & walls: led by Anne Harrison. RHS Members £6.95. Non-Members £7.95. ☎ 01270 625131.
Demonstration. 2 pm. Hadlow College, Tonbridge, Kent. 'Your garden in August' by Nick Egan. RHS Members £9.50. Non-Members £11. ☎ 01732 850551.

THU 5
Lecture. 2 pm. Pershore & Hindlip College, Worcester. 'Designing around the front door & drive' by David Everitt. RHS Members £5. Non-Members £10. ☎ 01386 554609.

AUGUST

FRI 6

Welsh Open Championships. Plant Fair. Picton Castle, Dyfed. £3. 3 days 6–8 August. ☎ 01834 861287.
Garden Walk. Meet the Gardener. 1.30 pm. Hutton-in-the-Forest, Cumbria. ☎ 017684 84449.
Jazz Concert & Fireworks. Kingston Lacy, Dorset. 6 pm. £12. ☎ 01985 843601.
Lecture. 6 pm. RHS Garden Rosemoor, Devon. 'Butterflies & moths' by Alec Worth. ☎ 01805 624067.
Shakespeare in the Garden. Leighton Hall, Lancs. 'The Taming of the Shrew'. ☎ 01524 734474.

SAT 7

Demonstration. 10 am. Pershore & Hindlip College, Worcester. 'Your garden in August' by Bob Hares. RHS Members £5. Non-Members £10. ☎ 01386 554609.
Organic Gardening Weekend. 2 – 6 pm. Deans Court, Dorset (with HDRA). 2 days 7–8 August. ☎ 01202 888478.
Manchester Garden Show. Platts Fields Park, Manchester. 2 days 7–8 August. ☎ 0161 224 2902.
Ripley Show. 9.30 am – 5 pm. Ripley Castle, North Yorkshire. ☎ 01423 770152.
Workshop. 10 am – 4 pm. Surrey Wildlife Trust. Nower Wood Reserve, Leatherhead. 'Gardening for wildlife'. ☎ 01372 379509.
British Fuchsia Society Northern Show. Little Hulton Community School, Salford, Manchester. ☎ 0161 799 6257.
Organic Gardening Weekend. HDRA, Ryton, Warks. 2 days 7–8 August. ☎ 01203 303517.
Shakespeare in the Garden. Leighton Hall, Lancs. 'The Taming of the Shrew'. ☎ 01524 734474.
Garden Walk. Meet the gardener. Coughton Court, Warwicks. ☎ 01789 400777.
Children's Weekend. Plant centre, RHS Garden Wisley, Surrey. 2 days 7–8 August.

SUN 8

Evening Garden Tour. 7.30 pm Belsay Hall, Northumberland, with Head Gardener Paul Harrigan. £6. ☎ 01661 881636.
Herefordshire Country Fair. Whitfield. ☎ 01981 240168.
Garden Open. Brook Lodge Farm Cottage, Surrey 2 – 5 pm.

NOTES

'I CANNOT IMAGINE ANYTHING MORE DEPRESSING TO THE GARDEN LOVER, MORE ANTI-ENGLISH, THAN THE HABIT OF THE EIGHTEENTH-CENTURY 'LANDSCAPE' SCHOOL OF CARRYING HUMPS AND SERPENTINES RIGHT UP TO THE FOUR WALLS OF THE HOUSE AND ALLOWING NOTHING BUT LAWNS AND TREES TO BE VISIBLE — BANISHING ALL FLOWERS TO A FAR-OFF PLACE'.
H. AVRAY TIPPING, *THE GARDEN OF TODAY*, 1933.

AUGUST

NOTES

MON 9

TUE 10

RHS Flower Show. 11 am – 7 pm. (10 am – 5 pm 2nd day.) RHS New Hall, Westminster. Ornamental Plant Competition. Gladiolus Competition. Botanical Photographs. 2 days 10–11 August.
RHS London Lecture. 2.15 pm. RHS Halls, Westminster. 'Euphorbias in the wild & in the garden' by Timothy Walker.
Demonstration. 2 pm. Pershore & Hindlip College, Worcester. 'Summer pruning' by Bob Hares. RHS Members £5. Non-Members £10. ☎ 01386 554609.
Garden Walk with John Anderson. Mount Usher, Co Wicklow. 7.30 pm. 'The white Knights of Summer'. £5.
☎ 00 353 404 40116.

WED 11

Eclipse of the Sun. 11.11 am. Cornwall. Special events at several gardens, including Chyverton, Mount Edgcumbe. See also *www.cornwalleclipse99.com*
Demonstration. Flower Arranging. 10 am – 12.30 pm. RHS Garden Wisley, Surrey. 'My world of flowers' with John Chennell. ☎ 01483 224234.
Garden Walk. RHS Garden Wisley, Surrey. 'Drought-resistant plants' with Dean Peckett. RHS Members £5. Non-Members £10. ☎ 01483 224234.
South Show. Guernsey. Sausmarez Manor, St Martin. 2 days 11–12 August. ☎ 01481 723552.
Garden Walk. 2 pm. Claremont Landscape Garden, Surrey.
Garden Open. Brook Lodge Farm Cottage, Surrey 2 – 5 pm.
Lecture. 2 pm. Scottish Agricultural College, Auchincruive, Ayr. 'Searching for the super tree' by Dr Glynn Percival. RHS Members £5.95. Non-Members £7.95. ☎ 01292 525393.

THU 12

Children's Concert. Chyverton, Cornwall. ☎ 01872 540324.
Lakeside Walk. 2 pm. Harewood House, W Yorks. Meet in gift shop. ☎ 0113 288 6331.
Battle of the Flowers. Jersey. 2 days 12–13 August.
☎ 01534 500700.

AUGUST

Shrewsbury Flower Show. 2 days 13–14 August.
☎ 01743 364051.

FRI 13

NOTES

Hampshire Flower Show. Broadlands, Romsey. 2 days 14–15 August. ☎ 01794 505010.
Cactus Sale. British Cactus & Succulent Society. Tropical World, Canal Gardens, Leeds. 2 days 14–15 August. ☎ 0113 266 1850.
Northumberland Fuchsia Society Show. 12 noon. Belsay Hall. 2 days 14–15 August. ☎ 01661 881636.
Fireworks & Laser Concert. 7.30 pm. Bowood, Wiltshire.
☎ 01625 56000.
Chili Fiesta. West Dean, West Sussex. 2 days 14–15 August.
☎ 01243 811205.
British Fuchsia Society London Show. Uxbridge College, Uxbridge. ☎ 01252 29731.

SAT 14

'I FIRMLY BELIEVE THAT EACH OF US IS ABLE TO ASSIMILATE ONLY ONE PROFESSION IN A LIFETIME. THAT IS BECAUSE OF THE COMPLEXITY OF WHAT WE HAVE TO ABSORB. I WAS INTO GARDENING RIGHT FROM THE START...' CHRISTOPHER LLOYD, *GARDENER COOK*, 1997.

Budding Day. Brogdale, Kent. Budding fruit trees while you wait. Morning only. ☎ 01795 535286.
Concert. Capesthorne Hall, Cheshire. Fireworks & lasers.
Summer Plant Fair. Pashley Manor Gardens, East Sussex.
☎ 01580 200692.
Summer Picnic. 12 noon. Wiltshire Gardens Trust. South Wraxall Lodge. ☎ 01225 722267.
Gardens Open. Greenways, Oxford 2 – 6 pm; Home Covert, Wilts. 2 – 6 pm.
Garden Walk. 2 pm. Cragside, Northumberland.
☎ 01669 620150.

SUN 15

AUGUST

NOTES

MON 16

On This Day
Eight and a half inches (216mm.) of rain fell in 4½ hours at Cannington in Somerset on 18 August 1924.

TUE 17

Guided Tour of Terraces. 2 pm. Harewood House, W Yorks. Meet in gift shop. ☎ 0113 288 6331.

WED 18

Jersey Summer Flower Show. Howard Davis Park. 2 days 18–19 August. ☎ 01534 866555.
Plantsman's Day. RHS Garden Rosemoor, Devon. 'Colour in the garden' by Christopher Bailes. ☎ 01805 624067.
West Show. Guernsey. L'Erée, St Pierre du Bois. 2 days 18–19 August. ☎ 01481 723552.
Garden Tour. 6 pm. Reaseheath College, Cheshire. Led by Anne Harrison. RHS Members £6.95. Non-Members £7.95. ☎ 01270 625131.

THU 19

Southport Flower Show. 3 days 19–21 August. ☎ 01704 547147.

FRI 20

Demonstration. 11.30 am. RHS Garden Hyde Hall, Essex. 'Propagation of half-hardies' with Julie Dixon & Jo Cobb. RHS Members £5. Non-Members £10. ☎ 01245 400256.

SAT 21

Craft Fair. 11 am – 6 pm. Nymans Garden, West Sussex. ☎ 01444 400321.
British Fuchsia Society Welsh Show. New Lodge Club, Gorseinon, Swansea. ☎ 01792 891939.
Skelton Horticultural & Agricultural Show. Hutton-in-the-Forest. ☎ 01768 483032.
Garden Walk. 2.15 pm. Hinton Ampner, Hants. 'Meet the gardener'. Numbers limited. £1. ☎ 01962 771305.
British Gladiolus Show. Capel Manor, London. 2 days 21–22 August. ☎ 0181 366 4442.

SUN 22

Gentian Time & Craft Demonstrations. 10.30 am – 5 pm. High Beeches, West Sussex. ☎ 01444 400589.
British Fuchsia Society Southern Show. Pelham's Community, Bournemouth. ☎ 01202 386517.
Falconry Demonstrations. Penshurst Place, Kent.
Music & Fireworks. Shugborough, Stafford. ☎ 01889 881388.
International Conifer Conference. Wye College, Kent. 4 days 22–25 August. ☎ 0181 332 5198.

'I HAVE HEARD TRAVELLERS ASSERT THAT THEY NEVER ATE A GOOD APPLE IN THE SOUTH OF EUROPE WHERE THE HEATS ARE SO GREAT AS TO RENDER THE JUICES VAPID AND INSIPID'. *GILBERT WHITE, THE NATURAL HISTORY OF SELBOURNE.*

AUGUST

MON 23

TUE 24
Wisley Flower Show. RHS Garden Wisley, Surrey. 10 am – 5.30 pm. 3 days 24–26 August. ☎ 01483 224234.
Guided Tour of Terraces. 2 pm. Harewood House, W Yorks. Meet in gift shop. ☎ 0113 288 6331.

WED 25
North Show. Guernsey. Saumarez Park. 2 days 25–26 August. ☎ 01481 723552
Wisley Flower Show. RHS Garden Wisley, Surrey. 10 am – 5.30 pm. 2nd day. ☎ 01483 224234.

THU 26
Ayr Flower Show. Ayr Racecourse. 3 days 26–28 August. ☎ 01292 616695.
Lakeside Walk. 2 pm. Harewood House, W Yorks. Meet in gift shop. ☎ 0113 288 6331.
Plantarium Trade Show. Boskoop, Netherlands. 9 am – 6 pm. 4 days 26–29 August. ☎ 0031 172 235 400.
Wisley Flower Show. RHS Garden Wisley, Surrey. 10 am – 5 pm. Last day. ☎ 01483 224234.

FRI 27

SAT 28
British Orchid Growers' Association. Orchid Fayre. Jarvis Elcot Park Hotel, Kintbury, Berkshire. 9 am – 5 pm. £2. 2 days 28–29 August. ☎ 01626 352233.
Belsay Hall Flower Show, Northumberland. North of England Rose, Carnation and Sweet Pea Society. 12 noon. 3 days 28–30 August. ☎ 01661 881636.
Gardeners' Weekend at Audley End, Essex. 3 days 28–30 August. ☎ 0121 682 0862.
Wrest Park Garden Show. Silsoe, Beds. 3 days. ☎ 01234 345725.
Plant Fair. Savill Gardens, Windsor Great Park. ☎ 01753 847518.
British Fuchsia Society South-western Show. Filton High School, Bristol. ☎ 01394 283454.
British Fuchsia Society Border Show. Queen Elizabeth High School, Hexham. ☎ 0191 386 1709.
Festival of Wood. Westonbirt Arboretum, Glos. 3 days 28–30 August. ☎ 01666 880220.

SUN 29
Swallowfield Horticultural Show. Reading, Berks. 2 days 29–30 August. ☎ 0118 988 2736.

NOTES

'*KITCHEN GARDEN:* RADISHES, SOW THE NINTH AND LAST CROP. *FLOWER GARDEN:* SEEDS OF ALL SORTS GATHER AS THEY RIPEN. *FRUIT GARDEN:* FRUIT GATHER EARLY IN THE MORNING'. RICHARD WESTON ESQ., *THE GARDENER'S POCKET CALENDAR*, 1783.

AUGUST • SEPTEMBER

NOTES

MON 30
Concert. Capesthorne Hall, Cheshire. Whaley Bridge Brass Band.
Valley Gardens Arts Fair, Harrogate. ☎ 01423 500600.

TUE 31
Guided Tour of Terraces. 2 pm. Harewood House, W Yorks. Meet in gift shop. ☎ 0113 288 6331.

WED 1
Coffee Morning. Friends of RBG, Kew. Cambridge Cottage. ☎ 0181 332 5922.
Lecture. 6.30 pm. Reaseheath College, Cheshire. 'Lawn maintenance' by Bryan Jones. RHS Members £6.95. Non-Members £7.95. ☎ 01270 625131.

'I HAVE NEVER LIKED THE RED BORDERS AT HIDCOTE. PINK WOULD BE FINE, ORANGE DANDY, BUT FULL-BLOODED RED SOMEHOW FALLS FLAT. PERHAPS IT ABSORBS TOO MUCH LIGHT'. HUGH JOHNSON, *RHSJ*, DECEMBER 1988.

THU 2
Lecture. 2 pm. Pershore & Hindlip College, Worcester. 'Late summer delights for your garden' by Duncan Coombs. RHS Members £5. Non-Members £10. ☎ 01386 554609.
Lecture. 7.30 pm. Dorset AGS. Lytchett Matravers Village Hall. 'An introduction to alpines' by Alan Cook.

SEPTEMBER

FRI 3

National Amateur Gardening Show. Bath & West Showground. Incorporating the **National Dahlia Society Show**. 3 days 3–5 Sept.
☎ 01460 66616.
Dundee Flower Show. Camperdown Country Park. 3 days 3–5 Sept. ☎ 01382 434000.
Garden Walk. Meet the Gardener. 1.30 pm. Hutton-in-the-Forest, Cumbria. ☎ 017684 84449.

NOTES

'I KNOW I CANNOT MAKE ANYTHING NEW, IT HAS ALL BEEN DONE BEFORE'. ROSEMARY VEREY, *THE ENGLISHWOMAN'S GARDEN*, 1980.

SAT 4

Chatsworth Country Fair. Bakewell, Derbys. 2 days 4–5 Sept.
☎ 01263 711736.
Harbottle Horticultural & Poultry Show. Northumberland.
☎ 01669 650216.
British Fuchsia Society South-eastern Show. Orwell High School, Felixstowe. 2 days 4–5 Sept. ☎ 01394 283454.
Garden Walk. Meet the gardener. Coughton Court, Warwicks.
☎ 01789 400777.

SUN 5

Charities Day. Mannington Gardens, Norfolk. ☎ 01263 584175.
Kildale Agricultural & Horticultural Show. North Yorkshire.
☎ 01642 724214.
NCCPG Plant Sale. University of Leicester Botanic Garden.
11 am – 4 pm.
Garden Open. Brook Lodge Farm Cottage, Surrey 2 – 5 pm.
Garden Walk. 2 pm. Hillier Arboretum, Hants.
☎ 01794 368787.

SEPTEMBER

NOTES

MON 6
Lecture. 7 pm. Rosecarpe. 'The orchards & gardens of Singapore' by Don Charlton. Civic Centre, Gateshead. ☎ 0191 252 7052.
Lecture. 7.30 pm. Bedfordshire AGS. Wilstead Village Hall. 'Silver & grey plants' by Eric Jarrett. ☎ 01462 711295.
Specialist Day. RHS Garden Wisley, Surrey. 'Plantsman's day' ☎ 01483 224234.

TUE 7
Demonstration. 2 pm. Pershore & Hindlip College, Worcester. 'Your garden in September' by Bob Hares. RHS Members £5. Non-Members £10. ☎ 01386 554609.

WED 8
Demonstration. Flower Arranging. 10 am – 12.30 pm. RHS Garden Wisley, Surrey. 'September splendour' with Anne Blunt. ☎ 01483 224234.
Demonstration. RHS Garden Rosemoor, Devon. 'Hedges in the garden'. ☎ 01805 624067.
Lecture. 1.30 pm. Houghall College, Durham. 'Rejuvenating your lawn.' RHS Members £4. Non-Members £5. ☎ 0191 386 1351.
Lecture. 2 pm. Scottish Agricultural College, Auchincruive, Ayr. 'The naivety of a knowledgeable novice' by Dr Neil McRoberts. RHS Members £4.95. Non-Members £5.95. ☎ 01292 525393.
Garden Walk. 2 pm. Claremont Landscape Garden, Surrey.
Lecture. 2 pm. Writtle College, Chelmsford, Essex. 'Lawn pests, diseases & disorders' by Stewart Brown. ☎ 01245 424200.

'FRUIT GARDEN: GRAPES, PUT INTO BAGS OF CRAPE, GAUZE OR PAPER. *GREENHOUSE:* ORANGE-TREES, FRESH EARTH, THIN THE FRUIT, AND TAKE INTO THE HOUSE AT THE END OF THE MONTH'. RICHARD WESTON ESQ., *THE GARDENER'S POCKET CALENDAR,* 1783.

THU 9
Lecture. 1 pm. Welsh College of Horticulture, Northop, Flintshire. 'Bulbs for spring colour' by Anne Lewis. RHS Members £8. Non-Members £10. ☎ 01352 841000.

FRI 10

Garden Opera. 'Così fan tutte' with the Garden Opera Company. RHS Garden Rosemoor, Devon. ☎ 01805 624067.
Country Lifestyle Fair. Hatfield House, Herts. 3 days 10–12 Sept. ☎ 01707 262823.
Lecture. 7.30 pm. Chilterns AGS. Great Kingshill Village Hall. 'Rock garden construction & maintenance' by Keith Moorhouse. ☎ 01628 486709.

SAT 11

Flower Arranging Weekend. Plant centre, RHS Garden Wisley, Surrey. 2 days 11–12 Sept.
Romsey Show. Broadlands, Romsey, Hampshire. ☎ 01794 505056.
Plant Sale. Friends of Ventnor Botanic Garden, IOW. ☎ 01983 855397.
NCCPG Plant Sale. RHS Garden Rosemoor, Devon. ☎ 01805 624067.
Harvest Gardening Festival. Ragley Hall, Warwicks. 2 days 11–12 Sept. ☎ 0121 682 ☎ 0860.
Lecture. 9.30 am. Welsh College of Horticulture, Northop, Flintshire. 'Bulbs for spring colour' by Anne Lewis. RHS Members £8. Non-Members £10. ☎ 01352 841000.
Demonstration. 10 am. Pershore & Hindlip College, Worcester. 'Your garden in September' by Bob Hares. RHS Members £5. Non-Members £10. ☎ 01386 554609.
Early Chrysanthemum Show. County Showground, Stafford. 2 days 11–12 Sept. ☎ 01827 310311.
Cider & Perry Festival. Brogdale, Kent. 2 days 11–12 Sept. ☎ 01795 535286.

SUN 12

Country Fair. Frampton Court, Glos.
Prize giving. Photographic competition. RHS Garden Rosemoor, Devon. ☎ 01805 624067.
British Fuchsia Society Midland Show. County Show Ground, Stafford. ☎ 01527 875958.
Rare Plant Fair. 11 am – 5 pm. Borde Hill, West Sussex. £2. Plus £2 for gardens. ☎ 0117 969 1570.
Garden Open. Cowdray Park, West Sussex 2 – 6 pm.

NOTES

SEPTEMBER

NOTES

MON 13

TUE 14

RHS Great Autumn Show. 10 am – 7 pm. (10 am – 5 pm 2nd day.) RHS New Hall, Westminster. 2 days 14–15 Sept.
RHS London Lecture. 2.15 pm. RHS Halls, Westminster. 'Gardening on Canada's Pacific coast' by David Tarrant (Vancouver Botanic Garden).
Plantsman's Day. 'Grasses'. RHS Garden Rosemoor, Devon. ☎ 01805 624067.
Course. 9.30 am – 12 noon. 'How to enjoy your herbaceous perennials'. Friends of Ness Gardens, Cheshire. Visitor Centre, Ness. £6.50. ☎ 0151 353 0123.
RHS Regional Lecture. RHS Garden Rosemoor, Devon. 'Planting style for historic gardens' by John Sales. ☎ 0171 821 3049.
Lecture. 2 pm. Pershore & Hindlip College, Worcester. 'Salvias for late summer' by John Sutton. RHS Members £5. Non-Members £10. ☎ 01386 554609.
RHS London Lecture. Jointly with the Worshipful Gardeners' Company. 6 pm. RHS Halls, Westminster.

WED 15

RHS London Lecture. 2.15 pm. RHS Halls, Westminster. 'Street cred: gardening where others can see it' by Nigel Colborn.
Lecture. 'Plants & People & the Kew collections' by Hew Prendergast. Friends of Wakehurst Place, West Sussex. £2. ☎ 01444 894035.
Garden Tour. 2 pm. 'Meet the gardener'. Mottisfont Abbey, Hants.
Garden Walk. 2.30 pm. Sizergh Castle, Cumbria. With Head Gardener.
Demonstration. RHS Garden Wisley, Surrey. 'The mixed border' with David Jewell. RHS Members £5. Non-Members £10. ☎ 01483 224234.
Lecture. 2 pm. Writtle College, Chelmsford, Essex. 'Four seasons in the garden – autumn' by Marion Polley. ☎ 01245 424200.

'IF ONE'S PLOT IS OF SMALL DIMENSIONS, IT IS ALMOST AS IMPORTANT TO KNOW WHAT NOT TO GROW AS WHAT TO GROW'. SIR ARTHUR HORT, *THE UNCONVENTIONAL GARDEN*, 1928.

THU 16

Demonstration. 2 pm. Pershore & Hindlip College, Worcester. 'Success with seeds in autumn' by Bob Hares. RHS Members £5. Non-Members £10. ☎ 01386 554609.
NAFAS Exhibition. RHS Garden Rosemoor, Devon. 4 days 16–19 Sept. ☎ 01805 624067.

September

FRI 17

19th British Orchid Congress. Llandudno. 3 days 17–19 Sept.
Harrogate Autumn Flower Show. 3 days 17–19 Sept.
☎ 01423 561049.
Garden Craft Fair. RHS Garden Rosemoor, Devon. 3 days
17–19 Sept. ☎ 01805 624067.
Giardini in Fiera. Italian garden fair. Fattoria Le Corti, San
Casciano Val di Pesa, near Florence. 3 days 17–19 Sept.
☎ 00 44 055 820123.
Flormart. Trade Show. Padua, Italy. 3 days 17–19 Sept.
☎ 00 39 049 840111.

SAT 18

City of Belfast Horticultural Fair. Botanic Gardens, Belfast.
2 days 18–19 Sept.
Borders Country Living Fair. Kailzie Gardens, Peebles. 2 days
18–19 Sept. ☎ 01721 720007.
Annual Show. National Pot Leek Society. Pelaw & District Social
Club, Heworth. 2 days 18–19 Sept. ☎ 0191 549 4274.
Lecture. 10 am. Reaseheath College, Cheshire. 'Demonstration
fruit garden: the tastes of summer' by Bert Davis. RHS Members
£6.95. Non-Members £7.95. ☎ 01270 625131.
Fungi Foray. 10 am. Pershore & Hindlip College, Worcester. Led
by Diana & Tim Bateman. ☎ 01386 554609.
NCCPG Plant Sale. 11 am. RHS Garden Hyde Hall, Essex.
☎ 01245 400256.
Workshop Weekend. Intermediate Level Photography.
10 am – 5 pm. RHS Garden Wisley, Surrey. 2 days 18–19 Sept.
☎ 01483 224234.
Late Bulb Show. Scottish Rock Garden Club. Dundee.
10 am – 4 pm. ☎ 01224 314533.
Demonstration. 2 pm. Otley College, Ipswich, Suffolk. 'Winter
hanging baskets' by Zara Martin. RHS Members £5.
Non-Members £6. ☎ 01473 785543.
Craft fair. Capesthorne Hall, Cheshire. 2 days 18–19 Sept.
Garden Walk. 2.15 pm. Hinton Ampner, Hants. 'Meet the
gardener'. Numbers limited. £1. ☎ 01962 771305.

SUN 19

Autumn Plant Fair. Newby Hall, North Yorks. ☎ 01423 322583.
Norton Priory Horticultural Show. Runcorn, Cheshire.
☎ 01928 569895.
Rare Plant Fair. 12 noon – 5 pm. The Royal Free Hospital,
Hampstead. £3. ☎ 0117 969 1570.
Gardens Open. Dam House Farm, Derbys. 11 am – 4 pm;
Hillbarn House, Wilts. 2 – 6 pm.
Rare Plant Sale. Ickworth, Suffolk. ☎ 01284 735270.
Garden Walk. 2 pm. Cragside, Northumberland.
☎ 01669 620150.

On This Day
*'1766 Sept 19 at Filton Park, Whitehaven, a cabbage was cut, and
weighed four stone and seven ounces, among many hundreds of
nearly the same weight'.* Peter Collinson, Memoranda, 1766.

Notes

'IF ONLY WE COULD
HAVE THE LAST TWENTY
YEARS ALL OVER AGAIN!
WE WOULDN'T MAKE ANY
CHANGES IN THE DESIGN,
BUT I WOULD LIKE TO GO
BACK AND MAKE A GREAT
MANY CHANGES IN THE
PLANTING. BEASTLY
GARDEN
(SISSINGHURST).' VITA
SACKVILLE-WEST,
LETTER TO HAROLD
NICOLSON, 1954.

SEPTEMBER

NOTES

MON 20

TUE 21
Demonstration. 2 pm. Pershore & Hindlip College, Worcester. 'The potager in autumn' by Bob Hares. RHS Members £5. Non-Members £10. ☎ 01386 554609

WED 22
Lecture. 2 pm. Writtle College, Chelmsford, Essex. 'Introduction to botany & systematics' by Jean Halfhide. ☎ 01245 424200.
Demonstration. RHS Garden Wisley, Surrey. 'Lawn maintenance' with Greg Arthur. RHS Members £5. Non-Members £10. ☎ 01483 224234.

THU 23
Lecture. 1 pm. Welsh College of Horticulture, Northop, Flintshire. 'Seed collecting & sowing' by Anne Lewis. RHS Members £8. Non-Members £10. ☎ 01352 841000.
Lecture. 2 pm. Pershore & Hindlip College, Worcester. 'The *Iris sibirica* Collection' by Kim Davis. RHS Members £5. Non-Members £10. ☎ 01386 554609.
Botanical Art Course. RHS Garden Wisley, Surrey. Intermediate level. 4 days 23–26 Sept. ☎ 01483 224234.

FRI 24
Workshop. 11.30 am. RHS Garden Hyde Hall, Essex. Tree walk, with Jo Cobb. RHS Members £5. Non-Members £10. ☎ 01245 400256.
Hortec '99 Trade Fair. Karslruhe, Germany. 3 days 24–26 Sept. ☎ 00 49 721 9325874.

SAT 25
Malvern Autumn Show. 9 am – 6 pm. (9 am – 5 pm 2nd day.) Three Counties Showground, Malvern, Worcs. 2 days 25–26 Sept. ☎ 01684 584900.
Lecture. 9.30 am. Welsh College of Horticulture, Northop, Flintshire. 'Seed collecting & sowing' by Anne Lewis. RHS Members £8. Non-Members £10. ☎ 01352 841000.
Lecture. 10 am. Reaseheath College, Cheshire. 'Winter Containers & Baskets' by Anne Harrison. RHS Members £6.95. Non-Members £7.95. ☎ 01270 625131.

'IF ONE'S PLOT IS OF SMALL DIMENSIONS, IT IS ALMOST AS IMPORTANT TO KNOW WHAT NOT TO GROW AS WHAT TO GROW'. SIR ARTHUR HORT, *THE UNCONVENTIONAL GARDEN*, 1928.

SUN 26
Workshop. 10.30 am – 3.30 pm. Brogdale, Kent. 'Planning & planting a fruit garden'. Friends of Brogdale £20. Others £30. ☎ 01795 535286.
Garden Open. Great Barfield, Bucks. 2 – 5 pm.
Demonstration. RHS Garden Wisley, Surrey. 'Lawn maintenance' with Greg Arthur. RHS Members £5. Non-Members £10. ☎ 01483 224234.
Malvern Autumn Show. 9 am – 5 pm. Last day.

MON
27

TUE
28

Demonstration. 2 pm. Pershore & Hindlip College, Worcester. 'Decking in your garden' by David Everitt. RHS Members £5. Non-Members £10. ☎ 01386 554609.

WED
29

Photography Workshop. 1.30 pm. Houghall College, Durham. 'Plant portraits.' RHS Members £4. Non-Members £5. ☎ 0191 386 1351.
Garden Tour. Myerscough College, Preston, Lancs. Led by Jeff Hodson. RHS Members £6. Non-Members £7.50. ☎ 01995 640611.

THU
30

Specialist Day. RHS Garden Wisley, Surrey. 'Plantsman's day'. ☎ 01483 224234.
Lecture. 2 pm. Pershore & Hindlip College, Worcester. 'A feast of herbs' by Kim Hurst. RHS Members £5. Non-Members £10. ☎ 01386 554609.

FRI
1

Fungal Foray. Bedgebury National Arboretum, Kent. Led by Roger Phillips. ☎ 01580 211044.

SAT
2

Apple Tasting Weekend. Plant centre, RHS Garden Wisley, Surrey. 2 days 2–3 Oct.
Lecture. 2 pm. Orchid Society of Great Britain. 'Little orchids for little places' by John Davison. Napier Hall, Hide Place, London. ☎ 01483 421423.

SUN
3

Lecture. 2 pm. 'Red-flowered plants: an asset or liability?' by P L Cunnington. Friends of Ness Gardens, Cheshire. Visitor Centre, Ness. Free to RHS Members.
Fungus Foray. 10.30 am. Belsay Hall, Northumberland. Led by Dr Gordon Beakes. £6. Pre-book. ☎ 01661 881636.
Conker Day. 11 am – 3 pm. Barrington Court, Somerset. ☎ 01935 823289.
NCCPG Plant Fair. 12 noon – 4 pm. Felley Priory, Notts. ☎ 01773 810230.
Garden Walk. 2 pm. Hillier Arboretum, Hants. ☎ 01794 368787.

NOTES

'IF WE ALLOWED THEM TO, PLANTS WOULD DO MUCH OF THE HARD WORK WE HAVE BEEN TAUGHT IS AN ESSENTIAL PART OF GARDENING. PLANTS WOULD REPLACE THE SPADE, RAKE AND HOE AS THE CONTROLLERS OF WHAT GOES ON IN THE GARDEN – FOR WITHOUT CONTROL, GARDENING OF ANY KIND IS DIFFICULT'. PETER THOMPSON, *THE SELF-SUSTAINING GARDEN*, 1997.

OCTOBER

NOTES

MON 4
Plant Sale. 7.30 pm. Bedfordshire AGS. Wilstead Village Hall.
☎ 01462 711295.

TUE 5
RHS Flower Show. 11 am – 7 pm. (10 am – 5 pm 2nd day.) RHS New Hall (& additional venue) Westminster. Autumn Fruit & Vegetable Competition. Ornamental Plant competition. 2 days 5–6 Oct.
RHS London Lecture. 2.15 pm. RHS Halls, Westminster. 'The myth & mystery of herbs' by Jekka McVicar.
Garden Tour. 2 pm. 'Meet the gardener'. Mottisfont Abbey, Hants.
Demonstration. 2 pm. Pershore & Hindlip College, Worcester. 'Your garden in October' by Bob Hares. RHS Members £5. Non-Members £10. ☎ 01386 554609.

WED 6
Jersey Autumn Show. St Helier. Fruit, flowers & vegetables. 2 days 6–7 Oct. ☎ 01534 866555.
Practical Demonstrations: Jobs for Autumn. Kingston Lacy, Dorset. 11 am – 1 pm. Meet in car park. Donation. No dogs.
Lecture. 1.30 pm. Reaseheath College, Cheshire. 'Autumn colour' by Stephen Davies. RHS Members £6.95. Non-Members £7.95. ☎ 01270 625131.
Garden walk. RHS Garden Rosemoor, Devon. 'Autumn flowers, fruit & foliage'. RHS Members £5. Non-Members £10. ☎ 01805 624067.

'IN A WOOD AT WISLEY, NEAR WEYBRIDGE, MR WILSON HAS MADE A WOOD-GARDEN. BUT IT IS NOT A GARDEN, IT IS STILL A WOOD AND, AS IT IS FOUR MILES FROM THE HOUSE, IT IS CERTAINLY NOT A HOME-GARDEN'.
CANON HENRY ELLACOMBE, *IN A GLOUCESTERSHIRE GARDEN*, 1895.

THU 7
Lecture. 1 pm. Welsh College of Horticulture, Northop, Flintshire. 'Creating a cottage garden' by Julia White. RHS Members £8. Non-Members £10. ☎ 01352 841000.
Lecture. 2 pm. Pershore & Hindlip College, Worcester. 'Incorporating formal features into your garden'. RHS Members £5. Non-Members £10. ☎ 01386 554609.

On This Day
Seven and a fifth inches (182mm.) of rain fell in 5 hours at Horncastle in Lincolnshire on 7 October 1960.

OCTOBER

FRI 8

RHS Regional Lecture. Cannington College, Somerset. 'The conservation & restoration of historic gardens' by Jim Marshall.
☎ 0171 821 3049.

NOTES

'IT IS A GREATER ACT OF FAITH TO PLANT A BULB THAN TO PLANT A TREE'.
CLARE LEIGHTON, *FOUR HEDGES*, 1935.

SAT 9

Lecture. 9.30 am. Welsh College of Horticulture, Northop, Flintshire. 'Creating a cottage garden' by Julia White. RHS Members £8. Non-Members £10. ☎ 01352 841000.
Demonstration. 10 am. Pershore & Hindlip College, Worcester. 'Your garden in September' by Bob Hares. RHS Members £5. Non-Members £10. ☎ 01386 554609.
Garden Walk with John Anderson. Mount Usher, Co Wicklow. 5 pm. 'Autumn Colour at Mount Usher'. £5 pre-book:
☎ 00 353 404 40116.
Joint Show. Scottish Rock Garden Club & Alpine Garden Society. Ponteland, Northumberland. ☎ 01224 314533.
AGM. National Primula & Auricula Society (Southern Section). RHS Garden Wisley, Surrey.

SUN 10

Garden Walk. 2 pm. Hillier Arboretum, Hants.
☎ 01794 368787.
Garden Walk. RHS Garden Wisley, Surrey. 'Autumn colour' with Jim Gardiner. RHS Members £5. Non-Members £10.
☎ 01483 224234.
Autumn Colour Sunday. Capel Manor, London.
☎ 0181 366 4442.

OCTOBER

NOTES

'IT IS THE FASHION, ESPECIALLY AMONG BOTANISTS, TO DESPISE VARIEGATED PLANTS; THEY ARE SAID TO BE DISEASED, AND TO SHOW THEIR DISEASE BY THEIR SICKLY APPEARANCE. THIS MAY BE TRUE, BUT IT DOES NOT PREVENT THEM FROM BEING VERY BEAUTIFUL AND VERY USEFUL'.
CANON HENRY ELLACOMBE, *IN A GLOUCESTERSHIRE GARDEN*, 1895.

MON 11

TUE 12

WED 13
Lecture. 1.30 pm. Houghall College, Durham. 'Choosing plants for winter effect.' RHS Members £4. Non-Members £5. ☎ 0191 386 1351.
Lecture. 1.30 pm. Myerscough College, Preston, Lancs. 'Propagating woody plants from seed' by Peter Wiseman. RHS Members £6. Non-Members £7.50. ☎ 01995 640611.
Lecture. 2 pm. Scottish Agricultural College, Auchincruive, Ayr. 'A horticulturist's guide to 'surfing'' by Dr Richard Jefferies. RHS Members £4.95. Non-Members £5.95. ☎ 01292 525393.
Lecture. Writtle College, Chelmsford, Essex. 'Glass & pot painting for horticulturists' by Jackie Larner. ☎ 01245 424200.
Garden Walk. RHS Garden Wisley, Surrey. 'Autumn colour' with Colin Crosbie. RHS Members £5. Non-Members £10. ☎ 01483 224234.
NAFAS AGM. Central Hall, Westminster. ☎ 0171 828 5145.

THU 14
Lecture. 2 pm. Pershore & Hindlip College, Worcester. 'Mountain ash & its relatives' by Hugh McAlister. RHS Members £5. Non-Members £10. ☎ 01386 554609.
RHS Regional Lecture. RHS Garden Rosemoor, Devon. 'Planting style for historic gardens' by John Sales. ☎ 0171 821 3049.
Botanical Art Course. RHS Garden Wisley, Surrey. Advanced level. 4 days 14–17 Oct. ☎ 01483 224234.

OCTOBER

FRI 15

Journées des Plantes de Courson. Garden show 35 km south of Paris. 3 days 15–17 Oct. ☎ 00 33 164 58 90 12.

SAT 16

AGM. 12.45 pm. Friends of Ness Gardens, Cheshire. Visitor Centre, Ness.
Lecture. 2 pm. Otley College, Ipswich, Suffolk. 'Trees for autumn colour' by Nick Holmes. RHS Members £5. Non-Members £6.
☎ 01473 785543.
Lecture. 2.30 pm. Wiltshire Gardens Trust. Calne. Donald Everitt.
☎ 01225 722267.
AGS Show. 11.30 am– 4.30 pm. Horsham, West Sussex.
☎ 01323 420975.
Weekend Garden Design Course. 10 am – 4.30 pm. Pershore & Hindlip College, Worcester. ☎ 01386 554609.
Craft Fair. Rockingham Castle, Leics. 2 days 16–17 Oct.
☎ 01536 770240.

SUN 17

Herbaceous Plant Sale at Benington Lordship, Herts.
☎ 01438 869228.
Apple Day celebrations at Acorn Bank gardens, Cumbria,
☎ 01763 61893; West Dean, West Sussex, ☎ 01243 811205; RHS Garden Rosemoor, Devon, ☎ 01805 624067.
Garden Open. Coates Manor, West Sussex 11 am – 5.30 pm.
Garden Walk. 2 pm. Hillier Arboretum, Hants.
☎ 01794 368787.
Woodland Walk & Talk. Kingston Lacy, Dorset. 11 am – 1 pm. Meet in car park.

NOTES

'*KITCHEN GARDEN:* AS OCTOBER IS THE ONLY TIME TO CROP A GARDEN BEFORE WINTER, OMIT NOT ANYTHING ORDERED NOW TILL NEXT MONTH. SEEDS OF ALL SORTS SHOULD BE THRESHED OUT, DRIED, AND PUT INTO BAGS. *FRUIT GARDEN:* APPLES AND PEARS GATHER IN THE MIDDLE OF FINE DRY DAYS, AND PLANT THE TREES AT THE END OF THE MONTH'. RICHARD WESTON ESQ., *THE GARDENER'S POCKET CALENDAR*, 1783.

OCTOBER

NOTES

MON 18
Garden Open. Coates Manor, West Sussex 11 am – 5.30 pm.
Apple Celebrations. RHS Garden Wisley, Surrey. Until 21 Oct. ☎ 01483 224234.

TUE 19
Lecture. 2 pm. Pershore & Hindlip College, Worcester. 'Historic gardens of Worcestershire' by David Everitt. RHS Members £5. Non-Members £10. ☎ 01386 554609.

WED 20
Autumn Festival. Flowers & Produce. NFU Floristry team at Leeds Castle, Kent. 5 days 20–24 Oct. ☎ 01622 765400.
Workshop. Flower Arranging. 10 am – 3.30 pm. RHS Garden Wisley, Surrey. 'Now what can I do with these?' with Monica Trigg. ☎ 01483 224234.
Workshop. 1.30 pm. Reaseheath College, Cheshire. Flower arranging with June Shallcross. RHS Members £6.95. Non-Members £7.95. ☎ 01270 625131.
RHS Regional Lecture. RBG, Edinburgh.

THU 21
Apple Day. Celebrations. 2 pm. Pershore & Hindlip College, Worcester. Led by John Edgeley. RHS Members £5. Non-Members £7. ☎ 01386 554609.
RHS Regional Lecture. Welsh College of Horticulture, Northop, Flintshire. 'Roses: yesterday, today & tomorrow' by John Mattock. ☎ 0171 821 3049.

OCTOBER

FRI 22

Lecture. 11 am. 'Cactus Country, USA' by Peter Brandham. Friends of Wakehurst Place, West Sussex. £2. ☎ 01444 894035
Demonstrations. 11.30 am and 2 pm. RHS Garden Hyde Hall, Essex. 'Pruning roses – ramblers, shrubs & climbers' with Andrew Lodge & Ian LeGros. RHS Members £5. Non-Members £10. ☎ 01245 400256.
Floodlit Garden Walks. 5 – 8.30 pm. Abbotsbury Subtropical Gardens, Dorset. Daily until end of month. ☎ 01305 871387.
Apple Celebrations. Brogdale, Kent. Over 300 cultivars on show. 3 days 22–24 Oct. ☎ 01795 535286.
The Beautiful Homes & Gardens Show. Poole, Dorset. 3 days 22–24 Oct. ☎ 01202 604306.

SAT 23

Lecture. 1.30 pm. Myerscough College, Preston, Lancs. 'Hardy herbaceous perennials' by Jeff Hodson. RHS Members £6. Non-Members £7.50. ☎ 01995 640611.
Workshop Weekend. 10 am – 5 pm. RHS Garden Wisley, Surrey. Intermediate level photography. 2 days 23–24 Oct. ☎ 01483 224234.

SUN 24

Autumn Splendour. Plants Stalls, produce & garden furniture. 10.30 am – 5 pm. High Beeches, West Sussex. ☎ 01444 400589.
Pumpkin Day. Pumpkin & sunflower competitions. RHS Garden Rosemoor, Devon. ☎ 01805 624067.
RHS Regional Lecture. 2 pm. 'Making the most of your greenhouse' by Ray Waite. Visitor Centre, Ness Botanic Gardens, Cheshire. Info: ☎ 0171 821 3049.

NOTES

'IT MUST BE ADMITTED THAT ONE OF THE GREAT DRAWBACKS TO GARDENING AND WEEDING IS THE STATE INTO WHICH ONE'S HANDS AND FINGERS GET'. MRS C W EARLE, *POT POURRI FROM A SURREY GARDEN*, 1897.

OCTOBER

NOTES

MON 25
Floodlit Garden Walks. 5 pm – 8.30 pm. Daily for 7 days 25–31 Oct. Abbotsbury.

TUE 26
Lecture. 2 pm. Pershore & Hindlip College, Worcester. 'The new breed of heathers'. RHS Members £5. Non-Members £10. ☎ 01386 554609.

WED 27
Demonstration. RHS Garden Wisley, Surrey. 'Soil management for gardeners' with Jon Pickering. RHS Members £5. Non-Members £10. ☎ 01483 224234.

THU 28
Lecture. 1 pm. Welsh College of Horticulture, Northop, Flintshire. 'Your garden in autumn' by Anne Lewis. RHS Members £8. Non-Members £10. ☎ 01352 841000.
Lecture. 2 pm. Pershore & Hindlip College, Worcester. 'Screening with trees & shrubs'. RHS Members £5. Non-Members £7. ☎ 01386 554609.

FRI 29
Roseweek '99. Centenary of Rose Society of Victoria. Melbourne. 7 days 29 Oct–4 Nov. ☎ 00 61 3 9842 1886.

SAT 30
Lecture. 9.30 am. Welsh College of Horticulture, Northop, Flintshire. 'Your garden in autumn' by Anne Lewis. RHS Members £8. Non-Members £10. ☎ 01352 841000.
RHS Regional Lecture. Windermere, Cumbria. 'What makes a garden grow?' by Allen Paterson. ☎ 0171 821 3049.
Cyclamen Society Autumn Show. RHS Garden Wisley, Surrey. ☎ 01483 224234.

SUN 31
Garden open. Last opening of the season 'Monks & Mysteries'; Michelham Priory, East Sussex; 10.30 am – 4 pm.
Autumn Orchid Show. Birmingham Botanical Gardens. ☎ 0121 454 1860.
Garden Walk. 2 pm. Hillier Arboretum, Hants. ☎ 01794 368787.
Plant Sale. Norton Priory, Runcorn, Cheshire. ☎ 01928 569895.

NOVEMBER

MON 1
AGM. 7 pm. Rosecarpe (The North of England Rose, Carnation & Sweet Pea Society). Civic Centre, Gateshead. ☎ 0191 252 7052.

TUE 2
RHS Flower Show. 11 am – 7 pm. (10 am – 5 pm 2nd day.) RHS New Hall, Westminster. Ornamental Plant competition. Botanical Paintings. 2 days 2–3 Nov.
RHS London Lecture. 2.15 pm. RHS Halls, Westminster. 'The development of the garden at The Garden House' by Keith Wiley.
Demonstration. 2 pm. Pershore & Hindlip College, Worcester. 'Your garden in November' by Bob Hares. RHS Members £5. Non-Members £10. ☎ 01386 554609.

WED 3
Garden Walk. RHS Garden Wisley, Surrey. 'The charm of Wisley under glass' with Nick Morgan. RHS Members £5. Non-Members £10. ☎ 01483 224234.
Lecture. 1.30 pm. Myerscough College, Preston, Lancs. 'Commercial Micropropagation' by Dr David Elphinstone. RHS Members £6. Non-Members £7.50. ☎ 01995 640611.
Workshop. 1.30 pm. Houghall College, Durham. 'Winter pruning.' RHS Members £4. Non-Members £5. ☎ 0191 386 1351.
Lecture. 1.30 pm. Reaseheath College, Cheshire. 'Garden design – modern approaches into the millenium' by Alison Evans. RHS Members £6.95. Non-Members £7.95. ☎ 01270 625131.

THU 4
Demonstration. 2 pm. Pershore & Hindlip College, Worcester. 'Pools, stream & bog' by Frank Hardy. RHS Members £5. Non-Members £7. ☎ 01386 554609.

FRI 5
Late Chrysanthemum Show. County Showground, Stafford. 2 days 5–6 Nov. ☎ 01827 310311.
Floodlit Garden Walks. 5 pm – 8.30 pm. Abbotsbury Subtropical Gardens, Dorset. Daily for 3 days 5–7 Nov. ☎ 01305 871387.

SAT 6
Lecture. 9.30 am. Welsh College of Horticulture, Northop, Flintshire. 'Planting & caring for trees & shrubs' by David Toyne. RHS Members £8. Non-Members £10. ☎ 01352 841000.

SUN 7
Lecture. 2 pm. 'Friends & foes of plants' by Dr K Hardwick. Friends of Ness Gardens, Cheshire. Visitor Centre, Ness. Free to RHS Members.
Autumn Orchid Show. 2 pm. Orchid Society of Great Britain. Napier Hall, Hide Place, London. ☎ 01483 421423.
Woodland Walk. Kingston Lacy, Dorset. 2 pm. Meet in car park. £2. Dogs welcome.

NOTES

'MAJOR JOHNSTON MAINTAINS THAT IF YOU CRAM YOUR BEDS AND BORDERS WITH WHAT YOU DO WANT, THERE IS LESS ROOM FOR WHAT YOU DON'T WANT – WEEDS'. VITA SACKVILLE-WEST, WRITING ABOUT HIDCOTE IN *RHSJ*, 1949.

NOVEMBER

NOTES

'MATRIX PLANTING DEPENDS FOR ITS EFFECTS ON IMAGINATION RATHER THAN TIDINESS. IF YOU ARE DEDICATED TO GARDENING AS A FORM OF HOUSEWORK, YOU WILL NOT FIND MATRIX PLANTING AN APPEALING ALTERNATIVE. BUT IF YOU PREFER MORE RELAXED STYLES, WHERE HAPPENSTANCE PLAYS ITS PART, YOU MIGHT FIND IT A REWARDING PATH TO FOLLOW'. PETER THOMPSON, *THE SELF-SUSTAINING GARDEN*, 1997.

MON 8

TUE 9
RHS Regional Lecture. Glasgow Botanic Garden. 'Flowers of Central & South America' by Martin Gardner.
Lecture. 2 pm. Pershore & Hindlip College, Worcester. 'The recreation of Hanbury Hall Gardens' by Neil Cook. RHS Members £5. Non-Members £10. ☎ 01386 554609.

WED 10
Lecture. 2 pm. Scottish Agricultural College, Auchincruive, Ayr. 'Fragrant secrets of herbs' by Dr Katja Svoboda. RHS Members £4.95. Non-Members £5.95. ☎ 01292 525393.
Lecture. 'Autumn Colour'. RHS Garden Rosemoor, Devon. ☎ 01805 624067.

THU 11
RHS Regional Lecture. Norwich. 'Don't let your offspring be a nurseryman, Mrs Worthington: a nurseryman remembers' by Michael Jefferson-Brown. ☎ 0171 821 3049.
Demonstration. 2 pm. Pershore & Hindlip College, Worcester. 'Lighting for your garden'. RHS Members £5. Non-Members £10. ☎ 01386 554609.
Garden Design Course. RHS Garden Wisley, Surrey. Led by Robin Williams and Robin Templer Williams. 4 days 11–14 Nov. ☎ 01483 224234.

FRI 12
Lecture. 7.30 pm. Chilterns AGS. Great Kingshill Village Hall. 'Shade lovers for the rock garden' by Jack Elliott. ☎ 01628 486709.

SAT 13
Demonstration. 10 am. Pershore & Hindlip College, Worcester. 'Your garden in November' by Bob Hares. RHS Members £5. Non-Members £10. ☎ 01386 554609.
Workshop. 10.30 am – 3.30 pm. Brogdale, Kent. Traditional Orchards. Friends of Brogdale £20. Others £30. ☎ 01795 535286.
Christmas Craft Show. Broadlands, Romsey, Hampshire. 2 days 13–14 Nov. ☎ 01794 505056.

SUN 14
Lecture. 2 pm. 'Flowers of Crete' by L Wolstenholme. Friends of Ness Gardens, Cheshire. Visitor Centre, Ness. Free to RHS Members.

NOVEMBER

MON
15

TUE
16

Lecture. 10 am. Pershore & Hindlip College, Worcester. 'The principles of fruit tree pruning' by John Edgeley. RHS Members £5. Non-Members £10. ☎ 01386 554609.

WED
17

Lecture. 1.30 pm. Myerscough College, Preston, Lancs. 'Climbers & wall shrubs' by Joe Lamont. RHS Members £6. Non-Members £7.50. ☎ 01995 640611.
Demonstration. RHS Garden Wisley, Surrey. 'Pruning fruit trees & bushes' with Jim Arbury & Charlie Day. RHS Members £5. Non-Members £10. ☎ 01483 224234.
Lecture. 2 pm. Writtle College, Chelmsford, Essex. 'Hard landscaping'. ☎ 01245 424200.

THU
18

Lecture. 1 pm. Welsh College of Horticulture, Northop, Flintshire. 'Plants for winter interest' by Julia White. RHS Members £8. Non-Members £10. ☎ 01352 841000.
Demonstration. 2 pm. Pershore & Hindlip College, Worcester. 'Revitalising the herbaceous border'. RHS Members £5. Non-Members £7. ☎ 01386 554609.

FRI
19

RHS Regional Lecture. Belfast. 'The plant collections of the NCCPG' by Graham Pattison. ☎ 0171 821 3049.
Demonstration. RHS Garden Wisley, Surrey. 'Pruning fruit trees & bushes' with Jim Arbury & Charlie Day. RHS Members £5. Non-Members £10. ☎ 01483 224234.

SAT
20

Lecture. 9.30 am. Welsh College of Horticulture, Northop, Flintshire. 'Plants for winter interest' by Julia White. RHS Members £8. Non-Members £10. ☎ 01352 841000.
Lecture. 1.30 pm. Reaseheath College, Cheshire. 'The fruit garden displayed: practical pruning & maintenance' by Bert Davis. RHS Members £6.95. Non-Members £7.95. ☎ 01270 625665.
Christmas at Wisley. RHS Garden Wisley, Surrey. Until 28 Nov. ☎ 01483 224234.

SUN
21

Lecture. 2 pm. 'George Forrest – what a life' by Dr B McLean. Friends of Ness Gardens, Cheshire. Visitor Centre, Ness. Free to RHS Members.
Garden Walk. 2 pm. Cragside, Northumberland. ☎ 01669 620150.
Demonstration. RHS Garden Wisley, Surrey. 'Pruning fruit trees & bushes' with Jim Arbury & Charlie Day. RHS Members £5. Non-Members £10. ☎ 01483 224234.

NOTES

'MORE AND MORE I AM COMING TO THE CONCLUSION THAT RAIN IS A FAR MORE IMPORTANT CONSIDERATION TO GARDENS THAN SUN, AND THAT ONE OF THE LESSER ADVANTAGES THAT A GARDENER GAINS IN LIFE IS HIS THOROUGH ENJOYMENT OF A RAINY DAY'. MARGARET WATERFIELD, *FLOWER GROUPING IN ENGLISH, SCOTCH & IRISH GARDENS*, 1907

NOVEMBER

NOTES

MON
22

TUE
23
Workshop. 2 pm. Pershore & Hindlip College, Worcester. 'Winter cuttings' by Bob Hares. RHS Members £5. Non-Members £10. ☎ 01386 554609.

WED
24
Demonstration. RHS Garden Wisley, Surrey. 'Winter treatment of grapes: indoors & out' with Jim Arbury & Ron Gilkerson. RHS Members £5. Non-Members £10. ☎ 01483 224234.
Workshop. RHS Garden Rosemoor, Devon. 'Preparing the garden & glasshouse for winter'. RHS Members £5. Non-Members £10. ☎ 01805 624067.
Demonstration. Flower Arranging. 10 am – 12.30 pm. RHS Garden Wisley, Surrey. 'Flowers for the festive season' with Robert Barlow. ☎ 01483 224234.
Demonstration. RHS Garden Wisley, Surrey. 'Festive plants' with Nick Morgan. RHS Members £5. Non-Members £10. ☎ 01483 224234.
Lecture. Shuttleworth College, Biggleswade, Bedfordshire. 'Hard landscaping skills' with David Campbell. ☎ 01245 424200.

KITCHEN GARDEN:
ANYTHING OMITTED LAST MONTH, PERFORM EARLY IN THIS, BEFORE THE RAIN PREVENT YOU.
FLOWER GARDEN:
LEAVES SHOULD BE CONSTANTLY SWEPT UP, AS THEY FALL, OR THEY WILL SPOIL THE WALKS.
GREENHOUSE: AIR GIVE IN THE MIDDLE OF THE DAY, EXCEPT WHEN IT IS VERY FOGGY; WATER WOODY PLANTS OFTEN, BUT GIVE THEM BUT A LITTLE AT A TIME, AS DAMPNESS IS MORE PREJUDICIAL IN A GREENHOUSE THAN COLD'. RICHARD WESTON ESQ., *THE GARDENER'S POCKET CALENDAR,* 1783

THU
25
Christmas Fayre. 2 pm. Pershore & Hindlip College, Worcester. ☎ 01386 554609.

FRI
26

SAT
27
Lecture. 1.30 pm. Myerscough College, Preston, Lancs. 'House plant propagation' by Dr Julie Youngs. RHS Members £6. Non-Members £7.50. ☎ 01995 640611.
Demonstration. 2 pm – 3.30 pm. Brogdale, Kent. 'Grafting fruit trees'. Friends of Brogdale £6. Others £10. ☎ 01795 535286.
Christmas Craft Fair. RHS Garden Rosemoor, Devon. 2 days 27–28 Nov. ☎ 01805 624067.

SUN
28
Lecture. 2 pm. 'Biodiversity – what is it and are we conserving it in our gardens?' by Dr Hugh McAllister. Friends of Ness Gardens, Cheshire. Visitor Centre, Ness. Free to RHS Members.

November • December

MON 29

TUE 30
Lecture. 2 pm. Pershore & Hindlip College, Worcester. 'A tree for every situation'. RHS Members £5. Non-Members £10. ☎ 01386 554609.

WED 1
Coffee Morning. Friends of RBG, Kew. Cambridge Cottage. ☎ 0181 332 5922.
Lecture. 1.30 pm. Roseheath College, Cheshire. 'Conservatory plants & their care' by Alexandra Baulkwill. RHS Members £6.95. Non-Members £7.95. ☎ 01270 625131.

THU 2
Lecture. 1 pm. Welsh College of Horticulture, Northop, Flintshire. 'Garden restoration' by David Toyne. RHS Members £8. Non-Members £10. ☎ 01352 841000.
Demonstration. 2 pm. Pershore & Hindlip College, Worcester. 'The care of houseplants during winter' by Howard Drury. RHS Members £5. Non-Members £10. ☎ 01386 554609

FRI 3

SAT 4
Christmas Craft Festival. Duncombe Park, North Yorkshire. 2 days 4–5 Dec. ☎ 01439 770213.
Lecture. 9.30 am. Welsh College of Horticulture, Northop, Flintshire. 'Garden restoration' by David Toyne. RHS Members £8. Non-Members £10. ☎ 01352 841000.
Lecture. 2 pm. Orchid Society of Great Britain. Napier Hall, Hide Place, London. ☎ 01483 421423.

SUN 5
Christmas Fayre. 1.30 pm. Houghall College, Durham. 'Bulbs for Christmas display'. RHS Members £4. Non-Members £5. ☎ 0191 386 1351.
Garden Walk. 2 pm. Hillier Arboretum, Hants. ☎ 01794 368787.

NOTES

'MY FATHER MISTRUSTED GARDENERS – THEY DIG UP ALL ONE'S PET PLANTS, HE AVOWED – AND WOULD NOT HAVE ONE ANYWHERE ABOUT THE PLACE, SO ALWAYS I WAS COMMANDEERED TO DO THE WEEDING AND CLEARING THAT BORED HIM. "WHEN I GROW UP, I'LL NEVER, NEVER, NEVER HAVE A GARDEN" I RESOLVED'. CLARE LEIGHTON, *FOUR HEDGES*, 1935.

DECEMBER

NOTES

MON 6
Lecture. 7.30 pm. Bedfordshire AGS. Wilstead Village Hall. 'The Altai Mountains' by Julia Corden. ☎ 01462 711295.

TUE 7
Demonstration. 2 pm. Pershore & Hindlip College, Worcester. 'Your garden in December' by Bob Hares. RHS Members £5. Non-Members £10. ☎ 01386 554609.

WED 8
Lecture. 1.30 pm. Myerscough College, Preston, Lancs. 'Planning the vegetable garden' by Philip Rhodes. RHS Members £6. Non-Members £7.50. ☎ 01995 640611.
Lecture. 2 pm. Scottish Agricultural College, Auchincruive, Ayr. 'Eco-friendly indoor pot plants' by Joanna Gough. RHS Members £4.95. Non-Members £5.95. ☎ 01292 525393.
Lecture. 2 pm. Writtle College, Chelmsford, Essex. 'Four seasons in the garden – winter' by Marion Polley. RHS Members £8. Non-Members £10. ☎ 01245 424200.
Winter Lecture. RHS Garden Rosemoor, Devon. 'The gardens at Abbotsbury' by Stephen Griffith. ☎ 01805 624067.

THU 9
Lecture. 2 pm. Pershore & Hindlip College, Worcester. 'Bark, stems & evergreens'. RHS Members £5. Non-Members £10. ☎ 01386 554609.

FRI 10

'KITCHEN GARDEN: TRAPS MUST BE SET TO CATCH MICE. FRUIT GARDEN: APPLES AND PEARS IN THE FRUITERY EXAMINE, AND PICK OUT THOSE WHICH BEGIN TO ROT. GREENHOUSE: FROST MUST BE GUARDED AGAINST, BY KEEPING THE DOORS AND WINDOWS CLOSE, WHEN IT BEGINS TO FREEZE'.
RICHARD WESTON ESQ., *THE GARDENER'S POCKET CALENDAR*, 1783.

SAT 11
Christmas Weekend. Plant centre, RHS Garden Wisley, Surrey. 2 days 11–12 Dec.
Demonstration. 10 am. Pershore & Hindlip College, Worcester. 'Your garden in December' by Bob Hare. RHS Members £5. Non-Members £10. ☎ 01386 554609.

SUN 12

December

MON
13

TUE
14

RHS Flower Show. 11 am – 7 pm. (10 am – 5 pm 2nd day.) RHS New Hall, Westminster. Christmas Show. Botanical Paintings. 2 days 14–15 Dec.
Workshop. 10 am. Pershore & Hindlip College, Worcester. 'Flower arranging for Christmas' with Sallie Campbell.
☎ 01386 554609.

WED
15

Demonstration. RHS Garden Rosemoor, Devon. 'Christmas Decorations'. RHS Members £5. Non-Members £10.
☎ 01805 624067.
Lecture. 1.30 pm. Reaseheath College, Cheshire. 'Plant arrangements for Christmas' by June Shallcross. RHS Members £6.95. Non-Members £7.95. ☎ 01270 625131.

THU
16

Christmas Plant Fayre. 2 pm. Pershore & Hindlip College, Worcester. ☎ 01386 554609.

FRI
17

SAT
18

SUN
19

NOTES

THE RAINFALL IN LONDON IN DECEMBER 1914 WAS 8.0IN. (203.2MM.)

December

NOTES

'No gardener can have a garden large enough for all the flowers that he would like to grow: we are compelled to do all we can to get the most out of our limited space'. Jason Hill, *The Curious Gardener*, 1932.

MON
20

TUE
21

WED
22

THU
23

FRI
24

SAT
25   **Christmas Day**

SUN
26

Part Three

Out And About

Gardens to Visit
Awards to Gardens
Holidays for Gardeners
Importing and Exporting Plants
European Nurseries
Courses for Amateurs

Gardens to Visit

THIS SECTION RECOMMENDS gardens in Great Britain and Ireland. Our aim is to supply sufficient detail to enable readers to decide whether and when to plan a visit. The list is not exhaustive. It offers a selection of the different types of garden which are open to the public: ancient and modern, large and small, public and private. The editors welcome suggestions for additions, deletions or alterations to entries. This year, for the first time, we have added about 100 nurseries and garden centres which are particularly rewarding to visit.

Our Garden Listings

Gardens are listed by county or region (for Scotland), and then alphabetically by name. The order is England, Wales, Scotland, Northern Ireland and Republic of Ireland. Our source for practical information about directions, opening times, admission charges, parking, loos, disabled facilities, shops and refreshments has been the owners or their staff, backed up by our own enquiries where appropriate. The accuracy of these details is not guaranteed, but is believed to be correct at the time of going to press. In order to assist readers who are hoping to arrange a group visit by special appointment, we have taken the unusual step of listing the telephone and fax numbers to which enquiries should be directed. In many cases this is the private telephone line of the owners: readers are strongly urged to respect their privacy. If telephone and fax numbers have been omitted, this is because the owners prefer to receive such requests by letter. A pre-booked group can often make a visit at a time when the garden is not open to individual visitors. Most gardens offer special rates and, if details are not given, it may be worth asking whether a reduction is available and what minimum number is acceptable. Not all gardens offer reductions for groups: popular gardens which already suffer from wear and tear may not welcome extra visitors. Special rates for families are sometimes available, especially at larger gardens attached to stately homes, where the garden is only one of many entertainments offered to the visitor. There are endless permutations on the numbers of adults and/or children which constitute a 'family' and the age at which a child becomes an adult and has to pay the full entry price. Season tickets are sometimes available, and good value for people who live near a large garden or stately home. National Trust members are usually admitted free to Trust properties. All readers are strongly recommended to join the National Trust in any event: its portfolio of blue-chip gardens is so comprehensive that no garden tour is complete without a visit to one or more of its properties. Remember too that members of the RHS enjoy free entry to many gardens throughout the country.

We generally give prices and times for visiting the garden only. If the house is open at the same time, a supplement may be payable. Entrance fees vary, and some owners have told us that they may increase fees in the middle of the season. Some have a high season for a month or so – like Leonardslee in May. Others have a special day of the week or open days for charity when the entrance fee is higher. A few owners had not yet fixed their 1999 times or admission charges and, with their agreement, we have therefore indicated that the times or prices quoted are for

"Many gardens have honesty boxes ... so take lots of change"

1998. All entrance fees are, in any event, liable to be changed: visitors would do well to take more money than they think they will need. Many gardens have honesty boxes, and it is also important to take lots of change, so that you are not forced to choose between paying too much or too little.

Remember that most gardens have a last admission time. Typically it will be 30 or 45 minutes before they close, but it can be much longer. The last admission to Stowe is one hour before it closes, while Stratfield Saye actually closes its gates to visitors at 4 pm, two hours before they are required to leave. The guide indicates whether parking is available: this may be at the garden itself or on a public road very close to it.

Parking may be at some distance from the house. At Saltram it is 500 yards away, and this is by no means exceptional. You can however expect better parking facilities at a popular property which offers a wide range of entertainments than at a small plantsman's garden in a country lane. In the case of refreshments, however, we have referred only to what is offered within the garden itself, and not to restaurants, tea-rooms and public houses nearby.

VISITORS WITH SPECIAL NEEDS

We have not specified the nature of the special facilities offered to the disabled, but in most cases it includes loos and ramps which are suitable for the wheelchair-bound. It is best to enquire in advance of a visit if particular items of special equipment are required. The National Trust is especially good at adapting its properties to accommodate the needs of disabled visitors and publishes an excellent free 56-page booklet called *Information for Visitors with Disabilities*, which details the many special facilities available at those of its properties which are suitable for disabled visitors. It is available from the National Trust's head office in London.

It is often a condition of admission that no photograph taken within a garden may be sold or used for public reproduction without the consent of the property owner. Visitors should also remember that almost all gardens accept dogs only if they are kept on leads. Some restrict dogs to particular areas of a property, like the car park, or the woods and parkland rather than the garden proper. Private owners are generally better disposed towards dogs than corporate owners like the National Trust or English Heritage.

Information about outsize trees is taken from a fascinating publication *Champion Trees in the British Isles* by Alan F Mitchell, Victoria E Schilling and John E J White (4th edition 1994, HMSO, £5). There are two ways of measuring trees: height and girth. Sometimes the tallest specimen will also have the thickest trunk – but not always. Both the tallest and the biggest can claim to be the champion tree, and we have made this distinction when noting record-breakers in gardens. Tree measurements can never be fully up to date: some records have not been verified since the great gales of 1987 and 1990. Nevertheless *Champion Trees in the British Isles* clearly indicates where the best collections of trees are: there are, for example, 101 record-breaking trees at Westonbirt Arboretum in Gloucestershire and 51 at the Sir Harold Hillier Gardens and Arboretum in Hampshire. Birr Castle has the leading collection in Ireland with 51 tree records, while in Scotland the largest number is at the Royal Botanic Garden in Edinburgh, which has 45. The dominance of conifers in western and central Scotland may also be noted. Further information about champion trees is available from the *Tree Register of the British Isles*, c/o Mrs Victoria Schilling, 2 Church Cottages, Westmeston, Hassocks, West Sussex BN6 8RJ.

We have noted those NCCPG National Collections which are held at the gardens and nurseries we list. Not all genera are the subject of a National Collection: there are still some horticulturally important groups of plants which have not yet been seriously collected and studied under the auspices of the NCCPG. Other genera have been split into a number of different collections. This is particularly necessary in the case of such a large genus as *Rhododendron* or those, like *Euphorbia*, which require a great variety of growing conditions. Moreover, the NCCPG has wisely introduced a system of duplicate collections so that plants are grown in two or more gardens. The need to maintain duplicate collections and split large genera explains why certain names occur several times in our list of National Collections. That list is taken from *The National Plant Collections Directory 1998*. The 1999 edition has now been published and lists over 600 National Plant Collections: copies are available from bookshops or directly from the NCCPG, c/o RHS Garden Wisley, Woking, Surrey GU23 6QB.

> *"... if a good garden is seldom open, it is all the more important to know when the opportunity to see it will arise"*

A word about our choice of gardens is appropriate. We aim to be comprehensive but realistic. All major gardens which are open regularly are listed as a matter of course. These include many gardens of the National Trust and the National Trust for Scotland as well as botanic and public gardens and those attached to stately homes. But many gardens do not open to visitors regularly: the National Gardens Scheme lists over 3,000. We have found space for a selection of these gardens which open only once a year or by appointment. Some guides would omit them on the grounds that it is not worthwhile to give publicity to gardens which so few people can visit.

We take the view that, if a good garden is seldom open, it is all the more important to know when the opportunity to see it will arise. And there are bound to be inconsistencies. We have, for example, omitted several excellent gardens where entry is free – Howth Castle Rhododendron Gardens in Co. Dublin and the Botanic Gardens Park in Belfast are two that spring immediately to mind – while we have included others such as The Royal Botanic Garden at Edinburgh and Chiswick House in London.

The starting point for garden visiting must be the 'Yellow Book' which the National Gardens Scheme publishes annually in February under the full title *Gardens of England & Wales Open to the Public*. The Yellow Book is a bestseller. Its sales immediately after publication exceed 5,000 copies per week, three times the success rate of its nearest rival among bestselling paperback reference books. It is wonderfully comprehensive and totally undiscriminating. The owners write their own garden entries, with the result that a really good garden may come across as self-deprecatingly boring, while an exciting description can often lead to disappointment. Beware of self-publicists: you can usually spot the hype. The Yellow Book lists nearly 3,500 gardens and is the single most important guide to visiting gardens in England and Wales, and the least expensive. Copies of *Gardens of England & Wales Open to the Public in 1999* are available from the end of February from bookshops or directly from the National Gardens Scheme, Hatchlands Park, East Clandon, Guildford, Surrey GU4 7RT.

Scotland has its own Yellow Book called *The Gardens of Scotland*, available from Scotland's Gardens Scheme, 31 Castle Terrace, Edinburgh EH1 2EL. It lists over 300 gardens throughout Scotland but, like the Yellow Book, does not always mention that some gardens are open at other times, not for the benefit of the Scheme. Indeed, some open for the Scheme only one day a year, and for their own funds for the other 364 days.

The leading guide to the whole of the British Isles is *The Good Gardens Guide 1999* by Peter King. Its quality is inevitably somewhat uneven because the entries are written by many different hands and the standard of their judgements varies. Nevertheless it accounts for many good gardens in more detail than any other book and, above all, it sorts out and evaluates many of the private gardens in the Yellow Book. *The Good Gardens Guide 1999* itself lists over 1,000 gardens, some across the Channel within a day's journey of the Tunnel. It saves so much time and money – not to mention good humour – which would otherwise be lost driving many miles to a disappointing garden, that *The Good Gardens Guide 1999* is worth every penny of its price.

The best of the garden guides is *The Daily Telegraph Gardener's Guide to Britain & Ireland 1998* by Patrick Taylor (Dorling Kindersley, £12.99) which is beautifully laid out and elegantly written. It is updated annually – the 1999 edition comes out in March – and receives a thorough biennial revision which keeps it fresh. It is also based on personal visits, and therefore utterly reliable: Patrick Taylor has a happy talent for tracking down new and interesting gardens which other writers have overlooked, and his judgements cannot be faulted – accurate, observant and intelligent. *The Daily Telegraph Gardener's Guide to Britain & Ireland* is especially valuable because it includes good nurseries: Patrick Taylor recognises that visiting new nurseries is just as enjoyable and important to a keen gardener as seeing other people's gardens.

VISITING IRISH GARDENS

The Northern Ireland Tourist Board has published a handsome brochure called *An Information Guide to Gardens and Historic Demesnes* which is illustrated and describes some 26 parks and gardens in considerable detail. It is available free from tourist offices in Northern Ireland, directly from NITB, 59 North Street, Belfast BT1 1NB, or from their offices in Glasgow and Dublin. The Irish Tourist Board (PO Box 273, Dublin 8) publishes an illustrated guide to *Great Houses, Castles & Gardens of Ireland*. In addition to 79 of the best places in Eire, it lists 16 Country House Hotels. The guide is invaluable, and whets the armchair visitor's appetite.

The Royal National Rose Society has published a very useful *Guide to Rose Gardens to Visit*, which lists all the best gardens for seeing roses and many of the leading rose nurseries too. The gardens include everything from such well-known places of pilgrimage as Mottisfont Abbey to several small gardens, seldom open, which nevertheless have amazing private collections of roses.

England

Bedfordshire

The Swiss Garden
Old Warden, Biggleswade
☎ 01234 228330   Fax 01234 228921
Owner Bedfordshire County Council
Location 1½ miles west of Biggleswade
Open 1 pm – 6 pm (but 10 am – 6 pm on Sundays & Bank Holidays); daily; March to September. 11 am – 3 pm; Sundays & 1 January; January, February & October
Admission Adults £2.50; Concessions £1.25 (1998 prices)
Facilities Parking; loos; facilities for the disabled; plants for sale; publications and souvenirs shop; restaurant at neighbouring Shuttleworth collection
Features Interesting for children; picturesque landscape; rhododendrons; Pulhamite grotto; fernery; Swiss cottage; new accessway (1998); much restoration & replanting (1997)
English Heritage Grade II*
Friends Details available at the entrance

A rustic, gothic landscape garden, largely developed by the Shuttleworth family in the 19th century. Winding paths and sinuous waterways; little cast-iron, ornamental bridges; picturesque huts and quaint kiosks; soaring ironwork arches; gullies and ferneries; vast conifers and cheerful rhododendrons; an early grotto-glasshouse (note the small panes of glass) planted as a fernery. In short – great fun to visit.

Woburn Abbey
Woburn MK43 0TP
☎ 01525 290666   Fax 01525 290271
Owner The Marquess of Tavistock
Location 1½ miles from Woburn on A4012
Open 10.45 am – 3.45 pm; daily; April to October. Private gardens open for NGS: 11 am – 5 pm; 18 April & 27 June. Maze open: 5 & 6 June & 22 August
Admission Park: £5 per car: NGS extra (1998 prices)
Facilities Parking; loos; facilities for the disabled; plants for sale; two shops; lunches & teas
Features Landscape designed by Capability Brown; fine conifers; lake; landscape designed by Humphry Repton; interesting for children; deer park; tallest *Zelkova sinica* (17m.) in the British Isles
English Heritage Grade I

Not a gardener's garden, though the park has many rare trees and there are more than 100 daffodil cultivars. The best way to see the famous redwood avenue is from the cable car. The private gardens are simple and formal, mainly 19th-century and Italianate, but they include the hornbeam maze with a Chinese pavilion in the centre.

Wrest Park
Silsoe MK45 4HS
☎ 01525 860152 (weekends)
Owner English Heritage
Location ¾ mile east of Silsoe
Open 10 am – 6 pm; Saturdays, Sundays & Bank Holiday Mondays; 2 April to 31 October
Admission Adults £3.20; Concessions £2.40; Children £1.60
Facilities Parking; dogs permitted; loos; gift shop; light refreshments
Features Landscape designed by Capability Brown; good architectural features; garden sculpture; grand parterres; long vistas; largest pink chestnut *Aesculus × carnea* in the British Isles
English Heritage Grade I

The 'English Versailles', dominated by a graceful long canal which runs down to the classical domed pavilion built by Thomas Archer in 1710. Capability Brown came here later, but worked around the earlier design. The house came later still, in the 1830s. A garden of grandeur.

Worth a Visit

Toddington Manor
Toddington LU5 6HJ ☎ 01525 872576. A newish garden, made by the owners in less than 20 years, around some magnificent old trees. It has some excellent features, notably a lime avenue which leads into a cherry walk, but some consider it overdesigned and underplanted – an agreeable garden that could do with more variety. However, we have never seen such a wonderfully high standard of maintenance in any garden.

Berkshire

Englefield House
Englefield, Theale, Reading RG7 5EN
☎ 0118 930 2221   Fax 0118 930 2226
Owner Sir William & Lady Benyon
Location On A340, 1 mile from M4 Jct 12
Open 10 am – dusk; Mondays (plus Tuesdays – Thursdays from April to October); all year. And on 15 May for NGS
Admission Adults £2; Children free
Facilities Parking; access for the disabled; plants for sale; refreshments on NGS days
Features Herbaceous plants; daffodils; rhododendrons and azaleas; old roses; woodland garden; deer park; 8ft grizzly bear carved from oak
English Heritage Grade II

A splendid woodland garden with underplantings of maples, viburnums, magnolias and many good shrubs. The Elizabethan house has a formal garden in front of it: wonderful colour borders along its walls.

THE OLD RECTORY, BURGHFIELD
Burghfield RG3 3TH
☎ 0118 983 3200

Owner R Merton
Location Right at Hatch Gate Inn and first entrance on right
Open 11 am – 4 pm; last Wednesday in month; February to October
Admission Adults £2; Children free
Facilities Parking; loos; facilities for the disabled; plants for sale; teas
Features Herbaceous plants; plantsman's garden; pond; rock garden; snowdrops; stone troughs; exotic displays in tubs; hellebores; lilies; new border of David Austin roses (1998)

Highly acclaimed garden, whose *tour de force* is a double herbaceous border where plants build up their impact through repetition, backed by yew hedges which get taller towards the end, to cheat the perspective. It leads to a pool framed by dense plantings of strong foliage – ferns, hostas, maples.

WYLD COURT RAINFOREST
Hampstead Norreys, Thatcham, Newbury
RG18 0TN
☎ 01635 202221   Fax 01635 202440

Owner The World Land Trust
Location Signed from Jct 13 on M4
Open 10 am – 5.15 pm; daily; all year. Closed 25 & 26 December
Admission Adults £3.50; Concessions £3; Children £2 (1998 prices)
Facilities Parking; loos; facilities for the disabled; plants for sale; gift shop; refreshments
Features Glasshouses; plantsman's garden; interesting for children

Three large landscaped glasshouses, computer-set to create three different rainforest climates. Each has a thickly planted collection of exotic plants of every kind, many of them endangered or vulnerable to extinction. Wonderful in winter, when the tropical orchids flower, and particularly rewarding in summer when *Victoria amazonica* fills one of the pools. But fascinating whatever the season or the weather outside.

WORTH A VISIT

BRESSINGHAM PLANT CENTRE
Dorney Court, Dorney, Windsor SL4 6QP
☎ 01628 669999. *Open 9 am – 5.30 pm, daily except 25 & 26 December. This plant centre offers the huge range of perennials and conifers for which the company is renowned. The quality is also outstanding. Weekly talks are held.*

FOLLY FARM
Sulhamstead, Reading RG7 4DF Open 2 – 6 pm; 11 April, 23 May, 20 June. Private bookings on written application (midweek only). One of the most enchanting gardens to come from the partnership between Sir Edwin Lutyens and Gertrude Jekyll, the structure of Folly Farm is intact. The most famous features are the canal garden, running up to a double-gabled wing of the house, and the sunken rose garden, where a cruciform bed of lavender rises from a tank of waterlilies. The plantings have been adapted to modern conditions and to the owners' taste for floribunda roses: Vernon Russell-Smith had a hand in it. Folly Farm is particularly lovely in spring when drifts of anemones flower under cherries and crab-apples.

FOXGROVE
Skinners Green, Enborne, Newbury RG14 6RE
☎ 01635 40554. *Open 2 – 6 pm; 20 February, 28 March & 2 May. Groups welcome by appointment. A plantsman's garden, linked to Louise Vockins' nursery next door. Bulbs, alpines and herbaceous plants are Audrey Vockins' great interest. The hellebores, crocuses and snowdrops give a great display in early spring. There are good shrubs, roses and handsome small trees too.*

HOLLINGTON NURSERIES
Woolton Hill, Newbury RG20 9XT ☎ *01635 253908. Open 10 am – 5 pm; Monday – Saturday; 11 am – 5 pm; Sundays and Bank Holidays; March to September. Please telephone October to February. Entrance fee to garden £1. The gardens are excellent: formally designed with handsome hard features and informally planted with herbs, roses and scented plants. The nursery stocks a large range of herbs and scented plants in containers, as well as roses to plant with them. See also www.herb-garden.co.uk*

OLD RECTORY COTTAGE
Tidmarsh, Pangbourne RG8 8ER ☎ *0118 984 3241. Open By appointment. This is the marvellous garden of a great plantsman who has collected in all four corners of the world – the introducer of such staples as Geranium palustre and Symphytum caucasicum. The garden is a treasure house of unusual species, forms and home-made hybrids. Snowdrops, crocuses, cyclamens, hellebores and winter stem colours justify a visit in February. Lilies are a special interest in early July – Bill Baker breeds them.*

BUCKINGHAMSHIRE

ASCOTT HOUSE & GARDENS
Wing, Leighton Buzzard LU7 0PS
☎ 01296 688242   Fax 01296 681904

Owner The National Trust
Location ½ mile east of Wing
Open Garden only: 2 pm – 6 pm; Tuesday – Friday; 1 – 30 April and 27 August to 27 September. Plus Wednesdays & last Sundays in month; 1 May to 25 August
Admission Garden only: £4 Adults; £2 Children
Facilities Parking; loos; access for the disabled

Features Herbaceous plants; fine conifers; lake; garden sculpture; good topiary; woodland garden; spring bulbs; Dutch garden; tallest *Cedrus atlantica* 'Aurea' in the British Isles
English Heritage Grade II*

Opulent late-Victorian extravaganza. Tremendous set-piece fountains by Story, grand terraces, magnificent trees and a giant sundial of box and golden yew. Almost too good to be true.

CHENIES MANOR
Chenies, Rickmansworth WD3 6ER
☎ 01494 762888

Owner Mrs A MacLeod Matthews
Location Centre of Chenies village
Open 2 pm – 5 pm; Wednesdays, Thursdays & Bank Holidays; April to October
Admission Garden only £2.20; House & garden £4.50
Facilities Parking; loos; access for the disabled; plants for sale; tea, coffee, home-made cakes
Features Fruit of special interest; herbs; good topiary; physic garden; award-winning maze
English Heritage Grade II*

Three acres of tightly designed gardens full of variety. Tudor bulb garden, modelled on Hampton Court; physic garden for herbs; Edwardian skittle alley; grass labyrinth; beautiful old lawns, yew hedges and walls alive with clever modern colour-conscious planting. Ethereally English.

CLIVEDEN
Taplow, Maidenhead SL6 0JA
☎ 01628 605069   Fax 01628 669461

Owner The National Trust
Location 2 miles north of Taplow, M4 Jct 7
Open 11 am – 6 pm (4 pm in November & December); daily; 13 March to 31 December
Admission Adults (Grounds) £5; Children £2.50
Facilities Parking; dogs permitted; loos; access for the disabled; National Trust shop, Wednesday – Sunday; light refreshments and meals, Wednesday – Sunday
Features Bluebells; herbaceous plants; fruit of special interest; modern roses; snowdrops; woodland garden; plantings by Graham Thomas; particularly interesting in winter; good autumn colour; tallest *Juglans cinerea* (24m.) in the British Isles; distinguished head gardener (Philip Cotton)
English Heritage Grade I
NCCPG National Collection *Catalpa*

A vast landscape garden, just stuffed with whatever money could buy: balustrading from the Villa Borghese in Rome, the dramatic 'Fountain of Love' and a huge parterre below the house. The best bits are the Arcadian ilex wood, quite magical, and newly restored rose garden, originally made by Geoffrey Jellicoe in 1932.

STOWE LANDSCAPE GARDENS
Stowe, Buckingham MK18 5EH
☎ 01280 822850   Fax 01280 822437

Owner The National Trust
Location 3 miles north-west of Buckingham
Open 10 am – 5 pm or dusk (last admissions 4 pm); daily; 20 March to 1 November, but closed on Tuesdays, Thursdays & Saturdays from 14 April to 4 July and from 5 September to 31 October
Admission Adults £4.50
Facilities Parking; dogs permitted; loos; facilities for the disabled; plants for sale at weekends; light meals 11 am – 5 pm
Features Landscape designed by Capability Brown; worked on by Kent; particularly interesting in winter; tallest *Fraxinus angustifolia* var. *lentiscifolia* (24m.) and largest × *Crataemespilus grandiflora* (9m.) in the British Isles
English Heritage Grade I

Mega landscape, considered by some the most important in the history of gardens. The National Trust acquired control from the boys' public school in 1989 and the restoration will take many years. Go if you have not been already, and go again if you have. Stowe is not obvious: stomp round slowly, and contemplate the history and symbolism of each feature. Read the National Trust's excellent guide and then go round again, this year, next year, every year, and commune with the *genius loci*.

TURN END
Townside, Haddenham, Aylesbury HP17 8BG
☎ 01844 291383

Owner Mr & Mrs Peter Aldington
Location Turn at Rising Sun in Haddenham, then 300 yds on left. Park in street
Open 10 am – 4 pm; 2, 9, 16, 23 & 30 June. 2 – 6 pm; 4 April, 3 May & 19 September for NGS. Groups by appointment
Admission Adults £2; Children 50p
Facilities Loos; plants for sale; refreshments on NGS days
Features Plantsman's garden; rock garden; old roses; ferns; grasses; brilliant design

Only one acre, but never was space so used to create an illusion of size. A brilliant series of enclosed gardens, sunken or raised, sunny or shady, each different and yet harmonious, contrasts with lawns, borders and glades. Much featured in the glossies, and deservedly. Visitors are requested to park well away from the house, please.

WADDESDON MANOR
Aylesbury HP18 0JH
☎ 01296 651226   Fax 01296 651142

Owner The National Trust
Location A41 Bicester & Aylesbury; 20 miles from Oxford
Open 10 am – 5 pm; Wednesday – Sunday & Bank Holiday Mondays; 3 March to 24 December. Guided tours every Thursday, Saturday & Sunday
Admission Grounds only: Adults £3; Children £1.50; RHS members free in March & October

Facilities Parking; loos; facilities for the disabled; plants for sale; gift & wine shop; tea-room
Features Herbaceous plants; daffodils; lake; new spring walk with 80,000 crocuses (1998); new tropical mound (1998)
English Heritage Grade II*

A grand Victorian park, splendid formal gardens, a rococo aviary and extravagant bedding are the first fruits of restoring the grounds of this amazing Rothschild palace. An exciting addition to the National Trust's portfolio of historic gardens.

WEST WYCOMBE PARK
West Wycombe HP14 3AJ
☎ 01494 488675

Owner The National Trust
Location West end of West Wycombe on A40
Open 2 pm – 6 pm; Sunday – Thursday; June to August. Plus, gardens only, Sundays, Wednesdays & Bank Holidays in April & May
Admission Adults £2.50
Facilities Parking; loos; facilities for the disabled
Features Good architectural features; garden sculpture
English Heritage Grade I

Early landscape park, with a lake in the shape of a swan. Classical temples and follies, plus three modern eye-catchers designed by Quinlan Terry. Celebrating 300 years since the Dashwoods first bought the estate in 1698.

WORTH A VISIT

BLOSSOMS
Cobblers Hill Great Missenden ☎ *01494 863140. Open By appointment only. A large modern plantsman's garden: five acres of very varied habitats from beech woods to lakes and from screes to cutting borders.*

BUCKINGHAM NURSERIES AND GARDEN CENTRE
10 Tingewick Road, Buckingham MK18 4AE
☎ *01280 813556. Open Summer: 8.30 am – 6 pm (5.30 pm in winter); Monday – Friday; 10 am – 4 pm; Sundays. The nursery produces bare-root hedging and tree plants for ornamental and forestry use. There are some interesting varieties of trees and shrubs, with a growing list of herbaceous plants and a good selection of container plants.*

BUTTERFIELDS NURSERY
Harvest Hill, Bourne End SL8 5JJ ☎ *01628 525455. Open 9 am – 5 pm; usually. NCCPG National Collection: Pleione. Butterfields has two main but very different specialities: pleiones and dahlias. The pleiones (over 100 cultivars) are best from March to May: the dahlia show garden is open from August to the first frost.*

GREAT BARFIELD
Bradenham, High Wycombe HP14 4HP ☎ *01494 563741. Open 2 pm – 5 pm; 21 February; 2 pm – 5.30 pm; 4 April; 2 pm – 6 pm; 4 July; 2 pm – 5 pm; 26 September.*

And by appointment. NCCPG National Collections: Iris unguicularis; Leucojum; Ranunculus ficaria. One of the best modern plantsman's gardens in southern England, not least because it is beautifully designed, labelled and maintained. Whatever the season, Great Barfield amazes the visitor by the number and variety of plants in flower and their thoughtful placing.

HUGHENDEN MANOR
High Wycombe HP14 4LA ☎ *01494 532580. Open 1 pm – 5 pm; Saturdays & Sundays in March; Wednesday – Sunday plus Bank Holiday Mondays from 31 March to 31 October. Closed 2 April. Not a great garden, but interesting for its association with Disraeli. The garden was made by his wife c. 1860 and is a classic formal design of its period. Recently restored, using photographs taken in 1881, the parterre is once again planted with Victorian bedding.*

THE MANOR HOUSE, BLEDLOW
Bledlow, Princes Risborough HP27 9PB Open 2 pm – 6 pm; 2 May & 20 June for NGS. And by appointment. One of the best gardens of our times: beautifully planted and well maintained. There are three parts: first, the garden 'proper' round the house (kitchen garden is particularly impressive, with a gazebo in the middle); second, a modern sculpture garden, fluidly landscaped and planted; and, last but not least, a water garden in the modern style, densely planted around two lakes and a dozen springs, and open daily (and free) from dawn to dusk.

CAMBRIDGESHIRE

ANGLESEY ABBEY
Lode CB5 9EJ
☎ 01223 811200

Owner The National Trust
Location Off B1102
Open 11 am – 5.30 pm (last entry 4.30 pm); Wednesday – Sunday, plus Bank Holiday Mondays; 27 March to 31 October. Plus Mondays & Tuesdays from 5 July to 13 September. Winter Walk open 11 am – 4 pm, Thursday – Sunday from 2 January to 26 March and from 1 November to 19 December
Admission Gardens: Adults £3.50; Children £1.75. Winter Walk: Adults £3; Children £1.50
Facilities Parking; loos; facilities for the disabled; plants for sale; National Trust shop; licensed restaurant & picnic area
Features Herbaceous plants; garden sculpture; snowdrops; landscaping on the grandest scale; long avenues of trees; dahlias; cyclamen; good autumn colour; new winter walk (1999)
English Heritage Grade II*

Seventy years old, no more, but the grounds at Anglesey already deserve to be famous, for they are the grandest made in England this century. Majestic avenues and 35 acres of grass are the stuff of it: visit Anglesey when the horse chestnuts are out and tulips glow in the meadows.

Large formal gardens, carved out of the flat site by yew hedges, house the first Lord Fairhaven's collection of homoerotic sculpture. Then there are smaller gardens, said to be more intimate, where thousands of dahlias and hyacinths hit the eye: glorious or vainglorious, Anglesey has no match.

CAMBRIDGE UNIVERSITY BOTANIC GARDEN

Cory Lodge, Bateman Street, Cambridge CB2 1JF
☎ 01223 336265   Fax 01223 336278
Owner University of Cambridge
Location Entrance on Bateman Street, 1 mile to the south of the City Centre
Open 10 am – 4 pm in winter (5 pm in spring & autumn, 6 pm in summer); daily, except 25 & 26 December
Admission Adults £2; OAPs & children £1.50
Facilities Loos; facilities for the disabled; light refreshments
Features Good collection of trees; herbaceous plants; ecological interest; glasshouses; particularly good in July–August; particularly interesting in winter; important rock garden; species roses; new 'dry' garden (1998); new 'genetic' bed (1999); tallest *Broussonetia papyrifera* (15m.) in the British Isles (and 22 other record trees)
English Heritage Grade II*
NCCPG National Collections *Alchemilla*; *Bergenia*; *Fritillaria*; *Geranium*; *Lonicera*; *Ribes*; *Ruscus*; *Saxifraga*; *Tulipa*
Friends A very active association – contact the Friends Administrator 01223 336271

One of the best botanic gardens in the world for the way it matches amenity and public recreation to education, research, conservation, ecology, systematic taxonomy and horticultural excellence. The two rock gardens, one limestone and the other sandstone, are particularly successful and alone worth a long journey. For all-round interest, Cambridge B G runs close to Kew, Wisley and Edinburgh.

CLARE COLLEGE FELLOWS' GARDEN

Clare College, Cambridge CB2 1TL
☎ 01223 333222   Fax 01223 333219
Owner The Master & Fellows
Location Enter from Clare Old Court, Trinity Lane or Queens Road
Open 10.30 am – 4.30 pm; daily; 29 March to 30 September. Closed 12–18 & 26 June
Admission £1.75

Two acres of views and vistas, walks and Hidcote-style enclosures filled with exquisite spring bulbs, spectacular hot-colour borders dating from the 1950s and brilliant bedding which is changed twice a year.

CROSSING HOUSE GARDEN

Meldreth Road, Shepreth, Royston SG8 6PS
☎ 01763 261071

Owner Mr & Mrs D G Fuller
Location 8 miles south of Cambridge off A10
Open Dawn to dusk; daily; all year
Admission Donation to NGS
Facilities Parking; dogs permitted; access for the disabled
Features Plantsman's garden

One of the wonders of modern gardening, the Crossing House celebrates the achievements of its makers over the last 30 years, on an unpropitious site right beside the main line to Cambridge. It contains over 5000 varieties of plant, densely planted in the cottage style. Peat beds, screes, arches, topiary, pools and raised beds are some of the features which add variety to the most intensely and intensively planted small garden in England. And every few minutes a London express whizzes past.

DOCWRA'S MANOR

Shepreth, Royston SG8 6PS
☎ 01763 260235/261557
Owner Mrs John Raven
Location Off A10 to Shepreth
Open 10 am – 4 pm; Wednesdays and Fridays; all year; 2 pm – 4 pm, first Sunday of April to October. 10 May for NGS. And by appointment
Admission £2 (£3 for special openings)
Facilities Parking; loos; access for the disabled; plants for sale; teas for NGS openings
Features Herbaceous plants; plantsman's garden; modern roses; old roses; Mediterranean plants

Very much a plantsman's garden, whose lush profusion defies the dry, cold site. Docwra's Manor is a series of small gardens – walled, wild, paved and so on – each brimming with interesting plants and good combinations. There is a sense of abundance, whatever the season. Do read John Raven's charming and erudite *The Botanist's Garden*, now in print again.

ELTON HALL

Peterborough PE8 6SH
☎ 01832 280468   Fax 01832 280584
Owner Mr & Mrs William Proby
Location A605, 8 miles west of Peterborough
Open 2 pm – 5 pm; Wednesdays; June to August. Also Thursdays & Sundays in July & August, plus 30 & 31 May and 30 August
Admission Garden only: Adults £2.50; Children free
Facilities Parking; loos; plants for sale; Bressingham Plant Centre on site; tea-room
Features Good collection of trees; herbaceous plants; old roses; handsome hedges; good colour plantings
English Heritage Grade II*

The house is a castellated extravaganza, but the Victorian gardens have been energetically restored in recent years and make Elton highly visitable. The knot garden and the collection of old roses are the high spots, best in June.

PADLOCK CROFT
West Wratting CB1 5LS
☎ 01223 290383

Owner Peter & Susan Lewis
Location 2½ miles off B1307 (was A604) between Linton & Horseath
Open By appointment, any day except Sunday. And for NGS
Admission £1
Facilities Parking; access for the disabled; plants for sale
Features Plantsman's garden; rock garden
NCCPG National Collections *Adenophora*; *Campanula*; *Platycodon*; *Symphyandra*

One acre of plantsmanship, 'interesting' rather than 'exquisite' say the owners. But they do themselves an injustice, because this is a fascinating garden. Plants are crammed in, growing where they will do best. There are four National Collections of Campanulaceae. Visit from mid-June onwards, when the campanulas are a knockout.

PECKOVER HOUSE
North Brink, Wisbech PE13 1JR
☎ & Fax 01945 583463

Owner The National Trust
Location Signposted from Wisbech
Open Garden only: 12.30 pm – 5.30 pm; Saturdays – Thursday; 27 March to 31 October
Admission £3.50
Facilities Parking; loos; facilities for the disabled; plants for sale
Features Victorian shrubberies; orangery; fernery; Malmaison carnations; tallest *Acer negundo* (18m.) in the British Isles
English Heritage Grade II

Charming example of a not-too-grand Victorian garden, complete with monkey puzzle, fernery and spotted laurel shrubberies. One of the orange trees in the conservatory is 200 years old.

WIMPOLE HALL
Arrington, Royston SG8 0BW
☎ 01223 207257   Fax 01223 207838

Owner The National Trust
Location On A603, south-west of Cambridge
Open 10.30 am – 5 pm; daily except Monday & Friday (but open Good Friday & Bank Holiday Mondays); 13 March to 31 October
Admission Garden: £2.50. Park: free
Facilities Parking; loos; facilities for the disabled; National Trust shop; restaurant & tea-room
Features Landscape designed by Capability Brown; daffodils; landscape designed by Humphry Repton; old roses; woodland garden; interesting for children; Chinese bridge; major replanting of traditional fruit trees in walled garden (1998)
English Heritage Grade I
NCCPG National Collection *Juglans*

A classical 18th-century landscape where Bridgeman, Brown and Repton have all left their mark. The grand Victorian parterres have 72 flower beds arranged as eight Union Jack patterns and bright with 24,000 bedding plants.

WORTH A VISIT

ABBOTS RIPTON HALL
Abbots Ripton ☎ 01487 773555.   Open For NGS. Humphrey Waterfield, Lanning Roper and Jim Russell all worked here, and few garden owners have had as many gardening friends as Lord and Lady De Ramsey, who made and remade this garden over more than 50 years. The result is a garden of stylish individuality – witness the gothic trellis work and the bobbles of yellow philadelphus – but also of great unity: pure enchantment.

HARDWICKE HOUSE
High Ditch Road, Fen Ditton, Cambridge CB5 8TF
☎ 01223 292246.   Open 2 pm – 5.30 pm, 23 May for NGS & by appointment April to July.   NCCPG National Collection: Aquilegia.   Essentially a plantsman's garden with an emphasis on herbaceous plants, roses and bulbs. The owner has a particular interest in Asia Minor: there is an area devoted to Turkish bulbs.

MONKSILVER NURSERY
Oakington Road, Cottenham CB4 4TW
☎ 01954 251555.   Open 10 am – 4 pm; Friday – Saturday; March to June and October. Plus Open Day 11 am – 5 pm; 19 September. Galanthus gala 13 February. NCCPG National Collections: Galeobdolon; Lamium; Lathyrus (part); Vinca.   This remarkable nursery is deservedly fashionable. Monksilver specialises in finding and rescuing some really rare plants. Much of the stock is herbaceous, though there are also some desirable shrubs. A fifth of the catalogue changes each year.

CHESHIRE

ARLEY HALL & GARDENS
Great Budworth, Northwich CW9 6NA
☎ 01565 777353   Fax 01565 777465

Owner Viscount Ashbrook
Location 5 miles west of Knutsford
Open 11 am – 5 pm; Tuesday – Sunday; 2 April to 26 September
Admission Adults £4; OAPs £3.50; Children (5–16) £2
Facilities Parking; dogs permitted; loos; access for the disabled; plants for sale; shop; lunches & light refreshments
Features Herbaceous plants; old roses; good topiary; woodland garden; newly restored kitchen garden (1999); HHA/Christie's Garden of the Year in 1987
English Heritage Grade II*
Friends *Friends of Arley Hall & Gardens*. Talks, events and voluntary projects. Details from The Membership Secretary, 54 High Street, Great Budworth, Cheshire CW9 6HF

Arley has pleached limes, red *Primula florindae*, clipped holly cylinders (30 feet high) and pretty old roses. But its claim to fame is the double herbaceous border, backed and buttressed by yew hedges, one of the oldest and still one of the best in England.

BRIDGEMERE GARDEN WORLD
Bridgemere, Nantwich CW5 7QB
☎ 01270 521100   Fax 01270 520215
Owner J Ravenscroft
Location M6 Jct 15 & 16: follow signs
Open 8.30 am – 8 pm (5 pm in winter); daily; all year except 25 & 26 December
Admission Garden World: free. Television Gardens: Adults £1.50; Children & OAPs £1
Facilities Parking; loos; access for the disabled; plants for sale; several shops, as well as the famous garden centre; refreshments
Features Herbaceous plants; fruit of special interest; glasshouses; herbs; plantsman's garden; rock garden; modern roses; old roses; woodland garden; young garden; particularly good in July–August

More than twenty immaculate show gardens in different styles and the television set of *Gardeners' Diary* are just some of Bridgemere's innumerable attractions: definitely worth a visit, whatever the season.

CAPESTHORNE HALL
Siddington, Macclesfield SK11 9JY
☎ 01625 861221   Fax 01625 861619
Owner W A Bromley-Davenport
Location A34, 3 miles south of Alderley Edge
Open 12 noon – 6 pm; Wednesdays, Sundays & Bank Holidays; April to October. Plus 5 August for NGS
Admission Adults £3; OAPs £2.50; Children £1.50
Facilities Parking; loos; facilities for the disabled; small gift shop; tea-rooms
Features Good collection of trees; woodland garden; historic park

Classic English landscape, with some pretty modern planting by Vernon Russell-Smith by the lakes, a 19th-century arboretum and formal gardens.

CHOLMONDELEY CASTLE GARDENS
Malpas SY14 8AH
☎ 01829 720383   Fax 01829 720519
Owner The Marchioness of Cholmondeley
Location Off A49 Tarporley–Whitchurch road
Open 11.30 am – 5.30 pm; Wednesdays, Thursdays, Sundays & Bank Holiday Mondays. 2 April to 30 September
Admission Adults £3; OAPs £2.50; Children £1
Facilities Parking; dogs permitted; loos; facilities for the disabled; plants for sale; gift shop; tea-room, light lunches, home-made teas
Features Good collection of trees; herbaceous plants; good architectural features; lake; rock garden; woodland garden; Japanese cherry walk; rhododendrons
English Heritage Grade II

Handsome early 19th-century castle in rolling parkland, redeveloped since the 1960s with horticultural advice from Jim Russell. The new plantings have been well integrated into the classical landscape. The exquisite temple garden, curling the whole way around a small lake, is breathtakingly beautiful. Highly recommended.

DORFOLD HALL
Nantwich CW5 8LD
☎ 01270 625245   Fax 01270 628723
Owner R C Roundell
Location 1 mile west of Nantwich on A534
Open 2 pm – 5 pm; Tuesdays & Bank Holiday Mondays; April to October. Also 2 pm – 5.30 pm on 23 May for NGS
Admission House & gardens: Adults £4; Children £2. NGS day: Adults £2; Children 75p
Facilities Parking; dogs permitted; teas & plants for sale on 23 May
Features Bluebells; rhododendrons and azaleas; woodland garden; millennium parterre planned for 2000
English Heritage Grade II

William Nesfield designed the formal approach but the main reason for visiting the gardens is the new woodland garden of rhododendrons and other shrubs, leading down to a stream where *Primula pulverulenta* has naturalised in its thousands. Do not miss the incredible hulk of an ancient Spanish chestnut in the stable yard.

GRANADA ARBORETUM
Jodrell Bank, Macclesfield SK11 9DL
☎ 01477 571339   Fax 01477 571695
Owner Manchester University
Location On A535 between Holmes Chapel and Chelford
Open 10.30 am – 5.30 pm; daily; 15 March to 31 October. 11 am – 4.30 pm; Tuesday – Sunday; 1 November to 14 March
Admission Grounds, Science Centre & Planetarium: Adults £4.30; Concession £3; Children £2.10
Facilities Parking; loos; access for the disabled; shop; self-service cafeteria
Features Good collection of trees; Heather Society's *Calluna* collection; new sculpture (1998)
NCCPG National Collections *Malus*; *Sorbus*

Originally known as the Jodrell Bank Arboretum and founded by Sir Bernard Lovell in 1971, this wonderful arboretum specialises in alders, birches, crab apples, pine and *Sorbus*. Long straight drives lead spaciously into the distance, by way of large collections of heaths (*Erica*) and heathers (*Calluna*). The plantings are young and vigorous, the groupings imaginative. A huge radio telescope dominates the site: an awesome presence.

HARE HILL GARDEN
Garden Lodge, Over Alderley, Macclesfield SK10 4QB
☎ 01625 828981
Owner The National Trust

Location Between Alderley Edge and Prestbury
Open 10 am – 5.30 pm; Wednesdays, Thursdays, Saturday, Sundays & Bank Holiday Mondays (but daily from 10 to 30 May); 3 April to 30 October
Admission Adults £2.50; Children £1.25
Facilities Parking; loos
Features Herbaceous plants; plantsman's garden; rock garden; woodland garden

Basically, a woodland garden, thickly planted with trees and underplanted with rhododendrons, azaleas and shrubs by Jim Russell in the 1960s. In the middle is a walled garden which has been developed as a flower garden with a pergola, arbour and tender plants against the walls. Planting continues: much *Rhododendron ponticum* has been cleared recently and replaced by new cultivars. Best in May but there are still some rhododendrons to flower with the roses in July.

LITTLE MORETON HALL
Congleton CW12 4SD
☎ 01260 272018

Owner The National Trust
Location 4 miles south of Congleton on A34
Open 11 am – 5 pm; Wednesday – Sunday & Bank Holiday Mondays; 20 March to 31 October. 11 am – 5 pm; Saturdays & Sundays; 6 November to 28 December
Admission Adults £4.20; Children £2. Free 4 to 19 December
Facilities Parking; loos; access for the disabled; plants for sale; restaurant – lunches, coffee, teas
Features Herbaceous plants; fruit of special interest; herbs; plantings by Graham Thomas
English Heritage Grade I

Little Moreton Hall is the handsomest timber-framed house in England. When the National Trust asked Graham Thomas to design and plant a suitable period garden, he specified box-edged parterres with yew topiary and gravel infilling – and very fine they are too. In the kitchen garden, a speciality has been made of old varieties of fruit and vegetables. Peaceful, charming and orderly.

LYME PARK
Disley SK12 2NX
☎ 01663 762023   Fax 01663 765035

Owner The National Trust
Location 6½ miles south-east of Stockport on A6, just west of Disley
Open 11 am – 5 pm (but 1 pm – 5 pm on Wednesdays & Thursdays); daily; 26 March to 31 October. 12 noon – 3 pm; Saturdays & Sundays; 1 November to 20 December
Admission Garden only: Adults £2; Children £1
Facilities Parking; loos; facilities for the disabled; shop; light refreshments from Easter to October
Features Herbaceous plants; good architectural features; lake; old roses; spring bulbs; bedding-out; orangery by Wyatt; 'Dutch' garden
English Heritage Grade II*
NCCPG National Collection Vicary Gibbs plants

There is much of horticultural interest at Lyme, as well as the razzmatazz of a country park: traditional bedding-out, two enormous camellias in the conservatory, and a Jekyll-type herbaceous border by Graham Thomas whose colours run from orange to deepest purple. Best of all is the sunken Dutch garden whose looping box and ivy parterres contain the most extravagant bedding displays. The National Trust has now assumed full control of the garden and begun to restore the structure. Lyme Park featured as Pemberley in the BBC's *Pride & Prejudice*.

NESS BOTANIC GARDENS
Neston L64 4AY
☎ 0151 353 0123   Fax 0151 353 1004

Owner University of Liverpool
Location Signed off A540, Chester to Hoylake
Open 9.30 am – dusk (4 pm from November to February); daily; all year
Admission Adults £5; Concessions £3.50; RHS members free
Facilities Parking; loos; facilities for the disabled; plants for sale; gift shop; two restaurants
Features Good collection of trees; fine conifers; glasshouses; rock garden; old roses; 30-metre laburnum arch; tallest *Alnus cremastogyne* (3.3m.) in the British Isles
English Heritage Grade II
Friends Membership of the 7,500-strong Friends of Ness Gardens gives lectures, a newsletter, and a seed list (max. 10 packets). Contact Dr Joanna Sharples

Ness was started 100 years ago by A.K. Bulley, who sponsored George Forrest the plant collector, and it was here that many Chinese plants were first grown in Europe – notably candelabra primulas. It retains the sense of being a private garden not a botanic one. The borders and shrubberies team with interesting plants: rhododendrons, *Sorbus*, lilies, willows, roses, heathers and conifers – including a magnificent *Sequoia sempervirens* 'Adpressa'. The rock garden is particularly well planted, and the mild climate and acid soil allow a wide variety of different plants to flourish. Ness is one of those gardens where you tend to spend much longer than you intended.

NORTON PRIORY MUSEUM & GARDENS
Tudor Road, Runcorn WA7 1SX
☎ 01928 569895

Owner Norton Priory Museum Trust (Cheshire County Council)
Location Well signposted locally
Open 12 noon – 5 pm (but 4 pm in March, and 6 pm at weekends & Bank Holidays from April on); daily; March to October
Admission Adults £3.10; OAPs £1.80
Facilities Parking; loos; facilities for the disabled; plants for sale; garden produce shop; refreshments at museum site
Features Herbaceous plants; fruit of special interest; herbs; rock garden; modern roses; old roses; current holder of Sandford Award
NCCPG National Collection *Cydonia oblonga*

A new layout in the old walled garden, modelled on 18th-century precedents and intended to instruct and please modern visitors. A cottage garden border, medicinal herb garden and orchard rub shoulders with colour borders, children's gardens and a scented garden. Beyond are 16 acres of woodland garden with Georgian summerhouses and glades by the stream.

REASEHEATH COLLEGE
Nantwich CW5 6DF
☎ 01270 625131   Fax 01270 625665
Owner Reaseheath College
Location 1 mile north of Nantwich on A51
Open 2 pm – 4 pm; Wednesdays; 26 May to 28 July. College Open Days 12.30 pm – 5.30 pm on 22 & 23 May
Admission Donation
Facilities Parking; loos; Reaseheath Garden Centre, open daily, all year; shop; restaurant & coffee lounge
Features Good collection of trees; herbaceous plants; rhododendrons and azaleas; modern roses; woodland garden; heather garden; candelabra primulas

Reaseheath's 12 hectares have been thoroughly replanted recently: there is an enormous amount to enjoy and learn here. Highlights include woodland garden, rose garden, heather garden, rock garden, good bedding on the formal terraces and splendid mixed borders.

RODE HALL
Church Lane, Scholar Green, Stoke on Trent ST7 3QP
☎ 01270 882961   Fax 01270 882962
Owner Sir Richard Baker Wilbraham
Location 5 miles south-west of Congleton between A34 and A50
Open 2 pm – 5 pm; Tuesday – Thursday & Bank Holidays; 2 March to 30 September. Plus 1.30 pm – 5.30 pm on 9 May for NGS and 12 noon – 4 pm from 14 to 21 February for snowdrops
Admission Garden only: £2
Facilities Parking; dogs permitted; loos; plants for sale; garden produce
Features Fine conifers; good architectural features; fruit of special interest; old roses; snowdrops; good topiary; woodland garden; ice house; rhododendrons; grotto
English Heritage Grade II

Landscaped by Repton c. 1790 and given a formal garden by Nesfield in 1860, the main horticultural interest comes from the massed banks of azaleas and rhododendrons in the late Victorian 'Wild Garden'.

STAPELEY WATER GARDENS LTD
London Road, Stapeley, Nantwich CW5 7LH
☎ 01270 623868   Fax 01270 624919
Owner Stapeley Water Gardens Ltd
Location A51, 1 mile south of Nantwich

Open 10 am – 5.30 pm (5 pm in winter); daily; all year except 25 December. Nursery opens at 9 am Monday – Friday & 10 am on Saturdays & Sundays; closes at 6 pm (but 4 pm on Sundays, 7 pm on winter Wednesdays & 8 pm on summer Wednesdays)
Admission Palms Tropical Oasis: Adults £3.50; OAPs £2.75; Children £1.80
Facilities Parking; loos; facilities for the disabled; major nursery & garden centre; cafeteria & terrace restaurant
Features Glasshouses; interesting for children; particularly interesting in winter; collection of hardy water lilies; *Victoria regia*, the giant water lily
NCCPG National Collection *Nymphaea*

Part entertainment, part nursery and part display garden, the Palms Tropical Oasis is worth a visit in its own right. A long rectangular pool in the Moorish style is flanked by tall palms, strelitzias and other showy tropical flowers. Visit in winter.

TATTON PARK
Knutsford WA16 6QN
☎ 01565 750780   Fax 01565 650179
Owner The National Trust (managed by Cheshire County Council)
Location Off M6 Jct 19 and M56 Jct 7 – well signposted
Open 10.30 am – 6 pm (but 11 am – 4 pm from 2 November to 31 March); Tuesday – Sunday, plus Bank Holiday Mondays; all year
Admission Adults £2.80; Children £1.80 (1998 prices)
Facilities Parking; loos; facilities for the disabled; plants for sale; shop; hot meals & snacks (summer only)
Features Good collection of trees; herbaceous plants; landscape designed by Capability Brown; good architectural features; lake; landscape designed by Humphry Repton; rhododendrons & azaleas in May; biggest *Quercus* × *schochiana* in the British Isles; current holder of Sandford Award; Europa Nostra award for restored orangery & fernery
English Heritage Grade II*
NCCPG National Collections *Adiantum*; *Inula*

Humphry Repton laid out the parkland. Joseph Paxton designed both the formal Italian garden and the exquisite fernery, claimed as the finest in the United Kingdom. Later came a Japanese garden and Shinto temple, such follies as the African hut, and the mass plantings of rhododendrons and azaleas. Tatton Park is wonderfully well organised for visitors, and gets better every year. Be prepared for a long and absorbing visit.

WORTH A VISIT

ADLINGTON HALL
Macclesfield SK10 4LF ☎ 01625 829206. *Open By prior appointment only. An old avenue of lime trees, planted in 1688 to celebrate the accession of William and Mary, leads to a woodland wilderness with follies. These include a Shell Cottage, a Temple to Diana, a Chinese bridge and a Hermitage. The young owners are restoring these buildings, and have plans for further developments.*

FOXHILL ARBORETUM
Tarvin Road, Frodsham WA6 6XD ☎ *01928 739189.*
Open Saturdays & Sundays from April to October. A 40-acre arboretum, with fine views and many good garden features including a Japanese garden and a physic garden.

GROSVENOR GARDEN CENTRE
Wrexham Road, Belgrave, Chester CH3 9EB
☎ *01244 682856. Open 9 am – 6 pm (5 pm in winter), Monday – Saturday; 10 am – 4 pm, Sundays. This large garden centre has a full range of plants and products, plus monthly lectures, and a design service.*

PEOVER HALL
Over Peover Knutsford ☎ *01565 722656. First a classic 18th-century parkland, then an Edwardian overlay of formal gardens – yew hedges and brick paths. Now Peover has modern plantings too – borders in colour combinations, a herb garden, and a rhododendron dell in the woods.*

TIRLEY GARTH TRUST
Utkinton, Tarporley CW6 0LZ ☎ *01829 732301. Open 2 pm – 6 pm; 16, 30 & 31 May & 6 June. Famous example of Thomas Mawson's work: wonderful terraces, paths, retaining walls and garden buildings. Good rhododendrons and azaleas in the woodland below.*

CORNWALL

ANTONY HOUSE
Torpoint PL11 2QA
☎ & Fax 01752 812364

Owner The National Trust
Location 5 miles west of Plymouth, 2 miles north-west of Torpoint
Open 1.30 pm – 5.30 pm; Tuesday – Thursday & Bank Holidays; 1 April to 28 October; also Sundays from June to August
Admission Adults £4; Children £2
Facilities Parking; loos; access for the disabled; tea-room
Features Herbaceous plants; landscape designed by Capability Brown; fine conifers; landscape designed by Humphry Repton; magnolias; yew hedges; tallest Japanese loquat *Eriobotrya japonica* (8m.) in the British Isles (and two other tree records)
English Heritage Grade II
NCCPG National Collection *Hemerocallis*

A classic 18th-century landscape, influenced by Humphry Repton, in a superb position above the Tamar estuary. Yew hedges nearer the house enclose modern plantings while the kitchen garden houses the vast NCCPG National Collection of *Hemerocallis* or day lilies – some 575 cultivars! The neighbouring Woodland Garden still belongs to the Carew Poles and is planted with the best modern forms of rhododendrons, azaleas, magnolias and camellias.

BOSVIGO
Bosvigo Lane, Truro TR1 3NH
☎ & Fax 01872 275774

Owner Wendy & Michael Perry
Location ¾ mile from Truro centre. Turn off A390 at Highertown near Sainsbury roundabout then 500 yds down
Open 11 am – 6 pm; Thursday – Saturday; 4 March to 2 October
Admission Adults £2; Children 50p
Facilities Parking; loos; excellent small herbaceous nursery
Features Herbaceous plants; plantsman's garden; vegetables of interest; woodland garden; young garden; unusual perennials; Victorian conservatory; colour borders

Not a typical Cornish garden, the emphasis at Bosvigo is upon herbaceous plants, chosen for all their qualities and planted in fine colour combinations. Many are rare: some are for sale.

BURNCOOSE NURSERIES & GARDENS
Gwennap, Redruth TR16 6BJ
☎ 01209 861112   Fax 01209 860011

Owner F J Williams CBE
Location On A393 between Lanner and Ponsanooth
Open 8.30 am – 5 pm (open 11 am on Sundays); Monday to Saturday; all year
Admission Adults £2; Children free
Facilities Parking; dogs permitted; loos; access for the disabled; important nursery (major RHS gold medal winner); teas & light refreshments
Features Bluebells; camellias; plantsman's garden; rhododendrons and azaleas; woodland garden; magnolias; rare trees & shrubs

Thirty acres of traditional Cornish woodland garden, planted with ancient rhododendrons and handsome trees, but re-invigorated by extensive shrub planting since 1981 – the result of a partnership between the Williams family and Cornwall's leading nurseryman.

CAERHAYS CASTLE GARDENS
Gorran, St Austell PL26 6LY
☎ 01872 501310   Fax 01872 501870

Owner F J Williams
Location Between Mevagissey & Portloe
Open 11 am – 4 pm; Monday – Friday; 15 March to 14 May. Plus 17 April. Charity openings: 4 & 18 April & 3 May
Admission Adults £3.50; Children £1.50
Facilities Parking; dogs permitted; loos; plants for sale; tea-rooms & beach shop/café in car park
Features Good collection of trees; fine conifers; plantsman's garden; woodland garden; camellias; magnolias; rhododendrons; tallest specimen of *Emmenopterys henryi* (17m.) in the British Isles, and 37 further record-breaking trees (including eight *Acer* species)
English Heritage Grade II*

The Williams family subscribed to many of the great plant-collecting expeditions and the fruits of their labours flourish at Caerhays. Wilson and Forrest are represented by thousands of trees and shrubs, and one of the joys of Caerhays is to stumble upon magnificent old specimens deep in its 100 acres of woodland. There are splendid collections of *Nothofagus* and *Lithocarpus* as well as the three genera for which Caerhays is famous – magnolias, camellias and rhododendrons. The original × *williamsii* camellias still flourish, including 'J.C. Williams', 'Mary Christian' and 'Saint Ewe'. There is much to discover at Caerhays: allow plenty of time.

COTEHELE
St Dominick, Saltash PL12 6TA
☎ 01579 351346   Fax 01579 351222

Owner The National Trust
Location 14 miles from Plymouth via Saltash
Open 11 am – 5.30 pm (dusk if earlier); daily; all year
Admission £3.20 from 27 March to 31 October; rest of year, donation
Facilities Parking; loos; facilities for the disabled; plants for sale; National Trust gift shop; restaurant for meals and drinks
Features Good collection of trees; daffodils; modern roses; good topiary; woodland garden; palms; ferns; pretty dovecote; largest *Davidia involucrata* in the British Isles
English Heritage Grade II

Broad Victorian terraces below the house support many tender climbers such as *Jasminum mesnyi* while the beds beneath have wallflowers and roses. Down the wooded valley are camellias, rhododendrons and shade-loving plants which thrive in an ancient woodland, kept damp by a small stream. Much gentle restoration and renewal in recent years.

GLENDURGAN GARDENS
Helford River, Mawnan Smith, Falmouth
TR11 5TR
☎ 01326 250906

Owner The National Trust
Location 1 mile west of Mawnan Smith, west to Trebah
Open 10 am – 5.30 pm (last admissions 4.30 pm); Tuesday – Saturday, plus Bank Holidays except Good Friday; 2 March to 30 October
Admission Adults £3.40; Children £1.70
Facilities Parking; loos; plants for sale; small shop; teas & light lunches
Features Fine conifers; subtropical plants; woodland garden; laurel maze; wildflowers; huge tulip tree; tallest *Eucryphia lucida* (13m.) in the British Isles; new Bhutanese valley planting (1996)
English Heritage Grade II

A steep, subtropical valley garden on the Helford River with a good collection of old rhododendrons and camellias. Glendurgan also boasts an extraordinary 1830s maze of clipped cherry laurel, recently restored and best seen from the new viewing platform above. Indeed, the whole garden is almost best when viewed from the top – but the temptation to wander down and into it is irresistible!

THE LOST GARDENS OF HELIGAN
Pentewan, St Austell PL26 6EN
☎ 01726 844157/843566   Fax 01726 843023

Owner Heligan Gardens Ltd
Location St. Austell to Mevagissey Road, following brown tourist signs
Open 10 am – 6 pm; daily; all year except 24 & 25 December
Admission Adults £5; OAPs £4.50; Children £2.50
Facilities Parking; dogs permitted; loos; facilities for the disabled; plants for sale; tea-room with sandwiches, salads, etc.
Features Good architectural features; rhododendrons and azaleas; rock garden; subtropical plants; woodland garden; beautiful ferny gully; splendid kitchen garden
English Heritage Grade II
Friends Friends subscription £15 includes newsletters

Heligan calls itself 'The Lost Gardens of Heligan' and has been spectacularly rescued since 1990 from a jungle of neglect. To date the restoration team has uncovered the Italian garden, the Crystal Grotto, the wishing well, the Bee Boles, the Sundial Garden and other authentic features. Newly recovered features emerge with incredible speed: recent restorations include the Northern Summerhouse garden and several rides within the Lost Valley. The enthusiasm of the restorers is infectious and their achievements are already substantial. The owners are brilliant at getting financial support and publicity – with the result that the garden can get very crowded.

KEN CARO
Bicton, Liskeard PL14 5RF
☎ 01579 362446

Owner Mr & Mrs K R Willcock
Location Signed from A390, midway between Callington & Liskeard
Open 2 pm – 6 pm; Sunday – Wednesday; 11 April to 30 June; plus Tuesdays & Wednesdays in July & August
Admission Adults £2; Children 50p
Facilities Parking; loos; plants for sale
Features Herbaceous plants; fine conifers; oriental features; plantsman's garden; aviary and waterfowl; new water-lily pond (1998)

Started in 1970 as two acres of intensely planted formal gardens in different styles, and extended in 1993 by taking in a further two acres. Very much a plantsman's garden with good herbaceous plants and shrubs, not at all a typical Cornish garden. The owners are flower-arrangers: look for architectural plants and original combinations.

LAMORRAN HOUSE
Upper Castle Road, St Mawes TR2 5BZ
☎ 01326 270800   Fax 01326 270801

Owner Mr & Mrs Robert Dudley-Cooke
Location ½ mile from village centre

Open 10.30 am – 5 pm; Wednesdays, Fridays & the first Saturday of the month; April to September
Admission Adults £2.50; Children free
Facilities Parking; loos; plants for sale
Features Good collection of trees; herbaceous plants; good architectural features; plantsman's garden; subtropical plants; young garden; extensive new plantings of Australian & South African plants (1998)

Made since 1980 on a steep site above the sea and tightly designed in the Italian style, but also full of unusual plants. An English Mediterranean garden in Cornwall, say the owners, a mainland Tresco. One of their latest ventures is a bank planted with cacti and succulents. The collection of different palm trees is simply amazing.

LANHYDROCK
Bodmin PL30 5AD
☎ 01208 73320   Fax 01298 74084

Owner The National Trust
Location 2½ miles south-east of Bodmin
Open 11 am – 5.30 pm (dusk, if sooner); daily; all year
Admission Garden only £3.20
Facilities Parking; loos; plants for sale; National Trust shop; restaurant & bar, cream teas
Features Bluebells; herbaceous plants; good topiary; woodland garden; Victorian parterres; spring bulbs
English Heritage Grade II*
NCCPG National Collection *Crocosmia*

A grand mansion, mainly 19th-century with one of the best formal gardens in Cornwall – clipped yews, box parterres and bedding-out, as well as large herbaceous borders which contain the NCCPG National Collection of *Crocosmia*. The woodlands behind are impressive for their size and colourful rhododendrons in spring. But it is the magnolias which impress the visitor most: 140 different species and cultivars.

MOUNT EDGCUMBE GARDENS
Cremyll, Torpoint PL10 1HZ
☎ 01752 822236   Fax 01752 822199

Owner Cornwall County Council & Plymouth City Council
Location At the end of the B3247 in south-east Cornwall, or by ferry from Plymouth
Open Formal gardens & park: dawn to dusk; all year. House & Earl's Garden: 11 am – 5 pm; Wednesday – Sunday & Bank Holiday Mondays; April to mid-October
Admission House & Earl's Garden: Adults £4; OAPs £3; Children £2. Formal gardens & park: free
Facilities Parking; dogs permitted; loos; facilities for the disabled; gift and book shops; camellias for sale; orangery restaurant in formal gardens
Features Good collection of trees; herbaceous plants; daffodils; good architectural features; glasshouses; subtropical plants; summer bedding; deer park; formal gardens; fern dell; genuine Victorian rose garden; tallest cork oak *Quercus suber* (26m.) in the British Isles
English Heritage Grade I
NCCPG National Collection *Camellia*

Friends Contact Mrs C Gaskell Brown (01752 822236)

A long, stately grass drive runs down from the house to Plymouth Sound, through oak woods interplanted with large ornamental trees. Here is the NCCPG National Collection of *Camellia*, meticulously labelled, which will eventually include all 32,000 known cultivars. The formal gardens are right down on the waterside, protected by a clipped holly hedge 30 feet high. There are no less than ten acres of gardens here, including an Italian garden (*c.* 1790), a French garden (early Victorian), an American garden, a modern New Zealand garden complete with geyser, Milton's Temple, an orangery, a conservatory and the fern dell. Allow plenty of time to do justice to these majestic pleasure gardens.

PENCARROW
Washaway, Bodmin PL30 3AG
☎ 01208 841369

Owner The Trustees of the Molesworth-St Aubyn Family
Location 4 miles north-west of Bodmin – signed off the A389 at Washaway
Open 10 am – 6 pm; daily; 1 April to 15 October. House open 1.30 pm – 5 pm, Sunday – Thursday, but opens at 11 am on Bank Holiday Mondays & from 1 June to 10 September
Admission Garden only: Adults £2; Children free
Facilities Parking; dogs permitted; loos; facilities for the disabled; plants for sale; craft centre; light lunches, cream teas
Features Fine conifers; rock garden; old roses; Italian garden; rhododendrons; camellias
English Heritage Grade II

A long drive through rhododendrons and vast conifers leads to the pretty Anglo-Palladian house. Below is an Italian garden, laid out in the 1830s, and next to it a great granite rock garden where boulders from Bodmin Moor lie strewn among the trees and shrubs. Pencarrow is famous for its conifers: an ancestor planted one of every known variety in the mid-19th century and the survivors are so venerable that the great Alan Mitchell wrote a guide to them. Recent plantings have concentrated upon planting rhododendrons (over 700 of the best modern varieties) and adding new conifers to the old. It is good to see the fortunes of such a distinguished garden revived.

PENJERRICK
Budock Water, Falmouth TR11 5ED
☎ 01872 870105

Owner Mrs Rachel Morin
Location 3 miles south-west of Falmouth, entrance at junction of lanes opposite Penmorvah Manor Hotel
Open 1.30 pm – 4.30 pm; Wednesdays, Fridays & Sundays; March to September. 11.30 am – 4.30 pm for charity on 11 & 25 April & 2 May
Admission Adults £1.50; Children 50p
Facilities Parking; dogs permitted
Features Woodland garden; rhododendrons; camellias; tree ferns; new paths restored in valley (1997); waterfall improved (1998)

English Heritage Grade II

Famous for the Barclayi and Penjerrick hybrid rhododendrons and now a mature woodland garden recovering well from a period of neglect: very Cornish. Last year the lower pond in the valley was reclaimed and restored.

PINE LODGE GARDENS
Cuddra, St Austell PL25 3RQ
☎ 01726 73500

Owner Mr & Mrs Raymond Clemo
Location East of St Austell between Holmbush and Tregrehan
Open 2 pm – 5 pm; Wednesday – Sunday, plus Bank Holidays; April to September. And by appointment for groups at any time of year
Admission Adults £3.50; Children £1.75
Facilities Parking; loos; access for the disabled; garden nursery; tea-room
Features Good collection of trees; herbaceous plants; fine conifers; fruit of special interest; plantsman's garden; garden sculpture; woodland garden; bog gardens; Japanese garden (1997)
NCCPG National Collection *Grevillea*

A modern garden, rather different from the typical Cornish garden. There are rhododendrons and azaleas, of course, but they are planted and underplanted with other shrubs and herbaceous plants to create lasting colour effects. The pace of the garden's development is very exciting.

ST MICHAEL'S MOUNT
Marazion TR17 0HT
☎ 01736 710507 Fax 01736 711544

Owner Lord St Levan & The National Trust
Location 1 mile south of Marazion
Open 10.30 am – 5.30 pm; Monday – Friday; April to October
Admission £1.50
Facilities Loos; plants for sale; refreshments
Features Herbaceous plants; ecological interest; rock garden; subtropical plants; woodland garden; wild narcissus; naturalised kniphofias and agapanthus
English Heritage Grade II

A triumph of man's ingenuity in the face of Atlantic gales, salt spray and bare rock with sand for a garden soil. Careful experiment over the generations has enabled the owners to plant a remarkable garden of plants which resist the elements: *Luma apiculata*, rugosa roses, correas, nerines, Hottentot figs and naturalised agapanthus. On the north side, a sparse wood of sycamores and pines gives protection to camellias, azaleas and hydrangeas. Nigel Nicolson calls it 'the largest and loveliest rock-garden in England'. There is nothing rare about the plants: the wonder is that they grow at all.

TREBAH GARDEN TRUST
Mawnan Smith, Falmouth TR11 5JZ
☎ 01326 250448 Fax 01326 250781
Website www.trebah-garden.co.uk

Owner The Trebah Garden Trust
Location 4 miles south-west of Falmouth, signposted from Hillhead roundabout on A39 approach to Falmouth
Open 10.30 am – 5 pm (last admission); daily; all year
Admission Adults £3.50; OAPs £3.20; Children (5 – 15) & disabled visitors £1.20; Children (under 5) free; RHS members free
Facilities Parking; dogs permitted; loos; access for the disabled; excellent nursery; coffee shop & picnic area
Features Good collection of trees; plantsman's garden; subtropical plants; woodland garden; interesting for children; particularly interesting in winter; Tarzan camp and Tarzan trails for children; access to private beach; massed hydrangeas; lilies and candelabra primulas; extensive new plantings of palms & succulents at the top of the water garden; resident sculptor (1999); tallest hardy palm *Trachycarpus fortunei* (15m.) in the British Isles and three other tree records
English Heritage Grade II
Friends The Trebah Trust is a registered charity which aims to preserve the gardens for posterity: details from 01326 250448

Glorious Trebah! This lost garden has been vigorously restored and improved since the Hibberts bought it in 1980. The view from the top is magical – a secret valley which runs right down to the Helford estuary. Vast trees, natural and exotic, line the steep sides, while the central point is held by a group of elegant tall palms. Trebah is popular with children, whose curiosity is aroused by trails, quizzes and educational games. But it is a garden for all people and for all seasons – open *every day of the year*.

TREGREHAN
Par PL24 2SJ
☎ 01726 812438 Fax 01726 814389

Owner T C Hudson
Location 1 mile west of St Blazey on A390
Open 10.30 am – 5 pm; daily except Easter Sunday; mid-March to June
Admission Adults £3; Children free
Facilities Parking; loos; access for the disabled; plants for sale; teas
Features Woodland garden; camellias; pinetum; walled garden; sunken garden
English Heritage Grade II*

An old Cornish garden whose 20 acres include a fine range of Victorian conservatories, tall conifers and lanky rhododendrons. But Tregrehan is best known for the camellias bred there by the late Gillian Carlyon, especially 'Jennifer Carlyon' which won her the Cory Cup from the RHS.

TREHANE
Probus, Truro TR2 4JG
☎ 01872 520270

Owner David & Simon Trehane
Location Signposted from A39 by Tresillian Bridge
Open 2 pm – 5 pm; 28 March; 11, 18 & 25 April; 9, 16 & 23 May; 13 June; 4 July; 19 September

Admission Adults £2; Children 50p
Facilities Parking; dogs permitted; loos; plants for sale; refreshments
Features Herbaceous plants; fine conifers; plantsman's garden; woodland garden; bluebells

You would expect camellias from anyone called Trehane, and their eponymous garden has a fine collection. There is, however, no limit to their interests and there are many other good things here, especially magnolias, crocosmias, geraniums and other herbaceous plants.

TRELISSICK GARDEN
Feock, Truro TR3 6QL
☎ 01872 862090   Fax 01872 865808

Owner The National Trust
Location Take B3289 off main Truro – Falmouth Road
Open 10.30 am – 5.30 pm, Monday – Saturday; 12.30 pm – 5.30 pm, Sunday; 27 February to 31 October. Closes at 5 pm in February, March & October
Admission Adults £4.20; Children £2.10
Facilities Parking; loos; facilities for the disabled; gift and plant shop; refreshments
Features Fine conifers; plantsman's garden; garden sculpture; woodland garden; particularly good in July–August; particularly interesting in winter; aromatic plant garden; fig garden; hydrangeas; tallest tree fern *Dicksonia antarctica* (6m.) in the British Isles
English Heritage Grade II

Once famous for its fig garden, still maintained by the National Trust, Trelissick is particularly colourful in August and September when the hydrangeas are in full flower. There are over 100 varieties, some in a special walk. But venerable conifers and tender plants are also features: *Rosa bracteata* and *Yucca whipplei* are among the many good things to admire in summer, not to mention daffodils, rhododendrons and camellias in spring.

TRENGWAINTON GARDENS
Madron, Penzance TR20 8RZ
☎ 01736 363148   Fax 01736 368142

Owner Lt Col E T Bolitho & The National Trust
Location 2 miles north-west of Penzance, ½ mile west of Heamoor
Open 10.30 am – 5.30 pm (5 pm in March & October); Sunday – Thursday & Bank Holidays; 1 March to 31 October
Admission Adults £3; Children £1.50
Facilities Parking; dogs permitted; loos; facilities for the disabled; plants for sale; new National Trust shop; coffee, snacks, teas; new tea house (1999)
Features Old roses; subtropical plants; woodland garden; lilies; acacias; *Myosotidium hortensia*; tree ferns; tallest *Xanthoceras sorbifolium* (7m.) in the British Isles (and two record trees)
English Heritage Grade II

Trengwainton has the best collection of tender plants on the Cornish mainland, all thanks to the Bolitho family who started planting seriously only in 1925. Much came from original seed from such collectors as Kingdon-Ward: some rhododendrons flowered here for the first time in the British Isles, among them *R. macabeanum*, *R. elliottii* and *R. taggianum*. The plants in many Cornish gardens are past their best. Not so at Trengwainton, where so many are in their prime. It is a garden to wander through slowly, giving yourself as much time as you need to enjoy its riches.

TRERICE
Newquay TR8 4PG
☎ 01637 875404   Fax 01637 879300

Owner The National Trust
Location 3 miles south-east of Newquay – turn right off A3058 at Kestle Mill
Open 11 am – 5.30 pm (5 pm in October); daily except Tuesdays & Saturdays (but open every day from 28 July to 7 September); 1 April to 31 October
Admission House: £4; Garden: free
Facilities Parking; loos; access for the disabled; plants for sale; National Trust shop; restaurant & tea-room
Features Oriental features; modern roses; colour borders; good collection of apple trees; new summerhouse in orchard (1997)

A perfect West Country manor house with pretty Dutch gables, Trerice is unusual among Cornish gardens. It is small and comparatively formal: the design and herbaceous plantings are its best points. It is not surrounded by swirling rhododendron woodland. There is a perfect harmony between the Jacobean architecture and the gardens. Somewhat anomalously, it boasts the largest collection of mid-Victorian to current-day lawn mowers in the country. They are both interesting and fun.

TRESCO ABBEY
Isles of Scilly TR24 0QQ
☎ 01720 422849   Fax 01720 422807

Owner Robert Dorrien Smith
Location Direct helicopter flight from Penzance
Open 10 am – 4 pm; daily; all year
Admission Adults £5; Children (under 14) free (1998 prices)
Facilities Dogs permitted; loos; facilities for the disabled; plants for sale; shop; light refreshments
Features Fine conifers; good architectural features; plantsman's garden; subtropical plants; interesting for children; particularly good in July–August; particularly interesting in winter; cacti; succulents; South African, Australian and New Zealand plants; tallest *Luma apiculata* (20m.), *Metrosideros excelsus* (20m.) and *Cordyline australis* (15m.) in the British Isles
English Heritage Grade I
NCCPG National Collection *Acacia*

These legendary gardens have been extensively replanted in recent years, with hundreds of exotic plants from Kew, all protected by extensive new shelterbelts. The profusion is amazing while the standards of maintenance are exemplary. The helicopter service makes access easier than ever, but it does distract you while actually visiting the garden.

TREWITHEN

Grampound Road, Truro TR2 4DD
☎ 01726 883647   Fax 01726 882301
Owner A M J Galsworthy
Location A390 between Probus and Grampound
Open 10 am – 4.30 pm; Monday – Saturday (& Sundays in April & May); March to September
Admission Adults £3; OAPs £2; Children £1.50; Groups (12+) £2.80; RHS members free
Facilities Parking; dogs permitted; loos; facilities for the disabled; excellent nursery & garden shop; tea-room with light refreshments
Features Good collection of trees; herbaceous plants; camellias; plantsman's garden; rhododendrons and azaleas; woodland garden; magnolias; quarry garden; cyclamen; new fountain (1999); tallest *Magnolia campbellii* subsp. *mollicomata* (19m.) in the British Isles and sixteen more record-breaking tree species
English Heritage Grade II*

Trewithen's setting is magnificent. Instead of the steep terraces of most Cornish gardens, there is a spacious flat lawn that stretches 200 yards into the distance, with gentle banks of rhododendrons, magnolias and rare shrubs on all sides. It sets the tone for the garden's grandeur, which was entirely the work of George Johnstone in the first half of this century. Johnstone was a great plantsman. He subscribed to plant-hunting expeditions, such as those of Frank Kingdon-Ward. Note how he used laurel hedges to divide up the woodland and give structure to the garden. He also had an eye for placing plants to advantage. As a breeder, he gave us *Rhododendron* 'Alison Johnstone', *Ceanothus arboreus* 'Trewithen Blue' and *Camellia saluenensis* 'Trewithen White'. The Michelin Guide gives Trewithen its top award of three stars – *vaut le voyage*!

WORTH A VISIT

CARCLEW GARDENS
Perran-ar-Worthal, Truro TR3 7PB ☎ *01872 864070. Open 2 pm – 5.30 pm; 2, 9, 16 & 23 May. The gardens first opened to the public in 1927 and have continued to do so for charity every year since then. Vast hummocks of old rhododendrons, some grown from Sir Joseph Hooker's Himalayan collections nearly 150 years ago. Good trees, including a large ginkgo and a Quercus × hispanica which looks different from 'Lucombeana'.*

CARWINION
Mawnan Smith, Falmouth TR11 5JA ☎ *01326 250258. Ten acres of Cornish jungle, exotically thick with rhododendrons, camellias, drimys and the largest collection of bamboos in the south-west.*

CHYVERTON
Zelah, Truro TR4 9HD ☎ *01872 540324. Open By appointment; March to June. The garden of a distinguished plantsman who calls it 'a magic jungle'. Magnolias are a special interest: several Chyverton seedlings now bear cultivar names. Many other established plants have also been grown from seed: rhododendron hybrids from Brodick, for instance, and Eucalyptus nicholii from a wild collection. But there is much more to interest the plantsman. A large Berberidopsis corallina and a lanky red-stemmed hedge of Luma apiculata below the house are both outstanding. And the planting continues.*

HEADLAND
Polruan-by-Fowey PL23 1PW ☎ *01726 870243. Open 2 pm – 6 pm; Thursdays; May to July. A cliff garden with the sea on three sides and its own sandy beach, Headland is a lesson in what will tolerate salt-laden winds: aloes, eucalyptus, acacias, foxgloves, columbines and junipers. Only 1¼ acres, but it seems much larger.*

LANTERNS
Restronguet, Mylor Bridge TR11 5ST ☎ *01326 372007. Plantsman's half-acre garden with a wide range of subjects that flourish in the mild climate but tolerate salt-bearing winds.*

PROBUS GARDENS
Probus ☎ *TR2 4HQ. Open 10 am – 4 pm; daily; all year. Closed for winter weekends. A wonderful modern garden – eight acres of experimental designs and plantings designed to inspire visitors and show them what they can grow in their own gardens. Every imaginable type of plant is here: highly recommended.*

CUMBRIA

ACORN BANK GARDEN
Acorn Bank, Temple Sowerby, Penrith CA10 1SP
☎ 017683 61893
Owner The National Trust
Location North of Temple Sowerby, 6 miles east of Penrith on A66
Open 10 am – 5 pm; daily; 27 March to 31 October
Admission Adults £2.30; Children £1.20
Facilities Parking; loos; facilities for the disabled; plants for sale; National Trust shop; light refreshments
Features Herbaceous plants; fruit of special interest; herbs; old roses; woodland garden; spring bulbs; woodland walk past Mill

Acorn Bank boasts the largest collection (250 varieties) of culinary and medicinal plants in the north, but it is almost better visited in spring when thousands and thousands of daffodils fill the woodland slopes, and the fruit trees flower in the old walled garden. Best of all is the huge quince tree, a wondrous sight in flower or fruit.

BRANTWOOD
Coniston LA21 8AD
☎ 015394 41396
Owner The Brantwood Trust
Location East side of Coniston Water, 2½ miles from Coniston, 4 miles from Hawkshead

Open 11 am – 5.30 pm; daily; mid-March to mid-November; 11 am – 4 pm; Wednesday – Sunday; mid-November to mid-March
Admission Garden only: £2
Facilities Parking; dogs permitted; loos; plants for sale; bookshop & craft gallery; meals, light refreshments & drinks all day
Features Lake; rhododendrons and azaleas; woodland garden; daffodils; bluebells
Friends Friends of Brantwood, very active, ring 015394 41396 for details

Twenty acres of woodland garden, laid out by John Ruskin from 1871 onwards and restored with a grant from the European Community. Working with natural materials, Ruskin accentuated the natural character of the site with woodland plantings and rhododendrons. Open plantings at the front of the house frame wonderful views across Coniston Water.

DALEMAIN
Penrith CA11 0HB
☎ 017684 86450   Fax 017684 86223
Owner Robert Hasell-McCosh
Location M6 (Jct 40), A66 (West 1m), A592
Open 10.30 am – 4.30 pm (5 pm on Sundays & Bank Holiday Mondays); Sunday – Thursday; 5 April to 4 October
Admission Gardens only: £3
Facilities Parking; loos; facilities for the disabled; gift shop; small plant centre; morning coffee, light lunches, afternoon teas
Features Herbs; old roses; woodland garden; interesting for children; meconopsis; old flower and fruit varieties; adventure playground; biggest *Abies cephalonica* in the British Isles
English Heritage Grade II*

This historic garden has a 16th-century terrace and a kitchen garden with fruit trees planted 250 years ago, but it feels Edwardian. The mixed borders and roses are dreamily English. Plants are well labelled and well grown. In the wild garden below are drifts of meconopsis and martagon lilies.

GRAYTHWAITE HALL
Ulverston, Hawkshead LA12 8BA
☎ 015395 31248   Fax 015395 30060
Owner Graythwaite Estate Trustees
Location Between Newby Bridge and Hawkshead
Open 10 am – 6 pm; daily; April to June
Admission Adults £2; Children free
Facilities Parking; dogs permitted; loos
Features Good collection of trees; rock garden; modern roses; old roses; good topiary

Thomas Mawson on home ground and at his best. Formal gardens by the house drop down to sweeping lawns; beyond the stream is a woodland with rhododendrons and azaleas. Further developments are planned.

HOLEHIRD GARDENS
Lakeland Horticultural Society, Patterdale Road, Windermere LA23 1NP
☎ 01539 446008
Owner Lakeland Horticultural Society
Location 1 mile north of Windermere town, off A592
Open Dawn to dusk; daily; all year
Admission Donation (min. £1)
Facilities Parking; loos
Features Glasshouses; herbs; rock garden; woodland garden; heathers; roses; hostas; ferns; Victorian garden; walled garden; new pergola in walled garden (1998)
NCCPG National Collections *Astilbe*; *Hydrangea*; *Polystichum*
Friends The Lakeland Horticultural Society is a registered charity: details from the Secretary

A demonstration and trial garden, maintained almost entirely by local volunteers to promote appropriate horticultural practices for the Lake District. Particularly good to see what flourishes in a cool damp climate: alpines, azaleas, heathers, ferns and much, much more.

HOLKER HALL
Cark-in-Cartmel, Grange-over-Sands LA11 7PL
☎ 015395 58328   Fax 015395 58776
Owner Lord Cavendish of Furness
Location Jct 36 off M6, follow brown and white tourist signs
Open 10 am – 6 pm (last admission 4.30 pm); Sunday – Friday; April to October
Admission Adults £3.35; Children £1.90
Facilities Parking; loos; facilities for the disabled; plants for sale; shop; clocktower cafeteria (licensed)
Features Modern roses; old roses; woodland garden; rhododendrons; formal gardens; fine limestone cascade & fountain; HHA/Christie's Garden of the Year in 1991; tallest *Ilex latifolia* (15m.) in the British Isles (and two other tree records)
English Heritage Grade II*
NCCPG National Collection Styracaceae

The 19th-century formal gardens below the house are scrumptiously planted as herbaceous borders, the first of many imaginative modern designs and plantings throughout this extensive garden. The woodland has foxgloves, rhododendrons and splendid trees: Joseph Paxton supplied a monkey puzzle and Lord George Cavendish the cedars grown from seeds he brought back from the Holy Land.

HUTTON-IN-THE-FOREST
Skelton, Penrith CA11 9TH
☎ 017684 84449   Fax 017684 84571
Owner Lord Inglewood
Location 3 miles from Exit 41 of M6 on B5305
Open Gardens: 11 am – 5 pm; all year except Saturdays
Admission Gardens only: Adults £2.50; Children free
Facilities Parking; dogs permitted; loos; refreshments when house open, from 12.30 pm

CUMBRIA GARDENS 153

Features Herbaceous plants; good topiary; woodland garden; rhododendrons; herbaceous borders in the walled garden
English Heritage Grade II

Handsomely sited house with high Victorian terraces and grand views across the valley. Romantic parkland and good modern plantings. A garden to watch.

LEVENS HALL
Kendal LA8 0PD
☎ 015395 60321   Fax 015395 60669
Owner C H Bagot
Location 5 miles south of Kendal on A6
Open 10 am – 5 pm; Sunday – Thursday; 1 April to 14 October
Admission Garden only: Adults £3.90; Children £2.10
Facilities Parking; loos; access for the disabled; gift shop and plant centre; light lunches & teas
Features Good topiary; interesting for children; spring & summer bedding; new fountain garden; HHA/Christie's Garden of the Year in 1994
English Heritage Grade I

Levens means topiary: huge overgrown chunks of box and yew left over from a simple formal parterre laid out in 1694 and supplemented by golden yews in the 19th century. The arbours and high yew hedges, some of them crenellated, are spangled with *Tropaeolum speciosum* and the parterres planted annually with 15,000 plants, which makes Levens one of the best places to study the expensive art of bedding-out. Well maintained.

MUNCASTER CASTLE
Ravenglass CA18 1RQ
☎ 01229 717614   Fax 01229 717010
Website www.users.globalnet.co.uk/-acrhodos
Owner Mrs P R Gordon-Duff-Pennington
Location A595 1 mile east of Ravenglass on west coast of Cumbria
Open Grounds: 11 am – 5 pm; daily; all year. Castle: 12.30 pm – 4 pm; Sunday – Friday; 21 March to 7 November
Admission Gardens: Adults £3.50; Children £2 (1998 prices)
Facilities Parking; dogs permitted; loos; facilities for the disabled; plants for sale; two gift shops; good specialist plant centre; snacks & full meals
Features Fine conifers; woodland garden; rhododendrons; camellias; maples; masses of new plantings; tallest *Nothofagus obliqua* (31m.) in the British Isles; lots of new plantings
English Heritage Grade II*

Visit Muncaster in May, when the rhododendrons are at their peak. Many are grown from the original seed introduced by such plant-hunters as Forrest and Kingdon-Ward in the 1920s and 1930s. Muncaster also has a developing collection of hardy hybrid rhododendrons and a nursery which sells 500+ cultivars. The castle was revamped 150 years ago: its steep slopes and the lakeland hills behind create an intensely romantic landscape.

RYDAL MOUNT
Ambleside LA22 9LU
☎ 015394 33002   Fax 015394 31738
Owner Rydal Mount Trust (Wordsworth Family)
Location 1½ miles north of Ambleside on A591, turn up Rydal Hill
Open 9.30 am – 5 pm, March to October; 10 am – 4 pm, November to February
Admission Adults £3.50. Garden only: £1.50
Facilities Parking; dogs permitted; loos
Features Bluebells; daffodils; trees; rhododendrons; Dora Wordsworth's terrace undergoing restoration (1997)
English Heritage Grade II

Kept very much as it was in the poet's day, the garden at Rydal Mount is a memorial to William Wordsworth. He believed that a garden should be informal in its design, harmonise with the country and keep its views open.

SIZERGH CASTLE
Kendal LA8 8AE
☎ 015396 60070
Owner The National Trust
Location 3½ miles south of Kendal
Open 12.30 pm – 5.30 pm; Sunday – Thursday; 28 March to 31 October
Admission Garden only: Adults £2.20; Children £1.10
Facilities Parking; loos; facilities for the disabled; plants for sale; tea-room from 1.30 pm
Features Herbaceous plants; wildflower meadow; tender plants
English Heritage Grade II*
NCCPG National Collections *Asplenium scolopendrium*; *Cystopteris*; *Dryopteris*; *Osmunda*

One of the best National Trust gardens, with lots of interest from wild daffodils and alpines in April to hydrangeas and a hot half-hardy border in September – *Beschorneria yuccoides*, *Buddleja colvilei*. Best of all is the 1920s rock garden, made of local limestone, and home to an important (and beautiful) collection of ferns.

WORTH A VISIT

HARTSIDE NURSERY GARDEN
Alston CA9 3BL ☎ 01434 381372. Open 9 am – 4.30 pm; Monday – Friday; 12.30 pm – 4 pm; Saturdays, Sundays & Bank Holidays; March to October. Other months by appointment. The nursery specialises in alpines, particularly primulas, gentians, dwarf shrubs and conifers, and hardy ferns: all grown in the North Pennines at altitude. The substantial gardens are also open, and there is a self-catering cottage available.

WINDERWATH
Temple Sowerby, Penrith CA10 2AG ☎ 01768 88250. This garden has fine old trees, naturalised bulbs and a working Victorian walled garden.

DERBYSHIRE

BLUEBELL NURSERY & ARBORETUM
Annwell Lane, Smisby, Ashby-de-la-Zouch
LE65 2TA
☎ 01530 413700   Fax 01530 417600

Owner Mr & Mrs Robert Vernon
Location 200 yds south of Smisby Church. Follow brown tourist signs to arboretum
Open 9 am – 5 pm (4 pm from November to February); Monday – Saturday; all year. 10.30 am – 4.30 pm; Sundays; March to October
Admission Adults £1; Children free; RHS members free
Facilities Parking; loos; important tree & shrub nursery
Features Good collection of trees

Bluebell Nursery is a stalwart supporter of RHS shows and has won many medals for its displays of rare trees and shrubs. The arboretum has been planted and expanded every year since it was first planted in 1993. Highlights include an avenue of witch-hazel cultivars (*Hamamelis*) and the largest collection of deciduous hollies, *Ilex verticillata*, in Europe. The nursery sells many more plants than those in its excellent catalogue.

CALKE ABBEY
Ticknall DE7 1LE
☎ 01332 863822

Owner The National Trust
Location 10 miles south of Derby in village of Ticknall
Open 11 am – 5 pm; Saturday – Wednesday; 27 March to 31 October
Admission £2.30
Facilities Parking; loos; facilities for the disabled; National Trust gift shop; restaurant
Features Herbaceous plants; fruit and vegetables of special interest; dahlias; good Victorian-style bedding; deer park; horse-chestnut trees; local varieties of apples & soft fruit; vinery fully restored (1997)
English Heritage Grade II*

The 'sleeping beauty' house is not really matched by its garden, but when funds are available it will be replanted in the early 19th-century style, with period ornamental and fruit varieties, a physic garden and an orangery. The drive runs along a magnificent avenue of ancient limes. In the walled garden is the only surviving Auricula Theatre, originally built to display the perfection of these beautiful 'florist's' plants.

CHATSWORTH
Bakewell DE45 1PP
☎ 01246 582204   Fax 01246 583536

Owner Chatsworth House Trust
Location 8 miles north of Matlock off B6012
Open 11 am – 5 pm; daily; 17 March to 31 October
Admission Adults £3.75; OAPs £3; Children £1.75; Family ticket £9.20
Facilities Parking; dogs permitted; loos; facilities for the disabled; plants for sale in Potting Shed shop, in Orangery; self-service restaurant, licensed
Features Good collection of trees; landscape designed by Capability Brown; rhododendrons and azaleas; rock garden; modern roses; garden sculpture; good topiary; woodland garden; interesting for children; pinetum; maze; tulip tree avenue; adventure playground; tallest *Pinus strobus* (42m.) in the British Isles
English Heritage Grade I

Everyone knows of Chatsworth: 105 acres of Capability Brown, a 'conservative wall' to keep the heat and ripen fruit trees, Paxton's rockeries (huge boulders surrounded by conifers), a serpentine hedge with yews of different hues, enormous *Camellia reticulata* 'Captain Rawes' with trunks 80 cm. thick, and of course the famous long cascade. But there is so much more: well run and fun for all the family.

ELVASTON CASTLE COUNTY PARK
Borrowash Road, Elvaston DE72 3EP
☎ 01332 571342   Fax 01332 758751

Owner Derbyshire County Council
Location 5 miles south-east of Derby. Signed from A6 and A52
Open Dawn to dusk (Old English Garden, 9 am – 5 pm); daily; all year
Admission Gardens free. Car park 70p midweek, £1.30 weekends
Facilities Parking; dogs permitted; loos; facilities for the disabled; two gift shops; restaurant open all year 10 am – 4.30 pm
Features Herbaceous plants; lake; old roses; good topiary; particularly interesting in winter
English Heritage Grade II*

A historic garden, once famous for its topiary, and saved from oblivion by Derby County Council in the 1970s. The parterres have been replaced and the walled garden replanted with roses and herbaceous plants, and renamed the Old English Garden.

HADDON HALL
Bakewell DE45 1LA
☎ 01629 812855   Fax 01629 814379

Owner The Duke of Rutland
Location 1½ miles south of Bakewell on A6
Open 11 am – 5 pm; daily; April to September. Plus Monday – Thursday in October
Admission House & garden: Adults £5.50; OAPs £4.75; Children £3
Facilities Parking; loos; coffee, lunch, afternoon teas
Features Herbaceous plants; good topiary; roses of every kind; clematis; delphiniums; Christie's/HHA Garden of the Year in 1994
English Heritage Grade I

Terraced neo-Tudor gardens to complement a castellated Elizabethan prodigy house. Fine balustrading and old yews, spring bulbs and herbaceous borders but, above all, roses, roses, roses. The family's private gardens, leading

DERBYSHIRE GARDENS 155

down to the River Wye, are open for the first time this year (1999).

Hardwick Hall
Doe Lea, Chesterfield S44 5QJ
☎ 01246 850430   Fax 01246 854200
Owner The National Trust
Location Signposted from M1 Jct 29
Open Gardens: 12 noon – 5.30 pm; daily; 27 March to 31 October
Admission Garden only: Adults £3; Children £1.50
Facilities Parking; loos; facilities for the disabled; weekend plant sales only; refreshments Wed/Thurs/Sat/Sun when Hall is open
Features Herbaceous plants; herbs; old roses; daffodils; fine hedges; mulberry walk; hollies
English Heritage Grade I
NCCPG National Collection *Scabiosa caucasica*

The formal gardens are extensive: avenues of hornbeam and yew and a newly restored 'Elizabethan' (actually 1970s) herb garden (lavender and eglantine) in the kitchen garden. Hardwick has wonderful old fruit trees, nutteries, a mulberry avenue, old roses and modern borders in the Jekyll style. In the park are fine cedars and Hungarian oaks. This is one of the best National Trust gardens, and getting still better.

Kedleston Hall
Derby DE22 5JH
☎ 01332 842191   Fax 01332 841972
Owner The National Trust
Location 5 miles north-west of Derby
Open 11 am – 6 pm; Saturday – Wednesday; 27 March to 31 October
Admission Adults £4.90; Children £2.40. Park & garden only: £2.10
Facilities Parking; loos; access for the disabled; National Trust shop; lunches & teas, licensed
Features Rhododendrons and azaleas; modern roses; handsome Adam orangery
English Heritage Grade I

The landscaped park runs down to a long lake. The house is matched by an Adam summerhouse in the circular garden: impressive and important.

Lea Gardens
Lea, Matlock DE4 5GH
☎ 01629 534380   Fax 01629 534260
Owner Mr & Mrs J Tye
Location 3 miles south-east of Matlock
Open 10 am – 7 pm; daily; 20 March to early July
Admission Adults £3; Children 50p; Season ticket £4; Wheelchair-bound free
Facilities Parking; dogs permitted; loos; plants for sale; light lunches & teas
Features Rhododendrons and azaleas

This is the garden of a rhododendron lover: over 650 varieties as well as kalmias, magnolias, maples and dwarf conifers. Best in May, when it is frankly spectacular.

Melbourne Hall
Melbourne DY3 1EN
☎ 01332 862502   Fax 01322 862263
Owner Lord Ralph Kerr
Location 8 miles south of Derby
Open 2 pm – 6 pm; Wednesdays, Saturdays, Sundays & Bank Holiday Mondays; April to September
Admission Adults £3; OAPs £2
Facilities Parking; loos; access for the disabled; shop; refreshments
Features Herbaceous plants; garden sculpture; turf terracing; grand avenues; new Visitors' Centre
English Heritage Grade I

Near-perfect example of an early 18th-century garden, influenced by Le Nôtre. Statues, gravel, *bassins*, lumpy old hedges and the famous yew tunnel.

Renishaw Hall
Renishaw, Sheffield S31 9WB
☎ 01246 432042/0777 860755
Owner Sir Reresby Sitwell
Location 2½ miles from M1 Jct 30
Open 10.30 am – 4.30 pm; Friday – Sunday, plus Bank Holiday Mondays; 2 April to 30 September
Admission Adults £3; OAPs £2; Children £1
Facilities Parking; dogs permitted; loos; access for the disabled; plants for sale; small tea-rooms
Features Herbaceous plants; fine conifers; modern roses; old roses; woodland garden; daffodils; Italian garden
English Heritage Grade II*

Lots of modern colour, including a magnificent delphinium border, but best for the formal Italian garden laid out by Sir George Sitwell *c.* 1900. His meticulous and scholarly creation still dominates the horticultural splendours.

WORTH A VISIT

Abbey Brook Cactus Nursery
Bakewell Road, Matlock DE4 2QJ ☎ 01629 580306. Open 1 pm – 4 pm; weekdays; 1 pm – 5 pm; Saturdays; 12 noon – 5 pm; Sundays; daily. NCCPG National Collections: Conophytum; Haworthia; Lithops. The leading UK cactus nursery, now mainly wholesale (1,000,000 plants in stock) but their retail catalogue lists 2,000 species and the nursery is worth a visit at any time of the year.

Chatsworth Garden Centre
Calton Lees, Beeley, Matlock DE4 2NX ☎ 01629 734004. Open 9 am – 5 pm; weekdays. 10 am – 4 pm; Sundays. Times may vary according to season & weather. An excellent, bustling garden centre with a good range of indoor and outdoor plants, on the edge of the Chatsworth estate.

DAM FARM HOUSE
Ednaston, Ashbourne DE6 3BA ☎ *01335 360291.*
Open 11 am – 4 pm, 25 April & 19 September. 2 pm – 4.30 pm, 23 May & 18 July. Parties by arrangement from April to October. Mrs Player (born a Loder) has made this outstanding garden on a greenfield site since 1980. The design is firm, and the planting exuberant. Rare plants abound, but it is their treatment which makes the garden such an exciting place to visit and learn from: their planting, training and cultivation are a model for our times.

DARLEY HOUSE
Darley Dale, Matlock DE4 3BP ☎ *01629 733341.*
Open By appointment, May to September, for private visits and groups (not exceeding 15 people). Basically a modern, plantsman's garden, just over an acre, but planted with good colour sense and commendable restraint. Interesting too because it belonged to Sir Joseph Paxton in the 1840s and his layout still gives the whole garden its structure. Restoration continues.

DEVON

ARLINGTON COURT
Arlington, Barnstaple EX31 4LP
☎ 01271 850296   Fax 01271 850625

Owner The National Trust
Location 8 miles north of Barnstaple on A39
Open 11 am – 5.30 pm; Sunday – Friday; 28 March to 31 October. Open at noon on 11 August
Admission Gardens only: Adults £3.20
Facilities Parking; dogs permitted; loos; facilities for the disabled; National Trust shop; restaurant & tea-rooms
Features Fine conifers; huge old rhododendrons; Victorian walled garden restored & replanted (1997)
English Heritage Grade II

Arlington offers mature parkland on a dead flat site in front of a fine Georgian house. It has a pretty Victorian formal garden and conservatory. But watch the restoration of the walled garden: 19th-century fruit and vegetables grow alongside local cultivars.

BUCKLAND ABBEY
Yelverton PL20 6EY
☎ 01822 853607   Fax 01822 855448

Owner The National Trust
Location Signposted from A386 at Yelverton
Open 10.30 am – 5.30 pm; Friday – Wednesday; 27 March to 31 October. 2 pm – 5 pm; Saturdays & Sundays; November & December. Opens at noon on 11 August
Admission Adults £2.50
Facilities Parking; loos; facilities for the disabled; refreshments
Features Herbs; interesting for children; new Elizabethan herb garden begun (1999); current holder of Sandford Award

Originally a Cistercian Abbey, then the house of Sir Francis Drake, the main interest for garden lovers is the charming herb garden along the side of the Great Barn.

CASTLE DROGO
Drewsteignton EX6 6PB
☎ 01647 433306   Fax 01647 433186

Owner The National Trust
Location Drewsteignton village: signs from A30 & A382
Open 10.30 am – 5.30 pm (dusk in winter); Saturday – Thursday; 27 March – 31 December. Plus 2 April. Opens at noon on 11 August
Admission Adults £3.60
Facilities Parking; loos; facilities for the disabled; plants for sale; National Trust shop; self-service tea-room, waitress-service restaurant
Features Herbaceous plants; planted by Gertrude Jekyll; designed by Lutyens; rock garden; modern roses; old roses; woodland garden; interesting for children; tallest *Acer capillipes* (16m.) in the British Isles
English Heritage Grade II*

Major 1920s garden, 900 feet high on the edge of Dartmoor. Handsome yew hedges; formal design; vast and vivid herbaceous borders, contrasting with the austere castle on its windy bluff. Weather-beaten, lichen-heavy *Prunus* and acers on the slopes below. All on a heroic scale.

COLETON FISHACRE GARDEN
Coleton, Kingswear, Dartmouth TQ6 0EQ
☎ & Fax 01803 752466

Owner The National Trust
Location 3 miles from Kingswear off Lower-Ferry Road
Open 10.30 am – 5.30 pm (or dusk, if earlier); Wednesday – Sundays & Bank Holidays; 27 March – 31 October (plus Sundays in March). Open at noon on 11 August
Admission Adults £3.60
Facilities Parking; loos; facilities for the disabled; plants for sale; new visitor reception area & tea-room (1999)
Features Herbaceous plants; plantsman's garden; subtropical plants; woodland garden; rhododendrons; rare trees; tallest *Catalpa bungei* in the British Isles (and two other record trees); interesting new plantings in the 'Holiwell' area
English Heritage Grade II

Twenty acres of rhododendron and camellia woodland crashing down a secret valley to the sea. Almost frost-free, the range and size of Southern Hemisphere trees and shrubs is astounding. Rare bulbs in the warm terraces around the Lutyensesque house.

DARTINGTON HALL
Dartington, Totnes TQ9 6EL
☎ & Fax 01803 862367

Owner Dartington Hall Trust
Location 2 miles north-west of Totnes
Open Dawn to dusk; daily; all year. Groups by prior appointment only

Admission Donation (£2 min.)
Facilities Parking; loos; access for the disabled; plants for sale
Features Garden sculpture; good topiary; woodland garden; magnolias; rhododendrons; camellias; tilt-yard; new hot-coloured wild-flower meadows (1999)
English Heritage Grade II*

Grand mid-20th-century garden with some famous associations. Beatrix Farrand designed the terraces, including the so-called tilt-yard, and Percy Cane built the long staircase and spring plantings on either side. Henry Moore deposited a reclining woman. Some consider the garden grandiose and cold: we think it is magnificent, and wholly appropriate to the scale of house and landscape.

DOCTON MILL
Lymebridge, Hartland, Bideford EX39 6EA
☎ & Fax 01237 441369

Owner Mr & Mrs M G Bourcier
Location Take road from Hartland to Stoke and follow signposts towards Elmscott
Open 10 am – 6 pm; daily; March to October
Admission Adults £2.75; Children (under 14) 50p
Facilities Parking; dogs permitted; loos; plants for sale; light refreshments & cream teas
Features Fruit of special interest; woodland garden; apple orchards; new David Austin rose bed; bed & breakfast

The main attraction is a working water mill, but the garden is developing quickly and the new owners have already made further improvements. Worth watching.

ESCOT
Ottery St Mary, Exeter EX11 1LU
☎ 01404 822188   Fax 01404 822903

Owner John-Michael Kennaway
Location Signposted from A30 at Fairmile
Open 10 am – 6 pm (10.30 am – 4.30 pm from October to Easter); daily; all year
Admission Adults £2.95; OAPs & children £2.55; under-fives free
Facilities Parking; dogs permitted; loos; access for the disabled; water-plants for sale; home-cooked lunches & cream teas
Features Bluebells; fine conifers; rhododendrons and azaleas; snowdrops

An up-and-coming low-budget old/new garden, responding well to vigorous replanting. The house is an elegant Regency sugarlump, with distant views to East Hill (Capability Brown advised on the prospect), but the woodlands around the house are full of good Victorian rhododendrons and the walled garden sports a basic collection of old and English roses.

THE GARDEN HOUSE
Buckland Monachorum, Yelverton PL20 7LQ
☎ 01822 854769   Fax 01822 855358

Owner Fortescue Garden Trust

Location Signed off A386 on Plymouth side of Yelverton
Open 10.30 am – 5 pm; daily; March to October
Admission Adults £3.50; OAPs £3; Children £1; RHS members free
Facilities Parking; loos; plants for sale; tea-room with light lunches
Features Herbaceous plants; plantsman's garden; alpine bank; flowering cherries; wisterias; new 4-acre extension with *Acer* glade, spring garden, quarry garden, wildflower meadow

A plantsman's garden, made by the late Lionel Fortescue, who insisted on planting only the best forms of plants. The setting is awesome: a ruined abbey on the edge of Dartmoor, with stupendous views. Much of the effect is achieved through rigorous cultivation. Plants are well fed and firmly controlled: they flourish on the treatment. Exciting new developments on a huge scale.

HILL HOUSE NURSERY & GARDEN
Landscove, Ashburton, Newton Abbot TQ13 7LY
☎ & Fax 01803 762273

Owner Raymond, Valerie & Matthew Hubbard
Location Off A384, follow signs for Landscove
Open 11 am – 5 pm; daily; all year
Admission Free
Facilities Parking; dogs permitted; loos; facilities for the disabled; plants for sale; garden shop; Mother Hubbards Tea-Room (home made cakes)
Features Fine conifers; glasshouses; particularly interesting in winter; daffodils; cyclamen and snowdrops; two new herbaceous borders each 150 feet long (1997)

Victorian Old Vicarage made famous by Edward Hyams' *An Englishman's Garden*. Now the centre of an excellent plantsman's nursery.

KILLERTON
Broadclyst, Exeter EX5 3LE
☎ 01392 881345

Owner The National Trust
Location West side of B3181, Exeter to Cullompton Road
Open Dawn to dusk; daily; all year
Admission Adults £3.50 (but reduced rate in winter)
Facilities Parking; loos; facilities for the disabled; National Trust shop; small well-run plant centre; waitress-service restaurant and self-service tea-room
Features Good collection of trees; bluebells; daffodils; rhododendrons and azaleas; rock garden; snowdrops; particularly interesting in winter; tallest *Ostrya carpinifolia* (22m.) in the British Isles (and eight further record trees); magnolia; drifts of *Crocus tommasinianus*
English Heritage Grade II*

A historic giant among gardens, whose long connections with Veitch's Nursery have bequeathed a great tree collection. Innumerable record-breaking specimens, many from collectors' seed, but one's sense of awe is spoilt by droning traffic on the M5 below.

KNIGHTSHAYES GARDEN
Tiverton EX16 7RG
☎ 01884 254665   Fax 01884 253264

Owner The National Trust
Location Off A396 Tiverton to Bampton Road
Open 11 am – 5.30 pm; daily; 27 March to 31 October. Opens at noon on 11 August
Admission Adults £3.60; Children £1.80
Facilities Parking; loos; access for the disabled; plants for sale; National Trust shop; licensed restaurant; coffee, lunch & teas
Features Herbaceous plants; good topiary; woodland garden; plantings by Graham Thomas; hellebores; cyclamen; bulbs; peat beds; centenary planting of 100 trees along visitors' entrance; tallest *Quercus cerris* (40m.) in the British Isles
English Heritage Grade II*
Friends National Trust Culm & Eve Valleys Centre

Brilliant herbaceous plantings and stunning formal gardens, but Knightshayes is above all a garden in a wood, delightful at all seasons and notable for its rare plants and high standard of maintenance. Good new designs and plantings by the adventurous head gardener.

MARWOOD HILL GARDENS
Barnstaple EX31 4EB
☎ 01271 42528

Owner Dr J A Smart
Location Signed from A361 Barnstaple & Braunton Road
Open Dawn to dusk; daily; all year except 25 December
Admission Adults £3
Facilities Parking; dogs permitted; loos; plants for sale; teas, April to September, Sundays & Bank Holidays only
Features Alpines; good collection of trees; bog garden; herbaceous plants; camellias; daffodils; glasshouses; lake; plantsman's garden; rhododendrons and azaleas; climbing roses; old roses; particularly good in July–August; particularly interesting in winter; birches; eucalyptus; camellias; hebes; plants, more plants & yet more plants
NCCPG National Collections *Astilbe*; *Iris ensata*; *Tulbaghia*

A remarkable plantsman's garden, conceived on a grand scale and fast maturing, though it is still expanding along the long sheltered valley which gives such rewarding growth. Exciting for its scale, variety, and the energy of its owner. There is no better place in the south-west to learn about plants of every kind. Recent additions include a pergola with 12 different wisterias.

OVERBECKS MUSEUM & GARDEN
Sharpitor, Salcombe TQ8 8LW
☎ 01548 843238

Owner The National Trust
Location 2 miles south of Salcombe
Open 10 am – 8 pm (or dusk, if earlier); daily; all year
Admission Adults £2.70; Children £1.80
Features Bluebells; subtropical plants; palms; mimosas; cyclamen; *Magnolia campbellii*
English Heritage Grade II

A small, intensely planted, almost jungly garden, perched above the Salcombe estuary. The formal terraces (rather 1930s) are stuffed with interesting tender plants: *Musa basjoo*, phormiums, agapanthus, self-sown *Echium pininana* and every kind of South African daisy, all held together in a framework of *Trachycarpus* palms.

PAIGNTON ZOO & BOTANICAL GARDENS
Totnes Road, Paignton TQ4 7EU
☎ 01803 557479   Fax 01803 523457

Owner Whitley Wildlife Conservation Trust
Location On A385 Totnes Road, 1 mile from Paignton
Open 10 am – 5.30 pm (or dusk, if earlier); daily; all year
Admission Adults £5.40; OAPs £4.20; Children £3.75. Prices may vary in high season
Facilities Parking; loos; access for the disabled; shops; large self-service restaurant
Features Herbaceous plants; fine conifers; rock garden; interesting for children; glasshouses with tropical plants
NCCPG National Collections *Buddleja*; *Sorbaria*

Once a private garden devoted to blue-flowered and blue-leaved plants, now an inspiring combination of zoo, botanic collection, public park and holiday entertainment. Plans to increase the commitment to conservation have begun with six new habitats.

RHS GARDEN ROSEMOOR
Great Torrington EX38 8PH
☎ 01805 624067   Fax 01805 624717

Owner The Royal Horticultural Society
Location 1 mile south of Torrington on B3220
Open 10 am – 6 pm (but 5 pm October to March); daily except 25 December; all year. Open until 8.30 pm on 4 & 18 June and Fridays from 2 July to 13 August
Admission Adults £3.20; Children £1; Groups (10+) £2.75; RHS members free
Facilities Parking; loos; facilities for the disabled; plants for sale; good range of book & gifts; licensed restaurant
Features Plantsman's garden; modern roses; old roses; woodland garden; interesting for children; young garden; particularly interesting in winter; stream and bog garden; foliage garden; colour theme gardens; fruit and vegetable gardens; herb garden; cottage garden; tallest *Eucalyptus glaucescens* (21m.) in the British Isles (and seven further record trees)
NCCPG National Collections *Ilex*; *Cornus*

Rosemoor was created by Lady Anne Berry, who generously donated it to the RHS, with 32 acres of pastureland, in 1989. The RHS has made the new Rosemoor its West Country flagship through a wide-ranging development programme. The results are already impressive: good design, good plantings, an exceptionally high standard of maintenance, and the best-grown roses in England. But the people are the garden's making – friendly and helpful staff with a warm welcome for children, which makes a visit to Rosemoor so different from many grand gardens.

SALTRAM

Plympton, Plymouth PL7 3UH
☎ 01752 336546   Fax 01752 336474

Owner The National Trust
Location 2 miles west of Plympton
Open 11 am – 4 pm; Saturdays & Sundays; 6 to 21 March. 10.30 am – 5.30 pm; Sunday – Thursday; 27 March to 31 October. Also 2 April. Opens at noon on 11 August
Admission Adults £2.70; Children £1.35
Facilities Parking; loos; facilities for the disabled; National Trust shop in stable block; licensed restaurant 12 noon – 5.30 pm. Also light refreshments
Features Camellias; rhododendrons and azaleas; parkland; handsome orangery; lime avenue; 'melancholy' walk undergoing restoration (1998); tallest *Acer palmatum* 'Osakazuki' (13m.) in the British Isles
English Heritage Grade II*

Twenty acres of beautiful parkland, whose huge and ancient trees are underplanted with camellias and rhododendrons. Best in spring when the daffodils flower in hosts.

TAPELEY PARK

Instow EX39 4NT
☎ 01271 42371

Owner N D C I Ltd
Location Off A39 between Barnstaple & Bideford
Open 10 am – 5 pm; daily, except Saturdays; Good Friday to 31 October
Admission Adults £2.80; OAPs £2.30; Children £1.80
Facilities Parking; dogs permitted; loos; facilities for the disabled; plants for sale; gift shop; licensed lunches & cream teas
Features Good architectural features; fruit of special interest; glasshouses; woodland garden; interesting for children; British Jousting Centre; 1½-acre permaculture garden (1997)
English Heritage Grade II*

Fine Italianate formal garden laid out on several levels c. 1900 and planted with tender plants (*Sophora tetraptera* and *Myrtus communis* subsp. *tarentina*). Beyond are palm trees and a rhododendron woodland. All parts are undergoing restoration and replanting with advice from Mary Keen and Carol Klein. A garden to watch.

WORTH A VISIT

ANN & ROGER BOWDEN

Hostas, Sticklepath, Okehampton EX20 2NL
☎ 01837 840481.   Open Garden open for NGS 10.30 am – 5 pm; 1 & 2 May and 23 & 27 June. Otherwise, by appointment only.   NCCPG National Collection: Hybrid Hosta. Hostas only, from a handsome catalogue with excellent photographs. Prices are fair and range from £2 for basic species to £15 for the latest imported hybrids. But the choice is magnificent, and a large number are new or re-introduced.

BICTON PARK GARDENS

East Budleigh, Budleigh Salterton EX9 7DP
☎ 01395 443881.   Ring for opening times. Sixty acres of fascinating features, including: an Italian garden; important trees; the oriental garden; an American garden; a collection of dwarf conifers; more than 2,000 heathers; an avenue of monkey puzzles; a hermitage; and the finest pre-Paxton palm house built 1815-20 from thousands of tiny panes of glass. But the owners were looking for a new tenant as we went to press, so the times and dates of openings were not yet known.

EXETER UNIVERSITY GARDENS

Exeter EX4 4PX ☎ 01392 263059.   NCCPG National Collection: Azara.   One of the best University campuses, the gardens are educational, attractive and important. Based on the 19th-century Veitch collections of exotic trees, the plantings were supplemented by Chinese species collected 80 years ago by E H Wilson.

GIDLEIGH PARK HOTEL

Chagford TQ13 8HH ☎ 01647 432367.   Open Guests of the hotel & restaurant only. Forty-five acres of woodland (much of it recently replanted) on the edge of Dartmoor with a 1920s garden round the Tudorised house. Nothing very rare or special, but the position is stupendous and the sense of space, even grandeur, is enhanced by immaculate maintenance. Innumerable awards for the hotel and restaurant over many years.

GNOME RESERVE & WILDFLOWER GARDEN

The Pixie Kiln, West Putford, Bradworthy EX22 7XE
☎ 01409 241435.   Open 10 am – 6 pm; daily; 21 March to 31 October. There are four reasons to visit this remarkable conservation centre which has been featured on TV more than 50 times: first, the two-acre gnome reserve in a beech wood with a stream; second, the two-acre pixies' wildflower meadow, with 250 labelled species; third, the kiln where pottery gnomes and pixies are born; fourth, the museum of rare early gnomes.

KENWITH NURSERY

Blinsham, Torrington EX19 8NT ☎ 01805 603274. Open 10 am – 4.30 pm; daily; all year. Closed Sunday – Tuesday from November to February. Dwarf conifers are this nursery's speciality. Its garden, conveniently close to Rosemoor, is a good place to learn about the possibilities for small gardens.

PLEASANT VIEW NURSERY & GARDEN

Two Mile Oak, Denbury, Newton Abbot TQ12 6DG
☎ 01803 813388.   Open 10 am – 5 pm, Wednesdays & Fridays, 17 March to 16 October.   NCCPG National Collections: Abelia; Salvia.   This garden is a remarkable achievement: the collection of shrubs is exceptionally comprehensive – and it has all been achieved from open pasture since 1988. The nursery carries rare shrubs for gardens and conservatories, and a number of Salvia from the National Collection.

POWDERHAM CASTLE

Exeter EX6 8JQ ☎ *01626 890243. Open 10 am – 5.30 pm; daily; March to 1 October. Not a major garden, but the 18th-century landscaped park is serenely English, the woodland garden is stupendous in March and there is a cheerful modern rose garden all along the front of the house.*

SILVER DALE NURSERIES

Shute Lane, Combe Martin EX34 0HT ☎ *01271 882539. Open 10 am – 6 pm; daily; all year. NCCPG National Collection: Fuchsia hardy cvs. This fuchsia nursery, long known for its mail-order service, now has a display garden where the National Collection (and many other fuchsia cultivars) may be studied and admired.*

SOUTHCOMBE GARDENS

2 Willens Cottages, Mamhead, Kenton EX6 8HQ ☎ *01626 888947. Open By appointment. This youngish nursery is beginning to make an impact at RHS shows. It specialises in plants for small gardens, especially rock-garden plants, grasses and ferns.*

THORNHAYES NURSERY

Dulford, Cullompton EX15 2DF ☎ *01884 266746. Open By appointment only. A retail and wholesale nursery. The stock is both open-ground and container-grown, and covers a broad spectrum of interesting ornamental and fruit trees, including some hard-to-get West Country apples (for cider, cooking and eating). The Sorbus, Pyrus and Crataegus are also good: dendrophiles should take a closer look.*

WYLMINGTON HAYES GARDENS

Wilmington, Honiton EX14 9JZ ☎ *01404 831751. An Edwardian house in the Tudor style, with a formal Italian garden and 90 acres of ornamental woodland planted with rhododendrons, azaleas, camellias, acers and magnolias.*

DORSET

ABBOTSBURY SUBTROPICAL GARDENS
Abbotsbury, Weymouth DT3 4LA
☎ 01305 871387   Fax 01305 871902

Owner Ilchester Estates
Location B3157, on coast, in village
Open 10 am – 6 pm (4 pm from November to March); daily; all year. Closed 1 January, 25 & 26 December
Admission Adults £4.20; OAPs £3.80; Children £1.50; RHS members free in January & February
Facilities Parking; dogs permitted; loos; access for the disabled; plants for sale; shop; new restaurant (1998)
Features Good collection of trees; bluebells; camellias; plantsman's garden; rhododendrons and azaleas; modern roses; subtropical plants; woodland garden; particularly interesting in winter; magnolias; candelabra primulas; rare trees; free-standing loquat *Eriobotrya japonica*; tallest English oak *Quercus robur* (40m.) in the British Isles; five other record trees

English Heritage Grade I
NCCPG National Collections *Hebe* (large-leaved); *Hoheria*

A 20-acre woodland garden of splendid specimens and trees of great rarity which has enjoyed a spectacular renaissance in recent years. Palms, eucalyptus, pittosporum and camellias all grow lushly in the sheltered valley and romantic walled garden. A stylish Visitors' Centre and excellent nursery make for added value.

ATHELHAMPTON HOUSE & GARDENS
Dorchester DT2 7LG
☎ 01305 848363   Fax 01305 848135
Website www.athelhampton.co.uk

Owner Patrick Cooke
Location 1 mile east of Puddletown on A35
Open 10.30 am – 5 pm; Sunday – Friday; March to October. Plus Sundays from November to February
Admission House & garden: £4.95. Garden only: £3.50
Facilities Parking; loos; access for the disabled; plants for sale; shop; refreshments
Features Good topiary; gazebos; beautiful walls and hedges; winner of HHA/Christie's Garden of the Year Award for 1997; two *Metasequoia glyptostroboides* from the original seed
English Heritage Grade I

Inigo Thomas designed this about 100 years ago as the perfect garden for the perfect manor house. Sharply cut pyramids of yew, a long canal with water lilies, and rambling roses in early summer.

CHIFFCHAFFS
Chaffeymoor, Bourton, Gillingham SP8 5BY
☎ 01747 840841

Owner Mr & Mrs K R Potts
Location At Wincanton end of Bourton, off A303
Open 2 pm – 5.30 pm; Wednesdays & Thursdays, plus first & third Sundays of the month & Bank Holiday weekends; 31 March to 30 September
Admission Adults £2; Children 50p
Facilities Parking; excellent nursery attached, open 10 am – 1 pm and 2 pm – 5 pm, Tuesday to Saturday; for groups, by appointment
Features Plantsman's garden; woodland garden; spring bulbs; dwarf rhododendrons

A pretty cottage, with an excellent small nursery attached, and just off the A303. Only 15 years old, the garden has a flowing design, exploits a great variety of habitats and burgeons with good plants. A bluebell-lined path leads to the woodland garden, which boasts a splendid collection of rhododendrons, drifts of daffodils and candelabra primulas, and yet more carpets of bluebells.

COMPTON ACRES GARDENS
Canford Cliffs Road, Poole BH13 7ES
☎ 01202 700778   Fax 01202 707537

Owner L Green
Location Well signposted locally

Open 10 am – 6 pm; daily; March to October
Admission Adults £4.95; OAPs £3.35
Facilities Parking; loos; access for the disabled; plants for sale; several shops; tea-rooms & light lunches
Features Fine conifers; good architectural features; oriental features; rock garden; modern roses; garden sculpture; subtropical plants; woodland garden
English Heritage Grade II*

Very touristy and very 1920s. Compton Acres offers ten totally unconnected but highly entertaining gardens, all in different styles but joined by tarmac paths. Best are the Italian garden, the palm court, the white azaleas in the watery glen which runs down to the harbour, and the stupendous Japanese garden. There is opulence, vulgarity, overcrowding and blatant commercialism, but the standards are among the highest in any garden: no visitor could fail to be cheered up by the bravura of it all. We love it.

CRANBORNE MANOR
Cranborne, Wimborne BH21 5PP
☎ 01725 517248   **Fax** 01725 517862

Owner Viscount Cranborne
Location 10 miles north of Wimborne on B3078
Open 9 am – 5 pm; (7 pm in May & June) Wednesdays; March to September. Plus 10 am – 5 pm on 13 June for NGS
Admission Adults £3; Concessions £2.50; Children (under 16) 50p
Facilities Parking; loos; garden centre
Features Herbaceous plants; old roses; good topiary; Jacobean mount
English Heritage Grade II*

The garden at Cranborne is modern, but employs Elizabethan elements. The mixed borders in the charming courtyard are good. Much of the structure dates from the 1960s and 1970s, but you would never know it.

FORDE ABBEY
Chard TA20 4LU
☎ 01460 220231   **Fax** 01460 220296

Owner The Trustees of the G D Roper settlement
Location 4 miles south of Chard
Open 10 am – 4.30 pm; daily; all year
Admission Adults £3.75; OAPs £3.50; Children & RHS members free October to April
Facilities Parking; dogs permitted; loos; facilities for the disabled; plants for sale; new shop (1998); cafeteria
Features Good collection of trees; bog garden; herbaceous plants; lake; rock garden planted by Jack Drake; new Ionic temple (Ham stone); HHA/Christie's Garden of the Year in 1993; tallest *Cornus controversa* (16m.) in UK
English Heritage Grade II*

A garden of great variety around the rambling house, part Jacobean, part Gothick. The planting is modern, and includes rhododendrons, azaleas, acers, magnolias, irises, meconopsis and candelabra primulas. But there are also mature Victorian conifers (*Sequoia sempervirens*,

Calocedrus decurrens), lakes, ponds, streams, cascades, bogs and such oddities as a Beech House.

IVY COTTAGE
Aller Lane, Ansty, Dorchester DT2 7PX
☎ 01258 880053

Owner Anne & Alan Stevens
Location Midway between Blandford & Dorchester
Open 10 am – 5 pm; Thursdays; April to October. And 2 pm – 5.30 pm on 29 August for NGS
Admission Adults £2; Children free (but £2.50 & 50p for NGS)
Facilities Parking; plants for sale
Features Herbaceous plants; plantsman's garden
NCCPG National Collection *Trollius*

One and a half acres of cottage garden made (and immaculately maintained) by the present owners over the last 30 years and crammed with interesting things, particularly moisture-loving plants. Springs and streams, combined with greensand soil, multiply the possibilities – drifts of marsh marigolds, astilbes and candelabra primulas.

KINGSTON LACY
Wimborne Minster BH21 4EA
☎ 01202 883402

Owner The National Trust
Location 1½ miles from Wimborne on B3082 to Blandford
Open 11 am – 6 pm; daily; 27 March to 31 October. 11 am – 4 pm; Friday – Sunday; November & December. Closed 16 July, 6 & 20 August
Admission Adults £2.50; Children £1.25
Facilities Parking; loos; access for the disabled; plants for sale; lunches & teas
Features Fine conifers; garden sculpture; snowdrops; Victorian fernery; Dutch parterre; huge cedars of Lebanon planted by visiting royalty
English Heritage Grade II
NCCPG National Collections *Anemone nemorosa*; *Convallaria*

Two hundred and fifty acres of classic 18th-century parkland, with a cedar avenue, Egyptian obelisk and laurel walk dating from Victorian times, to which the National Trust is adding modern horticultural excitements.

KNOLL GARDENS
Stapehill Road, Wimborne BH21 7ND
☎ 01202 873931   **Fax** 01202 870842

Owner John & Jane Flude & Neil Lucas
Location Signposted from B3073 at Hampreston
Open 10 am – 4 pm; Wednesday – Sunday; 3 March – 1 April. 10 am – 5.30 pm (4.30 in October); daily; 2 April to 31 October. November & December: phone for times
Admission Adults £3.50; OAPs £3; Children £1.75
Facilities Parking; loos; access for the disabled; plants for sale; good shop; restaurant & refreshments

Features Herbaceous plants; fine conifers; rhododendrons and azaleas; rock garden; eucalyptus; new gravel garden (1998)
NCCPG National Collections *Ceanothus; Phygelius*

Around the massive new rock garden of Purbeck stone are the relics of an intimate and enclosed collection of tender exotics. The modern plantings lower down offer less to the discriminating plantsman. But there is a fine open area of lawn at the bottom which gives onto a gravel garden, a conifer collection, a small pond and sinuous herbaceous plantings. Well maintained.

MAPPERTON GARDENS
Beaminster DT8 3NR
☎ 01308 862645   Fax 01308 863348
Owner The Earl & Countess of Sandwich
Location 2 miles south-east of Beaminster
Open 2 pm – 6 pm; daily; March to October
Admission Adults £3; Children (5–18) £1.50 (under-fives free)
Facilities Parking; loos; plants for sale; small shop selling terracotta pots; soft drinks
Features Good collection of trees; good topiary
English Heritage Grade II*

Mapperton has spectacular hanging gardens that you see laid out in their entirety from the lawn beside the house. First comes an enchanting steep formal valley-garden, running down from a pinnacled orangery to a handsome pool surrounded by terracing and gardens of clipped yew. Below are two canals and a long dell garden, with an excellent collection of spring-flowering trees and shrubs.

MINTERNE
Minterne Magna, Dorchester DT 7AU
☎ 01300 341370   Fax 01300 341747
Owner Lord Digby
Location On A352, 2 miles north of Cerne Abbas
Open 10 am – 7 pm; daily; 28 March to 10 November
Admission Adults £3; Children free
Facilities Parking; dogs permitted; loos
Features Rhododendrons and azaleas; subtropical plants; woodland garden; cherries; cyclamen; *Lathraea clandestina*; tallest *Chamaecyparis pisifera* 'Filifera' (25m.) in the UK
English Heritage Grade II

A woodland garden, best in spring, and well integrated into the park around the hideous Edwardian house. The oldest rhododendrons came from Hooker's collection, but the remarkable late Lord Digby also supported Farrer, Forrest, Rock and Kingdon-Ward, which makes Minterne one of the best Himalayan collections. The walk down a greensand valley to the woodland stream is ravishing.

PARNHAM HOUSE
Beaminster DT8 3NA
☎ 01308 862204   Fax 01308 863494
Owner Mr & Mrs J Makepeace
Location On A3066 north of Bridport
Open 10 am – 5 pm; Tuesday – Thursday, Sunday & Bank Holidays; April to October; groups by appointment
Admission House & garden: Adults £5; Children £2
Facilities Parking; dogs permitted; loos; facilities for the disabled; woodware & contemporary crafts; tea, coffee, hot & cold lunches
Features Old roses; good topiary
English Heritage Grade II*

A handsome wisteria-clad Jacobean mansion, approached through a courtyard, with formal terraces running down to lakes and bluebell woods. The gardens have been restored and imaginatively replanted with mixed borders and, above all, roses. But Parnham offers much more beside: iris borders, a meadow of fritillaries, an Italian garden, topiary, gazebos, rhododendrons, acres of *Allium ursinum* and splendid modern sculptures including a larger-than-life Morecambe and Wise.

STAPEHILL ABBEY
Stapehill, Wimborne BH21 2EB
☎ 01202 861686
Owner Stapehill Enterprises Ltd
Location Signed from A31
Open 10 am – 5 pm; daily; Easter to September. Plus 10 am – 4 pm; Wednesday – Sunday; October to Easter
Admission Adults £5; OAPs £4.50; Children £3.50
Facilities Parking; loos; facilities for the disabled; plants for sale; licensed coffeeshop
Features New Japanese garden (1999)
Friends Friends of Stapehill started: ring for details

A modern leisure development with vintage tractors to admire and lots of plants to sell. The design is rather uncoordinated but the individual gardens are richly planted and there are some handsome features: a small rose garden, a laburnum pergola, a water garden, a small tropical house and an extensive rock garden, more noteworthy for its design and size than for its plantings. Not a botanical collection, but a good horticultural one.

STICKY WICKET
Buckland Newton, Dorchester DT2 7BY
☎ 01300 345476
Owner Peter & Pam Lewis
Location 11 miles from Dorchester & Sherborne
Open 10.30 am – 8 pm; Thursdays; June to September. Plus 20 June & 22 August for NGS (2 pm – 8 pm)
Admission Adults £2.50; Children £1
Facilities Parking; loos; access for the disabled; plants for sale; tea, coffee & home-made cakes
Features Ecological interest; young garden; made since 1987; good colour associations

An original garden, worth watching. The owners are both designers and conservationists, and their devotion to ecology guides their garden-making. A scented garden, a white garden and a colour wheel are secondary to the need to attract birds, insects and other wildlife. Yet it is also one of the most photographed and admired of modern gardens for the subtlety and integrity of Pam Lewis's colour combinations.

WORTH A VISIT

BENNETTS WATER GARDENS
Putton Lane, Chickerell, Weymouth DT3 4AF
☎ 01305 785150. Website: www.waterlily.co.uk
Open 10 am – 5 pm; Tuesday – Sunday; April to August. 10 am – 5 pm; Tuesday – Saturday; September. NCCPG National Collection: Nymphaea. Water lilies, pond plants and marginals in abundance, as well as extensive display ponds. The flowering season is from June to late September. They also have tropical varieties to tempt conservatory owners.

C W GROVES & SON
Nursery & Garden Centre, West Bay Road, Bridport DT6 4BA ☎ 01308 422654. Open 8.30 am – 5 pm, Monday – Saturday; 10.30 am – 4.30 pm, Sundays. This traditional, family-run nursery-cum-garden centre is worth knowing. The firm was founded by the present owner's great-great-grandfather in 1866. They also specialise in named cultivars of Victorian violets. These named violet cultivars, but only sold by mail order.

DEAN'S COURT
Wimborne BH21 1EE ☎ 01202 888478. Open 2 pm – 6 pm; 4 April, 2 May, 28 August & 19 September. Plus 10 am – 6 pm; 5 April, 3 May & 30 August. A very wholesome garden: everything, including 150 different herb varieties, is grown without artificial fertilisers, pesticides or herbicides.

EDMONDSHAM HOUSE
Edmondsham, Wimborne BH21 5RE ☎ 01725 517207. Open 2 pm – 5 pm; Wednesdays, Sundays & Bank Holiday Mondays; April to October. The walled garden is maintained organically, with borders round the sides – go in August to see the vast patches of white crinums. It is intensively cultivated and brims with interesting vegetables and fruit houses. Fine trees around the main lawns.

HORN PARK
Beaminster DT8 3HB ☎ 01308 862212. Open 2 pm – 6 pm; Sunday – Thursday; April to October. A garden of rare plants, including such tender exotics as carpenterias and myrtles, and a wildflower meadow listed as a nature conservation site.

KINGSTON MAURWARD GARDENS
Kingston Maurward College, Dorchester DT2 8PY
☎ 01305 215003. Kingston Maurward belonged to the Hanbury family who owned La Mortola on the Riviera, and laid out the formal garden here in the Italian style (c. 1920). It is being restored in the country house style with herbaceous borders and old-fashioned roses, but the old kitchen garden is a splendid modern teaching garden with innumerable demonstrations of what can be grown in Dorset. Highly instructive.

MACPENNYS NURSERIES
154 Burley Road, Bransgore, Christchurch BH23 8DB
☎ 01425 672348. Open 9 am – 5 pm; Monday – Saturday. 2 pm – 5 pm; Sundays (but 10 am – 5 pm on Sundays from April to June). Long-established nursery with a reliable general range across the plant spectrum. The large woodland garden next to the nursery is open for the National Gardens Scheme at the same times and full of good plants.

RED HOUSE MUSEUM & GARDENS
Quay Road, Christchurch BH23 2NF ☎ 01202 482860. Open 10 am – 5 pm; Tuesday – Saturday & Bank Holiday Mondays; all year. Plus 2 pm – 5 pm; Sundays. Small and simple, a setting for the museum, this half-acre oasis in Christchurch's conservation area concentrates on plants of historic interest and contemporary sculpture.

TREHANE NURSERY & CAMELLIA CENTRE
Stapehill Road, Hampreston, Wimborne BH21 7NE
☎ 01202 873490. Open 9.30 am – 4.30 pm; Monday – Friday; all year. 10 am – 4 pm; Saturday – Sunday; spring & autumn. Excellent wholesale and retail camellia growers. They have a wide choice of camellia hybrids, and kalmias, magnolias, pieris and azaleas.

CO. DURHAM

THE BOWES MUSEUM GARDEN & PARK
Barnard Castle DL12 8NP
☎ 01833 690606   Fax 01833 637163
Owner Durham County Council
Location ½ mile west of Barnard Castle town
Open Dawn to dusk; daily; all year
Admission Free
Facilities Parking; dogs permitted; loos; facilities for the disabled; shop; museum café
Features Good collection of trees; old roses; parterre; large monkey puzzle
English Heritage Grade II
Friends Friends of Museum & Park, ring 01833 690606 for details

Twenty-one acres of Victorian splendour, now maintained by the County Council as a public amenity. The formal gardens are good and fine trees pepper the park, especially conifers.

HOUGHALL COLLEGE GARDENS
Durham DH1 3SG
☎ 0191 386 1351   Fax 0191 386 0419
Owner Durham College of Agriculture & Horticulture
Location Follow A177 from A1 to Durham
Open 12.30 pm – 4.30 pm; daily; all year
Admission Free
Facilities Parking; loos; facilities for the disabled; plants for sale; shop; tea-room (closed in winter)
Features Alpines; good collection of trees; bog garden; herbaceous plants; glasshouses; rock garden; modern roses; heathers; hardy fuchsias; seasonal bedding; fuchsias; excellent young pinetum
NCCPG National Collection *Sorbus*

Friends Houghall Horticultural Society linked to the college

A well-run teaching garden attached to the County horticultural college. Many trials are conducted here, for example on the hardiness of fuchsias: 'if it grows at Houghall it will grow anywhere'. The arboretum has more than 500 different trees.

UNIVERSITY OF DURHAM BOTANIC GARDEN
Hollingside Lane, Durham DH1 3TN
☎ 0191 374 7971   Fax 0191 374 7478
Owner University of Durham
Location In the south of the City of Durham
Open 10 am – 5 pm; daily; March to October. 11 am – 4 pm; daily; November to February
Admission Adults £1; Concessions 50p
Facilities Parking; loos; facilities for the disabled; plants for sale; tea, coffee, cold drinks & snacks
Features Good collection of trees; old roses; primulas; meconopsis; autumn colour; sculpture by Ian Hamilton Findlay
Friends 300 members and a full programme – details from the curator

Moved to its present site in 1970, this garden impresses with its youthful energy. The new 'American arboretum' was planted to copy natural associations 15 years ago. A woodland garden dates from 1988, a wetland one from 1989, and 1992 saw the opening of the 'Prince Bishop's Garden' with statues transferred from the Gateshead garden festival.

WESTHOLME HALL
Winston, Darlington DL2 3QL
☎ 01325 730442   Fax 01325 730946
Owner Mrs J H McBain
Location On B6274 north towards Staindrop
Open 2 pm – 6 pm; 23 May, 11 July & 29 August
Admission Adults £2; Children 50p
Facilities Parking; dogs permitted; loos; access for the disabled; plants for sale; tea-rooms
Features Old roses; rhododendrons

Five acres of late-Victorian gardens, recently restored and revived, around a smashing Jacobean house. Designed and planted for all seasons: there are parts for spring (bulbs and azaleas), summer (roses and lilacs) and autumn (herbaceous borders). All is maintained by the owners' own hard work and enthusiasm. Worth a long detour to see.

ESSEX

AUDLEY END
Saffron Walden
☎ 01799 522842/520052   Fax 01799 522131
Owner English Heritage
Location On B1383, 1 mile west of Saffron Walden
Open Garden: 11 am – 6 pm; Wednesday – Sunday, plus Bank Holiday Mondays; April to September
Admission Gardens: Adults £4; OAPs £3; Children £2
Facilities Parking; dogs permitted; loos; access for the disabled; plants for sale; shop; restaurant & picnic site
Features Landscape designed by Capability Brown; good architectural features; bedding-out; parterre; magnificent plane trees
English Heritage Grade I

Capability Brown landscaped the park (rather too many Canada geese) but the recent excitement at Audley End has been the rejuvenation of the formal garden behind the house. This dates from the 1830s and has 170 geometric flower beds crisply cut from the turf and planted with simple perennials for late summer effect. Work continues.

THE BETH CHATTO GARDENS
Elmstead Market, Colchester CO7 7DB
☎ 01206 822007   Fax 01206 825933
Owner Beth Chatto
Location 7 miles east of Colchester
Open 9 am – 5 pm; Monday – Saturday; March to October. 9 am – 4 pm; Monday – Friday; November to February. Closed on Bank Holidays
Admission Adults £3; Children free
Facilities Parking; loos; big nursery adjacent to the garden; drinks machine
Features Herbaceous plants; lake; colour contrasts; new gravel garden (1998)

Superb modern planting, particularly good for herbaceous plants, chosen for foliage as much as flower: all made by Beth Chatto since 1960. There are two types of planting here and it is the contrast between them which makes the garden. First, there are the parts on dry gravelly soil, where Mediterranean plants flourish; second, there are the water- and bog-gardens made on clay. But gardens are only one of Beth Chatto's gifts: her writings and nearby nursery have made her famous.

RHS GARDEN HYDE HALL
Rettendon, Chelmsford CM3 8ET
☎ 01245 400256   Fax 01245 401363
Owner Royal Horticultural Society
Location 6 miles south-east of Chelmsford, signposted from A130
Open 11 am – 6 pm (5 pm in September & October); Wednesday – Sunday and Bank Holidays; 24 March to 26 October
Admission Adults £3; Children (6 – 16) 70p; Groups (10+) £2.50
Facilities Parking; loos; access for the disabled; plants for sale; licensed restaurant serving hot & cold lunches, afternoon teas
Features Herbaceous plants; plantsman's garden; woodland garden; bearded irises; magnolias; South African bulbs; peonies; spring bulbs; ponds; heathers; roses of every kind
NCCPG National Collections *Malus*; *Viburnum*

Acquired by the RHS in 1993, this outstanding modern garden (started in 1955) was developed by Mr and Mrs R H M Robinson from a greenfield site. The Society has an extensive programme of refurbishment of the garden in hand. Both ponds have been re-modelled and accommodate an increased range of plants. The new Entrance Garden opened last year and further developments are planned for 1999 and 2000. The Society intends to build upon the strengths of the Robinsons' original design while creating opportunities to extend the range of garden styles and plantings represented.

SALING HALL
Great Saling, Braintree CM7 5DT

Owner Mr & Mrs Hugh Johnson
Location 2 miles north of the Saling Oak on A120
Open 2 pm – 5 pm; Wednesdays; May, June & July. Plus 2 pm – 6 pm on 30 May. Groups by appointment on weekdays
Admission Adults £2; Children free
Facilities Parking; loos; access for the disabled
Features Good collection of trees; herbaceous plants; lake; oriental features; plantsman's garden; new standing stone (1998)
English Heritage Grade II

A thinking man's garden, Saling also provokes thought in its visitors. The plantsmanship is impressive, particularly the choice and placing of trees and shrubs. Few modern gardens are conceived on such a scale, or mix classical and Japanese elements so smoothly. The moods, and the lessons, are endless.

WORTH A VISIT

COUNTY PARK NURSERY
384 Wingletye Lane, Hornchurch RM11 3BU
☎ *01708 445205. Open 9 am – 6 pm, Monday – Saturday; 10 am – 5 pm, Sundays; from March to October. Closed Wednesdays. Open in winter by appointment only. NCCPG National Collections: Coprosma; Parahebe. A small nursery for Antipodean plants, many of them grown from native seed. Look out for hebes and* Parahebe, *as well as clematis and* Coprosma.

CROWTHER NURSERIES AND LANDSCAPES
Ongar Road, Abridge RM4 1AA ☎ *01708 688581. Open 9 am – 5.30 pm, daily; closed over Christmas. Nursery and garden centre with a good general range, a garden design and a working garden which doubles as the BBC Essex Garden: Ken Crowther broadcasts for BBC Essex.*

EASTON LODGE
Great Dunmow CM26 2BB ☎ *01371 876979. Open 11 am – 6 pm; daily; mid-March to mid-October. And in February for snowdrops. Twenty acres of Peto gardens, abandoned in 1950 and lovingly restored since 1971. Good modern gardens, too.*

GLEN CHANTRY
Ishams Chase, Wickham Bishops CM8 3LG
☎ *01621 891342. Open 10 am – 4 pm; Friday & Saturday; 26 March to 15 October. Plus several Sundays & Mondays for charity. Three and a half acres of gardens, all planted since 1976 and much featured on TV and in magazines. Good plants: good plantings. The nursery specialises in unusual perennials and alpines.*

LANGTHORNS PLANTERY
Little Canfield, Dunmow CM6 1TD ☎ *01371 872611. Open 10 am – 5 pm; daily. Closed Christmas to New Year. This nursery offers hardy plants at reasonable prices in a very varied and interesting range. The herbaceous section is especially good, and there are interesting alpines, shrubs and trees here too. Langthorns Garden is open the last week of each month.*

OLIVERS
Olivers Lane, Colchester CO2 0HJ ☎ *01206 330575. Open 10 am – 6 pm; 25 April. And by appointment. Quite a modern garden, started in 1960 around two small lakes, with an eye-catching walk to one side leading down to a statue of Bacchus. Good plants and planting everywhere, from the parterres by the house to the woodland where roses and rhododendrons flourish. The main borders have just undergone a highly successful major re-design. This is the garden of enthusiastic and energetic owners: an inspiration.*

PARK FARM
Chatham Hall Lane, Great Waltham, Chelmsford CM3 1BZ ☎ *01245 360871. A fast-maturing garden, constantly developing and well maintained, with good colour combinations and a willingness to experiment. Derek Bracey is an architect: his wife Jill Cowley is an artist and plantswoman. Rooms are enclosed by hedges of box and yew for solidity and there is a winter garden of hellebores, snowdrops and aconites. Add in a Chinese garden, a garden of the Giants (outsize plants), a hot garden, an arid garden and a Russian garden, and you have the measure of Park Farm's variety. Good design and inventive details pull it together. If only it were open more often!*

RHODES & ROCKLIFFE
2 Nursery Road, Nazeing EN9 2JE ☎ *01992 463693. Open by appointment only. NCCPG National Collection: Begonia. The begonia specialists are renowned for their out-of-the-way species and hybrids.*

VOLPAIA
54 Woodlands Road, Hockley SS5 4PY ☎ *01702 203761. Open 2.30 pm – 6 pm; Thursdays & Sundays; 18 April to 27 June, or by appointment. This is the woodland garden of a keen plantsman who has now turned his hobby into a nursery. Rhododendrons, camellias and magnolias are the main shrubs, underplanted with erythroniums and woodland herbaceous plants, plus candelabra primulas in the boggy bits.*

GLOUCESTERSHIRE

BARNSLEY HOUSE
Barnsley, Cirencester GL7 5EE
☎ & Fax 01285 740561
Owner Charles Verey
Location On B4425 in Barnsley village
Open 10 am – 6 pm; Mondays, Wednesdays, Thursdays & Saturdays; all year except January. Groups by appointment only
Admission Adults £3.50; OAPs £2.50; Children free
Facilities Parking; loos; access for the disabled; plants for sale
Features Herbaceous plants; good architectural features; fruit of special interest; herbs; plantsman's garden; old roses; ornamental potager; Simon Verity's sculpture

Rosemary Verey's own garden: compact, modern, much copying and much copied. Barnsley is interesting at all seasons, but best when the little laburnum walk and the purple alliums underneath are in flower together. Influential.

BATSFORD ARBORETUM
The Estate Office, Moreton-in-Marsh GL56 9QF
☎ 01608 650722   Fax 01608 650290
Owner The Batsford Foundation (a Registered Charity)
Location Off A44 between Moreton-in-Marsh & Burton-on-the-Hill
Open 10 am – 5 pm; daily; 1 March to 6 November
Admission Adults £3.50; OAPs & children (5–16) £3
Facilities Parking; dogs permitted; loos; facilities for the disabled; plants for sale; shop; light meals & refreshments
Features Good collection of trees; fine conifers; oriental features; bluebells; maple glade; tallest *Betula platyphylla* (19m.) in the British Isles (and 12 other tree records)
English Heritage Grade I

Batsford has an openness which makes its hillside a joy to wander through, passing from one dendrological marvel to the next. Begun in the 1880s, the Arboretum also has several oriental curiosities brought from Japan by Lord Redesdale – a large bronze Buddha and an oriental rest-house for instance. Lord Dulverton has renewed the plantings over the last 30 years: both the collection and the amenities are improving all the time.

BERKELEY CASTLE
Berkeley GL13 9BQ
☎ 01453 810332
Owner R J G Berkeley
Location Off A38
Open 1 pm – 5 pm; Tuesday – Sunday; April & May. 11 am – 5 pm, Tuesday – Saturday; also 1 pm – 5 pm, Sundays; May to September. Plus Mondays in July & August. 1 pm – 5 pm; Sundays; October. 11 am – 5 pm; Bank Holiday Mondays
Admission Garden only: Adults £1.85; Children 90p
Facilities Parking; loos; plants for sale; shop at Castle Farm; light lunches & afternoon tea
Features Herbaceous plants; fine conifers; plantsman's garden; old roses
English Heritage Grade II*

The grim battlements of Berkeley Castle are host to an extensive collection of tender plants. On three terraces are *Cestrum*, *Cistus* and *Rosa banksiae* among hundreds of plant varieties introduced by the owner's grandfather, a nephew of Ellen Willmott. An Elizabethan-style bowling green and a water-lily pond fit well into the overall scheme.

BOURTON HOUSE
Bourton-on-the-Hill, Moreton-in-Marsh GL56 9AE
☎ 01386 700121   Fax 01386 701081
Owner Mr & Mrs Richard Paice
Location On A44, 1½ miles west of Moreton-in-Marsh
Open 12 noon – 5 pm; Thursdays & Fridays; 27 May to 22 October, plus 30 & 31 May, 29 & 30 August
Admission Adults £3; Children free
Facilities Parking; loos; plants for sale; self-service tea & coffee
Features Herbaceous plants; modern roses; old roses; good topiary; new parterre & gazebo in front of house (1998)
English Heritage Grade II

First laid out by Lanning Roper in the 1960s, but consistently improved by the present owners, the garden at Bourton House is both fashionable and a delight. A knot garden, a small potager, a raised pond, the topiary walk, white-painted trellis work, a croquet lawn, exuberant climbing roses and borders bulging with good colour schemes – purple-leaved *Prunus* with yellow roses, for instance.

DYRHAM PARK
Chippenham SN14 8ER
☎ 0117 937 2501
Owner The National Trust
Location On A46, 8 miles north of Bath
Open 11 am – 5.30 pm; Friday – Tuesday; 27 March to 31 October. Closed 2 & 3 July
Admission Park & garden: £2.50; Children £1.25
Facilities Parking; loos; access for the disabled; plants for sale; tea-room
Features Herbaceous plants; deer park; handsome orangery restored (1998)
English Heritage Grade II*

Fascinating for garden historians, who can study the Kip plan and trace the lines of the 17th-century formal garden which Humphry Repton turned into classic English parkland. Not a Mecca for the dedicated plantsman, but the impressive orangery (newly restored) is full of colour and scent.

GLOUCESTERSHIRE GARDENS

HIDCOTE MANOR GARDEN
Hidcote Bartrim, Chipping Campden GL55 6LR
☎ 01386 438333   Fax 01386 438817
Owner The National Trust
Location Signposted from B4632, Stratford/Broadway Road
Open 11 am – 7 pm (6 pm in October); daily except Tuesday & Friday; 27 March to 31 October. Plus Tuesdays in June
Admission Adults £5.60; Children £2.80; RHS members free
Facilities Parking; loos; facilities for the disabled; plants for sale; National Trust shop; licensed restaurant, coffee & lunches 11 am – 2 pm; teas 2.15 pm – 5 pm
Features Herbaceous plants; good architectural features; plantsman's garden; rock garden; modern roses; old roses; good topiary; woodland garden; plantings by Graham Thomas; tallest pink acacia *Robinia* × *ambigua* 'Decaisneana' (19m.) in the British Isles
English Heritage Grade I
NCCPG National Collection *Paeonia*

Probably the most influential 20th-century garden in the world – certainly the most important and most copied. Essential visiting for all garden owners.

HODGES BARN
Shipton Moyne, Tetbury GL8 8PR
☎ 01666 880202   Fax 01367 880373
Owner Mrs Charles Hornby
Location 3 miles south of Tetbury on Malmesbury Road from Shipton Moyne
Open 2 pm – 5 pm; Mondays, Tuesdays & Fridays; 1 April to 19 August. Plus 11 April & 6 June for NGS
Admission Adults £3; Children free
Facilities Parking; dogs permitted; loos; teas by arrangement
Features Herbaceous plants; plantsman's garden; climbing roses; old roses; good topiary; woodland garden; daffodils; bluebells; cyclamen

A big garden – six acres – and all intensively planted. Terraces, courtyards and gardens enclosed by stone walks or yew hedges are planted to give year-round colour. One has *rugosa* roses underplanted with hellebores, forget-me-nots and early bulbs for winter. Shrub roses and climbers are another Hornby passion. The woodland garden is almost an arboretum of ornamental trees – birches, maples, whitebeams and magnolias – underplanted with daffodils and primroses. Hodges Barn is a garden of great energy and loveliness.

HUNTS COURT
North Nibley, Dursley GL11 6DZ
☎ 01453 547440
Owner T K & M M Marshall
Location Signposted in centre of village
Open 9 am – 5 pm; Tuesday – Saturday & Bank Holiday Mondays in spring; all year, except August. Also 13, 20 & 27 June and 4 & 11 July for NGS
Admission Adults £2; OAPs £1.50; Children free

Facilities Parking; loos; access for the disabled; first-rate nursery attached; refreshments on NGS days
Features Plantsman's garden; climbing roses; modern roses; old roses

The best collection of old roses in the west of England, still expanding, and underplanted with geraniums and penstemons. Keith and Margaret Marshall say they have 'the collector's touch of madness': the result is charming, peaceful and educational.

KIFTSGATE COURT
Chipping Campden GL55 6LW
☎ & Fax 01386 438777
Owner Mr & Mrs J Chambers
Location 3 miles from Chipping Campden opposite Hidcote Manor
Open 2 pm – 6 pm; Wednesdays, Thursdays, Sundays & Bank Holiday Mondays; April, May, August & September; plus 12 noon – 6 pm on Wednesdays, Thursdays, Saturdays & Sundays in June & July
Admission Adults £3.50; Children £1
Facilities Parking; loos; plants for sale; tea-room in the house
Features Herbaceous plants; plantsman's garden; woodland garden; roses of every kind; colour plantings
English Heritage Grade II*

Famous for its roses, especially the eponymous *Rosa filipes* 'Kiftsgate', Kiftsgate is all about plants and the use of colour. The best example is the yellow border, where gold and orange are set off by occasional blues and purples. After some dull years, everything about Kiftsgate has revived again: new thinking, new plantings and new enthusiasm have more than restored its excellence.

LYDNEY PARK GARDENS
Lydney Park GL15 6BU
☎ 01594 842844   Fax 01594 842027
Owner Viscount Bledisloe
Location Off A48 between Lydney & Aylburton
Open 11 am – 6 pm; Sundays, Wednesdays & Bank Holidays; 4 April to 6 June. Plus daily 31 May to 5 June
Admission £2.50, but £1.50 on Wednesdays; Children free
Facilities Parking; dogs permitted; loos; plants for sale; some souvenirs for sale; light teas
Features Fine conifers; woodland garden; deer park; rhododendrons, azaleas & camellias

A remarkable collection of rhododendrons planted over the last 50 years is the backbone to this extensive woodland garden. And not just rhododendrons, but azaleas and camellias too, all carefully planted to create distinct effects from March to June. The numbers are still growing, and include plants grown from collected seed and hybrids from distinguished breeders, many as yet unnamed, while others have yet to flower. Lydney is now recognised as one of the best rhododendron gardens in England.

MISERDEN PARK
Miserden, Stroud GL6 7JA
☎ 01285 821303   Fax 01285 821530

Owner Major M T N H Wills
Location Signed from A417, or turn off B4070 between Stroud & Birdlip
Open 9.30 am – 4.30 pm; Tuesday – Thursday; April to September. Plus 28 March & 27 June for NGS and 4 April for Red Cross
Admission Adults £3
Facilities Parking; dogs permitted; loos; access for the disabled; excellent garden nursery by entrance
Features Herbaceous plants; fine conifers; planted by Gertrude Jekyll; good topiary; fritillaries; martagon lilies; roses, old & new; domed yew hedges; cyclamen; new water feature (1998)
English Heritage Grade II*

The Jacobean Cotswold house has wide views across the Golden Valley, while the open spacious gardens lie to the side. Most were laid out in the 1920s – a charming rose garden, the long yew walk and expansive herbaceous borders, but there is also an older arboretum and an Edwardian shrubbery. Very peaceful.

OWLPEN MANOR
Uley, Dursley GL11 5BZ
☎ 01453 860261   Fax 01453 860819

Owner Nicholas Mander
Location Off B4066 near Uley
Open 2 pm – 5 pm; Tuesday – Sunday & Bank Holiday Mondays; April to October
Admission Adults £3.25; Children £1
Facilities Parking; loos; plants, guidebooks & postcards for sale; licensed restaurant (noon – 5 pm)
Features Old roses; good topiary; standard gooseberries
English Heritage Grade II

Dreamy Cotswold manor house whose loveliness depends upon its site, but there is a small terraced garden with box parterres and overgrown topiary yews and plantings of roses and herbs, most of them added since 1980 by the present owners. The aim is to suggest an earlier garden 're-ordered conservatively' in about 1700. Owlpen is perhaps not worth a special journey by keen plantsmen, but the restaurant, the setting and the house all add up to a good place for an outing.

PAINSWICK ROCOCO GARDEN
Painswick, Stroud GL6 6TH
☎ 01452 813204

Owner Painswick Rococo Garden Trust
Location Outside Painswick on B4073
Open 11 am – 5 pm; Wednesday – Sunday; 13 January to 30 November. Daily in July & August
Admission Adults £3; OAPs £2.70; Children £1.60
Facilities Parking; dogs permitted; loos; plants for sale; gift shop; licensed restaurant, coffee, teas & light snacks
Features Good architectural features; garden sculpture; woodland garden; snowdrop wood; new plant nursery; new maze (planted 1998)

English Heritage Grade II*
Friends The Painswick Rococo Gardens Trust was established in 1988 to preserve the gardens in perpetuity. Details from Lord Dickinson

Only ten years of restoration work lie behind the unique rococo garden at Painswick which has re-emerged from back-to-nature woodland. A white Venetian gothic exedra, a Doric seat, the plunge pool, an octagonal pigeon house, a gothic gazebo called the Eagle House, a bowling green, the fish pond and a gothic alcove have all been reconstructed in their original positions thanks to the efforts of Lord Dickinson and the Painswick Rococo Garden Trust. A remarkable garden and brilliant theatrical achievement.

THE PRIORY
Kemerton GL20 7JN
☎ 01386 725258

Owner The Hon Mrs Healing
Location In Kemerton village
Open 2 pm – 6 pm; Thursdays; May to September. Plus 30 May, 20 June, 11 July, 1 & 29 August & 12 September
Admission £1.50 in May & June, then £2
Facilities Parking; dogs permitted; loos; access for the disabled; plants for sale; teas on open Sundays
Features Herbaceous plants; plantsman's garden; old roses; particularly good in July–August; new knot garden (1998)

The Priory is a late-summer comet, brilliant in August and September when annuals and tender plants supplement the perennial colour planting. The late Peter Healing spent 50 years perfecting his colour gradings. The results are worth a long journey to see and to study: the crimson border is the best there has ever been.

RODMARTON MANOR
Rodmarton, Cirencester GL7 6PF
☎ 01285 841253

Owner Simon Biddulph
Location Off A433 between Cirencester & Tetbury
Open 2 pm – 5 pm; Wednesdays & Saturdays; 12 May to 28 August
Admission Adults £2.50; Children free
Facilities Parking; loos; access for the disabled
Features Herbaceous plants; fine conifers; plantsman's garden; modern roses; old roses; good topiary; woodland garden; much renovation and replanting, including herbaceous borders, white border & wild garden (1998)
English Heritage Grade II*

A splendid arts and crafts garden, with a strong design and exuberant planting. Simon Biddulph says there are 18 different areas within the garden, from the trough garden for alpine plants to the famous double herbaceous borders, now entirely renovated, which lead to a Cotswold summerhouse. Highly original – contemporary, but made without any contact with Hidcote. Very photogenic.

SEZINCOTE
Moreton-in-Marsh GL56 9AW
Owner Mr & Mrs D Peake
Location On A44 to Evesham, 1½ miles out of Moreton-in-Marsh
Open 2 pm – 6 pm (or dusk, if earlier); Thursdays, Fridays & Bank Holiday Mondays; January to November
Admission Adults £3; Children £1
Facilities Parking; loos
Features Good collection of trees; good architectural features; lake; oriental features; landscape designed by Humphry Repton; garden sculpture; subtropical plants; woodland garden; plantings by Graham Thomas; tallest maidenhair tree *Ginkgo biloba* (26m.) in the British Isles (and five other record trees)
English Heritage Grade I

The house was the model for Brighton Pavilion, and seems inseparable from the cruciform Moghul garden that sets off its Indian façade so well: yet this brilliant formal garden was designed as recently as 1965. On the other side are sumptuous borders planted by Graham Thomas and a luscious water garden of candelabra primulas and astilbes around the Temple to Surya, the Snake Bridge and Brahmin bulls. Humphry Repton had a hand in the original landscape, but the modern gardens are far more satisfying.

SNOWSHILL MANOR
Broadway WR12 7JU
☎ & Fax 01386 852410
Owner The National Trust
Location In Snowshill village
Open 1 pm – 5 pm; daily except Tuesday; April to October, except Good Friday
Admission Gardens only: £2.50 (1998 price)
Facilities Parking; loos; National Trust shop; refreshments
Features Herbaceous plants; good architectural features; old roses
English Heritage Grade II

Praised for its changes of levels and collection of curious artefacts – an armillary sphere and a gilt figure of St George and the Dragon, for instance. Snowshill is as curious as its maker, Charles Wade, and the spooky bric-a-brac which fills his house, but many visitors find it 'charming' or 'interesting'. Snowshill was the National Trust's first all-organic garden.

SUDELEY CASTLE & GARDENS
Winchcombe GL54 5JD
☎ 01242 602308   Fax 01242 602959
Owner Lady Ashcombe
Location 8 miles north-east of Cheltenham B4632
Open 10.30 am – 5.30 pm (4.30 pm in March); daily; 6 March to 31 October
Admission Adults £4.50; OAPs £3.50; Children £2.25
Facilities Parking; loos; plants for sale; good shop, rather upmarket; restaurant & tea-rooms
Features Herbaceous plants; fine conifers; good architectural features; herbs; modern roses; old roses;

good topiary; ruins of banqueting hall, now a pretty garden; new 'Victorian' kitchen garden (all organic); adventure playground
English Heritage Grade II*

This large commercially run garden has features by many top garden designers: Jane Fearnley-Whittingstall did the roses and Rosemary Verey planted some borders. There are fine old trees, magnificent Victorian topiary (mounds of green and gold yew) and a raised walk around the pleasure gardens that may be Elizabethan in origin. Not our favourite garden, but popular and successful.

UNIVERSITY OF BRISTOL BOTANIC GARDEN
Bracken Hill, North Road, Leigh Woods, Bristol BS8 3PF
☎ 0117 973 3682   Fax 0117 973 3682
Owner University of Bristol
Location Take M5 Jct 19 towards Clifton, left into North Road before suspension bridge
Open 9 am – 5 pm; Monday – Friday; all year except public holidays
Admission Free, but open on 10 June & 5 September from 10 am for NGS (Adults £1; Children 50p)
Facilities Parking; loos; teas & plants for sale on NGS days
Features Good collection of trees; ecological interest; glasshouses; plantsman's garden; rock garden; cistus; hebes; sempervivums; peonies; aeoniums; salvias
Friends £15. Good programme and privileges (e.g. seed list). Details from Membership Secretary c/o address above

An educational and accessible garden that bridges the gap between botany and horticulture. The unusual climatic conditions in its position above the Avon gorge have made possible some fine new plantings of South African and New Zealand plants. And of course there is the rare endemic *Sorbus bristoliensis*.

WESTBURY COURT
Westbury-on-Severn GL14 1PD
☎ 01452 760461
Owner The National Trust
Location 9 miles south-west of Gloucester on A48
Open 11 am – 6 pm, Wednesday – Sunday & Bank Holiday Mondays; 27 March to 31 October. Closed Good Friday
Admission Adults £2.70; Children £1.35
Facilities Parking; loos; facilities for the disabled; picnic area
Features Herbaceous plants; fruit of special interest; herbs; old roses; garden sculpture; good topiary; biggest holm oak *Quercus ilex* in the British Isles; new restoration of pool & fountain as shown by Kip in 1712
English Heritage Grade II*

Restored over the last 20 years to become the best example of a 17th-century Dutch garden in England. A pretty pavilion, tall and slender, looks down along a long tank of water. On the walls are old apple and pear varieties. Parterres, fine modern topiary and a T-shaped tank with a statue of Neptune in the middle make up the rest of the garden, with an opulent rose garden (old varieties only) underplanted with pinks, tulips and herbs. Immaculately maintained.

Westonbirt Arboretum
Westonbirt, Tetbury GL8 8QS
☎ 01666 880220   Fax 01666 880559
Owner Forestry Commission
Location 3 miles south of Tetbury on A433
Open 10 am – 8 pm (or dusk if earlier); daily; all year. Visitor centre open 10 am – 5 pm; daily; March to December
Admission Adults £4; OAPs £3; Children £1; RHS members free
Facilities Parking; dogs permitted; loos; facilities for the disabled; plants for sale; gift shop; cafeteria
Features 101 species of record-breaking trees, including 25 *Acer* and 21 *Sorbus*
English Heritage Grade I
NCCPG National Collections *Acer*; *Salix*

The finest and largest arboretum in the British Isles: 500 acres, 17 miles of paths, 4,000 species, 18,000 trees. The maple glade is famous, and so are the bluebells in the part known as Silk Wood. Brilliantly managed by the Forestry Commission, whose Visitor Centre is a marvel of helpfulness. Brightest perhaps in spring and autumn, but the best place we know for a long winter walk.

WORTH A VISIT

Abbotswood
Stow-on-the-Wold, Cheltenham GL54 1LE
☎ *01451 830173.   Open 1.30 pm – 6 pm; for NGS.* One of the most interesting gardens in the Cotswolds. Handsome formal gardens in front of the house: very Lutyens, very photogenic. A magnificent rock garden with a stream (artificially pumped, but you would never know) which meanders through alpine meadows, bogs and moraines, past dwarf azaleas, primulas, lysichitons, heaths and heathers until it disappears again. There is also a small arboretum, rather overgrown, but with some unusual forms, fascinating to browse around.

Cowley Manor
Cowley, Cheltenham GL53 9NL ☎ *01242 870540. Open 10 am – 6 pm; Tuesday – Thursday, Saturdays, Sundays & Bank Holidays; 1 May to 31 October.* A new garden which seeks to pioneer the modern principles of planting worked out in Germany. It uses broad masses of naturalistic plantings in ecological mixes which enable a balance to be maintained between cultivated and wild plants. It is intended to be bold, striking, effective and labour-saving: watch it develop and decide on its value for yourself.

The Ernest Wilson Memorial Garden
High Street, Chipping Campden GL55 6AF
☎ *01386 840764.   Open Dawn to dusk; daily; all year.* A collection of plants all introduced by Ernest H Wilson,

the greatest of European plant-hunters in China: Chipping Campden was his birthplace. *Acer griseum, Clematis montana var. rubens* and the pocket-handkerchief tree *Davidia involucrata* are among his best-known introductions: all are represented here.

Frampton Court
Frampton-on-Severn GL2 7EU ☎ *01452 740698. Open By appointment all year.* Beautiful and mysterious garden, little changed since 1750. The Dutch water garden – a long rectangular pool – reflects the orangery of Strawberry Hill Gothic design. But do also ask to see the collection of botanical watercolours known as the *Frampton Flora*.

Goldney Hall
Lower Clifton Hill, Clifton, Bristol BS8 1BH
☎ *0117 926 5698.   Open 2 pm – 6 pm; 25 April & 9 May.* A Bristol merchant's extravagance, nearly 300 years ago. Ten acres in the middle of the city, with an elegant orangery, a gothic folly tower and the gorgeous Goldney Grotto, which sparkles with crystalline rocks among the shells and follies.

The Old Manor
Twyning GL20 6DB ☎ *01684 293516.   Open By appointment on weekdays & for the NGS.* This alpine nursery, in a splendid plantsman's garden, is slowly winding down. Visit it this year, and give thanks for the thousands of good plants which found their way into our gardens from it over the last 30 years.

Stancombe Park
Dursley GL11 6AU ☎ *01453 542815.   Open Groups by appointment.* Stancombe has everything: a handsome house above a wooded valley, a flower garden of wondrous prettiness, and a gothic horror of an historic Folly Garden at the valley bottom. Start at the top. Peter Coates, Lanning Roper and Nadia Jennett all worked on the rose gardens and mixed borders by the house: there is more to learn about good modern design and planting here than any garden in Gloucestershire. Then wander down the valley where the path narrows and the incline steepens to a ferny tunnel, and start the circuit of the follies, best described as an open-air ghost train journey without the ghosts. Highly recommended.

Stanway House
Stanway, Cheltenham GL54 5PQ ☎ *01386 584469. Open 2 pm – 5 pm; Tuesdays & Thursdays; August & September. And by appointment.* The important water gardens are undergoing restoration. A pyramidal folly dominates the hillside behind the house. Repairs have begun on the 170-metre cascade which runs down to a long still tank known as the Canal. Worth another visit.

Stowell Park
Northleach GL54 3LE ☎ *01285 720308.   Open 2 pm – 5 pm; 16 May & 27 June.* A historic landscape in a magnificent position, with a pleasure garden and walled garden, stylishly replanted with advice from Rosemary Verey of nearby Barnsley.

GREATER MANCHESTER

DUNHAM MASSEY
Altrincham WA14 4SJ
☎ 0161 941 1025   Fax 0161 946 9291
Owner The National Trust
Location 3 miles south-west of Altrincham off A56, well signposted (Dunham Massey Hall and Park)
Open 11 am – 5 pm (4 pm in October); daily; 27 March to 31 October
Admission Gardens only: Adults £3; Children £1.50
Facilities Parking; loos; facilities for the disabled; plants for sale; garden shop; large restaurant
Features Herbaceous plants; good architectural features; good topiary; interesting for children; hydrangeas; skimmias; Edwardian parterre; current holder of Sandford Award
English Heritage Grade II*

Dunham Massey's 250 acres include an ancient deer park, a medieval moat made into a lake in the 18th century, an Elizabethan mount, an 18th-century orangery and some early landscape avenues. All remain as features of the grounds, but the National Trust has decided to major on its even more interesting Victorian relics – evergreen shrubberies, ferns and colourful bedding-out schemes. Even that does not preclude the Trust from planting the most modern forms, such as the hybrids of *Rhododendron yakushimanum* and latest *occidentale* hybrid azaleas. The result is a potent cross-section of historical and modern styles with a solid core of Victorian excellence, while the standard of maintenance is perhaps the highest in any National Trust garden.

FLETCHER MOSS BOTANICAL GARDENS
Mill Gate Lane, Didsbury M20 8SD
☎ 0161 434 1877
Owner Manchester City Council
Open 8 am (9 am at weekends & Bank Holidays) to dusk; daily; all year. Orchid house open 8 am – 4 pm, weekdays only
Admission Free
Facilities Parking; dogs permitted; loos; facilities for the disabled; plants for sale; cafeteria
Features Fine conifers; lake; rock garden; bulbs; heathers; rhododendrons; orchid house

A model municipal botanic garden, beautifully maintained but free to the public. There are good collections of small conifers, maples and aquatics. Excellent autumn colour: almost as good in spring.

HAMPSHIRE

BRAMDEAN HOUSE
Bramdean, Alresford SO24 0JU
☎ 01962 771214   Fax 01962 771095
Owner Mr & Mrs H Wakefield
Location On A272 between Winchester & Petersfield
Open 2 pm – 5 pm; 4 & 5 April, 9 May, 13 June, 11 July, 8 August, 12 September and by appointment
Admission Adults £2.50; Children free
Facilities Parking; loos; plants for sale; refreshments
Features Herbaceous plants; daffodils; fruit of special interest; climbing roses; old roses; good topiary; handsome cedars; peonies; winter aconites; flowering cherries
English Heritage Grade II

Beautifully designed by the late Mrs Feilden and immaculately maintained by her daughter, the gardens at Bramdean are much admired, and rightly so. Two wide herbaceous borders lead up from the terrace behind the house, against a backdrop of mature beeches and cedars. At the end of the central axis, steps lead to a walled kitchen garden whose central bed is planted with 'Catillac' pears, perennials and annuals. The vista runs yet further, through an orchard to a gazebo some 300 yards from the house. The views in both directions are stunning.

BROADLANDS
Romsey
☎ 01794 517888   Fax 01794 518884
Owner Lord & Lady Romsey
Location On Romsey by-pass by town centre roundabout
Open 12 noon – 5.30 pm (last admissions 4 pm); daily; 14 June to 3 September
Admission Adults £5.50; OAPs £4.70; Children (12–16) £3.85
Facilities Parking; loos; facilities for the disabled; plants for sale; gift shop; tea-rooms & picnic area by river
Features Good collection of trees; herbaceous plants; landscape designed by Capability Brown; lake; woodland garden; tallest swamp cypress *Taxodium distichum* (36m.) in the British Isles
English Heritage Grade II*

Classic Capability Brown landscape, handsome old trees and an open park which runs slowly down to a lake and the River Test.

EXBURY GARDENS
Exbury, Southampton SO4 1AZ
☎ 01703 891203   Fax 01703 243350
Owner Edmund de Rothschild
Location 3 miles south of Beaulieu
Open 10 am – 5.30 pm (or dusk if earlier); daily; 28 February to 1 November
Admission Adults £3.50; OAPs £3; Children £2.50. But Adults £5; OAPs £4.50; Children £4 in high season (approximately mid-March to mid-June)

Facilities Parking; dogs permitted; loos; facilities for the disabled; plants for sale; gift shop; artist's studio; hot & cold lunches, cream teas; new tea-room
Features Herbaceous plants; lake; landscape designed by Humphry Repton; rock garden; old roses; woodland garden; candelabra primulas; rare trees; new herbaceous & grasses garden (1998); tallest shagbark hickory *Carya ovata* (21m.) in the British Isles (and five other tree records)
English Heritage Grade II*

Rhododendrons, rhododendrons, rhododendrons: over one million of them in 200 acres of natural woodland. More than 40 have won awards from the Royal Horticultural Society. But there are magnolias, camellias and rare trees too, many grown from the original seed introduced by famous plant-collectors. A place of wonder in May.

FURZEY GARDENS
Minstead, Lyndhurst SO4 7GL
☎ 01703 812464   Fax 01703 812297

Owner Furzey Gardens Charitable Trust
Location Off A31 or A337 to Minstead
Open 10 am – 5 pm (dusk in winter); daily except 25 & 26 December
Admission March – October: Adults £3; OAPs £2.50; Children £1.50. November – February: Adults £1.50; OAPs £1; Children 50p
Facilities Parking; loos; plants for sale; small shop
Features Bluebells; bog garden; camellias; fine conifers; rhododendrons and azaleas; interesting for children; naturalised dieramas; heathers; spring bulbs; heather garden & fern garden replanted & extended (1997)
Friends No Friends organisation but the gardens are owned by a charitable trust

Furzey demonstrates how woodland garden effects can be created in quite small areas. Parts are a maze of narrow curving paths running between hedges of Kurume azaleas, unforgettable in April–May, but the late-summer flowering of eucryphias runs them close and the autumn colours of nyssas, parrotias and enkianthus are worth a visit in October.

HIGHCLERE CASTLE
Highclere, Newbury RG15 9RN
☎ 01635 253210   Fax 01635 810193

Owner The Earl of Carnarvon
Location South of Newbury off A34
Open 11 am – 5 pm; Tuesday – Sunday & Bank Holiday Mondays; 1 July to 5 September
Admission Gardens only: Adults £3; Children £1.50
Facilities Parking; loos; facilities for the disabled; plants for sale; shop; good restaurant
Features Herbaceous plants; landscape designed by Capability Brown; good architectural features; rhododendrons and azaleas; particularly good in July–August; good collection of cedars; long avenues
English Heritage Grade I
NCCPG National Collection *Rhododendron*

A major historic garden – when Capability Brown landscaped it in the 1770s he left intact the avenues and follies of the early 18th century, but the park is dominated now by hundreds of huge cedars. Salvin's imposing house has 365 windows. Jim Russell advised on the planting in the walled garden, though the 'Secret Garden' is not among his best.

HINTON AMPNER HOUSE
Bramdean, Alresford SO24 0LA
☎ & Fax 01962 771305

Owner The National Trust
Location On A272 1 mile west of Bramdean
Open 1.30 pm – 5.30 pm; Tuesdays, Wednesdays, Saturdays, Sundays & Bank Holiday Mondays; 21 & 28 March, then 3 April to 30 September
Admission Adults £3.20; Children £1.60
Facilities Parking; loos; facilities for the disabled; teas & home-made cakes
Features Garden sculpture; subtropical plants; good topiary; daffodils; yew trees
English Heritage Grade II

The gardens at Hinton Ampner were laid out by the scholarly Ralph Dutton in the middle of this century with great regard to line, landscape and historical propriety. Statues, buildings, axes and views have been restored with exquisite judgement to lead you subtly along the exact route that Dutton intended. Good plantings, too.

HOUGHTON LODGE GARDEN & HYDROPONICUM
Houghton, Stockbridge SO20 6LQ
☎ & Fax 01264 810177
Website www.hydroponicum.co.uk

Owner Martin Busk
Location Off A30 at Stockbridge
Open 2 pm – 5 pm; Mondays, Tuesdays, Thursdays & Fridays. 10 am – 5 pm; Saturdays, Sundays & Bank Holidays. March to September. The hydroponicum may remain open after September
Admission £3 for garden; £2 for hydroponicum. Groups at special rates
Facilities Parking; dogs permitted; loos; facilities for the disabled; plants for sale; hydroponics shop; refreshments
Features Good architectural features; glasshouses; good topiary; daffodils; cyclamen; new herb garden (1996)
English Heritage Grade II*

A lovely Gothic *cottage ornée* on a ledge above the River Test, with long spacious views down the river and across the watermeadows. Part of the film *Wilde* was shot here. Houghton also boasts the leading hydroponic greenhouse in England, where plants are grown in nutrient-rich solutions instead of soil – salad vegetables and some 50 different herbs, as well as bougainvillaeas and bananas.

LONGSTOCK WATER GARDENS
Longstock, Stockbridge SO20 6EH
☎ 01264 810894   Fax 01264 810439

HAMPSHIRE   GARDENS   173

Owner John Lewis Partnership
Location 1½ miles north-east of Longstock Village
Open 2 pm – 5 pm; 1st & 3rd Sunday in the month; April to September
Admission Adults £3; Children 50p
Facilities Parking; loos; facilities for the disabled; plants for sale
Features Herbaceous plants; ecological interest; lake; plantsman's garden; woodland garden; interesting for children
NCCPG National Collection *Buddleja*

Quite the most extraordinary and beautiful water garden in England, a little Venice where dozens of islands and all-but-islands are linked by small bridges and intensely planted with water-loving plants. Drifts of astilbes, primulas, kingcups, hemerocallis, musks, water irises and lilies. The ground is so soft that the islands seem to float, and a remarkable accumulation of peat has allowed such calcifuge plants as *Meconopsis betonicifolia* and *Cardiocrinum giganteum* to flourish in this chalky valley. But there is also a walled garden with an archway of rambling roses, herbaceous borders and a six-acre arboretum.

LONGTHATCH
Lippen Lane, Warnford, Southampton SO32 3LE
☎ 01730 829285

Owner Peter & Vera Short
Location 1 mile south of West Meon on A32, turn right by George & Falcon, & right again, 400m on right
Open 10 am – 5 pm; Wednesdays; 3 March to 25 August. And 2 pm – 5 pm; 7, 14 & 21 March; 18 April, 30 & 31 May, 27 June, 22 August for NGS
Admission Adults £2; Children free
Facilities Parking; loos; access for the disabled; plants for sale; tea & coffee; cake on NGS days
Features Alpines; plantsman's garden; new woodland area; damp-loving plants
NCCPG National Collection *Helleborus*

Three acres of plantsmanship, this garden had been developed by the Shorts over many years. It is perhaps best in spring when the garden is busy with hellebores, pulmonarias, primulas and bog plants.

MOTTISFONT ABBEY
Romsey SO51 0LJ
☎ 01794 340757   Fax 01794 341492

Owner The National Trust
Location 4 miles north-west of Romsey
Open 12 noon – 6 pm; Saturday – Wednesday; 27 March to 31 October. Plus 11 am – 8.30 pm; daily; 12 to 27 June
Admission £4.50 (but £5 in rose season)
Facilities Parking; loos; facilities for the disabled; plants for sale; good shop selling books and National Trust smellies; light refreshments
Features Herbaceous plants; plantsman's garden; climbing roses; old roses; plantings by Graham Thomas;

guided walks and 'rose clinics' in season; tallest *Paulownia tomentosa* (13m.) in the British Isles
English Heritage Grade II
NCCPG National Collections *Platanus*; *Rosa*

The park and gardens near the house are stately: Russell Page, Geoffrey Jellicoe and Norah Lindsay all worked here. But it is the old rose collection in the walled garden which has made Mottisfont's name. It is Graham Thomas's best-known work, a collection of all the roses he has discovered, assembled, preserved and made popular through his writings. Surely the loveliest rose garden in Britain, but expect some temporary slippage as it is thoroughly overhauled for the first time since the walled garden was planted in 1972.

SIR HAROLD HILLIER GARDENS & ARBORETUM
Jermyns Lane, Ampfield, Romsey SO51 0QA
☎ 01794 368787   Fax 01794 368027

Owner Hampshire County Council
Location Signposted from A31 & A3057
Open 10.30 am – 6 pm (5 pm, or dusk if earlier, from November to March); every day except Bank & Public Holidays over Christmas. Open at 9.30 at weekends at Bank Holidays
Admission April to October: Adults £4.25; OAPs £3.75; Children £1. November to March: Adults £3.25; OAPs £2.75; Children £1; RHS members free
Facilities Parking; loos; facilities for the disabled; plants for sale; light refreshments from Easter to end of October, & most weekends
Features Good collection of trees; herbaceous plants; fine conifers; plantsman's garden; old roses; interesting for children; particularly good in July–August; particularly interesting in winter; new winter garden (1998); Gurkha memorial garden (1997); 1993 winner of Sandford Award; 51 record trees, including 11 *Sorbus*
NCCPG National Collections *Carpinus*; *Cornus*; *Corylus*; *Cotoneaster*; *Hamamelis*; *Ligustrum*; *Lithocarpus*; *Photinia*; *Pinus*; *Quercus*; 'Hillier' plants
Friends Details of the Friends scheme are available from the Curator: benefits include trips to other gardens, coffee mornings and a quarterly newsletter

Quite the most important modern arboretum in the UK, for the number of its taxa – over 11,000 in 160 acres and totalling 40,000 plants. Every part of the garden is an education and a pleasure whatever the season or weather. Exemplary labelling and helpful guidebooks available. Hillier's nursery shares a car park with the arboretum. Guided walks are given at 2 pm on the first Sunday in each month, and on Wednesdays in May to October.

SPINNERS
Boldre, Lymington SO4 5QE
☎ 01590 673347

Owner Diana & Peter Chappell
Location Signed off A337 between Brockenhurst & Lymington

Open 10 am – 5 pm; Tuesday – Saturday; all year. Other days by appointment
Admission £1.50 from 1 April to 14 September; free at other times
Facilities Parking; loos; plants for sale
Features Good collection of trees; plantsman's garden; woodland garden; rhododendrons; woodland plants; rarities and novelties; new peat beds & bog garden; biggest *Eucalyptus perriniana* in the British Isles

Only two acres, but what a garden! Spinners is a plantsman's paradise, where the enthusiast can spend many happy hours browsing at any time of the year. Everything is well labelled and Peter Chappell's nursery sells an extraordinary range of good plants: you always come away with a bootful of novelties.

STRATFIELD SAYE HOUSE
Stratfield Saye, Basingstoke RG7 2BT
☎ 01256 882882   Fax 01256 882345
Owner The Duke of Wellington
Location 1 mile west of A33 between Reading and Basingstoke
Open 11.30 am – 6 pm (last admissions 4 pm); daily, except Friday; June to August. Plus Saturdays, Sundays & Bank Holiday Mondays in May & September
Admission Garden only: £2
Facilities Parking; dogs permitted; loos; facilities for the disabled; plants for sale; gift shop; light refreshments
Features Herbaceous plants; fine conifers; lake; modern roses; camellia house in walled garden; American garden; tallest Hungarian oak *Quercus frainetto* (33m.) in the British Isles
English Heritage Grade II

Not a great garden, but there are some fine features: a huge kitchen garden, a large and cheerful rose garden, rhododendrons in the park, and magnificent trees, including wellingtonias, named after the Iron Duke.

WEST GREEN HOUSE
Hartley Wintney, Basingstoke RG27 8JB
☎ 01252 844611
Owner Marylyn Abbott
Location In West Green village
Open 10.30 am – 3.30 pm; Thursday – Sunday & Bank Holiday Monday; 20 May to 16 August. Also for the National Trust
Admission £3
Facilities Parking
Features Good architectural features; woodland garden; parterres, exuberant plantings

Marylyn Abbott is restoring and remaking the garden at West Green with all the energy she showed in the garden she made in her native Australia. Formality, variety, invention and sheer beauty are here in abundance. The potager is especially stylish. Visit it, if you can, and see one of the greatest modern gardens come to life again.

WORTH A VISIT

BLACKTHORN NURSERY
Kilmeston, Alresford SO24 0NL ☎ *01962 771796. Open 9 am – 5 pm, Friday and Saturday only, March to June. Hellebore breeders and specialists with several strains called Blackthorn. The most striking are semi-doubles called Party Dress Group. Look out for new and unusual* Epimedium *species and cultivars.*

BRANDY MOUNT HOUSE
East Street, Alresford SO24 9EG ☎ *01962 732189. Open 11 am – 4 pm; 6, 7 & 10 February. 2 pm – 5 pm; 14 March, 11 April, 9 May, 26 June, and by appointment. NCCPG National Collections:* Daphne; Galanthus. *Essentially a plantsman's garden, but a plantsman who is also a distinguished plant collector and exhibitor of alpine plants. The garden is fascinating, immaculately maintained, and linked to a thriving small nursery which has propagated* Galanthus *by twin-scaling.*

FAIRFIELD HOUSE
Hambledon, Waterlooville PO7 4RY ☎ *01705 632431. Open 2 pm – 6 pm; 4 April, 16 May, 27 June, and by appointment. Fairfield is one of the best private rose gardens in England. Old roses and climbers were the late Peter Wake's main interest and he grew them unusually well. The shrubs are trained up a cat's cradle of string drawn between five wooden posts. The results make you gasp – 'Charles de Mills' 10 feet high.*

FAMILY TREES
Botley SO3 2EA ☎ *01329 834812. Open 9.30 am – 12.30 pm; Wednesday and Saturday; mid-October to mid-April. Many varieties of organically grown dessert apples, pears, plums and peaches. They are available field-grown as bushes or trained.*

HARDY'S COTTAGE GARDEN PLANTS
Priory Lane, Freefolk, Whitchurch RG28 7NT ☎ *01256 896533. Open 10 am – 5 pm; daily; March to October. This family-run nursery has a large range of pretty cottage-garden perennials and flowering shrubs. Watch out for their attractive exhibits at shows.*

THE LOYALTY GARDEN
Basing House Ruins, Redbridge Lane, Basing, Basingstoke RG24 7HB ☎ *01256 467294. A charming modern garden in the ruins of Old Basing castle: parterres of sage, santolina and box, and the motto of the Paulet family* Aymez Loyautei, *from which it takes its name.*

THE MANOR HOUSE, UPTON GREY
Upton Grey, Basingstoke RG25 2RD ☎ *01256 862827. Ros Wallinger has restored this Jekyll garden since 1984 using the original planting plans (now at Berkeley University, California). She has gone to great pains to recreate it exactly in all its Edwardian loveliness. Some of the roses were extinct here until re-introduced from private gardens in France and Italy after years of searching. The rich herbaceous borders drift from cool blues, white and pinks at either end to hot reds, oranges and yellows in the*

middle. There is no better place to study Gertrude Jekyll's plantings, but what makes it so special is that it is a 'young' garden again.

PETERSFIELD PHYSIC GARDEN
c/o 32 College Street, Petersfield GU31 4AF
☎ 01730 268583. Open Dawn to dusk; daily except 25 December. A small town garden, surrounded by walls and planted with the fruit trees, roses, herbs and other plants that were known in the 17th century. An initiative of that most energetic and successful organisation, the Hampshire Gardens Trust.

SOUTHVIEW NURSERIES
Chequers Lane, Eversley Cross, Hook RG27 0NT
☎ 0118 973 2206. Open 9 am – 4.30 pm; Thursday – Saturday; March – October. NCCPG National Collection: Dianthus old cultivars. The garden opens for the NGS, but the nursery is worth knowing all summer. Hardy plants are its speciality, and there is a splendid selection of old pinks, chosen from the collection in the garden.

STEVEN BAILEY LTD
Silver Street, Sway, Lymington SO41 6ZA
☎ 01590 682227. Open 9 am – 1 pm & 2 pm – 4 pm; Monday – Friday; all year, plus Saturdays from March to June. Also 10 am – 4 pm, Sundays, March to June only. Long-established specialists for carnations, pinks and alstroemerias. Active on the show circuit, so look out for them.

TUDOR HOUSE GARDEN
Bugle Street, Southampton SO14 2AD ☎ 01703 635904. Open 10 am – 12 noon and 1 pm – 5 pm (4 pm on Saturdays), Tuesday – Saturday; 2 pm – 5 pm, Sundays. All year. Sylvia Landsberg's unique reconstruction of a Tudor garden with knot garden, fountain, secret garden and contemporary plantings of herbs and flowering plants all crammed into a tiny area. Some call it a pastiche, others a living dictionary of Tudor garden language.

WHITE WINDOWS
Longparish, Andover SP11 6PB ☎ 01264 720222. Open 2 pm – 6 pm; by appointment from March to September on Wednesdays. And for NGS. NCCPG National Collection: Helleborus. One of the best small modern plantsman's gardens on chalk, remarkable for the way Jane Sterndale-Bennett arranges her material. Layer upon layer, White Windows bulges with good plants. Leaves and stems are as important as flowers, especially in the combinations and contrasts of colour – gold and yellow, blue and silver, and crimsons, pinks and purples. Much use is made of evergreens and variegated plants. Perhaps the most luxuriant chalk garden in Hampshire and all made since 1979.

HEREFORD & WORCESTER

ABBEY DORE COURT GARDEN
Abbey Dore, Hereford HR2 0AD
☎ 01981 240419   Fax 01981 240279
Owner Mrs Charis Ward
Location 3 miles west of A465, midway between Hereford & Abergavenny
Open 11 am – 6 pm; daily except Wednesdays; 6 March to 17 October
Admission Adults £2.50; Children 50p
Facilities Parking; loos; facilities for the disabled; county gift gallery, teddy bears loft, good nursery; licensed restaurant, coffee, lunch & tea; all food home-made
Features Herbaceous plants; plantsman's garden; rock garden; handsome wellingtonias; ferns; hellebores

Plantsman's garden on a damp cold site, with fine borders leading down to the ferny river walk. Mrs Ward says it has 'stopped getting any bigger', but the garden grows, changes and improves with every visit: very exciting.

ARROW COTTAGE
Weobley HR4 8RN
☎ 01544 318468   Fax 01544 318468
Owner Jane & Lance Hattatt
Location 1 mile from Weobley: off Wormsley road, signposted Ledgemoor & second right, first house on left
Open 2 pm – 5 pm; Wednesday – Friday & Sundays; April to September
Admission Adults £2. Unsuitable for children
Facilities Parking; loos; plants for sale; refreshments
Features Herbaceous plants; plantsman's garden; old roses; stream; featured on Channel 4 (1997)

Young and expanding garden, or series of gardens, in the modern style. Garden rooms create the space for different styles, but all are maintained to the highest standard. Much plantsmanship and artistry.

BERRINGTON HALL
Leominster HR6 0DW
☎ 01568 615721   Fax 01568 613263
Owner The National Trust
Location On A49, 3 miles north of Leominster
Open 12.30 pm – 6 pm (5 pm in October); Saturday – Wednesday; 27 March to 31 October
Admission £2
Facilities Parking; loos; facilities for the disabled; National Trust shop; licensed restaurant for lunch & teas
Features Landscape designed by Capability Brown; fruit of special interest
English Heritage Grade II*
NCCPG National Collection Malus (Hereford apples)

This majestic park is classic Capability Brown. The National Trust has laid out a one-mile parkland walk which takes in the best vantage points and shows you how the landscape would have looked when young. In the old walled garden, a comprehensive collection of Hereford Pomona is supplemented by old pear varieties, quinces and medlars.

Bryan's Ground
Stapleton, Presteigne LD8 2LP
☎ 01544 260001   Fax 01544 260015

Owner David Wheeler & Simon Dorrell
Location On minor road between Stapleton and Kinsham
Open 2 pm – 5 pm; Saturday – Monday; 1 May to 27 September. Groups at any time by appointment
Admission Adults £2; Children 50p
Facilities Parking; loos; access for the disabled; plants for sale; tea-rooms
Features Young garden; good modern design

A young garden: incredibly, the owners moved here as recently as November 1993. They have made wonderfully good use of the inherited structure (yew hedges and mature trees around the Surrey stockbroker house) and filled it with good plants. Recent additions include an auricula theatre, a belvedere and a Garden Club Room furnished with books, magazines and sofas to dawdle in if it rains. Full of original ideas, Bryan's Ground is already an influential and fashionable garden.

Burford House Gardens
Treasures of Tenbury, Tenbury Wells WR15 8HQ
☎ 01584 810777   Fax 01584 810673

Owner Treasures of Tenbury Ltd
Location A456 between Tenbury Wells and Ludlow
Open 10 am – 5 pm (dusk in winter); daily; all year
Admission Adults £2.50; Children £1; Groups (10+) £2 (by prior arrangement)
Facilities Parking; loos; facilities for the disabled; tea-rooms (light lunches, afternoon teas), beverages
Features Herbaceous plants; fine conifers; plantsman's garden; climbing roses; old roses; *Rosa* 'Treasure Trove'; new wildflower garden; new collection of bamboos
NCCPG National Collection *Clematis*

Glamorous four-acre modern garden to complement a stylish Georgian house. The fluid design is enhanced by interesting plants, imaginatively used and comprehensively labelled. There are good roses and herbaceous borders, and a magnificent series of water gardens, but Burford means *Clematis* – over 200 varieties – cleverly trained, grown and displayed among shrubs.

Dinmore Manor
Hereford HR4 8EE
☎ 01432 830322   Fax 01432 830503

Owner Dinmore Manor Estate Ltd
Location 6 miles north of Hereford on A49
Open 10 am – 5.30 pm; daily; all year
Admission Adults £3; Children under 14 free
Facilities Parking; loos; access for the disabled; plants for sale; plant centre; refreshments by arrangement
Features Pond; rock garden; old roses; 1,200-year old yew

The 1920s rock garden is cheerfully planted with dwarf conifers and Japanese maples. The 1,200-year old yew is an impressive sight.

Eastgrove Cottage Garden & Nursery
Sankyns Green, Shrawley, Little Witley, Worcester WR6 6LQ
☎ 01299 896389
Website www.hughesmedia.co.uk/eastgrove/

Owner Malcolm & Carol Skinner
Location On road between Great Witley & Shrawley
Open 2 pm – 5 pm; Thursday – Monday; April to July. Also Thursday – Saturday; 2 September to 9 October. Also 19 September & 3 October
Admission Adults £2
Facilities Parking; loos; access for the disabled; attached to good small nursery
Features Herbaceous plants; herbs; plantsman's garden; old roses

A cottage garden attached to a cottage-garden nursery. The scale is small, but the quality and variety of the plantings are stunning. Herbs, dwarf conifers, a developing arboretum, a bog garden, a 'secret garden' and, above all, thickly planted herbaceous plants.

Eastnor Castle
Eastnor, Ledbury HR8 1RL
☎ 01531 633160   Fax 01531 631776

Owner Mr James & The Hon Mrs Hervey-Bathurst
Location 2 miles east of Ledbury
Open 11 am – 5 pm; Sundays & Bank Holiday Mondays; April to September. Also daily except Saturdays in July & August
Admission Adults £2.75; Children £1.50
Facilities Parking; dogs permitted; loos; access for the disabled; plants for sale; souvenirs and gift shop
Features Good collection of trees; fine conifers; lake; spring bulbs; tallest deodar *Cedrus deodara* (38m.) in the British Isles, plus 11 more record trees
English Heritage Grade II*

Eastnor is all about trees. The arboretum planted by Lord Somers 150 years ago is now mature, and full of champion specimens. Many are rare. The conifers are particularly fine in early spring and complement the shaggy neo-Norman castle.

Hergest Croft Gardens
Kington HR5 3EG
☎ 01544 230160   Fax 01544 230160

Owner W L Banks
Location Signposted from A44
Open 1.30 pm – 6 pm; daily; April to October
Admission Adults £3.50; Children free
Facilities Parking; dogs permitted; loos; plants for sale; home-made teas
Features Good collection of trees; herbaceous plants; fruit of special interest; old roses; rhododendrons; tallest

HEREFORD & WORCESTER — GARDENS — 177

Cercidiphyllum japonicum (25m.), *Toona sinensis* (27m.) and *Corylus colurna* (27m.) in the British Isles, among 17 record trees
English Heritage Grade II*
NCCPG National Collections *Acer*; *Betula*; *Zelkova*
Wonderful woodland garden and arboretum around a whopping Edwardian house. There is no end to the garden's marvels: huge conifers, magnificent birches, scores of interesting oaks, many acres of billowing rhododendrons. Plus good herbaceous borders, alpine collections, autumn gentians and kitchen garden, all on a scale that most of us have forgotten.

HOW CAPLE COURT GARDENS
How Caple, Hereford HR1 4SX
☎ 01989 740626   Fax 01989 740611
Owner Mr & Mrs Roger Lee
Location Signposted on B4224 & A449 Jct
Open 9.30 am – 5 pm; daily; all year
Admission Adults £2.50; Children £1.25
Facilities Parking; dogs permitted; loos; facilities for the disabled; clothes shop; nursery; dried flower shop; ice-cream & soft drinks
Features Fine conifers; old roses; garden sculpture; good topiary; woodland garden; Italian terraces surrounded by restored pergola
Friends New Friends Association: ask for details

Spectacular formal gardens laid out at the turn of the century (some Italianate, others more Arts and Crafts), and now undergoing restoration. Pergolas, loggias, dramatic terraces and *giardini segreti* with stunning views across a lushly wooded valley. How Caple is a garden of national importance, unjustly ignored by English Heritage and little known even locally.

THE MANOR HOUSE, BIRLINGHAM
Birlingham, Pershore WR10 3AF
☎ & Fax 01386 750005
Owner Mr & Mrs David Williams-Thomas
Location In village
Open 11 am – 5.30 pm; 2, 3, 30 & 31 May; Thursdays from 1 June to 15 July; Thursdays in September. Plus 11 am – 5 pm on 27 June Rare Plant Specialist Nurseries Fair
Admission Adults £2; Children free
Facilities Parking; loos; access for the disabled; plants for sale; teas
Features Herbaceous plants; plantsman's garden; walled garden

The outbuildings and paddocks around this old farmhouse have been laid out in the Lutyens style and lavishly planted in the nostalgic style. Rare plants are used in unusual combinations to bring out contrasts and harmonies of form and colour.

QUEEN'S WOOD ARBORETUM & COUNTRY PARK
Dinmore Hill, Leominster HR6 0PY
☎ 01568 797052   Fax 01568 879305
Owner Hereford & Worcester County Council
Location Midway between Leominster & Hereford on A49
Open 9 am – dusk; daily; all year
Admission Free, but small charge for parking
Facilities Parking; dogs permitted; loos; facilities for the disabled; gift shop; light meals from 9 am to 5 pm
Features Bluebells; fine conifers; woodland garden; interesting for children; wood anemones

A vigorous young arboretum, planted over the last 40 years with public amenity in mind. Wonderful for walking, whatever the season, and well run in a friendly, efficient manner so that visitors get the most from it.

SPETCHLEY PARK
Worcester WR5 1RS
☎ 01905 345224
Owner R J Berkeley Esq
Location 2 miles east of Worcester on A422
Open 11 am – 5 pm; Tuesday – Friday & Bank Holiday Mondays (plus 2 pm – 5 pm on Sundays); April to September
Admission Adults £3; OAPs £3; Children £1.50
Facilities Parking; loos; access for the disabled; teas & refreshments
Features Good collection of trees; herbaceous plants; daffodils; plantsman's garden; rhododendrons and azaleas; modern roses; old roses; particularly good in July–August; deer park; good new plantings in the kitchen garden; naturalised lilies
English Heritage Grade II*

In a classic English landscaped park, three generations of Berkeleys have created one of the best plantsman's gardens in the Midlands. Ellen Willmott was the owner's great aunt and many of the most exciting trees and shrubs date from her time. The planting continues: this garden offers something to everyone.

STONE HOUSE COTTAGE GARDEN
Stone, Kidderminster DY10 4BG
☎ & Fax 01562 69902
Owner Mr James & The Hon Mrs Arbuthnott
Location In village, 2 miles from Kidderminster on A448
Open 10 am – 5.30 pm; Wednesday – Saturday; March to mid-October. Plus 5 April, 2, 3, 30 & 31 May, 20 June, 29 & 30 August
Admission Adults £2; Children free
Facilities Parking; loos; access for the disabled; excellent nursery attached
Features Alpines; herbaceous plants; herbs; plantsman's garden; climbing roses; old roses; young garden; particularly good in July–August; unusual climbing plants

The garden of a famous nursery, which it matches for the range of beautiful and unusual plants it offers. Exquisite plantings, and an eccentric collection of follies built as towers in the garden walls. Bliss.

WITLEY COURT
Great Witley, 1 WR6 7JT
☎ 01299 896636
Owner English Heritage
Location 10 miles north of Worcester on A443
Open 10 am – 6 pm (5 pm in October); daily; April to October. 9 am – 4 pm; Wednesday – Sunday; November to March. Closed 24–26 December. Open 1 January 2000
Admission Adults £3.50; Concessions £2.30; Children £1.80
Facilities Parking; loos; access for the disabled; café
Features Classical landscape
English Heritage Grade II*

Glorious parkland surrounds this Jacobean house but English Heritage has also begun to restore the formal gardens round the house.

WORTH A VISIT

BODENHAM ARBORETUM
Wolverley ☎ *DY11 5SY. Open 11 am – 5 pm; daily; May to October. This 40-acre arboretum within a working farm of 135 acres opened to the public for the first time last year. Among 2,000 different taxa are collections of alder and poplar, long laurel walks, rhododendrons and azaleas, and a 70-yard laburnum arch wide enough to drive a tractor down the middle!*

KENCHESTER WATER GARDENS
Church Road, Lyde, Hereford HR1 3AB
☎ *01432 270981. Open 9 am – 6 pm; Monday to Saturday; March to October. 9 am – 5.30 pm; daily; November to February. Open Sundays 11 am – 5 pm in summer & 10.30 am – 4.30 pm in winter. NCCPG National Collection: Nymphaea. This retail and wholesale aquatic specialist has a series of striking water gardens. The nursery offers over 130 varieties of Nymphaea and stocks everything for ponds and pools.*

MARSTON EXOTICS
Brampton Lane, Madley, Hereford HR2 9LX
☎ *01981 251140. Open 8 am – 4.30 pm; Monday – Friday; all year; 1 pm – 5 pm; Saturday – Sunday; March to October. NCCPG National Collection: Sarracenia. A formidable collection of carnivorous plants – the largest in Europe, they claim. The range of rare Sarracenia species is quite exceptional.*

OLD COURT NURSERIES
Walwyn Road, Colwall, Malvern WR13 6QE
☎ *01684 540416. Open 11 am – 5.30 pm; Wednesday – Sunday; June to October. NCCPG National Collection: Aster. Holders of National Collection of Michaelmas daisies which are grown in the Picton garden adjoining this nursery. The extensive collection is fully described in A Guide to the Asters grown by Old Court Nurseries. There are also many other interesting perennials and cottage-garden plants here.*

OVERBURY COURT
Overbury, Tewkesbury GL20 7NP ☎ *01386 725312. Open For groups by appointment. A peaceful and expansive garden laid out around the large, handsome, Georgian house, with a view of the Parish church worked in. Geoffrey Jellicoe, Aubrey Waterfield and Russell Page all worked on the design and planting: the result is a garden of exceptional harmony.*

RICKARDS HARDY FERNS LTD
Kyre Park, Tenbury Wells WR15 8RP ☎ *01885 410282. Open 11 am – 5 pm; Wednesday – Monday; April to October. NCCPG National Collections: Cystopteris, Polypodium. Specialists in hardy ferns. They have a great number for sale, and over 900 different varieties in their own collection. Half-hardy tree ferns are also sold. The garden has five lakes, waterfalls and magnificent old trees: well worth a visit.*

RUSHFIELDS OF LEDBURY
Ross Road, Ledbury HR8 2LP ☎ *01531 632004. Open 11 am – 5 pm, Wednesday – Saturday, and by appointment. This nursery offers a good choice of perennials, especially geraniums, hardy osteospermums, hostas and Helen Ballard hellebore cultivars.*

WEBBS OF WYCHBOLD
Wychbold, Droitwich WR9 0DG ☎ *01527 861777. Open 9 am – 6 pm; Monday – Friday (8 pm April to September); 9 am – 6 pm; Saturdays and Bank Holidays; 10.30 am – 4.30 pm; Sundays. NCCPG National Collection: Potentilla fruticosa. Forward-looking garden centre and nursery, with an extensive range of good plants and all sorts of sundries and equipment. The Potentilla collection is grown in a special garden.*

WHITFIELD
Allensmore HR2 9BA ☎ *01981 570202. Open 2 pm – 6 pm; 6 June & 11 July. Groups by appointment. Whitfield has magnificent trees, planted by the Clives over the last 200 years. Zelkova serrata, a weeping oak, and a ginkgo planted in 1778 are some of the highlights, but there is nothing to beat the grove of 20 or so Sequoia sempervirens now pushing 150 feet in height.*

HERTFORDSHIRE

THE BEALE ARBORETUM
West Lodge Park, Cockfosters Road, Hadley Wood, Barnet EN4 0PY
☎ 0181 441 5159 ext. 304   Fax 0181 449 9916
Owner Trevor Beale
Location A111, halfway between M25 Jct 24 and Cockfosters station
Open 2 pm – 5 pm; Wednesdays; April to October. Plus 16 May & 24 October for NGS
Admission Adults £2; Children free
Facilities Parking; dogs permitted; loos; facilities for the disabled; refreshments

HERTFORDSHIRE GARDENS 179

Features Good collection of trees; fine conifers; woodland garden; 300-year-old specimen of *Arbutus unedo*
NCCPG National Collection *Carpinus*

Ten acres of young arboretum, begun 25 years ago and shortly to double in size. Among the older specimens – Victorian cedars and redwoods – is a fine collection of trees planted with a view to the overall effect and underplanted with rhododendrons. Little known as yet, but undoubtedly to be reckoned among the great late 20th-century gardens.

BENINGTON LORDSHIP
Benington, Stevenage SG2 7BS
☎ 01438 869228   Fax 01438 869622
Owner C H A Bott
Location Off A602 Stevenage to Hertford, in Benington village
Open 12 noon – 5 pm; Wednesdays; April to September. 2 pm – 5 pm; Sundays; April to August. Plus 17 October & Bank Holiday Mondays. Telephone for details of snowdrop openings
Admission Adults £2.80; Children free
Facilities Parking; loos; plants for sale
Features Herbaceous plants; rock garden; modern roses; old roses; snowdrops; heather garden; cowslip bank; many new roses planted (1997)
English Heritage Grade II

A sort-of-Georgian house with a mock-Norman gateway and the ruins of a real Norman castle in the grounds. The extensive gardens have been revived and replanted in recent years without destroying the older features: a Pulhamite folly, an Edwardian rock garden and a sense of spacious parkland. But the highlight of a visit today is the stupendous double herbaceous border that Mrs Bott has planted in gentle pastel shades: the best we know.

THE GARDENS OF THE ROSE
Chiswell Green, St Albans AL2 3NR
☎ 01727 850461   Fax 01727 850360
Owner The Royal National Rose Society
Location 1 mile from Jct of M1 & M25; 2 miles south of St Albans
Open 9 am – 5 pm (10 am – 6 pm on Sundays & Bank Holidays); daily; 5 June to 26 September. Plus Sundays & Bank Holiday Mondays from Easter to end of May
Admission Adults £4; OAPs £3.50; Children £1.50; Members free. Less from May to June
Facilities Parking; dogs permitted; loos; facilities for the disabled; plants for sale; shop with rose books & souvenirs; licensed cafeteria
Features Plantings by Graham Thomas; particularly good in July–August; new iris garden (1998); substantial plantings of bulbs and spring-flowering plants

The most comprehensive rose garden in Britain, with a 1960s design which emphasises modern roses but also has excellent collections of old roses (in a garden designed by Graham Stuart Thomas), shrub roses, climbers, ramblers, miniatures, ground cover and wild species of rose. 30,000 rose bushes and 1,750 varieties, plus a further 600 unnamed novelties in the trial grounds. Ambitious plans to expand to 60 acres began with the opening of the 'Peace' garden in 1995: more new features are promised.

HATFIELD HOUSE
Hatfield AL9 5NQ
☎ 01707 262823   Fax 01707 275719
Owner The Marquess of Salisbury
Location Off A1(M) Jct 4
Open 25 March to 26 September. West gardens: 11 am – 6 pm; daily except Mondays. East gardens: 11 am – 6 pm, Fridays
Admission House, park & garden: Adults £6
Facilities Parking; loos; facilities for the disabled; plants for sale; souvenirs and gift shop; licensed restaurant, coffee shop, snacks & hot lunches
Features Herbaceous plants; herbs; good topiary; knot gardens; physic garden; organic kitchen garden
English Heritage Grade I

Interesting old/new gardens to suit a historic stately home. An 1890s parterre, very pretty, is the main feature. The new knot garden has plants dating from the 17th century (Lady Salisbury is a stalwart of the Tradescant Trust), but there are *allées*, *rondpoints*, more knots and parterres: the complete design vocabulary for how-to-Tudorise your garden.

KNEBWORTH HOUSE
Knebworth, Stevenage SG3 6PY
☎ 01438 812661   Fax 01438 811908
Owner Lord Cobbold
Location Off A1(M) Jct 7
Open 11 am – 5.30 pm; daily; 27 March to 11 April and 29 May to 5 September; plus weekends and Bank Holidays 17 April to 23 May and weekends only 11 to 26 September
Admission £5
Facilities Parking; loos; plants for sale; licensed cafeteria
Features Herbaceous plants; planted by Gertrude Jekyll; designed by Lutyens; modern roses; sunken lawn; gold garden; wilderness
English Heritage Grade II*
Friends Knebworth House Education and Preservation Trust – details from the Secretary, c/o Knebworth House

Most of the garden was laid out by Lutyens, who married a daughter of the house. It has been well restored over the last 15 years with Jekyll plantings where appropriate. Inventive and harmonious, few gardens make such good use of space and perspective.

WORTH A VISIT

AYLETT NURSERIES LTD
North Orbital Road, London Colney, St Albans AL2 1DH
☎ *01727 822255.   Open 8.30 am – 5.30 pm; Monday – Friday; 8.30 am – 5 pm; Saturdays; 9.30 am – 5 pm; Bank Holidays; 10 am – 4 pm; Sundays in winter; 10.30 am – 4.30 pm; Sundays in summer. A huge (and very busy) general garden centre, in a prime trading position with a*

vast range of plants and every imaginable sundry. They also offer a design service and delivery. Their award-winning speciality is dahlias: the growing fields at Bowman's Farm are a sight in September.

HILL HOUSE
Stanstead Abbots, Ware SG12 8BX ☎ *01920 870013.*
Open 2 pm – 5 pm; 16 May, 6 & 13 June. Outstanding plantings in the old kitchen garden include colour borders of purple and gold, weeping pears, and vegetables all as neat as imaginable. Pretty woodland garden and lush growth around the small lake.

HOPLEYS PLANTS LTD
High Street, Much Hadham SG10 6BU ☎ *01279 842509.*
Open 9 am – 5 pm, daily except Tuesdays; 2 pm – 5 pm, Sundays. Hopleys have an extensive choice of hardy shrubs and perennials and are particularly strong on diascias, osteospermums, penstemons and salvias. The garden is a true show garden for the nursery, which has been responsible for such introductions as Lavatera 'Barnsley' and Potentilla fruticosa Red Ace. The tradition continues.

PRIORSWOOD CLEMATIS
Widbury Hill, Ware SG12 7QH ☎ *01920 461543.*
Open 8 am – 5 pm (9 am – 3 pm from November to March); Tuesday – Sunday; all year. This nursery has a long list of clematis species and hybrids – many of them new and some of their own raising. Honeysuckles and passionflowers, too.

ST PAUL'S WALDEN BURY
Whitwell, Hitchin SG4 8BP ☎ *01438 871218.* Highly important as a unique example of the French 18th-century style – three hedged allées lead off into the woodland towards temples, statues and pools. The present owner's father (the Queen Mother's brother) was a past President of the RHS, and was able to blend rhododendrons, azaleas, maples and magnolias (plus much more besides) into parts of the woodland. A garden that appeals to historian, plantsman and artist equally.

VAN HAGE GARDEN COMPANY
Great Amwell, Ware SG12 9RP ☎ *01920 870811.*
Open 9.30 am – 6 pm, Mondays; 9 am – 6 pm, Tuesdays – Saturdays; 10.30 am – 4.30 pm, Sundays.
Long-established and award-winning garden centre and seed merchants. The garden centre is strong on houseplants, and has a large choice of plants and related products. There is a programme of lectures and demonstrations throughout the year.

ISLE OF WIGHT

MOTTISTONE MANOR
Newport
☎ 01983 740012
Owner The National Trust
Location On B3399 west of Brighstone

Open 2 pm – 5.30 pm; Tuesdays, Sundays & Bank Holiday Mondays; 28 March to 30 October
Admission £2.10
Facilities Parking; dogs permitted; loos; teas
Features Herbaceous plants; fine conifers; fruit of special interest; modern roses; bluebells; irises

A cleverly designed modern garden on a difficult site – steep and narrow. Much has been terraced and enclosed to allow a rose garden and good herbaceous borders. Most of the rest is given to a wide variety of fruit trees, trained to make avenues and underplanted with vegetables or spring bulbs. A model for this type of planting, and made long before the current fashion for ornamental potagers.

NUNWELL HOUSE
Brading, Ryde PO36 0JQ
☎ 01983 407240

Owner Colonel & Mrs J A Aylmer
Location Signed off A3055, 1 mile to the west of Brading
Open 1 pm – 5 pm; 30 & 31 May; then Monday – Wednesday from 28 June to 8 September. Plus 2 pm – 5 pm on 6 June for NGS
Admission Gardens only: £2.50
Facilities Parking; loos; plants for sale on 6 June
Features Good collection of trees; herbs; plantsman's garden; modern roses; garden sculpture; obelisks; walled garden re-opened (1999)
English Heritage Grade II

A pretty garden, largely replanted by Vernon Russell-Smith about 30 years ago: he also planted a small arboretum. The present owners have added some highly attractive garden ornaments and are restoring the fabric and the plantings after some years of neglect. Work continues.

OSBORNE HOUSE GARDEN
East Cowes PO32 0JY
☎ 01983 200022   Fax 01983 281380

Owner English Heritage
Location Follow the brown tourist signs
Open 10 am – 6 pm (5 pm in October); daily; April to October
Admission House & garden: Adults £6.90; Concessions £5.20; Children £3.50. Garden only: Adults £3.50; Concessions £2.60; Children £1.80
Facilities Parking; loos; facilities for the disabled; English Heritage shop; tea-room
English Heritage Grade II*
Friends Island Friends of Royal Osborne (telephone for details)

Prince Albert laid out stupendous Italianate terraces between this elegant Florentine palace and the parkland below.

VENTNOR BOTANIC GARDEN
Undercliff Drive, Ventnor PO38 1UL
☎ 01983 855397   Fax 01983 856154
Website www.botanic.co.uk

Owner Isle of Wight Council
Location 1½ miles west of Ventnor on A3055
Open Dawn to dusk; daily; 7 March to 31 October. Temperate House open 10 am – 5 pm, then 11 am – 4 pm in November & December
Admission Garden: free. Temperate House: 50p. Parking charges
Facilities Parking; dogs permitted; loos; access for the disabled; new nursery specialising in rare plants from the garden; cafeteria & bar with snacks, tea/coffee, lunches
Features Herbaceous plants; plantsman's garden; subtropical plants; interesting for children; particularly interesting in winter; palms; olives; bananas; medicinal herbs from all over the world; new xerophytic garden (1998); tallest *Peumus boldus* in UK; largest collection of New Zealand plants in UK
NCCPG National Collection *Pseudopanax*
Friends Friends of Garden (tel: 01983 855397), seed list distributions

Originally an offshoot of Hilliers Nursery, the Ventnor Botanic Garden is devoted to exotic plants. Many – perhaps most – are from the southern hemisphere but flourish in the unique microclimate of the 'Undercliff': widdringtonias from Zimbabwe and Tasmanian olearias, for instance. Almost destroyed by the gales of 1987 and 1990, the collection is rapidly forming again. The young head gardener has a wonderful eye for planting.

WORTH A VISIT

DEACON'S NURSERY
Moor View, Godshill PO38 3HW
☎ *01983 840750/522243. Open 8 am – 4 pm; Monday – Friday; all year. Plus 8 am – 1 pm on Saturdays from October to April. Fruit specialist, with tree and soft fruit of every size and variety. The very comprehensive list includes over 250 apple cultivars. All rootstocks are of virus-free origin.*

NORTH COURT
Shorwell PO30 3JG ☎ *01983 740415. Open 2.30 pm – 5 pm; dates to be announced; May & June. Groups at any time by appointment. The Harrison family which owns North Court inherited fine grounds with some magnificent trees and a clear stream at the bottom. John Harrison has extensively replanted it with a plantsman's enthusiasm and a special interest in tender exotica. Definitely a garden to watch in future.*

KENT

BEDGEBURY NATIONAL PINETUM
Goudhurst, Cranbrook TN17 2SL
☎ 01580 211044   Fax 01580 212423
Owner Forestry Commission
Location 1 mile east of A21 at Flimwell on B2079
Open 10 am – dusk; daily; all year

Admission Adults £2.20; OAPs £1.50; Children £1.20; RHS members free
Facilities Parking; dogs permitted; loos; plants for sale; cold drinks
Features Fine conifers; lake; particularly interesting in winter; rhododendrons; fungi; new Japanese maple glade; 18 record tree species, including two broadleaves
English Heritage Grade II*
NCCPG National Collections *Chamaecyparis lawsoniana* cvs; *Juniperus*; *Taxus*
Friends Details from the Curator

Take any of the trails through this magnificent woodland garden, or go to the excellent Visitors' Centre to see the cone collection, and the new exhibit which tells the story of the Great Storm of 1987. It is difficult to realise that all the plantings are less than 70 years old.

BELMONT PARK
Belmont, Throwley, Faversham ME13 0HH
☎ 01795 890202

Owner The Harris (Belmont) Charity
Location Signposted from A251 at Badlesmere
Open 2 pm – 5 pm; Saturdays, Sundays & Bank Holiday Mondays; 4 April to 26 September
Admission Garden: Adults £2.75; Children £1
Facilities Parking; dogs permitted; loos; facilities for the disabled; plants for sale; teas
Features Rock garden; shell grotto; rhododendrons; pets' cemetery; pinetum
English Heritage Grade II

Quiet parkland surrounds this handsome Samuel Wyatt house, while the pleasure gardens are so obviously for the pleasure of the owners, not for display, that they add considerably to the sense of domesticity. The old kitchen garden is being restored for the new millennium.

BROGDALE
Brogdale Road, Faversham ME13 8XZ
☎ 01795 535286   Fax 01795 531710
Owner Brogdale Horticultural Trust
Location 1 mile south-west of Faversham
Open 9.30 am – 5.30 pm; daily; Easter to Christmas. 10 am – 4.30 pm; daily; Christmas to Easter
Admission Adults £2.50; OAPs £2; Children £1.50; RHS members free
Facilities Parking; loos; access for the disabled; plants for sale; excellent shop with rare fruit varieties for sale in season; light lunches & teas
Features Fruit and vegetables of special interest; interesting for children
NCCPG National Collections *Corylus*; *Fragaria*; *Malus*; *Prunus* (cherry & plum); *Pyrus*; *Ribes*; *Vitis*

Brogdale describes itself as 'a living museum' and claims to have the largest collection of fruit cultivars in the world: more than 2,300 apples, 400 pears and 360 plums. There are demonstrations, exhibitions, workshops and events throughout the year. Fruit from the collections is sold, and scion wood supplied.

CHARTWELL
Westerham TN16 1PS
☎ 01732 866368   Fax 01732 868193

Owner The National Trust
Location A25 to Westerham then signposted from B2026
Open 11 am – 5 pm; Wednesday – Sunday & Bank Holiday Mondays (plus Tuesdays in July & August); 27 March to 31 October
Admission Gardens only: Adults £2.75; Children £1.40
Facilities Parking; dogs permitted; loos; facilities for the disabled; National Trust shop; restaurant
Features Modern roses
English Heritage Grade II*

The spacious and extensive gardens are well laid out and planted in a slightly old-fashioned style. One of the rose gardens has the cultivar 'Winston Churchill' but every part has a deep sense of history and all is maintained to a very high standard.

EMMETTS GARDEN
Ide Hill, Sevenoaks TN14 6AY
☎ 01732 750367/750429

Owner The National Trust
Location Between Sundridge and Ide Hill off B2042
Open 11 am – 5.30 pm (last ticket 4.30 pm); Wednesday – Sunday & Bank Holiday Mondays; 27 March to 30 May. Then Wednesdays, Saturdays, Sundays & Bank Holidays from June to October
Admission Adults £3; Children £1.50
Facilities Parking; dogs permitted; loos; tea-room 2 pm – 5 pm (may close in bad weather)
Features Bluebells; rock garden; Italianate rose garden; rare trees and shrubs; autumn colour; new azalea beds (1997)
English Heritage Grade II

A stiff walk up from the car park brings you to this windswept hilltop garden, laid out in Edwardian times and maintained on a slim budget. The formal Italianate rose garden is pretty in July, but better still is the informal woodland garden laid out with trees and shrubs in the William Robinson style. Best in bluebell time.

GODINGTON PARK
Ashford TN23 3BW
☎ 01233 632652

Owner The Godington House Preservation Trust
Location Godington Lane, Potters Corner A20
Open 2 pm – 5 pm; Thursday – Saturday; April to 30 October. Plus some Sundays for NGS
Admission Adults £4; children £2
Facilities Parking; loos
Features Daffodils; lake; garden sculpture; good topiary; formal Italianate garden; water lilies
English Heritage Grade I

Godington is perhaps the prettiest house in Kent, a Jacobean mansion reworked in the 1920s by Sir Reginald Blomfield, who made the charming Italian garden (statues, loggia, summerhouse). Add in the 18th-century park, the late 19th-century plantings and the woodland garden which the present owners have been making, and you have a garden of great charm and authenticity. Restoration continues.

GOODNESTONE PARK
Wingham, Canterbury CT3 1PL
☎ 01304 840107

Owner Lord & Lady FitzWalter
Location Follow brown tourist signs from B2046
Open 11 am – 5 pm; Mondays, Wednesday – Friday; April to October. Plus 12 noon – 6 pm on Sundays
Admission Adults £2.50; Children (under 12) 20p; Disabled in wheelchairs £1; Group (20+) £2.30; Guided group £3
Facilities Parking; loos; facilities for the disabled; plants for sale; teas
Features Herbaceous plants; old roses; snowdrops; good topiary; woodland garden; cedar walk; rhododendrons
English Heritage Grade II*

A handsome Palladian house associated with Jane Austen (her brother married a daughter of the house). Fine parkland, a formal garden in front of the house, a 1930s woodland garden (maples, camellias, azaleas) undergoing modern expansion, and good mixed plantings in the old kitchen garden.

GREAT COMP
St Mary's Platt, Borough Green, Sevenoaks TN15 8QS
☎ 01732 886154

Owner Great Comp Charitable Trust
Location 2 miles east of Borough Green B2016 off A20
Open 11 am – 6 pm; daily; April to October
Admission Adults £3; Children £1
Facilities Parking; loos; facilities for the disabled; plants for sale; gifts, plants and souvenirs; refreshments at weekends & Bank Holidays
Features Herbaceous plants; good architectural features; plantsman's garden; garden sculpture; woodland garden; ground cover; dwarf conifers
Friends Great Comp Society, mainly to support the annual music festival in July and September

Everyone admires the energy of the founder of this interesting garden, Roderick Cameron, and Clay Jones called it the best garden he had ever seen. There is much to admire in its seven acres, including 3,000 different plants.

GROOMBRIDGE PLACE GARDENS
Groombridge, Tunbridge Wells TN3 9QG
☎ 01892 863999   Fax 01892 863996

Owner Andrew de Candole
Location On B2110, 4 miles south-west of Tunbridge Wells
Open 9 am – 6 pm; daily; 31 March to 31 October
Admission Adults £6.50; OAPs & children £5.50

Facilities Parking; loos; facilities for the disabled; plants for sale; gift shops; light lunches and teas

Groombridge has lots to offer: a drunken garden where the yews lean at tipsy angles, an oriental garden, a draughtsman's garden and a chessboard garden. Best of all are the brilliant colour plantings. But some visitors feel that the price is quite steep for what you get.

HEVER CASTLE
Edenbridge TN8 7NG
☎ 01732 865224   Fax 01732 866796

Owner Broadland Properties Ltd
Location 3 miles south-east of Edenbridge, signposted from M25 Jct 6
Open 11 am – 5 pm (4 pm in winter); daily; March to November
Admission Adults £5.50; OAPs £4.70; Children (5–16) £3.60
Facilities Parking; dogs permitted; loos; facilities for the disabled; plants for sale; plant centre; shop; two restaurants
Features Bluebells; good architectural features; lake; rhododendrons and azaleas; old roses; good topiary; woodland garden; particularly good in July–August; Christie's/HHA Garden of the Year in 1995; new 120-yd herbaceous border and water-maze opened last year
English Heritage Grade I

One of the most important Edwardian gardens in England. The pretty moated castle sits in a park of oaks and firs (underplanted with rhododendrons) with a yew maze and formal neo-Tudor garden to one side. The best part is a spectacular Italian garden where a long pergola (cool dripping fountains all along) leads past a series of exquisite Italian gardens, stuffed with sculptures, urns, sarcophagi and other loot brought by William Waldorf Astor from Rome; it finally bursts onto a theatrical terrace and a 35-acre lake, hand-dug by 800 workmen.

LADHAM HOUSE
Goudhurst TN17 1DB
☎ 01580 211203

Owner Mr & Mrs Alastair Jessel
Location Left at Chequers Inn on Cranbrook Road, then right to Curtisdem Green
Open 1.30 pm – 5.30 pm; 2 & 16 May & 3 October. And by appointment
Admission Adults £2.50 (£3 for private visits); Children (under 12) 50p
Facilities Parking; dogs permitted; loos; teas
Features Good collection of trees; herbaceous plants; woodland garden; magnolias; new 200-metre ha-ha (1998)

Laid out by a botanist Master of the Rolls in the mid-19th century, and enthusiastically restored and updated by the present owner. Many new plantings and some fine specimens, especially a deep red form of *Magnolia campbellii* which has been named 'Betty Jessel'.

LEEDS CASTLE
Maidstone ME17 1PL
☎ 01622 765400   Fax 01622 735616

Owner Leeds Castle Foundation
Location Jct 8 off the M20
Open 10 am – 5 pm, March to October (but closed on 26 June & 3 July); 10 am – 3 pm, November to February
Admission Park & gardens: Adults £6; OAPs & students £4.80; Children £4
Facilities Parking; loos; facilities for the disabled; plants for sale; shop in Castle Greenhouse; refreshments in the 17th-century tithe barn
Features Herbaceous plants; herbs; lake; old roses; woodland garden; interesting for children; tallest *Acer cappadocicum* 'Aureum' (23m.) in the British Isles; new maze disappears into an underground grotto!
English Heritage Grade II*
NCCPG National Collections *Monarda*; *Nepeta*

More a romantic castle than a garden, best seen across the lake, Leeds is run by a high-profile charitable trust with a big advertising budget. The results are admirable. The latest development – opening this spring – is the 'Lady Baillie Garden', a series of sheltered terraces between the Culpeper Garden and the lake.

PENSHURST PLACE
Penshurst, Tonbridge TN11 8DG
☎ 01892 870307   Fax 01892 879866
Website www.seetb.org.uk/penshurst/

Owner Viscount De L'Isle
Location Follow brown tourist signs from Tonbridge
Open 11 am – 6 pm, Saturday & Sunday, 27 February to 26 March; then daily, 27 March to 31 October
Admission Gardens only: Adult £4.20; OAPs £3.70; Children £2.80
Facilities Parking; loos; access for the disabled; dried flowers for sale; garden restaurant
Features Herbaceous plants; daffodils; designed by Roper; climbing roses; modern roses; formal Italian garden; spring bulbs
English Heritage Grade I

A garden with substantial genuine Tudor remains, but well restored and developed in recent years. A vast Italianate parterre dominates the immediate pleasure garden: it is planted with scarlet polyantha roses – another is planted as a Union Jack. There are borders by Lanning Roper and John Codrington, a 100-yard bed of peonies, and a brand new garden for the blind, straight off the peg at the Chelsea Flower Show in 1994.

SCOTNEY CASTLE GARDEN
Lamberhurst, Tunbridge Wells TN3 8JN
☎ 01892 891081   Fax 01892 890110

Owner The National Trust
Location On A21, south of Lamberhurst

Open 11 am – 6 pm (but 2 pm – 6 pm on Saturdays & Sundays); Wednesday – Sunday; 27 March to 31 October. Plus 12 noon – 6 pm on Bank Holiday Mondays & preceding Sundays
Admission Adults £4; Children £2
Facilities Parking; loos; access for the disabled; shop
Features Lake; plantsman's garden; designed by Roper; woodland garden; rhododendrons; azaleas; water lilies; wisteria; good autumn colour; ruins of 14th-century castle
English Heritage Grade I

Moated and abandoned castle surrounded by rhododendrons and azaleas: very romantic and very photogenic. Among the ruins are a herb garden and cottage garden, surprisingly appropriate and effective. Lanning Roper had a hand in it.

Sissinghurst Castle Garden
Sissinghurst, Cranbrook TN17 2AB
☎ 01580 715330   Fax 01580 713911
Owner The National Trust
Location 1 mile east of Sissinghurst village, ½ mile off A262. Cross-country footpath from village
Open 1 pm – 6.30 pm; Tuesday – Friday; 27 March to 15 October. Plus 10 am – 5.30 pm; Saturdays, Sundays & Good Friday
Admission Adults £6; Children £3
Facilities Parking; loos; facilities for the disabled; plants for sale; National Trust gift shop; self-service restaurant
Features Herbaceous plants; herbs; plantsman's garden; old roses
English Heritage Grade I

Too well known to need description, Sissinghurst is part of every English gardener's education and a source of wonder and inspiration to which to return time and again. There is a 'timed ticket' system to restrict visitors to 400 at a time, which may mean waiting. Best visited out of season, in April, September or October.

Squerryes Court
Westerham TN16 1SJ
☎ 01959 562345   Fax 01959 565949
Owner J & A Warde
Location ½ mile from A25, signposted from Westerham
Open 12 noon – 5.30 pm; Wednesdays, Saturdays, Sundays & Bank Holiday Mondays; April to September
Admission Garden only: Adults £2.40; OAPs £2.10; Children £1.40
Facilities Parking; dogs permitted; loos; small shop in house; home-made teas
Features Old roses; good topiary; vegetables of interest; formal design; gazebo; ice-house; dovecote; Wolfe cenotaph
English Heritage Grade II

The gardens have been excellently restored with advice from Tom Wright since 1987, using a plan of the original garden made in 1731. Formal beds (box and santolina) lead to Edwardian borders, beautifully planted, and the 18th-century park beyond.

Stoneacre
Otham, Maidstone ME15 8RS
☎ 01622 862871   Fax 01622 862157
Owner The National Trust
Location 1 mile south of A20; north end of Otham village
Open 2 pm – 6 pm; Wednesdays & Saturdays; 27 March to 30 October
Admission Adults £2.50; Children £1.25
Facilities Parking
Features Spring bulbs, autumn colour, strong design

Stoneacre is particularly interesting because the tenant since 1989 has been Rosemary Alexander, Principal of the English Gardening School at the Chelsea Physic Garden. This is where she works out her ideas and shows her students how the principles of design and planting look 'on the ground'. It is one of the most exciting new gardens we know, and in perfect harmony with the Tudorised house.

Walmer Castle Gardens
Kingsdown Road, Deal CT14 7LJ
☎ 01304 364288
Owner English Heritage
Location Follow brown tourist signs
Open 10 am – 6 pm (or dusk, if earlier); daily; April to October. 10 am – 4 pm; Wednesday – Sunday; March, November & December. Also 10 am – 4 pm; Saturdays & Sundays in January & February. Closed 24–26 December and when the Lord Warden is in residence
Admission Adults £4.50; Concessions £3.40; Children £2.30
Facilities Parking; loos; facilities for the disabled; English Heritage shop; tea-room
Features Young garden; magnificent old yew hedges
English Heritage Grade II

The gardens at Walmer castle are well worth a visit. The castle looks onto a fine formal garden and terraces, with a kitchen garden and Penelope Hobhouse's new Queen Elizabeth the Queen Mother's Garden behind. Further away are drifts of daffodils, specimen trees planted by famous visitors, a thickly wooded quarry and a holm oak avenue.

Yalding Organic Gardens
Yalding, Maidstone
☎ & Fax 01622 814650
Owner Henry Doubleday Research Association
Location On B2162, ½ mile south of village
Open 10 am – 5 pm; Wednesday – Sunday; May to September. Also weekends in April & October and all Bank Holidays
Admission Adults £2.50; Concessions £2; Children £1.25; RHS members free
Facilities Parking; loos; plants for sale; café open from mid-morning to tea-time
Features Young garden; new thatched cottage in the Cobbett garden (1998)

Fourteen theme gardens run organically by the HDRA. They include a an apothecary's garden in the 13th-century style, a late-19th-century artisan's garden and a post-war allotment, all very stylish and educational.

WORTH A VISIT

ALAN C SMITH
127 Leaves Green Road, Keston BR2 6DG
☎ 01959 572531. *Open By appointment only. This nursery has an amazing range of sempervivums and jovibarbas, including species, hybrids and cultivars: there are about one thousand on offer, besides a more general selection of rock-garden plants.*

DOWNDERRY NURSERY
Pillar Box Lane, Hadlow, Tonbridge TN11 9SW
☎ 01732 810081. *Open 10 am – 5 pm; Wednesday – Saturday; 1 May to 3 October. 11 am – 5 pm on Sundays & Bank Holidays. NCCPG National Collection: Lavandula. Lavender specialist with a fascinating list of species and cultivars, old and new. Many are available as rooted cuttings and liners by post, wholesale and retail.*

HOLE PARK
Rolvenden, Cranbrook TN17 4JB ☎ 01580 241251. *Open By appointment. A great garden, and little known. The drive runs under an avenue of horse-chestnuts through classical parkland. The pleasure garden is Edwardian in origin, but revived and replanted by the present owner. Solid hedges and clipped specimens of yew are everywhere: backing the excellent herbaceous borders, around the water lily pond and framing a croquet lawn with standard wisterias. The flowery woodlands have palm trees in the dell, while the lake is surrounded by purple rhododendrons and orange azaleas. Bluebells, daffodils and wonderful views are added delights.*

IDEN CROFT HERBS
Frittenden Road, Staplehurst TN12 0DH
☎ 01580 891432. *Open 9 am – 5 pm; Monday – Saturday; all year; 11 am – 5 pm; Sundays and Bank Holidays; March to September only. NCCPG National Collections: Origanum; Mentha. The many themed gardens, built up over 30 years, include culinary, medicinal, patio, pot pourri and cottage gardens. All are designed for disabled access and worth a visit in their own right. Iden Croft calls itself a 'total herb centre' with some justification. The range of herbs and aromatic plants is both impressive and extensive. There are events, workshops and courses throughout the year.*

IGHTHAM MOAT
The National Trust, Ivy Hatch, Sevenoaks TN15 0NT
☎ 01732 810378. *Open 11 am – 5.30 pm; daily except Tuesdays & Saturdays; 28 March to 31 October. A moated medieval manor in a wooded Kentish valley, with borders of pinks, old roses and lilies. Nothing tremendously special, but dreamily English.*

J BRADSHAW & SON
Busheyfields Nursery, Herne, Herne Bay CT6 7LJ

☎ 01227 375415. *Open 10 am – 5 pm; Tuesday – Saturday and Bank Holidays; March to October. NCCPG National Collections: Lonicera (climbing); Clematis montana; Clematis chrysocoma. This family nursery specialises in climbing and wall plants. They have an exceptionally long list of climbing honeysuckles and cultivars of* Clematis montana.

KEEPERS NURSERY
Gallants Court, East Farleigh, Maidstone ME15 0LE
☎ 01622 726465. *Open By appointment at all reasonable times. Keeper's Nursery boasts the largest range of fruit trees in the country – over 600 cultivars: apples, pears, plums of all kinds, quinces, medlars, cherries and nuts, including some charmingly named old varieties. They offer a grafting service to propagate known and unknown varieties for customers.*

LONG BARN
Long Barn Road, Weald, Sevenoaks TN14 6NH
Open 2 pm – 5 pm; 20 June, 18 July. Chiefly of interest for its association with Harold Nicolson and Vita Sackville-West, and well restored to their period by the present owners. The strong designs and exuberant plantings of Sissinghurst are all here in their infancy.

MADRONA NURSERY
Pluckley Road, Betherden TN26 3DD ☎ 01233 820100. *Open 10 am – 5 pm; Saturday – Tuesday; 20 March to 2 November. Closed 4 to 20 August. Derek Jarman called this difficult-to-find nursery 'the most charming in England'. The emphasis is on interesting and attractive trees and shrubs, including new introductions, but there are also perennials, ferns, grasses and bamboos. Their catalogue has particularly helpful descriptions.*

RIVERHILL HOUSE GARDENS
Sevenoaks TN15 0RR ☎ 01732 458802. *Open 12 noon – 6 pm; Sundays, plus Bank Holiday weekends; April to June. Riverhill is a handsome Queen Anne house with grand views on a stately hillside, surrounded by billowing rhododendrons.*

STARBOROUGH NURSERY
Starborough Road, Marsh Green, Edenbridge TN8 5RB
☎ 01732 865614. *Open 10 am – 4 pm; Monday – Saturday. Closed Sundays; some Wednesdays; all January and July; and most of August. This nursery recently joined forces with G. Reuthe Ltd of Ightham, Sevenoaks. They now issue a single catalogue, combining Starborough's rare trees and shrubs with Reuthe's extensive list of rhododendrons and azaleas.*

LANCASHIRE

LEIGHTON HALL
Carnforth LA5 9ST
☎ 01524 734474   Fax 01524 720357
Owner R G Reynolds
Location Signed from A6 Jct M6

Open 2 pm – 5 pm; daily except Saturday & Monday (but open on Bank Holiday Mondays); May to September. Open at 11.30 am in August
Admission Not yet agreed as we went to press
Facilities Parking; loos; access for the disabled; plants for sale; gift shop; tea-rooms
Features Herbaceous plants; fruit of special interest; herbs; old roses; 'caterpillar' path maze

The handsome semi-castellated house is set in lush parkland with the moors as a backdrop, but the garden is in the old walled garden, where rose borders, herbs and the gravel maze bring a touch of fancy to the whole.

RUFFORD OLD HALL
Rufford, Ormskirk
☎ & Fax 01704 821254

Owner The National Trust
Location 7 miles north of Ormskirk on A59
Open 12 noon – 6 pm; Saturday – Wednesday; 27 March to October
Admission Garden only: Adults £2; Children £1
Facilities Parking; dogs permitted; loos; access for the disabled; National Trust shop; lunches & teas (no lunches on Sundays)
Features Herbaceous plants; rhododendrons and azaleas; old roses

One of the National Trust's most successful re-creations, the gardens are laid out in the Regency style around a remarkable 15th-century timber-framed house.

WORTH A VISIT

BANK HOUSE
Borwick, Carnforth LA6 1JR ☎ 01524 732768. Open By appointment. A successful private garden made over the last 30 years by the present owners. It manages to shoe-horn such features as a woodland garden, gravel garden, old-fashioned rose collection and a mini-arboretum into two acres. But it works.

CATFORTH GARDENS
Roots Lane, Catforth, Preston PR4 0JB ☎ 01772 690561. Open 10.30 am – 5 pm; mid-March – mid-September. NCCPG National Collection: Geranium. The nursery is sandwiched between three gardens which open at the same times. The list is strongest on hardy geraniums (both species and cultivars but many other perennials are also on offer.

HOGHTON TOWER
Hoghton, Preston PR5 0SH ☎ 01254 852986. Open 11 am – 4 pm; Tuesday – Thursday; July & August. 1 pm – 5 pm; Sundays; Easter to October. A series of spacious courtyards and walled gardens surround this fierce castellated house. Not a great garden, but the setting is impressive and there are fine spring walks in the rhododendron woods below.

HOLDEN CLOUGH NURSERY
Holden, Bolton by Bowland, Clitheroe BB7 4PF
☎ 01200 447615. Open 9 am – 5 pm; Monday –

Saturday; all year. A long-established working nursery, with a large and very hardy range of interesting alpines, perennials, dwarf conifers, shrubs, ferns and grasses.

REGINALD KAYE LTD
Waithman Nurseries, Silverdale, Carnforth LA5 0TY
☎ 01524 701252. Open 11 am – 5 pm; Thursday – Saturday; 1 – 5 pm Sunday; March to September. Alpine and fern specialists: good for hellebores and meconopsis in particular.

LEICESTERSHIRE

BELVOIR CASTLE
Belvoir, Grantham
☎ 01476 870262   Fax 01476 870443

Owner The Duke of Rutland
Location 6 miles west of Grantham
Open 11 am – 5 pm; Tuesday – Thursday, Saturdays, Sundays & Bank Holiday Mondays; 30 March to 30 September
Admission Castle & gardens: Adults £5; OAPs £4; Children £3
Facilities Parking; loos; gift shop; refreshments: lunches and teas; picnic site
Features Modern roses; woodland garden; tallest bird cherry *Prunus avium* (28m.) and yew tree *Taxus baccata* (29m.) in the British Isles
English Heritage Grade II

Formal gardens on the Victorian terraces beneath the castle. The Spring Garden, a pretty woodland garden, has recently been restored to its early 19th-century form and is open by appointment to groups at any time of the year.

LONG CLOSE
60 Main Street, Woodhouse Eaves, Loughborough LE12 8RZ
☎ 01509 890616 (daytime)

Owner Mrs George Johnson
Location 4 miles south of Loughborough
Open 9.30 am – 1 pm and 2 pm – 5.30 pm; Monday – Saturday; March to July. Also for NGS
Admission Adults £2; Children 20p. Tickets from Pene Crafts Gift Shop, opposite
Facilities Parking; dogs permitted; loos; access for the disabled; plants for sale, especially penstemons; teas on NGS days
Features Fine conifers; old roses; woodland garden; rhododendrons; azaleas; heathers

A plantsman's garden, made by the present owner over many years, and now magnificently mature. Five acres, crammed into a long narrow site that spreads out at the end into woodland, underplanted with massed rhododendrons and azaleas.

The University of Leicester Botanic Garden
Beaumont Hall, Stoughton Drive, Oadby LE2 2NA
☎ 0116 271 7725
Owner The University of Leicester
Location 3 miles south of Leicester on A6 London Road opposite Racecourse: badly signposted
Open 10 am – 4 pm (3.30 pm Friday); Monday – Friday; all year except Bank Holidays
Admission Free
Facilities Parking; loos; plants for sale
Features Fine conifers; glasshouses; rhododendrons and azaleas; rock garden; modern roses; old roses; cacti; succulents; heathers; fuchsias; tallest red maytree *Crataegus laevigata* 'Paul's Scarlet' (12m.) in the British Isles
NCCPG National Collections *Aubrieta*; *Chamaecyparis lawsoniana*; *Fuchsia*; *Hesperis*; *Skimmia*
Friends Membership offers newsletters, special access, plant exchanges, monthly meetings and guide. Application forms from: The Curator, Botany Dept., Leicester University, Leicester LE1 7RH

Sixteen acres, and one of the best modern botanic gardens, with a wide variety of plants from historic trees to an 1980s ecological meadow. A pretty Edwardian pergola draped with roses, a well-planted rock garden and a splendid display of hardy fuchsias from the National Collection all add to its interest.

Whatton House
Long Whatton, Loughborough LE12 SBG
☎ 01509 842302   Fax 01509 842268
Owner Lord Crawshaw
Location Jct 24, Kegworth A6 towards Hathern
Open 2 pm – 6 pm; Sundays & Bank Holiday Mondays; Easter to 31 August. And for NGS
Admission Adults £2; OAPs & children £1 (1998 prices)
Facilities Parking; dogs permitted; loos; facilities for the disabled; plants for sale; refreshments
Features Good collection of trees; herbaceous plants; good architectural features; fruit of special interest; rock garden; modern roses; old roses; climbing plants; bark temple; canyon garden; Chinese garden
English Heritage Grade II

Fifteen acres attached to a garden centre. Most of the features date from c. 1900 but there has been much replanting in recent years. The Chinese garden sports some extraordinary mythological figures. There is also a mysterious 'bogey hole'. Great fun to visit.

Worth a Visit

Barnsdale Plants and Gardens
The Avenue, Exton, Oakham LE15 8AH
☎ 01572 813200. Open 10 am – 5 pm (4 pm from November to March); daily; all year £5 for gardens (gardens open 1 March to 31 October). Barnsdale Garden, so familiar from Geoff Hamilton's TV series, is well worth a special journey to see. A wide selection of perennials, shrubs and trees is grown by the nursery. All are grown in peat-free compost.

Goscote Nurseries Ltd
Syston Road, Cossington LE7 4UZ ☎ 01509 812121.
Open 8 am – 5 pm (8 am – 4. 30 pm in winter), Monday – Friday; 9 am – 5 pm, Saturdays; 10 am – 5 pm, Sundays. This nursery has an extensive collection of trees and shrubs, with a particularly long list of azaleas, conifers and rhododendrons at reasonable prices.

The Herb Nursery
Thistleton, Oakham LE15 7RE ☎ 01572 767658.
Open 9 am – 6 pm (or dusk, if earlier); daily; all year. This nursery sells herbs, wildflowers, cottage-garden flowers and scented-leaf geraniums. Their list is written both in botanical Latin and common English.

Philip Tivey & Son
28 Wanlip Road, Syston LE7 8PA ☎ 0116 269 2968.
Open 9 am – 5 pm, Monday – Saturday; 9 am – 2.30 pm, Sundays. Well-known specialist growers of dahlias and chrysanthemums, including Korean and hardy border types.

Wartnaby Gardens
Wartnaby, Melton Mowbray LE14 3HY
☎ 01664 822549. Open 11 am – 4 pm; 27 June and by appointment (preferably weekdays). A model modern garden, where rare plants are displayed in an endless variety of situations and habitats. Roses feature significantly, with good herbaceous underplanting and satisfying colour schemes. Still expanding: recent additions include a knot garden, a rose garden and new herbaceous borders.

Lincolnshire

Belton House
Grantham NG32 2LS
☎ 01476 566116   Fax 01476 579071
Owner The National Trust
Location 3 miles north-east of Grantham on the A607
Open 11 am – 5.30 pm; Wednesday – Sunday plus Bank Holiday Mondays; 27 March to 31 October. Closed 2 April
Admission Adults £5.20; Children £2.80
Facilities Parking; loos; facilities for the disabled; gift shop; lunches, teas, licensed restaurant
Features Bluebells; herbaceous plants; good architectural features; snowdrops; good topiary; woodland garden; interesting for children; daffodils; statue walk re-instated (1997); biggest sugar maple *Acer saccharum* in the British Isles
English Heritage Grade I

Grandeur and amenity go hand in hand at Belton. There are 1,000 acres of wooded deer park, a Wyattville orangery, a Dutch garden and an Italian garden with statues and parterres. But the adventure playground and other facilities make it popular with all ages.

DODDINGTON HALL
Doddington, Lincoln LN6 4RU
☎ 01522 694308   Fax 01522 682584

Owner Anthony Jarvis
Location Signposted off the A46 Lincoln bypass
Open Garden only: 2 pm – 6 pm; Sundays; March & April. House & garden: Wednesdays, Sundays & Bank Holiday Mondays; May to September
Admission Garden only: £2.10; Children £1.05
Facilities Parking; loos; facilities for the disabled; licensed restaurant
Features Herbaceous plants; old roses; turf maze; spring bulbs; two new fountains in walled west garden (1998)
English Heritage Grade II*

A ravishing Elizabethan house around which successive generations have made a successful Tudor-style garden. Simple and open at the front, Edwardian knots and parterres in the walled garden (thickly and richly planted), and then a modern herb garden and pleached hornbeams. Wonderfully harmonious and strongly recommended in early summer.

GRIMSTHORPE CASTLE
The Estate Office, Grimsthorpe Castle, Bourne PE10 0NB
☎ 01778 591205   Fax 01778 591259

Owner Grimsthorpe & Drummond Castle Trust Ltd
Location On A151, 4 miles north-west of Bourne
Open 11 am – 6 pm; Thursdays, Sundays & Bank Holidays; 4 April to 26 September. Plus daily in August, except Friday & Saturday
Admission Adults £3; Concessions £2.
Facilities Parking; loos; access for the disabled; tea-rooms (licensed)
Features Good collection of trees; landscape designed by Capability Brown; lake; modern roses; good topiary
English Heritage Grade I

First Capability Brown, then a late-Victorian Italian garden, still maintained with summer bedding. The most interesting feature is a formal vegetable garden, made in the 1960s before the craze for potagers, right below the Italian garden.

GUNBY HALL
Gunby, Spilsby PE23 5SS
☎ 01909 486211

Owner The National Trust
Location 2½ miles north-west of Burgh-le-Marsh
Open 2 pm – 6 pm; Wednesdays (plus Thursdays for garden only); 27 March to 30 September
Admission Garden only: Adults £2.50, Children £1
Facilities Parking; dogs permitted; loos; access for the disabled; plants for sale
Features Herbaceous plants; fruit of special interest; herbs; old roses
English Heritage Grade II

Ignore the parkland and make for the two walled gardens. Here is all the action: rich herbaceous borders, an arched apple walk, shrub roses, herbs and vegetables.

SPRINGFIELDS SHOW GARDENS
Spalding PE12 6ET
☎ 01775 724843   Fax 01775 711209

Owner Springfields Horticultural Society Ltd
Location 1 mile from Spalding, off bypass
Open 10 am – 6 pm; daily; 19 March to 9 May
Admission Adults £3; OAPs £2.70; Children free
Facilities Parking; loos; facilities for the disabled; plants for sale; gift shop; restaurant and café
Features Modern roses; woodland garden; millions of bulbs
Friends Associate Membership available: £10

Originally a display garden for the Lincolnshire bulb trade, Springfields now offers fun and colour all through the season, with roses providing the midsummer display and bold bedding taking over until the autumn frosts. An eyeful of a garden, splendidly maintained.

WORTH A VISIT

BAYTREE NURSERIES & GARDEN CENTRE
High Road, Weston, Spalding PE12 6JU ☎ *01406 370242. Open 9 am – 6 pm, summer; 9 am – 5 pm, winter. This large, award-winning garden centre is worth knowing.*

HIPPOPOTTERING NURSERY
Orchard House, East Lound, Haxey, Doncaster DN9 2LR ☎ *01427 752185. Open By appointment only. This nursery specialises in Japanese maples, from selected colourful seedlings and bonsai material to mature specimens. Cultivars are selected from their collection of over 120; they also sell rootstocks.*

POTTERTON AND MARTIN
Moortown Road, Nettleton, Caistor LN7 6HX ☎ *01472 851792. Website www.users.globalnet.co.uk/~pottin01 Open 9 am – 5 pm; daily. This alpine, bulb and rock plant specialist has an impressive record of gold medals at Chelsea. It carries an interesting and extensive range, running from the easy to the unusual.*

RISEHOLME HALL
Lincolnshire College of Agriculture & Horticulture, Riseholme LN2 2LG ☎ *01522 522252. Open 10 am – 5 pm; 9 May. And by appointment. The old house has an 18th-century landscape – park, lake and broad trees. The Bishop's Walk is Edwardian: tender plants flourish between the yew hedge and brick wall. However the main garden is strictly educational, with demonstrations of roses, herbaceous plants, fruit and vegetables, alpine plants and annuals, all beautifully maintained and meticulously labelled.*

LONDON

CANNIZARO PARK
West Side Common, Wimbledon SW19
☎ 0181 946 7349
Owner London Borough of Merton
Location West side of Wimbledon Common
Open 8 am – sunset, Monday – Friday; 9 am – sunset, Saturday, Sunday & Bank Holidays; all year
Admission Free
Facilities Parking; loos; some refreshments at summer weekends
Features Herbaceous plants; fine conifers; modern roses; woodland garden; azaleas; magnolias; summer bedding; tallest *Sassafras albidum* (17m.) in the British Isles
English Heritage Grade II*

Famous for its azaleas, planted about 40 years ago and almost too much of a good thing when in full flower. Little known, even to Londoners, Cannizaro deserves recognition as one of the best Surrey-type woodland gardens in the country. A Friends group has just started: details from 0181 545 3657.

CAPEL MANOR
Bullsmoor Lane, Enfield EN1 4RQ
☎ 0181 366 4442
Owner Capel Manor Corporation
Location A10 by Jct 25 on M25
Open 10 am – 5.30 pm (or dusk if sooner); daily; March to October
Admission £4 Adults; £3.50 OAPs; £2 Children (1998 prices)
Facilities Parking; dogs permitted; loos; facilities for the disabled; small shop; refreshments
Features Alpines; good collection of trees; herbaceous plants; daffodils; ecological interest; fruit and vegetables of special interest; glasshouses; herbs; oriental features; plantsman's garden; good topiary; interesting for children; roses of every kind
NCCPG National Collections *Achillea*; *Sarcococca*

High profile demonstration garden attached to a horticultural college 'where the City meets the Countryside'. Brilliant for new ideas, especially for small gardens: there is a walled garden, herb garden, knot garden, disabled garden, shade garden, an Italianate holly maze, a pergola, alpine beds and some historical recreations.

CHELSEA PHYSIC GARDEN
66 Royal Hospital Road SW3 4HS
☎ 0171 352 5646   Fax 0171 376 3910
Owner Chelsea Physic Garden Company
Location Please look at your London A to Z
Open 11 am – 3 pm; 7 & 14 February for snowdrops. 12 noon – 5 pm, Wednesdays; 2 pm – 6 pm, Sundays; 4 April to 31 October. Plus 24 to 28 May for Chelsea Flower Show and 21 to 25 June for Chelsea Festival
Admission Adults £4; Concessions £2
Facilities Loos; facilities for the disabled; plants for sale; light refreshments
Features Herbaceous plants; glasshouses; herbs; 18th-century rock garden; new Pharmaceutical Garden (1999); largest *Koelreuteria paniculata* in England
English Heritage Grade I
NCCPG National Collection *Cistus*
Friends Friends have unrestricted rights of entry in office hours: worth considering if you live nearby

This oasis of peace between Royal Hospital Road and the Chelsea Embankment started life in 1673 as a pharmacological collection, and has kept its original design, but it also has the oldest rock garden in Europe, the largest olive tree in Britain, a vast number of rare and interesting plants, and probably the last known specimen of the 1920s' white hybrid tea rose 'Marcia Stanhope'.

CHISWICK HOUSE
Burlington lane, Chiswick W4 2RP
☎ 0181 742 1225
Owner English Heritage
Location South-west London on A4 and A316
Open 8 am – dusk; daily; all year
Admission Free
Facilities Parking; dogs permitted; loos; access for the disabled; refreshments
Features Camellias; good architectural features; glasshouses; worked on by Kent; parterres; summer bedding; luxuriant evergreens
English Heritage Grade I

Laid out by Bridgeman and Kent for Lord Burlington, Chiswick is the best baroque garden in Britain, and the exquisite house is pure Palladian. A Duke of Devonshire added an Italian renaissance garden early in the 19th century, and a Camellia House with slate benches and huge bushes, mainly of old *japonica* varieties. Forget the dogs and the joggers – almost all free-entry gardens have a municipal heart – but explore the *pattes d'oie*, *allées* and holly groves of the main garden on a hot July morning and you might be doing a Grand Tour of Italy 250 years ago.

FENTON HOUSE
Hampstead Grove NW3 6RT
☎ 0171 435 3471
Owner The National Trust
Location Entrances in Hampstead Grove near Hampstead Underground station
Open 2 pm – 5 pm; Wednesday – Friday; 7 April to 31 October. Plus 2 pm – 5 pm, Saturdays & Sundays; 6 March to 4 April. And 11 am – 5 pm; Saturdays & Sundays; March to October
Admission Adults £4.10; Children £2.05
Facilities Loos
Features Herbaceous plants; herbs; old roses; restored Edwardian garden; new greenhouse (1998)

A country garden in Hampstead. Neat, terraced gardens near the house, rather more informal at the bottom. Not outstandingly flowerful, but the hedges are good and plants are firmly trained: definitely worth knowing.

HAM HOUSE
Richmond TW10 7RS
☎ 0181 940 1950

Owner The National Trust
Location On River Thames, signed from A307
Open 10.30 am – 6 pm, or dusk, if earlier; daily except Thursdays, Fridays, 1 January & 25/26 December; all year
Admission Adults £1.50
Facilities Parking; loos; facilities for the disabled; National Trust shop; restaurant open when house open
Features Fruit of special interest; herbs; climbing roses; modern roses; parterres; holm oak avenue; new juniper walk (1998)
English Heritage Grade II*

A modern re-creation of the 17th-century original. The best bit is a grand series of hornbeam enclosures with white summerhouses and seats. There are plans to re-develop some of the other areas.

HAMPTON COURT PALACE
KT8 9AU
☎ 0181 781 9500

Owner Historic Royal Palaces Agency
Location North side of Kingston bridge over the Thames on A308 Jct with A309
Open Park: Dawn to dusk; daily; all year. King's Privy Garden: 9.30 am – 5.30 pm (April to mid-October) & 9.30 am – 4 pm (mid-October to March). Opens at 10.15 am on Mondays
Admission Parking £2. Privy Garden: Adults £2.10; Children £1.30
Facilities Parking; dogs permitted; loos; facilities for the disabled; shop
Features Herbaceous plants; fruit of special interest; herbs; modern roses; old roses; good topiary; interesting for children; particularly good in July–August; famous maze; laburnum walk; knot gardens
English Heritage Grade I

Sixty-six acres of famous garden and 600 acres of deer park. Here are some highlights: Charles II's Long Canal with radiating lime avenues to imitate the *pattes d'oie* at Versailles; the broad walk, now a herbaceous border 100 yards long; bowling alleys, tilt yards, the great maze and the Great Vine (actually 'Black Hamburgh'), the newly restored King's Privy Garden, the priory garden, knot garden and all those bulbs in spring. A ten-year plan for renovation has just been announced, starting with the great Maze: watch this space.

ISABELLA PLANTATION
Richmond Park, Richmond
☎ 0181 948 3209   Fax 0181 332 2730

Owner The Royal Parks Agency
Location Richmond Park
Open Dawn to dusk; daily; all year
Admission Free

Facilities Parking; dogs permitted; access for the disabled
Features Good collection of trees; fine conifers; lake; rhododendrons and azaleas; woodland garden; primulas
NCCPG National Collection *Rhododendron* (Kurume azaleas)
Friends Friends of Richmond Park. Secretary, Howard Stafford, 0181 789 4601

Forty-two acres of rhododendrons and azaleas under a deciduous canopy in Richmond Park. Best in May when the candelabra primulas flower and the hostas are in new leaf. Little known.

MYDDELTON HOUSE GARDENS
Bulls Cross, Enfield EN2 9HG
☎ 01992 717711   Fax 01992 651406

Owner Lee Valley Regional Park Authority
Location Off A10 onto Bullsmoor Lane: signposted at Bulls Cross. Or train to Turkey Street Station
Open 10 am – 4.30 pm; weekdays except Christmas Holidays; all year. 2 pm – 5 pm; Sundays & Bank Holidays; February to October
Admission Adults £1.80; Concessions £1.20
Facilities Parking; loos; access for the disabled; plants for sale
Features Good collection of trees; herbaceous plants; daffodils; plantsman's garden; pond; climbing roses; old roses; snowdrops; particularly interesting in winter
English Heritage Grade II
NCCPG National Collection *Iris*
Friends E A Bowles of Myddelton House Society, c/o The Secretary, 102 Myddelton Avenue, Enfield EN1 4AG

Holy ground for plantsmen with a sense of history, E A Bowles' garden was abandoned for 30 years. Lee Valley Regional Park Authority has started to restore it. The irises and roses are still impressive. In autumn, the colchicums and cyclamen match the carpets of crocuses and snowdrops of spring.

OSTERLEY PARK
Isleworth TW7 4RB
☎ 0181 560 5421

Owner The National Trust
Location 5 miles west of central London on A4
Open 9 am – 7.30 pm (or dusk, if earlier); daily; all year
Admission Park & pleasure grounds free
Facilities Parking; dogs permitted; loos; facilities for the disabled; new National Trust shop; tea-room
Features Fruit of special interest; herbs; lake; woodland garden; particularly interesting in winter; fine rare oaks; autumn colour; tallest variegated chestnut *Castanea sativa* 'Albomarginata' (16m.) in the British Isles
English Heritage Grade II*

Classical 18th-century landscape. Fine temple and semi-circular conservatory by Robert Adam. Good trees – especially cedars and oaks.

ROYAL BOTANIC GARDENS, KEW
Kew, Richmond TW9 3AB
☎ 0181 940 1171

Owner Trustees of the Royal Botanic Gardens
Location Kew Green, south of Kew bridge, or Underground Station
Open 9.30 am – 5.30 pm (7 pm at weekends) or 30 minutes before dusk, if earlier; daily; all year except 25 December & 1 January. Glasshouses close at 5.30 pm
Admission Adults £5; Concessions £3.50; Children £2.50 (under-fives free)
Facilities Parking; loos; facilities for the disabled; gift & book shop; orangery & pavilion restaurants & bakery
Features Alpines; good collection of trees; herbaceous plants; fine conifers; ecological interest; good architectural features; fruit of special interest; glasshouses; herbs; lake; oriental features; plantsman's garden; rock garden; climbing roses; modern roses; old roses; garden sculpture; snowdrops; subtropical plants; woodland garden; interesting for children; particularly interesting in winter; heather gardens; 138 record trees – more than any other garden in the British Isles – including 38 different oaks (*Quercus* spp.)
English Heritage Grade I
NCCPG National Collections Betula; *Hypericum*; *Nothofagus*; *Skimmia*
Friends Friends of Kew: very active and good value – write or telephone for details

Kew has such superstar status that it needs no description. Go in lilac time, if you wish, but go too in winter when there is much to see both in and out of the glasshouses. Visit the newly restored Palm House, as well as the new Princess of Wales Conservatory (worth a whole afternoon) and do not miss the alpine house. In summer there are very good bedding-out schemes, but the garden is somewhat bedevilled by Canada geese, which foul the grass, and by aircraft noise.

SYON PARK
Brentford TW8 8JF
☎ 0181 560 0881   Fax 0181 568 0936

Owner The Duke of Northumberland
Location Between Brentford and Isleworth, north bank of Thames
Open 10 am – 6 pm, or sunset if earlier; daily except 25 & 26 December; all year
Admission Adults £3; Concessions £2
Facilities Parking; loos; access for the disabled; plants for sale; Wyevale Garden Centre on site: 0181 568 0134; shops, restaurants, all the fun of the fair
Features Good collection of trees; herbaceous plants; landscape designed by Capability Brown; fine conifers; good architectural features; glasshouses; woodland garden; interesting for children; cacti; ferns; exhibition of gardening for the disabled; rose garden restored and replanted (1997); tallest *Catalpa ovata* (22m.) in the British Isles (and 14 further record trees); tropical butterfly house
English Heritage Grade I

Syon is a mixture of 18th-century landscape, 19th-century horticultural seriousness, 20th-century plantsmanship and 21st-century theme park. Splendid conservatories with good collections, worth visiting in winter.

WORTH A VISIT

CLIFTON NURSERIES
Clifton Villas, Little Venice W9 2PH ☎ 0171 289 6851. Open 8.30 am – 6 pm, Monday – Saturday; 10.30 am – 4.30 pm, Sundays; March to September. 8.30 am – 5.30 pm, Monday – Saturday; 10 am – 4 pm, Sundays; October to February. Smart, stylish source of good plants for London gardens. Particularly good for topiary, statuary, climbers and shrubs in specimen sizes, indoor and conservatory plants.

KENWOOD
Hampstead Lane NW3 7JR   Open 8 am to dusk (8.30 pm if sooner); daily; all year. These 100 acres of superb 18th-century parkland around two glittering lakes were recently half-restored to Repton's original designs, a haven of calm from London's busyness.

THE MUSEUM OF GARDEN HISTORY
Lambeth Palace Road SE1 7LB ☎ 0171 261 1891. Open 10.30 am – 4 pm (5 pm on Sundays); Sunday – Friday; 7 March to 12 December. The garden is small (and secondary to the Museum's collections and excellent exhibitions) but designed as a 17th-century knot garden and planted with plants associated with the Tradescants. A garden for contemplation.

WALPOLE HOUSE
Chiswick Mall W4 2PS ☎ 0181 994 1611.   Open 2 pm – 6 pm; 9 May. A large town garden, designed and planted in the Hidcote style and made to seem much larger than its 2/3rd acre. Big trees, a large lily-pond and densely planted herbaceous borders all contribute to the sense of rus in urbe.

MERSEYSIDE

CROXTETH HALL & COUNTRY PARK
Croxteth Hall Lane, Liverpool L12 0HB
☎ 0151 228 5311   Fax 0151 228 2817

Owner City of Liverpool
Location Muirhead Avenue East
Open 11 am – 5 pm; daily; Easter to September
Admission Walled garden: Adults £1.10; OAPs & children 60p. Grounds free
Facilities Parking; loos; facilities for the disabled; plants for sale; cafeteria
Features Herbaceous plants; fruit of special interest; glasshouses; herbs; interesting for children; current holder of Sandford Award
English Heritage Grade II
NCCPG National Collection *Fuchsia*
Friends Friends of Croxteth Hall & Country Park: details from Mrs Vickers

Very much a public amenity, Croxteth Hall majors on fruit, vegetables and herbs – showing in its walled garden what visitors can try at home. Good greenhouses. Heart-warming.

NORFOLK

BLICKLING HALL & GARDEN
Blickling, Norwich NR11 6NF
☎ 01263 733084   Fax 01263 734924
Owner The National Trust
Location 1 mile west of Aysham on B1354
Open 10.30 am – 5 pm; Wednesday – Sunday & Bank Holiday Mondays; 2 April to 31 October
Admission Adults £3.50; Children £1.75
Facilities Parking; loos; facilities for the disabled; plants for sale; National Trust shop; light snacks, lunches & teas
Features Bluebells; herbaceous plants; landscape designed by Capability Brown; old roses; subtropical plants; woodland garden; particularly good in July–August; herbaceous borders at peak July–August
English Heritage Grade II*

The garden with everything. Jacobean mansion, handsomely symmetrical; early landscape (Doric Temple, c. 1735); smashing conservatory by Samuel Wyatt; mid-19th-century parterre by Nesfield (topiary pillars); and 1930s herbaceous colour plantings by Nancy Lindsey (her masterpiece). Fabulous bluebells in the woods.

BRESSINGHAM GARDENS & STEAM MUSEUM
Bressingham, Diss IP22 2AB
☎ 01379 687386
Owner Alan Bloom
Location On A1066, 3 miles west of Diss
Open 10 am – 5.30 pm; daily; April to October. Adrian Bloom's garden is open on Mondays, Thursdays & the first Sunday of every month from April to October
Admission Gardens & Steam Museum: Adults £3.80 (1998 price)
Facilities Parking; loos; access for the disabled; plants for sale; refreshments in adjacent plant centre
Features Bog garden; herbaceous plants; fine conifers; plantsman's garden; particularly good in July–August
Friends Monthly lectures April – October

There is no better place to learn about herbaceous plants – what they look like, how they grow and how to place them. The Dell is a complex of island beds, which act as a trial ground for the herbaceous and alpine plants for which Alan Bloom is famous. Foggy Bottom contains Adrian Bloom's collection of conifers and exemplifies his ideas for planting them. Herbaceous interplantings are replacing the heathers: the results are fascinating.

EAST RUSTON OLD VICARAGE
East Ruston, Norwich NR12 9HN
☎ 01603 632350   Fax 01603 664217
Owner Graham Robeson & Alan Gray
Location 3 miles north of Stalham on Stalham to Happisburgh road. Ignore three signposts to East Ruston
Open 2 pm – 5.30 pm; Wednesdays, Sundays & Bank Holidays; 4 April to 31 October
Admission Adults £3; Children £1; RHS members free in September & October
Facilities Parking; loos; facilities for the disabled; plants for sale; tea-room
Features Young garden; architectural plants; 'tropical' borders; new one-acre gravel garden simulating a dried-up river bed (1999)

This is a modern garden on a grand scale: 12 acres of firm design, long vistas and extravagant plantings. Being close to the sea, the garden supports many plants that are usually too tender for East Anglia. The names of two of the garden rooms tell it all: the Tropical Border and the Mediterranean Garden.

ELSING HALL
Elsing, Dereham NR20 3DX
☎ & Fax 01362 637224
Owner Mr & Mrs D H Cargill
Location B1110 to North Tuddenham, then follow signs
Open 2 pm – 6 pm; Sundays; June to September; and by appointment
Admission Adults £3; children free
Facilities Parking; dogs permitted; loos; plants for sale
Features Good collection of trees; fruit of special interest; lake; old roses; kitchen garden; enlarged collection of old roses (1998); many rare trees planted (1999)

A garden of great charm, whose owners have planted many good trees, roses and a formal garden to enhance the medieval house and its romantic moat. An avenue of ginkgos, a collection of willows and a small arboretum of trees chosen for their coloured bark are some of the most recent additions. And the garden expands.

FAIRHAVEN GARDENS TRUST
South Walsham, Norwich NR13 6EA
☎ & Fax 01603 270449
Owner Fairhaven Garden Trust
Location 9 miles north-east of Norwich on the B1140
Open 11 am – 5.30 pm; Tuesday – Sunday, plus Bank Holidays; April to October
Admission Adults £3; OAPs £2.70; Children £1; RHS members free in April & May
Facilities Parking; dogs permitted; loos; access for the disabled; small shop; visitors' centre; excellent plant sales area; tea-room
Features Bluebells; lake; woodland garden; rhododendrons; lilies; candelabra primulas; new hydrangea walk (1998); boat trips on the broad

Basically an enormous plantsman's garden (200 acres) round one of the Norfolk broads. Rhododendrons and azaleas under a canopy of oak and alder, plus extensive plantings of candelabra primulas, lysichitons, astilbes, and other bog plants in and around the water. Splendid autumn colour.

FELBRIGG HALL
Roughton, Norwich NR11 8PR
☎ 01263 837444   Fax 01263 838297

NORFOLK GARDENS

Owner The National Trust
Location Entrance off B1436, signed from A148 & A140
Open 11 am – 5.30 pm; Saturday – Wednesday; 27 March to 31 October
Admission Adults £2.20; Children £1.10
Facilities Parking; loos; facilities for the disabled; plants for sale; National Trust shop; restaurant & tea-room
Features Herbaceous plants; fruit of special interest
English Heritage Grade II*
NCCPG National Collection *Colchicum*

The best bit of Felbrigg is the walled kitchen garden, oriented on a large brick dovecote flanked by Victorian vineries. Fruit trees are trained against the walls (figs, pears, plums) and the garden laid to neatly grown vegetables with herbaceous borders along the box-edged gravel paths.

HOLKHAM HALL
Holkham, Wells-next-the-Sea NR23 1AB
☎ 01328 710227 **Fax** 01328 711707

Owner The Earl of Leicester
Location Off A149, 2 miles west of Wells
Open 11.30 am – 5 pm; 4 & 5 April, 2, 3, 30 & 31 May. Then 1 pm – 5 pm; Sunday – Thursday; June to September. Park open daily
Admission House: Adults £4; Children £2. Park free
Facilities Parking; dogs permitted; loos; access for the disabled; gift shop; garden centre open daily all year 10 am – 5 pm; refreshments
Features Landscape designed by Capability Brown; garden sculpture
English Heritage Grade I

A big landscape garden, worked on by Kent, Brown and Repton. Mighty impressive. In the nearby garden centre is a walled garden with several demonstration gardens, including herbs, roses and perennials.

MANNINGTON GARDENS
Mannington Hall, Norwich NR11 7BB
☎ 01263 584175 **Fax** 01263 761214

Owner Lord Walpole
Location Signposted from B1149 at Saxthorpe
Open 12 noon – 5 pm; Sundays; May to September. And 11 am – 5 pm; Wednesday – Friday; June to August
Admission Adults £3; Concessions £2.50; Children free
Facilities Parking; loos; facilities for the disabled; roses for sale; light refreshments, teas
Features Climbing roses; old roses; new blue-and-silver herbaceous border (1998); new miniature rose collection (1998)
English Heritage Grade II

Mannington has a moated house, two lakes, a scented garden and handsome herbaceous borders, but the best part is the Heritage Rose Garden, made in association with Peter Beales, where thousands of old-fashioned roses are displayed to illustrate the History of the Rose.

OXBURGH HALL
Oxborough, King's Lynn PE33 9PS
☎ 01366 328258

Owner The National Trust
Location 7 miles south-west of Swaffham on Stoke Ferry Road
Open 11 am – 5.30 pm; Saturday – Wednesday; 27 March to 31 October. Daily in August
Admission Adults £2.50; Children £1.25
Facilities Parking; loos; facilities for the disabled; gift shop; light lunches & tea
Features Herbaceous plants; modern roses; French-style parterre; trained fruit trees
English Heritage Grade II

The baroque 19th-century parterre has been replanted by the National Trust with such herbs as rue and santolina making permanent companions for annuals and bedding plants. Good fruit trees in the walled garden: medlars, quinces, and mulberries. Not a great garden, but a good one.

SANDRINGHAM HOUSE
Sandringham, King's Lynn PE35 6EN
☎ 01553 772675 **Fax** 01485 541571

Owner H M The Queen
Location Signed from A148
Open 10.30 am – 5 pm; 1 April to 20 July and 5 August to 3 October
Admission Adults £4; OAPs £3.50; Children £2.50
Facilities Parking; loos; facilities for the disabled; plants for sale; gift shop; restaurant & tea-rooms
Features Herbaceous plants; rhododendrons; azaleas; maples; hydrangeas
English Heritage Grade II*

The best of the royal gardens. The woodland and lakes are rich with ornamental plantings, and the splendid herbaceous borders were designed by Geoffrey Jellicoe, but it is the scale of it all that most impresses, and the grandeur too.

SHERINGHAM PARK
Gardener's Cottage, Sheringham Park, Sheringham NR26 8TB
☎ 01263 823778

Owner The National Trust
Location Junction of A148 & B1157
Open Dawn to dusk; daily; all year
Admission Cars £2.60
Facilities Parking; dogs permitted; loos; facilities for the disabled; refreshments
Features Landscape designed by Capability Brown; fine conifers; landscape designed by Humphry Repton; woodland garden; rhododendrons
English Heritage Grade II*

One of the best Repton landscapes outstanding, but fleshed out with a great early 20th-century collection of rhododendrons and glorified by a classical temple, designed by Repton but not eventually built until 1975. Currently undergoing substantial restoration as the rhododendron woods are cleaned up and replanted: interesting to study.

WORTH A VISIT

AFRICAN VIOLET CENTRE
Station Road, Terrington St Clement, King's Lynn PE34 4PL ☎ *01553 828374. Open 10 am – 5 pm, all year, except for Christmas – New Year period. The specialists for saintpaulias, with a huge selection on offer. Weekend shows for other plants are held during the season.*

HOECROFT PLANTS
Severals Grange, Holt Road, Wood Norton, Dereham NR20 5BL ☎ *01362 684206. Open 10 am – 4 pm, Thursday – Sunday, April to September. Well-known specialist nursery for variegated and coloured foliage plants, and especially for decorative grasses – over 200 varieties.*

NORFOLK LAVENDER LTD
Caley Mill, Heacham, King's Lynn PE31 7JE ☎ *01485 570384. Open 10 am – 5 pm; daily; all year. NCCPG National Collection:* Lavandula. *Everything lavender is here: plants, hardy and tender, sold bare-root and in pots respectively; soaps, scents, dried flowers and the National Collection, as well as a large fragrant meadow.*

P W PLANTS
Sunnyside, Heath Road, Kenninghall NR16 2DS ☎ *01953 888212. Open 9 am – 5 pm; Fridays; and last Saturday of the month. P W Plants has a wide choice of general stock, and is strong on grasses. But its great speciality is bamboos, for long a major feature of RHS shows. The display gardens are extensive.*

PETER BEALES ROSES
London Road, Attleborough NR17 1AY ☎ *01953 454707. Open 9 am – 5 pm (4 pm in January); Monday – Friday; 9 am – 4.30 pm; Saturdays; 10 am – 4 pm; Sundays. NCCPG National Collection:* Rosa *(species). The display gardens of this specialist grower and collector of older and classic roses is well worth a visit. The extensive list has over 1,000 species and varieties, many not available elsewhere in UK. Among the popular and rare items, there is also an interesting selection of early hybrid teas.*

READS NURSERY
Hales Hall, Loddon NR14 6QW ☎ *0150 548395. Open 10 am – 5 pm; Tuesday – Saturday. Plus 11 am – 4 pm on Sundays & Bank Holiday Mondays from May to October. NCCPG National Collections:* Citrus; Ficus; Vitis vinifera. *Long-established family nursery (with the largest medieval barn in England) which specialises in citrus and conservatory plants. The mouth-watering list includes excellent collections of both of these, with vines, figs garden and greenhouse fruit trees, and topiary also.*

ROMANTIC GARDEN NURSERY
Swannington, Norwich NR9 4NW ☎ *01603 261488. Open 10 am – 5 pm; Wednesdays; Fridays; Saturdays.*

Well-known topiary specialists. Ornamental standards, bobbles and pyramids in Cupressus *and* Ilex, *as well as box in animal and other shapes. Clematis and half-hardy plants are also available.*

WYKE HOUSE
Mill Road, Bergh Apton, Norwich NR15 1BQ ☎ *01508 480322. Up-and-coming plantsman's garden in 3½ acres of old orchard, with an array of plants – eucalyptus, salvias and bamboos – that is unusual in this part of the country.*

NORTHAMPTONSHIRE

BOUGHTON HOUSE
Kettering NN14 1BJ
☎ 01536 515731   Fax 01536 417255
Website www.boughtonhouse.org.uk
Owner The Duke & Duchess of Buccleuch & The Living Landscape Trust
Location A43, 3 miles north of Kettering
Open 1 pm – 5 pm; Saturday – Thursday; 1 May to 1 September. Plus Fridays in August
Admission Adults £1.50; OAPs & children £1
Facilities Parking; dogs permitted; loos; facilities for the disabled; plants for sale; shop
Features Herbaceous plants; modern roses; interesting for children; current holder of Sandford Award; adventure playground
English Heritage Grade I

A seriously important landscaped park dating from the early 18th century. Rides, avenues, *allées*, pools, canals and prospects.

CANONS ASHBY HOUSE
Daventry NN11 3SD
☎ 01327 860044   Fax 01327 860168
Owner The National Trust
Location Signposted from A5 & A422
Open 12 noon – 5.30 pm; Saturday – Wednesday; 27 March to 31 October
Admission Adults £3.60; Children £1.80; Family £9
Facilities Parking; loos; facilities for the disabled; light lunches & teas
Features Herbaceous plants; fruit of special interest; good topiary
English Heritage Grade II*

A rare survivor among gardens. The Drydens, who owned it, never really took to the landscape movement. The early 18th-century layout is intact and has been carefully restored by the National Trust. The terraces below the house (*very* pretty) are planted with clipped Portugal laurel and period fruit trees. A place to contemplate old Tory values.

Castle Ashby Gardens
Castle Ashby, Northampton NN7 1LQ
☎ 01604 696187   Fax 01604 696516

Owner Marquess of Northampton
Location Off A428 between Northampton and Bedford
Open 10 am – dusk; daily; all year
Admission Adults £2.50; OAPs & children £1 (1998)
Facilities Parking; dogs permitted; facilities for the disabled; plants for sale; gift shops; refreshments
Features Good collection of trees; landscape designed by Capability Brown; glasshouses; good topiary; particularly interesting in winter
English Heritage Grade I

Much thought and money has been spent on restoring the gardens recently. The Italian formal gardens were among the first to be renewed, and the arboretum has been restocked. There are a stylish orangery and greenhouses by Sir Matthew Digby Wyatt but perhaps the best thing about Castle Ashby is the park – 200 acres of it, designed by Capability Brown.

Coton Manor
Guilsborough, Northampton NN6 8RQ
☎ 01604 740219   Fax 01604 740838

Owner Ian Pasley-Tyler
Location Signposted from A50 and A428
Open 12 noon – 5.30 pm; Wednesday – Sunday & Bank Holiday Mondays; April to September
Admission Adults £3.50; OAPs £3; Children £2
Facilities Parking; loos; access for the disabled; home produce & gifts; excellent small nursery; tea-room
Features Bluebells; herbaceous plants; lake; modern roses; woodland garden; waterfowl; 50 different hebes; lots of pots

A nicely designed and thoughtfully planted garden – rarities and common plants chosen for effect – made by three generations over 70 years. Highlights include a rose garden, herb garden, water garden, colour plantings and bluebell wood. The standard of maintenance is excellent, while the presence of a few ornamental birds adds another dimension to a visit.

Cottesbrooke Hall
Northampton NN6 8PF
☎ 01604 505808   Fax 01604 505619

Owner Captain & Mrs John Macdonald-Buchanan
Location 10 miles north of Northampton
Open 2 pm – 5 pm; Tuesday – Friday & Bank Holiday Mondays; 5 April to 30 September. Plus Saturdays & Sundays in September
Admission Garden only: Adults £2.50; Children £1.25
Facilities Parking; loos; plants for sale; tea/coffee & cold drinks
Features Herbaceous plants; old roses; garden sculpture
English Heritage Grade II

The garden with everything: a two-mile drive, majestic parkland, a classical bridge, a fabulously pretty house, an 18th-century park, lakes, waterfalls, bluebell woods, rhododendrons, acres of daffodils, 27 varieties of snowdrop, half-a-dozen garden rooms, Scheemaker's statues from Stowe, an armillary garden, pergolas, *allées*, 300-year old cedars, new developments every year, immaculate maintenance, an enlightened owner, a brilliant head gardener, plants a-plenty, and the signatures of Geoffrey Jellicoe and Sylvia Crowe among the designers who have helped to develop it. If only more people knew of it...

Holdenby House Gardens
Holdenby, Northampton NN6 8DJ
☎ 01604 770074   Fax 01604 770962

Owner Mr & Mrs James Lowther
Location 6 miles north-west of Northampton, off A50 or A428
Open 2 pm – 6 pm; Sunday – Friday; Easter to 30 September
Admission Adults £3; OAPs £2.25; Children £1.75
Facilities Parking; dogs permitted; loos; facilities for the disabled; plants for sale; souvenirs and crafts for sale; tea-room in original Victorian kitchen
Features Herbaceous plants; herbs; old roses; interesting for children; Elizabethan-style garden; fragrant and silver borders; current holder of Sandford Award
English Heritage Grade II*

Pretty modern gardens designed and planted by the present owners with help from Rosemary Verey and Rupert Golby. The Elizabethan-style garden uses only plants available in 1580.

Rockingham Castle
Market Harborough LE16 8TH
☎ 01586 770240   Fax 01586 771692

Owner Cdr L M M Saunders Watson
Location 2 miles north of Corby on A6003
Open 1 pm – 5 pm; Sundays, Thursdays, Bank Holiday Mondays & following Tuesdays (plus all Tuesdays in August); Easter Sunday to 17 October
Admission Adults £4.20; OAPs £3.70; Children £2.70
Facilities Parking; dogs permitted; loos; access for the disabled; tea-room
Features Good collection of trees; herbaceous plants; old roses
English Heritage Grade II*

Twelve acres around the historic castle. The formal circular rose garden on the site of the old keep is surrounded by a billowing 400-year-old yew hedge. The wild garden in a ravine was replanted 20 years ago as a mini-arboretum: very effective.

Sulgrave Manor
Sulgrave, Banbury OX17 2SD
☎ & Fax 01295 760205

Owner Sulgrave Manor Board
Location 7 miles from Banbury
Open 10.30 am – 1 pm (but mornings by appointment only on weekdays except in August) & 2 pm – 5.30 pm (4.30 pm in March, November & December); daily except Wednesdays (but weekends only in March,

November & December); 1 March to 24 December, plus 27 to 31 December
Admission Adults £3.75; Children £2
Facilities Parking; dogs permitted; loos; access for the disabled; plants for sale; tea-room
Features Herbaceous plants; fruit of special interest; herbs; modern roses; good topiary; splendid new visitor centre (1999)
English Heritage Grade II

Famous (and highly visitable) for two reasons: first, its association with George Washington; second, its formal design, unchanged since it was laid out by Sir Reginald Blomfield in 1921.

WORTH A VISIT

ALTHORP HOUSE
Althorp, Northampton NN7 4HQ ☎ *01604 770107.*
No opening arrangements at the time of our going to press. Interesting more for its ex-royal associations than as a great garden, which it is not. But the 19th-century formal gardens are impressive and the traditional parkland deeply pastoral.

THE OLD RECTORY, SUDBOROUGH
Sudborough NN14 3BX ☎ *01832 733247. Open for NGS & by appointment. Neat new garden, three acres in size, around a handsome Georgian rectory. Good snowdrops and hellebores; unusual vegetables. The garden is thickly and thoughtfully planted so that every season is rich in interest. Rosemary Verey and Rupert Bowlby had a hand in it.*

NORTHUMBERLAND

BELSAY HALL
Belsay, Newcastle-upon-Tyne NE20 0DX
☎ 01661 881636   Fax 01661 881043
Owner English Heritage
Location At Belsay on A696 Ponteland to Jedburgh road
Open 10 am – 6 pm (4 pm from 1 October to 31 March); daily except 24 to 26 December
Admission Adults £3.60; Concessions £2.70; Children £1.80 (1998 prices)
Facilities Parking; dogs permitted; loos; facilities for the disabled; plants for sale; gift shop; refreshments in summer and at weekends
Features Fine conifers; rhododendrons and azaleas; snowdrops; particularly interesting in winter; extraordinary quarry garden; tallest Portuguese laurel *Prunus lusitanica* (14m.) in the British Isles
English Heritage Grade I
NCCPG National Collection *Iris*

Wildly romantic Victorian gardens, including several acres of disused quarry with *Trachycarpus* palms, a sequence of gloomy chasms, splendid woodfuls of hardy hybrid rhododendrons, intensive modern herbaceous plantings, brooding conifers and the ruins of Belsay Castle. Superbly maintained.

BIDE-A-WEE COTTAGE
Stanton, Netherwitton, Morpeth NE65 8PR
☎ 01670772 262
Owner N M Robson
Location 7 miles north-west of Morpeth
Open 1.30 pm – 5 pm; Saturdays; May to August. And for NGS
Admission £2
Facilities Parking; new small nursery selling plants from garden
Features Plantsman's garden; rock garden

Mark Robson's youth has turned this newish garden into something of a cult, but deservedly so, for both design and plantings are brilliant. The situation is extraordinary: the entire garden is hidden in a disused quarry on the edge of a 500-foot ridge.

CHILLINGHAM CASTLE
Chillingham NE66 5NJ
☎ 01668 215359   Fax 01668 215463
Owner Sir Humphry Wakefield Bt
Location Off A1 between Alnwick and Berwick
Open 12 noon – 5 pm; daily except Tuesday; Easter weekend, then May to September. Plus Tuesdays from July to September
Admission Adults £3.90; OAPs £3.75; Children free (1998 prices)
Facilities Parking; loos; museum, antique and curio shop; tea-room
Features Herbaceous plants; fine conifers; modern roses; old roses; good topiary; woodland garden; daffodils; bluebells; vast yew trees and magnificent redwoods
English Heritage Grade II

Chillingham has made great efforts to smarten up for visitors. The results are very encouraging: a 19th-century Italianate garden by Wyattville, a modern herbaceous border in the old walled garden and splendid hardy hybrid rhododendrons in the woodland walks which surround the lake. Chillingham itself is a formidable medieval castle with amazing views down long 18th-century rides. There is an exhibition of old photographs in the castle which show the garden more than 100 years ago.

CRAGSIDE
Rothbury, Morpeth NE65 7PX
☎ 01669 620333
Owner The National Trust
Location 15 miles north-west of Morpeth off A697 & B6341
Open 10.30 am – 7 pm; Tuesday – Sunday; April to October. Plus Bank Holiday Mondays, and Mondays in June

Admission Adults £3.95; Children £1.95
Facilities Parking; loos; facilities for the disabled; plants for sale; National Trust shop; refreshments
Features Fine conifers; fruit of special interest; rock garden; old roses; interesting for children; massive rock garden; Armstrong's hydroelectric system fascinates adults and children alike; tallest *Abies nordmanniana* (50m.), *Chamaecyparis nootkatensis* (33m.) and *Picea glauca* (28m.) in the British Isles
English Heritage Grade II*

Two gardens. The newly acquired Italianate formal garden has splendid carpet bedding, ferneries and a fruit house with rotating pots. Even more impressive are the rhododendron woods – hundreds and hundreds of acres of 19th-century hybrids, plus trusty *R. ponticum* and *R. luteum*, breathtaking in late May.

HERTERTON HOUSE GARDENS & NURSERY
Hartington, Cambo NE61 4BN
☎ 01670 774278

Owner Mr & Mrs Frank Lawley
Location 2 miles north of Cambo (B6342)
Open 1.30 pm – 5.30 pm; daily except Tuesdays & Thursdays; April to September. For NGS on 19 June, 17 July & 7 August
Admission Adults £2.20; Children free
Facilities Parking; loos; first-class nursery attached
Features Herbaceous plants; herbs; plantsman's garden; knot garden; new gazebo at the top end (1998); Tudor rose garden under construction (1999)

A plantsman's garden attached to a small nursery. The knot garden is famous, and much photographed, full of herbs and pharmacological plants. More impressive still are the herbaceous plantings, all weaving through each other in beautiful colour-coordinated schemes. More new gardens are planned.

HEXHAM HERBS
Chesters Walled Garden, Chollerford, Hexham NE46 4BQ
☎ 01434 681483

Owner Mrs S White
Location 6 miles north of Hexham, off B6318 near Chollerford
Open 10 am – 5 pm; daily; April to October. Telephone for winter opening times
Admission Adults £1.50; Children (under 10) free
Facilities Parking; access for the disabled; nursery attached
Features Herbs; old roses; woodland garden; 'Roman' garden; grass garden (extended in 1998)
NCCPG National Collections *Origanum*; *Thymus*

An energetic and successful small modern nursery garden, strategically placed near the fort at Chesters. The herb collection is remarkable (over 900 varieties) and the design within a two-acre brick walled garden is charming. Dye plants, a Mediterranean garden, an astilbe bed and a knot garden are just some of the features.

HOWICK HALL GARDENS
Alnwick NE66 3LB
☎ & Fax 01665 577285

Owner Howick Trustees Ltd
Location Off B1399 between Longhoughton and Howick
Open 1 pm – 6 pm; daily; April to October
Admission Adults £2; OAPs & children £1
Facilities Parking; loos
Features Fine conifers; plantsman's garden; rhododendrons and azaleas; old roses; spring bulbs; eucryphias; biggest stone pine *Pinus pinea* in the British Isles
English Heritage Grade II

Rather an un-Northumbrian garden, because its closeness to the sea makes possible the cultivation of such tender plants as *Carpenteria* and *Ceanothus*. Formal terraces below the house are well planted, but the great joy of the garden at Howick is a small woodland which has acid soil. This was planted in the 1930s with a fine collection of rhododendrons and camellias: other plants are still added. The result looks more west coast than east.

WALLINGTON
Cambo, Morpeth NE61 4AR
☎ 01670 774283

Owner The National Trust
Location 6 miles north-west of Belsay (A696)
Open 10 am – 7 pm (4 pm or dusk, if earlier); daily; April to November
Admission Adults £3.80
Facilities Parking; dogs permitted; loos; access for the disabled; restaurant
Features Herbaceous plants; daffodils; glasshouses; rhododendrons and azaleas; climbing roses; old roses; woodland garden; plantings by Graham Thomas; particularly interesting in winter; new plantings in East Wood (1997); tallest *Sorbus discolor* (7m.) in the British Isles
English Heritage Grade II*
NCCPG National Collection *Sambucus*

There are three reasons to visit Wallington. First, because Capability Brown was born in nearby Kirkharle. Second, to gawp at the ancient tree-like specimen of *Fuchsia* 'Rose of Castille' in the conservatory. Third, to admire the modern mixed borders (*very* Graham Thomas) in the long, irregular, walled garden, in a sheltered valley far from the house. Worth the journey for any of them, but prepare for a longish walk to the walled garden.

NOTTINGHAMSHIRE

CLUMBER PARK
The Estate Office, Worksop S80 3AZ
☎ 01909 476592   Fax 01909 500721

Owner The National Trust

Location Off A614 Nottingham Road, 4 miles south of Worksop
Open Park: dawn to dusk; every day; all year. Walled garden, vineries and garden tool museum: 11 am – 5 pm; Saturdays, Sundays & Bank Holidays; April to October
Admission Park: free. Garden: Adults 70p; Children 30p. Car parking £3
Facilities Parking; dogs permitted; loos; facilities for the disabled; plants for sale; National Trust shop; restaurant
Features Landscape designed by Capability Brown; lake; woodland garden; autumn colour; vineries; old rhubarb cultivars; superb trees; tallest *Ilex aquifolium* 'Laurifolia' (20m.) in the British Isles
English Heritage Grade I

3,800 acres of thickly wooded parkland with a Gothic chapel, classical bridge, temples, an avenue of cedars, a heroic double avenue of limes and masses of rhododendrons. Good conservatories and a garden tools exhibition in the old walled garden. The scale is enormous: very impressive.

FELLEY PRIORY
Underwood NG16 5FL
☎ 01773 810230

Owner The Hon Mrs Chaworth-Musters
Location ½ mile west of M1 on A608
Open 9 am – 12.30 pm; Tuesdays, Wednesdays & Fridays; all year. Plus 9 am – 4 pm; 2nd & 4th Wednesday of every month; March to October. And 11 am – 4 pm; every 3rd Sunday of month; March to October. 11 am – 4 pm on 11 April for NGS. NCCPG plants fairs 12 noon – 4 pm; 6 June & 3 October
Admission Adults £1.50; Children free
Facilities Parking; loos; facilities for the disabled; nursery attached; tea-room
Features Herbaceous plants; modern roses; knot gardens, two pergolas and new rose garden; millions of daffodils; new pleached hedge of *Crataegus tanacetifolia;* rare shrubs; new rock garden (1997); new hydrangea border (1998)

Charming, modern, plantsman's garden, stylishly designed and planted, and attached to a small but promising nursery. Handsome yew hedges, less than 20 years old, with curvy tops and bobbles. There is a profusion of roses in high summer, with some varieties imported direct from French nurseries, while the red sandstone walls give shelter to an astonishing range of tender plants. And it gets better all the time.

HODSOCK PRIORY
Blyth, Worksop S81 0TY
☎ 01909 591204   Fax 01909 591578
Website www.courtfield.co.uk/hodsock

Owner Sir Andrew & Lady Buchanan
Location Signed off the B6045 Blyth – Worksop
Open Also 10 am – 4 pm; daily; February/March (telephone for exact dates) for snowdrops. Also 1 pm – 5 pm, 22 March
Admission Adults £2.50; Children free

Facilities Parking; loos; facilities for the disabled; tea-room
Features gardening courses

Richly planted modern garden on an ancient moated site surrounded by fine old trees. The snowdrops and aconites in February are spectacular and the Buchanans have been planting masses of different bulbs for late winter effect.

HOLME PIERREPONT HALL
Holme Pierrepont, Nottingham NG12 2LD
☎ & Fax 0115 933 2371

Owner Robin Brackenbury
Location 3 miles east of Trent Bridge
Open 2 pm – 5.30 pm; Easter, Spring & Summer Bank Holiday Sundays & Mondays; Thursdays in June; Wednesdays & Thursdays in July; Tuesday – Thursday in August
Admission House & gardens £3.50; Gardens £1.50
Facilities Parking; dogs permitted; loos; access for the disabled; plants for sale; teas in the long gallery
Features Old roses; young garden; formal gardens
English Heritage Grade II

The main attraction of this garden is a large courtyard garden, designed in 1875, whose box parterre is filled with modern plantings. But there are fine recent additions too: an old rose collection, splendid herbaceous borders and interesting fruit trees.

WORTH A VISIT

MILL HILL PLANTS
Mill Hill House, Elston Lane, East Stoke, Newark NG23 5QJ ☎ *01636 525460. Open 10 am – 6 pm; Wednesday – Sunday; and Bank Holiday Mondays; April to September. NCCPG National Collection: Berberis. The nursery stocks a range of hardy perennials and alpines: the speciality is bearded irises. The garden is planted for year-round interest and is open for the NGS on 14 April, 3 & 31 May, 16 June & 30 October.*

NATURESCAPE
Coach Gap Lane, Langar NG13 9HP ☎ *01949 851045. Open 11 am – 5.30 pm; daily; 1 April to 30 September. A wildlife centre, with a wildlife garden showing different habitats. Wildflowers, British native shrubs and trees, pond and marsh species and cottage-garden favourites, available as plants and seeds.*

NEWSTEAD ABBEY
Newstead Abbey Park NG15 8GE ☎ *01623 793557. Chiefly of interest for being the debt-ridden estate Lord Byron inherited and had to sell, but Newstead has a good modern garden. Best are the Japanese garden and substantial rockery. The Council has restored and replanted it all extensively as a public amenity: lots of cheerful roses and summer bedding.*

OXFORDSHIRE

BLENHEIM PALACE
Woodstock, Oxford OX20 1PX
☎ 01993 811091   Fax 01993 813577
Website www.blenheimpalace.com
Owner The Duke of Marlborough
Location 8 miles north of Oxford
Open 10.30 am – 5.30 pm; daily; 15 March to 31 October
Admission Park & gardens: Adults £5.60; Children £2.80. Maze extra (£1 in 1998)
Facilities Parking; loos; access for the disabled; plants for sale; good shops; one restaurant & two self-service cafés
Features Landscape designed by Capability Brown; good architectural features; lake; garden sculpture; interesting for children; formal gardens; new maze; current holder of Sandford Award
English Heritage Grade I

The grandest of grand gardens. Vanbrugh, Bridgeman, Hawksmoor and Wise worked here. The huge (2,000-acre) park was laid out by Capability Brown, and Achille Duchêne restored the formal baroque gardens in the 1920s; most impressive too are the eight acres of walled kitchen garden.

BROOK COTTAGE
Well Lane, Alkerton, Banbury OX15 6NL
☎ 01295 670303
Owner Mrs D M Hodges
Location 6 miles west of Banbury, ½ mile off A422
Open 9 am – 6 pm; Monday – Friday; 5 April to 31 October. Groups (& weekend visits) by appointment
Admission Adults £2.50; OAPs £2; Children free
Facilities Parking; dogs permitted; loos; plants for sale; DIY tea and coffee; groups by arrangement
Features Herbaceous plants; plantsman's garden; rock garden; old roses; 40 different clematis; new border of agapanthus & kniphofias (1997)

First-rate modern garden made by the present owner since 1964 on four acres of sloping pasture. Good plants and good plantings but, above all, a good sense of colour and form. Beautiful flowering trees in spring, opulent old roses in summer and fine autumn colour.

BROUGHTON CASTLE
Banbury OX15 5EB
☎ 01295 276070
Owner Lord Saye
Location 2½ miles west of Banbury on the B4035
Open 2 pm – 5 pm; Wednesdays & Sundays; 18 May to 14 September. Plus Thursdays in July & August and Bank Holiday Sundays and Bank Holiday Mondays (including Easter)
Admission Castle & gardens: Adults £4; OAPs & students £3.50; Children £2
Facilities Parking; dogs permitted; loos; facilities for the disabled; plants for sale; tea-room

Features Herbaceous plants; planted by Gertrude Jekyll; designed by Roper; climbing roses; old roses
English Heritage Grade II*

Mainly designed and planted by Lanning Roper 25 years ago, with a blue-yellow-white border contrasting with a pink-and-silver one. The neat knot garden with roses and lavender is best seen from the house: it was designed by Lady Algernon Gordon-Lennox in the 1890s.

BUSCOT PARK
Faringdon SN7 8BU
☎ 01367 240786   Fax 01367 241794
Owner The National Trust
Location On A417 west of Faringdon
Open House & garden: 2 – 6 pm; Wednesday – Friday, plus 2nd & 4th Saturday (& the Sunday immediately following) each month. Garden only: Monday – Friday (but not Bank Holidays). April to September
Admission Adults £4.40 house & garden; £3.30 garden only
Facilities Parking; loos; plants for sale; light refreshments
Features Herbaceous plants; good architectural features; fruit of special interest; old roses; good topiary; tallest *Pinus nigra* var. *cebennensis* (32m.) in the British Isles
English Heritage Grade II*

One of the most original gardens of this century, planned by Harold Peto as a water garden (long canals and bridges), with a *patte d'oie* groundplan. Peter Coats planted lush herbaceous borders in the 1970s and Tim Rees did a good conversion job in the walled garden ten years later: climbing vegetables as climbing plants and gooseberries grown as standards are among his quirkier features.

CLOCK HOUSE
Coleshill, Swindon SN6 7PT
☎ 01793 762476   Fax 01793 861615
Owner Denny Wickham
Location On B4019 between Highworth & Faringdon
Open 2 pm – 5 pm; Thursdays; April to October. Plus 16 May, 13 June, 12 September & 3 October. 2 pm – 8 pm on 4, 11, 18 & 25 June
Admission Adults £1.50; Children free
Facilities Parking; loos; plants for sale; teas & cakes
Features Herbaceous plants; herbs; old roses

A garden of charm and vigour, whose borders burgeon with good growth, unusual juxtapositions and original colour schemes. An inspiration.

MANOR HOUSE, STANTON HARCOURT
Stanton Harcourt, Witney OX8 1RJ
☎ 01865 881928
Owner The Hon Mrs Gascoigne
Location In village
Open 2 pm – 6 pm; 4, 5, 15, 18 April; 2, 3, 13, 16, 27, 30 & 31 May; 10, 13, 24, 27 June; 8, 11, 22, 25 July; 12, 15, 26, 29, 30 August; 9, 12, 23, 26 September

Admission Garden only: Adults £2.50; OAPs & children £1.50
Facilities Parking; loos; access for the disabled; plants for sale; teas
Features Herbaceous plants; daffodils; climbing roses; modern roses

Wonderful late-medieval manorhouse, surrounded by Edwardian gardens in the Elizabethan style. Parts are romantically overgrown. Others have been spruced up in contemporary taste with David Austin roses and espaliered fruit trees.

NUNEHAM COURTENAY ARBORETUM
Nuneham Courtenay
☎ 01865 276920

Owner University of Oxford
Location 6 miles south of Oxford on the Henley Road
Open 10 am – 5 pm; daily; May to October. 10 am – 4.30 pm; Monday – Friday; November to April
Admission Donation: £1 suggested
Facilities Parking
Features Good collection of trees; fine conifers; woodland garden
NCCPG National Collection Bamboos

Fifty-acre arboretum developed since 1950 around a nucleus of American conifers planted c. 1840. Experimental plantations and conservation areas rub along with cushioned rhododendrons, a bluebell wood and an *Acer* glade to match Westonbirt.

OXFORD BOTANIC GARDEN
High Street, Oxford OX1 4AX
☎ & Fax 01865 276920

Owner University of Oxford
Location East end of High Street next to river
Open 9 am – 5 pm (4.30 pm from October to March); daily; all year except 2 April & 25 December. Glasshouses open 2 pm – 4 pm
Admission Donation box, but £2 in summer
Facilities Facilities for the disabled
Features Fine conifers; glasshouses; herbs; rock garden; old roses; garden sculpture; vegetables of interest; interesting for children; systematic beds; huge service tree; new autumn border (1998); tallest *Diospyros virginiana* (18m.) in UK and five other record trees
English Heritage Grade I
NCCPG National Collection *Euphorbia*
Friends Very active Friends of Oxford Botanic Garden: details from the Secretary, c/o Oxford University Botanic Garden etc. Seed list, lectures, use of library, plant sales, visits

A beautifully laid-out, well-labelled, progressive, yet classical, botanic garden, founded in 1621. Everything you would expect, from ferns to carnivorous plants, but also a grace and calm that is far from the bustle outside.

ROUSHAM HOUSE
Steeple Aston, Bicester OX6 3QX
☎ & Fax 01869 347110

Owner C Cottrell-Dormer
Location A4260 then off the B4030
Open 10 am – 4.30 pm; daily; all year
Admission Adults £3. No children under 15
Facilities Parking; loos; access for the disabled
Features Worked on by Kent; early 18th-century landscape
English Heritage Grade I

Rousham is the most perfect surviving example of William Kent's landscaping: *Kentissimo*, according to Horace Walpole. The main axis brings you to Scheemakers's statue of a lion devouring a horse, high above the infant River Cherwell. Follow the circuit correctly: the serpentine landscape lies away to the side. Here are Venus' Vale, the Cold Bath and Townsend's Building, from which a lime walk will lead you to the Praeneste. Rousham is an Arcadian experience. The pretty herbaceous border in the walled garden and the modern rose garden by the dovecote seem almost an irrelevance.

STANSFIELD
49 High Street, Stanford-in-the-Vale SN7 8NQ
☎ 01367 710340

Owner Mr & Mrs D Keeble
Location Off A417 opposite Vale garage
Open 10 am – 4 pm; Tuesdays; 6 April to 24 August. 2 pm – 6 pm; Sundays; 9 May to 6 June. And by appointment
Admission Adults £1.50; Children free
Facilities Plants for sale; refreshments
Features Herbaceous plants; plantsman's garden; new rabbit-proof kitchen garden! (1997); new Mediterranean garden (1998)

A modern plantsman's garden, and a model of what enthusiastic collecting can produce in a few years. Over 2,000 different plants in just over one acre, with troughs, screes, open borders and endless micro-habitats. Fascinating.

STONOR PARK
Henley-on-Thames RG9 6HF
☎ & Fax 01491 638587

Owner Lord Camoys
Location 5 miles north of Henley-on-Thames
Open 2 pm – 5.30 pm; Sundays & Bank Holiday Mondays from April to September; Wednesdays in July & August
Admission £2.50
Facilities Parking; loos; access for the disabled; tea-room
Features Daffodils; rock garden; old roses
English Heritage Grade I

Stonor fills a hillside and can all be seen from the road below: classical parkland, the Elizabethan house, lawns, terraces, a walled garden, and finally the wood at the top. Nothing appears to have changed for 200 years: the effect is miraculous.

WATERPERRY GARDENS
Wheatley, Oxford OX33 1JZ
☎ 01844 339226   Fax 01844 339883

Owner School of Economic Science
Location Near Jct 8 on M40, well signed locally
Open 10 am – 5.30 pm (5 pm from November to March); daily; all year except 15–18 July & Christmas/New Year period
Admission April to October: Adults £3.25; OAPs £2.75; Children £1.75. November to March: all £1.50; RHS members free in October
Facilities Parking; dogs permitted; loos; access for the disabled; plants for sale; home produce, stoneware, books; tea-shop; wine licence
Features Herbaceous plants; glasshouses; herbs; rock garden; modern roses; dwarf conifer; citrus; soft fruit
NCCPG National Collection *Saxifraga*

Essentially a teaching garden with a commercial nursery grafted on, but the herbaceous borders and alpine collections are worth the journey.

WORTH A VISIT

BURFORD GARDEN CENTRE
Shilton Road, Burford OX18 4PA ☎ *01993 823117. Open 9 am – 6 pm, Monday – Wednesday & Saturdays, Thursdays & Fridays; 11 am – 5 pm, Sundays (earlier in January & February). Excellent garden centre with indoor and outdoor plants, and a wide range of associated product suppliers.*

GREENWAYS
40 Osler Road, Headington, Oxford OX3 9BJ
☎ *01865 767680 (after dark).   Open 2 pm – 6 pm; 16 May, 18 July, 15 August. Quite new, and totally different. The Cootes have emphasised the Provençal looks of the house by planting a rich Mediterranean garden – glittering evergreens, terracotta pots, old oil jars, gravel, parterres – with an exuberance of tender plants including olives, daturas, yuccas, oleanders, acanthus and Albizia julibrissin. Quite the most stylish garden we know, and intensively maintained to the highest standard.*

KELMSCOTT MANOR
Kelmscott, Lechlade GL7 3HJ ☎ *01367 252486. Open 11 am – 1 pm and 2 pm – 5 pm on Wednesdays; 2 pm – 5 pm on the 3rd Saturday of the month; April to September. Plus 2 pm – 5 pm; 3 & 17 July, 7 & 21 August. William Morris's garden is being remodelled and restored. Worth a visit if you are interested in the Arts and Crafts movement: the price of a ticket includes a tour of the house.*

LIME CLOSE
35 Henley's Lane, Drayton, Abingdon OX14 4HU
☎ *01235 531231.   Open 2 – 6 pm; 28 February & 16 May. This modern garden has been much praised, and deservedly, for its wide range of plants and the way in which they are grouped. As well as the rare plants, it can boast a recently planted shade border, a pond, an ornamental kitchen garden, a herb garden designed by Rosemary Verey and a wonderful selection of scree beds, gravel beds, raised beds and troughs planted by the owner's aunt Miss Christie-Miller. And all within three acres.*

MATTOCKS ROSES
Nuneham Courtenay, Oxford OX44 9PY
☎ *01865 343265.   Open 9 am – 5.30 pm (5 pm in winter), Monday – Saturday; 11 am – 5 pm, Sundays. Mattocks are particularly good for ground-cover roses and their own 'County' series. Now part of the Notcutts group.*

THE OLD RECTORY, FARNBOROUGH
Farnborough, Wantage OX12 8NX ☎ *01488 638298. Open 2 pm – 6 pm; 18 April, 16 May & 27 June. And by written appointment. Excellent modern garden, made by the owners on a high, cold, windy site over the last 25 years. Lots of hedges and thick planting were the keys to survival, but the effect now is of shelter and luxuriance. Splendid double herbaceous border and clever colour plantings.*

THE SKIPPET
Ramsden, Witney OX7 3AP ☎ *01993 868253.   Open By appointment for individuals & groups.   An alpine plantsman's collection, brimful with rarities in pots, troughs, screes, and raised beds. The owner considers that his garden maintenance is not as good as it used to be, but visitors disagree and find infinite interest in this beautifully sited two-acre treasure house for good plants. And not just alpines, but trees, shrubs, bulbs and herbaceous plants too.*

WESTWELL MANOR
Burford OX18 4JT ☎ *01993 823121.   Open 2 pm – 6.30 pm; 31 May.   A large and busy Cotswold garden with several distinct 'rooms' and well-used converted outbuildings. Roses in profusion, bulbs for spring and climbers draping the walls and hedges.*

WILCOTE HOUSE
Wilcote, Finstock OX7 3DY ☎ *01993 868606.   Open By appointment.   Fast-developing garden around a stunning Jacobean house. Courtyards and terraces with Mediterranean goodies and climbers. Borders with clever colours and wonderful roses. The arboretum is young and small, but promising.*

SHROPSHIRE

ATTINGHAM HALL
The National Trust, Attingham Park, Shrewsbury SY4 4TP
☎ 01743 709203   Fax 01743 709352

Owner The National Trust
Location 5 miles south-east of Shrewsbury on B4380
Open 8 am – 9 pm (5 pm from November to March); daily; all year except 25 December
Admission Adults £1.80; Children 90p
Facilities Parking; dogs permitted; loos; facilities for the disabled; National Trust shop; light lunches & teas

Features Daffodils; landscape designed by Humphry Repton; rhododendrons and azaleas; newly restored orangery
English Heritage Grade II*

No garden to speak of, but the classical late 18th-century parkland round the vast Georgian house is a joy to walk around at any time of the year.

BENTHALL HALL
Broseley TF12 5RX
☎ & Fax 01952 882159

Owner The National Trust
Location 1 mile north-west of Broseley (B4375)
Open 1.30 – 5.30 pm; Wednesdays, Sundays & Bank Holiday Mondays; April to September
Admission Adults £2
Facilities Parking; loos; facilities for the disabled
Features Herbaceous plants; herbs; old roses; garden sculpture; plantings by Graham Thomas

Smallish, but well restored with a Graham Thomas rose garden. Home of the 19th-century botanist George Maw. His Mediterranean collection is still the backbone of the garden – crocuses naturalised everywhere.

DAVID AUSTIN ROSES
Bowling Green Lane, Albrighton, Wolverhampton WV7 3HB
☎ 01902 373931

Owner David Austin
Location Signposted in village
Open 9 am – 5 pm; Monday – Friday. 10 am – 6 pm (or dusk if earlier); Saturdays & Sundays. All year
Admission Free
Facilities Parking; loos; important rose nursery; restaurant & light refreshments
Features Herbaceous plants; roses of every kind

David Austin has developed an entirely new strain of 'English' roses which combine the shape and scent of old-fashioned roses with the colours, health and floriferousness of modern types. The display gardens adjoining his nursery are impressive: five different sections, each extensive and thickly planted with old-fashioned roses and his own hybrids: magical in early July. Several new roses are introduced every year at Chelsea.

HODNET HALL GARDENS
Hodnet, Market Drayton TF9 3NN
☎ 01630 685202   Fax 01630 685853

Owner A E H Heber-Percy
Location Near junction of A53 & A442
Open 12 noon – 5 pm; Tuesday – Sunday & Bank Holiday Mondays; April to September
Admission Adults £3; OAPs £2.50; Children £1.20
Facilities Parking; dogs permitted; loos; facilities for the disabled; plants for sale; gift shop; 17th-century tea-rooms
Features Herbaceous plants; old roses; woodland garden; camellias; primulas; rhododendrons; HHA/Christie's Garden of the Year in 1985

English Heritage Grade II

A large garden – some 60 acres – still expanding and well maintained. Best known for the chain of lakes and ponds planted with primulas and aquatics, but the rhododendrons alone demand a visit. Good in late summer too, with hydrangeas and astilbes. One of the greatest 20th-century gardens.

WORTH A VISIT

THE DOWER HOUSE
Morville Hall, Bridgnorth WV16 5NB ☎ *01746 714407. Open 2 pm – 6 pm; Wednesdays & Sundays; April to September. A small modern garden or, rather, a series of them: a medieval turf maze, a cloister garden, an Elizabethan knot garden, a canal garden, a Victorian rose garden, and a 19th-century wilderness. And all of it made on 1½ acres since 1989.*

LOWER HALL
Worfield, Bridgnorth WV15 5LH ☎ *01746 716607. Lanning Roper helped to get this splendid garden going 30 years ago. It bestrides the River Worfe and every part has a distinct character. Lush streamside plantings, infinite colour schemes, and a woodland area at the bottom. Formal designs, straight brick paths, a pergola and more colour themes in the old walled garden. One of the best modern gardens and neatly kept.*

PREEN MANOR
Church Preen, Church Stretton SY6 7LQ
☎ *01694 771207. Open 2 pm – 6 pm; 2 May, 10, 24 & 27 June; 22 & 29 July; 3 October (closes at 4.30 pm). Groups by appointment in June & July. A new garden for an old site, with some original ideas. A chess garden, a collection of plants in handsome old pots, a fern garden and that symbol of the 1990s – a gravel garden. And it gets better every year.*

RUTHALL MANOR
Ditton Priors, Bridgnorth WV16 6TN ☎ *0174 634 608. Open For NGS, and by appointment. One-acre plantsman's garden, some 800 feet up, made over 20 years. Good trees, rare shrubs and lots of ground cover. Pretty pool with aquatics and marginals. Very satisfying.*

THE SHREWSBURY QUEST
193 Abbey Foregate, Shrewsbury SY2 6AH
☎ *01743 243324. Open 10 am – 5 pm (4 pm from November to March); daily; all year. Closed 1 January & 25 December. This interactive experience of medieval life includes a herb garden and a simple monks' garden of ancient plants. Particularly interesting for children.*

SWALLOW HAYES
Rectory Road, Albrighton, Wolverhampton WV7 3EP
☎ *01902 372624. Open 11 am – 4 pm; 24 January. Groups by appointment. NCCPG National Collections: Hamamelis; Lupinus (Russell strains). Swallow Hayes is a plantswoman's garden (3,000 plants) entirely made since 1966 and a model of its kind, where ground cover helps to minimise labour and maximise enjoyment.*

SOMERSET

THE AMERICAN MUSEUM
Claverton Manor, Bath BA2 7BD
☎ 01225 460503   Fax 01225 480726

Owner Trustees of the American Museum in Britain
Location Off A36 south of Bath
Open 1 pm – 6 pm, Tuesday – Friday; 12 noon – 6 pm, Saturdays, Sundays & Bank Holiday Mondays; 20 March to 7 November
Admission Adults £2.50; OAPs £2.25; Children £1.25. Private tours by prior arrangement
Facilities Parking; dogs permitted; loos; access for the disabled; plants for sale; book shop, herb shop and country store; light lunches at weekends; tea, coffee and American cookies
Features Good collection of trees; herbaceous plants; fruit of special interest; herbs; designed by Roper; old roses; good topiary
English Heritage Grade II
Friends Apply to Membership Secretary (01225 460503)

Fifteen immaculate and enchanting acres devoted to elements of American gardening, including a Colonial herb garden ('Colonial' = pre-1778), old roses (best in June), a well-labelled arboretum of American trees, and a pastiche of Mount Vernon.

BARRINGTON COURT
Barrington, Ilminster TA19 0NQ
☎ 01460 241480

Owner The National Trust
Location In Barrington village
Open 11 am – 5.30 pm; Saturdays & Sundays; 27 February to 14 March. Then Saturday – Thursday; 20 March to 31 October
Admission Adults £4.30; Children £2.10
Facilities Parking; loos; access for the disabled; plants for sale; tea-room & licensed restaurant
Features Good collection of trees; fruit of special interest; planted by Gertrude Jekyll; old roses; particularly good in July–August
English Heritage Grade II*

There is still an Edwardian opulence about Barrington. Massive plantings of irises, lilies and rich dark dahlias. And good design detail too: the patterns of the brick paving are a study in themselves.

BATH BOTANIC GARDENS
Royal Victoria Park, Bath
☎ 01225 448433   Fax 01225 480072

Owner Bath City Council
Location West of city centre by Upper Bristol Road
Open 9 am – dusk; daily; all year except 25 December
Admission Free
Facilities Parking; dogs permitted; facilities for the disabled

Features Good collection of trees; rock garden; autumn colour; fine bedding displays; good *Scilla* collection; tallest tree of heaven *Ailanthus altissima* (31m.) and tallest hornbeam *Carpinus betulus* (27m.) in England (and 11 other record trees)
Friends Very active – 330 members – telephone 01225 448433 for details. Quarterly newsletter; lectures and tours all through the year

Nine acres of trees, shrubs, borders, limestone-loving plants and scented walks. Not so much a botanic garden now, more of a public amenity. Standards are high, maintenance is good, and the seasonal highlights of bulbs and bedding are among the best. Some splendid old trees recall the garden's origin as a private garden. The excellent new guide-book is a model of visitor-friendliness.

CANNINGTON COLLEGE HERITAGE GARDEN
Cannington, Bridgwater TA5 2LS
☎ 01278 655000   Fax 01278 655055

Owner Cannington College
Location 3 miles west of Bridgwater on A39
Open 2 pm – 5 pm; daily; April to October
Admission Adults £2; OAPs & children £1.50
Facilities Parking; loos; plants for sale; student canteen open to visitors
Features Alpines; herbaceous plants; fine conifers; fruit of special interest; glasshouses; plantsman's garden; subtropical plants; roses of all sorts
NCCPG National Collections *Abutilon*; *Argyranthemum*; *Osteospermum*; *Wisteria*

Cannington has long been the leading West Country college for ornamental horticulture. The collections in its teaching gardens are very extensive and beautifully displayed. There is an excellent nursery on campus, specialising in tender exotics.

COTHAY MANOR
Greenham, Wellington TA21 0JR
☎ 01823 672283   Fax 01823 672345

Owner Mr & Mrs Alastair Robb
Location 1 mile west of Thorne St Margaret
Open 2 – 6 pm; Thursdays, Sundays & Bank Holiday Mondays; May to September. Groups (17+) by appointment
Admission £3 (in 1998)
Facilities Parking; loos; access for the disabled; plants for sale; cream teas
Features 1920s design; 1990s plants
English Heritage Grade II*

An exciting old/new garden on either side of the River Tone: eight acres of formal 1920s design by Reggie Cooper (friend of Lawrence Johnstone and Harold & Vita) now completely replanted, room by room, colour by colour, since the present owners came here in 1993. Cothay makes a model study of how a garden can be rejuvenated.

Dunster Castle
Minehead TA24 6SL
☎ 01643 821314

Owner The National Trust
Location 3 miles south-east of Minehead on A39
Open 11 am – 4 pm; daily; January to March. 10 am – 5 pm; daily; April to September. Closed 25 December
Admission Adults £2.90; Children £1.30
Facilities Parking; loos; facilities for the disabled; National Trust shop; tea-rooms at Dunster Mill
Features Subtropical plants; woodland garden; particularly interesting in winter; *Arbutus* grove; tallest *Taxodium ascendens* (23m.) in the British Isles
English Heritage Grade I
NCCPG National Collection *Arbutus*

A Victorian woodland on a steep slope, terraced in places and planted with tender exotica – mimosa, *Beschorneria* and a 150-year-old lemon tree in an unheated conservatory.

East Lambrook Manor Garden
East Lambrook, South Petherton TA13 5HL
☎ 01460 240328   Fax 01460 242344

Owner Mr & Mrs Andrew Norton
Location Signed from A303 at South Petherton
Open 10 am – 5 pm; Tuesday – Thursday & Saturdays; March to September
Admission Adults £2.50; Children & students 50p; Groups by arrangement £2
Facilities Parking; loos; plants for sale
Features Herbaceous plants; plantsman's garden; cottage garden plants; geraniums; 'ditch garden'
English Heritage Grade I
NCCPG National Collection *Geranium*

The archetypal super-cottage garden, made by Margery Fish, the popular and influential writer, and charmingly restored in recent years. Ground cover, narrow paths and, above all, plants, plants, plants.

Gaulden Manor
Tolland, Lydeard St Lawrence TA4 3PN
☎ & Fax 01984 667213

Owner James Starkie
Location 1 mile east of Tolland church, off B3224
Open 2 pm – 5 pm; Sundays, Thursdays & Bank Holidays; 6 June to 30 August. Groups by appointment at other times
Admission £2
Facilities Parking; loos; access for the disabled; plants for sale; book & gift shop; teas on Sundays & Bank Holidays
Features Herbaceous plants; herbs; modern roses; old roses; woodland garden; scent gardens; secret garden

A modern garden, and well planted. Small garden rooms, each devoted to a different theme (roses, herbs etc.), and a good stream garden made beneath the monks' pond, its sides planted with candelabra primulas, ferns and gunnera.

Greencombe Gardens
Porlock TA24 8NU

Owner Greencombe Garden Trust
Location ½ mile west of Porlock on left of road to Porlock Weir
Open 2 pm – 6 pm; Saturday – Tuesday; April to July and October to November
Admission Adults £3; Children (under 16) 50p
Facilities Parking; loos; access for the disabled; plants for sale; teas for large groups
Features Herbaceous plants; ecological interest; plantsman's garden; woodland garden
NCCPG National Collections *Erythronium*; *Gaultheria*; *Polystichum*; *Vaccinium*

Rather a cult garden, an organic showpiece, best for its woodland walks where stately gentleness dominates. Interesting plants galore: brilliant azaleas, roses, lilies and clematis – and all those National Collections!

Hadspen Garden
Castle Cary BA7 7NG
☎ & Fax 01749 813707

Owner N & S Pope
Location 2 miles east of Castle Cary on A371
Open 10 am – 5 pm; Thursday – Sunday & Bank Holiday Mondays; 4 March to 30 September
Admission Adults £2.50; Children 50p
Facilities Parking; loos; facilities for the disabled; nursery; light lunches & teas
Features Herbaceous plants; plantsman's garden; old roses; Eric Smith's *Hosta* collection
NCCPG National Collection *Rodgersia*

Part garden, part nursery specialising in colour-plantings and unusual plants. Little remains of Penelope Hobhouse's first garden: the Popes have remade it in the modern idiom, using a wide range of rare plants to create decorative effects. Rather a cult garden now, so we are probably alone in finding it rather disappointing. Certainly, the Popes' book *Colour by Design*, published by Conran Octopus and based on their work at Hadspen, was one of the best new gardening books of 1998.

Hestercombe House
Somerset County Council, Cheddon Fitzpaine, Taunton TA2 8LQ
☎ 01823 413923   Fax 01823 413030

Owner Somerset County Council Fire Brigade
Location 4 miles north of Taunton
Open 10 am – 5 pm; daily; all year
Admission Adults £3.50; Children £1
Facilities Parking; dogs permitted; loos; refreshments
Features Herbaceous plants; planted by Gertrude Jekyll
English Heritage Grade I

Famously restored garden with lots of Lutyens' hallmarks: iris-choked rills, pergolas, relieved staircases and pools where reflections twinkle on recessed apses. Gertrude Jekyll's planting is bold and simple, which adds to the vigour. Very photogenic. The secret Landscape Garden re-opened in 1997: 40 acres of lakes, temples and woodlands which have not been seen for 125 years.

LYTES CARY MANOR
Charlton Mackrell, Somerton TA11 7HU
☎ & Fax 01458 223297
Owner The National Trust
Location Near A303 junction with A372 & A37
Open 2 pm – 6 pm; Mondays, Wednesdays & Saturdays; 27 March to 30 October
Admission Adults £4; Children £2
Facilities Parking; loos; access for the disabled
Features Herbaceous plants; garden sculpture; good topiary; plantings by Graham Thomas
English Heritage Grade II

Neo-Elizabethan garden to go with the prettiest of manor houses. Yew hedges, hornbeam walks, alleys and lawns. Medlars, quinces and a simple Elizabethan flower border.

MILTON LODGE
Old Bristol Road, Wells BA5 3AQ
☎ 01749 672168
Owner D C Tudway Quilter
Location Old Bristol road off of A39
Open 2 pm – 6 pm; Sunday – Friday; 2 April to October
Admission Adults £2; Children (under 14) free
Facilities Parking; loos; plants for sale; teas on Sundays (May to August)
Features Good collection of trees; herbaceous plants; modern roses; tallest *Populus alba* (20m.) in the British Isles
English Heritage Grade II

Impressive Edwardian garden, terraced down against a backdrop of Wells Cathedral. Yew hedges, good modern plantings and an eight-acre arboretum in a combe, replanted in recent years. Excellently maintained and constantly improving.

MONTACUTE HOUSE
Montacute, Yeovil TA15 6XP
☎ 01935 823289
Owner The National Trust
Location In Montacute village
Open 11 am – 5.30 pm (dusk if earlier); daily except Tuesday; 24 March to 31 October. Then 11.30 am – 4 pm; Wednesday – Sunday; 4 November to 31 December
Admission Adults £3; Children £1.30
Facilities Parking; loos; facilities for the disabled; plants for sale; light lunches & teas, licensed restaurant
Features Herbaceous plants; old roses; exquisite gazebos
English Heritage Grade I

The garden is subsidiary to the amazing Elizabethan mansion, apart from a border started by Vita Sackville-West, worked over by Phyllis Reiss and finished by Graham Thomas. But it cannot be beaten for its sense of English renaissance grandeur.

PRIOR PARK
Bath
☎ 01225 833422
Owner The National Trust
Location 1½ miles south of Bath city centre
Open 12 noon – 5.30 pm; Wednesday – Monday; daily except 1 January and 25 & 26 December
Admission Adults £3.80; Children £1.90
Facilities Loos; facilities for the disabled
English Heritage Grade I

This great Palladian park is at last open to the public. There is a snag, however: the Trust can offer no onsite parking. Badgerline runs buses (Nos. 2 & 4) from the bus station or Dorchester Place, every 10 minutes.

SHERBORNE GARDEN
Pear Tree House, Litton BA3 4PP
☎ 01761 241220
Owner Mr & Mrs John Southwell
Location On B3114, ½ mile west of Litton village
Open 11 am – 6 pm; Mondays & Sundays; June to September. Other times by appointment
Admission Adults £2; Children free
Facilities Parking; dogs permitted; loos; access for the disabled; plants for sale; tea/coffee
Features Fine conifers; ecological interest; herbs; plantsman's garden; rock garden; modern roses; old roses; woodland garden; collection of hollies (180 varieties) and hardy ferns (250 varieties)

Plantsman's garden, started in a modest way in 1964 but now extending to nearly four acres. Thickly planted, and wild at the edges. The owners are particularly interested in trees and plant them closely in groups for comparison: hence the holly wood, the larch wood and the saliceum (*Salix* = willow). But there is much more than trees and it is a garden to dawdle in and learn from.

TINTINHULL HOUSE
Tintinhull, Yeovil BA22 8PZ
☎ 01935 822545
Owner The National Trust
Location In Tintinhull village
Open 12 noon – 6 pm; Wednesdays – Sunday; 27 March to 30 October
Admission Adults £3.70; Children £1.80
Facilities Parking; loos; refreshments
Features Herbaceous plants; old roses; good topiary; particularly good in July–August; colour borders
English Heritage Grade II

A series of formal garden rooms, beautifully designed to maximise a small site (only 1½ acres) and planted with rarities in exquisite colour combinations. No labels: they would spoil the dream.

WAYFORD MANOR
Crewkerne TA18 8QG
☎ 01460 73253
Owner Mr & Mrs R L Goffe

Location 3 miles south-west of Crewkerne off A30 or B3165
Open 2 pm – 6 pm; 11 April, 2, 17 & 30 May for NGS, or parties by appointment
Admission Adults £2; Children 50p
Facilities Parking; dogs permitted; loos; plants for sale; teas
Features Herbaceous plants; rhododendrons; spring bulbs; maples; tallest *Photinia davidiana* (13m.) in the British Isles
English Heritage Grade II

One of the best gardens designed by Harold Peto: terraces and courtyards, pools and arbours, balustrades and staircases, Tuscan and Byzantine. The whole garden is presently being restored by the enthusiastic and knowledgeable owners.

WORTH A VISIT

AMMERDOWN PARK

Kilmersdown, Radstock, Bath BA3 5SH ☎ *01761 437382. Open 11 am – 5 pm; 5 April & 31 May. Ammerdown's lay-out is Lutyens at his most ingenious. The lie of the land precludes right angles, but long straight views cover up the irregularities. Some nice plants, particularly trees, but the design is everything and there are good spring bulbs as well as some interesting new plantings.*

ARNE HERBS

Limeburn Nurseries, Chew Magna, Bristol BS18 8QW ☎ *01275 333399. Open 10 am – 4 pm; usually. Phone first. This nursery specialises in medieval and renaissance plants, both herbs and native species, which can be used for conservation schemes. Very reasonably priced. Fresh cut herbs available in season too.*

AVON BULBS

Burnt House Farm, Mid-Lambrook, South Petherton TA13 5HE ☎ *01460 242177. Open 9 am – 4.30 pm; Thursday – Saturday; 18 February to 31 March and 29 September to 30 October. Avon Bulbs offers an impressive variety of bulbs (and close relatives) covering all sizes, seasons and shapes. The nursery is well-run: plants are beautifully grown and immaculately displayed. Well worth a visit to see a wide range of stocks not listed in the catalogue.*

BLACKMORE & LANGDON

Stanton Nurseries, Pensford, Bristol BS18 4JL ☎ *01275 332300. Open 9 am – 5 pm; Monday – Saturday; 10 am – 4 pm; Sundays. Generations have admired the stupendous Chelsea displays of this family business, started in 1901 and still run by the founder's grandchildren. Theirs is a long tradition of huge begonias and tall delphiniums. All plants are grown on site.*

BROADLEIGH GARDENS

Bishops Hull, Taunton TA4 1AE ☎ *01823 286231. Open 9 am – 4 pm, Monday – Friday. £1 for charity. NCCPG National Collection: Narcissus (miniature). The gardens attached to this famous, mail-order, small-bulb nursery are now open to visitors, and especially colourful in spring and Autumn. Look out for foliage and woodland perennials, as well as the irises, snowdrops, miniature narcissus and wild tulips – and an amazing double green Muscari.*

CROWE HALL

Widcombe Hill, Bath BA2 6AR ☎ *01225 310322. Open 2 pm – 6 pm; 21 March, 18 April, 9 & 23 May, 13 June, 11 July & by appointment.* One of the most extraordinary gardens we know. It looks straight out at the Capability Brown landscape at Prior Park, and 'borrows' it. Below the house is an Italianate terrace, which leads to a ferny rock garden (real rocky outcrops here) and down into a modern garden in the woodland. Recent developments include a 'Sauce' garden, in memory of Lady Barratt, a former owner, and a 'Roman' garden.

HANNAYS OF BATH

Sydney Wharf Nursery, Bathwick, Bath BA2 4ES ☎ *01225 462230. Open 10 am – 5 pm; Wednesday – Sunday; plus Bank Holiday Mondays; March to September. The gardens are stuffed with rare and tender plants – definitely worth a visit in their own right – but the nursery is a rich source of herbaceous plants and shrubs, mainly species. Many plants come from seed collected by the Hannays and the Compton, d'Arcy, Rix expeditions.*

KELWAYS LTD

Langport TA10 9EZ ☎ *01458 250521. Open 9 am – 5 pm, Monday – Friday; 10 am – 5 pm on Saturdays; 10 am – 4 pm on Sunday. Long famous for their herbaceous and tree peonies, Kelways also has a stupendous range of irises and day lilies. Their catalogue is a handsome publication and a joy to read.*

LOWER SEVERALLS HERB NURSERY

Crewkerne TA18 7NX ☎ *01460 73234. Open 10 am – 5 pm; daily; all year mornings & Thursdays. Herbs of all kinds, as you would expect, but there are also good selections of the hardy geraniums and salvias. The garden has fine herbaceous borders and herb gardens.*

MALLET COURT NURSERY

Curry Mallet, Taunton TA3 6SY ☎ *01823 480748. Open 10 am – 4 pm; Mondays to Fridays. Other days by appointment. Mallet Court offers a stupendous number of rare trees. Particularly good for Quercus and Acer, and also strong on species from China and Korea. They have a very large number of Japanese maples from the late J. D. Vertrees' collection in the USA.*

NATIONAL COLLECTION OF PASSIFLORA

Greenholm Nurseries Ltd, Kingston Seymour, Clevedon BS21 6XS ☎ *01934 833350. Open 9 am – 1 pm; 2 pm – 5 pm; Monday – Saturday; all year. Closed Bank Holidays. NCCPG National Collection: Passiflora. Passion flowers only, but what a collection! 220 cultivars, and still growing. The nursery's catalogue is detailed, and includes precise temperature requirements. A fascinating proposition for anyone in a position to grow them.*

STAFFORDSHIRE — GARDENS — 207

Scotts Nurseries Ltd
Merriott TA16 5PL ☎ *01460 72306. Open 9 am – 5 pm, Monday – Saturday; 10.30 am – 4.30 pm on Sundays. A first-rate, long-established and respected nursery-cum- garden centre, with a wide range of plants but especially ornamental trees, top fruit and shrubs. Excellent quality and reasonable prices.*

Ston Easton Park
Ston Easton, Bath BA3 4DF ☎ *01761 241631. Open 10 pm – 4 pm; Wednesdays; June to August. A country house hotel, voted Hotel of the Year in 1992, with a Humphry Repton landscape. His 'red book' still exists. A sham castle and ruined grotto are two of the features he built, but there are fine trees, spacious lawns and the highest standard of maintenance to enjoy, too.*

The Manor House, Walton-in-Gordano
Walton-in-Gordano, Clevedon, Bristol BS21 7AN ☎ *01275 872067. Open by appointment, on weekdays only. A really interesting plantsman's garden on a substantial scale, offering something for every taste, from autumn-flowering bulbs to rare conifers. The range of the Wills' interests is breath-taking and there is always much for the visitor to learn and enjoy, whatever the season. Beautifully maintained, too.*

STAFFORDSHIRE

Alton Towers
Alton, Stoke-on-Trent ST10 4DB
☎ 0990 204060   Fax 01538 704099
Website www.alton-towers.co.uk
Owner Tussauds Group
Location Signposted for miles around
Open 9.30 am – 5/6/7 pm depending on season; daily; all year
Admission Adults £19.50; Children £15.50. Gardens free to hotel guests in winter
Facilities Parking; loos; facilities for the disabled; many restaurants
Features Herbaceous plants; fine conifers; good architectural features; oriental features; rock garden; modern roses; woodland garden; interesting for children; particularly good in July–August
English Heritage Grade I

Three hundred acres of dotty and exuberant display, best seen from the cable-car. Ignore the theme park: the gardens are by and large detached from the razzmatazz. Splendid Victorian conifers and gaudy bedding, magnificently done. A Swiss Cottage, Roman bridge, Chinese pagoda, flag tower, and corkscrew fountain. Excellent entertainment but not for contemplative souls. Best in term time.

Biddulph Grange Garden
Biddulph, Stoke-on-Trent ST8 7SD
☎ 01782 517999

Owner The National Trust
Location ½ mile north of Biddulph, 3½ miles south-east of Congleton
Open 12 noon – 6 pm, Wednesday – Friday (closed Good Friday); 11 am – 6 pm; Saturdays, Sundays & Bank Holiday Mondays; 27 March to 31 October. Also 12 noon – 4 pm; Saturdays & Sundays; 6 November to 19 December
Admission Adults £4.20; Children £2.10 (but £2 & £1 respectively in November & December)
Facilities Parking; loos; plants for sale; gift shop; tea-room
Features Fine conifers; good architectural features; oriental features; interesting for children; mosaic parterre restored (1997); Mrs Bateman's Garden replanted (1998)
English Heritage Grade I

A fantastic folly garden, very Victorian, energetically restored by the National Trust. Yew hedges cut to make an Egyptian temple; a statue of a sacred cow; a Scottish glen; a four-acre Chinese garden complete with Great Wall of China and look-out tower; a dahlia walk; a bowling green, quoits ground and 'stumpery'. Work continues.

The Dorothy Clive Garden
Willoughbridge, Market Drayton TF9 4EU
☎ 01630 647237
Owner Willoughbridge Garden Trust
Location A51, midway between Nantwich and Stone
Open 10 am – 5.30 pm; daily; April to October
Admission Adults £3; OAPs & groups (20+) £2.50; Children £1
Facilities Parking; dogs permitted; loos; facilities for the disabled; tea-room with beverages & home-baked food
Features Herbaceous plants; camellias; fine conifers; rock garden; woodland garden; rhododendrons; azaleas; heather; cyclamen

Meticulously maintained and still expanding, this 40-year-old garden seems ageless. Made on an unpromising site, a cold windy hilltop, it is best perhaps in May, when the woodland quarry is brilliant with rhododendrons. But the scree garden (replanted in 1998) and rock garden (reflected in the lake) are hard to beat at any season. Highly recommended.

Moseley Old Hall
The National Trust, Moseley Old Hall Lane, Fordhouses WV10 7HY
☎ & Fax 01902 782808
Owner The National Trust
Location South of M54 between A449 & A460
Open 1.30 pm – 5.30 pm (but 11 am – 5 pm on Bank Holiday Mondays); Saturdays, Sundays, Bank Holiday Mondays & the following Tuesdays (except 4 May); plus Wednesdays from June to October and Tuesdays in July & August. Also 1.30 pm – 4 pm on Sundays from November to 19 December
Admission Adults £3.90
Facilities Parking; dogs permitted; loos; access for the disabled; plants for sale; gift shop; tea-room

Features Herbs; snowdrops; good topiary; current holder of Sandford Award

Modern reconstruction of a 17th-century town garden. Neat box parterres, a nut walk and an arched pergola hung with clematis. Plantings all of a period. Quietly inspirational.

SHUGBOROUGH HALL
c/o The Estate Office, Milford, Stafford ST17 0XB
☎ 01889 881388   Fax 01889 881323

Owner The National Trust
Location Signed from Jct 13 M6
Open 11 am – 5 pm; daily; 27 March to 26 September, plus Sundays in October. And parties by appointment
Admission Vehicles £2; Coaches free
Facilities Parking; dogs permitted; loos; facilities for the disabled; garden centre; lunches, snacks, tea & evening dinners
Features Herbaceous plants; good architectural features; lake; oriental features; old roses; woodland garden; plantings by Graham Thomas; interesting for children; current holder of Sandford Award
English Heritage Grade I

Classical and neo-classical landscape with Chinese additions and a handsome Nesfield terrace dominated by dumplings of clipped golden yew. Fifty oaks in the new arboretum. Rose garden restored by Graham Thomas. All very popular with the locals.

TRENTHAM PARK GARDENS
Stone Road, Stoke-on-Trent ST4 8AX
☎ 01782 657341

Owner Trentham Leisure Ltd
Location Signposted from M6
Open 11 am – 5 pm (4 pm in winter); daily; all year
Admission Adults £2; Children £1
Facilities Parking; dogs permitted; loos; facilities for the disabled; gift shop; coffee lounge; plus a diner in summer
English Heritage Grade II*

This is the grandest of grand Victorian gardens, designed by Barry and Nesfield, and set within a Capability Brown park. Colourful summer bedding recalls its 19th-century heyday.

WESTON PARK
Weston-under-Lizard, Shifnal TF11 8LE
☎ 01952 850207   Fax 01952 850430

Owner The Weston Park Foundation
Location Off the A5 to Telford
Open 11 am – 7 pm (last admissions 5 pm); 2 – 5 April; Saturdays, Sundays & Bank Holidays in May & June; daily in July & August; 4, 5, 11, 12, 18 & 19 September
Admission Garden only: Adults £3.50; OAPs £2.50; Children £2 (1998 prices)
Facilities Parking; dogs permitted; loos; facilities for the disabled; gift shop; tea-rooms

Features Good collection of trees; landscape designed by Capability Brown; woodland garden; landscaped park; rhododendrons
English Heritage Grade II*

18th-century landscape with 19th-century Italianate parterre, a temple of Diana and an handsome orangery by Paine. But best for its trees, some of them record-breakers, and the collection of *Nothofagus* planted by the late Lord Bradford.

WORTH A VISIT

OULTON HOUSE
Oulton, Stone ST15 8UR   ☎ 01785 813556.   Open By appointment, April to June.   Newish three-acre garden, made for private enjoyment and full of good plants – roses, rhododendrons, geraniums and clematis – arranged in colour groupings.

SUFFOLK

EUSTON HALL
Euston, Thetford IP24 2QP
☎ 01842 766366   Fax 01842 766764

Owner The Duke of Grafton
Location On A1088 3 miles south of Thetford
Open 2.30 pm – 5 pm; Thursdays; 3 June to 30 September, plus 27 June & 5 September
Admission House & garden: Adults £3; OAPs £2.50; Children 50p
Facilities Parking; loos; access for the disabled; craft shop; home-made teas
Features Landscape designed by Capability Brown; lake; old roses; William Kent temple and summerhouse
English Heritage Grade II*

Classic 18th-century parkland on a sweeping site, formal terraces by the house and a pretty modern garden with shrub roses. Not spectacular, but satisfying.

HELMINGHAM HALL
Stowmarket IP14 6EF
☎ 01473 890363   Fax 01473 890776

Owner Lord Tollemache
Location 9 miles north of Ipswich on B1077
Open 2 pm – 6 pm; Sundays; 25 April to 5 September; plus individuals & groups on Wednesday afternoons by prior arrangement
Admission Adults £3.50; OAPs £3; Children £2
Facilities Parking; dogs permitted; loos; access for the disabled; plants for sale; shop; tea-rooms
Features Herbaceous plants; old roses; deer park; moat; fine walled garden
English Heritage Grade I

Most of the garden is modern, but cleverly done with old flowers and knot gardens to suit the Elizabethan house. Wonderful modern planting in the walled garden:

billowing, chunky shrub roses and triumphant herbaceous borders.

ICKWORTH
National Trust Office, Horringer, Bury St Edmunds
IP29 5QE
☎ & Fax 01284 735270

Owner The National Trust
Location 3 miles south-west of Bury St Edmunds
Open 10 am – 5 pm (4 pm in winter); daily; all year. Closed at weekends in November & December. 12 September for NGS
Admission Adults £2.20; Children 70p
Facilities Parking; dogs permitted; loos; facilities for the disabled; plants for sale; National Trust shop; large licensed restaurant, self-service
Features Landscape designed by Capability Brown; autumn colour; Italian garden; Victorian 'stumpery'; new display of lemon trees in orangery (1998); tallest *Quercus pubescens* (29m.) in the British Isles
English Heritage Grade II*
NCCPG National Collection *Buxus*

An extraordinary garden for an extraordinary house: the main borders follow the curves of the house. There is also an Italian garden in front of the house, and long vistas in the park, but the old kitchen garden is bare.

SHRUBLAND HALL
Coddenham, Ipswich IP6 9QP
☎ 01473 830221   Fax 01473 832202

Owner Lord de Saumarez
Location Between Claydon and Coddenham: come by A14 or A140
Open 2 pm – 5 pm; Sundays & Bank Holiday Mondays; 4 April to 12 September
Admission Adults £2.50; OAPs & children £1.50
Facilities Parking; loos; tea-tent
Features Herbaceous plants; good architectural features; modern roses; woodland garden; box maze; Swiss châlet
English Heritage Grade I

A grand Victorian garden designed by Charles Barry and famous for its spectacular Italianate staircase which connects the terrace around the house with the formal gardens below. William Robinson later helped with the planting, both around the formal garden and in the park and woodland gardens beyond. Much restoration and recovery has been completed in recent years: Shrubland is getting better and better.

SOMERLEYTON HALL & GARDENS
Somerleyton, Lowestoft NR32 5QQ
☎ 01502 730224   Fax 01502 732143

Owner Lord & Lady Somerleyton
Location 4 miles north-west of Lowestoft on B1074
Open 12.30 pm – 5.30 pm; Thursdays, Sundays & Bank Holiday Mondays, plus Tuesdays & Wednesdays in July & August; Easter Sunday to 26 September

Admission Adults £4.50; OAPs £4.20; Children £2.20 (1998 prices)
Facilities Parking; loos; facilities for the disabled; souvenir gift shop; light lunches & teas
Features Glasshouses; modern roses; maze; miniature railway
English Heritage Grade II*

A grand formal garden around the monstrous Victorian house. Nesfield laid out the terraces, and Paxton built the curving greenhouses which have just been re-roofed. Good 19th-century maze (not too difficult) and masses of cheerful bedding and roses.

WYKEN HALL
Stanton, Bury St Edmunds IP31 2DW
☎ 01359 250287   Fax 01359 252256

Owner Sir Kenneth & Lady Carlisle
Location Stanton, 9 miles north-east from Bury St Edmunds; brown signs from A143 at Ixworth to Wyken Vineyard
Open 10 am – 6 pm; Thursdays, Fridays, Sundays & Bank Holiday Mondays; 1 April to 1 October
Admission Adults £2.50; OAPs £2; Children free
Facilities Parking; dogs permitted; loos; facilities for the disabled; plants for sale; country store shop; lunches & teas at excellent Vineyard Restaurant
Features Herbaceous plants; fine conifers; fruit of special interest; herbs; plantsman's garden; modern roses; old roses; woodland garden; new shrub border (1999); award-winning seven-acre vineyard

The garden is ingeniously designed: a series of old-style gardens to complement the Elizabethan house. These include a knot garden, herb garden, traditional English kitchen garden, wildflower meadows, nuttery and a copper beech maze. All are in scale with the house and the farmland around. Stylish and well maintained, this is one of the best modern private gardens in the country. The restaurant gets three stars in the *Good Food Guide*.

WORTH A VISIT

EAST BERGHOLT PLACE
East Bergholt CO7 6UP ☎ *01206 299224. Open 10 am – 5 pm; Tuesday – Sunday & Bank Holiday Mondays; March to October. Fifteen acres laid out by Charles Eley 100 years ago and still owned by his family. Fine trees and shrubs, many from the famous plant-hunters' seed, especially camellias, rhododendrons and magnolias. Good plants for sale.*

FISK'S CLEMATIS NURSERY
Westleton, Saxmundham IP17 3AJ ☎ *01728 648263. Open 9 am – 5 pm; Monday – Friday; March to October; 9 am – 4 pm; Monday – Friday; November to February; 10 am – 1 pm; 2 pm – 5 pm; Saturdays & Sundays; April to October. Well-known clematis breeders and nursery with an extensive list of large-flowered hybrids and species.*

GOLDBROOK PLANTS
Hoxne, Eye IP21 5AN ☎ *01379 668770. Open 10.30 am – 6 pm; Thursday – Sunday; April to*

September. Saturdays & Sundays from October to March. Closed January; and around Chelsea and Hampton Court Shows. An exceptional choice of hostas for sale (over 400 from a collection of over 850 different cultivars), with a good choice of Hemerocallis and shade-loving plants too. As exhibitors they have an impressive unbroken run of Chelsea gold medals from 1988 to 1998.

HAUGHLEY PARK
Stowmarket IP14 3JY ☎ *01359 240205. Parkland round a Jacobean mansion with competent modern flower gardens and fine trees (Davidia involucrata). The walled garden is undergoing conversion to a flower garden. But the acres of lily-of-the-valley in the woodland garden are worth the journey no matter how far.*

MILLS FARM PLANTS AND GARDENS
Norwich Road, Mendlesham IP14 5NQ
☎ *01449 766425. Open 9 am – 5.30 pm, daily. Closed Tuesdays, and all January. Mills Farm specialise in Dianthus (new and old hybrids, species and rock-garden types) and old roses: there is a helpful catalogue for each genus and one for garden perennials – most of them modern classics.*

NOTCUTTS NURSERIES
Ipswich Road, Woodbridge IP12 4AF ☎ *01394 383344. Website: www.notcutts.co.uk Open 9 am – 6 pm, Monday – Saturday; 10.30 am – 4.30 pm, Sundays. Closes at 8 pm on Thursdays. Large wholesale nurseries with a garden centre chain. They are strongest on flowering shrubs and trees, including roses. Quality is first class. They have a design capability through Nottcutts Landscapes.*

PARADISE CENTRE
Twinstead Road, Lamarsh, Bures CO8 5EX
☎ *01787 269449. Website: www.software-technics.co.uk/paradise-centre Open 10 am – 5 pm, Saturday – Sunday, and Bank Holidays; Easter to October. And by appointment. This garden nursery specialises in bulbs, herbaceous plants and shade and damp lovers. The adjoining gardens are superb: five acres of light woodland where thousands of bulbs give colour at every season.*

PARK GREEN NURSERIES
Wetheringsett, Stowmarket IP14 5QH ☎ *01728 860139. Open 10 am – 5 pm; daily; March to September. This nursery specialises in Hosta and Hemerocallis, with new cultivars each year. Other specialities include astilbes and ornamental grasses and primulas.*

PEARL SULMAN
54 Kingsway, Mildenhall, Bury St Edmunds IP28 7HR
☎ *01638 712297. Open Open weekend; 12 – 13 June. A small nursery which specialises in dwarf and miniature pelargoniums (500). Only open on the second weekend in June, otherwise by mail order.*

ROUGHAM HALL NURSERIES
A14 Rougham, Bury St Edmunds IP30 9LZ
☎ *01359 270577. Open 10 am – 4 pm; daily; March to*

October. NCCPG National Collections: Delphinium; Ribes (gooseberries). Breeders, introducers and growers of an extensive and interesting range of perennials. The selection of delphiniums and asters is particularly good. Mouthwatering gooseberries.

SURREY

CHILWORTH MANOR
Chilworth, Guildford
☎ 01483 561414

Owner Lady Heald
Location In middle of village, up Blacksmiths Lane
Open 2 pm – 6 pm; 10 & 11 April, 8 & 9 May, 12 & 13 June, 10 & 11 July, 7 & 8 August; or by appointment
Admission £2
Facilities Parking; dogs permitted; loos; plants for sale; teas & cakes
Features Herbaceous plants; woodland garden; rhododendrons; interesting new shrub plantings; flower arrangements in the house; sculpture exhibitions; tallest *Ilex aquifolium* 'Bacciflava' (10.5m.) and largest *Ilex aquifolium* 'Pendula' in the British Isles

A remarkable garden, tiered up seven distinct levels, the top three being *c.* 1700 and walled around (beautiful brickwork). Good climbers and shrubs against the walls, and a bog garden in the woods at the bottom. The main herbaceous border has recently been replanted by a Dutch designer.

CLANDON PARK
West Clandon, Guildford GU4 7RQ
☎ 01483 222482   **Fax** 01483 223479

Owner The National Trust
Location Off the A247 at West Clandon
Open 9 am – dusk; daily; all year
Admission Free
Facilities Parking; loos; access for the disabled; Clandon Park Garden Centre is nearby; restaurant
Features Landscape designed by Capability Brown; daffodils; parterres; grotto; Dutch garden; Maori summerhouse; new herbaceous border (1997)
English Heritage Grade II

Capability Brown's magnificent mature beeches are now underplanted with sombre Victorian shrubberies and slabs of comfrey, bergenias and *Geranium macrorrhizum* – the apotheosis of National Trust ground cover. There is a modern pastiche of a Dutch garden in front of the house but the daffodils in spring are breathtaking.

CLAREMONT LANDSCAPE GARDEN
Portsmouth Road, Esher KT10 9JG
☎ 01372 469421

Owner The National Trust
Location On southern edge of town (A307)

Open 10 am – 6 pm, but 5 pm from November to March and 7 pm on Saturdays, Sundays & Bank Holiday Mondays from April to October (sunset, if earlier); all year. Closed 13 July and at 2 pm from 14 to 18 July. Also closed 1 January & 25 December
Admission Adults £3
Facilities Parking; loos; access for the disabled; shop; restaurant
Features Landscape designed by Capability Brown; good architectural features; worked on by Kent; lake; plantings by Graham Thomas; particularly interesting in winter; laurel lawns; tallest service tree *Sorbus domestica* (23m.) in the British Isles, and two further record trees
English Heritage Grade I

This vast historic landscape – now much reduced – was worked over by Vanburgh, Bridgeman, Kent and Capability Brown and has been energetically restored in recent years. The elegant green theatre is best seen flanked by spreading cedars from across the dark lake. Very popular locally, and apt to get crowded at summer weekends.

HATCHLANDS
East Clandon, Guildford GU4 7RQ
☎ 01483 222482   Fax 01483 223479
Owner The National Trust
Location Off A246 Guildford to Leatherhead
Open 2 pm – 5.30 pm; Tuesday – Thursday, Sundays & Bank Holiday Mondays; 1 April to 31 October. Also Fridays in August. Park walks in Repton Park open daily 11.30 am – 6 pm
Admission Adults £1.75
Facilities Parking; loos; facilities for the disabled; National Trust shop; restaurant
Features Landscape designed by Capability Brown; planted by Gertrude Jekyll; landscape designed by Humphry Repton; woodland garden

Apart from the Jekyll garden (roses, lupins, box and columbines), Hatchlands is an 18th-century landscape with parkland. But the garden buildings are charming and the National Trust has made good progress with restoration and replanting.

PAINSHILL PARK
Portsmouth Road, Cobham KT11 1JE
☎ 01932 868113   Fax 01932 868001
Owner Painshill Park Trust
Location Signposted from M25 Jct 10
Open 10.30 am – 6 pm (last tickets 4.30 pm); Tuesday – Sunday & Bank Holiday Mondays; April to October. Telephone for details of winter openings
Admission Adults £3.80; Concessions £3.30; Children (under 16) £1.50
Facilities Parking; loos; facilities for the disabled; plants for sale; souvenirs, books, cards, etc.; light refreshments
Features 'American' garden; grotto; Turkish tent; tallest *Juniperus virginiana* (26m.) in the British Isles
English Heritage Grade I

Charles Hamilton went bust making this extravagant Gothic landscape in the 1770s. It has been industriously restored over the last ten years and now looks as new and stagey as ever. A £848,000 grant from the Heritage Lottery Fund has transformed the future of this historic park.

POLESDEN LACEY
Great Bookham, Dorking RH5 6BD
☎ 01372 458203   Fax 01372 452023
Owner The National Trust
Location Off A246 between Leatherhead & Guildford
Open 11 am – 6 pm; daily; all year
Admission Adults £3
Facilities Parking; dogs permitted; loos; facilities for the disabled; plants for sale; large National Trust shop; self-service restaurant & tea-rooms
Features Herbaceous plants; climbing roses; modern roses; old roses; snowdrops; plantings by Graham Thomas
English Heritage Grade II*

Best for the long terraced walk, laid out by Sheridan, and the return through an Edwardian-style rose garden whose pergolas drip with ramblers.

RAMSTER
Chiddingfold GU8 4SN
☎ 01428 644422   Fax 01428 658345
Owner Mr & Mrs Paul Gunn
Location 1½ miles south of Chiddingfold on A283
Open 11 am – 5.30 pm; daily; 17 April to 11 July. Parties by appointment at other times
Admission Adults £2.50; Children free
Facilities Parking; dogs permitted; loos; access for the disabled; plants for sale; home-made teas in May
Features Good collection of trees; fine conifers; rhododendrons; camellias; azaleas; bluebells; largest *Euonymus europaeus* (6m.) in the British Isles; new bog garden (1998); extensive new plantings (1999)

Twenty acres of Surrey woodland underplanted with camellias, rhododendrons and all manner of rare shrubs by Mrs Gunn's grandmother 70 years ago. She was the second Lord Aberconway's sister and many of her plants came from Bodnant: some of the rhododendrons and azaleas are her hybrids, but the Gunns are adding to her plantings with enthusiasm and sensibility. There is a special display-cum-sale of pots and plants from specialist nurseries daily between 15 & 31 May and an embroidery exhibition at the same time.

RHS GARDEN WISLEY
Woking GU23 6QB
☎ 01483 224634   Fax 01483 211750
Owner The Royal Horticultural Society
Location Near M25 Jct 10
Open 10 am (but 9 am at weekends) to 6 pm or dusk if earlier; daily; all year except 25 December. Sundays reserved for RHS members only
Admission Adults £5; Children £1.75; RHS Members free. Discounts for groups (pre-booked 21 days) – contact Sally Hallum

Facilities Parking; loos; facilities for the disabled; plants for sale; marvellous bookshop and souvenir shop; restaurant & café
Features Good collection of trees; herbaceous plants; fine conifers; fruit of special interest; glasshouses; lake; plantsman's garden; rock garden; modern roses; old roses; snowdrops; subtropical plants; woodland garden; interesting for children; particularly good in July–August; particularly interesting in winter; heather garden; herb garden; horticultural trials; vegetable gardens; tallest *Ostrya virginiana* (15.5m.) in the British Isles, and 19 further record trees
English Heritage Grade II*
NCCPG National Collections *Bruckenthalia*; *Calluna vulgaris*; *Crocus*; *Daboecia*; *Epimedium*; *Erica*; *Galanthus*; *Pulmonaria*; *Rheum*

Sir Thomas Hanbury bought the Wisley estate in 1903 and gave it to the RHS for 'the encouragement and improvement of the science and practice of horticulture in all its branches'. The Society has been true to that purpose, so that the 200-acre garden now offers something for everyone: Wisley is a garden to delight, instruct and inspire. Its unmissable highlights include:

The Alpine Meadow, a carpet of hoop-petticoat narcissi in early spring, and later with autumn-flowering crocus.

The Rock Garden, completed in 1912 and now perhaps the finest in England. Its year-long floral display rises majestically above the massive rock-work.

The landscaped Alpine House, with its unique planting schemes, and the Alpine Pan House where ever-changing displays of flowering alpines are maintained throughout the year, a complement to the sheer scale of the nearby Rock Garden.

Battleston Hill, a beautifully laid-out woodland garden underplanted with innumerable rhododendrons, azaleas, magnolias and camellias.

The Mediterranean Garden on Battleston Hill, where the great gale of 1987 has made possible an extensive collection of plants with a reputation for tenderness to show what can be grown successfully on light, well-drained soil.

The Glasshouses, with their extensive collections of ornamental exotics, many of which are suitable for home cultivation. Flamboyant display houses give colour at every season of the year, even in November when the 'Charm' and 'Cascade' chrysanthemums provide their own fireworks.

The Mixed Borders which face each other along the 128m. walk up to Battleston Hill. Shrubs form the framework for all the traditional perennials of the English herbaceous border. Bulbs extend the season but the borders are best from July to September.

The Model Gardens, which grow and develop every year. Each takes a theme and shows you how to apply it on a small scale: inspiration for Wisley's 700,000 annual visitors. The model fruit, vegetable and herb gardens also show interested visitors just what can be achieved in a small garden.

The Fruit Fields, where over 1,400 cultivars of top, bush and soft fruit are grown: the Society has long been associated with the cultivation of fruit.

The main Trials area in Portsmouth Field, where seeds and plants of vegetables and flowers are grown. The best may be awarded the Award of Garden Merit, the Society's 'Kitemark' of plant quality.

The Heather Collection in Howard's Field, and the tranquil, less frequented Pinetum along the River Wey.

The Canal and Walled Gardens, designed by Geoffrey Jellicoe and Lanning Roper in front of the laboratory building which houses the Society's offices. The pool is a formal setting for water lilies: the walled enclosures have spectacular summer and winter bedding displays. But time does not stand still at Wisley. The Great Storm of 1987 made possible a major reshaping of the garden, from which it has benefited enormously. There is a rolling programme of development: a Country Garden by Penelope Hobhouse is due to be opened this year.

THE SAVILL GARDEN

c/o Crown Estate Office, Great Park, Windsor SL4 2HT
☎ 01753 860222   Fax 01753 859617
Owner Crown Property
Location At Englefield Green, 3 miles west of Egham off the A30 & 5 miles from Windsor
Open 10 am – 6 pm (4 pm from November to February); daily except 25 & 26 December
Admission Adults £3.80; OAPs £3.30; Children free
Facilities Parking; plants for sale; gift and book shop; lavatories; licensed restaurant & picnic area
Features Good collection of trees; camellias; lake; plantsman's garden; modern roses; woodland garden; particularly good in July–August; particularly interesting in winter; Kurume azaleas; mahonias; magnolias; magnificent late-summer borders; tallest silver birch *Betula pendula* (30m.) in the British Isles (& 13 other record trees)
English Heritage Grade I
NCCPG National Collections *Ilex*; *Magnolia*; *Mahonia*; *Pernettya*; *Pieris*; *Rhododendron*; Ferns; Dwarf conifers
Friends Active Friends Organisation: details from John Bond

Quite simply the finest woodland garden in England, crammed with rhododendrons, magnolias, azaleas, maples, mahonias and hydrangeas and underplanted with drifts of meconopsis, primulas and wild narcissus. The primulas come in monospecific masses, from the earliest *P. rosea* and *P. denticulata* through to *P. florindae* in July and August. But the late-summer herbaceous borders are also an inspiration and the gravel garden is one of England's oldest and largest.

THE VALLEY GARDENS

c/o Crown Estate Office, Great Park, Windsor SL4 2HT
☎ 01753 860222
Owner Crown Property

Location At Englefield Green, 5 miles from Windsor, off A30: follow signs for Savill Garden
Open 8 am – 7 pm, or sunset if earlier; daily; all year
Admission Car & occupants £3 (£4 in April, May & October)
Facilities Parking; loos; dogs permitted; shop; refreshments at the Savill Garden
Features Good collection of trees; plantsman's garden; rhododendrons and azaleas; woodland garden; magnolias; heathers; hydrangeas
NCCPG National Collections *Ilex*; *Magnolia*; *Mahonia*; *Pernettya*; *Pieris*; *Rhododendron*; Dwarf conifers

A bigger and better Savill Gardens: all is planted on a royal scale in a wilder woodland setting. Best known is the Punch Bowl, where massed ranks of Kurume azaleas fill a natural combe with amazingly garish mixtures. Other parts are underplanted with hostas, ferns, bergenias and candelabra primulas. There is also a fine pinetum and a good collection of hydrangeas. But the gardens extend to 300 acres: not to be undertaken by the frail or faint-hearted.

VANN

Hambledon, nr Godalming GU8 4EF
☎ 01428 68 3413   Fax 017267 9344
Owner Mr & Mrs Martin Caroe
Location 2 miles from Chiddingfold. Signs from A283 at Hambledon on NGS days
Open 10 am – 6 pm; daily; 6 to 11 April, 4 to 9 May, 1 to 6 June. Also 2 pm – 6 pm on 5 April & 3 May
Admission Adults £2.75; Children 50p. Pre-booked groups welcome
Facilities Parking; loos; teas by arrangement
Features Bluebells; herbaceous plants; planted by Gertrude Jekyll; lake; woodland garden; wood anemones; new south-end garden (1997)
English Heritage Grade II

High-profile Jekyll garden, well restored and meticulously maintained by the present Caroes, the third generation to live here. Start at the back of the house and move along the Arts and Crafts pergola which leads straight to the lake. This is the heart of the garden, from which five or six distinct gardens lead from one to the next and melt into the Surrey woods: among them, a yew walk, a water garden, a woodland cherry walk, a hazel coppice and a woodland garden under vast oaks. The plantings are dense and thoughtful.

WINKWORTH ARBORETUM

Hascombe Road, Godalming GU8 4AD
☎ 01483 208477
Owner The National Trust
Location 2 miles south-east of Godalming, off B2130
Open All year; Dawn to dusk. Groups *must* pre-book in writing
Admission Adults £2.70; Children (5 – 16) £1.25
Facilities Parking; dogs permitted; loos; shop; tea-room
Features Good collection of trees; lake; woodland garden; plantings by Graham Thomas; bluebells; wood

anemones; autumn colour; boathouse restored (1998); tallest *Acer davidii* (19m.) in the British Isles, and five further record trees
NCCPG National Collection *Sorbus* (Aria & Micromeles groups)

Beautiful arboretum, planted with particularly decorative species (maples, *Sorbus*, magnolias and *Hamamelis*) in large groups for maximum effect. Good in May when the azaleas are underscored by bluebells: better still for autumn colour in October.

WORTH A VISIT

BRIAN & HEATHER HILEY

25 Little Woodcote Estate, Wallington SM5 4AU
☎ 0181 647 9679.   Open 9 am – 5 pm; Wednesday – Saturday.   The Hileys offer a stylish collection of tender perennials and shrubs: the salvias and penstemons are particularly good. The Hileys are regulars at RHS shows where their brilliant exhibits – and Brian Hiley's waistcoats – have gained the recognition they deserve.

BROOK LODGE FARM COTTAGE

Blackbrook, Dorking RH5 4DT ☎ 01306 888368. Open 2 pm – 5 pm; 13 & 16 June, 18 & 21 July, 8 & 11 August, 5 September. And by appointment.   Planted by the present owner over many years, this garden has matured into a fine plantsman's garden with much variety: shrub roses, a rockery, a woodland walk, herbaceous borders and two cottage gardens.

GREEN FARM PLANTS

Bentley, Farnham GU10 5JX ☎ 01420 23202. Open 10 am – 6 pm; Wednesday – Saturday; mid-March to October.   This nursery is full of interesting plants, including the results of recent collecting trips. The main groups are hardy and half-hardy perennials, with an increasing number of woodland plants and sun-loving shrubs. Piet Oudolf's interesting and provocative garden is worth a visit in its own right.

KNAP HILL NURSERY LTD

Barrs Lane, Knaphill, Woking GU21 2JW
☎ 01483 481214. Open 9 am – 5 pm; Monday – Friday.   This famous old nursery specialises in rhododendrons and azaleas. its extensive list includes hybrids, dwarf, semi-dwarf and R. yakushimanum cultivars, as well as deciduous and evergreen azaleas. The old stock grounds contain a very large number of famous specimen trees.

MILLAIS NURSERIES

Crosswater Lane, Churt, Farnham GU10 2JN
☎ 01252 792698. Open 10 am – 1 pm; 2 pm – 5 pm; Monday – Friday. Also Saturdays in March; April; October & November. And daily in May.   Leading rhododendron and azalea specialist with nearly 1,000 species and cultivars, including some new Himalayan species. In addition to the garden (six acres, ponds, stream and companion plantings – open in May for £1.50) there is a trials garden where hundreds of new cultivars are labelled and tested.

Munstead Wood
Heath Lane, Busbridge, Godalming GU7 1UN
☎ 01483 417867. *Open 2 pm – 6 pm; 25 April, 30 May & 18 July. Gertrude Jekyll's own garden was nearly lost before the Clarks bought it but they have successfully restored much to its original state. The roses and colour plantings are inspirational. Work continues, and the lawns still end where the birches begin, to make Munstead 'a garden in a wood'.*

Pantiles Plant & Garden Centre
Almners Road, Lyne, Chertsey KT16 0BJ
☎ 01932 872195. *Open 8.30 am (9 am on Sundays) – 6 pm (5.30 pm in winter); daily; all year. One of the best places for outsize container-grown specimens (up to 8m.), including Dicksonia antarctica (tree fern). Awesome to visit.*

Pinewood House
Heath House Road, Worplesdon Hill, Woking GU22 0QU
☎ 01483 473241. *Open Parties by appointment, April to October. Four acres of old garden, to go with a new house. Lovely woodland, lakes and underplantings with rhododendrons.*

Toobees Exotics
Blackhorse Road, Woking GU22 0QT ☎ *01483 797534. Website: www.demon.co.uk/mace/toobees/toobees.html Open 10 am – 5 pm; Wednesday – Sunday & Bank Holiday Mondays; 27 February to 2 October. And by appointment. Toobees have a constant flow of new and rare succulents from Africa and Madagascar, including species of* Euphorbia, *carnivorous plants, palms and cycads.*

Vale End
Albury Guildford ☎ *01483 202296. Open 10 am – 5 pm; 27 June & 1 August. A modern plantsman's garden, the best we know on Bagshot sand, where a love of plants has not been allowed to obscure either the design or the landscape beyond.*

Vernon Geranium Nursery
Cuddington Way, Cheam, Sutton SM2 7JB
☎ 0181 393 7616. *Open 9.30 am – 5.30 pm; Monday – Saturday; 10 am – 4 pm; Sundays; March to July. Specialist growers of pelargoniums (1,100 – the number speaks for itself) and fuchsias (100). Plants are available as rooted cuttings by post, and pot-grown plants can be had from the nursery. A delight to visit.*

East Sussex

Bateman's
Burwash, Etchingham TN19 7DS
☎ 01435 882302
Owner The National Trust
Location Signposted at west end of village
Open 11 am – 5.30 pm; Saturday – Wednesday; 27 March to 31 October
Admission Adults £5; Children £2.50
Facilities Parking; loos; access for the disabled; National Trust shop; restaurant & café
Features Herbaceous plants; herbs; old roses; interesting for children; arcade planted with pears and clematis; water mill
English Heritage Grade II

Ten acres on the banks of the River Dudwell, where Rudyard Kipling lived from 1902 until his death in 1936. Fun for children, because there is a working flour mill, but not spectacular for the knowledgeable gardener, except for the *Campsis grandiflora* on the house.

Bates Green Farm
Arlington, Polegate BN26 6SH
☎ & Fax 01323 482039

Owner Mr & Mrs J R McCutchan
Location 3 miles south-west of Hailsham
Open 10 am – 6 pm; Thursdays; April to September. Also for NGS and by appointment
Admission Adults £2; Children free
Facilities Parking; loos; access for the disabled; plants for sale; refreshments by arrangement
Features Herbaceous plants; woodland garden; colour borders; bluebells; rockery replanted (1998)

Made by the present owners over the last 20 years. Several different areas: a large rock garden (renovated last winter), a shady garden, and wonderful mixed borders planted for year-round colour associations. The owners seek perfection, but wonder if they will ever achieve it.

Cabbages & Kings Garden
Wilderness Farm, Wilderness Lane, Hadlow Down TN22 4HU
☎ 01825 830552   Fax 01825 830736

Owner Andrew & Ryl Nowell
Location ½ mile south of A272
Open 10.30 am – 5.30 pm; Thursday – Saturday; March to October
Admission Adults £3; Concessions £2
Facilities Parking; loos; access for the disabled; plants for sale; tea, coffee, home-made cakes
Features Good modern design & planting

Subtitled 'The Centre for Garden Design', this is the show garden of a leading modern garden designer. It is conceived as a series of interlinking garden-rooms, terraces and incidents, lushly and vividly planted. Lots of ideas for your own garden.

Great Dixter
Dixter Road, Northiam TN31 6PH
☎ 01797 252878   Fax 01797 252879
Owner Christopher Lloyd
Location Off A28 at Northiam Post Office

Open 2 pm – 5 pm; Tuesday – Sunday; 1 April to 25 October, plus Bank Holiday Mondays. Open at 11 am at Bank Holiday weekends
Admission Adults £4; Children £1
Facilities Parking; loos; plants for sale; gift shop
Features Herbaceous plants; herbs; plantsman's garden; modern roses; old roses; subtropical plants; good topiary; particularly good in July–August; meadow garden; colour schemes
English Heritage Grade I

Several well-defined enclosures surround the Lutyens house but they change constantly as Christopher Lloyd rethinks, reworks and replants. Dixter is a living lesson in the choice and use of plants, a garden to revisit frequently – provocative, adventurous and inspirational.

MERRIMENTS GARDENS
Hawkhurst Road, Hurst Green TN19 7RA
☎ 01580 869666   Fax 01580 869324
Owner Mrs Peggy Weeks
Location On A229
Open 9.30 am – 5.30 pm; daily; 2 April to 31 October. Nursery open every day except 24 December to 4 January
Admission £2.50
Facilities Parking; loos; access for the disabled; first-rate nursery attached; garden café
Features Herbaceous plants; plantsman's garden; young garden; brilliant modern design

The gardens at this nursery are young – started in 1991 – but the tail is already wagging the dog. Four remarkable acres of imaginative design and striking planting are kept meticulously tidy. They include a Monet garden, foliage borders, a blue garden – and dozens more. The nursery is good, too.

MICHELHAM PRIORY
Upper Dicker, Hailsham BN27 3QS
☎ 01323 844224   Fax 01323 844030
Owner The Sussex Archaeological Society
Location Signposted from A22 and A27
Open 10.30 am – 4 pm; Wednesday – Sunday; 15 to 31 March & October. 10.30 am – 5 pm; Wednesday – Sunday; April to July & September. 10.30 am – 5.30 pm; daily; August
Admission Adults £4.20; OAPs £3.50; Children £2.20
Facilities Parking; loos; facilities for the disabled; plants for sale; restaurant & tea-room
Features Herbaceous plants; fine conifers; herbs; modern roses; old roses

The old Augustinian priory has an Elizabethan barn, blacksmith shop, rope museum and moat. A Physic Garden is planted with medieval herbs.

PASHLEY MANOR GARDEN
Ticehurst, Wadhurst TN5 7NE
☎ 01580 200692   Fax 01580 200102
Owner James A Sellick
Location On B2099 between A21 and Ticehurst

Open 11 am – 5 pm; Tuesday – Thursday, Saturday & Bank Holiday Mondays; 10 April to 30 September. Plus gardens (but no facilities) 10 am – 4 pm; Monday – Friday; October
Admission Adults £4.50; OAPs & children £4
Facilities Parking; loos; plants for sale; fresh produce for sale; lunches & teas
Features Fine conifers; climbing roses; old roses; Victorian shrubberies; hydrangeas; irises; new late-summer herbaceous borders (1998); new plantings in water & bog gardens (1999)

A new/old garden, made or remade in the Victorian style over the last ten years with advice from Tony Pasley. The results are gentle shapes, spacious expanses, harmonious colours and solid plantings. It gets better every year.

SHEFFIELD PARK GARDEN
Uckfield TN22 3QX
☎ 01825 790231
Owner The National Trust
Location Between East Grinstead & Lewes on A275
Open 10.30 am – 4 pm; Saturdays & Sundays; January & February. 10.30 am – 4 pm; Tuesday – Sunday; March, November & December. 11 am – 6 pm; Tuesday – Sunday & Bank Holidays; April to October
Admission Adults £4.20; Children £2.10; RHS members free
Facilities Parking; loos; facilities for the disabled; National Trust shop; refreshments nearby
Features Good collection of trees; bluebells; landscape designed by Capability Brown; fine conifers; lake; landscape designed by Humphry Repton; plantings by Graham Thomas; daffodils; kalmias; autumn crocuses; rhododendrons; tallest *Nyssa sylvatica* (21m.) in the British Isles, plus two other record tees
English Heritage Grade I
NCCPG National Collection *Rhododendron* (Ghent azaleas)

Little remains of Capability Brown and Repton except the lakes which now reflect the plantings of exotic trees – landscaping on the grandest of scales. Wonderful leaf colours whatever the season, plus gentians in autumn.

STANDEN
East Grinstead RH19 4NE
☎ 01342 323029   Fax 01342 316424
Owner The National Trust
Location 2 miles south of East Grinstead, signposted from B2110
Open 12.30 pm – 6 pm; Wednesday – Sunday & Bank Holiday Mondays; 24 March to 7 November. 1 pm – 4 pm; Friday – Sunday; 10 November to 19 December
Admission Adults £5; Children £2.50
Facilities Parking; loos; plants for sale; National Trust shop; restaurant
Features Herbaceous plants; fine conifers; rock garden; old roses; rhododendrons; azaleas; woodland shrubs

Small Edwardian garden with magnificent views across the valley. A series of enclosed gardens around the house gives way to woodland slopes and an old quarry furnished with ferns.

WORTH A VISIT

BRICKWALL HOUSE & GARDENS
Frewen College, Northiam TN31 6NL
☎ 01797 223329. *Open By appointment for groups (guided tours). Designed as a Stuart garden, to match the house, Brickwall has borders planted exclusively with old-fashioned plants and a chess garden where green and yellow yew shapes are grown in squares of black or white chips. The bluebells in the arboretum are magnificent.*

CLINTON LODGE
Fletching, Uckfield TN22 3ST ☎ 01825 722952.
Open 2 – 6 pm; 13, 14, 23 & 30 June. A rising star among new gardens, designed round a handsome 17th-century house. Six acres of formal gardens of different periods, starting with a 'medieval' potager and an Elizabethan herb garden. The most successful parts are the pre-Raphaelite walk of lilies and pale roses, and the Victorian herbaceous borders in soft pastel shades.

COBBLERS
Mount Pleasant, Jarvis Brook, Crowborough TN6 2ND
☎ 01892 655969. *Open 2.30 – 5 pm. For NGS (see Yellow Book) and by appointment for groups of 15+. Tightly planned and beautifully planted garden made by an architect who is also a plantsman. There is a great variety of habitats and plants (bog, alpine, hot-coloured, shade-loving etc.) within a design which opens out its perspectives slowly.*

PARADISE PARK
Avis Road, Newhaven BN9 0DH ☎ 01273 616001.
Open 10 am – 6 pm (but 5.30 pm in winter), Monday – Saturday; 9 am – 6 pm, Sundays; daily; all year except 25 December. Part of a leisure complex attached to a garden centre, the most interesting features are a tropical house and a cactus house, each landscaped with handsome species chosen for display. A haven in winter.

WEST SUSSEX

BORDE HILL GARDEN
Haywards Heath RH16 1XP
☎ 01444 450226   Fax 01444 440427
Website www.bordehill.co.uk
Owner Borde Hill Garden Ltd
Location 1½ miles north of Haywards Heath
Open 10 am – 6 pm; daily; all year
Admission Adults £4; Children £1.50
Facilities Parking; dogs permitted; loos; facilities for the disabled; plants for sale; small gift shop; Bressingham Plant Centre; tea-rooms, restaurant & pub
Features Good collection of trees; plantsman's garden; woodland garden; interesting for children; rhododendrons; azaleas; magnolias; plants from original seed; new Italian Garden made with Lottery money (1999); 48 different record trees, one of the largest collection in the British Isles
English Heritage Grade II*

This important woodland garden has a significant collection of rhododendron species grown from such introducers as Forrest and Kingdon-Ward. It has recently been revamped for the recreation market and is all the better for the new capital. There are good new borders, a lake, and all sorts of facilities like an adventure playground and a smart restaurant: very cockle-warming to see Borde Hill on the up again.

DENMANS
Fontwell, Arundel BN18 0SU
☎ 01243 542808   Fax 01243 544064
Location Off A29 or A27, near Fontwell racecourse
Open 9 am – 5 pm; daily; March to October. Or by appointment
Admission Adults £2.80; OAPs £2.50; Children (over 5) £1.50
Facilities Parking; loos; access for the disabled; shop; garden centre; lunches & teas
Features Herbaceous plants; herbs; old roses; spring bulbs

This small modern garden is a showpiece for John Brookes' ideas and commitment to easy care. He uses foliage, gravel mulches, contrasts of form, coloured stems, winter bark and plants as elements of design. Garden decoration *in excelsis*.

THE HIGH BEECHES
Handcross RH17 6HQ
☎ 01444 400589
Owner High Beeches Gardens Conservation Trust
Location South of B2110, 1 mile east of M23 at Handcross
Open 1 pm – 5 pm; daily, except Wednesdays; April to June, September & October. Plus Mondays & Tuesdays in July & August
Admission Adults £3.50. Coaches by appointment
Facilities Parking; loos; drinks & ice-creams
Features Good collection of trees; fine conifers; ecological interest; plantsman's garden; woodland garden; rhododendrons; tallest *Stewartia monodelpha* (11m.) in the British Isles
English Heritage Grade II*
NCCPG National Collection *Stewartia*
Friends High Beeches Gardens Conservation Trust is an active organisation with many events of interest to gardeners throughout the year: details from the Curator

One of the best of the famous Sussex gardens, a valley of ponds and woodland glades, with splendid rhododendrons, azaleas, magnolias and camellias, but wonderful spring and autumn colours too, and a policy of letting good plants naturalise – wild orchids, willow gentians and *Primula helodoxa*. A great credit to the Boscawens who have devoted 25 years to its maintenance and improvement.

WEST SUSSEX GARDENS 217

HIGHDOWN
Littlehampton Road, Goring-by-Sea BN12 6NY
☎ 01903 239999 ext 2539   Fax 01903 821384
Owner Worthing Borough Council
Location Signposted from A259
Open 10 am – 6 pm (4.30 pm October & November, 4 pm December & January, 4.30 pm February & March); daily (but not weekends from October to March); all year. Closes at 8 pm at weekends and on Bank Holiday Mondays from April to September
Admission Free – donations welcome
Facilities Parking; loos; refreshments in high season
Features Good collection of trees; herbaceous plants; fine conifers; plantsman's garden; rock garden; old roses; woodland garden; tallest specimen of *Carpinus turczaninowii* in the UK, a handsome tree
English Heritage Grade II*

A very important garden. Its maker, Sir Frederick Stern, was determined to try anything that might grow on chalk. Eighty years on, the results are some handsome trees, vigorous roses, and long-forgotten peony hybrids. Best of all are the naturalised hellebores, tulips, daffodils and anemones.

LEONARDSLEE GARDENS
Lower Beeding, Horsham RH13 6PP
☎ 01403 891212   Fax 01403 891305
Owner R R Loder
Location 4 miles south-west of Handcross at junction of A279 & A281
Open 9.30 am – 6 pm (8 pm in May); daily; April to October
Admission Adults £4 (£5 in May); Children £2.50
Facilities Parking; loos; plants for sale; gift shop; licensed restaurant & café
Features Bluebells; fine conifers; glasshouses; oriental features; plantsman's garden; rhododendrons and azaleas; rock garden; woodland garden; new alpine house; wallabies; summer wildflower walk; new millennium plantings (120 oak species; 240 maple cultivars; many flowering *Cornus*); Victorian motor cars; tallest fossil tree *Metasequoia glyptostroboides* (28m.) and *Magnolia campbellii* (27m.) in the British Isles, and five further champion trees
English Heritage Grade I

A spectacular collection of rhododendrons and azaleas is the essence of Leonardslee, and the way they are planted in drifts of one colour. But there are magnolias, camellias and innumerable rare plants, as well as a formidable bonsai collection. The 80 acres open to the public are laced with lakes, dells and groves; they have just been extended to 240 acres. Ravishing in May.

NYMANS GARDEN
Handcross, Haywards Heath RH17 6EB
☎ 01444 400321   Fax 01444 400353
Owner The National Trust
Location Handcross, off the main road
Open 11 am – 6 pm; Wednesday – Sunday, plus Bank Holiday Mondays; 3 March to 31 October. 11 am – 4 pm; Saturdays & Sundays; November to February 2000. Closed 25 December & 1 January 2000
Admission Adults £5; Children £2.50; RHS members free
Facilities Parking; loos; facilities for the disabled; shop; plant centre open daily 11 am – 6 pm; teas
Features Good collection of trees; herbaceous plants; plantsman's garden; old roses; good topiary; woodland garden; eight different record-breaking trees
English Heritage Grade II*

Nymans has made a brilliant recovery since the Great Storm of 1987. There are opulent yellow-and-blue herbaceous borders in the walled garden, a pioneering collection of old roses, a stupendous wisteria pergola and vast collections of magnolias and camellias.

PARHAM
Parham House, Pulborough RH20 4HS
☎ 01903 742021   Fax 01903 746557
Owner Parham Park Trust
Location On A283 midway between Pulborough and Storrington
Open 12 noon – 6 pm; Wednesdays, Thursdays, Sundays & Bank Holiday Mondays; April to October
Admission Gardens only: Adults £3; Children 50p
Facilities Parking; dogs permitted; loos; plants for sale; shop; light lunches & teas
Features Herbaceous plants; fruit of special interest; plantsman's garden; old roses; new children's garden behind the Wendy House (1999); HHA/Christie's Garden of the Year in 1990
English Heritage Grade I

An ethereal English garden for the loveliest of Elizabethan manor houses. In the park are a landscaped lake and a cricket ground. The fun for garden-lovers is in the old walled garden: lush borders, colour plantings in yellow, blue and mauve, old and new fruit trees, and all maintained to the highest standard. The aim is to achieve 'Edwardian opulence... without being too purist'.

PETWORTH HOUSE
Petworth GU28 0AE
☎ 01798 342207
Owner The National Trust
Location At Petworth, well signed
Open Garden: 12 noon – 6 pm; 20 & 21 March; then Saturday – Wednesday; 27 March to 31 October. Also 2 April. Opens 11 am in July & August. Park: 8 am – 9 pm, or dusk if sooner; daily; all year (but closes at noon 25 to 27 June)
Admission Garden: £1. Park: free
Facilities Parking; dogs permitted; loos; facilities for the disabled; shop; restaurant; tea-rooms
Features Herbaceous plants; landscape designed by Capability Brown; lake; woodland garden; particularly interesting in winter; deer park; one million daffodils; nine record-holding trees all felled by the Great Gale of 1987

English Heritage Grade I
One of the best Capability Brown landscapes in England sweeps up to the windows of the house itself. The National Trust has decided to add modern attractions: herbaceous borders and acres of azaleas in a new woodland garden. Both park and garden have enjoyed a renaissance since the Great Gale.

WAKEHURST PLACE
Ardingly, Haywards Heath RH17 6TN
☎ 01444 894066   Fax 01444 894069

Owner National Trust, but leased to RBG, Kew
Location On B2028 between Turner's Hill & Ardingly
Open 10 am – 7 pm (6 pm in March & October, 5 pm in February & 4 pm from November to January); daily except 25 December & 1 January; all year
Admission Adults £5; OAPs £3.50; Children £2.50
Facilities Parking; loos; access for the disabled; gift-shop; plant sales (March to October); light refreshments & new restaurant
Features Alpines; good collection of trees; bluebells; bog garden; camellias; daffodils; ecological interest; lake; plantsman's garden; rhododendrons and azaleas; climbing roses; old roses; woodland garden; particularly interesting in winter; Asian heath garden; pinetum; cardiocrinums; good autumn colour; new *Iris ensata* dell (1998); tallest *Ostrya japonica* (15m.) in the British Isles, plus 25 further tree records
English Heritage Grade II*
NCCPG National Collections *Betula*; *Hypericum*; *Nothofagus*; *Skimmia*
Friends The Friends of Kew have a branch at Wakehurst: ring Amanda Millar on 01444 894035

Allow plenty of time for Wakehurst: it is very big, and there is much to see. Near the house are the winter garden, two ponds, the new Asian heath garden and the southern hemisphere garden. No garden combines so perfectly the function of a major botanic institute with the sense of being a private garden still.

WEST DEAN GARDENS
West Dean, Chichester PO18 0Q2
☎ 01243 811301   Fax 01243 811342

Owner The Edward James Foundation
Location 6 miles north of Chichester on A286
Open 11 am – 5 pm; daily; March to October
Admission Adults £4; OAPs £3.50; Children £2
Facilities Parking; loos; facilities for the disabled; plants for sale; licensed restaurant
Features Glasshouses; old roses; museum of old lawn mowers; tallest *Cupressus goveniana* (22m.) and *Ailanthus vilmoriniana* (26m.) in UK; amazing kitchen garden
English Heritage Grade II*
NCCPG National Collections *Aesculus*; *Liriodendron*

Laid out in the 1890s and 1900s, West Dean has now been extensively restored: Harold Peto's 100-m. pergola has been replanted with roses; much of the damage to the arboretum caused by the 1987 storm has been made good; and the great range of glasshouses in the walled garden has been repaired – the garden itself planted as a working kitchen garden. We know of no private garden with so many beautifully grown fruit and vegetables.

WORTH A VISIT

ARCHITECTURAL PLANTS
Cooks Farm, Nuthurst, Horsham RH13 6LH
☎ *01403 891772. Open 9 am – 5 pm, Monday – Saturday. This stylish and charming nursery is worth a visit in its own right, quite apart from the exotic-looking, evergreen foliage plants, often with architectural shapes. Almost as good is their catalogue: breezily written and exceptionally helpful.*

COATES MANOR
Fittleworth, Pulborough RH20 1ES ☎ *01798 865356. Open 11 am – 6 pm; 17 & 18 October for autumn colour, and by appointment at other times. A small, neatly designed and intensely planted garden which crams a lifetime's learning into its plantings. Long-term colour effects are its outstanding quality: leaves, berries, trunks, stems, form, shadow and texture are all individually exploited to the maximum. A model of its kind and beautifully maintained.*

COOKE'S HOUSE
West Burton, Pulborough RH20 1HD ☎ *01798 831353. Open By appointment. A neat and well-maintained garden, pretty in spring when the primulas and bulbs are out. Even better at midsummer when the roses and herbaceous plants crammed into small enclosures create a sense of great richness and harmony.*

COWDRAY PARK
Midhurst GU29 0AQ ☎ *01730 812461. Open 2 pm – 6 pm; 16 May & 12 September. Seldom open, but worth a long journey to see the extraordinarily overwrought house and its contemporary (100 years old) collection of trees, particularly conifers. Some are now record-breakers, and the sweeps of rhododendrons and azaleas, especially the hardy hybrids down The Dell, are on the grand scale too. Pretty awesome.*

CROFTWAY NURSERY
Yapton Road, Barnham, Bognor Regis PO22 0BH
☎ *01243 552121. Open 9 am – 5 pm; March – November; daily. This family business specialises in bearded irises, of which they have a very large selection. But they also sell other iris types, and herbaceous perennials, including hardy geraniums.*

GRAVETYE MANOR HOTEL
East Grinstead RH19 4LJ ☎ *01342 810567. Open Hotel guests only; all year. The perimeter path is open to the public free of charge from 10 am to 5 pm on Tuesdays & Fridays. William Robinson's own garden, very influential 80 years ago, and scrupulously maintained by Peter Herbert as it was in its prime. Gravetye is still a garden to learn from: there is much to admire and copy.*

HOLLY GATE CACTUS GARDEN
Billingshurst Road, Ashington RH20 3BA
☎ 01903 892930. *Open 9 am – 5 pm; daily. Closed 25 – 26 December.* One of the largest of the cacti and succulent nurseries in Europe: 30,000 plants growing in landscaped glasshouses extending to 10,000 sq. ft (£1.50 for adults, £1 for OAPs). The extensive retail and wholesale lists includes all types of cacti, with over 50,000 specimens in stock, fascinating for cognoscenti and an eye-opener for the uninitiated.

STONEHURST
Ardingly RH17 6TN ☎ 01444 892052. *Open 11 am – 5 pm; 11 April & 3 May.* Stonehurst is in a rock-lined secret valley, where springs issue to form a series of small lakes, and rare liverworts have special scientific interest. The Strausses have made it known as a garden for rhododendrons, camellias and rare trees and shrubs which regularly win prizes at RHS shows in London. Well maintained.

W E TH INGWERSEN LTD
Birch Farm Nursery, Gravetye, East Grinstead RH19 4LE
☎ 01342 810236. *Open 9 am – 1 pm, 1.30 pm – 4 pm, daily, March to September. Opens at 10 am on Saturdays, Sundays & Bank Holidays.* This long-established alpine nursery has an excellent range of popular and less common rock-garden plants, including dwarf shrubs and conifers. There is an annual plant sale in late September, but the nursery is worth a browse at any season. Excellent value.

YEW TREE COTTAGE
Crawley Down, Turners Hill RH10 4EY
☎ 01342 714633. *Open By appointment from April to August.* This miraculous small garden (⅓ acre) has been designed, planted and maintained by the nonagenarian owner over many years and won infinite plaudits for its display of plants in the Jekyll manner. There is no better example of the cottage-garden style.

TYNE & WEAR

WORTH A VISIT

BEDE'S WORLD HERB GARDEN
Bede's World, Church Bank, Jarrow NE32 3DY
☎ 0191 489 2196. *Open Dawn to dusk; daily; all year.* A herb garden based on 9th-century descriptions: a small part of an ambitious enterprise which seeks to impart a feeling for the Anglo-Saxon world. In front of the new museum are four raised beds planted as a late medieval formal garden.

WARWICKSHIRE

ARBURY HALL
Nuneaton CV10 7PT
☎ 01203 382804   Fax 01203 641147

Owner Viscount Daventry
Location 3 miles south-east of Nuneaton off the B4102
Open 2pm – 6 pm; Saturdays & Sundays; Easter Sunday to September
Admission Adults £4.50; Children £2.50
Facilities Parking; dogs permitted; loos; access for the disabled; gift & crafts shop; tea-rooms
Features Bluebells; daffodils; good architectural features; rhododendrons and azaleas; modern roses; woodland garden
English Heritage Grade II*

Good trees (especially purple beeches), handsome parkland, lakes and ponds – Arbury has good bones for a garden. Then there are bluebell woods, pollarded limes, a large rose garden, a walled garden and a huge wisteria. Nothing is outstanding in itself, but the ensemble is an oasis of peace on the edge of industrial Daventry and worth the journey from far away.

CHARLECOTE PARK
Wellesbourne, Warwick CV35 9ER
☎ 01789 470277   Fax 01789 470544

Owner The National Trust
Location Signed from A429
Open 11 am – 6 pm; Friday – Tuesday; 20 March to 31 October. Closed Good Friday
Admission House & garden: £4.90
Facilities Parking; loos; facilities for the disabled; National Trust shop; restaurant
Features Landscape designed by Capability Brown; fine conifers; glasshouses; lake; good topiary; deer park; orangery
English Heritage Grade II*

Fine cedars and a Capability Brown park are the main claims to Charlecote's fame, but the young William Shakespeare is reputed to have poached deer from the park, so the National Trust has planted a border with plants mentioned in his works.

COUGHTON COURT
Alcester B49 5JA
☎ 01789 400777   Fax 01789 765544

Owner Mrs Clare Throckmorton
Location 2 miles north of Alcester on A435
Open 11 am – 5.30 pm; Saturdays & Sundays, 15 to 31 March and 1 to 17 October; Wednesday – Sunday, 3 April to 30 September. Plus Bank Holiday Mondays, 6 April, 1 June and Tuesdays in August
Admission Adults £4.50; Children £2.25
Facilities Parking; loos; access for the disabled; gift shop & plant centre; restaurant/café
Features New bog garden (1997)

The garden is new, and designed by Christina Birch, the owner's daughter. An Elizabethan-style knot garden fills the courtyard, and extensive new plantings beyond lead the eye out to the distant landscape. There are a new rose labyrinth and a herb garden, as well as an orchard planted with local varieties of fruit.

FARNBOROUGH HALL
Banbury OX17 1DU
☎ 01295 690002

Owner The National Trust
Location Off A423, 6 miles north of Banbury
Open 2 pm – 6 pm; Wednesdays & Saturdays; April to September. Also 2 & 3 May
Admission Grounds £1.50; Terrace Walk £1 (Thursdays & Fridays only)
Facilities Parking; dogs permitted; loos; access for the disabled
Features Good architectural features; lake; old roses; good topiary; woodland garden
English Heritage Grade I

Sanderson Millar's masterpiece – grand vistas, classical temples and a dominating obelisk. Plus a long curving terraced walk to the adjoining estate of Mollington. No flowers, but space and peace.

THE MILL GARDEN, WARWICK
55 Mill Street, Warwick CV34 4HB
☎ 01926 492877

Owner Arthur Measures
Location Off A425, beside castle gate
Open 9 am – dusk; daily; Easter to mid-October
Admission Adults £1; Children free. Groups by appointment
Facilities Access for the disabled; plants for sale
Features Plantsman's garden; water plants

No garden has such an idyllic setting, on the banks of the Avon at the foot of Warwick castle: the views in all directions are superb. The garden is planted in the cottage style and seems much larger than its one acre: it burgeons with plants, and the use of annuals to supplement the varied permanent planting enables it to have colour and form, contrasts and harmonies, at every season.

PACKWOOD HOUSE
Packwood Lane, Lapworth, Solihull B94 6AT
☎ 01564 782024   Fax 01564 782014

Owner The National Trust
Location 2 miles east of Hockley Heath: signposted from A3400
Open 2 pm – 6 pm; Wednesday – Sunday & Bank Holiday Mondays; 27 March to 30 September. Plus 12.30 pm – 4.30 pm in October
Admission Garden only: Adults £2.20; Children £1.10
Facilities Parking; loos; access for the disabled; National Trust shop; refreshments available at peak times
Features Good topiary
English Heritage Grade I

Long famous for its topiary, but Packwood also has magnificent herbaceous borders which make a visit in July or August particularly rewarding.

RYTON ORGANIC GARDENS
Henry Doubleday Research Association,
Ryton-on-Dunsmore, Coventry CV8 3LG
☎ 01203 303517   Fax 01203 639229

Owner The Henry Doubleday Research Association (HDRA)
Location 5 miles south-east of Coventry off A45
Open 10 am – 5.30 pm; daily; all year except Christmas week
Admission Adults £2.50; Concessions £2; Children £1.25; RHS members free
Facilities Parking; loos; facilities for the disabled; plants for sale; shop with gardening products, books, food, wine & gifts; organic whole-food restaurant
Features Ecological interest; fruit and vegetables of special interest; glasshouses; herbs; interesting for children; new 'Cook's Garden' (1998); new Paradise Garden, built as a memorial to Geoff Hamilton (1999)
Friends Join the HDRA – details above

Ryton is the UK centre for organic gardening where experiments are made in using only natural fertilisers and trying to operate without pesticides. It is very well laid out, with dozens of different small gardens, all highly instructive. The staff's commitment is also impressive. You may not be convinced by what you see, but it will make you think. The excellent restaurant and substantial shop will add considerably to your enjoyment.

UPTON HOUSE
Banbury OX15 6HT
☎ 01295 670266

Owner The National Trust
Location A422, 7 miles north-west of Banbury
Open 2 – 6 pm; Saturday – Wednesday; 27 March to 31 October
Admission Adults £2.60; Children £1.30
Facilities Parking; loos; facilities for the disabled; plants for sale; National Trust shop; tea-room
Features Herbaceous plants; fruit of special interest; new soft fruit plantings in kitchen garden (1997)
English Heritage Grade II*
NCCPG National Collection Aster

High on a ridge near the site of the battle of Edgehill, Upton is terraced right down to the pool at the bottom. The centrepiece is a kitchen garden, reached by flights of Italianate stairs. There are also modern formal gardens, one with standard *Hibiscus* 'Bluebird' underplanted with eryngiums, another a rose garden. Further down are a bog garden, a cherry garden and grand herbaceous borders to lead you back to the house. Fascinating, and not at all what you expect when you first see the house.

WARWICK CASTLE
Warwick CV34 4QU
☎ 01926 495421   Fax 01926 401692

Owner Tussauds Group
Location In town centre

Open 10 am – 6 pm (5 pm in winter); daily; all year except 25 December
Admission Adults £9.25; OAPs £6.65; Children £5.60 (prices will be reviewed in March)
Facilities Loos; shop; refreshments
Features Fine conifers; rhododendrons and azaleas; old roses; good topiary; Capability Brown landscape; handsome conservatory
English Heritage Grade I

A classic 18th-century landscape, looking good after recent restoration, to which have been added a late-19th-century formal garden, a Backhouse rock garden, and a rather 1980s Victorian-style rose garden.

WORTH A VISIT

FIBREX NURSERIES LTD
Honeybourne Road, Pebworth, Stratford-upon-Avon CV37 8XT ☎ *01789 720788. Open 10.30 am – 5 pm; Monday – Friday; all year. Noon – 5 pm; Saturdays & Sundays from March to July. NCCPG National Collections: Hedera; Pelargonium. Specialists in pelargoniums, ferns and ivies: their exhibits at RHS shows are famous. A recent addition to their range is hellebore hybrids: definitely worth a visit, quite apart from the fern garden and ivy garden.*

THE HILLER GARDEN CENTRE
Dunnington Heath Farm, Alcester B49 5PD
☎ *01789 490991. Open 10 am – 5 pm; daily; all year. A two-acre garden (free admission) planted for year-round interest and centring on a Victorian-style rose-garden. Good plant centre.*

SHERBOURNE PARK
Sherbourne, Warwick CV35 8AP ☎ *01926 624506. A splendid post-war garden planned and planted to produce a series of smallish enclosed gardens around the house, each distinct and beautifully planted. The shelter of walls and hedges allows such tender genera as Olearia and Carpenteria to survive, and sometimes to flourish.*

WOODFIELD BROS
Wood End, Clifford Chambers, Stratford on Avon CV37 8HR ☎ *01789 205618. Open 10 am – 1 pm and 2.30 pm – 4.30 pm; daily; all year. 10 am – 12.30 pm on Sundays. A good nursery for traditional herbaceous plants: they specialise in perpetual flowering carnations, delphiniums and lupins. Phlox, Hosta and Begonia cultivars are usually available too.*

WEST MIDLANDS

BIRMINGHAM BOTANICAL GARDENS & GLASSHOUSES
Westbourne Road, Edgbaston, Birmingham B15 3TR
☎ 0121 454 1860   **Fax** 0121 454 7835
Owner Birmingham Botanical & Horticultural Society
Location Follow brown tourist signs in Edgbaston
Open 9 am (Sunday 10 am) – 7 pm, or dusk if earlier; daily; all year except 25 December
Admission Adults £4.20; Concessions £2.30
Facilities Parking; loos; facilities for the disabled; plants for sale; gift shop; restaurant & light refreshments
Features Herbaceous plants; fine conifers; fruit of special interest; glasshouses; plantsman's garden; rock garden; modern roses; old roses; interesting for children; new fern walk (1997); new alpine yard (1998); children's gardens; adventure playground; three new 'historic' gardens – Roman, Medieval & Tudor
English Heritage Grade II*
NCCPG National Collections *Verbascum*; *Solenostemon*; Bonsai
Friends Membership details available from Reception

Part botanic garden, part public park, wholly delightful, the Birmingham Botanical Gardens can boast a historic layout (John Loudon), rare trees and shrubs, gardens for rhododendrons, roses, herbs and alpines, and four glasshouses (tropical, palm house, orangery and cacti house) as well as a good restaurant, brilliant standards of maintenance and a brass band playing on Sunday afternoons in summer. Last year it hosted the G8 Summit dinner party: pictures of the Blairs and Clintons were on every front page.

CASTLE BROMWICH HALL
Chester Road, Castle Bromwich B36 9BT
☎ 0121 749 4100   **Fax** 0121 749 4100
Owner Castle Bromwich Hall Gardens Trust
Location 5 miles from city centre just off A47
Open 1.30 – 4 30 pm; Tuesday – Thursday; May to September. 2 – 6 pm; Saturdays, Sundays & Bank Holiday Mondays; Easter to September
Admission Adults £2.50; OAPs £1.50; Children 50p
Facilities Parking; dogs permitted; loos; facilities for the disabled; plants for sale; gift shop; refreshments
Features Interesting for children; green walks; fruit garden; maze; wilderness; Lady Bridgeman's Physic Garden (1997); historic garden undergoing restoration
English Heritage Grade II*
Friends Friends of the Gardens organisation

Garden archaeology at work. Castle Bromwich is being restored as it was in 1700 by a privately funded trust. Quietly awe-inspiring, and the tiny orangery, little more than a summerhouse, is very covetable.

WIGHTWICK MANOR
Wightwick, Wolverhampton WV6 8EE
☎ 01902 761108   **Fax** 01902 764663
Owner The National Trust
Location 3 miles west of Wolverhampton on A454
Open 11 am – 6 pm on Wednesdays & Thursdays; 1 pm – 6 pm on Saturdays & Bank Holidays; March to December
Admission Adults £2.40
Facilities Parking; dogs permitted; loos; access for the disabled; coffee & soft drinks

Features Herbaceous plants; rock garden; climbing roses; old roses; good topiary; current holder of Sandford Award; Thomas Mawson herbaceous borders restored (1997)

A substantial Victorian garden, designed by Thomas Mawson and planted by Alfred Parsons. Topiary, a rose arbour, avenues of Irish yews and a Poets' Corner where all the plants were taken as cuttings from the gardens of literary men – Keats, Tennyson and Dickens among them.

WORTH A VISIT

ASHWOOD NURSERIES LTD
Greensforge, Kingswinford DY6 0AE ☎ *01384 401996. Open 9 am – 6 pm; Monday – Saturday; 9.30 am – 6 pm; Sundays. Closed 25 & 26 December. NCCPG National Collections:* Lewisia; Cyclamen *hardy. This large nursery carries a very extensive range of fruit trees, conifers, heathers, trees and shrubs – one of the best in England – but its specialities are* Lewisia, Cyclamen, Helleborus *and* Primula auricula, *for each of which there is an active programme of hybridisation and selection. Ashwood lewisias and hellebores are a spectacle at the spring RHS shows at Westminster.*

WILTSHIRE

AVEBURY MANOR
Avebury, Marlborough
☎ 01672 539203

Owner The National Trust
Location In the village, well signposted
Open 11 am – 5.30 pm; daily except Mondays & Thursdays; 2 April to 31 October
Admission Adults £2.25; Children £1
Facilities Parking; access for the disabled; shop just outside the garden; refreshments in village
Features Herbaceous plants; rock garden; old roses; good topiary; double lavender walk

A recent owner did much to revive this great Edwardian garden. The National Trust is continuing the work of restoration: the results are well worth another visit.

BOWOOD HOUSE
Calne SN11 0LZ
☎ 01249 812102   **Fax** 01249 821757

Owner The Earl of Shelburne
Location Off A4 in Derry Hill village between Calne and Chippenham
Open 11 am – 6 pm; daily; 27 March to 31 October
Admission Adults £5.50; OAPs £4.50; Children £3.20. Rhododendron walks – starting mid-May – £3: on 23 May for NGS
Facilities Parking; loos; facilities for the disabled; plants for sale; gift shop; buffet lunches & afternoon teas in licensed restaurant
Features Landscape designed by Capability Brown; fine conifers; good architectural features; lake; landscape designed by Humphry Repton; rhododendrons and azaleas; good topiary; woodland garden; interesting for children; bluebells; immodest sculpture; adventure playground; tallest *Thuja occidentalis* 'Wareana' in the UK
English Heritage Grade I

Beautifully maintained and welcoming, Bowood has something from every period of English garden history. Capability Brown made the lake and Charles Hamilton the famous cascade. There are an important 19th-century pinetum laid out on pre-Linnaean principles, handsome Italianate formal gardens (replanted by Mary Keen), and modern rhododendron drives in a bluebell wood. Be sure to miss the reclining nude above the formal gardens.

BROADLEAS
Devizes SN10 5JQ
☎ 01380 722035

Owner Broadleas Gardens Charitable Trust
Location 1 mile south of Devizes
Open 2 pm – 6 pm; Wednesdays, Thursdays & Sundays; April to October
Admission Adults £3; Children £1
Facilities Parking; dogs permitted; loos; access for the disabled; plants for sale; teas on summer Sundays
Features Good collection of trees; herbaceous plants; plantsman's garden; modern roses; old roses; woodland garden
English Heritage Grade II

Broadleas has a rose garden, a grey border, a rock garden and a 'secret' garden, all near the Regency house. But the main attraction is the Dell, a greensand combe that stretches down to the valley below, its sides just stuffed with good things – rare trees, vast magnolias, sheets of *Primula whitei* and cyclamen.

CORSHAM COURT
Corsham SN13 0BZ
☎ 01249 701610/701611   **Fax** 01249 444556

Owner Trustees of the Methuen Estate
Location Signposted from A4 Bath to Chippenham
Open 11 am – 5.30 pm; Tuesday – Sunday & Bank Holiday Mondays; 20 March to 30 September. Plus 2 – 4.30 pm; Saturdays & Sundays; 1 October to 19 March
Admission Adults £2; OAPs £1.50; Children £1
Facilities Parking; dogs permitted; loos; access for the disabled; plants for sale
Features Good collection of trees; designed by Capability Brown and Humphry Repton; amazing oriental plane *Platanus orientalis* whose sweeping limbs have rooted over a huge area.
English Heritage Grade II*

Major 18th-century landscape garden, with pretty 1820s flower garden and ambitious modern arboretum: strongly recommended.

THE COURTS
Holt, Trowbridge BA14 6RR
☎ 01225 782340

Owner The National Trust
Location In the middle of Holt village
Open 1.30 pm – 5.30 pm; Sunday – Friday; 28 March to 31 October
Admission Adults £3; Children £1.50
Facilities Parking; access for the disabled
Features Good collection of trees; herbaceous plants; plantsman's garden; good topiary
English Heritage Grade II

1920s masterpiece in the Hidcote style. Rich colour plantings in a series of garden rooms. Excellent plants, beautifully used: well maintained by the new Head Gardener who has come from Sissinghurst.

HEALE HOUSE
Middle Woodford, Salisbury SP4 6NT
☎ 01722 782504

Owner Guy Rasch
Location Signposted off the western Woodford valley road, and from A345 & A360
Open 10 am – 5 pm; daily; all year
Admission Adults £3; Children free
Facilities Parking; dogs permitted; loos; access for the disabled; large plant centre; garden & gift shop
Features Herbaceous plants; fruit of special interest; oriental features; old roses; snowdrops; Christie's/HHA Garden of the Year in 1984
English Heritage Grade II*

A Peto garden round the prettiest house in Wiltshire. Formal walks, ponds, lawns and balustrading. Rich colours and clever planting. Japanese garden around genuine tea-house. Pure enchantment.

IFORD MANOR
Bradford-on-Avon BA15 2BA
☎ 01225 863146

Owner Mrs E Cartwright-Hignett
Location 7 miles south-east of Bath, signed from A36 and Bradford-on-Avon
Open 2 – 5 pm; Sundays & Easter Monday; April & October. Plus Tuesday – Thursday, Saturdays, Sundays & Bank Holiday Mondays from May to September
Admission Adults £2.50; OAPs & children (over 10) £1.90
Facilities Parking; dogs permitted; loos; teas on Bank Holidays and some weekends
Features Good architectural features; garden sculpture; Italian cypresses and handsome *Phillyrea*; martagon lilies; cyclamen
English Heritage Grade I
NCCPG National Collection *Acanthus*

Harold Peto's own Italianate garden on a steep wooded hillside is meticulously maintained and imaginatively planted. Peto bought the estate in 1899, so there will centenary celebrations this year. Highlights include a Romanesque cloister, an octagonal cloister, a gloriously colonnaded terrace and much architectural bric-à-brac. Every detail is wonderfully photogenic.

LACKHAM COUNTRY ATTRACTIONS
Lacock, Chippenham
☎ 01249 466800   Fax 01249 444474

Owner Lackham College
Location 3 miles south of Chippenham on A350
Open 10 am – 4 pm; 13 & 14 March, 23 May and possibly some other days. Ring for information
Admission Adults £3; OAPs £2; Children £1
Facilities Parking; dogs permitted; loos; access for the disabled; plants for sale; souvenirs for sale; refreshments
Features Alpines; good collection of trees; bluebells; herbaceous plants; daffodils; fruit and vegetables of special interest; glasshouses; herbs; plantsman's garden; interesting for children; particularly good in July–August; roses of every kind; adventure playground; farm museum
NCCPG National Collection *Populus*
Friends Friends of Lackham Charitable Trust. Also Lackham Garden Club. Details on 01249 443111

Among the best of county college gardens, Lackham is a living monument to the knowledge and initiative of Oliver and the late Ann Menhinnick. A major extension was opened in 1996 but the heart of Lackham is the walled garden, beautifully laid out to educate and delight, with a magnificent glasshouse collection of orchids, tropical fruits and bulbs. New building works mean that the garden will probably be open very little this year.

LONGLEAT HOUSE
Warminster BA12 7NW
☎ 01985 844400   Fax 01985 844885
Website www.longleat.co.uk

Owner The Marquess of Bath
Location Off A362 Warminster to Frome road
Open Daylight hours; daily; all year except 25 December. Maze and other attractions open from 13 March to 31 October
Admission Grounds & gardens: Adults £2; OAPs & children 50p
Facilities Parking; dogs permitted; loos; access for the disabled; shops; cafeterias & restaurants
Features Good collection of trees; herbaceous plants; landscape designed by Capability Brown; lake; rhododendrons and azaleas; climbing roses; modern roses; old roses; good topiary; woodland garden; interesting for children; particularly good in July–August; Safari Park; orangery; world's largest maze; new Maze of Love with saucily named roses; newly planted Sun Maze & Lunar Labyrinth
English Heritage Grade I

Forget the lions and the loins, Longleat has a classic 18th-century landscape by Capability Brown, a home park of 600 acres best seen from Heaven's Gate and a grand Victorian garden reworked by Russell Page in the 1930s. The new Lord Bath has conserved the best and is invigorating the rest of Longleat. Worth another visit.

Pound Hill House
West Kington, Chippenham SN14 7JG
☎ 01249 782822   Fax 01249 782953

Owner Mr & Mrs Philip Stockitt
Location Signposted in village
Open 2 pm – 5 pm; daily; April to October
Admission Adults £2
Facilities Parking; loos; access for the disabled; adjacent to West Kington Nurseries Plant Centre; refreshments
Features Alpines; fruit of special interest; modern roses; old roses; woodland garden; play area for children; new walled area for topiary & specimen plants (1999)

The private garden of a discriminating nurseryman, Pound Hill has been developed as a year-round showplace. Stylish new plantings make it a garden to watch: *Parrotia persica* underplanted with white colchicums, and *Betula jacquemontii* with pulmonarias and 'Queen of Night' tulips.

Sharcott Manor
Pewsey SN9 5PA
☎ 01672 563485

Owner Captain & Mrs David Armytage
Location Off A4345, one mile south-west of Pewsey
Open 11 am – 5 pm; first Wednesday of every month; April to October. Plus 2 – 6pm; 11 April & 4 July
Admission Adults £2; Children free
Facilities Parking; loos; good plant sales area, all propagated from garden; home-made teas
Features Herbaceous plants; plantsman's garden

This extensive modern garden has been quite transformed over the last 20 years into a densely planted plantsman's paradise. There is much to see and you move gently from garden room to garden room. There are harmonies and contrasts to please the most colour-conscious, while the dark shady lake at the bottom is a haven of romantic broodiness. An excellent garden: why do so few people know of it?

Stourhead
Stourton BA12 6QD
☎ & Fax 01747 841152

Owner The National Trust
Location 3 miles north of Mere, signposted off the A303/B3092
Open 9 am – 7 pm, or dusk if earlier (4 pm, 22 to 25 July); daily; all year
Admission Adults £4.30; Children £2.50
Facilities Parking; loos; facilities for the disabled; National Trust shop near entrance; new plant centre; famous hotel/pub opposite gate
Features Good collection of trees; bluebells; fine conifers; good architectural features; lake; rhododendrons and azaleas; garden sculpture; snowdrops; interesting for children; good autumn colour; tallest tulip tree *Liriodendron tulipifera* (37m.) in the British Isles, and 12 other record tree species
English Heritage Grade I

Whatever the weather or season, Stourhead conveys a sense of majesty and harmony. Try it early on a May morning, before it opens officially, when the air is sweet with azaleas. Or scuff the fallen leaves in late November. Think of it 200 years ago, without the rhododendrons, when all the beech trees were interplanted with spruces. Ponder the 18th-century aesthetic, which esteemed tones and shades more highly than colours. Spot the change from classical to Gothic, from Pope to Walpole. And wonder at the National Trust's ability to maintain it so well with only six gardeners.

Stourton House
Stourton, Warminster BA12 6QF
☎ 01747 840417

Owner Mrs Anthony Bullivant
Location Next to Stourhead, 2 miles north of A303 at Mere
Open 11 am – 6 pm; Wednesdays, Thursdays, Sundays & Bank Holiday Mondays; April to November
Admission Adults £2.50; Children 50p; Groups (12+) £1.50
Facilities Parking; loos; facilities for the disabled; plants & dried flowers for sale all year; teas; light lunches; sticky cakes
Features Herbaceous plants; particularly good in July–August; Victorian conservatory; elegantly curving hedges; 270 different hydrangeas; hosts of daffodils, in innumerable shapes, sizes and colours

This five-acre Old Vicarage garden, next to Stourhead, is famous for its dried flowers, thanks to the energy and personality of Elizabeth Bullivant. Strongly recommended at any season: fascinating collection of split-corona daffodils in spring.

Wilton House
Wilton, Salisbury SP2 0BJ
☎ 01722 746720   Fax 01722 744447

Owner Earl of Pembroke/Wilton House Trust
Location In village, 3 miles west of Salisbury on A30
Open 10.30 am – 5.30 pm; daily; 27 March to 31 October
Admission Adults £3.75; Children £2.50
Facilities Parking; loos; access for the disabled; plants for sale in adjoining Wilton House garden centre; self-service restaurant
Features Old roses; interesting for children; handsome cedars; famous Palladian bridge; magnificent golden-leaved oak; new 'cloister garden' within the inner courtyard of the house (1996); adventure playground
English Heritage Grade I

Sublime 18th-century park around classical Inigo Jones pile famous for its paintings. Wilton also has a pretty new rose garden and water garden.

WORTH A VISIT

BOLEHYDE MANOR
Allington Chippenham ☎ 01249 652105. *Open By appointment, and for the NGS. Charming series of enclosed gardens around old stone-built house. Brilliantly developed by the owners over the last ten years.*

BOTANIC NURSERY
Bath Road, Atworth, Melksham SN12 8NU
☎ 01225 706597. *Open 10 am – 12.30 pm & 2 pm – 5 pm; Wednesday – Monday; February – December. NCCPG National Collection: Digitalis. A splendid nursery for browsing – not the tidiest we know, but full of good things. Their many specialities include lime-tolerant plants and foxgloves, which are a highlight of the RHS summer flower shows.*

CONOCK MANOR
Devizes SN10 3QQ ☎ 01380 840227. *Open 2 pm – 6 pm; 23 May. Beautiful parkland surrounds this covetable Georgian house. Behind the copper-domed stables an elegant shrub walk meanders past Sorbus, maples and magnolias.*

HILLBARN HOUSE
Great Bedwyn, Marlborough SN8 3NU *Open 2 pm – 6 pm; 20 June & 19 September. Lanning Roper's masterpiece makes brilliant use of a small steep site by dividing space to create an illusion of size. Well maintained.*

HOME COVERT
Roundway, Devizes SN10 2JA ☎ 01380 723407. *Open 2 pm – 6 pm; 3 May, 15 August for NGS; groups by appointment. One of the finest and largest (33 acres) plantsman's gardens in England; 'a botanical madhouse' say the owners. Rare trees (Cercis racemosa) and shrubs (Heptacodium jasminoides): Lathraea clandestina and swathes of candelabra primulas in the bog garden.*

OARE HOUSE
Oare, Marlborough SN8 4JQ ☎ 01672 62428. *Open 2 pm – 6 pm; 25 April & 25 July. Oare has an approach along lime avenues and tall hedges whose grandeur is echoed by the main garden behind: a huge apron of walled lawn, with majestic mixed borders at the sides, lead the eye over a half-hidden swimming pool to a grand ride beyond and on to the Marlborough Downs beyond. Intimacy exists only in some small enclosed gardens to the side and in the kitchen garden. Here are a magnificent herbaceous border in reds and yellows, a tunnel of fruit trees and vegetables in neat rows. A delight.*

THE OLD VICARAGE
Edington, Westbury BA13 4QF ☎ 01380 830512. *Open 2 pm – 6 pm; 13 June. NCCPG National Collection: Oenothera. Two acres of intensively cultivated plantsman- ship. The owner is a distinguished plant-collector: his garden is immaculately maintained and bristles with new species (Salvia darcyi) and living holotypes.*

ROCHE COURT
East Winterslow, Salisbury SP5 1BG ☎ 01980 862244. *Open 11 am – 4 pm; daily; all year except 25 December. As a garden, nothing special, but a show place for Lady Bessborough's contemporary sculpture shop. Everything is for sale, so the garden is ever changing. The Sculpture Park runs to 20 acres, and many of the pieces are modern classics.*

SHERSTON PARVA NURSERY LTD
Malmesbury Road, Sherston SN16 0NX
☎ 01666 841066. *Open 10 am – 5 pm; daily; all year. Clematis (over 200 cultivars), climbers and wall-shrubs are this nursery's speciality. Their list is impressive – and growing.*

THOMPSON'S HILL
Sherston, Malmesbury SN16 0PZ ☎ 01666 840766. *Half-acre modern garden, growing up quickly and changing all the time. Well planted and neatly maintained by owners' own efforts. Much featured in the glossies.*

WESTDALE NURSERIES
3 Westdale Nurseries, Holt Road, Bradford on Avon BA15 1TS ☎ 01225 863258. *Open 9 am – 6 pm; daily. Closed 25 December. A West Country source of Bougainvillea in numerous varieties.*

NORTH YORKSHIRE

BENINGBROUGH HALL
Shipton-by-Beningbrough, York YO30 1DD
☎ 01904 470666   Fax 01904 470002
Owner The National Trust
Location 8 miles north-west of York off the A19
Open 11 am – 5 pm; Saturday – Wednesday, plus Good Friday & Fridays in July & August; 27 March to 31 October
Admission Adults £3.50; Children £1.70
Facilities Parking; loos; facilities for the disabled; National Trust gift shop; morning coffee; hot & cold lunches; afternoon teas
Features Herbaceous plants; fruit of special interest; plantings by Graham Thomas; American garden; good conservatory on house; traditional Victorian kitchen garden undergoing restoration (1997); 'Lady Downe's Seedling' grape, raised at Beningbrough in 1835; vast Portuguese laurel *Prunus lusitanica*
English Heritage Grade II

Beningbrough is approached by an avenue of limes through stately parkland. Apart from a gloomy Victorian shrubbery, the gardens are modern – and pretty in a National Trust sort of way. Two small formal gardens, one with reds and oranges and the other with pastel shades, lie on either side of the early Georgian house. A sumptuous mixed border, graded from hot colours to cool, runs right to the gate of the walled kitchen garden. Restoration has begun here in earnest: there are exciting plans for further developments.

BURNBY HALL GARDENS
Pocklington YO4 2QF
☎ 01759 302068

Owner Stewarts Trust
Location Off A1079 13 miles east of York
Open 10 am – 6 pm; daily; 2 April to 4 October
Admission Adults £2.20; OAPs £1.70; Children 80p (subject to review)
Facilities Parking; loos; facilities for the disabled; plants for sale; snacks & salads, home-made cakes
Features Herbaceous plants; fine conifers; lake; rock garden; new secret garden (1998); winner of *Age Concern* award; fortnightly band concerts
NCCPG National Collection *Nymphaea*

Famed for its water lilies, planted by Frances Perry in the 1930s and now totalling over 80 different cultivars. But there is much more to Burnby Hall: a rock garden, cheerful modern rose garden and good collection of conifers all contribute to its visitor-friendly style. Follow the tarmacadam path around the lake: Burnby is a grand place for a promenade.

BURTON CONSTABLE HALL
Hull HU11 4LN
☎ 01964 562400   Fax 01964 563229

Owner Burton Constable Foundation
Location Via Hull B1238 to Sproatley follow HH (Historic House) signs
Open 12 noon – 5 pm (last admission 4.15 pm); Saturday – Thursday; Easter Sunday to 31 October
Admission Grounds: free
Facilities Parking; dogs permitted; loos; facilities for the disabled; shop; light snacks
Features Herbaceous plants; landscape designed by Capability Brown; woodland garden; interesting for children; fine 18th-century orangery; Victorian parterre restored (1999)
English Heritage Grade II
Friends Details from The Secretary, Friends of Burton Constable, Burton Constable, Hull HU11 4LN

Essentially a Capability Brown landscape (his original plans are still shown), but the 19th-century pleasure gardens are being restored and the whole estate will undoubtedly develop excitingly in future.

CASTLE HOWARD
York YO6 7DA
☎ 01653 648444   Fax 01653 648501

Owner Castle Howard Estates Ltd
Location 15 miles north-east of York, off A64
Open 10 am – 4.30 pm (last entry); daily; March to October
Admission Adults £4.50; Children £3
Facilities Parking; dogs permitted; loos; access for the disabled; shop and plant centre; cafeteria
Features Herbaceous plants; good architectural features; modern roses; old roses; garden sculpture; woodland garden; tallest elm *Ulmus glabra* (37m.) in British Isles
English Heritage Grade I

Heroic megapark (1,200 hectares) laid out with five axes by the 3rd Earl of Carlisle, Vanbrugh and Hawksmoor with important buildings (Temple of the Four Winds, Mausoleum). Grand 1980s rose gardens (slightly Surrey) designed by Jim Russell, with every type of rose from ancient to modern. Ray Wood is a fine and historic collection of rhododendrons and other ericaceous plants, meticulously labelled, and destined to develop as one of the greatest woodland gardens in Europe. A must for botanist and gardener alike – be prepared to spend all day here – and essential visiting for anyone with a sense of history.

DUNCOMBE PARK
Helmsley YO6 5EB
☎ 01439 770213   Fax 01439 771114
Website www.duncombepark.com

Owner Lord Feversham
Location Off A170; signed from Helmsley
Open 11 am – 6 pm or dusk if earlier; Saturday – Thursday; 7 April to 31 October. Plus Fridays from May to September
Admission Adults £3.75; Children £1.75
Facilities Parking; loos; access for the disabled; plants for sale; gift shop; restaurant
Features Good architectural features; garden sculpture; Rysbrack statue of Old Father Time
English Heritage Grade I

Major early 18th-century landscape, a grass terrace which sweeps between Vanburgh's Ionic rotunda and a Tuscan temple with views across the valley to Helmsley and the moors, matched only by views from its sister terrace at Rievaulx, in the care of the National Trust.

HARLOW CARR BOTANICAL GARDENS
Beckwithshaw, Harrogate HG3 1QB
☎ 01423 565418   Fax 01423 530663

Owner Northern Horticultural Society
Location Crag Lane off Otley Road (B6162), 1½ miles from Harrogate centre
Open 9.30 am – 6 pm, or dusk if earlier; daily; all year
Admission Adults £3.60; OAPs £2.70; Students £1.80; Children (under 16) free; Groups (20+) £2.60; RHS members free
Facilities Parking; loos; facilities for the disabled; gift shop; plant centre open every day 10.30 am – 5 pm; licensed restaurant
Features Good collection of trees; bluebells; daffodils; fruit and vegetables of special interest; herbs; rock garden; heathers and alpines; good autumn colour; tallest native rowan tree *Sorbus aucuparia* in the British Isles
NCCPG National Collections *Calluna*; *Dryopteris*; *Hypericum*; *Polypodium*; *Rheum*

Harlow Carr is quite the best place for northern gardeners to learn about gardening: the Wisley of the north.

MOUNT GRACE PRIORY
Staddlebridge, Northallerton DL6 3JG
☎ 01609 883494   Fax 01609 883361

NORTH YORKSHIRE — GARDENS

Owner The National Trust (managed by English Heritage)
Location 12 miles north of Thirsk on A19
Open 10 am – 6 pm; daily; April to September. 10 am – 4 pm; daily; October. 10 am – 1 pm and 2 pm – 4 pm; Wednesday – Sunday; November to March 2000
Admission Adults £2.80; Concessions £2.10; Children £1.50; RHS members free
Facilities Parking; loos; access for the disabled
Features Herbs

The herb garden, designed by Stephen Anderton in 1994, is of most interest to gardeners. It is a recreation of a 15th-century monastic garden. Around the house, the 1920s flower borders are being restored.

NEWBY HALL
Ripon HG4 5AE
☎ 01423 322583   Fax 01423 324452
Owner Robin Compton DL, VMH
Location Off B6265, 2 miles from A1
Open 11 am – 5.30 pm; Tuesday – Sunday & Bank holiday Mondays; April to September
Admission Adults £4.30; OAPs £3.70; Children & disabled £2.90 (1998 prices)
Facilities Parking; loos; facilities for the disabled; shop and plant stall; licensed restaurant
Features Herbaceous plants; daffodils; plantsman's garden; rock garden; climbing roses; old roses; woodland garden; HHA/Christie's Garden of the Year in 1986; tallest *Acer griseum* (15m.) in UK; adventure playground
English Heritage Grade II*
NCCPG National Collection *Cornus*

The garden with everything: firm design, an endless variety of features, great plantsmanship, immaculate maintenance. Its axis is a bold, wide, double border stretching endlessly down to the River Ure. Second only to Hidcote as an example of 20th-century gardening, but very much grander. Visit Newby at any season and expect to spend all day there.

PARCEVALL HALL GARDENS
Skyreholme, Skipton BD23 6DE
☎ 01756 720311
Owner Walsingham College (Yorkshire Properties) Ltd
Location Off B6160 from Burnsall
Open 10 am – 6 pm; daily; Good Friday to October; winter visits by appointment
Admission Adults £2; Children (5–12) 50p
Facilities Parking; dogs permitted; loos; plants for sale
Features Fine conifers; rhododendrons and azaleas; rock garden; climbing roses; woodland garden; candelabra primulas; refurbished rose garden (1999)

Breathtaking architectural layout, and views. Planted by Sir William Milner in 1927 and best now for its woodland walks where rhododendrons grow alongside limestone outcrops, daffodils (including 'W. P. Milner') and *Primula florindae* given by Kingdon-Ward now naturalised round the lily pond.

RIPLEY CASTLE
Ripley, Harrogate HG3 3AY
☎ 01423 770152   Fax 01423 771745
Owner Sir Thomas Ingilby Bt
Location 3½ miles north of Harrogate, off A61
Open 10 am – 5 pm (or dusk if earlier); daily; all year
Admission Adults £2.50; OAPs £2; Children £1
Facilities Parking; loos; facilities for the disabled; gift shop with plants, fruit and vegetables; castle tea-room
Features Bluebells; herbaceous plants; landscape designed by Capability Brown; subtropical plants; interesting for children; particularly interesting in winter; birds of prey sanctuary
English Heritage Grade II
NCCPG National Collection *Hyacinthus orientalis*

14th-century castle (restored); temples; smashing Regency conservatory; Victorian formal garden; evergreen shrubberies (handsome yews); rare vegetables from HDRA; hundreds of thousands of bulbs (daffodils in hosts). A garden with something for everyone.

SLEDMERE HOUSE
Sledmere, Driffield YO25 0XG
☎ 01377 236637   Fax 01377 236560
Owner Sir Tatton Sykes
Location Off A166 between York & Bridlington
Open 11.30 am – 5.30 pm; daily except Mondays & Saturdays; Easter weekend plus May to September
Admission Adults £1.75; Children £1
Facilities Parking; dogs permitted; loos; facilities for the disabled; craft & gift shop; tea-terrace & cafeteria
Features Landscape designed by Capability Brown; fine conifers; climbing roses; deer park
English Heritage Grade I

Sledmere has a classical Capability Brown landscape: his originals plans can be seen in the Library. An Italianate formal garden was added in 1911, with Greek and Roman busts swathed in climbing roses. A new knot garden is growing up quickly. Definitely a garden on the up.

STUDLEY ROYAL
Fountains, Ripon HG4 3DZ
☎ 01765 608888   Fax 01765 608889
Owner The National Trust
Location 3 miles west of Ripon off B6265, via the Visitor Centre
Open 10 am – 5 pm (7 pm in summer) or dusk if sooner; daily; all year, except Fridays from November to January & 24 & 25 December. Closes at 4 pm on 9 & 10 July & 7 August
Admission Adults £4.30; Children £2.10
Facilities Parking; dogs permitted; loos; facilities for the disabled; National Trust visitor centre shop; tea-room
Features Lake; snowdrops; good topiary; particularly interesting in winter; World Heritage site; 400-acre deer park; newly restored (1997) water garden; biggest *Prunus avium* (bird cherry) in British Isles
English Heritage Grade I

Inextricably linked to Fountains Abbey, which forms the focus of an unsurpassed surprise view from Anne Boleyn's Seat, Studley is a classical, geometrical landscape of major importance. Best seen high up from the banqueting house lawn and the Octagon tower – the formal canal, Moon pools, Grotto Springs, rustic bridge and Temple of Filial Piety.

SUTTON PARK
Sutton-in-the-Forest, York YO6 1DP
☎ 01347 810249   Fax 01347 811251

Owner Sir Reginald & Lady Sheffield
Location 8 miles north of York on B1363
Open 11 am – 5 pm; daily; Easter to 30 September
Admission Adults £2; OAPs £1.50; Children 50p
Facilities Parking; loos; plants for sale occasionally; refreshments on Sundays in summer
Features Herbaceous plants; landscape designed by Capability Brown; plantsman's garden; old roses; woodland garden; frequent Yorkshire & Humberside in Bloom winner; new fern garden & herb garden (1998)

Capability Brown was here 200 years ago, but the joy of Sutton is the formal garden laid out on terraces below the house by Percy Cane in the 1960s and planted by Mrs Sheffield with exquisite taste. Quite the prettiest garden in Yorkshire.

THORP PERROW ARBORETUM
Bedale DL8 2PR
☎ & Fax 01677 425289

Owner Sir John Ropner Bt
Location On the Bedale-Ripon road, 2 miles south of Bedale
Open Dawn to dusk; daily; all year
Admission Adults £3.50; OAPs & students £2.50; Children £2
Facilities Parking; dogs permitted; loos; facilities for the disabled; plants for sale; shop; information centre; tea-room
Features Good collection of trees; bluebells; daffodils; new Millennium Glade (1999); 18 different champion trees – tallest or largest in the UK
English Heritage Grade II
NCCPG National Collections *Fraxinus*; *Juglans*; *Tilia*
Friends Friends of Thorp Perrow (details from Administrator)

This important modern arboretum is one of the finest and largest (85 acres) in private ownership. Wonderful avenues of laburnum, glades of cherries and coniferous groves.

THE VALLEY GARDENS, HARROGATE
Harrogate Borough Council, Harrogate
☎ 01423 500600 ext. 3211   Fax 01423 504426

Owner Harrogate Borough Council
Location Harrogate
Open Dawn to dusk; daily; all year
Admission Free
Facilities Dogs permitted; loos; access for the disabled; small cafeteria

Features Herbaceous plants; rock garden; interesting for children; wonderful meconopsis & primulas alongside the stream; children's play area; band concerts most Sunday afternoons all summer
English Heritage Grade II

The best example of plantsmanship in a public garden in England, laid out 1880–1910: the Sun Pavilion has just been reopened after repairs with a grant from the Lottery. Alpine rarities in spring, a romantic dell, magnificent dahlia display in late summer and the best colour bedding in Yorkshire.

WORTH A VISIT

BURTON AGNES HALL GARDENS
Burton Agnes, Driffield YO25 0ND ☎ *01262 490324. NCCPG National Collection:* Campanula. *The old walled garden has been redesigned with such unconventional features as a life-size games board for snakes and ladders, and exuberantly planted with herbaceous plants. A remarkable garden, strongly recommended.*

R V ROGER LTD
The Nurseries, Pickering YO18 7HG ☎ *01751 472226. Open 9 am – 5 pm, Monday – Saturday; 1 pm – 5 pm, Sundays. NCCPG National Collections:* Erodium; Erythronium. *This substantial and well-established nursery has a first-rate, all-round range including alpines, bulbs, conifers, perennials, roses, and trees and shrubs. They are especially good on tree fruit and soft fruit, including gooseberries.*

SLEIGHTHOLMEDALE LODGE
Fadmoor, Kirkbymoorside YO6 6JG ☎ *01751 431942. This family garden – Mrs James is the third generation to garden here – is a plantsman's paradise right on the edge of the moors. As well as magnificent meconopsis and hardy herbaceous plants, it has Mexican and Mediterranean rarities (a cistus walk, for example) which are a triumph for good cultivation and manipulation of the microclimate. And there are roses of every sort – hundreds of them, perhaps thousands.*

STILLINGFLEET LODGE NURSERIES
Stillingfleet, York YO19 6HP ☎ *01904 728506. Open 10 am – 4 pm; Tuesday – Wednesday, Friday – Saturday; 1 April to 18 October. NCCPG National Collection:* Pulmonaria. *Excellent herbaceous list with a high proportion of unusual plants from a nursery on top form. Particularly good for geraniums and pulmonarias. The Pulmonaria collection is open 1.30 pm – 5 pm, 18 April.*

SOUTH YORKSHIRE

BRODSWORTH HALL
English Heritage, Brodsworth, Doncaster
☎ 01302 722598   Fax 01302 337165
Owner English Heritage

Location 6 miles north-west of Doncaster
Open 12 noon – 6 pm; Tuesday – Sunday & Bank Holiday Mondays; 1 April to 1 November. Then 11 am – 4 pm; weekends only; until Christmas
Admission Garden only: Adults £2.60; OAPs £2; Children £1.30. Cheap rates in winter
Facilities Parking; loos; facilities for the disabled; shop; licensed restaurant
Features Fine conifers; Victorian bedding
English Heritage Grade II

English Heritage's recent acquisition, unkempt for 50 years and now restored as first laid out in the 1860s. Brodsworth offers Italianate terraces, statues and classical follies, a rose garden where ramblers are trained on ironwork arcades, magnificent trees, including monkey puzzles and 30-foot *Arbutus* trees, and bright Victorian bedding. There are garden walks and talks throughout the season: ring for details.

SHEFFIELD BOTANICAL GARDENS
Clarkehouse Road, Sheffield S10 2LN
☎ 0114 250 0500   Fax 0114 255 2375
Owner Sheffield Town Trust (administered by City Council)
Location Jct 33 of M1, follow A57 signs to Glossop, left at Royal Hallamshire Hospital, 500m. on left
Open 7.30 am (10 am at weekends) – 7.45 pm (4 pm in winter); daily; all year
Admission Free
Facilities Dogs permitted; loos; facilities for the disabled
Features Herbaceous plants; fine conifers; rock garden; modern roses; particularly interesting in winter; conservatories by Paxton; peat garden; heath garden
NCCPG National Collections *Diervilla*; *Weigela*
Friends Friends (ring 0114 250 0500); good lecture programme

Founded in 1833 by public subscription and still burgeoning with civic pride. Good camellias and magnolias, ericas and *Sorbus*. Splendid summer bedding too, and lots of seats and waste bins: an exemplary combination of botany and amenity. The garden has been awarded a £5.1m Lottery grant: watch this space!

WENTWORTH CASTLE GARDENS
Lowe Lane, Stainborough, Barnsley S75 3ET
☎ 01226 731269
Owner Barnsley Metropolitan District Council
Location Signed 'Northern College'. 3 miles south of Barnsley; 2 miles from M1
Open 10 am – 5 pm; 30 & 31 May. Groups by arrangement. Guided tours on Tuesdays at 10 am and Thursdays at 2 pm in May & June
Admission Adults £2; Unwaged, OAPs & students £1
Facilities Parking; dogs permitted; loos; access for the disabled; refreshments and plants for sale at Spring Bank Holiday
Features Rhododendrons and azaleas; woodland garden; interesting for children; newly excavated 19th-century rock garden; educational collection of rhododendrons

English Heritage Grade I
NCCPG National Collections Rhododendron (*falconeri* series); *Magnolia* species
Friends Friends of the Gardens Society

Major landscape garden currently undergoing development as an educational and cultural resource. Twinned with the Kun-ming Academy of Sciences. A garden to watch.

WEST YORKSHIRE

BRAMHAM PARK
Wetherby LS23 6ND
☎ 01937 844265   Fax 01937 845923
Owner George Lane Fox
Location 5 miles south of Wetherby on A1
Open 1.15 pm – 5 pm; Tuesday – Thursday & Sundays; 20 June to 5 September. Plus 3–5 April, 1–3 May, 29–31 May & 30 August
Admission Gardens only: Adults £2.50; OAPs £2; Children £1
Facilities Parking; dogs permitted; loos; facilities for the disabled
Features Herbaceous plants; daffodils; good architectural features; garden sculpture
English Heritage Grade I

Very important pre-landscape formal gardens, laid out in the grand manner in the style of Le Nôtre in the early 18th century. Long straight rides cut through dense woodland, with ornamental ponds, cascades, loggias, temples and an obelisk. The standard of maintenance is exemplary: all credit to the Lane Foxes for the care they have lavished upon Bramham over such a long period.

CANAL GARDENS
Roundhay Park, Street Lane, Leeds LS8 2ER
☎ 0113 266 1850   Fax 0113 237 0077
Owner Leeds City Council
Location 3 miles north-west of city centre, off A6120 ring road
Open Open 10 am all year. Closes at 4 pm in January & December; 5 pm in February & November; 6 pm in March & October; 7 pm in April & September; 8 pm from May to August
Admission Tropical World: Adults £1; Children 50p. Gardens free
Facilities Parking; dogs permitted; loos; access for the disabled; souvenirs; cafeteria by lakeside
Features Glasshouses; modern roses; subtropical plants; particularly interesting in winter; good carpet bedding; orchids; new floral clock (1998); new French & Spanish gardens (May 1999); new Desert & Nocturnal Houses
English Heritage Grade II

Tropical World glasshouses containing South American rainforest plants, bromeliads, hoyas, cacti and Butterfly House. A wonderful retreat from a Yorkshire winter and a triumph of municipal horticultural excellence.

GOLDEN ACRE PARK
Otley Road, Bramhope, Leeds LS16 5NZ
☎ 0113 267 3729

Owner Leeds City Council
Location 4 miles north on A660 Otley Road
Open Dawn to dusk; daily; all year
Admission Free
Facilities Parking; dogs permitted; loos; access for the disabled; gifts/souvenirs; restaurant
Features Rock garden; large heather garden
NCCPG National Collections *Primula auricula*; *Syringa*

Part historic park, part botanic collection, part demonstration garden, part test ground for Fleuroselect and *Gardening Which?*; perhaps the best of the five impressive public gardens in Leeds.

HAREWOOD HOUSE
The Estate Office, Harewood, Leeds LS17 9LQ
☎ 0113 288 6331   Fax 0113 288 6467

Owner The Earl of Harewood
Location Between Leeds and Harrogate on A61
Open 10 am – 6 pm; daily; 9 March to 31 October
Admission Grounds: Adults £5.75; OAPs £4.75; Children £3.25
Facilities Parking; dogs permitted; loos; access for the disabled; plants for sale; refreshments
Features Landscape designed by Capability Brown; oriental features; woodland garden; interesting for children; adventure playground; Japanese garden; rhododendrons; current holder of Sandford Award
English Heritage Grade I
NCCPG National Collection *Hosta*

Capability Brown landscaped Harewood, but Repton and Loudon also had a hand in this grandest of Yorkshire gardens. Charles Barry added the grand Italianate terrace, recently restored with an EC grant. Harewood is well maintained, welcomingly run, and gets even better every year. There are guided walks of the lakeside on Thursdays at 2 pm from 15 April to 26 August and of the terrace gardens at 2 pm on Tuesdays from 15 June to 14 September.

THE HOLLIES PARK
Weetwood Lane, Leeds LS16 5NZ
☎ 0113 278 2030   Fax 0113 247 8277

Owner Leeds City Council
Location 3 miles north of city off A660
Open Dawn to dusk; daily; all year
Admission Free
Facilities Parking; dogs permitted; loos
Features Woodland garden; rhododendrons; eucryphias
NCCPG National Collections *Deutzia*; *Hemerocallis* (Coe hybrids); *Hosta* (large-leaved); *Philadelphus*; *Syringa*

This public park is made in a plantsman's garden, and is well run by a hard-pressed and enthusiastic team. Visitors wishing to see the National Collections are advised to make a prior appointment.

LOTHERTON HALL
Aberford, nr Leeds LS25 3EB
☎ 0113 281 3259   Fax 0113 281 3068

Owner Leeds City Council
Location Off A1, ¾ mile east on B1217
Open 8 am – 8 pm or dusk, if earlier; daily; all year
Admission Free
Facilities Parking; loos; facilities for the disabled; shop; cafeteria
Features Oriental features; modern roses
English Heritage Grade II

Edwardian showpiece garden, given to the Council in 1968 and now recovering from neglect. It offers gazebos, formal walks, yew hedging, rose gardens, and a lily pond recently replanted with period varieties. A garden that is on the move again: last year saw the opening of a woodland trail for disabled users.

TEMPLE NEWSAM PARK
Leeds 15
☎ 0113 264 5535

Owner Leeds City Council
Location 3 miles south-east of city, off A63 Selby Road
Open Dawn to dusk; daily; all year
Admission Free. Admission charge to house
Facilities Parking; dogs permitted; loos; access for the disabled; plants for sale; souvenirs; restaurant
Features Herbaceous plants; landscape designed by Capability Brown; glasshouses; modern roses; old roses; rhododendrons
English Heritage Grade II
NCCPG National Collections *Aster*; *Delphinium*; *Phlox paniculata*

A prodigious house on a windy bluff, surrounded by 1,200 acres of parkland, now a 'green lung' for Leeds. Massive rhododendron rides in the woodland, and austere borders in the old walled garden. Somewhat dilapidated in the past, now improved by some recent softening plantings.

WORTH A VISIT

LAND FARM GARDENS
Colden, Hebden Bridge, Halifax HX7 7PJ
☎ 01422 842260. *A pioneering plantsman's garden, 1,000 feet up in the Pennines. Now four acres with a range of plants that is an eye-opener.*

YORK GATE
Back Church Lane, Adel, Leeds LS16 8DW
☎ 0113 267 8240. *Open 2 pm – 5 pm; Thursdays; May to July. Plus 14 February, 14 March, 11 April, 9 May, 6 & 20 June, 4 & 18 July, 15 August. 6 – 9 pm, 15 June & 9 July. Now safely in the care of the Gardeners' Royal Benevolent Fund, this is quite the busiest small garden in England. It is a masterpiece of tight design, invention, colour sense and sheer creative opportunism.*

Scotland

Borders

Abbotsford
Melrose TD6 9BQ
☎ 01896 752043   Fax 01896 752916
Owner The Maxwell-Scott family
Location Off A7, 2 miles from Melrose
Open 10 am – 5 pm (but 2 pm – 5 pm on Sundays in April, May & October); daily; 15 March to 31 October. And on 8 August for SGS
Admission Adults £3.50; Children £1.80
Facilities Parking; loos; access for the disabled; gift shop; self-service tea-room
Features Fine walled garden; orangery

Sir Walter Scott laid out the gardens at Abbotsford in the 1820s: he designed the formal Court garden by the house and planted the surrounding woodlands. The walled garden centres on a handsome orangery, with roses, fruit trees and herbaceous borders planted for late-summer effect.

Dawyck Botanic Garden
Stobo EH45 9JV
☎ 01721 760254   Fax 01721 760214
Owner Royal Botanic Garden, Edinburgh
Location 8 miles south-west of Peebles on B712
Open 9.30 am – 6 pm; daily; March to October
Admission Adults £3; Concessions £2.50p; Children £1; Family £7
Facilities Parking; loos; plants for sale; gift shop; light refreshments
Features Herbaceous plants; particularly interesting in winter; meconopsis; Chinese conifers; Dawyck beech; Douglas fir from original seed; tallest *Fagus crenata* (21m.) in the British Isles, and 18 further record trees

A woodland garden, run as an annexe of the Royal Botanic Garden in Edinburgh and long famous for its trees. The Dawyck beech is the upright, fastigiate form, first found in the policies in the mid-19th century. Edinburgh have underplanted with interesting shrubs, and some herbaceous plants. Dawyck can also boast the first Cryptogamic Sanctuary.

Floors Castle
Roxburghe Estates Office, Kelso TD5 7SF
☎ 01573 223333   Fax 01573 226056
Owner The Duke of Roxburghe
Location Signposted in Kelso
Open 10 am – 4.30 pm (4 pm in October); daily; 2 April to 31 October
Admission £3
Facilities Parking; dogs permitted; loos; access for the disabled; garden centre in walled garden; licensed restaurant & shop
Features Herbaceous plants; new woodland garden (1997); new children's play area (1999)

Not a great garden, but there are handsome traditional herbaceous borders in the walled garden and the siting of the castle in its parkland is very impressive.

Kailzie Gardens
Kailzie, Peebles EH45 9HT
☎ 01721 720007
Owner Lady Angela Buchan-Hepburn
Location On B7062, 2 miles east of Peebles
Open 11 am – 5.30 pm; daily; all year
Admission Adults £2.50; Children 75p (but £2 & 50p respectively from November to May)
Facilities Parking; dogs permitted; loos; access for the disabled; plants for sale; shop; restaurant & teas
Features Daffodils; snowdrops; woodland garden

Kailzie has been revived over the last 20 years. The large walled garden has a mixture of flowers and produce: a laburnum alley, a rose garden and double herbaceous borders are some of the attractions. There are meconopsis and primulas in the rhododendrons woodland walks outside.

Manderston
Duns TD11 3PP
☎ 01361 883450   Fax 01361 882010
Owner Lord Palmer
Location On A6105, 2 miles east of Duns
Open 2 pm – 5.30 pm; Sundays & Thursdays; 14 May to 27 September, plus 25 May & 31 August. Groups at any time by appointment
Admission Gardens only: Adults £3.50; Children £1.50
Facilities Parking; dogs permitted; loos; cream teas & ice-cream
Features Herbaceous plants; fine conifers; rhododendrons and azaleas; good topiary; woodland garden; good bedding-out

The house is sort-of-Georgian. Below it are four expansive terraces, with rich planting around clipped yews and hollies. Unfortunately it is possible to visit only a small part of this formal garden. Below are a small lake, a Chinese-style bridge (18th-century) and a woodland garden with modern rhododendrons and azaleas. All is planted and maintained in the grand manner.

Mellerstain
Gordon TD3 6LG
☎ 01573 410225   Fax 01573 410636
Owner Mellerstain Trust

Location 1 mile west of A6089 Kelso to Edinburgh road
Open 12.30 pm – 4.30 pm; 2 to 5 April. Then daily, except Saturdays; May to September
Admission Adults £4.50; OAPs £3.50; Children £2
Facilities Parking; dogs permitted; loos; access for the disabled; tweed and gift shop; licensed restaurant
Features Modern roses; good topiary; Italian terraced garden by Sir Reginald Blomfield (1909); lake restored (1997/98)

The house has extensive views south to the Cheviots. Below it lies Blomfield's formal garden planted with floribundas and lavender. Beneath it runs the landscape laid out by William and Robert Adam, sauntering down to a lake. Uncompromisingly grand.

MERTOUN GARDENS
St Boswells, Melrose TD6 0EA
☎ 01835 823236   Fax 01835 822474
Owner Mertoun Gardens Trust
Location B6404, 2 miles north-east of St Boswells
Open 2 pm – 6 pm; Saturdays, Sundays & Bank Holiday Mondays; 28 March to 26 September
Admission Adults £1.50; Children 50p
Facilities Parking; loos; access for the disabled
Features Herbaceous plants; daffodils; glasshouses; herbs; vegetables of interest

Originally part of the Duke of Sutherland's estates, Mertoun is best known for its traditional kitchen garden. A long herbaceous border within it has recently been replanted.

MONTEVIOT HOUSE GARDENS
Jedburgh TD8 6UQ
☎ 01835 830380   Fax 01835 830288
Owner Private
Location Off A68 north of Jedburgh & B6400 to Nisbet
Open 12 noon – 5 pm; daily; April to October
Admission Adults £2; OAPs £1; under-14s free
Facilities Parking; dogs permitted; loos; plants for sale; tours for pre-booked groups
Features Good collection of trees; water garden; Victorian rose garden

A substantial garden, attached to a large estate and open at weekends for the first time this year. The rose garden, recently replanted, is Victorian in origin: much of the rest came from Percy Cane in the 1930s. The modern water garden is good. But the trees in the arboretum are exceptional and recent clearing has displayed them in their glory.

PRIORWOOD GARDEN
Melrose TD6 9PX
☎ 01896 822493
Owner The National Trust for Scotland
Location Next to Melrose Abbey
Open 10 am (1.30 pm on Sundays) – 5.30 pm; daily; 1 April to 30 September. 10 am (1.30 pm on Sundays) – 4 pm; daily; 1 October to 24 December

Admission £1 in honesty box
Facilities Parking; dogs permitted; access for the disabled; plants for sale; dried flower shop and NTS gift shop
Features Herbaceous plants; fruit of special interest; herbs; new woodland walkway (1997)

Best known for its shop, which was recently extended and improved. Everything at Priorwood is geared towards dried flowers. Inspirational.

TRAQUAIR HOUSE
Innerleithen EH44 6PW
☎ 01896 830323   Fax 01896 830639
Owner Mrs Maxwell Stuart
Location Signposted from Innerleithen
Open 10.30 am – 5.30 pm; daily; Easter to 30 September. Plus 12.30 pm – 5.30 pm, Friday – Sunday in October
Admission Grounds only: Adults £2; Children £1
Facilities Parking; dogs permitted; loos; access for the disabled; plants for sale; gift shop; restaurant serving lunch & tea; Traquair ale
Features Herbaceous plants; modern roses; woodland garden

The main attraction is a large maze, planted in 1980 of beech and Leyland cypress. The house is a Catholic time-warp: the Bear Gates in the park, once the main entrance to the estate, have been closed ever since Bonnie Prince Charlie passed through them for the last time in 1746.

WORTH A VISIT

EDROM NURSERIES
Coldingham, Eyemouth TD14 5TZ   ☎ *01890 771386.*
Open 10 am – 4.30 pm; Monday – Friday; 1 March to 1 October. This well-known alpine nursery specialises in woodlanders and peat plants and carries a particularly comprehensive list of primulas and gentians which includes many forms not available elsewhere. Many are new to commerce or grown under collectors' numbers.

DUMFRIES & GALLOWAY

ARBIGLAND
Kirkbean DG2 8BQ
☎ 01387 880283
Owner Arbigland Estate Trust
Location South of Kirkbean on A710 Solway Coast road
Open 2 – 6 pm; Tuesday – Sunday, and Bank Holiday Mondays; May to September
Admission Adults £2; OAPs £1.50; Children 50p
Facilities Parking; dogs permitted; loos; access for the disabled; plants for sale; home-made teas
Features Old roses; woodland garden; interesting for children; rhododendrons; maples

A woodland garden, with many different features. Best is the area called Japan, where ancient Japanese maples surround a water garden. But there are also a hidden rose garden, splendid large-leaved rhododendrons, and paths down to the sandy shore. The house will be open 22 to 31 May 1999.

BROUGHTON HOUSE & GARDENS
National Trust for Scotland, 12 High Street, Kirkcudbright DG6 4JX
☎ & Fax 01557 330437

Owner Hornel Trust (managed by National Trust for Scotland)
Location Signed in centre of Kirkcudbright
Open 1 pm – 5.30 pm; daily; April to October
Admission Adults £2.50; Concessions £1.65
Facilities Parking; loos
Features Oriental features

E A Hornel the artist laid out the Japanese garden, which is the best-known part of the garden here and featured in many of his portraits. Most of the rest is a 'Scottish' garden.

CASTLE KENNEDY GARDEN
Stair Estates, Rephad, Stranraer DG9 8BX
☎ 01776 702024   Fax 01776 706248

Owner Lochinch Heritage Estate
Location 5 miles east of Stranraer on A75
Open 10 am – 5 pm; daily; April to September
Admission Adults £2; OAPs £1.50; Children £1 (1998 prices)
Facilities Parking; dogs permitted; loos; access for the disabled; plants for sale; plant centre; tea-rooms
Features Herbaceous plants; woodland garden; rhododendrons; embothriums; eucryphias; monkey puzzle avenue; tallest *Pittosporum tenuifolium* (17m.) in the British Isles, tallest *Rhododendron arboreum* (16m.) and three other record-breaking trees

A huge garden, with early 18th-century rides, avenues and *allées*, a complete 19th-century pinetum, rhododendrons from Hooker's Himalayan expedition, a vast collection of trees and shrubs, and handsome herbaceous plantings in the walled garden. Important and impressive.

GALLOWAY HOUSE GARDENS
Garlieston, Newton Stewart DG8 8HF
☎ 01988 600680

Owner Galloway House Gardens Trust
Location Off B7004 at Garlieston
Open 9 am – 5.30 pm; daily; March to October
Admission Adults £1.50; Concessions 50p; Family £2.50
Facilities Parking; dogs permitted; access for the disabled
Features Camellias; daffodils; rhododendrons and azaleas; snowdrops; camellia house restored (1999); extensive new plantings; holiday cottage to let

Galloway House is where Neil McEacharn learnt to garden, before moving to Lake Maggiore to create the great gardens of Villa Taranto. A vast *Davidia involucrata* dates from his ownership.

GLENWHAN GARDEN
Dunragit, by Stranraer DG9 8PH
☎ 01581 400222

Owner Mr & Mrs William Knott
Location 1 mile off A75 at Dunragit Village
Open 10 am – 5 pm; daily; 15 March to 15 October
Admission Adults £2.50; OAPs £2; Children £1; Seasonal concessions to RHS members
Facilities Parking; dogs permitted; loos; facilities for the disabled; shop; nursery with interesting plants; garden restaurant
Features Plantsman's garden; old roses; woodland garden; bluebells; trees and shrubs; many new *Rhododendron* species planted (1997)

A young garden on a large scale (12 acres and still growing), started by the owners in 1979 and worked by them and one gardener. Very much a plantsman's garden, but it uses plants to create effects, and capitalises upon the lie of the land to produce different habitats. The achievement to date is commendable: definitely a garden to visit and revisit as it expands and matures year by year.

LOGAN BOTANIC GARDENS
Port Logan, Stranraer DG9 9ND
☎ 01776 860231   Fax 01776 860333

Owner Royal Botanic Garden, Edinburgh
Location 14 miles south of Stranraer on B7065
Open 9.30 am – 6 pm; daily; March to October
Admission Adults £3; Concessions £2.50; Children £1; Family £7
Facilities Parking; loos; facilities for the disabled; plants for sale; shop selling books, gifts and local crafts; light meals & refreshments
Features Herbaceous plants; garden sculpture; subtropical plants; particularly good in July–August; tree ferns; cardiocrinums; gunnera; cordylines; trachycarpus palms
Friends Part of the Friends of the Royal Botanic Garden at Edinburgh

The extraordinary effects of Logan are created by palms, cordylines and tree ferns within the semi-formal setting of a walled garden. Huge gunneras and cardiocrinums pile on the message, but the richness extends also to diversity, for here is one of the great botanic collections of tender exotica, worth a long journey on a sunny day in summer.

THREAVE GARDEN
Castle Douglas DG7 1RX
☎ & Fax 01556 502575

Owner The National Trust for Scotland
Location 1 mile west of Castle Douglas
Open 9.30 am – sunset; daily; all year. Visitor Centre open 9.30 am – 5.30 pm, April to October
Admission Adults £4.40; Concessions £2.90
Facilities Parking; loos; facilities for the disabled; plants for sale; shop; restaurant & snacks
Features Good collection of trees; herbaceous plants; fruit of special interest; glasshouses; plantsman's garden; rock garden; modern roses; old roses; woodland garden;

peat garden; heath garden; tallest *Alnus rubra* (23m.) in the British Isles, and two other record trees

A teaching garden with a very wide range of attractions – something to interest every gardener, in fact. Developed over the last 30 years with the needs of students at the School of Horticulture, garden-owners and tourists all in mind, Threave has quickly acquired the reputation of a Scottish Wisley. The modern designs are inspirational and there are plans to build a Victorian-style conservatory in the walled garden.

WORTH A VISIT

CALLY GARDENS
Gatehouse of Fleet, Castle Douglas DG7 2DJ.
Open 2 pm – 5.30 pm, Tuesday – Friday; 10 am – 5.30 pm, Saturdays & Sundays; 3 April to 25 September. A nursery for the horticultural avant-garde. It specialises in perennials from collected and botanic garden seed. Culled from a collection of over 3,500 varieties, the catalogue changes by as much as half each year.

CRAIGIEBURN GARDEN
Moffat DG10 9LF ☎ 01683 221250. Open 12.30 – 7 pm; Tuesday – Sunday; 2 April to 31 October; plus Bank Holidays. Adults £2; Children free. NCCPG National Collection: Meconopsis. An eight-acre garden is being developed alongside this nursery with many different habitat plantings and a new formal garden. The nursery carries an attractive range of perennials, with an emphasis on woodlanders. Meconopsis and primulas are among the specialities.

ELIZABETH MACGREGOR
Ellenbank, Tongland Road, Kirkcudbright DG6 4UU
☎ 01557 330620. Open 10.30 am – 5.30 pm; Fridays and Saturdays; May to October. Violas – over 100 of them – are the speciality at this excellent nursery, complemented by a lively selection of perennials and shrubs for cottage-garden and mixed border planting.

J TWEEDIE FRUIT TREES
Maryfield Road Nursery, Maryfield, Terregles DG2 9TH
☎ 01387 720880. Open 9.30 am – 2 pm; Saturdays; mid-October to March. Other times by appointment. A good choice of fruit trees and bushes and soft fruit in new varieties, with a few old ones also in the list.

FIFE

FALKLAND PALACE
Falkland KY15 7BU
☎ 01337 857397
Owner The National Trust for Scotland
Location On A912, 11 miles north of Kirkcaldy; 10 miles from M90, Jct 8
Open 11 am – 5 pm, Monday – Saturday; 1.30 pm – 5 pm, Sundays; 1 April to 31 October
Admission Adults £2.50; Concessions £1.70

Facilities Parking; loos; facilities for the disabled; gift shop
Features Herbaceous plants; fruit of special interest; autumn colour; spectacular delphinium border

Percy Cane's reconstruction of a Scottish renaissance garden, with a herb garden, an astrolabe walk and formal parterres prettily planted in pastel colours.

HILL OF TARVIT
Cupar KY15 5PB
☎ 01334 653127
Owner The National Trust for Scotland
Location Off A916, 2½ miles south of Cupar
Open 9 am – sunset (or 9 pm if earlier); daily; all year round
Admission £1 in honesty box
Facilities Parking; loos; facilities for the disabled; shop; tea-room in house (open in summer)
Features Herbaceous plants; plantsman's garden; old roses; woodland garden; heathers

Essentially a plantsman's garden, opulently planted and maintained in keeping with the Lorimer house. The Edwardian plantings, now splendidly mature, have been complemented by modern additions. The Trust has begun to restore and replant the borders on the top terrace in the Edwardian style. Highly satisfying.

KELLIE CASTLE
Pittenween KY10 2RF
☎ 01333 720271
Owner The National Trust for Scotland
Location Signposted from main roads
Open 9.30 am – sunset; daily; all year
Admission £1 in honesty box
Facilities Parking; loos; access for the disabled; gift shop; tea-room
Features Herbaceous plants; fruit of special interest; old roses; particularly good in July–August; strong design; extended collection of historic vegetables

Sir Robert Lorimer's family house: it was he who remade the garden in its present form and designed both the Secret Garden and Robin's Corner, though much of the planting is modern. Only one acre, but strong lines and thick planting create a sense of both space and enclosure. The yew hedges are threaded with scarlet *Tropaeolum speciosum*.

ST ANDREWS BOTANIC GARDEN
The Canongate, St Andrews KY16 8RT
☎ 01334 477178/476452
Owner Fife Council
Location A915, Largo Road, then entrance in The Canongate
Open 10 am – 7 pm (4 pm October to April); daily; all year. Greenhouses closed at weekends October to April
Admission Adults £2; OAPs & children £1.50p; Seasonal concessions for RHS members
Facilities Parking; loos; access for the disabled; plants for sale

Features Good collection of trees; glasshouses; rhododendrons and azaleas; rock garden; woodland garden; interesting for children; particularly interesting in winter; peat beds; ferns; heath garden; order beds; new landscaped orchid house (1996)
Friends Very active Friends organisation, with lectures, workshops, garden visits, a newsletter and seed scheme: details from Honorary Curator, St. Andrews Botanic Garden, St. Andrews KY16 8RT

The University botanic garden has taken a new lease of life since the Council took on its administration. The garden's main asset, the peat, rock and water complex (crag, scree, moraine, alpine meadow and bog) is being repaired and replanted. The cactus house has been completed, a new alpine house is now open, and the orchid house reopened last year too. The garden caters particularly well for children.

WORTH A VISIT

CAMBO GARDENS
Kingsbarns, St Andrews KY16 8QD ☎ *01333 450054. Open 10 am – dusk; daily; all year. 21 February for snowdrops. Victorian walled garden built around the Cambo Burn with a waterfall and elegant oriental bridge. Spectacular when the snowdrops and snowflakes flower.*

GRAMPIAN

BRODIE CASTLE
Brodie, Forres, Moray IV36 0TE
☎ 01309 641371   Fax 01309 641600
Owner The National Trust for Scotland
Location Signposted from A96
Open Grounds: 9.30 am – sunset; daily; all year
Admission £1 in honesty box
Facilities Parking; dogs permitted; loos; facilities for the disabled; NTS shop; Brodie-bred daffodils for sale; small tea-room in castle
Features Daffodils; pond; rhododendrons and azaleas; woodland garden
NCCPG National Collection *Narcissus*

Famous for its daffodils, many bred here at the turn of the century and a glorious sight when they bloom in the lawns around the baronial castle.

CRATHES CASTLE
Banchory AB31 5QJ
☎ 01330 844 525   Fax 01330 844 797
Owner The National Trust for Scotland
Location 15 miles west of Aberdeen
Open 9 am – sunset; daily; all year
Admission Adults £4; Concessions £2.50
Facilities Parking; loos; facilities for the disabled; plants for sale; NTS shop; restaurant/café open April to October
Features Fine conifers; plantsman's garden; modern roses; old roses; woodland garden; two ice houses;

specimen trees; colour borders; current holder of Sandford Award; tallest *Zelkova* × *verschaffeltii* in the British Isles, and four further tree records
NCCPG National Collections *Viburnum*; *Dianthus* (Malmaison carnations)

Famous for its walled garden, with eight distinct theme gardens: a white border, a yellow enclosure, a blue garden, and dreamy high summer borders with pastel shades for long Highland evenings. Only four acres but intensively planted and constantly improved.

CRUICKSHANK BOTANIC GARDEN
University of Aberdeen, Dept of Plant and Soil Science, St Machar Drive, Aberdeen AB24 3UU
☎ 01224 272704   Fax 01224 272703
Owner Aberdeen University
Location Follow signs for Aberdeen University and/or Old Aberdeen
Open 9 am – 4.30 pm; Monday – Friday; all year. Plus 2 pm – 5 pm; Saturdays & Sundays; May to September
Admission Free
Facilities Dogs permitted; loos; access for the disabled
Features Good collection of trees; herbaceous plants; rock garden; old roses; stone troughs; peat beds; Scottish upland plants
Friends Active and well established Friends group, with plant sales, lectures, excursions and a seed list. Contact 01224 272704

Twelve acres of classic botanic garden, with every educational element: rock gardens, an arboretum, collections of native plants, beds which illustrate the history of the rose, water plants and systematic beds. Well worth exploration.

DRUM CASTLE
Drumoak, Banchory AB31 3EY
☎ 01330 811406
Owner The National Trust for Scotland
Location Off A93, 10 miles west of Aberdeen
Open Grounds: 9.30 am – sunset; daily; all year. Garden: 10 am – 6 pm; daily; 2 to 5 April, then 1 May to 3 October
Admission Adults £4.40; Concessions £2.90
Facilities Parking; dogs permitted; loos; plants for sale; small tea-room
Features Old roses

A historic garden of roses, with the best collection of Scottish roses (hybrids of *Rosa pimpinellifolia*) in Britain.

KILDRUMMY CASTLE GARDENS
Kildrummy, Alford AB33 8RA
☎ 019755 71203/71277
Owner Kildrummy Castle Garden Trust
Location On A97, off A944
Open 10 am – 5 pm; daily; April to October
Admission Adults £2; Children free
Facilities Parking; dogs permitted; loos; access for the disabled; plants for sale; tea & coffee

Features Good collection of trees; plantsman's garden; old roses; interesting for children; autumn colour; heathers; water garden & rock garden replanted (1998); play area & nature trails

A romantic glen-garden, laid out nearly 100 years ago. Richly planted pools and ponds, a plantsman's collection on the hillside, and a large mature rock garden made from the natural sandstone. One of the most romantic gardens in Scotland.

LEITH HALL
Kennethmont, Huntly AB54 4NQ
☎ 01464 831 269

Owner The National Trust for Scotland
Location On B9002 west of Kennethmont
Open 9.30 am – sunset; daily; all year
Admission Adults £4.40; Concessions £2.90
Facilities Parking; loos; refreshments from May to 3 October, 1.30 pm – 5.30 pm
Features Herbaceous plants; rock garden; modern roses; particularly good in July-August; bluebells; ice house; recent restorations & improvements; garden walks throughout the season (telephone for dates); new sculptures in woodland walk

Richly planted borders are the pride of Leith Hall: they are full of colour all through the summer. Also impressive is the rock garden, restored and replanted by that most successful of societies, the Scottish Rock Garden Club. Leith gets better and better.

PITMEDDEN
Ellon AB4 7PD
☎ 01651 842352

Owner The National Trust for Scotland
Location 1 mile west of Pitmedden on A920
Open 10 am – 5 pm; daily; May to September
Admission Adults £3.90; Concessions £2.60
Facilities Parking; loos; facilities for the disabled; plants for sale; tea-room
Features Herbs; gazebos; parterres

A 17th-century formal garden meticulously created by the National Trust for Scotland 40 years ago. It has three miles of box hedging and uses 40,000 bedding plants every summer. The result may lack authenticity, but is impressive, satisfying and peaceful.

HIGHLAND

CAWDOR CASTLE
Cawdor Castle, Nairn IV12 5RD
☎ 01667 404615   Fax 01667 404674

Owner The Dowager Countess Cawdor
Location Between Inverness and Nairn on B9090
Open 10 am – 5.30 pm; daily; 1 May to 10 October
Admission £2.80

Facilities Parking; loos; facilities for the disabled; gift shop; licensed restaurant in castle
Features Herbaceous plants; fruit of special interest; old roses; woodland garden; good late-summer plantings

A Victorian garden which has been replanted and, in part, redesigned in recent years by the addition of a holly maze, laburnum walk and colour schemes. Earth, Purgatory and Paradise are somehow represented in the new plantings, but they are best enjoyed as colours and shapes. The effect is neither cranky nor grand, just extremely charming, while the house is as Scottish a castle as ever was seen.

DOCHFOUR GARDENS
Inverness IV3 6JY
☎ 01463 861218   Fax 01463 861336

Owner Lord & Lady Burton
Location 5 miles south-west of Inverness on the A82
Open 10 am – 5 pm; daily; April to September
Admission Adults £1.50; Concessions £1
Facilities Parking; access for the disabled; plants for sale; no shop, but pick-your-own fruit in season
Features Rhododendrons and azaleas; good topiary; naturalised daffodils; parterres; water gardens; tallest *Thuja occidentalis* 'Lutea' in the British Isles, plus three further tree records

A substantial garden, landscaped and terraced down to the River Ness. Best when the daffodils and rhododendrons colour the hillside, but famous for the size and number of its 19th-century conifers.

DUNROBIN CASTLE GARDENS
Golspie, Sutherland KW10 6RR
☎ 01408 633177   Fax 01408 634081

Owner The Sutherland Trust
Location 1 mile north of Golspie on A9
Open Dawn to dusk; daily; all year round. Castle: 10.30 am (12 noon on Sundays) – 5.30 pm (4.30 pm in April, May & October); daily, but Sundays only in July & August; 1 April to 15 October
Admission Castle & garden: Adults £5.50; OAPs £4; Reductions for groups. Gardens free when castle closed
Facilities Parking; loos; gift shop; tea-room in castle
Features Herbaceous plants; modern roses; good topiary; woodland garden; formal gardens

Grand terrace gardens, designed by Nesfield, striding down to the Dornoch Forth. Recently replanted and partially restored. New rhododendrons have been added: last year another ten wooden pyramids were planted with clematis and climbing roses – very pretty.

INVEREWE
Poolewe, Ross and Cromarty IV22 2LQ
☎ 01445 781200   Fax 01445 781497

Owner The National Trust for Scotland
Location On A832, 6 miles north of Gairloch
Open 9.30 am – 9 pm (5 pm from 1 November to 14 March); daily; all year
Admission Adults £5; Concessions £3.40

Facilities Parking; loos; facilities for the disabled; plants for sale; large shop; excellent new restaurant
Features Good collection of trees; herbaceous plants; fine conifers; fruit of special interest; plantsman's garden; rock garden; subtropical plants; woodland garden; particularly good in July–August; autumn colour; meconopsis; candelabra primulas; lilies; tallest *Eucalyptus cordata* (30m.) in the British Isles, and three further record trees
NCCPG National Collections *Olearia*; *Brachyglottis*; *Ourisia*; *Rhododendron barbatum*

One of the wonders of the horticultural world, a subtropical garden in the north–west Highlands and exceptionally well maintained. Fabulous large-leaved Himalayan rhododendrons, magnolias, eucalyptus, tree ferns, palms and tender rarities underplanted with drifts of blue poppies and candelabra primulas. Best on a sunny dry day in May, before the midges breed.

LOCHALSH WOODLAND GARDEN
Balmacara, By Kyle of Lochalsh, Ross IV40 8DN
☎ 01599 566376
Owner The National Trust for Scotland
Location On A87, 3 miles from Kyle
Open 9 am – dusk; daily; all year
Admission £2 in honesty box
Facilities Parking; dogs permitted; loos
Features Fine conifers; plantsman's garden; subtropical plants; woodland garden

This woodland garden is becoming much better known, and deservedly. The structure is about 100 years old – tall pines, oaks and larches with ornamental underplantings started about 30 years ago. Rhododendrons from Euan Cox at Glendoick came first: newer plantings include collections of hardy ferns, bamboos, fuchsias, hydrangeas and *maddenii* rhododendrons, as well as plants from Tasmania and New Zealand. The season of interest extends from early spring well into autumn.

WORTH A VISIT

ABRIACHAN GARDEN NURSERY
Loch Ness Side, Inverness IV3 6LA ☎ 01463 861232. Open 9 am – 7 pm (or dusk if earlier); daily; February to November. This terraced garden in the woods above Loch Ness has a fine collection of hardy plants. The nursery is particularly good for helianthemums, primulas and anything hardy in such a northerly latitude.

ACHILTIBUIE HYDROPONICUM
Achiltibuie IV26 2YQ ☎ 01854 622202. Open 10 am – 6 pm; daily; Easter to September. This Hydroponicum is one of the oldest and best-known in Britain. It has three climatic zones where you can see everything from subtropical fruit trees to salad herbs grown in a soilless medium under glass.

ALLANGRANGE
Munlochy, Black Isle IV8 8NZ ☎ 0146 3811249. Colour gardening by Mrs Cameron, a botanical artist, has made this one of the loveliest summer gardens in the British Isles. Good spring flowers, too.

ARDFEARN NURSERY
Bunchrew, Inverness IV3 6RH ☎ 01463 243250/223607. Open 9 am – 5 pm; daily. Alpines and small ericaceous shrubs in quantity are produced at this nursery in a lovely Highland setting. Particularly good for celmisias, gentians and, above all, primulas. The sales area has easy wheelchair access.

JACK DRAKE
Inshriach Alpine Plant Nursery, Aviemore, Inverness-shire PH22 1QS ☎ 01540 651287. Open 9 am – 5 pm Monday – Friday; 9 am – 4 pm, Saturdays. Closed Sundays. This famous Highland nursery is Mecca for devotees of alpine and rock-garden plants. True alpines rub shoulders with species for wild and bog gardens. Mail order and an excellent seed list are also available.

LOTHIAN

DALMENY HOUSE
Rosebery Estates, South Queensferry EH30 9TQ
☎ 0131 331 1888 **Fax** 0131 331 1788
Owner The Earl of Rosebery
Location B924 off A90
Open 12 noon (1 pm on Sundays) – 5.30 pm; Sunday – Tuesday; July & August. And for SGS in snowdrop time
Admission Grounds only: free
Facilities Parking; loos; access for the disabled; refreshments
Features Fine conifers; snowdrops; woodland garden; rhododendrons & azaleas; wellingtonias; landscaped pond & new planting in Garden Valley (1997)

The grounds at Dalmeny are extensive, and visitors are encouraged to see the valley walk with rhododendrons, wellingtonias and other conifers.

INVERESK LODGE GARDEN
24 Inveresk Village, Musselburgh EH21 7TE
☎ 0131 665 1855
Owner The National Trust for Scotland
Location A6124 south of Musselburgh, 6 miles east of Edinburgh
Open 10 am – 4.30 pm, Monday – Saturday; 2 pm – 5 pm, Sundays; all year. Closed Saturdays from October to March
Admission £1 in honesty box
Facilities Parking; loos
Features Herbaceous plants; old roses; plantings by Graham Thomas; raised beds; peat beds

A modern garden, tailor-made for a modest NTS estate and maintained to a high standard. Graham Thomas designed the rose borders. Good climbing plants.

MALLENY HOUSE GARDEN
Balerno EH14 7AF
☎ 0131 449 2283

Owner The National Trust for Scotland
Location In Balerno, south-west of Edinburgh, off A71
Open 9.30 am – 7 pm (4 pm from November to March); daily; all year
Admission £1 in honesty box
Facilities Parking; loos; access for the disabled
Features Herbaceous plants; glasshouses; climbing roses; old roses; good topiary; particularly good in July–August; Scottish National Bonsai Collection
NCCPG National Collection *Rosa* (19th-century shrubs)
Friends The Friends of Malleny enjoy garden visits, lectures and other benefits. The Secretary is Mrs Evlyne Danskin, 13 Marchbank Drive, Balerno EH14 7ER. Tel: 0131 449 2826.

One of the NTS's best gardens, much praised for its 'personal' quality. The 19th-century shrub roses are underplanted with herbaceous plants which take the display into the autumn. The bonsai collection creates quite another dimension, as do the magnificent conservatory and the huge cones of yew topiary. Very peaceful.

ROYAL BOTANIC GARDEN, EDINBURGH
Inverleith Row, Edinburgh EH3 5LR
☎ 0131 552 7171   Fax 0131 552 0382

Owner Scottish Office Board of Trustees
Location 1 mile north of Princes Street
Open 9.30 am – 7 pm; daily; April to August. Closes at 6 pm in March & September, 5 pm in February & October, 4 pm from November to January. Closed 25 December & 1 January
Admission Free. Guided tours at 11 am & 2 pm, daily from April to September
Facilities Parking; loos; facilities for the disabled; shop; recently enlarged plant sales area; licensed terrace café
Features Alpines; good collection of trees; herbaceous plants; fine conifers; ecological interest; glasshouses; herbs; oriental features; rhododendrons and azaleas; rock garden; modern roses; old roses; garden sculpture; subtropical plants; woodland garden; interesting for children; particularly interesting in winter; peat beds; excellent new guide book (1997); 45 UK record-breaking trees, more than any other Scottish garden
Friends Active Friends of the RBG. Lectures, newsletter, seeds: details from the Friends' Office at the garden

Edinburgh outclasses Kew in several ways – better rock gardens, peat beds, rhododendrons and woodland gardens. And entry is free. Wonderful cantilevered glasshouses and good facilities for people with special needs – children, disabled persons and the blind. Edinburgh also has the highest standards of maintenance. No visitor can fail to respond, above all, to the friendly welcome and helpfulness of all the staff.

SUNTRAP GARDEN
43 Gogarbank, Edinburgh EH12 9BY
☎ 0131 339 7283

Owner Oatridge Agricultural College
Location 1 mile west of Edinburgh bypass, between A8 & A71
Open 10 am – 4.30 pm; daily; all year, but weekdays only from October to March, and closed for Christmas fortnight
Admission Adults £1; Children free
Facilities Parking; dogs permitted; facilities for the disabled
Features Alpines; herbaceous plants; daffodils; glasshouses; oriental features; pond; modern roses; vegetables of interest; woodland garden; 'Italian' garden; peat walls
Friends Friends of Suntrap. Annual subscription £3. Events & visits. Details from Edwin Arthur: 01875 815541

Three acres of demonstration gardens attached to Oatridge Agricultural College, one of the best places in Lothian to learn how to be a better gardener. Island beds, a rock garden, a peat garden, sculptures, vegetable plots, a rose garden, annual borders – and much more.

STRATHCLYDE

ACHAMORE GARDENS
Isle of Gigha PA41 7AD
☎ 01583 505254

Owner Holt Leisure Parks Ltd (Mr D N Holt)
Location Take Gigha ferry from Tainloan (20 mins) then easy walking for 1½ miles
Open Dawn to dusk; daily; all year
Admission Adults £2; Children £1
Facilities Parking; dogs permitted; loos; lunches & teas at Gigha Hotel
Features Subtropical plants; woodland garden; rhododendrons; azaleas; biggest *Larix gmelinii* in the British Isles

One of the best rhododendron gardens in the British Isles, and only 50 years old. Mainly planted by Sir James Horlick with advice from Jim Russell. The collection of large-leaved Himalayan rhododendrons is breathtaking.

AN CALA
Isle of Seil PA34 4RF
☎ & Fax 01852 300237

Owner Mr & Mrs T Downie
Location In village of Easdale
Open 10 am – 6 pm; daily; April to September
Admission Adults £1; Children free
Facilities Parking; dogs permitted
Features Bog garden; rock garden; new sheep sculptures by Rupert Till (1998)

Sheltered garden on the wild west coast, with a natural rock garden and several streams which have been dammed and planted with moisture-loving species. The result is a garden of great lushness.

Angus Garden
Barguillean, Taynuilt PA35 1HY
☎ 01866 822254

Owner Sam Macdonald
Location Turn south off A85 at Taynuilt: 3 miles on right
Open Dawn to dusk; daily; all year
Admission Adults £2; Children free
Facilities Parking; dogs permitted; Barguillean Nursery adjoins the garden
Features Rhododendrons and azaleas; woodland garden

This young garden in a beautiful setting on the shores of Loch Angus has a particularly fine collection of modern rhododendrons in light oak woodland. It doubles up as a test ground for new hybrids introduced from USA by the adjacent Barguillean Nurseries. There are plans for a substantial expansion of the gardens to create more summer and autumn interest. Rather short on labels, but a garden to watch.

Ardanaiseig Hotel Garden
Ardanaiseig, Kilchrenan, by Taynuilt PA35 1HE
☎ 01866 833333   Fax 01866 833222

Owner Bennie Gray
Location On Loch Awe, 4 miles up from Kilchrenan
Open 9 am – 9 pm, or dusk if earlier; daily; all year
Admission Adults £2; Children free
Facilities Parking; dogs permitted; loos; hotel open to garden visitors
Features Bluebells; herbaceous plants; daffodils; rhododendrons and azaleas; woodland garden; maples; magnolias

A fine woodland garden with an important collection of rhododendrons and azaleas in a stunning position on a promontory. The hotel is famous for its good food (three AA rosettes).

Ardchattan Priory
Connel, Oban PA37 1RQ
☎ 01631 750274

Location 5 miles east of Connel Bridge, on the north shore of Loch Etive
Open 9 am – 6 pm; daily; April to October
Admission Adults £1.50; Children free
Facilities Parking; dogs permitted; loos; facilities for the disabled; craft shop; light lunches & teas daily 11 am – 6 pm
Features Herbaceous plants; daffodils; old roses; good collection of *Sorbus* species; huge *Hebe* bushes

Best in spring, when daffodils flower in light ornamental woodland, but Ardchattan is also planted for high summer, with an emphasis on roses and herbaceous borders.

Ardkinglas Woodland Garden
Cairndow PA26 8BH
☎ & Fax 01499 600263

Owner S J Noble Esq
Location On A83 at Cairndow
Open Daylight hours; daily; all year
Admission £2
Facilities Parking; dogs permitted; loos; excellent nursery
Features Fine conifers; rhododendrons and azaleas; woodland garden; tallest tree in all Europe *Abies grandis* (63m.), and seven further UK record trees

Formerly known as Strone Gardens, Ardkinglas is famous for its magnificent conifers but has been substantially improved by recent plantings. Among the rhododendrons are many hybrids bred by the late Lord Ardkinglas, when he was Secretary of State for Scotland.

Ardtornish Garden
Lochaline, Morvern by Oban PA34 5VZ
☎ 01967 421288   Fax 01967 421211

Owner Mrs John Raven
Location 2 miles north of Lochaline
Open 10 am – 5 pm; daily; May to October
Admission £2
Facilities Parking; dogs permitted; loos; plants for sale
Features Bluebells; fine conifers; plantsman's garden; kitchen garden; gunnera; rhododendrons; new pools (1998)

This is Faith Raven's other garden – see Docwra's Manor in Cambridgeshire – and a complete contrast: 28 acres of rocky hillside full of Edwardian hybrid rhododendrons like 'Pink Pearl' and 'Cynthia'. Mrs Raven has actively improved it with a great range of interesting plants. Remote, but worth every inch of the journey.

Arduaine Garden
Arduaine, by Oban, Argyll PA34 4XQ
☎ & Fax 01852 200366

Owner The National Trust for Scotland
Location On A816 between Oban & Lochgilphead
Open 9.30 am – sunset; daily; all year
Admission Adults £2.50; Concessions £1.70
Facilities Parking; loos; access for the disabled; no refreshments in the garden, but Loch Melfort Hotel is next door
Features Subtropical plants; rhododendrons; tallest *Nothofagus antarctica* (26m.) in the British Isles and six further records
NCCPG National Collections *Ampelopsis*; *Parthenocissus*

A luxuriant woodland garden in a sheltered, south-facing valley at the edge of the sea. Stout conifers and 40-foot thickets of *Griselinia* protect the rhododendrons which two nurserymen planted in the 1970s. *Primula denticulata* and *Narcissus cyclamineus* have naturalised in grassy glades. Arduaine is in excellent condition and handsomely maintained.

Brodick Castle
Isle of Arran KA27 8HY
☎ 01770 302202   Fax 01770 302312

Owner The National Trust for Scotland
Location Ferry from Ardrossan to Brodick, follows signs
Open 9.30 am – dusk; daily; all year
Admission Adults £2.50; Concessions £1.70

Facilities Parking; dogs permitted; loos; facilities for the disabled; plants for sale; NTS shop; tea-rooms open Easter to October
Features Good collection of trees; herbaceous plants; subtropical plants; interesting for children; candelabra primulas; meconopsis; lilies; four new garden trails; good bedding; tallest *Drimys winteri* (21m.) and *Embothrium coccineum* (20m.) in the British Isles (& three further records); new streamside trail for the disabled
NCCPG National Collection *Rhododendron* (subsections *Falconera*, *Grandia* and *Maddenia*)

Ravishing 60-acre rhododendron garden on sloping woodland in a mild wet climate. Good magnolias, camellias, crinodendrons and olearias too, but they are never a match for the rhododendrons, many from collectors' seed (Forrest, Kingdon-Ward etc.).

COLZIUM WALLED GARDEN
Colzium-Lennox Estate, Stirling Road, Kilsyth G65 0RZ
☎ & Fax 01236 823281

Owner North Lanarkshire Council
Location Signposted from Kilsyth on B803
Open Noon – 8 pm; daily; Easter to 27 September. Noon – 4 pm; Saturdays & Sundays; rest of year
Admission Free
Facilities Parking; loos; access for the disabled
Features Trees & shrubs

An up-and-coming young garden, which the Council has developed on an ancient site since 1978. A wide range of plants is grown within the protection of high walls, particularly ornamental trees and shrubs, and the standards of maintenance and labelling are excellent.

CRARAE GARDENS
Crarae, by Inverary PA32 8YA
☎ 01546 886614
Website www.crarae-gardens.org

Owner The Crarae Garden Charitable Trust
Location South of Inverary on A83
Open 9 am – 6 pm; daily; Easter to October. Daylight hours; daily; 1 November to Easter
Admission Adults £3; Children £2
Facilities Parking; dogs permitted; loos; plants for sale; small shop selling books, china & local crafts; light refreshments
Features Woodland garden; camellias; rhododendrons; autumn colour; tallest *Acer pensylvanicum* in the British Isles (and 12 further tree records)
NCCPG National Collection *Nothofagus*
Friends Major appeal ongoing

Fifty acres of romantic woodland, centred on a steep glen spanned by wooden bridges. The long narrow climb up the glen is a pilgrim's progress for plantsmen, past all manner of exotic plants displayed for effect, but especially large-leaved rhododendrons. At the top, you pass out of the enchanted garden into wild moorland: no other garden offers such catharsis. Best in the morning, and in late May.

CULZEAN CASTLE & COUNTRY PARK
Maybole, Ayrshire KA19 8LE
☎ 01655 760269   Fax 01655 760615

Owner The National Trust for Scotland
Location Off A719, west of Maybole & South of Ayr
Open 9.30 am – dusk; daily; all year
Admission Park & garden only: Adults £3.50; Concessions £2.50
Facilities Parking; dogs permitted; loos; facilities for the disabled; plants for sale; good shop; self-service restaurant; light refreshments in car park
Features Herbaceous plants; good architectural features; glasshouses; herbs; lake; woodland garden; interesting for children; deer park; formal garden; adventure playground; pagoda renovated (1997); tallest Irish yew *Taxus baccata* 'Fastigiata' (19m.) in the British Isles (plus two further tree records); current holder of the Sandford Award

An important historic landscape, the flagship of the NTS, recently restored and seriously open to the public (400,000 visitors a year). Good trees as well as a Gothic camellia house, an ice house, gazebos and a pagoda.

FINLAYSTONE
Langbank PA14 6TJ
☎ 01475 540 285

Owner George Macmillan
Location On A8, 10 mins west of Glasgow
Open 10.30 am – 5 pm; daily; all year. And on 11 April for SGS (plant stall)
Admission Adults £2.50; OAPs & children £1.50
Facilities Parking; dogs permitted; loos; access for the disabled; gift shop; light meals, 11 am – 5 pm, March to September
Features Bluebells; daffodils; rhododendrons and azaleas; 1900s peach house carefully restored (1997)

A traditional west-coast garden of woodland walks and rhododendrons which has been transformed by the present owner's imaginative new designs and plantings, including a Celtic paving garden, a 'smelly garden' and a modern folly.

GLASGOW BOTANIC GARDEN
730 Great Western Road, Glasgow G12 0UE
☎ 0141 334 2622   Fax 0141 339 6964

Owner Glasgow City Council
Location On A82, 2 miles from city centre
Open Grounds: 7 am – dusk; daily; all year. Glasshouses & Kibble Palace: 10 am – 4.45 pm (4.15 pm in winter); daily; all year. Main range open during afternoon only at weekends
Admission Free
Facilities Dogs permitted; loos; facilities for the disabled
Features Good collection of trees; herbaceous plants; fine conifers; glasshouses; herbs; rock garden; modern roses; old roses; good topiary; particularly interesting in winter; beautiful glasshouse (the 'Kibble Palace'); systematic beds; new orchid houses (1998)
NCCPG National Collections *Begonia*; *Dendrobium*; Dicksoniaceae

STRATHCLYDE — GARDENS — 241

Friends Active Friends organisation with lectures, garden visits and a bi-monthly newsletter. Details from the Gardens' office

Most of the elements of the botanic garden are here, including systematic beds and chronological beds, but the glory of Glasgow is the two glasshouses – the Kibble Palace and the Main Range. From tree ferns to palms and from cacti to orchids, the Main Range is an essay in plant types. The Kibble Palace however is divided between geographical areas – South Africa, Australia, China, South America, the Canaries and so on. There is no better place to enjoy a winter's day in Glasgow.

GLENARN
Rhu, Helensburgh G84 8LL
☎ 01436 820493   Fax 0141 21 8450

Owner Mr & Mrs Michael Thornley
Location Turn up Pier Road at Rhu Marina, first right is Glenarn Road
Open Dawn to dusk; daily; 21 March to 21 September
Admission Adults £1.50; OAPs & children £1. £2 on 2 May for SGS
Facilities Dogs permitted; access for the disabled; plants for sale; refreshments may be booked in advance
Features Fine conifers; plantsman's garden; rock garden; rhododendrons; embothriums; new greenhouse (1997)

Ten acres of woodland garden, with some rhododendrons dating from Sir Joseph Hooker's Himalayan expedition and others from the 1930s trips of Kingdon-Ward and Ludlow and Sheriff. Good hybrids too – the original Gibson plants. But plenty of magnolias, camellias, pieris, and other good plants.

GREENBANK GARDEN
Flenders Road, Clarkston, Glasgow G76 8RB
☎ 0141 639 3281   Fax 0141 616 0550

Owner The National Trust for Scotland
Location 1 mile along Mearns Road from Clarkston Toll, take 1st left
Open Garden: 9.30 am – sunset; daily; all year. Closed 1 & 2 January, 25 & 26 December
Admission Adults £3.20; Concessions £2.20
Facilities Parking; dogs permitted; loos; facilities for the disabled; plants for sale; NTS gift shop; light refreshments & drinks (Easter to October)
Features Herbaceous plants; fruit of special interest; rock garden; woodland garden; garden for the disabled; roses of every kind
Friends Friends of Greenbank organise events throughout the year. The chairman is Mrs Kathy Rice, 23 Langtree Avenue, Glasgow G46 7LJ. Tel: 0141 638 7361

Greenbank is a demonstration garden: it was left to the Trust in 1976 on condition that it was developed as a teaching resource for people with small gardens. The walled garden has therefore been divided into a great number of sections which represent different interests and skills: rock garden, fruit garden, dried flower plot, raised beds, winter garden, and so on. Does it *work*? Yes, definitely.

MOUNT STUART
Isle of Bute PA20 9LR
☎ 01700 503877   Fax 01700 505313

Owner The Mount Stuart Trust
Location 5 miles south of Rothesay
Open 10 am – 5 pm; daily except Tuesdays & Thursdays; May to mid-October. Plus April weekends
Admission Adults £3.50; Children £2; Family £9 (1998 prices)
Facilities Parking; loos; facilities for the disabled; plants for sale; audio-visual room; tea-room
Features Fine conifers; glasshouses; rhododendrons and azaleas; woodland garden

A vast and fascinating garden for a sumptuous house. Its 300 acres include: a Victorian pinetum, recently expanded by a further 100 acres dedicated to RBG Edinburgh's Conifer Conservation Programme; a two-acre rock garden designed by Thomas Mawson and stuffed with rare collected plants; a 'wee' garden of five acres, planted with tender exotics from Australia and New Zealand; and a kitchen garden recently redesigned by Rosemary Verey and planted with David Austin's roses. Add in the relics of an 18th-century landscape, a tropical greenhouse, acres of bluebells and established rhododendrons, and you have the measure of a long and fascinating visit.

TOROSAY CASTLE & GARDENS
Craignure, Isle of Mull PA65 6AY
☎ 01680 812421   Fax 01680 812470

Owner Mr C James
Location 1 mile from Craignure on A849 to Iona
Open 10.30 am – 5.30 pm; daily; all year
Admission Adults £3.50; Concessions £2.75; Children £1
Facilities Parking; dogs permitted; loos; facilities for the disabled; plants for sale; shop; tea-room (summer only) with light lunches
Features Oriental features; rock garden; garden sculpture; water garden; *Eucalyptus* walk; new conservation plantings with conifers from RBG Edinburgh

The best feature of the gardens at Torosay is the Italian Statue Walk, lined with 19 figures by Antonio Bonazza. The Japanese garden and rock garden add to the sheer variety. The woodland garden is stuffed with interesting specimens: *Eucryphia*, *Embothrium* and *Crinodendron* among many.

THE YOUNGER BOTANIC GARDEN, BENMORE
Dunoon PA23 8QU
☎ 01369 706261   Fax 01369 706369

Owner Board of Trustees/Royal Botanic Garden, Edinburgh
Location 7 miles north of Dunoon on A815
Open 9.30 am – 6 pm; daily; March to October
Admission Adults £3; OAPs £2.50; Children £1; Family £7
Facilities Parking; dogs permitted; loos; facilities for the disabled; plants for sale; gift shop; tea-room

Features Good collection of trees; fine conifers; woodland garden; interesting for children; giant redwood avenue planted in 1863; rhododendrons; ferns; red squirrels; new Chilean plant collection

Benmore has been an annexe of the Royal Botanic Garden at Edinburgh since 1929. The mild, wet climate makes possible the cultivation of tender plants from lower altitudes of the Sino-Himalaya, Bhutan, Japan and the New World. Benmore is a living textbook of the genus *Rhododendron*. Their background is of conifers planted early in the 19th century, perhaps the best collection in Scotland. But the whole garden is spacious, educational and beautifully maintained.

WORTH A VISIT

ACHNACLOICH
Connel, Oban PA37 1PR ☎ *01631 710221. A substantial woodland garden made in three stages. First there were the Victorian conifers, which have grown to great heights. Then came the large-scale plantings of rhododendrons, particularly the Triflorum series which have begun to naturalise. The latest stage has been the creation of a plantsman's garden using the tender shrubs and trees which flourish on the west coast on Argyll. Some of the embothriums are taller than the native oaks.*

BIGGAR PARK
Biggar ML12 6JS ☎ *01899 221085. Open By appointment for groups; 1 May to 20 August. Ten acres of plantsmanship, with drifts of naturalised fritillaries in spring, and deep traditional herbaceous borders in summer.*

TAYSIDE

BRANKLYN GARDEN
Dundee Road, Perth PH2 7BB
☎ 01738 633199

Owner The National Trust for Scotland
Location Off Dundee Road, on eastern edge of Perth, ½ mile from Queen's Bridge
Open 9.30 am – sunset; daily; March to October
Admission Adults £2.50; OAPs £1.70
Facilities Parking; loos; access for the disabled; plants for sale; small NTS gift shop
Features Plantsman's garden; rock garden; rhododendrons; alpines; *Meconopsis grandis* 'Branklyn'
NCCPG National Collections *Cassiope; Paeonia*

The apotheosis of Scottish rock gardening, a suburban garden absolutely stuffed with rare plants in an ideal microclimate.

CLUNY HOUSE
by Aberfeldy, Perthshire PH15 2JT
☎ 01887 820795

Owner Mr J & Mrs W Mattingley
Location 3½ miles from Aberfeldy, on the Weem to Strathtay Road
Open 10 am – 6 pm; daily; March to October
Admission Adults £2.50; Children under 16 free
Facilities Parking; plants for sale
Features Good collection of trees; plantsman's garden; meconopsis; primulas; cardiocrinums; tallest *Prunus maackii* in the British Isles

A plantsman's garden, largely made in the 1950s by Mrs Mattingley's father, who subscribed to the Ludlow and Sherriff expeditions. Superb rhododendrons and, above all, candelabra primulas – sheets of them from April to July.

DRUMMOND CASTLE GARDENS
Muthill, Crieff PH7 4HZ
☎ 01764 681257   Fax 01764 681550

Owner Grimsthorpe & Drummond Castle Trust Ltd
Location South of Crieff on A822
Open 2 – 6 pm; daily; 2 to 5 April, then from May to October
Admission Adults £3; OAPs £2; Children £1.50
Facilities Parking; dogs permitted; loos; teas on 1 August for SGS
Features Fruit of special interest; important formal garden

Drummond has probably the most important formal garden in Scotland, laid out *c*. 1830 as a St Andrew's cross, with complex parterres filled with roses, statues, clipped cones, herbaceous plants, gravel and lots more beside. The result is order, shape, structure, mass, profusion and colour. Parts of *Rob Roy* were shot in the gardens.

EDZELL CASTLE
Edzell, Angus DD9 7VE
☎ 01356 648631
Owner Historic Scotland
Location On B966 to Edzell Village, then signed for 1 mile
Open 9.30 am – 6.30 pm; daily; April to November. But not open until 2 pm on Sundays in October & November. Some openings in December too
Admission Adults £2.30; OAPs £1.75; Children £1
Facilities Parking; dogs permitted; loos; access for the disabled; plants for sale; shop
Features Formal garden
Friends Historic Scotland

A 1930s formal garden in the 17th-century style, designed to be seen from the ruined keep. A quincunx, of sorts, with yew bobbles, box edging and roses in the beds. The four main segments have the motto of the Lindsey family *DUM SPIRO SPERO* cut round their edges in box. Fun, though not a garden to linger in.

HOUSE OF DUN
Montrose, Angus DD10 9LQ
☎ 01674 810264
Owner The National Trust for Scotland
Location On A395, halfway between Montrose & Brechin
Open 9.30 am – dusk; daily; all year
Admission £1 in honesty box
Facilities Parking; loos; facilities for the disabled; plants for sale; NTS shop; tea-room, open with house
Features Fine conifers; daffodils; fruit of special interest; old roses; snowdrops; woodland garden; ice house; new woodland garden (1997)

The first thing you notice at House of Dun, particularly in winter, is the magnificent line of mature wellingtonias, but there are sheets of spring bulbs, a Victorian rose garden for summer, a border of *Nerine bowdenii* over 100m. long, and a collection of old fruit trees of interest in autumn.

HOUSE OF PITMUIES
by Forfar, Angus DD8 2SN
☎ 01241 828245
Owner Mrs Farquhar Ogilvie
Location Off A932 Forfar to Arbroath Road
Open 10 am – 5 pm; daily; April to October
Admission £2
Facilities Parking; dogs permitted; loos; access for the disabled; plants for sale; home-raised plants & produce in season
Features Herbaceous plants; fruit of special interest; glasshouses; modern roses; old roses; alpine meadow; ferns; colour schemes; tallest *Ilex aquifolium* '*Argentea Marginata*' in the British Isles

One of the most beautiful modern gardens in Scotland, and still expanding. Laid out and planted in the Hidcote style, Pitmuies has wonderful shrub roses in mixed plantings, clever colour schemes, and innumerable different gardens within the garden: a delphinium border, a cherry walk, an alpine meadow for wildflowers, rhododendrons glades, vast hollies and splendid monkey puzzles inherited from Victorian times. Enchanted and enchanting.

KINROSS HOUSE
Kinross KY13 7ET
Owner Sir David Montgomery Bt
Location In Kinross
Open 10 am – 5 pm; daily; May to September
Admission Adults £2; Children 50p
Facilities Parking; access for the disabled
Features Walled garden; beautiful situation

Kinross is the most beautiful house in Scotland, with extensive views across Loch Leven. It is approached along a magnificent avenue of lime trees. The elegant walled garden has herbaceous borders and roses and, above all, a 17th-century sense of proportion.

SCONE PALACE
Perth PH12 6BD
☎ 01738 552300   Fax 01738 552588
Owner The Earl of Mansfield
Location Signed from A93
Open 9.30 am – 5.45 pm; daily; 2 April to 25 October
Admission Gardens only: Adults £2.70; Children £1.60
Facilities Parking; dogs permitted; loos; facilities for the disabled; gift shop; plants in adjoining garden centre; restaurant in old kitchens; self-service coffee-shop
Features Fine conifers; daffodils; rhododendrons and azaleas; new 'Murray' maze (1998), easy to get lost in!; tallest *Tilia platyphyllos* (37m.) in the British Isles, and four further record trees

Famous for its pinetum and for the Douglas firs (*Pseudotsuga menziesii*) grown from original seed sent back by their discoverer David Douglas, who was born on the estate here.

UNIVERSITY OF DUNDEE BOTANIC GARDEN
Riverside Drive, Dundee DD2 1QH
☎ 01382 566939   Fax 01382 640574
Owner University of Dundee
Location Signposted from Riverside Drive (A85), near its Jct with Perth Road
Open 10 am – 4.30 pm (3.30 pm from November to February); Monday – Saturday; all year. Plus 11 am – 4 pm (3 pm from November to February); Sundays; all year
Admission Adults £1.50; OAPs & children 75p
Facilities Parking; loos; access for the disabled; plants for sale; new shop (1998); new café (1998)
Features Fine conifers; ecological interest; glasshouses; herbs; subtropical plants; drought-resistant plants; carnivorous plants
Friends Friends: Newsletters, botanical excursions and illustrated lectures

A fine botanic garden which caters well for visitors. As well as historic plant collections, systematic and chronological borders, there are areas which illustrate native plant communities, including both montane and coastal habitats.

WORTH A VISIT

BELL'S CHERRYBANK GARDENS
Cherrybank, Perth PH2 0NG ☎ *01738 627330. Open 9 am – 5 pm; daily; Easter to September (in 1998). NCCPG National Collection: Erica. This garden is undergoing substantial alterations in 1998–99. Ring to check when it is open. Eighteen acres of immaculately maintained show gardens which make good use of water and incorporate some striking modern sculptures. Best known for its collection of heaths and heathers, the most comprehensive in the British Isles (over 900 cultivars).*

GLENDOICK GARDENS
Glendoick, Perth PH2 7NS ☎ *01738 860205. Open 2 pm – 5 pm; 2 & 16 May. NCCPG National Collections: Kalmia; Enkianthus. Everyone knows of the Glendoick nursery, but the garden is even more important. Started by Farrer's friend Euan Cox in the 1920s, it has one of the best collections of plants, especially rhododendron species, forms and hybrids, in the British Isles. More's the pity that it is so seldom open.*

GOWRANES
Kinnaird, by Inchture PH14 9QY ☎ *01828 686752. A newish plantsman's garden on a steeply sloping site above a burn which has been dammed to create pools and waterfalls. Rhododendrons, camellias, pieris and similar shrubs in the woodland parts: gunneras and candelabra primulas down among the boggy bits.*

MEGGINCH CASTLE
Errol PH2 7SW ☎ *01821 642222. Open 2 – 5 pm; Wednesdays; all year. And daily in August. The gardens are a mixture of old and new: vast ancient yew trees, a Victorian kitchen garden (double-walled), an astrological garden and charming rose garden.*

WALES

CLWYD

BODNANT GARDENS
Tal-y-Cafn, Colwyn Bay LL28 5RE
☎ 01492 650460   Fax 01492 650448
Owner The National Trust
Location 8 miles south of Llandudno and Colwyn Bay on A470. Entrance ½ mile along Eglwysbach Road
Open 10 am – 5 pm; daily; 13 March to 31 October
Admission Adults £4.60; Children £2.30; RHS members free
Facilities Parking; loos; access for the disabled; Plant Centre open 10 am – 5 pm; light lunches, teas, refreshments 11 am – 5 pm
Features Good collection of trees; herbaceous plants; camellias; good architectural features; plantsman's garden; rhododendrons and azaleas; magnolias; good autumn colour; tallest Californian redwood *Sequoia sempervirens* (47m.) in the British Isles and 18 further record-breaking tree species – more than any other garden in Wales
NCCPG National Collections *Embothrium*; *Eucryphia*; *Magnolia*; *Rhododendron forrestii*

The greatest garden in Wales, some would say in all Britain. The grand Italianate terraces above a woodland 'dell' are only part of its renown: Bodnant is famous for its laburnum tunnel, white wisterias, vast *Arbutus* × *andrachnoides*, the 1730s gazebo called the Pin Mill, the green theatre, *Viburnum* × *bodnantense*, hybrid camellias, huge rhododendrons, flaming embothriums, the two Lords Aberconway, father and son, both past-Presidents of the Royal Horticultural Society, and the three generations of the Puddle family who have been Head Gardeners.

CHIRK CASTLE
Chirk LL4 5AF
☎ 01691 777101   Fax 01691 774706
Owner The National Trust
Location 1½ miles west of Chirk off A5
Open 11 am – 6 pm (last admission 4.30 pm); Wednesday – Sunday, plus Bank Holiday Mondays; 27 March to 30 September. Saturdays & Sundays from 3 October to 1 November
Admission Adults £2.60; Children £1.30
Facilities Parking; loos; facilities for the disabled; shop; restaurant & tea-room
Features Herbaceous plants; good architectural features; rhododendrons and azaleas; rock garden; modern roses; old roses; garden sculpture; snowdrops; good topiary; woodland garden; eucryphias; hydrangeas; lime avenue; current holder of Sandford Award
English Heritage Grade I

Chirk has handsome 19th-century formal gardens, one planted with roses and another with billowing yew topiary. There is also a good 1930s collection of trees and shrubs, the relics of a garden by Norah Lindsay. But some say the whole garden is 'a little too National Trust' now.

ERDDIG
Wrexham LL13 0YT
☎ 01978 355314   Fax 01978 313333
Owner The National Trust
Location Signposted from A483 and A525
Open 11 am – 6 pm; Saturday – Wednesday; 20 March to 31 October. Opens at 10 am in July & August; closes at 5 pm in October
Admission Gardens only: Adults £4; Children £2
Facilities Parking; loos; access for the disabled; plants for sale; restaurant, tea-room
Features Fruit of special interest; lake; old roses; woodland garden; spring bulbs; current holder of Sandford Award
English Heritage Grade I
NCCPG National Collection *Hedera*

More of a re-creation than a restoration, Erddig today majors on domestic life in the early 18th century. There are old-fashioned fruit trees, an avenue of pleached limes, and a long canal to frame the house, but all are slightly awed by the Victorian overlay – avenues of monkey puzzles and wellingtonias.

WORTH A VISIT

CELYN VALE NURSERIES
Allt-y-Celyn, Carrog, Corwen LL21 9LD
☎ 01490 430671. *Open 9 am – 4.15 pm; Monday – Friday; all year except Bank Holidays. Specialist growers of eucalyptus and acacias: they use seed from high-altitude specimens to maximise hardiness and will advise on suitable species. Retail and wholesale.*

DIBLEYS
Efenechtyd Nurseries, Llanelidan, Ruthin LL15 2LG
☎ 01978 790677. *Open 9 am – 5 pm; daily; April to September. NCCPG National Collection: Streptocarpus. Varieties and species of Streptocarpus are the main speciality here, but the choice extends to other gesneriads, coleus and foliage begonias. Active on the show circuit: they attend more than 50 each year.*

DYFED

CAE HIR
Cribyn, Lampeter SA48 7NG
☎ 01570 470839

Owner W Akkermans
Location In village
Open 1 pm – 6 pm; daily except Mondays (but open on Bank Holiday Mondays). Closed in winter
Admission Adults £2.50; OAPs £2; Children 50p
Facilities Parking; dogs permitted; loos; plants for sale; light refreshments
Features Bog garden; herbaceous plants; colour gardens; bonsai

Vigorous and expanding garden, begun in 1985 and already featured ten times on television. Six acres have been taken from meadows and made into a series of beautiful colour-conscious gardens by the present owner. Trees, shrubs and herbaceous plants, often used in original ways. Immaculately tidy: Mr Akkermans' energy and achievement are an inspiration.

COLBY WOODLAND GARDEN
Amroth, Narberth SA67 8PP
☎ 01834 811885
Owner The National Trust
Location Signposted from A477
Open 10 am – 5 pm; daily; April to October
Admission Adults £2.80; Children £1.40
Facilities Parking; dogs permitted; loos; access for the disabled; plants for sale; shop; light refreshments
Features Fine conifers; rhododendrons and azaleas; woodland garden

A grand woodland garden, best in May when the rhododendrons are in full flower.

PICTON CASTLE TRUST
Picton Castle, Haverfordwest, Pembrokeshire SA62 4AS
☎ & Fax 01437 751326
Owner Picton Castle Trust
Location 4 miles east of Haverfordwest off A40
Open 10.30 am – 5 pm; Tuesday – Sunday & Bank Holidays; April to September
Admission Adults £2.75; OAPs £2.50; Children £1; Seasonal concessions to RHS members
Facilities Parking; dogs permitted; loos; facilities for the disabled; plants for sale; garden shop selling surplus garden produce; restaurant
Features Camellias; rhododendrons and azaleas; woodland garden

Essentially a 40-acre woodland garden, best in May and June when the rhododendrons are at their peak, but the walled garden has roses, herbaceous borders, a fernery and a herb garden – all recently planted and growing well. Visitors can expect further improvements.

WORTH A VISIT

THE DINGLE
Crundale, Haverfordwest SA62 4DJ ☎ 01437 764370. NCCPG *National Collection*: Gunnera. *This excellent young garden was started in 1982 to display the plants* which Mrs Jones grows in the adjoining nursery – roses, clematis, herbaceous plants and alpines – but it has the feel of a private garden. Plants are arranged to show off their form as well as their flowers and leaf-colours. 'Secret, peaceful and romantic' the owners say.

PEN-Y-BANC NURSERY
Crwbin, Pontyberem, Kidwelly SA17 5DP
☎ 01269 871729. Open 9 am – 5 pm; Monday – Friday. 10 am – 5 pm; Saturdays & Sundays. March to August. *Eight hundred cultivars of* Fuchsia *in more than 4500 sq. ft. of glass. New hybrids are introduced every year, some from Holland.*

SOUTH GLAMORGAN

DYFFRYN BOTANIC GARDEN
St Nicholas, Cardiff CF5 6SU
☎ 01222 593328   Fax 01222 591966
Owner Vale of Glamorgan Council
Location Jct 33 M4 on A48 then follow signs
Open 10 am – 5.30 pm; daily; 2 April to 30 September. 10.30 am – dusk; Wednesday – Saturday; October to March
Admission Adults £3; OAPs & children £2.50
Facilities Parking; dogs permitted; loos; access for the disabled; plants for sale on Bank Holidays; refreshments
Features Herbaceous plants; rhododendrons and azaleas; modern roses; woodland garden; spring bulbs; summer bedding; tallest purple birch *Betula pendula* 'Purpurea' in the British Isles (and ten other record trees)
NCCPG **National Collection** *Salvia*

Fifty-five acres of sumptuous gardens designed by Thomas Mawson around an Edwardian prodigy house and now being restored with a chunky £3.23m millennium grant. Intended partly for display – there is even a Roman garden with a temple and fountain – and partly for the owners' own pleasure, Dyffryn has a huge collection of good plants built up by Reginald Cory in the early years of this century. Watch it revive over the next year or so: the garden as a status symbol.

WEST GLAMORGAN

CLYNE GARDENS
Mumbles Road, Black Pill, Swansea
☎ 01792 298637   Fax 01792 635408
Owner City & County of Swansea
Location 3 miles west of Swansea on coast road
Open Dawn to dusk; daily; all year
Admission Free
Facilities Parking; dogs permitted; loos; facilities for the disabled; occasional light refreshments

Features Herbaceous plants; lake; oriental features; rhododendrons and azaleas; woodland garden; band concerts on Sunday afternoons in May
NCCPG National Collections *Pieris; Enkianthus; Rhododendron* (*Triflora* & *Falconera* subsections)
Friends Details of Friends organisation from Julie Bowen

Clyne is a stupendous woodland garden, the best in South Wales, well cared for by enthusiastic and knowledgeable staff. Best as a magic rhododendron valley in May, but the range of rare and tender plants provides interest all year. The car park is small, and tends to fill up early in the day. There are band concerts on Sunday afternoons in summer.

PLANTASIA
Parc Tawe, Swansea SA1 2AL
☎ 01792 474555/298267   Fax 01792 652588
Owner Swansea City Council
Location Off main Eastern approach to Swansea
Open 10 am – 5 pm; Tuesdays – Sundays & Bank Holidays; all year. Closed 1 January, 25 & 26 December
Admission Adults £1.95; Concessions £1.25
Facilities Parking; loos; access for the disabled; plants for sale; souvenirs; soft drinks
Features Glasshouses; interesting for children; particularly interesting in winter; aviary and tropical fish

A major modern amenity commitment by the go-ahead City Council. Plantasia is a large glasshouse (1,600 sq. m.) with three climatic zones (arid, tropical, and rainforest) and each is stuffed with exotic plants – palms, strelitzias, tree ferns, nepenthes, cacti and such economic plants as coconuts and pineapple. The perfect goal for a winter expedition, and not expensive.

WORTH A VISIT

MARGAM PARK
Port Talbot SA13 2TJ ☎ *01639 881635. A popular country park with lots to interest the garden historian and plantsman. A wonderful range of conservatories and glasshouses, including the orangery for which Margam is famous, big trees and rhododendrons (some grown from Kingdon-Ward's seed), and cheerful bedding-out. Recent additions include a collection of dwarf conifers, a permanent exhibition of modern sculptures, a maze (one of the largest in Europe) and a new pergola 450 yards long: further work is promised.*

GWENT

WORTH A VISIT

LOWER HOUSE FARM
Nantyderry, Abergavenny NP7 9DP ☎ *01873 880257. Open 2 & 3 May for NGS, and by appointment to end of July. A modern garden, substantially made by the present owners. Many good features, notably the bog garden and fern island, and unusual young trees.*

PENPERGWM LODGE
Abergavenny NP7 9AS ☎ *01873 840208. The show garden attached to an established garden school. Clever design and satisfying planting. Recommended.*

GWYNEDD

BODYSGALLEN HALL
Llandudno LL30 1RS
☎ 01492 584466   Fax 01492 582519
Owner Historic House Hotels Ltd
Location On right, off A470 to Llandudno
Open Daily; all year
Admission Open only to Hotel Guests. Children over 8 welcome
Facilities Parking; loos; access for the disabled; refreshments at hotel
Features Good architectural features; fruit of special interest; herbs; rock garden; old roses; woodland garden; knot garden; parterres

Good gardens and good grounds for a good hotel. Partly 1920s and partly modern, the gardens include a knot garden divided into eight segments, an extremely busy kitchen garden, woodland walks, a little sunken garden with a lily pond and a modern parterre with white floribundas in the old walled garden. Handy for Bodnant.

PENRHYN CASTLE
Bangor LL57 4HN
☎ 01248 353084   Fax 01248 371281
Owner The National Trust
Location 3 miles east of Bangor on A5122, signposted from A55 – A5 Jct
Open 11 am – 6 pm; daily except Tuesday; 24 March to 31 October. Opens at 10 am in July & August
Admission Adults £3; Children £1.50
Facilities Parking; dogs permitted; loos; facilities for the disabled; plants for sale; light lunches in licensed tea-room
Features Fine conifers; subtropical plants; woodland garden; 1920s walled garden; rhododendrons; trees planted by royals; *Fuchsia* pergola walk; new 'wet' garden

A Norman castle (actually a Victorian fake) with a distant walled garden of parterres and terraces merging into the slopes of rhododendrons and camellias. There is much of dendrological interest (ancient conifers, holm oaks and naturalised arbutus trees) and a 'dinosaur landscape' of tree ferns, gunneras and aralias.

PLAS BRONDANW GARDENS
Llanfrothen, Panrhyndeudraeth LL48 6SW
☎ 01766 770484
Owner Trustees of the Second Portmeirion Foundation
Location On Croesor road off A4085
Open 9 am – 5 pm; daily; all year
Admission Adults £1.50; Children 25p
Features Good topiary; folly

Highly original and architectural Edwardian garden laid out by Clough Williams-Ellis 17 years before he began Portmeirion, and now assiduously restored by his granddaughter Menna. One of the best-kept secrets in North Wales, full of slate stonework and such original design ideas as the arbour of four red-twigged limes. The garden rooms are inward-looking and almost cottagey in their planting, but the mountain peaks are ever present.

PLAS NEWYDD
Llanfairpwll, Anglesey LL61 6EQ
☎ 01248 714795   Fax 01248 713673
Owner The National Trust
Location 2 miles south-west of Llanfairpwll on A4080
Open 11 am – 5.30 pm; Saturday – Wednesday; 27 March to 31 October
Admission Garden only: £2.20
Facilities Parking; loos; access for the disabled; plants for sale; National Trust shop; tea-room
Features Fine conifers; good architectural features; landscape designed by Humphry Repton; azaleas; magnolias; rhododendrons; maples; spectacular agapanthus

A grand collection of rhododendrons (plus azaleas, magnolias and acers) within a Repton landscape on a spectacular site above the Menai Straits. The rhododendrons came as a wedding present to Lord & Lady Anglesey from Lord Aberconway at Bodnant. The fine Italianate garden below the house is 1930s, most surprising.

PLAS PENHELIG COUNTRY HOUSE HOTEL
Aberdovey LL35 0NA
☎ 01654 767676   Fax 01654 767783
Owner The Richardson family
Location On the hillside above Aberdovey Bay
Open 10.30 am – 5.30 pm; Wednesday – Sunday & Bank Holiday Mondays; 1 April to 24 October
Admission Adults £1.50
Facilities Parking; dogs permitted; loos; Country House Hotel; light meals to full restaurant fare
Features Herbaceous plants; fruit of special interest; glasshouses; rock garden; old roses; subtropical plants; woodland garden; rhododendrons; azaleas; bluebells

Fourteen acres of woodland garden around a hotel on the west coast of Wales. The Richardsons have been reclaiming and replanting it after years of neglect: the results are admirable.

PLAS-YN-RHIW
Rhiw, Pwllheli LL53 8AB
☎ 01758 780219
Owner The National Trust
Location 12 miles from Pwllheli on south-coast road to Aberdarow
Open 12 noon – 5 pm; daily except Tuesday; 27 March to 30 September. Closed on Wednesdays between 27 March & 18 May
Admission Adults £3.20; Children £1.60; Family £8
Facilities Parking; loos

Features Herbaceous plants; formal gardens

Pretty garden, small and formal, with box-edged parterres filled with rambling roses and billowing cottage-garden flowers. Tender trees and shrubs flourish in the mild coastal climate.

PORTMEIRION
LL48 6ET
☎ 01766 770228   Fax 01766 771331
Owner Portmeirion Ltd
Location Between Penrhyndeudraeth and Porthmadog
Open 9.30 am – 5.30 pm; daily; all year
Admission Adults £4; OAPs £3.20; Children £2
Facilities Parking; loos; plants for sale; several shops; refreshments, and hotel
Features Good architectural features; rhododendrons and azaleas; subtropical plants; woodland garden; giant yuccas; exuberant summer bedding; tallest *Maytenus boaria* (18m.) in the British Isles

Portmeirion is where the architect Clough Williams-Ellis worked out his Italianate fantasies. The gardens are carved out of a rhododendron woodland but formal, with a mixture of Mediterranean plants and exotic palms, and full of architectural bric-a-brac of every period. Wyevale Garden Centres are using Portmeirion as the inspiration for their stand at this year's Chelsea Flower Show.

WORTH A VISIT

BRYN BRAS CASTLE
Llanrug, Caernarfon LL55 4RE   ☎ *01286 870210. Open Groups by arrangement. There is much to commend the gardens at Bryn Bras: excellent herbaceous borders, an old/new knot garden and delicious walks through 30 acres of rhododendron woodland. If only more people knew of it.*

CEFN BERE
Cae Deintur, Dolgellau LL40 2YS   ☎ *01341 422768. Open By appointment from early spring to late autumn. A plantsman's garden within a disciplined design: the owners say that it encapsulates their own development as gardeners over the last 40 years. A great variety of rare plants within a small compass, especially alpines, dwarf conifers, ferns and evergreens. Wonderful views.*

CRÛG FARM PLANTS
Griffith's Crossing, Caernarfon LL55 1TU
☎ *01248 670232. Website: www.crug-farm.demon.co.uk Open 10 am – 6 pm; Thursday – Sunday & Bank Holidays; 27 February to 26 September. This exciting nursery is unusual in specialising in plants for shade: perennials, shrubs and climbers. The range is extensive and interesting. Their selection of hardy geraniums equals many specialists in the genera. The fruits of recent collecting expeditions to Korea, Sikkim and Taiwan are now being released.*

POWYS

DINGLE NURSERIES & GARDEN
Welshpool
☎ 01938 555145   Fax 01938 555778

Owner Mr & Mrs Roy Joseph
Location Left turn to Nurseries off A490 to Llanfyllin
Open 9 am – 5 pm; daily except Tuesdays; all year except Christmas week
Admission Adults £1.50; Groups £1. All for charity
Facilities Parking; dogs permitted; loos; access for the disabled; first-rate nursery attached; cold drinks & ice-creams
Features Fine conifers; rhododendrons and azaleas; rock garden; woodland garden; colour borders; new plantings or unusual trees & shrubs

Steep and stony garden attached to a successful nursery, but essentially a plantsman's private garden still. Mainly trees and shrubs, mulched with bark, but some herbaceous plants too, and all planted to create the best colour effects.

DOLWEN
Cefn Coch, Llanrhaeadr-ym-Mochnant SY10 0BL
☎ 01691 780411

Owner Bob Yarwood & Jeny Marriott
Location Right at Three Tuns Inn, 1 mile up lane
Open 2 pm – 4.30 pm; Fridays, plus last Sunday of month; May to September
Admission £1.75
Facilities Parking; loos; plants for sale; tea-room
Features Herbaceous plants; plantsman's garden; old roses; garden sculpture; woodland garden

Old garden: new owners. This plantsman's garden on a steep four-acre site, energetically made by Mrs Denby in the 1980s, continues to be open under the enthusiastic guidance of the new owners. Beautiful plantings around three large ponds, fed by natural springs and connected by waterfalls. One of the best gardens in Wales, of ever-growing interest.

GLANSEVERN GARDENS
Glansevern, Berriew, Welshpool SY21 8AH
☎ 01686 640200   Fax 01686 640829

Owner Neville Thomas
Location On A483, 4 miles south-west of Welshpool
Open 2 pm – 6 pm; Saturdays, Sundays & Bank Holiday Mondays; May to September
Admission Adults £2; OAPs £1.50; Children free
Facilities Parking; dogs permitted; loos; access for the disabled; plants for sale; garden shop; galleried tea-room
Features Herbaceous plants; rock garden; modern roses; good trees; much recent tree-planting (1997); water garden extended (1997)

The handsome Greek-revival house sits in a landscaped park (1802), complete with its lake, rhododendrons and splendid Victorian specimen trees. The 1840s rock garden incorporates a spooky grotto. But it is the modern planting which distinguishes Glansevern: luxuriant primulas in the water garden, island beds around the house and roses in the walled garden.

POWIS CASTLE
Welshpool SY21 8RF
☎ & Fax 01938 554336

Owner The National Trust
Location 1 mile south of Welshpool off the A483
Open 11 am – 6 pm; Wednesday – Sunday plus Bank Holiday Mondays; 27 March to 31 October. Plus Tuesdays in July & August
Admission Adults £5; Children £2.50
Facilities Parking; loos; facilities for the disabled; plant shop & gift shop; restaurant for light lunches & teas
Features Herbaceous plants; good topiary; woodland garden; plantings by Graham Thomas; particularly good in July–August; tender climbers; colour plantings; good autumn colour; largest (i.e. thickest trunk) sessile oak *Quercus petraea* in the British Isles, and four other record trees
NCCPG National Collections *Aralia*; *Laburnum*

Famous hanging terraces swamped by bulky overgrown yews and wonderfully rich with colour planting by Graham Thomas. Smashing in early autumn when maples colour the lower slopes and again in May when rhododendrons fill the surrounding woodland. Rare and tender plants on the walls include a hefty *Acca sellowiana*. The aspect is south-east, so Powis is best seen in the morning light: photographers please note.

Northern Ireland

Co. Derry

WORTH A VISIT

GUY WILSON DAFFODIL GARDEN
University of Ulster, Coleraine BT52 1SA
☎ 01265 44141. *Open Dawn to dusk; daily; all year.*
NCCPG National Collection: Narcissus. *The name says it all – this is both a celebration of Guy Wilson as a daffodil breeder and a museum of his hybrids. Drifts of his hybrids, and others of Irish raising, sweep through the university gardens.*

Co. Down

CASTLEWELLAN NATIONAL ARBORETUM
Castlewellan Forest Park, Castlewellan BT25 9KG
☎ 01396 778664   Fax 01396 771762

Owner Department of Agriculture, Forest Services
Location 30 miles south of Belfast, 4 miles west of Newcastle
Open Dawn to dusk; daily; all year
Admission £3.50 per car
Facilities Parking; dogs permitted; loos; access for the disabled; light refreshments at peak times
Features Good collection of trees; fine conifers; woodland garden; particularly interesting in winter; autumn colours; embothriums; eucryphias; tallest *Chamaecyparis nootkatensis* 'Lutea' (22m.) in the British Isles, plus 39 other tree records; new 'fragrant garden' around a Lutyensesque tea house

Castlewellan means trees: 40 record-breakers and many rarities. The heart of the collection is in a huge walled garden, interplanted with rhododendrons and other shrubs. The central path has mixed borders at the top: dwarf rhododendrons are prominent even here. Labelling is good, and the standard of maintenance high. There are plans to make the collections of *Taxus* and *Eucryphia* comprehensive.

MOUNT STEWART
The National Trust, Mount Stewart Estate, Grey Abbey, Newtownards BT22 2AD
☎ 012477 88387

Owner The National Trust
Location East of Belfast on A20
Open 11 am – 6 pm; Wednesday – Monday; May to September; plus weekends & Bank Holidays in April & October
Admission Adults £3.50; Children £1.75
Facilities Parking; dogs permitted; loos; facilities for the disabled; souvenir shop; refreshments from 12.30 pm
Features Good collection of trees; bluebells; herbaceous plants; good architectural features; lake; old roses; snowdrops; good topiary; vegetables of interest; woodland garden; plantings by Graham Thomas; rare and tender shrubs galore
NCCPG National Collection *Phormium*

One of the best gardens in the British Isles and very little known outside Ireland. The formal gardens by the house are utterly original: a Spanish garden, statues of mythical beasts, and the red hand of Ulster set in a shamrock surround. Good plants too: *Rosa gigantea* grows on the house walls, and the herbaceous and woodland plantings are brilliant with colour and variety. Better still is the walk around the lake, where rhododendrons flood the woodlands. They are underplanted in places with meconopsis and candelabra primulas and, at one point, you catch a glimpse of a white stag in a glade. For design, variety, plants and plantings, Mount Stewart is a place of miracles. Allow lots of time for your visit.

ROWALLANE GARDEN
Saintfield, Ballynahinch BT24 7LH
☎ 01238 510131   Fax 01238 511242

Owner The National Trust
Location One mile south of Saintfield on A7
Open 10.30 pm – 6 pm, Monday – Friday; 2 – 6 pm, Saturday & Sunday; April to October. 10.30 am – 5 pm; Monday – Friday; November to March
Admission Adults £2.50; Children £1.25; Groups £1.75
Facilities Parking; dogs permitted; loos; facilities for the disabled; National Trust shop; new Information Centre; light refreshments 2 pm – 6 pm May to August & weekends in April & September
Features Good collection of trees; plantsman's garden; rhododendrons and azaleas; rock garden; snowdrops; particularly interesting in winter; good autumn colour; tallest *Cupressus duclouxiana* (14m.) in the British Isles
NCCPG National Collection *Penstemon*

Fifty-two acres of rhododendrons and azaleas, which started near the house and expanded into the fields beyond as the seedlings came and needed to be planted. No garden can match it on a sunny day in April or May, as you amble from a glade of *Rhododendron augustinii* forms to a line of *R. macabeanum* or back through *R. yakushimanum* hybrids.

WORTH A VISIT

BALLYROGAN NURSERIES
The Grange, Ballyrogan, Newtownards BT23 4SD
☎ 01247 810451 *(evenings). Open By prior arrangement. NCCPG National Collections:* Celmisia;

Crocosmia; Euphorbia. *A small part-time nursery selling stock derived from their own large collections of herbaceous plants and bulbs. As well as the National Collections, there are interesting* Agapanthus, Dierama *and* Kniphofia.

CASTLE WARD
Strangford, Downpatrick BT30 7LS ☎ *01396 881204. Open Dawn to dusk; daily; all year. Castle Ward offers bluebells, cordylines, giant rhododendrons and a stately parkland with stupendous views across Strangford Lough. And the dotty two-faced house is well worth a visit, too.*

SEAFORDE GARDENS
Seaforde, Downpatrick BT30 8PG ☎ *01396 811225. Open 10 am – 5 pm; Monday – Saturday; 1 pm – 6 pm; Sundays. Open Monday – Friday only; November to February. NCCPG National Collection:* Eucryphia. *If this nursery were in the south of England, it would be the darling of discriminating plantsmen. The list was built up on Irish specialities (*Eucryphia × intermedia *'Rostrevor') and tender taxa, but now includes a magnificent number of rhododendrons grown from Patrick Forde's own collecting expeditions to Bhutan, Yunnan, Tibet and Vietnam. The gardens are extensive, and include a hornbeam maze, Victorian conifers, hardy hybrid rhododendrons and a tropical butterfly house, as well as drifts of primulas, camassias and bluebells, and both pink forms of* Eucryphia lucida.

CO. FERMANAGH

FLORENCE COURT
The National Trust, Florence Court, Enniskillen BT92 1DB
☎ 01365 348249   Fax 01365 348873
Owner The National Trust
Location 8 miles south-west of Enniskillen
Open 1 pm – 6 pm; daily except Tuesday; 1 May to 31 August; plus Saturday, Sunday & Bank Holidays in April & September. Grounds: 10 am – 7 pm (4 pm October to March); daily. Closed 25 December
Admission Adults £2.80; Children £1.40; Family £7; Garden/Estate: £2 per car
Facilities Parking; dogs permitted; loos; facilities for the disabled; National Trust shop; light lunches & teas, picnics welcome
Features Good collection of trees; woodland garden; interesting for children; ice house; water-powered sawmill; current holder of Sandford Award

Classic 18th-century parkland, with stupendous views and magnificent trees, notably the original 'Irish Yew' *Taxus baccata* 'Fastigiata' and a beautiful form of weeping beech with a broad curving crown. The sawmill is fun for children.

Republic of Ireland

Co. Carlow

Altamont Garden
Altamont Garden Trust, Altamont, Tullow
☎ 00 353 503 59128/59302
Fax 00 353 503 59128

Owner Mrs North
Location Signed from N80 & N81
Open 2 pm – 6 pm; Sundays & Bank Holidays; April to October. And by appointment
Admission Adults I£3; Children (under 10) I£1
Facilities Parking; loos; access for the disabled; large garden centre; craft shop; art gallery; home-made teas
Features Rhododendrons and azaleas; woodland garden; cyclamen; new temple folly (1999); new wisteria pergola (1999)

Charming and romantic woodland gardens, stretching to nearly 100 acres, and full of huge specimens of rare plants. Lakes, islands, a bog garden and a shady glen: Altamont is a place of contemplation and wonder, and very old-world Irish.

Co. Cork

Annes Grove Gardens
Castletownroche, Mallow
☎ 00 353 22 26145

Owner Patrick Annesley
Location 1 mile north of Castletownroche on N72
Open 10 am – 5 pm, Monday – Saturday; 1 – 6 pm, Sundays; 17 March to 30 September
Admission Adults I£3; OAPs & students I£2; Children I£1
Facilities Parking; dogs permitted; loos; plants for sale; lunches & teas by arrangement for groups
Features Herbaceous plants; plantsman's garden; woodland garden; rhododendrons from wild seeds; rare trees; self-catering accommodation available; tallest *Azara microphylla* (11m.) in the British Isles

Annes Grove has long been famous for its 30-acre garden, begun in 1907: 'Robinsonian' is the word most often used to describe it. The walled garden is a flower garden, with a 17th-century mount and a Victorian gothic summer house on top. The river garden is lushly wild with lysichiton, gunnera and candelabra primulas around the pools. In the glen garden lies a wonderfully dense collection of rhododendrons and azaleas, many from Kingdon-Ward's seed.

Creagh Gardens
Skibbereen
☎ & Fax 00 353 28 22121

Owner Gwendoline Harold-Barry Trust
Location 4 miles from Skibbereen on the Baltimore road
Open 10 am – 6 pm; daily; March to September
Admission Adults I£3; Children I£2
Facilities Parking; loos; access for the disabled; refreshments for groups by arrangement
Features Camellias; pond; rhododendrons and azaleas; subtropical plants; woodland garden; serpentine mill pond; traditional organic walled garden; new fern glade with tree ferns (1997)

Twenty acres of exotic woodland on the edge of a sea estuary and lushly planted by the late Peter and Gwendoline Harold-Barry in the style of a Douanier Rousseau painting. Recent restorations confirm it as one of the great gardens of southern Ireland.

Fota
Fota Island, Carrigtwohill
☎ 00 353 21 812728   Fax 00 353 21 270244

Owner Fota Trust Company Ltd
Location 9 miles from Cork city, off Cobh road
Open 10 am (11 am on Sundays) – 6 pm (5 pm in winter); daily; all year. Closed for Christmas holidays
Admission Cars I£1; Pedestrians free of charge
Facilities Parking; dogs permitted; loos; facilities for the disabled
Features Good collection of trees; fine conifers; ecological interest; lake; woodland garden; interesting for children; 165 Irish-bred daffodil cultivars (1998); wildlife park; tallest Italian cypress *Cupressus sempervirens* (25m.) in the British Isles, plus 18 other record trees

Fota has a handsome formal garden and walled garden, now undergoing restoration, but is famous above all for its trees. As well as a fine collection of Victorian conifers (huge redwoods and wellingtonias), there are flowering mimosas, a wonderful *Cornus capitata* and such tender trees as the Canary Islands palm *Phoenix canariensis*. And the collection is now growing again with additions from central America.

WORTH A VISIT

Ballymaloe Cookery School Garden
Ballymaloe Shanagarry ☎ 00 353 21 646785.
Open 9 am – 6 pm; daily; 1 April to 1 October. The garden attached to the famous Ballymaloe cookery school is full of unusual fruit, vegetables and herbs. Seldom is a functional garden so stylishly designed and planted, or so extensive.

HILLSIDE
Annmount Glounthane ☎ 00 353 21 353119.
Open 9 am – 6 pm; daily. And by appointment throughout the summer. Intensely cultivated garden in a setting of mature trees and rhododendrons, but burgeoning with alpines in every part – stone troughs, a scree bed and gravel areas.

CO. DONEGAL

WORTH A VISIT

ARDNAMONA
Lough Eske ☎ 00 353 73 22650. A wilderness of huge rhododendrons, some as much as 60 feet high, like a Himalayan forest, now taken in hand and cleared of almost 40 acres of Rhododendron ponticum.

GLENVEAGH CASTLE
Churchill Letterkenny ☎ 00 353 74 37040. NCCPG National Collection: Pieris. Glenveagh was built for its view down the rocky slopes of Lough Veagh, and part of the gardens is known as the View Garden. Lanning Roper laid out a formal Italianate courtyard garden. Jim Russell advised on planting. There are wonderful borders and conservatories as well as rhododendrons and camellias. The unusual shrubs are magnificent: tree-like griselinias and Michelia doltsopa, for instance. New plantings from RBG Edinburgh and a trip to Yunnan in 1996.

CO. DUBLIN

ARDGILLAN PARK
Balbriggan
☎ 00 353 1 8727777   Fax 00 353 1 8727530
Owner Fingal County Council
Location Coast road between Skerries and Balbriggan
Open 10 am – 5 pm; daily; all year
Admission Free
Facilities Parking; loos; facilities for the disabled; refreshments
Features Herbaceous plants; good architectural features; fruit of special interest; herbs; rock garden; modern roses; old roses; ice house; 200-year-old yew walk; restored Victorian glasshouse in rose garden

Ardgillan was all but lost in the troubles, but restored ten years ago by the Council as a public amenity. A new rose garden and herbaceous borders have been added. The four-acre walled garden is being developed too – it has a herb garden now and fruit trees grown against the walls.

DILLON GARDEN
Ranelagh, Dublin 6
☎ 00 353 1 4971308   Fax 00 353 1 4971308
Owner Helen & Val Dillon
Location 45 Sandford Road
Open 2 pm – 6 pm; daily; March, July & August. Plus Sundays, April to June, & September. Groups by appointment
Admission Adults I£3; OAPs I£2
Facilities Loos; access for the disabled; plants for sale
Features Herbaceous plants; glasshouses; plantsman's garden; redesigned garden around oval lawn (1998); front garden replanted (1998); raised beds

This much acclaimed plantsman's garden offers a fantastic range of rarities, from snowdrops and hellebores in spring, to tropaeolums in autumn. Unlike some collectors' gardens, Helen Dillon's is immaculately maintained, strictly planted according to colour and beautifully designed as a series of garden rooms.

FAIRFIELD LODGE
Monkstown Avenue, Monkstown
☎ & Fax 00 353 1 2803912
Owner John Bourke
Location In Monkstown village
Open 2 pm – 6 pm; Sundays; June to August. And by appointment
Admission Adults: I£2.50
Facilities Parking; loos; plants for sale; refreshment
Features Herbaceous plants; climbing roses; old roses; colour combination

A small town garden, made to appear much larger by division into a series of outdoor rooms. Formal design, informal planting and clever colour combinations: a modern classic.

FERNHILL
Sandyford
☎ 00 353 1 295 6000
Owner Mrs Sally Walker
Location 7 miles south of central Dublin on the Enniskerry Road
Open 11 am – 5 pm (2 pm – 6 pm on Sundays & Bank Holidays); Tuesday – Sunday (& Bank Holidays); March to October
Admission Adults I£3; OAPs I£2; Children I£1
Facilities Parking; loos
Features Good collection of trees; herbaceous plants; rock garden; woodland garden; sculpture exhibitions; rhododendrons

A popular garden on the outskirts of Dublin, with a good collection of rhododendrons and other woodland plants and some magnificent trees 150 years old. Steep woodland walks and an excellent nursery thrown in.

NATIONAL BOTANIC GARDENS, DUBLIN
Glasnevin, Dublin 9
☎ 00 353 1 837 4388   Fax 00 353 1 836 0080
Owner Office of Public Works
Location 1 mile north of Dublin near Glasnevin cemetery
Open 9 am – 6 pm (4.30 pm in winter); daily except 25 December. Open at 11 am on Sundays

Admission Free
Facilities Loos; facilities for the disabled; refreshments by arrangement
Features Good collection of trees; herbaceous plants; fine conifers; ecological interest; fruit of special interest; glasshouses; lake; plantsman's garden; rock garden; old roses; subtropical plants; particularly interesting in winter; carpet-bedding; fern house; tallest variegated plane tree *Platanus* × *hispanica* 'Suttneri' (21m.) in the British Isles, plus 25 further tree records
NCCPG National Collections *Garrya*; *Potentilla fruticosa*

Glasnevin garden greets you with beautiful old-fashioned summer bedding and a bed of *Rosa chinensis* 'Parson's Pink', known here as 'The Last Rose of Summer'. Very much a botanic garden in the old tradition: public education and amenity hand in hand. Richard Turner's elegant curvilinear range of glasshouses, built in 1847, has recently been restored. Interesting plant collections and some good trees, most notably a weeping Atlantic cedar: allow a full day to do its 48 acres justice.

PRIMROSE HILL
Primrose Lane, Lucan
☎ 00 353 6280373

Owner Robin & Cicely Hall
Location Lucan village, at top of Primrose Lane, through black iron gates
Open 2 pm – 6 pm; daily; 1 February to 1 March and mid-June to mid-August. And by appointment
Admission I£3
Facilities Parking; loos; plants for sale
Features Herbaceous plants; plantsman's garden; snowdrops

Four acres of intensive plantsmanship, particularly interesting for its rare forms of herbaceous plants and its snowdrops. The planting continues, and includes a small arboretum.

TALBOT BOTANIC GARDENS
Malahide Castle, Malahide
☎ 00 353 1 8727777   Fax 00 353 1 8727530

Owner Fingal County Council
Location 10 miles north of Dublin on Malahide Road
Open 2 pm – 5 pm (or by appointment); daily; May to September
Admission I£2 (1998 price)
Facilities Parking; loos; facilities for the disabled; souvenir shop in castle; restaurant
Features Good collection of trees; fine conifers; plantsman's garden; woodland garden; Tasmanian plants; excellent new alpine section (1997)
NCCPG National Collection *Olearia*

The garden at Malahide was the work of Milo Talbot, a passionate amateur botanist with a particular interest in Tasmanian flowers. He built up a collection of 5,000 different taxa and, since the soil is limey, all are calcicole. Best visited at 2 pm on Wednesday afternoons when guided tours are offered of the walled garden (not otherwise open).

WORTH A VISIT

ST ANNE'S PARK
Dublin ☎ 00 351 1 8331859. Open Dawn to dusk; daily; all year. *The rose garden is the best in southern Ireland. It includes the international trial grounds and the eponymous Bourbon rose 'Souvenir de Saint Anne's'.*

TRINITY COLLEGE BOTANIC GARDEN
Palmerston Park, Dartry Dublin 6 ☎ 00 353 1 4972070. *A charming old-fashioned botanic garden, full of interesting plants, including a collection of Irish natives.*

CO. KERRY

DERREEN
Lauragh, Killarney
☎ 00 353 64 83103

Owner The Hon David Bigham
Location 15 miles from Kenmare on the Castletown Road
Open 11 am – 6 pm; daily; April to September
Admission Adults I£3; Children I£1.50
Facilities Parking; dogs permitted; loos; facilities for the disabled; tea-room
Features Rock garden; subtropical plants; woodland garden; tree ferns; rhododendrons; natural rock garden

Derreen is quite extraordinary. The rocky outcrops come right to the front door, but the fast lush growth of its trees and shrubs is boundless. Tree ferns *Dicksonia antarctica* and myrtles *Myrtus communis* have gone native, and seed themselves everywhere. Moss, lichen and ferns abound. Large-leaved rhododendrons grow to great heights. Wonderful on a sunny day in late April.

MUCKROSS HOUSE & GARDENS
Muckross, Killarney
☎ 00 353 64 31440   Fax 00 353 64 33926

Owner Office of Public Works
Location 4 miles south of Killarney on N71
Open Dawn to dusk; daily; all year except one week at Christmas
Admission Free
Facilities Parking; dogs permitted; loos; facilities for the disabled; lunches, hot & cold snacks daily
Features Good collection of trees; fine conifers; rock garden; woodland garden; rhododendrons; azaleas; extensive conifer plantings in arboretum (1997)

Killarney National Park provides a most beautiful setting for the gardens of Muckross House. There is a young arboretum (25 acres and now fully open to visitors) and some enormous old rhododendrons, but the native woodland is of Scots pines and arbutus trees and, even more exciting for a garden-visitor, the rock garden is a natural one, of carboniferous limestone. Well maintained.

Co. Kildare

Japanese Gardens
Tully, Kildare Town
☎ 00 353 45 521617   Fax 00 353 45 522129
Owner Irish National Stud
Location Signposted in Kildare
Open 9.30 am – 6 pm; daily; 12 February to 12 November
Admission I£6 Adults; I£4.50 OAPs; I£3 Children
Facilities Parking; loos; plants for sale; souvenir shop; light refreshments
Features Famous Japanese garden

The garden is a sequence which symbolises Man's journey through life. It was made for Lord Wavertree by Japanese gardeners in the early years of this century. This year (1999) sees the opening of a new garden dedicated to St Fiacre, the patron saint of gardeners.

Worth a Visit

Coolcarrigan Gardens
Coolcarrigan Naas ☎ *00 353 45 863512. Open By appointment only, from April to August. This garden owes everything to a gale which knocked the heart out of the established plantings in 1974. Harold Hillier advised on the replanting and the result is one of the best modern collections of trees and shrubs in Ireland. The owners, keen plantsmen, have added late-summer borders and a rock garden.*

Lodge Park Walled Garden
Straffan ☎ *00 353 1 628 8412. Open 2.30 pm – 5.30 pm; Tuesday – Friday (plus Sunday in June & July); June to August. An 18th-century walled garden planted for the owners' use and pleasure, with everything from fruit, herbs and vegetables to sweet peas and roses.*

Co. Kilkenny

Worth a Visit

Kilfane Glen & Waterfall
Thomastown ☎ *00 353 56 24558. A romantic landscape garden laid out in the 1790s and vigorously restored by the present owners. Sit in the tiny cottage, admire the exquisite form of the waterfall across the ravine, and dream of Rousseau.*

Co. Laois

Gash Gardens
Gash, Castletown, Portlaoise
☎ 00 353 502 32217

Owner Noel Kennan
Location ½ mile from main Dublin-Limerick road
Open 10 am – 5 pm; daily; May to September
Admission I£2.50. Group rates by appointment. Not suitable for children
Facilities Parking; loos; nursery at entrance, open all year
Features Plantsman's garden; rhododendrons and azaleas; rock garden; old roses; new 150m. boundary border (1998)

Young award-winning plantsman's garden, full of unusual plants and maintained to very high standard. Four acres, on either side of the River Nore, with streams and other water features.

Worth a Visit

Heywood Gardens
Ballinakill ☎ *00 353 502 33563. A ravishing garden, originally designed by Lutyens, which was taken into State care late in 1993 and is in the middle of careful restoration and replanting by Graham Thomas. Go now, to see what an Edwardian garden looked like when newly made.*

Co. Limerick

Glin Castle
Glin
☎ 00 353 68 34173   Fax 00 353 68 34364
Owner Desmond Fitzgerald, Knight of Glin
Location On N69, 32 miles west of Limerick
Open 10 am – noon & 2 pm – 4 pm; daily; May & June. Groups by appointment
Admission Adults I£3; Groups I£2; Children I£1
Facilities Parking; loos; facilities for the disabled; gate shop
Features Bluebells; camellias; daffodils; rhododendrons and azaleas; subtropical plants; vegetables of interest; grotto & shell-house restored (1997)

Simple formal gardens run down towards the park and merge with the surrounding woodland. Not a great garden but, taken with the Gothicised castle and magnificent position on the Shannon estuary, a place of rare enchantment.

Worth a Visit

Ballynacourty
Ballysteen ☎ *00 353 61 396409. Open By appointment A fine modern family garden: four densely planted acres won from open farmland. Interesting, too, for its selection of lime-tolerant trees and shrubs.*

Co. Meath

Butterstream
Kildalkey Road, Trim
☎ 00 353 46 36017   Fax 00 353 46 31702
Owner Jim Reynolds
Location Outskirts of Trim on Kildalkey Road
Open   11 am – 6 pm; daily; April to September
Admission   Adults I£3; Children I£1
Facilities   Parking; loos; plants for sale
Features   Herbaceous plants; fruit of special interest; plantsman's garden; modern roses; old roses; colour borders

Ireland's Sissinghurst, only 20 years old, and still expanding. A series of garden rooms (13 at the last count) in the modern style around an old farmhouse. Each is different but connected to the next. They include a green garden, a white garden, a hot-coloured garden, a Roman garden, a pool garden (with Tuscan portico reflected in it), an obelisk garden, and many others. The plants are determined by the soil – heavy, cold, limy clay.

Co. Offaly

Birr Castle Demesne
Birr
☎ 00 353 509 22154   Fax 00 353 509 21583
Website www.ireland.iol.ie/birr-castle
Owner Earl of Rosse
Location Rosse Row in Birr, Co. Offaly
Open 9 am – 6 pm or dusk; daily; all year
Admission   Adults I£4; OAPs I£3.20; Children I£2.50
Facilities   Parking; dogs permitted; loos; access for the disabled; plants for sale; craft shop; good guide books; morning coffee, lunch & tea at gates
Features   Good collection of trees; herbaceous plants; herbs; lake; plantsman's garden; old roses; good topiary; *Paeonia* 'Anne Rosse'; *Magnolia* 'Anne Rosse'; winner of all-Ireland Property of the Year Award in 1992; tallest *Acer monspessulanum* (15m.) and boxwood *Buxus sempervirens* (12m.) in the British Isles, plus 49 other record species
Friends   Friends of the Birr Castle Demesne organisation

The best garden in the Irish Midlands. Birr has 50 hectares of grounds, a huge collection of trees and shrubs, and a wonderful walled garden with a tunnel down the middle. Many of the plants are grown from original collectors' material: some were collected in the wild by the owner's parents, Michael and Anne Rosse. Birr also has the tallest box hedges in the world. In the grounds is the famous telescope, once the largest in the world, now fully restored and witness to the polymath abilities of the owner's family over the generations.

Co. Waterford

Curraghmore
Portlaw
☎ 00 353 51 387102   Fax 00 353 51 387481
Owner The Marquess of Waterford
Location 14 miles west of Waterford: enter by Portlaw gate
Open 2 pm – 5 pm; Thursdays & Bank Holidays; Easter to mid-October. Groups by appointment may visit the handsome Palladian house too
Admission   I£3
Facilities   Parking; loos; access for the disabled
Features   Good collection of trees; landscaped park

A magnificent estate, with a classical landscape garden, a fine Victorian arboretum, and the pretty baroque shellhouse (1754). Curraghmore deserves to be better known.

Lismore Castle
Lismore
☎ 00 353 58 54424   Fax 00 353 58 54896
Owner Lismore Estates
Location Centre of Lismore
Open 1.45pm – 4.45 pm; daily; 3 April to 26 September
Admission   Adults I£2.50; Children I£1.30
Facilities   Parking; dogs permitted; loos
Features   Old roses; woodland garden; magnolias; spring bulbs; herbaceous borders replanted (1997)

Best for the castellated house: the gardens are interesting rather than exceptional, but there is a pretty grove of camellias and a double yew walk planted in 1707. The upper enclosure is even older, a Jacobean survivor. Visit the walled garden for some fine traditional kitchen gardening: the vinery was designed by Paxton.

Co. Westmeath

Tullynally Castle Gardens
Castlepollard
☎ 00 353 44 61159   Fax 00 353 44 61856
Owner The Hon Mr & Mrs Thomas Pakenham
Location Signposted from Castlepollard
Open 2 pm – 6 pm; daily; May to September
Admission   Adults I£3; Children I£1
Facilities   Parking; dogs permitted; loos; access for the disabled; plants for sale; tea-room open mid-May to the end of August
Features   Bluebells; daffodils; woodland garden; grotto; new Tibetan garden (1999); biggest beech tree *Fagus sylvatica* in the British Isles and tallest *Griselinia littoralis* (20m.)

A grand garden for a grandly turreted house. Formal terraces lead down to the park and into the woodland gardens. A fine avenue of centennial Irish yews is the centrepiece of the walled garden. Tom Pakenham wrote the acclaimed *Meetings with Remarkable Trees* (Weidenfeld, 1996, £25), some of whose photographs were taken at Tullynally. And he is starting to introduce exotics from his travels abroad. Watch this space.

CO. WEXFORD

THE JOHN F KENNEDY ARBORETUM
New Ross
☎ 00 353 51 388171   Fax 00 353 51 388172
Owner The Office of Public Works
Location 8 miles south of New Ross off R733
Open 10 am – 8 pm, May to August; 10 am – 6.30 pm, April and September; 10 am – 5 pm, October to March. Closed 2 April & 25 December
Admission Adults I£2; OAPs I£1.50; Children & students I£1
Facilities Parking; dogs permitted; loos; facilities for the disabled; souvenirs; cafeteria for teas/refreshments in summer
Features Good collection of trees; fine conifers; interesting for children; eight different tree records for the British Isles

A memorial arboretum founded in 1968 by Irish/American citizens on 623 acres adjoining the Kennedy home town. Thirty years on, the statistics are impressive: 4,500 types of trees and shrubs arranged on 200 plots both taxonomically and by geographical distribution, and planted with artistry. All meticulously labelled. There are picnic areas, viewpoints, signposted walks, a vigorous visitors' centre, plots of experimental forestry and a miniature railway which runs through plantings that represent each continent.

JOHNSTOWN CASTLE GARDENS
Wexford
☎ 00 353 53 42888   Fax 00 353 53 42004
Owner TEAGASC (Food & Agriculture Development Authority)
Location 4 miles south-west of Wexford
Open 9 am – 5.30 pm; daily; all year except 25 December
Admission I£3 per car & passengers
Facilities Parking; dogs permitted; loos; access for the disabled; plants for sale; coffee-shop with snacks, July and August only
Features Fine conifers; glasshouses; woodland garden; walled gardens; tallest *Cupressus macrocarpa* (40m.) in the British Isles

Fifty acres of ornamental grounds with good trees, tall cordylines, three lakes and the Irish Agricultural Museum.

RAM HOUSE GARDEN
Coolgreany, Gorey
☎ 00 353 402 37238   Fax 00 353 402 37238
Owner Godfrey & Lolo Stevens

Location N11 to Inch and turn inland 1½ miles to Coolgreany
Open 2.30 pm – 6 pm; Fridays to Sundays & Bank Holidays; May to August
Admission Adults I£3; OAPs I£2.50; Children I£2
Facilities Parking; loos; paintings for sale; seeds for sale; tea-room
Features Herbaceous plants; pond; climbing roses; woodland garden; water garden; over 60 clematis

Two acres laid out in the modern style as a series of garden rooms, full of good plants and clever plantings. Utterly charming and forever expanding and improving.

CO. WICKLOW

MOUNT USHER GARDENS
Ashford
☎ 00 353 404 40205   Fax 00 353 404 40116
Owner Mrs Madelaine Jay
Location Ashford, 30 miles south of Dublin on the N11
Open 10.30 am – 6 pm; daily; 12 March to 2 November. Open to 8 pm on 25 April and 2 & 9 May
Admission Adults I£3.50; OAPs & children I£2.50. Guided tours for groups available
Facilities Parking; loos; access for the disabled; courtyard shops with pottery, books, furniture, etc.; tea-room with home-baked food
Features Good collection of trees; fine conifers; plantsman's garden; subtropical plants; woodland garden; spring bulbs; pretty bridges across the river; tallest *Cornus capitata* (18m.) in the British Isles, plus 28 other record tree species

Twenty acres of garden with the River Vartry through the middle, crowded with unusual trees and shrubs – 5,000 different species, some *very* rare. The self-sown *Pinus montezumae* are justly famous. Good herbaceous plants too, and lilies in July. A truly remarkable plantsman's garden made by four generations of Walpoles 1868–1980 and extensively restored by the present owner.

POWERSCOURT GARDENS
Powerscourt Estate, Enniskerry
☎ 00 353 1 2867676   Fax 00 353 1 2863561
Owner Powerscourt Estate
Location 12 miles south of Dublin off N11
Open 9.30 am – 5.30 pm (dusk in winter); daily; all year
Admission Adults I£3.50; Students I£3.20; Children I£2
Facilities Parking; dogs permitted; loos; access for the disabled; plants for sale; garden centre; tea-rooms with light lunches
Features Good collection of trees; fine conifers; lake; oriental features; garden sculpture; woodland garden; interesting for children; much recent restoration, including the Bamberg gates, and a remodelling of the Japanese garden; tallest *Abies spectabilis* (32m.) in the British Isles, plus ten other record tree specimens

Powerscourt is a wonderful mixture of awesome grandeur and sheer fun. It is also extremely well organised for visitors. The main Italianate garden, a stately 1860s staircase down to a lake, has Great Sugarloaf Mountain as an off-centre backdrop. It is lined with bedding plants, statues and urns (look out for the sulky cherubs). To one side is the Japanese garden – not strongly Japanese – but full of twists and hummocks and scarlet paintwork. In the arboretum, Alan Mitchell designed a tree trail. Powerscourt is busy in summer, but you can escape into solitude along the avenue of monkey puzzles. The magnificent house has been restored and is now open to visitors again.

WORTH A VISIT

NATIONAL GARDEN EXHIBITION CENTRE
Kilquade Kilpedder ☎ *00 353 1 2819890. Open 10 am (1 pm on Sundays) – 6 pm (dusk in winter); daily; all year.*
Permanent exhibition of contemporary styles attached to a garden centre. Seventeen linked but distinct gardens: the Herb Garden; the Geometric Garden; the Contemplative Garden; the Seaside Garden; the 'Pythagoras at Play' Garden; and so on. Each was made by a different designer and construction team. The best of modern Irish design for small gardens: a shop window for ideas on style, plants and materials.

VALCLUSA GARDENS & NURSERY
Waterfall Road Enniskerry ☎ *00 353 1 286 9485. The garden has a plum position by the famous waterfall.* Among its established trees (huge specimens of redwood, embothriums, Cornus capitata *and a weeping form of Liriodendron tulipifera) is a modern plantsman's garden of rhododendrons, grasses, hostas and over 100 geraniums.*

Awards to Gardens

The Garden of the Year Award

The Garden of the Year Award was introduced jointly by the Historic Houses Association (HHA) and Christie's in 1984. It is designed to recognise the importance of gardens, either in their own right or as settings for historic houses. It reflects public enjoyment of those privately owned gardens which are open regularly to the public, rather than their horticultural excellence, although many winners can claim that too. The award winners since its institution have been:

1984 Heale House, Wiltshire
1985 Hodnet Hall, Shropshire
1986 Newby Hall, North Yorkshire
1987 Arley Hall, Cheshire
1988 Barnsley House, Gloucestershire
1989 Brympton d'Evercy, Somerset
1990 Parham Park, West Sussex
1991 Holker Hall, Cumbria
1992 Forde Abbey, Dorset
1993 Haddon Hall, Derbyshire
1994 Levens Hall, Cumbria
1995 Hever Place, Kent
1996 Sudeley Castle, Gloucestershire
1997 Athelhampton House, Dorset

Details of the 1998 winner will be revealed when the award is presented in spring 1999.

The Sandford Awards

The Sandford Awards are given by the Heritage Education Trust to historic properties in recognition of the educational facilities they offer school parties. The awards are a measure of how well adapted a house or garden is to ensuring that visitors get maximum educational value. An award is based on properties meeting five educational criteria:

1. Good liaison between the owners and potential school visitors.
2. Imagination applied to developing the educational potential.
3. The design of educational materials and facilities.
4. Encouraging preparation for a visit, managing that visit effectively and offering good follow-up.
5. The use of interpretative facilities to relate the visit to a school curriculum, and to encourage exciting and imaginative work.

The Heritage Education Trust is principally concerned with historic buildings. It follows that a property can get an award even though it does not use its garden for educational purposes. In practice that happens rarely: educational facilities are usually offered both inside and outside the house.

Two or three properties with gardens receive a Sandford Award every year. Current holders, with the year of their award, include: Blenheim Palace, Oxfordshire (1997); Boughton House, Northamptonshire (1998); Buckland Abbey, Devon (1996); Chirk Castle, Clwyd (1994); Crathes Castles, Grampian (1997); Croxteth Hall and Country Park, Merseyside (1994); Culzean Castle, Strathclyde (1994); Dunham Massey, Cheshire (1994); Erdigg Hall, Clwyd (1996); Florence Court, Co. Fermanagh (1995); Glamis Castle (1997); Harewood House, West Yorkshire (1994); Holdenby House, Northamptonshire (1995); Moseley Old Hall, Staffordshire (1994); Norton Priory, Cheshire (1997); Shugborough Hall, Staffordshire (1997); Sir Harold Hillier Gardens, Hampshire (1998); Tatton Park, Cheshire (1996); Wightwick Manor, West Midlands (1996).

The places which have given thought to the educational needs of visiting children are just as interesting for grown-ups. It saves a great amount of disappointment if everyone can be sure that the place will be well equipped. The presence of a Sandford Award is a guarantee that all manner of educational aids will be available for you to learn more from your visit and thus to enjoy it more fully.

Further details are available from: The Heritage Education Trust, Boughton House, Kettering, Northamptonshire NN14 1BJ. Tel/Fax 01327 877943. Secretary: David Hill.

Holidays for Gardeners

The emergence of comfortable middle-class tourism for garden-lovers has been one of the great growth areas of the last five years. Before then, there was little to choose between luxury tours of five-star gardens by top-of-the-market operators, cheap coach-trips to see the Dutch bulbfields, and camping holidays for plant enthusiasts happy to survive under canvas for a fortnight in pursuit of the perfect photograph of a rare plant. All that has changed. Any keen gardener now has a wealth of opportunities and destinations from which to choose. The enthusiasts' holidays still exist, and so do trips to outlandish places in the utmost comfort. But there is now a host of holidays for people who enjoy plants and enjoy visiting gardens, but do not want to be too bothered by Latin names – people who want some shopping and sight-seeing and like to remember that they are on holiday. Many are arranged through affinity marketing groups based on a newspaper like the *Daily Telegraph* or an organisation like the National Trust.

The following list includes a number of specialised garden and botanical tour operators. In addition to the companies below, some general tour operators will organise holidays which include a significant number of interesting gardens in their itinerary.

ACE Study Tours
Babraham, Cambridge CB2 4AP
☎ 01223 835055

Destinations: South Africa, French Riviera, the Campagna, Italian lakes, Tuscany, Ireland, Norfolk, Northants, Lincolnshire & Yorkshire

A.C.E. stands for Association for Cultural Exchange and is an educational charity, specialising in study tours and courses. The venues, facilities and leaders are all high quality.

Boxwood Tours: Quality Garden Holidays
56 Spring Road, Abingdon, Oxfordshire OX14 1AN
☎ 01235 532791

Destinations: Cornwall and Tresco, North Wales and the Welsh Marches, Andalucia

Boxwood offer visits to private and better-known gardens and good hotels. Distinguished leaders accompany each tour: both partners are themselves Kew-trained.

Brightwater Holidays
Eden Park House, Cupar, Fife KY15 4HS
☎ 01334 657155

Destinations: Argentina, China (Beijing), Durban & Cape Town, Madeira, Crete, Loire Valley, Riviera, Normandy, Andalucia, Rhodope Mountains, Prague, Tuscany, Italian lakes, Ninfa, Sorrento & Ischia, Dutch bulbfields, the Highlands & Islands, the north of Scotland (& the Castle of Mey), Tresco, Ninfa

Brightwater is a fast-expanding company which now runs tours for the National Trust for Scotland, *The Scotsman*, *The Guardian*, *The Observer*, and *The Daily Telegraph*, among others. Some are based round specific flower shows: Chelsea, Hampton Court, Harrogate (Spring), Southport, Courson & Scotland's new National Gardening Show.

Cox & Kings Travel
Fourth Floor, Gordon House, 10 Greencoat Place, London SW1P 1PH
☎ 0171 873 5000

Destinations: New Zealand, South Africa, Seychelles, Costa Rica, High Atlas, Iceland, Cyprus (north or south), Crete, Lesbos, Corfu, Algarve, Andalucia, Picos de Europa, Spanish Pyrenees, Slovenia, Hungary, Carinthia, Wengen, the Lot

Specialised botany and wild flower tours with top tour leaders, including Mary Briggs. Destinations this year include many of the classic botanical areas of Europe.

David Sayers Travel
10 Barley Mow Passage, London W4 4PH
☎ 0181 995 3642

Destinations: Ecuador, Madagascar, Andalucia, the Lot Valley

HOLIDAYS FOR GARDENERS

Specialist botanical tours, operated by Andrew Brock Travel. Kew-trained horticulturist David Sayers accompanies most of the tours.

ENTERPRISE TRAVEL
P O Box 1, Bradford BD1 2QE
☎ 01756 710507

Destinations: Cornwall, Devon, Wessex, Surrey & Sussex, Kent, Chilterns, Norfolk, Welsh Marches, Cotswolds, Peak District, Lincolnshire, Yorkshire, Northumberland, Snowdonia & the Wicklow Mountains, Wicklow, Guernsey, Fife, Argyll, Rhine cruises, Danube cruises, Bavaria

Although it is now running trips to Europe, Enterprise is particularly strong on short tours in the British Isles, often themed to include a major show like Chelsea, Hampton Court, BBC Gardener's World, Harrogate (Spring & Autumn), Tatton Park or Southport. More information on *www.igarden.co.uk/enterprisetravel/*

FINE ART TRAVEL LTD
15 Savile Row, London W1X 1AE
☎ 0171 437 8553

Destinations: Florence, Lucca, Sicily, Granada

There are no tours specifically for gardeners, but this top-end of the market firm has the *entrée* to many fine gardens. Robin Lane-Fox leads the tour of Sicilian villas & gardens.

GARDENERS' DELIGHT HOLIDAYS
Garden House, 45 Church Road, Saxilby, Lincoln LN1 2HH
☎ 01522 703773

Destinations: Paris, Tayside & Borders, Cornwall, Lincoln, Waltham Abbey

The UK tours tend to be long weekends or Monday to Friday, often with lectures and talks in the evening from well-known gardening personalities. Tours abroad are longer: all go to excellent gardens, public and private.

GREENTOURS NATURAL HISTORY HOLIDAYS
Pines Farm, Biddulph Park, Biddulph, Stoke-on-Trent, Staffordshire
☎ 1260 272837

Destinations: Ceylon, Tien Shan, Georgia, Turkish lakes, Morocco, Crete, Dolomites, Spanish Pyrenees, Andalucia, Alpes Maritimes, Peloponnese

Greentours offer relaxed and friendly natural history holidays with expert guides – Ian Green and Paul Cardy among them.

MOTTS LEISURE LTD
4 Buckingham Street, Aylesbury, Buckinghamshire HP20 2LD
☎ 01296 336666

Destinations: Brittany, Cornwall, Shrewsbury Flower Show

Inexpensive coach tours, including a growing number to visit gardens at home and abroad.

NATURETREK
Chautara, Bighton, Alresford, Hampshire SO24 9RB
☎ 01962 733051

Destinations: South Africa (Cape and Namaqualand), Sikkim, the Tien Shan, Nepal, Crete, Wengen, Slovakia, the Cévennes, Madeira, eastern Portugal, Cyprus, Sorrento peninsular, French Pyrenees, Minorca, western Andalucia

Specialist treks for wildlife enthusiasts with some exciting venues. These trips are primarily for botanists. Treks are graded for difficulty. For the adventurous.

PAGE & MOY
136-140 London Road, Leicester LE2 1EN
☎ 0116 250 7000

Destinations: Normandy, French Riviera, Italian Lakes, Tuscany, Rome & Lazio, Madrid & New Castille, Lisbon, Holland, Ireland

Page & Moy are official tour operators to the National Trust. They offer tours for lovers of art and architecture as well as great gardens. All are accompanied by two leaders.

SAGA HOLIDAYS LTD
The Saga Building, Middelburg Square, Folkestone, Kent CT20 1AZ
☎ 0800 300500

Destinations: South Africa, Mauritius, Portugal, Azores, Madeira, French Riviera, Tenerife, Malta, Galicia, Dolomites, Guernsey, Jersey, Cornwall, North Wales, Cambridge, Ripon

Saga has a special Garden Holidays brochure for the young-at-heart over-50s. It offers a very wide choice of UK destinations, particularly in the West Country, and leisurely tours abroad.

SPECIALTOURS
81a Elizabeth Street, London SW1W 9PG
☎ 0171 730 2297

Destinations: Mauritius, Tuscany, Corsica, Bernese Oberland, Gardens of Cork

Specialtours runs tours for the National Art Collections Fund, mainly to see good architecture, but the trips to Tuscany and Cork are for *Gardens Illustrated*. Specialtours also run many made-to-measure garden tours.

TRAVELSCENE LTD
11-15 St. Ann's Road, Harrow, Middlesex HA1 1AS
☎ 0181 427 8800

Destinations: Dutch bulbfields
Moderately priced short breaks to see the bulbfields.

TROSSACHS GARDEN TOURS
Orchardlea House, Callander, Perthshire FK17 8BG
☎ 01877 330798

Destinations: Harrogate, Argyll & Bute (several), Fife, Biggar (see the Jencks garden), Melrose, Dumfries & Galloway; Harrogate; Callander and the Trossachs

Attractively packaged weekend and midweek visits for small groups to private and public Scottish gardens. They have the *entrée* to many gardens that other operators overlook.

VICTORIA TRAVEL
30 Hewell Road, Barnt Green, Birmingham B45 8NE
☎ 0121 445 5656

Destinations: Mauritius, Chile, Caribbean, South Africa, Zimbabwe, Madeira, Mediterranean, Italian Lakes, the Rhine, Paris, Normandy, Loire Valley, Ireland

Specialists in garden tours around the world, Victoria Travel organises holidays for *BBC Gardeners' World Magazine*. They have an impressive list of tour guides, including Roy Lancaster, Nigel Colborn and Pippa Greenwood. They also run a trip to Madeira for Hilliers Garden Centre.

VOYAGES JULES VERNE
Travel Promotions Ltd., 21 Dorset Square, London NW1 6QG
☎ 0171 616 1000

Destinations: Madeira, Tenerife, Tuscany, Riviera

Most of Voyages Jules Verne's tours are not specifically for garden-lovers, but the trips to these destinations have a distinct horticultural interest.

WILDLIFE TRAVEL
Green Acre, Wood Lane, Oundle, Peterborough PE8 5TP

Destinations: Costa Rica, Nepal, Ethiopia, Central China, Azores, Estonia, St Petersburg & Murmansk, Cyprus, Andalucia, Dolomites, Sardinia, Shetlands, The Burren, Scilly Isles, Sussex

Wildlife Travel is a charity which supports the Wildlife Trusts. They advertise very little, so their prices are very reasonable. They specialise in small groups, from 8 people to 20 (at the most).

Tour companies each have their own place in the market, which varies enormously. Some concentrate on gardens, others on wild flowers. Some are completely devoted to the pursuit of things horticultural or botanical: others make time for private sight-seeing or offer a mixed menu to their customers – stately homes and gardens, for example, or wild flowers and bird-watching. Only by detailed study of the brochures can you know just where an operator makes its market pitch. Things to look for include the method of travel, the size of the group and the level of accommodation you can expect. It is also essential, of course, to check that your holiday or your money is safe if a tour company should run into problems.

Several horticultural societies organise holidays for their members. Pride of place must go to the RHS tours, organised on its behalf by Arena Travel (01394 691201), because they aim to offer some trips which concentrate upon gardens (public and private) and others which visit the classic plant-hunting areas of the world. All incorporate interesting countryside as an essential ingredient, while the accommodation is of a very high standard without being over-the-top. Destinations in 1999 include: the Caribbean in February, 15 days to follow in the footsteps of the *Gardens of the Caribbean* video; Marrakech in March, a five-day trip which combines a visit to leading gardens with a trip into the Atlas mountains; Malaysia, Brunei and Singapore in April, a two-week adventure which includes a visit to the tropical rainforests of the Kimbalu National Park; 12 days in Japan in April to see classic and modern gardens at the peak season for their beauty; northern Italy in April, from Lake Garda and the gardens of Verona to the secret gardens of Venice; Andalucia in May, a week to see the gardens of Seville, Cordoba and, above all, Granada; Giverny and the Journées des Plantes at Courson in May – five days; an eight-day tour of Benelux gardens in June, to include a trip to the rose festival at Château Hex in Belgium; Gardens of New York in June – a mere five days to see the glories of the botanic gardens (New York & Brooklyn); a long trip to see gardens of the Pacific coast in June, 17 days to visit everything from the Huntington Botanic Gardens to the Vancouver (just the names of the stop-over places are enough to make one's mouth water: Pasadena, Santa Barbara, San Francisco, Napa Valley, Portland, Seattle, Victoria, Vancouver); Castles & Gardens of Denmark in July – an eight-day tour; Mexico and Belize in September; South Africa – a fortnight's tour at the best time of the year to take in the Drakensberg, the Garden Route and Port Elizabeth before ending at Kirstenbosch in Cape Town; Chile in November, an adventurous tour of the extraordinarily varied coastline which also dips over the border into Argentina; and a western Mediterranean cruise in October which visits some fascinating gardens in Italy, Spain, Tunisia and Malta.

The RHS Fruit Group is planning a tour of Holland and Belgium from 19 to 23 June to visit Kalmthout Arboretum, Het Loo, Breda and various experimental fruit stations. The Alpine Garden Society will be running tours for people who wish to visit mountains and see the flowers. Their destinations in 1999 include: Japan, Australia, Namaqualand, East Africa, the Tien Shan, the Peloponnese and the Savoy Alps. Further details are available from the AGS Director of Tours: Bryan Wardley, 19 Polstead Road, Oxford, OX2 6TW. Tel: 01865 516000. The Friends of Kew have an exciting list of destinations this year, all arranged through different travel agents who are experts in running holidays to particular parts of the world. 1999's destinations are: the Brazilian Amazon; the Pantanal; the Seychelles; Yunnan; Jordan. Please ring 0181 332 5917 for further details. Members of the International Dendrology Society have access to many otherwise closed gardens through the IDS tours to Portugal (March), Crete (April), Northern Ireland (May), North-east England (May), California (June), September (Madagascar) and a millennium tour to Taiwan.

HOTELS WITH GOOD GARDENS

SOME OF THE HOUSES attached to historic landscapes have become hotels. In several cases the gardens themselves have been well-maintained or even improved by the new owners. Sometimes the gardens remain in good condition but in different ownership: the house is sold separately as a hotel. Many people find the idea of staying in a hotel with a beautiful garden particularly attractive. Here is a selection of hotels with gardens which are good enough to mention in their own right. Their size and services vary considerably, from simple B & B to 5-Star ratings.

THE BEECHES HOTEL & PLANTATION GARDEN
4-6 Earlham Road, Norwich Norfolk NR2 3DB
☎ 01603 621167

Famous Victorian garden in the Italian style (with gothic details), lost within the 3 acres of grounds until uncovered in the 1980s. It is being restored by a registered charity, the Plantation Preservation Trust.

CANNIZARO HOUSE
West Side, Wimbledon Common, London SW19 4UF
☎ 0181 879 14641

An elegant Georgian house right on the edge of Cannizaro Park: see Gardens chapter.

CLIVEDEN HOUSE HOTEL
Taplow, Maidenhead, Berkshire SL6 0JF
☎ 01628 668561

One of the greatest gardens in the Thames Valley: see Gardens chapter.

CONGHAM HALL HOTEL
Lynn Road, Grimston, King's Lynn, Norfolk PE32 1AH
☎ 01485 600250

Forty acres of parkland and a good kitchen garden: best for its herb garden, with over 300 varieties, many available for purchase.

FIVE ARROWS HOTEL
High Street, Waddesdon, Buckinghamshire HP18 0JE
☎ 01296 651727

On the edge of the Waddesdon estate, with access not only to the gardens (see Gardens chapter), but also to the Rothschild cellars.

GLIFFAES COUNTRY HOUSE HOTEL
Crickhowell, Powys NP8 1RH
☎ 01874 730371

Twenty-nine acres of grounds; wonderful rhododendrons, maples and conifers dating from the 19th century.

GRAVETYE MANOR
Vowels Lane, East Grinstead, West Sussex RH19 4LJ

This wonderful hotel has a seriously important garden – William Robinson's own. It has been imaginatively restored and replanted by Peter Herbert and is immaculately maintained: see Gardens chapter.

GREYWALLS
Muirfield, Gullane, Lothian EH31 2EG
☎ 01620 842144

Designed by Lutyens, planted by Jekyll: beautifully maintained and restored. Roses everywhere, and innumerable architectural jokes.

HANBURY MANOR HOTEL
Ware, Hertfordshire SG12 0SD
☎ 01921 487722

Extensive parkland and immaculately maintained gardens: the walled garden is *extremely* pretty, but there are a secret garden, rose garden, woodland walk and arboretum too.

HARTWELL HOUSE
Oxford Road, Aylesbury, Buckinghamshire HP17 8NL
☎ 01296 747444

Hartwell's grounds were landscaped by a disciple of Capability Brown in the 1770s, building on an earlier version which included the handsome equestrian statue of Frederick, Prince of Wales (1757). Geoffrey Jellicoe restored and revived the whole garden in the 1980s.

HAWKSTONE PARK HOTEL
Weston-under-Redcastle, Shrewsbury, Shropshire SY4 5UY
☎ 01939 20061

Hawkstone is a historic Grade I park, laid out in the 18th century by Sir Rowland Hill and covering 100 acres of rugged cliffs and exotic follies. Chief among them are the Swiss Bridge and the Grotto but they are tacked together by sinuous paths and precipitous walks. The monkey puzzles and rhododendrons are a Victorian bonus.

HOPE END HOTEL
Ledbury, Hereford & Worcester HR8 1JQ
☎ 01531 633613

Late Georgian landscape garden, laid out by John Loudon for Elizabeth Barrett Browning's father in 1809. Temple, grotto, wooded walks, carp pool and shady seats. Splendid walled garden, all organic.

LAINSTON HOUSE HOTEL & RESTAURANT
Sparsholt, Winchester, Hampshire SO21 2LT
☎ 01962 863588

Sixty-three acres of parkland surround this very handsome William & Mary house with a spectacular lime avenue, but the modern flower gardens by the house are a model of mixed planting: small trees, shrubs, roses and herbaceous plants all mixed.

LE MANOIR AUX QUAT' SAISONS
Church Road, Great Milton, Oxford OX44 7PD
☎ 01844 278881

World famous restaurant: 19 rooms. Beautiful flower gardens in the English romantic style and impressive kitchen gardens.

LEEMING HOUSE HOTEL
Watermillock, Ullswater, Penrith, Cumbria CA11 0JJ
☎ 017684 86622

Leeming House has 20 splendid acres of Victorian park and garden above the lake: there are mature conifers and magnificent billowing clumps of rhododendrons.

LITTLE THAKENHAM HOTEL
Merrywood Lane, Storrington, West Sussex RH20 3HE
☎ 01903 744416

Lutyens house, with a period garden; paved walks and courtyards, a rose pergola and magnificent flowering trees and shrubs.

LONG CROSS HOTEL
Trelights, Port Isaac, Cornwall PL29 3TF
☎ 01208 880243

Dramatic gardens, substantially remade in the late Victorian style, with many tender plants. Being so close to the sea, the plants were chosen for their resistance to sea spray – Monterey pine and glossy evergreens in particular.

MEUDON HOTEL
Mawnan Smith, Falmouth, Cornwall TR11 5HT
☎ 01326 250541

Eight acres of lushly planted valley running down to its own private beach on the Helford estuary: tree ferns, bananas, cordylines, drimys, camellias and vast clumps of *Gunnera*. Members of the German rose society who stayed there on their 1995 tour and said it was the best garden in Cornwall!

MIDDLETHORPE HALL
Bishopthorpe Road, York, North Yorkshire YO2 1QB
☎ 01904 641241

Handsome modern gardens (and a small arboretum) in the formal style, to complement the William & Mary house: splendid old cedar of Lebanon on the lawn.

RHINEFIELD HOUSE HOTEL
Rhinefield, Brockenhurst, Hampshire S042 7QB
☎ 01590 622922

Grand Italian garden (actually late Victorian), well restored recently: magnificent conifers.

RIBER HALL HOTEL
Matlock, Derbyshire DE4 5JU
☎ 01629 582795

Very pretty rock garden, herbaceous borders and mixed plantings near the hotel; splendid bluebell walks in the woods.

SOUTH LODGE HOTEL
Lower Beeding, Horsham, West Sussex RH13 6PS
☎ 01403 891711

HOLIDAYS FOR GARDENERS 265

Ninety acres of grounds surround this wisteria-clad mansion, including a fine collection of mature rhododendrons, conifers, ponds and a rock garden.

STON EASTON PARK
Ston Easton, Somerset BA3 4DF
☎ 01761 241631

Humphry Repton landscape, carefully restored by the hotel owners: see Gardens chapter.

SUMMER LODGE HOTEL
Evershot, Dorchester, Dorset DT2 0JR
☎ 01935 83424

Thomas Hardy, as a young architectural draughtsman, designed the drawing-room. Penny Hobhouse has been replanting the luscious mixed borders.

THE LYGON ARMS
Broadway, Hereford & Worcester WR12 7DU
☎ 01386 852255

Beautiful walled garden of roses and fruit trees: magnificent summer bedding.

THORNBURY CASTLE HOTEL
Thornbury, Bristol, Avon BS12 1HH
☎ 01454 281182

High Victorian formal garden within the castellated enceinte.

TYLNEY HALL HOTEL
Rotherwick, Hook, Hampshire RG27 9AZ
☎ 01256 764881

67 acres of late Victorian exotica: avenues of wellingtonias, Italian garden, lakes and massive rhododendrons. Gertrude Jekyll designed the rock garden.

WILLAPARK MANOR HOTEL
Bossiney, Tintagel, Cornwall PL34 0BA
☎ 01840 770782

Fourteen acres on a magnificent headland. The owner is a keen gardener: he inherited good rhododendrons and spring flowers, and is extending the display.

YNYSHIR HALL
Eglwysfach, Machynlleth, Powys SY20 8TA
☎ 01654 781209

The drive runs past giant wellingtonias: 14 acres of Victorian woodland gardens with splendid old rhododendrons and azaleas.

In addition, we recommend the following hotels which are listed in the Gardens chapter: Ardnamona, Co Donegal; Loch Melfort Hotel, Arduaine, Strathclyde; Gidleigh Park, Devon; Kildrummy Castle, Grampian; Owlpen Manor, Gloucestershire; West Park Lodge, Beale Arboretum, Herts. If a garden is not separately listed in the Gardens section of *The Gardener's Handbook*, you should first ask whether it is ever open to non-patrons. The owners' attitudes to visitors who are not guests of the hotel differ greatly. Cliveden and Waddesdon are examples of hotels whose associated gardens may freely be visited most of the year. But some owners are concerned to emphasise that their gardens are never open to the public, but reserved entirely for the pleasure of visitors to the hotel or restaurant: at Graveyte Manor and Gidleigh Park, for example, the delights of the garden may only be known to guests of the business.

OTHER ACCOMMODATION

SEVERAL ORGANISATIONS offer Bed & Breakfast accommodation to keen gardeners. The Hardy Plant Society publishes a list of about 120 members who have a B & B business: this list is however only available to members of the HPS, who should please send a SAE for a copy to Mrs Pam Adams, Little Orchard, Great Comberton, Pershore, Hereford & Worcester, WR10 3DP. Among the owners of important gardens who are listed by the Hardy Plant Society are: Jane Sterndale-Bennett of White Windows, Hampshire and Alan Bloom of Bressingham Hall, Norfolk. The list also includes several members in Europe and overseas. We also strongly recommend a pamphlet called *Bed and Breakfast for Garden Lovers*: please send a SAE to Mrs S. Colquhoun, Handywater Farm, Sibford Gower, Banbury, Oxfordshire OX15 5AE which lists garden owners all over the country who do B & B. The guide also identifies those which are mentioned in the Yellow Book or *The Good Gardens Guide*, so that would-be visitors can do their holiday homework before deciding where to stay. Wolsey Lodges, 17 Chapel Street, Bildeston, Suffolk, IP9 7EP Tel 01449 741297 is a marketing organisation for up-market B & B in private houses throughout Britain. Several of the properties listed in the Gardens section of *The Gardener's Handbook* appear in the pages of *The Wolsey Lodges Guide*, including Docton Mill in Devon. We also recommend the Irish equivalent, an excellent booklet called *The Hidden Ireland* which is available for £3 from Bord Fáilte (The Irish Tourist Board) and from the Northern Irish Tourist Board, as well as from The Secretary, The Hidden Ireland, P O Box 5451, Dublin 2 (Telephone 00 353 1 6627166. Website: *www.indigo.ie/hiddenireland/*). The 40 or so houses, manors, lodges and demesnes tend to be grander than their British equivalents, and there is a sprinkling of English and Irish titles among the owners. Some properties, such as Ardnamona in Co Donegal, have gardens that qualify for an entry in the Gardens chapter of *The Gardener's Handbook*.

Working holidays are becoming increasingly popular, especially the chance to take a break from day to day to a semi-educational course attached to environmental conservation. The National Trust alone offers about 400 week-long and week-end projects every year and has about 3,000 holiday makers. Other organisations offering working holidays include: National Trust Working Holidays (Tel: 01285 644727); the National Trust for Scotland (0131 226 5922); and the British Trust for Conservation Volunteers, Natural Break Department (Tel: 01491 839766). Recent BTCV projects include garden restoration work at Heligan in Cornwall and Stanway in Gloucestershire.

We recommend The National Trust 1999 Holiday Cottage Brochure, available in return for a donation of £2: please telephone 01225 791133. The lets may be cottages on the estate, converted lodges, water towers, estate buildings or stables, or even a flat in part of the house itself. Prices vary from about £142 pw for a modest property in the low season to £1,411 pw for a top one in high season, which is actually a measure of just how good the best ones really are. There are over 1,400 lets available in 1999, including the following properties with good gardens: Cliveden, Buckinghamshire; Cotehele, Cornwall; Glendurgan, Cornwall; Trelissick, Cornwall; Acorn Bank, Cumbria; Castle Drogo, Devon; Coleton Fishacre, Devon; Mottistone Manor, Isle of Wight; Felbrigg Hall, Norfolk; Beningbrough, North Yorkshire; Studley Royal, North Yorkshire; Bodnant, Clwyd; Colby Woodland Garden, Dyfed; Powis Castle, Powys; Florence Court, Co Fermanagh. The National Trust for Scotland offers holiday lets in a number of its properties. It also has up-market apartments on the top floor of Culzean Castle, which it runs as a private hotel. Readers may also like to know that the Gothick orangery at Frampton Court in Gloucestershire has been converted into a holiday self-catering home. It is right at the heart of the famous gardens, at the head of the Dutch Canal, and is available for short or long lets. Write for a copy of the illustrated brochure (see Gardens chapter).

WHEN YOU GO AWAY

WHETHER YOU'RE soaking up sun and sangria in Spain during the winter months or just cruising the Norfolk Broads for a long weekend, how will the garden manage without you? The answer depends on how well it manages when you are there. Work out how much time you spend tending your plot each week and you'll have a pretty good idea what sort of arrangements, if any, will be needed in your absence. After all, if a grudging hour or so at the weekend is par for the course, then it probably won't even notice you're not there. If, on the other hand, hour upon hour, week in, week out, go to grooming the garden to perfection, then either you'll need someone else to keep up the standard till you return, or else you should think about going away at a quieter season horticulturally.

Should you fall somewhere in between, then there is a choice of steps you can take to keep the upper hand. So, given that most people go away in summer, the main problem is protecting your plants from English heat and drought. It helps if you can remove pots and hanging baskets to a place of shade and shelter while you are away. Plants in pots fare even better if you plunge them in the ground and water the earth around them well.

Consider introducing any or all of the following: mulches on the borders, and especially around newly planted trees and shrubs, to reduce the amount of water lost through evaporation; shade netting; capillary matting or plunge beds for pots, inside and out; a time-controlled watering system. This last need not be as expensive as it sounds. Use seepage hoses and/or an electronic clock which switches on after dusk when watering is most effective. And remember that no system is suitable for long periods.

After water, the main problem is growth. Puritanical journalists will advise you to cut the heads of flowers which have not yet faded, or perhaps not even opened, before you leave. Necessary or not, the grass won't cut itself and produce will not pick itself, so you'll have to get a friend or neighbour to fight this battle by proxy. Don't expect them to spare as much time as you would: their little will make all the difference.

For bigger gardens and more intensive cultivation, you will probably need to rely on expert help.

HOLIDAYS FOR GARDENERS   267

Greenhouse gardening is a high-risk activity. Precious specimens are best entrusted to the safe custody of an experienced gardening friend to look after in his or her own greenhouse. If this is impossible, you must find a knowledgeable person to water and ventilate your greenhouse as frequently as you do yourself. Remember that the usual fault of inexperienced caretakers is to overwater everything. Leave long and detailed instructions in writing, run through them point by point, and give a practical demonstration of your requirements. If you don't have a gardener already, consider arranging for contract gardeners to fill in for you. You will have to set out their duties precisely, and expect to pay from £10 an hour for their time. Alternatively, you can ask one of the specialist agencies to find you a residential houseminder.

Houseminders carry out the basic domestic and garden duties that you would normally perform yourself. These usually involve caring for pets, answering the telephone, and providing the security of a presence in the house, as well as watering the tomatoes and mowing the lawn. Large gardens or greenhouses which demand hours of commitment may require a higher fee. Most agencies are happy to make special arrangements to accommodate your particular needs. The terms they offer differ enormously, not so much in price, but more in the smaller details. Agencies include:

ANIMAL AUNTS
Smugglers Cottage, Rogate, Petersfield, Hampshire GU31 5DA
☎ 01730 821529   **Fax** 01730 821057

Founded in 1987. Mainly for people with pets and other animals, particularly those with special requirements.

COUNTRY COUSINS
10a Market Square, Horsham, West Sussex RH12 1EX
☎ 01403 210415   **Fax** 01403 217827

Founded more than 30 years ago, they specialise in the care of the elderly, but individual carers may be willing to undertake some light garden duties while you are away.

HOLIDAY HOMEWATCH
Nursery Cottage, Penybont, Llandrindrod Wells, Powys LD1 5SP
☎ 01597 851840

Founded in 1988. Supply supervisors who specialise in assignments where there are horses and farm livestock as well as domestic pets to look after.

HOME & PET CARE
Greenrigg Farm, Caldbeck, Wigton, Cumbria CA7 8AH
☎ 01697 478515

Founded in 1988. Primarily a House Sitting company, and particularly for people with pets, but they are also quite happy to maintain gardens.

HOMESITTERS LTD
Buckland Wharf, Buckland, Aylesbury, Buckinghamshire HP22 5LQ
☎ 01296 630730

Founded in 1980. Perhaps the largest agency, Homesitters are particularly conscious of the problems of garden owners who wish to go on holiday. 'When you take a spring break, they will nurture the seedlings and ventilate the greenhouse; while you relax on your summer holiday, they will mow the lawn regularly and water the hanging baskets'.

HOUSEWATCH LTD
Little London, Berden, Bishops Stortford, Hertfordshire CM23 1BE
☎ 01279 777412   **Fax** 01279 777049

Housewatchers will care for your animals and undertake basic domestic and garden duties.

Importing & Exporting Plants

Thanks to the EU's single market, plants can now in general be moved freely between all the countries of the European Union. This is very good news for British gardeners. To see why, browse through the section of European nurseries in this book. There are some exceptionally good lists there, opening up access to many cultivars that are unavailable in the UK. We think many gardeners will find this prospect exciting. For this reason, this chapter concentrates on private individuals who want to bring plants into the UK, although we also touch on the more complicated situation for exporters and the wholesale trade.

Some controls remain, and it is necessary to understand how these work in order to take full advantage of what has been a significant relaxation in import controls. There are three overlapping systems of control.

- The first distinguishes between the status of the importer. Individuals bringing plants in for their own use face the least restriction. Plants which are imported ready for immediate retail sale are more tightly controlled, but have a number of exemptions from the stricter régime which is applied to plants passing between wholesalers.
- There are distinctions based on origin. A generally permissive régime applies within the EU, with the exception of particular protected zones (usually designated to protect disease-free areas). For the rest of the world, more restrictions exist, although these are relaxed sometimes for other European and Mediterranean countries. Where diseases are localised, especially for economic species, very complex and specific regulations can apply.
- Species which are considered to be endangered are subject to CITES – the Convention on International Trade in Endangered Species of wild fauna and flora. Permits are required to move species covered by CITES. Wild plants may also be covered by national protection legislation.

Private Individuals: Moving Plants Within the EU

As a general rule, there are no restrictions on private individuals buying plants for their personal use anywhere in the EU. That is a direct result of the coming of the Single Market: Europe is one country now. Plants must be carried in your personal baggage (e.g. in your car) and be for your own household use. They must also be free from signs of pests or diseases.

People who live in protected zones will have to comply with the higher plant health standards which exist there. Protected zones are exceptions to the free movement policy which have been negotiated by individual member states. They are areas (usually countries) which are substantially free from a particular harmful pest or disease and where, as a result, a higher level of plant health control is required to keep them free. It is not possible, for example, to import poinsettia cuttings from elsewhere in the EU because the UK is a protected zone for *Euphorbia pulcherrima*: this was imposed to protect British crops from infection with a pest called *Bemisia tabaci*. If in doubt contact MAFF. The main application of protected zones to the UK are to seed potatoes, conifers and potential carriers of fireblight.

Private Individuals: The Rest of the World

Contrary to widespread belief, individuals are free to bring back small quantities of plants and propagating material from anywhere in the world. Again, they must be for personal use, be carried in your baggage and be free from pests and diseases. 'Small quantities' means:

- up to 2kg of fruit and raw vegetables (no potatoes);
- one bouquet of cut flowers or parts of plants;
- five packets of retail seed (not potatoes)

These can be imported from any part of the world.

In addition, two categories may be imported from 'non-EU countries of the Euro-Mediterranean area':
- 2kg of bulbs, corms tubers and/or rhizomes;
- five plants.

This applies to all European countries, plus Algeria, Cyprus, Egypt, Israel, Jordan, Lebanon, Libya, Malta, Morocco, Tunisia and Turkey.

These allowances extend to children as well as to adults. The regulations make no distinction between wild-collected and cultivated plants, but see the note on CITES and conservation below. Nor is there any restriction on the import of flower seeds from any part of the world: the 'five packets' rule therefore applies only to non-flower seeds.

Similar rules apply in the rest of the EU and in Northern Ireland (they derive from the same EU directive), but it is always worth checking first before taking plants from the UK to other parts of the EU in case protective zones apply.

Further advice on personal allowances is available from the Plant Health Division, MAFF, Room 340, Foss House, 1–2 Peasholme Green, Kings Pool, York YO1 2PX. MAFF also publishes a leaflet entitled *Travellers! Plants brought back to Britain from abroad could carry serious pests and diseases* which is available free on request: contact 0645 556000.

CITES

CITES regulates the trade in wild plants which are listed in its schedules. The agreement was originally signed by 21 countries in 1975: now it has over 140 signatories, including the UK. 'Trade' is not limited to commerce: any movement of specimens across international frontiers constitutes trade for CITES purposes. Failure to comply with the rules is a criminal offence. CITES is administered in the UK by the Department of the Environment, Wildlife Licensing Branch, Tollgate House, Houlton Street, Bristol BS2 9DJ (0117 9878168).

The list of species is regularly revised and amounts to more than 20,000 plant taxa. CITES forbids the import or export of those species which are listed as endangered (Appendix I) and restricts trade in those which are at risk of becoming endangered (Appendix II). The principal genera protected by CITES are *Aloe, Cyclamen, Galanthus, Nepenthes, Sternbergia* and all orchids, cycads and cacti, but it is essential that anyone wishing to buy, sell or collect plants should know what is protected and what is not. That said, you can assume that any plant offered by a reputable nurseryman may legitimately be bought.

As far as most international conservation controls are concerned, there is no distinction between wild and cultivated plants. Many species have been endangered by careless or unscrupulous collectors in the past, and we suggest that plant-collecting is best left to the experts. If you do collect, the guiding principles are: do not touch anything unless (i) you are sure it is not protected and (ii) you have the permission of the owner. Moreover, you should never endanger the plant community from which you collect, nor take material which you will not be able to grow or use. To avoid introducing pests and diseases from foreign countries, remember that seed is generally the best way of bringing back plants because it can be cleaned, although some viruses are seed-borne. The recent infestation of gypsy moths in South Norwood is thought to have entered the country as eggs laid on the underside of a vehicle. But there is no danger of introducing gypsy moths or Colorado beetles with a packet of seeds.

FURTHER READING

The basis of all the rules about importing and exporting plants is *The Plant Health (Great Britain) Order 1993* (SI 1993 No. 1320) and its amending instruments. CITES has an extremely helpful website (*www.wcmc.org.uk/CITES/*).

European Nurseries

Austria

Alpengarten Zenz
Rosenhain 5, A–8071 Grambach b. Graz
☎ 00 43 316 401239
Specialities Alpines
Catalogue Yes
Mail order Yes

This excellent traditional alpine nursery is a good source of unusual species and forms. Their stock is not confined to alpine plants: we noticed *Rosa watsoniana* and *Decaisnea fargesii* among the shrubs which they offer. They also issue an annual seed list: many of the items are collected in the wild.

Baumschule Franz Praskac
Praskacstr. 101–108, Postfach 242, A–3430 Tulln
☎ 00 43 2272 62460   **Fax** 00 43 2272 63816
English-speaking contact Wolfgang Praskac
Specialities Herbaceous perennials; shrubs; trees
Catalogue ÖS 50
Mail order Yes

The most famous Austrian nursery, with an excellent general range and high-quality plants. They also have a garden centre in Vienna. They grow all types of perennials, shrubs and trees, including conifers and fruit. Their highly illustrated catalogue is invaluable to anyone who needs to know what will survive the bitter winters of central Europe and thrive.

Fuchsien Kulturen Lakonig
Niederdorf 37, A–9591 Treffen
☎ 00 43 4248 3685   **Fax** 00 43 4248 3688
English-speaking contact Harald or Caroline Lakonig
Specialities Fuchsias
Catalogue ÖS 30
Mail order Yes

The range at this fuchsia nursery extends to some 1,000 cultivars with 200 new introductions last year. A nursery to watch.

Sarastro
Christian Kress, A–4974 Ort im Innkreis
☎ 00 43 7751 424   **Fax** 00 43 7751 424
English-speaking contact Christian or Fritzi Kress
Specialities Alpines; herbaceous perennials
Catalogue One international reply coupon
Mail order Yes

Young nursery being built up by enthusiastic plantsman to specialise in species perennials and forms. Christian Kress also writes and lectures on perennials.

Silvia Tunkl
Hauptplatz 8A, A–2242 Prottes
☎ 00 43 2282 3958   **Fax** 00 43 2282 5178
English-speaking contact Frau Silvia Tunkl
Specialities Mediterranean plants; seeds; citrus; tropical fruit
Catalogue ÖS 20
Mail order Yes

Tropical, subtropical and Mediterranean plants and seeds. There are *Passiflora*, *Citrus* in both small and specimen sizes up to 2m., including such varieties as *Citrus medica* and 'Lipo', and *Ficus* 'White Adriatic' and 'San Pedro'. Some plants which require protection in Austria would probably be hardy in milder parts of Britain.

Stauden Feldweber
im Innkreis 139, A–4974 Ort
☎ 00 43 7751 8320   **Fax** 00 43 7751 7223
English-speaking contact Mrs Suzanne Platz
Specialities Alpines; herbaceous perennials
Catalogue ÖS 70 for main catalogue and collectors' list

Founded in 1896, this nursery lists a wide range of alpines and perennials in two catalogues, published in January, one their general list and the other for plantsmen. They are particularly good for peonies, irises, hostas and grasses, of which they stock large numbers. There are also some interesting *Primula* hybrids and cultivars, e.g. *P.* × *seriana* 'Oberschlesien'. Coming from Austria, everything is extremely hardy, and the list contains a good number of cultivars not grown in the UK. Recommended.

Wirth Dahlien
Leschetitzkygasse 11, A–1100 Wien
☎ 00 43 222 479 5383
Fax 00 43 222 479 1083
Specialities Dahlias
Catalogue Free
Mail order Yes

Every serious dahlia-grower should know this important nursery, founded in 1929. Dr Wirth is the leading breeder of new dahlias in Austria, and a useful source of interesting new material, both for showing and for garden use. He lists over 200 cultivars, and indicates which have won prizes at the international trials in several countries.

BELGIUM

ARBORETUM WAASLAND
Kriekelaarstraat 29, B–9100 Nieuwkerken-Waas
☎ 00 32 3 775 93 09   Fax 00 32 3 755 36 50
English-speaking contact Michel Decalut
Specialities Shrubs; trees
Catalogue BF 300
Mail order Yes

The best tree and shrub nursery in Belgium, perhaps in all Europe. The sheer number of forms and varieties they offer is amazing – some 10,000 taxa, and chosen for their hardiness down to –20°C. Obviously it includes hundreds which have never been grown in the UK, let alone offered for sale. The rarer ones are propagated to order, so you may have to wait a while for delivery. The catalogue is essential reading for any serious dendrophile, National Collection holder, or seeker after novelty. Among recent introductions are *Fagus sylvatica* 'Montefiore' and *Quercus cerris* 'Waasland'.

BOOMKWEKERIJ DE LINDE
Nieuwstraat 70, B–8956 Kemmel
☎ 00 32 57 44 63 49   Fax 00 32 57 44 82 94
English-speaking contact Bart Dequidt
Specialities Fruit
Catalogue BF 50

This nursery has a good list of tree fruit and soft fruit, and a particularly interesting selection of apples. Many are indigenous varieties of Flanders and the Pas de Calais, obtained from the Belgian *Ressources Génétiques Fruitières* and the French *Espace Naturel Régional*: they should do well in southern England. Collection only.

FUCHSIAS MICHIELS-DE SMEDT
Kruisstraat 51, B–2500 Lier-Koningshooikt
☎ 00 32 3 482 25 62   Fax 00 32 3 482 02 14
English-speaking contact Yes
Specialities Fuchsias
Catalogue BF 140

The best *Fuchsia* nursery we know, with 2,000 cultivars for sale out of a total grown at the nursery of over 3,500 cultivars. Not only do they seek to be comprehensive, and grow every new variety, but they actively seek out old hybrids to propagate and preserve. Every year the new additions total some 200 items. There is no mail order, but it is worth a special journey to Antwerp to collect. Open daily, except Sunday afternoons and public holidays. Strongly recommended.

KAWANA
Wijnegembaan, B–2520 Ranst
☎ 00 32 3 3540270   Fax 00 32 3 3530158

English-speaking contact Koen Engelen
Specialities Iris
Catalogue Free

Iris mega-nursery, with an amazing list of all the main groups: hundreds tall bearded, c.80 remontant, over 100 dwarf bearded, hundreds of Japanese irises *Iris ensata* and so on. Essential reading for anyone interested in irises, and a fascinating read for any keen plantsman. They also list about 120 Japanese peonies.

LENS ROSES
Redinnestraat 11, B–8460 Oudenburg
☎ 00 32 59 267 830   Fax 00 32 59 265 614
English-speaking contact Yes
Specialities Roses
Catalogue BF 50
Mail order Yes

Probably the best-known rose-breeders in Belgium, Lens have also been responsible for reviving interest in the old and shrub roses. Their list is impressive, and essential reading for all keen rosarians. Its 700 cultivars include many that are not known in Britain. Among the most exciting are the wonderful series of modern hybrid musks which they have bred over the last 15 years, updating the work of Rev. Pemberton 80 years ago.

DENMARK

ARNE KR. JORGENSEN
Kirkebjergvej 22, Roerslev, DK–5466 Asperup
☎ 00 45 6448 1073
English-speaking contact Arne Kr Jorgensen
Specialities Alpines; herbaceous perennials
Catalogue Free
Mail order Yes

Alpine and perennial nursery. The closely printed catalogue lists 1,800 species but up to 4,500 are available from the nursery in small quantities.

ASSENS PLANTESKOLE
Fåborgvej 10, DK–5610 Assens
☎ 00 45 64 71 16 99   Fax 00 45 7 06 46 59
English-speaking contact Ole Madsen
Specialities Alpines; bog plants; fruit; herbaceous perennials; roses; shrubs; trees
Catalogue Yes, five separate catalogues
Mail order Yes

A first-rate all-round nursery, particularly strong on roses, fruit trees (200 apples), irises and shrubs. Here are a few of the hundreds of cultivars which are not available in the UK: *Rosa* 'Thor', 'Wilhelm Hansman' and 'Président Dutailley'; *Anemone nemorosa* 'Italica', *Armeria maritima* 'Arvi' and *Aster alpinus* 'Blue Star'; *Maddenia hypoleuca*, *Malus ioensis* 'Fimbriata', and *Menziesia pilosa*. This nursery is strongly recommended.

HORNING FUCHSIARI: V/H. OG B. HOJER
Alléen 2, DK–8362 Horning
☎ 00 45 869222230

English-speaking contact Troels Have Kristensen
(☎ 00 45 40568664, 6 – 8 pm)
Specialities Fuchsias
Catalogue Dkr. 20
Mail order Yes

Fuchsia specialist with a range of over 1,000 cultivars. There are new introductions every year.

LYNGE STAUDEGARTNERI
Lynge Mellevej 4, DK–3540 Lynge
☎ 00 45 4218 7248 **Fax** 00 45 4218 8126

English-speaking contact Grethe Petersen
Specialities Herbaceous perennials
Catalogue Dkr. 25
Mail order Yes

Perennial nursery with a range of 1,800 different kinds. Collection preferred, but mail order is possible.

RHODODENDRON-HAVEN PLANTESKOLE
Viborg Hovedvej 114, Hammer, DK–7160 Torring
☎ 00 45 7580 0555 **Fax** 00 45 7580 0333

English-speaking contact Claus Jorgensen
Specialities Rhododendrons
Catalogue Dkr. 50
Mail order Yes

A first-rate rhododendron nursery with one of the best collections of species in Europe (second only to Muncaster Plants) and a good list of rhododendron and azalea hybrids, many of them unknown and ungrown in the UK. The highly informative catalogue is in Danish only, but beautifully illustrated.

ROSENPLANTESKOLEN I LOVE
Plantevej 3, Love, DK–4270 Hong
☎ 00 45 53569313 **Fax** 00 45 53569019

English-speaking contact All staff
Specialities Roses
Catalogue Dkr. 120
Mail order Yes

The most important plants at this nursery (previously Petersen) are the vast collection of roses. There is a long list of all types, with a bias towards older and rare kinds. Species roses are especially good – several forms are listed according to provenance in some cases. Rosarians should study it carefully: the list is longer than any rose nursery's in the UK and there is an impressive number of cultivars unavailable from other sources.

SONDERBORG PLANTESKOLE
Spang, DK–6400 Sonderborg
☎ 00 45 74425080

English-speaking contact Jorgen Thagaard Jensen
Specialities Rhododendrons; shrubs; trees
Catalogue Dkr. 52

Mail order Yes

A good nursery, especially for trees and shrubs, including conifers – some of them quite unusual. The main speciality, however, is ericaceous plants: the excellent long list of hardy Rhododendron and azalea varieties contains many German and Danish hybrids not available in Britain.

FRANCE

ARBORETUM NATIONAL DES BARRES
F–45290 Nogent-sur-Vernisson
☎ 00 33 2 38 95 02 74 **Fax** 00 33 2 38 95 02 78

English-speaking contact Jean-Christophe Reuter or Thierry Lamant
Specialities Shrubs; trees
Catalogue FF 10

The nurseries attached to the National Arboretum divide their catalogue into two parts: plants grown from seed, grafts or cuttings taken at the arboretum (or other botanical collection), and those grown from seed collected in the wild. Provenance is listed in the latter section. Both parts contain much to interest the dendrologist, including *Syringa × henryi*, *Fagus sylvatica* 'Faux de Versy', and *Alnus trabeculosa*. Collection only; orders must be placed at least eight days ahead.

BAMBOUS DE PLANBUISSON
Rue Montaigne, F–24480 Le Buisson
☎ & **Fax** 00 33 5 53 22 01 03

English-speaking contact Michel Bonfils
Specialities Bamboos; grasses
Catalogue FF 25
Mail order Yes

Youngish nursery stocking bamboos and grasses. The first-class collection consists of about 150 varieties of each: more are added every year. They have an enthusiastic approach to their speciality which they like to convey to customers.

BERNARD BOUREAU
28 bis, rue du Maréchal Galliéni B.P. 8, F–77169 Grisy-Suisnes
☎ 00 33 1 64 05 91 83 **Fax** 00 33 1 64 05 97 66

Specialities Roses
Catalogue Yes
Mail order Yes

Alas, this famous old rose nursery is closing down. Some stock remains: ring to see what is available.

BONSAÏ RÉMY SAMSON
25, rue de Chateaubriand, F–92290 Châtenay-Malabry
☎ 00 33 1 47 02 91 99 **Fax** 00 33 1 47 02 61 75

English-speaking contact Mr or Mrs Samson

Specialities Bonsai
Mail order Yes

Bonsai for indoors, outdoors and conservatories as well as accessories, pots and books. There is a second shop at 10 Rue de la Comète, 75007, Paris.

CACTUS ESTEREL

Chemin de Maupas, F–83600 Bagnols en Fôret
☎ 00 33 4 94 40 66 73 **Fax** 00 33 4 94 40 69 11
English-speaking contact Vincent Cerutti
Specialities Cacti and succulents
Catalogue FF 25 or five international reply coupons
Mail order Yes

Remarkably comprehensive list of cacti and succulents with a large proportion of unusual species and varieties.

CAYEUX SA

La Carcaudière, F–45500 Poilly-Lèz-Gien
☎ 00 33 2 38 67 05 08 **Fax** 00 33 2 38 67 84 98
English-speaking contact Mr Richard Cayeux
Specialities *Iris; Hemerocallis*
Catalogue FF 14
Mail order Mail order only

This distinguished old nursery was founded in 1892 and now specialises in the highly popular *Iris* and *Hemerocallis*. Their iris fields are a breathtaking sight towards the end of May: they grow and test many more than the 350 bearded cultivars offered in their excellent catalogue. Sibiricas, japonicas and water-irises are other specialities. Recommended.

DELBARD

16, quai de la Mégisserie, F–75054 Paris Cedex 01
☎ 00 33 1 44 88 80 10 **Fax** 00 33 1 40 26 36 25
English-speaking contact Christian Ledeux
Specialities Fruit; roses
Catalogue Free
Mail order Yes, France and EU countries

To many people Delbard means roses, and rightly so, but they are equally accomplished breeders of fruit trees. They introduce a new cultivar most years: last year it was an apple called 'Tentation' ('une pomme secrète, un peu timide mais qui contient tous les plaisirs'), which follows on 'Delbard Jubilé' and 'Papi Delbard'. Their new roses include a line of striped HTs named after artists ('Camille Pissarro', 'Claude Monet' etc.), scented roses ('Dioressence', 'Crêpe de Chine' etc.), shrub roses, climbers and many others. Few, if any, are known and grown in Britain: we cannot think why.

DINO PELLIZZARO

290, chemin de Léouse, F–06220 Vallauris
☎ 00 33 4 93 64 18 43 **Fax** 00 33 4 93 64 40 14
English-speaking contact Dino Pellizzaro
Specialities Mediterranean plants
Catalogue FF 20 in stamps or notes
Mail order No

Dino Pellizzaro does not offer mail order, but his remarkable list merits a special journey. His nursery is a legend among Mediterranean garden-owners.

E.A.R.L. DES CAILLOUX VIVANTS

F–46360 Saint-Cernin
☎ 00 33 5 65 31 31 51 **Fax** 00 33 5 65 31 32 66
English-speaking contact Jean-Luc Marcénac
Specialities Fuchsias; shrubs
Catalogue FF 15
Mail order Yes

Fuchsias for collectors: there are about 500 cultivars in this catalogue, stylishly printed on hand-made paper. The list of species is particularly impressive. Recommended.

E.A.R.L. RIBANJOU

Zone Horticole du Rocher, Briollay, F–49125 Tiercé
☎ 00 33 2 41 42 65 19 **Fax** 00 33 2 41 42 66 45
Specialities Soft fruit
Mail order Yes

Soft fruit. The nursery has many cultivars of that are not known in England. One example is a raspberry called 'Bois Blanc' from the Savoy, said to have superb flavour, if disease-prone. They also stock many unusual minor fruits, including forms of elderberry, *Aronia* and *Amelanchier* selected for their fruit. Good blueberries and blackberries.

ÉTS. HORT. HODNIK

Le Bourg, F–45700 St Maurice s/Fessard
☎ 00 33 2 38 97 84 59 **Fax** 00 33 2 38 97 89 39
Specialities Conservatory plants; Mediterranean plants
Catalogue FF 30
Mail order Yes

Mediterranean, half-hardy and conservatory plants. There is a wide choice, but they have two impressive specialities. One is species and hybrid *Begonia*, of which they list about 100. The other is *Hibiscus rosa-sinensis* cultivars, which they have introduced to cultivation in France in large numbers: they now list over 100 cultivars.

ÉTS. KUENTZ: LE MONDE DES CACTUS

327, rue du Général-Brosset, F–83600 Fréjus
☎ 00 33 4 94 51 48 66 **Fax** 00 33 4 94 95 49 31
Specialities Cacti and succulents
Catalogue FF 30
Mail order Yes

One of the best nurseries for cacti and succulents in Europe. The range is impressive: 39 haworthias, 55 euphorbias, 20 agaves, 29 aloes, and nearly 80 opuntias as well as hundreds of lesser genera. Large specimens, at least ten years old, are also available for the impatient, though here the range is smaller.

GAEC DE CHAMPAGNE M. BOURDILLON

B P 2, F–41230 Soings-en-Sologne
☎ 00 33 2 54 98 71 06 **Fax** 00 33 2 54 98 76 76

EUROPEAN NURSERIES

Specialities *Iris; Hemerocallis*
Catalogue FF 10
Mail order Yes

Iris and *Hemerocallis* are still not as popular in Britain as they deserve. It is different in France where people visit iris gardens in the same spirit as we flock to Mottisfont. There is a splendid selection of bearded iris and dramatic daylilies to tempt possible converts in this catalogue. And although sales are by mail order at the appropriate time of year, they have a show garden which can be visited. Best around 20 May, they say.

IRIS EN PROVENCE
B P 53, Route de l'Appie
☎ 00 33 4 94 65 98 30 Fax 00 33 4 94 35 24 91

Specialities *Iris; Hemerocallis*
Catalogue FF 14
Mail order Mail order only

Iris and *Hemerocallis* in profusion. They are breeders as well as growers of both. The brilliantly coloured catalogue lists a huge variety of their own and American cultivars with regular new introductions. Besides the tall bearded iris so popular in France, there also hybrids of *Iris spuria*, *I. sibirica* and *I. Louisiana* Hybrids. Mail order only, but the gardens can be visited in late April and May.

JARDIN AQUATIQUE
Chemin de Maupas, F-83600 Bagnols en Fôret
☎ 00 33 4 94 40 62 32 Fax 00 33 4 94 40 69 11

Specialities Aquatic plants
Catalogue FF 25
Mail order Yes

Specialists in water lilies with over 100 from which to choose, including 30 tropical hybrids and eight night-flowering varieties (*Nelumbo*) and aquatics: two new lotuses introduced fairly recently are 'Shirokunshi' and 'Sharon'.

LA BAMBOUSERAIE DE PRAFRANCE
Générargues, F-30140 Anduze
☎ 00 33 4 66 61 70 47 Fax 00 33 4 66 61 64 15

English-speaking contact Martine Bouret
Specialities Bamboos
Catalogue FF 40
Mail order No

The Bambouseraie is the sort of place which needs superlatives. Everything is immensely stylish and done on a large scale: the catalogue (there are English and French editions), the bamboo nursery (the biggest in Europe), the gardens and the bamboos themselves. An impressive selection is available container-grown, ranging from rare varieties for collectors to those suitable for massed planting. If you have a chance to visit the garden (strongly recommended) you can see established plantations and examples of how to use bamboo for everything and anything, from all-bamboo houses to tiny ornaments.

LATOUR MARLIAC SA
F-47110 Temple s/Lot
☎ 00 33 5 53 01 08 05 Fax 00 33 5 53 01 02 30

English-speaking contact Mr Chris Farmer
Specialities Aquatic plants
Catalogue Free
Mail order Yes

Proud of being the oldest water lily nursery in the world, Latour Marliac can boast of supplying Monet at Giverny. The current catalogue lists some 120 hardy varieties, besides tropical kinds, *Nelumbo* and a range of other aquatic plants.

LES ROSES ANCIENNES DE ANDRÉ EVE
Morailles, F-45300 Pithiviers-le-Vieil

Specialities Roses
Catalogue Yes
Mail order Mail order only

André Eve's catalogue lists a tempting selection of old roses plus a few modern varieties and some good climbers bred by him. His selection of old climbers and ramblers is particularly attractive and includes such varieties as 'Alexandre Tremouillet', 'Château de la Juvenie' and 'Primevère'. His own garden can be visited during the rose season.

LUMEN
Les Coutets, F-24100 Creysse Bergerac
☎ 00 33 5 53 57 62 15 Fax 00 33 5 53 58 54 88

English-speaking contact Bernadette Cross or Michel Lumen
Specialities Ferns; grasses; herbaceous perennials
Catalogue FF 20
Mail order Yes

This nursery near Bergerac has an extensive range of garden-worthy perennials, ferns and grasses and lots of *Sempervivum*. Most plants are open-ground but a container selection is always available. Useful for Dordogne dwellers who want an English border or cottage garden.

MARCEL LECOUFLE
5 Rue de Paris, F-94470 Boissy St Léger
☎ 00 33 1 45 95 25 25 Fax 00 33 1 45 98 34 19

English-speaking contact Isabelle Bert
Specialities Orchids
Catalogue FF 24
Mail order Yes

This old-established firm (founded in 1888) is one of the leading orchid breeders and propagators in Europe and a welcome exhibitor at RHS shows last year. They also trade under the name Vacherot & Lecoufle. Popular hybrids are their main line but these include novelties of their own raising and they also have a collection of 2,000 different taxa which may be visited most days of the year.

Meilland Richardier
B P 2, F–69815 Tassin-la-Demi-Lune Cedex
☎ 00 33 4 78 34 46 52 **Fax** 00 33 4 72 38 09 97
Specialities Roses
Mail order Yes

Roses bred by the Meilland dynasty form the bulk of the catalogue: an interesting way of seeing how rose breeding has moved since the war. The newest varieties are very floriferous, and open flat to give an abundance of colour. Three modern climbers are among them: 'César', 'Tchin Tchin' and 'Domaine de Courson'. The catalogue also includes companion plants and sundries.

Nature et Paysages
F–32360 Peyrusse-Massas
☎ 00 33 5 62 65 52 48 **Fax** 00 33 5 62 65 50 44
Specialities Carnivorous plants
Catalogue Ten international reply coupons
Mail order Yes

This name, with its echoes of Rousseau, belongs to a carnivorous plant nursery. The catalogue is informative and clear, the range impressive. It includes such curiosities as *Brocchinia reducta*, *Roridula dentata*, some 30 *Pinguicula* species and a good selection of *Sarracenia*. The minimum value for mail order outside France is FF 1,000.

Pép. Botanique Jean Thoby
Château de Gaujacq, F–40330 Amou
☎ 00 33 5 58 89 24 22 **Fax** 00 33 5 58 89 06 62
English-speaking contact Jean Thoby (a little)
Specialities Camellias; shrubs; trees; *Hosta*; *Hydrangea*; *Wisteria*
Catalogue FF 55
Mail order Yes

This is one of the most dynamic plantsman's nurseries in Europe. The catalogue alone is a collectors' piece, stylishly produced on handmade paper bound with raffia, quite apart from the treasures it contains. Jean Thoby summarises the contents as 'Camellias (550), Hydrangeas (240), Hosta (220), Wisteria (40) as well as 4,000 other taxa, trees, shrubs, climbers and perennials'.

Pép. Charentaises
Route de Beauregarde, F–16310 Montemboeuf
☎ 00 33 5 46 65 02 61 **Fax** 00 33 5 45 65 14 40
English-speaking contact Roland Meynet
Specialities Climbers; conifers; fruit; roses; shrubs; trees
Catalogue FF 40 (1995)
Mail order Mainland France only

Long-established and very big nurseries. The large glossy catalogue lists an extensive and well-chosen range of trees and shrubs, conifers, roses, climbers and fruit trees, from the familiar favourite to the collectors' rarity, such as *Rosa* 'Lorenzo Pahissa'. Indeed, a fair number of their plants are available from no other source. Recommended if you can visit them or have a house in France: they do not do mail order abroad.

Pép. Christophe Delay
Les Combes, F–38780 Estrablin
☎ 00 33 4 74 57 14 42 **Fax** 00 33 4 74 57 14 29
Specialities Fruit
Catalogue FF 10
Mail order Yes

Here are old cultivars of tree fruits, mainly of French origin, apples, plums, pears, cherries and peaches, chosen for their good flavour. Organic methods of cultivation are used.

Pép. Claude Thoby
BP 113, Route de Paris, F–44471 Carquefou Cedex
☎ 00 33 2 40 50 88 48 **Fax** 00 33 2 40 77 91 92
Specialities Camellias
Catalogue FF 50
Mail order Yes

Quite simply, the best camellia nursery in Europe. Thoby grows hundreds of different varieties, from the newest species to the oldest *japonica* hybrids. His beautiful catalogue lists and re-lists them, first alphabetically, then according to their time of flowering and their colour and finally botanically, according to their species and groups. Compulsory reading for all camellia-lovers.

Pép. Côte Sud des Landes
Route départ. 12, F–40230 Saint Geours de Maremme
☎ & **Fax** 00 33 5 58 57 33 30
Specialities Shrubs; trees
Catalogue FF 30
Mail order Yes

This excellent nursery in the south-west of France specialises in ornamental trees and shrubs for acid soils. They have a particularly long list of *Acer*, *Camellia*, *Cornus*, *Hydrangea*, *Rhododendron* and *Viburnum*. Among recent additions to their list are 15 forms of *Hydrangea macrophylla* including 'Bergfink' and 'Buntspech'.

Pép. de L'Arboretum de Balaine
Château de Balaine, F–03460 Villeneuve-sur-Allier
☎ 00 33 4 70 43 50 07 **Fax** 00 33 4 70 43 36 91
English-speaking contact Louise Courteix-Adanson
Specialities Rhododendrons; shrubs; trees
Catalogue FF 15
Mail order Yes

The nursery attached to this world-famous arboretum specialises in ericaceous shrubs and rare trees, many of them not available in Britain. The list of *Magnolia* species and *Quercus* is quite exceptional. Among recent novelties are *Quercus* 'Warburgii' and *Fagus sylvatica* 'Brocklesby'. The arboretum, about 17 km. north of Moulins on the N7, is open 9 am – 12 noon and 2 pm – 7 pm from April to November.

PÉP. DE LA FOUX
Chemin de la Foux, F–83220 Le Pradet
☎ 00 33 4 94 75 35 45 **Fax** 00 33 4 94 08 17 13
Specialities *Salvia*
Catalogue Yes
Mail order No

Best known for their National Collection of *Salvia*, which is growing fast and now dominates their list. It has over 160 of them. They also have a good general stock of plants suitable for the south of France or English conservatories. They only deliver locally and do not do mail order, but they attend many of the best garden fairs in France like Courson, St Jean de Beauregard and Gaujacq, and are willing to bring plants for collection.

PÉP. DE LA VALLÉE DE L'HUVEAUNE
CD 2, Route de Gémenos, F–13400 Aubagne
☎ 00 33 4 42 82 36 00 **Fax** 00 33 4 42 82 97 55
English-speaking contact Robert Pélissier
Specialities Conservatory plants
Catalogue FF 35
Mail order Yes

This nursery east of Marseilles specialises in plants for a Mediterranean climate. The means (to English eyes) a mixture of the familiar and the exotic. *Elaeagnus* and *Cupressus* rub along with palms, cycads and fruiting cultivars of jujube. The catalogue lists almost all the staple plants of traditional gardens, together with some good modern additions. Recent additions include a collection of *Agapanthus* and more cycads from South Africa and Australia.

PÉP. ERIC DUMONT
42, avenue des Martyrs, F–10800 Buchères
☎ 00 33 3 25 41 84 87 **Fax** 00 33 3 25 41 96 59
English-speaking contact Eric Dumont or Christine Mangin
Specialities Fruit
Mail order Delivery can be arranged

Fruit trees in old and new varieties. They specialise in producing specimens which are ready to fruit, trained in traditional styles, fans, cordons, espaliers, and pyramids. Rare varieties can be grafted to order. There is a general nursery on site too. Eric Dumont comes from a long tradition of nurserymen: he is the 13th generation.

PÉP. FILIPPI
RN 113, F–34140 Mèze
☎ 00 33 4 67 43 88 69 **Fax** 00 33 4 67 43 84 59
English-speaking contact Olivier Filippi
Specialities Mediterranean plants; *Nerium oleander*
Catalogue FF 40
Mail order Yes

This catalogue sets out to inspire drought-conscious gardeners everywhere, as well as those who garden around the Mediterranean. And it succeeds. There is a wealth of plant material for dry gardens, including over 100 *Nerium oleander* cultivars (the best collection in Europe), all of which are fully described. More *Cistus, Artemisia, Teucrium,* and *Callistemon* have just been added to the range. Highly recommended, particularly to lovers of conservatory plants.

PÉP. JEAN REY
Route de Carpentras, F–84150 Jonquières
☎ 00 33 4 90 70 36 00 **Fax** 00 33 4 90 70 35 21
English-speaking contact J Paul Charvin
Specialities Conservatory plants; Mediterranean plants
Mail order Wholesale only

Wholesale nursery specialising in Mediterranean and conservatory plants – everything from cistus to palms. They introduced several new cultivars of *Nerium oleander* last year. Retail sales are from their garden centre on RN98 83250 La Londe les Maures.

PÉP. MARIE-PIERRE FOURNIER
Patrie, F–32110 Magnan
☎ 00 33 5 62 69 01 15
English-speaking contact Marie-Pierre Fournier
Specialities *Salvia*
Catalogue Free
Mail order Yes

Small nursery offering a collection of nearly 150 *Salvia* species and forms from all over the world.

PÉP. RHÔNE-ALPES A. GAYRAUD
3.549, route de Paris, F–01440 Viriat
☎ 00 33 4 74 25 36 55
Specialities Fruit; hedging; shrubs; trees
Catalogue FF 30
Mail order Yes

The main catalogue lists the nursery's specialities of ornamental trees and shrubs, hedging and a good range of roses of all types, old and new. The collections of *Cornus* and *Magnolia* include some good varieties. But separately, in a special catalogue called *Fruits Oubliés* (FF 40), are listed and described with clarity and Gallic charm many old kinds of fruit trees: apples, pears, plums, cherries, figs and peaches. Recipes, some in rhyme, will help customers to enjoy the crop.

PÉPINIÈRES TRAVERS
Rue Cour-Charette, F–45650 Saint-Jean-le-Blanc
☎ 00 33 2 38 66 37 53 **Fax** 00 33 2 38 51 90 18
English-speaking contact Arnaud Travers
Specialities Clematis; climbers
Catalogue Leaflet free on request for France only
Mail order France only

This nursery specialises in climbing plants and soft fruit. Its list of clematis is particularly good: some 200 cultivars, including a regular supply of new introductions. 'Golden Tiara' is their latest, a new form of *Clematis tangutica*. No mail order outside France: collection only.

Pivoines Michel Rivière
La Plaine, F–26400 Crest
☎ 00 33 4 75 25 44 85 Fax 00 33 4 75 76 77 38
English-speaking contact Jean-Luc Riviere
Specialities Peonies
Catalogue FF 25
Mail order Yes

Famous peony nursery. They still breed and introduce new varieties besides continuing to seek out older cultivars. Their collection of over 600 varieties is recognised as a French National Collection. The list also includes plants bred by Sir Peter Smithers.

Pommiers du Pays d'Auge
La Redoute, St Germain de Livet, F–14100 Lisieux
☎ 00 33 2 31 31 68 65
English-speaking contact Denis Jacques
Specialities Fruit
Catalogue FF 15
Mail order Yes

Apple trees only, new and old, dessert and cider varieties. Recent introductions include 'Faras', 'Belle Joséphine' and 'Verité'.

Roseraies Pierre Guillot
Domaine de la Plaine, F–38460 Chamagnieu
☎ 00 33 4 74 90 27 55 Fax 00 33 4 74 90 27 17
English-speaking contact Martine Guillot
Specialities Roses
Catalogue Free
Mail order Yes

Rose breeders and growers with a proud tradition stretching back to 1829, who introduced the first polyantha and the first hybrid tea, Guillot specialises in old roses, especially those bred by his ancestors, such as 'Emotion' (before 1862), and 'Renée Danielle' (1913). They also introduce the new roses which Massad breeds in the old style – a specifically French answer to David Austin's English roses. Three new cultivars were issued in 1998: more are due this year.

Santonine
Tout y Faut, F–17260 Villars en Pons
☎ 00 33 5 46 94 26 94 Fax 00 33 5 46 94 62 36
English-speaking contact Christine Verneuil
Specialities Herbaceous perennials
Catalogue FF 5
Mail order Yes

A charming list of herbaceous plants. Most are varieties popular in England but adapted to the climate of south-west France. The list is strong on *Salvia* species, of which they have the French National Collection: *S. nevadensis*, *S. moelleri*, *S. trijuga* and *S. tubifera* are recent additions to their list. Worth investigating.

Schryve Jardin
1.315, route du Steentje, F–59270 Bailleul
☎ 00 33 3 28 49 27 40 Fax 00 33 3 28 49 27 42
English-speaking contact Delphine Quilliot (00 33 20 54 32 02)
Specialities Bulbs
Catalogue FF 30
Mail order Yes

All types of flowering bulbs are catalogued according to time of flowering. You can start with *Colchicum* 'Attlee' in the autumn and continue until *Eremurus* × *isabellinus* 'Cleopatra' flowers in July. There is a new display garden, open from 2 – 6 pm on Thursday and 10 am – 6 pm at weekends from mid-May to mid-September. Roses and perennials are stocked too.

Germany

Alpengarten Pforzheim
Auf dem Berg 6, D–75181 Pforzheim-Würm
☎ 00 49 7231 70590   Fax 00 49 7231 788626
English-speaking contact M Carl
Specialities Alpines; shrubs

Alpine nursery in a hillside garden, worth seeking out and visiting for its interesting collection of alpines, particularly *Primula*, rock-garden plants and dwarf shrubs.

Alpine Staudengärtnerei Siegfried Geißler
OT Gorschmitz Nr 14, D–04703 Leisnig/Sachsen
☎ 00 49 34321 14623
Specialities Alpines
Catalogue Yes
Mail order Yes

Really rare alpines from a collector turned professional. There is a pretty, small display garden, arranged geographically. Stock changes constantly: Herr Geißler is the most adventurous alpine nurserymen in Germany. There is a remarkable list of rare alpine willows. Worth a long detour.

Arboretum Altdorf
Sachsenstr. 6, D–91052 Erlangen
☎ & Fax 00 49 9131 301004
English-speaking contact Gisela Dönig
Specialities Trees
Catalogue Free
Mail order Yes

Specialists in just one genus, *Fagus*. Arboretum Altdorf grows every form of common beech known to man, and offers them all for sale. There are over 60 of them: we particularly recommend the prostrate-growing 'Süntelensis', but Altdorf sells dozens of cultivars not yet grown in the UK.

BAMBUSCHULEN JANSSEN
Stöckheimerstr. 11, D–50259 Pulheim
☎ 00 49 2238 965530   **Fax** 00 49 2238 9655355
Specialities Bamboos
Catalogue DM 5
Mail order Yes

An excellent list of bamboos: nearly 300 of them, most of them unknown to bamboo enthusiasts in Britain. Strongly recommended.

BAUMSCHULE BÖHLJE
Oldenburgerstr. 9, D–26655 Westerstede
☎ 00 49 4488 2203   **Fax** 00 49 4488 71286
English-speaking contact G D Böhlje
Specialities Conifers; rhododendrons; shrubs; trees
Catalogue DM 10
Mail order Yes

Large wholesale nurseries (though retail customers can be seen by appointment) with an impressive list of trees and shrubs, including some good conifers. Recent new introductions include *Tsuga canadensis* 'Wintergold', *Prunus spinosa* 'Pendula' and *Chaenomeles japonica* 'Cido'.

BAUMSCHULE H. HACHMANN
Brunnenstr. 68, D–25355 Barmstedt in Holstein
☎ 00 49 4123 2055/2470   **Fax** 00 49 4123 6626
English-speaking contact Holger Hachmann
Specialities Rhododendrons
Catalogue DM 32
Mail order Yes

Baumschule Hachmann is a serious rhododendron nursery and has been responsible for the recent surge of interest in the genus in Germany and central Europe. Hans Hachmann has been breeding new cultivars for over 40 years: he specialises in hybrids that are low-growing and very hardy. The magnificent catalogue offers over 500 cultivars, together with a good range of conifers. It will be of interest to every rhododendron enthusiast.

BAUMSCHULE RÖHLER
Auf der Bult 20, D–31789 Heuerßen – OT Kobbensen
☎ 00 49 5725 5065   **Fax** 00 49 5725 5879
Specialities Shrubs; trees; *Fagus*; *Quercus*
Catalogue DM 3 in stamps

Wholesale and retail nursery with a range of container-grown trees and shrubs. The special list of *Fagus* and *Quercus* contains many rare forms and species such as *Fagus* × *moesiaca*, *Fagus sylvatica* 'Süntelensis', *Quercus petraea* 'Giesleri' and 'Spessart'.

BLATTGRÜN
Willstätterstr. 1, D–38116 Braunschweig
☎ 00 49 531 512529   **Fax** 00 49 531 515364
English-speaking contact Gaby Braun-Nauerz
Specialities *Hosta*
Catalogue Free
Mail order Yes

One of the great *Hosta* nurseries, which specialises in sending young plants by mail order. They also have a nursery which is open from 8 am to 12 noon from Monday to Friday and between 6 pm and 8 pm on Wednesdays from May to September: the address is Am Bülten, 38176-Wendeburg. They bring out about 25 new cultivars every year: hostamaniacs, please note.

BONSAI CENTRUM
Mannheimerstr. 401, D–69123 Heidelberg
☎ 00 49 6221 84910   **Fax** 00 49 6221 849130
Specialities Bonsai
Catalogue Free
Mail order Yes

A splendid centre for good bonsai, including some unconventional types: *Crassula arborescens* and *Portulaca afra* for example. The centre also offers a wide range of accessories and Japanese garden ornaments. The nursery is open every day except Sunday.

BOTANISCHE RARITÄTEN
Oberkohlfurth, D–42349 Wuppertal-Cronenberg
☎ 00 49 202 470443   **Fax** 00 49 202 4780119
English-speaking contact Bernd Wetzel
Specialities Alpines; bulbs; herbaceous perennials; orchids
Catalogue DM 7
Mail order Yes

An extensive list of alpines, herbaceous plants, bulbs and terrestrial orchids. Almost all are species, forms and natural varieties – few hybrids. A high percentage of what they offer is unavailable in the UK. Seriously interesting.

BOTANISCHER ALPENGARTEN F. SÜNDERMANN
Aeschacher Ufer 48, D–88131 Lindau/Bayern
☎ 00 49 8382 5402   **Fax** 00 49 8382 21539
Specialities Alpines
Catalogue Price list free
Mail order Yes

A famous old firm of alpine nurserymen, founded in 1886, with an excellent traditional range. Good for saxifrages, dianthus and primulas, and reasonably priced.

FA. TREFFINGER-HOFMANN
Am Stadion 20, D–75038 Oberderdingen
☎ 00 49 7045 2214   **Fax** 00 49 7045 90237
Specialities Roses
Catalogue Free
Mail order Yes

This firm is the main outlet for roses bred by Hetzel, who has begun to revolutionise German rose breeding in the same way that David Austin has in England. Most of the list consists of Hetzel hybrids, including 'Super Dorothy' and 'Super Excelsa', the repeat-flowering ramblers which have been so successful on the continent.

FLORA MEDITERRANEA
Königsgütler 5, D–84072 Au/Hallertau
☎ 00 49 8752 1238   Fax 00 49 8752 9930
English-speaking contact Christoph or Maria Köchel
Specialities Conservatory plants; Mediterranean plants, specimen sizes
Catalogue DM 8
Mail order To German-speaking countries only

This is a substantial nursery, with five enormous glass-houses, each maintained with different climatic conditions. They produce an extensive range of container-grown half-hardy and subtropical plants for conservatories and interior landscapes. Many are available in specimen sizes but mail order is offered only within Germany.

FRIESLAND STAUDENGARTEN (UWE KNÖPNADEL)
Husumer Weg 16, D–26441 Jever/Rahrdum
☎ 00 49 4461 3763   Fax 00 49 4461 2307
Specialities Herbaceous perennials; irises; peonies, *Hosta*; *Hemerocallis*
Catalogue DM 22 for general catalogue; DM 35 for hemerocallis, hosta and iris catalogue
Mail order Yes, but DM 500 minimum to the UK

When we first heard of this nursery, we wondered what would grow in the bleak windswept town of Husum. The answer is everything! This nursery has one of the longest and richest lists of any, including over 2,000 hemerocallis cultivars, 600 hostas, 500 irises (*excluding* bearded cultivars) and hundreds of peonies of every kind, hollies (*Ilex*), clematis, narcissus and rhododendrons. They reckon to have about 10,000 taxa in stock at any time. The high minimum order is a turn-off, but specialist societies, National Collection holders, small nurseries and plantsmen in search of novelty should all club together to access this nursery's remarkable list. More's the pity that they say their minimum mail order for UK is DM 500.

GARTENBAU F. WESTPHAL
Peiner Hof 7, D–25497 Prisdorf
☎ 00 49 4101 74104   Fax 00 49 4101 781113
English-speaking contact Mr Manfred or Mrs Sabine Westphal
Specialities Clematis
Catalogue Free
Mail order Yes, throughout Europe

The nursery lists some 350 clematis species, hybrids and cultivars in both large- and small-flowered varieties. Many originated in the Baltic States and former USSR. These are identified in the list of varieties and are particularly interesting. Examples include 'Maerjamaa', 'Mefistofel', 'Roogoja' and 'Sakala'. Strongly recommended.

GARTENBAUBETRIEB ENGELHARDT
Güterbahnhofstr. 53, D–01809 Heidenau bei Dresden
☎ 00 49 5329 512069
Specialities Dahlias
Catalogue Free
Mail order Yes

Long-established (founded in 1914) nursery specialising in dahlias. They have introduced a large number of their own seedlings over the years, specialising in pompon and cactus types. Their current lists offers over 200 cultivars, many of which are not known in the UK. A thoroughly recommended nursery.

GEORG ARENDS
Monschaustr. 76, D–42369 Wuppertal-Ronsdorf
☎ 00 49 202 464610   Fax 00 49 202 464957
English-speaking contact Anja Maubach
Specialities Herbaceous perennials; *Astilbe*
Catalogue DM 10
Mail order Yes

A famous name, but did you know that Georg Arends worked in England over 100 years ago? He exhibited at Chelsea a plant which he raised and which is still deservedly popular today: *Sedum telephium* 'Herbstfreude' ('Autumn Joy'). Now run by the fourth generation, the nursery continues to be an excellent source of good perennials including *Astilbe* and *Phlox* raised there. There are lectures and courses all through the year.

GRÜBELE BAUMSCHULEN
Martin-Luther-Weg 14, D–71804 Weissach im Tal-Unterweissach
☎ 00 49 7191 51234   Fax 00 49 7191 52513
Specialities Acers; conifers; trees
Catalogue DM 10
Mail order Yes

This nursery has an excellent list of unusual trees: dendrologists, please note. One of their specialities is *Ginkgo* (14 cultivars); another is *Acer* (150 cultivars, including 100 *palmatum*). But every part of their list has rare taxa. Take *Syringa* × *prestoniae*, for instance: they offer 'Coral', 'Donald Wymann', 'Nocturne' and 'Royalty', none of them available from UK nurseries.

GÄRTNEREI HERMANN ERMEL
Kurpfalzstraße, D–67308 Zellertal-Harxheim
☎ 00 49 6355 639   Fax 00 49 6355 3462
Specialities Fuchsias
Catalogue DM 10
Mail order Yes

An excellent fuchsia nursery, with a list of some 2,500 varieties. They are particularly good at introducing new cultivars bred by German hybridisers. Their catalogue is strongly recommended to any fuchsia enthusiast who is looking for new and unusual stock.

Ingwer J. Jensen GMBH
Am Schloßpark 2b, D–24960 Glucksberg
☎ 00 49 4631 60100

Specialities Roses
Catalogue Yes, several, costing between DM 17.50 and DM 27.50
Mail order Yes

Long list of old and new roses, besides clematis, climbers, rhododendrons and azaleas. The list of varieties of old roses available from Jensen is one of the most extensive anywhere. There is a good selection of modern roses too, including many English roses from David Austin. Efficient mail order.

Kakteen Haage
Blumenstr. 68, D–99092 Erfurt
☎ 00 49 361 2261014   Fax 00 49 361 2119320

English-speaking contact Ulrich Haage
Specialities Cacti and succulents; hoyas; tillandsias
Catalogue Free
Mail order Yes

Haage is the oldest cactus nursery in Europe, dating from 1822. The present head of the family, H-F Haage, has a distinguished collection, in the best German tradition of scholar-nurserymen. The excellent list of cacti and succulents includes over 100 *Mammillaria* and more than 50 succulent *Euphorbia*, as well as a vast selection of epiphytic cacti, some 70 hoyas and 60 tillandsias. The nursery is a focus for cactophiles throughout Europe, and hosts such events as an annual 'Hoyafest'. They sell seeds, too.

Kakteengärtnerei Max Schleipfer
Sedlweg 71, D–86356 Neusäß bei Augsburg
☎ 00 49 821 464450

Specialities Alpines; cacti and succulents; herbaceous perennials
Catalogue Cacti list free; perennials DM 3
Mail order Yes, all year round for cacti. Other plants collection only

Combined specialities of cacti and perennials, each listed separately. Cacti are of garden origin, not imported. The range is extensive. They list 70 named varieties of *Echinopsis* among their specialities, with more available in small quantities. In the list of alpines and perennials enthusiasts should note named forms of *Geranium cinerium* var. *subcaulescens* 'Glühwein', 'Signa' and 'Giuseppina', an improved 'Giuseppe'.

Karl Foerster-Stauden GMBH
Am Raubfang 6, D–14469 Potsdam-Bornim
☎ 00 49 331 520294   Fax 00 49 331 520124

Specialities Herbaceous perennials

This famous wholesale nursery has been responsible for many good introductions and well-known for its influence on the history of garden design and planting over the last 100 years. Post-war introductions are now being introduced here by discerning nurseries.

Klaus Oetjen
Oberbühlhof, D–78337 Schienen/Bodensee
☎ 00 49 7735 2247   Fax 00 49 7735 3734

English-speaking contact Klaus Oetjen (written English preferred)
Specialities Alpines; herbaceous perennials
Catalogue DM 3
Mail order Yes

Alpine and herbaceous plants are the specialities of this owner-run nursery, particularly campanulas, geraniums and peonies. Among their recent introductions are *Campanula persicifolia* 'Duett', *Rosmarinus officinalis* 'Blaulippe', *Lavandula angustifolia* 'Siesta', *Campanula cochlearifolia* 'Seekampf' and *Geranium himalayense* 'Larissa': enough to show that this is an excellent source of new and interesting forms of popular herbaceous genera. Recommended.

Michael von Allesch
Ackermannstr. 21, D–22087 Hamburg
☎ 00 49 40 723 2141   Fax 00 49 40 220 9458

English-speaking contact Michael von Allesch
Specialities Camellias; passionflowers
Catalogue Yes
Mail order Yes

Michael von Allesch issues two specialised catalogues, one for camellias and the other for passionflowers. Both depend for their excellence upon his particular ability to winkle out new forms and hybrids and introduce them to cultivation in Europe. His novelties come from such breeders as Ackermann (new *Camellia oleifera* hybrids) and Parks (the late-flowering *C. japonica* strain) but he also imports old/new cultivars directly from Japan. Recommended.

Naturwuchs
Bardenhorst 15, D–33739 Bielefeld
☎ 00 49 521 8751500   Fax 00 49 521 85356

English-speaking contact Th. Reichelt
Specialities Fruit; herbaceous perennials; roses; shrubs; trees
Catalogue DM 5 or £2
Mail order Yes, Germany only

This nursery specialises in native plants, forms and hybrids for habitat planting as well as old and traditional varieties of fruit, shrubs, bulbs and perennials for cottage-garden planting. They will advise, design and plant these for you too, and offer an intriguing roof planting kit.

Osnabrücker Staudenkulturen P. und B. zur Linden
Linner Kirchweg 2, D–49143 Bissendorf – Linne
☎ 00 49 5402 5618   Fax 00 49 5402 4706

English-speaking contact P and B zur Linden

Specialities Herbaceous perennials; *Phlox*
Catalogue DM 5 in stamps

Perennial breeders and growers with a particular interest in introducing and popularising new species and cultivars. Their breeding work with such genera as *Aster* and *Phlox* has resulted in the introduction of some 20 new named cultivars in recent years. Definitely a nursery to watch. Collection only.

RÖLLKE ORCHIDEENZUCHT

Füssweg 11, Stukenbrock, D–33758 Schloß Holte-Stukenbrock
☎ 00 49 5207 6647   Fax 00 49 5207 6697

English-speaking contact Lutz Röllke
Specialities Orchids
Catalogue Free
Mail order Yes

Top German orchid breeder and grower. There is a range of species and hybrids with lots of regular new introductions. They also sell companion plants and accessories.

ROSEN VON SCHULTHEIS

Rosenhof, D–61231 Bad Nauheim Steinfurth
☎ 00 49 6032 81013   Fax 00 49 6032 85890

Specialities Roses
Catalogue DM 10
Mail order Yes

Schultheis is one of the most famous rose nurseries in Germany, and still run by the family after 125 years. It specialises in old and rare roses, although the long and interesting list includes a representative selection of modern ones too.

ROSENSCHULE MARTIN WEINGART

Hirtengasse 16, D–99947 Bad Langensalz-Aufhoven
☎ 00 49 3603 813926

English-speaking contact Martin Weingart
Specialities Roses
Catalogue Yes
Mail order Yes

Martin Weingart's list of old, rare and species roses includes many unobtainable elsewhere. He has a good selection of varieties bred by the Austro-Hungarian Rudolf Geschwind such as 'Freya', 'Ernst G. Dörell' and 'Gilda'. Much of his budwood comes from the great Rosarium at Sangerhausen. Strongly recommended.

RUDOLF U. KLARA BAUM (FUCHSIENKULTUREN)

Scheffelrain 1, D-71229 Leonberg
☎ 00 49 7152 27558   Fax 00 49 7152 28965

English-speaking contact Frau Woller speaks some English
Specialities Conservatory plants; fuchsias; houseplants
Catalogue DM 13

Mail order Germany only

Fuchsias and exotic conservatory and houseplants. Very basic descriptions for the true plantsman seeking to enlarge his collection from the 1,000 fuchsias, over 100 *Brugmansia* (daturas), nearly 200 *Passiflora* and other species offered. A remarkable list, which gets better every year, and worth the journey to collect.

SCHIMANA STAUDENKULTUREN UND WASSERGÄRTEN

Waldstr. 21, D–86738 Deiningen bei Nördlingen
☎ & Fax 00 49 9081 28074

English-speaking contact Eckhard & Walter Schimana
Specialities Aquatic plants; ferns; grasses; herbaceous perennials
Catalogue DM 8
Mail order Yes

Good all-round list of aquatic plants, ferns, grasses and perennials with an impressive list of 13 named forms of *Yucca filamentosa*. Recent introductions include *Helictotrichon sempervirens* 'Robust' and *Veronica longifolia* 'Rosenkerze'.

SCHÖPPINGER IRISGARTEN (WERNER REINERMANN)

Bürgerweg 8, D–48624 Schöppingen
☎ 00 49 2555 1851   Fax 00 49 2861 85145

Specialities *Iris; Hemerocallis; Hosta*
Mail order Mail order only

Well-known breeder of *Hemerocallis* who also specialises in *Hosta* and *Iris*. Each year the list includes a number of his introductions. Mail order only, but there are two open weekends each year. Open 9 am – 5 pm Saturday, 9 am – 2 pm Sunday.

STAUDENGÄRTNER KLOSE

Rosenstr. 10, D–34253 Lohfelden bei Kassel
☎ 00 49 561 515555   Fax 00 49 561 515120

English-speaking contact Heinz Richard Klose
Specialities Delphiniums; herbaceous perennials; peonies; *Hosta*
Catalogue DM 18
Mail order Yes

A large nursery, best-known as a breeder and grower of hostas, peonies and other perennials: their peony fields are a marvellous sight in June. Recent introductions include *Delphinium* 'Gewitterstimmung', *Hosta* 'Schwarzer Ritter' and 'Violetta' all bred here.

STAUDENGÄRTNEREI DIETER GAISSMAYER

Jungvielweide 3, D–89257 Illertissen
☎ 00 49 7303 7258   Fax 00 49 7303 42181

English-speaking contact Mr Gaißmayer or Mr Mayer
Specialities Herbaceous perennials
Catalogue DM 5
Mail order Yes

The general catalogue is stylish and helpful, indicating whether a plant can be used in cookery, is attractive to bees and butterflies, can be cut and dried, as well as detail of size, height, colour, cultural conditions and delightful descriptions of a plant's special peculiarities. There is an extra herbaceous list, with a wide range and many varieties not available in the UK – particularly *Astilbe* × *arendsii* and *Phlox paniculata* forms. Recommended.

STAUDENGÄRTNEREI GRÄFIN VON ZEPPELIN
Laufen am Südschwarzwald, D–79295 Sulzburg (Baden)
☎ 00 49 7634 69716   Fax 00 49 7634 6599

English-speaking contact Cai von Rumohr
Specialities Herbaceous perennials; irises; peonies; sempervivums; *Papaver orientalis*
Catalogue DM 10
Mail order Yes, worldwide

Famous nursery in pretty setting on the southern edge of the Black Forest now run by Gräfin von Zeppelin's daughter and son-in-law Aglaia and Cai von Rumohr who speak excellent English. The well-produced and informative catalogue lists around 3,000 species and cultivars. The best times to visit are mid-May to mid-June, July and September. Their open weekend at the end of May features guided tours and lectures on their specialities. New introductions raised by them recently include: *Clematis heracleifolia* 'Cassandra', *Papaver orientale* 'Abu Hassan', 'Aslahan', 'Effendi', 'Khedive' and 'Prinz Eugen'.

STAUDENGÄRTNEREI WOLFGANG SPRICH
Papierweg 20, D–79400 Kandern
☎ 00 49 7626 6855/7443

Specialities Grasses; herbaceous perennials
Catalogue DM 10
Mail order Yes

Perennial nursery. Grasses and hardy geraniums are the main specialities. New lines introduced recently include *Geranium renardii* 'Tschelda', and *Geranium* × *cantabrigiense* 'Vorjura'.

STAUDENGÄRTNEREI ZINSER
Burgwedelerstr. 48, D–30916 Isernhagen HB
☎ 00 49 511 732385

English-speaking contact Irene, Petra & Dr R Zinser
Specialities Grasses; herbaceous perennials
Mail order No

Perennial nursery with a good range, including lots of cultivars not well known here.

STAUDENKULTUREN STADE
Beckenstrang 24, D–46325 Borken-Marbeck
☎ 00 49 2861 2604

Specialities Grasses; herbaceous perennials
Mail order Yes

Stade offers coloured catalogues for their water plants and perennials, but it is best to ask for the price list, which has a very wide range of alpines, perennials and grasses. Among some 4,000 different lines, there are particularly good lists of asters, astilbes, delphiniums, phlox and saxifrages. Recommended.

SÜDFLORA BAUMSCHULEN
Stutsmoor 42, D–22607 Hamburg
☎ 00 49 40 8991698   Fax 00 49 40 8901170

English-speaking contact Peter Klock
Specialities Fruit; Mediterranean plants; *Citrus*; subtropical fruit
Catalogue Free
Mail order Yes

This nursery specialises in Mediterranean plants, citrus and subtropical fruit, understocks and fruit trees: the list of oranges and tangerines is particularly interesting. There is a range of fruit selected for growing in containers, on a balcony, terrace or in a garden.

TROPEN EXPRESS
Familie Steininger, Dr Winklhofer Straße 22, D–94036 Passau
☎ 00 49 851 81831   Fax 00 49 851 87687

English-speaking contact Hubert & Gudrun Steininger
Specialities Palms; tropical plants
Catalogue DM 3 and international reply coupon
Mail order Yes

An amazing list of tender tropical plants, including palms, bananas and gingers. The list is in two parts: plants available from stock and the real rarities which are available only by special advance order. Tucked in at the end of their catalogue is a list of the *Crinum* species and cultivars which they offer: a mere 28 of them! Strongly recommended.

W LINNEMANN STRAUCHPÄONIEN
Rheindorferstr. 49, D–53225 Bonn
☎ 00 49 228 471488   Fax 00 49 228 471247

English-speaking contact Wolfgang Linnemann
Specialities Peonies
Catalogue Three international reply coupons
Mail order Yes

Wolfgang Linnemann imports tree peonies from Japan, China, the USA and Europe. The range extends to nearly 300 cultivars. Recent introductions include winter-flowering tree peonies to grow in a cool greenhouse and *Paeonia delavayi* Potaninii group 'Alba'.

W. KORDES' SÖHNE
D–25365 Klein Offenseth-Sparrieshoop
☎ 00 49 4121 48700   Fax 00 49 4121 84745

Specialities Roses
Catalogue Yes
Mail order Yes

An important firm of breeders and growers, one of the largest in Europe. They sell mainly modern roses and maintain a regular stream of excellent new introductions, many of which are not introduced in the UK because our market is too small. Their sumptuous catalogue suggests a large and efficient mail-order service, which we can vouch for. Their plants are exceptionally healthy and well-grown.

Wolff's Pflanzen
Hauptstr. 19, D–74541 Vellberg-Großaltdorf
☎ 00 49 7907 89752   Fax 00 49 7907 23865
Specialities Herbaceous perennials; roses, general range
Catalogue Free
Mail order Yes

An nursery for herbaceous plants, with a useful sideline in old-fashioned roses. Most of the roses are available in the UK, but there a few which are not: 'Zoë', 'Tom Wood' and 'La Reine Rosarien', for example. Among the herbaceous plants, however, are many good cultivars which have yet to be introduced to the UK: pink-flowered *Lychnis chalcedonica* 'Morgenrot', pale pink *Geranium sanguineum* 'Apfelblüte' and *Veronica spicata* 'Spielarten', for instance.

Italy

Bassi Vivai
Via Tonello 17, I–12100 Cuneo
☎ 00 39 171 402149   Fax 00 39 171 634351
English-speaking contact Dr Guido Bassi
Specialities Fruit
Catalogue Free
Mail order Yes

Specialists in old fruit cultivars, with one of the best lists of apples, pears, peaches and plums in Italy. Dr Bassi is a champion of the local varieties of fruit and his catalogue offers a wonderful choice of names which are unknown in the UK. Minor crops are not forgotten: there are apricots, cherries, walnuts, Japanese chestnuts, and some 20 Italian chestnuts as well as fungal spawn for *Boletus* and truffle species. Strongly recommended to anyone interested in traditional varieties.

Calvisi Manlio
I–33040 Perteole (UD), Via Verdi, 74
☎ 00 39 431 99413   Fax 00 39 431 99413
English-speaking contact Calvisi Manlio (written English only)
Specialities Aquatic plants
Catalogue Free
Mail order Yes

A first-class nursery for aquatics, Calvisi lists more than 90 hardy water lilies and 15 forms of the lotus lily *Nelumbo nucifera*. The list of bog plants and marginals is likewise excellent. Highly recommended.

Camelie Borrini SNC
Via della Torre, I–55065 Sant'Andrea di Compito (LU)
☎ 00 39 583 977066   Fax 00 39 586 501920
English-speaking contact Giulio Cattolica
Specialities Camellias
Catalogue Free
Mail order In special circumstances

This camellia nursery specialises in pot-grown cultivars, old and new. They are busy breeding new hybrids, the first of which may find their way into their next catalogue. They are also experimenting with the cultivation of tea-plants. Guido Cattolica is the joint author of the modern classic *Camelie dell'800 in Italia* (Pacini, Pisa) and organiser of the annual Old Camellias Show at Pieve di Compito.

Capitanio Stefano
Contrada Conghia, 298, I–70043 Monopoli (BA)
☎ 00 39 80 801720   Fax 00 39 80 801720
Catalogue 5,000 lire, plus postage
Mail order Yes

Specialises in Mediterranean and aromatic plants, especially unusual ones. Recent novelties include *Galvezia speciosa* and *Ruellia amoena*. The list is forever changing and improving as Sig. Capitanio travels around looking for new plants. Strongly recommended.

Cellarina di Maria Luisa Sotti
Via Montà, 65, I–14100 Cellarengo (AT)
☎ & Fax 00 39 141 935258
English-speaking contact Dr Carola Lodari (00 39 11 8127267)
Specialities Aromatic and scented plants, grey-leaved perennials
Catalogue Two: aromatic plants & grey-leaved
Mail order Yes

Maria Luisa Sotti is the *grande dame* of Italian plantswomen. She trained first as a botanist, and is still one of the experts on the flora of Piemonte, but her great love is aromatic plants and her expertise as a tutor is sought by gardens and gardeners throughout Italy. Recent introductions include *Chenopodium umbrosum*, *Micromeria juliana*, *M. dalmatica* and *Satureja thymbra*. Maria Luisa Sotti is the author of *Le Piante Perenni* (Mondadori, 1991) the classic Italian book on herbaceous plants which is based entirely upon her own experiences and has none of the regurgitated Graham Stuart Thomas you normally get in Italian gardening books.

Coltivazione Riviera del Conero di Oste Lucio
Via G Pascoli, 12, I–60020 Loreto (AN)
☎ & Fax 00 39 71 978384
English-speaking contact Federico Oste
Specialities Palms
Catalogue Free
Mail order Palms only

This is a traditional general nursery which sells a good selection of trees, shrubs and herbaceous plants, including some 120 irises. However, it is also the centre for an amazing collection of palm trees, the largest selection in Europe. As well as trialling some 80 species for hardiness in eastern Italy, where winter temperatures descend to –15°C, they broker some 900 different palm species from all over the world, and a long list of cycads too. It is essential reading for anyone who is interested in palms. Naturally the nursery also acts as a European centre of knowledge and research.

Flora 2000
Via Zenzalino Sud, 19/A, I–40054 Budrio (BO)
☎ 00 39 51 800406   Fax 00 39 51 808039
English-speaking contact Andrea Pagani (evenings)
Specialities Fruit; peonies; roses
Catalogue 5,000 lire
Mail order Yes

Specialists in old varieties of roses, peonies and fruit. Recent introductions include the downy cherry *Prunus tomentosa* and a giant jujube *Ziziphus jujuba* 'Lee'.

Floricultura Hillebrand
Viale Azari, 95, I–28048 Verbania Pallanza (NO)
☎ & Fax 00 39 323 503802
English-speaking contact Piero Hillebrand
Specialities Camellias; rhododendrons; shrubs; trees
Catalogue Free
Mail order Yes

This tree and shrub nursery specialises in ericaceous and calcifuge taxa. Their list of camellias is particularly good, with many modern US hybrids alongside traditional 19th-century Italian cultivars. Among their recent introductions are *Arbutus unedo* 'Quercifolia' and *Stewartia pteropetiolata*. One of the most botanically minded of Italian nurseries.

Il Giardino delle Higo
Via Jerago, 18, I–21010 Besnate (VA)
☎ & Fax   00 39 331 274096
English-speaking contact Dr Franco Ghirardi
Specialities Camellias
Catalogue On request
Mail order Yes

Dr Ghirardi is an amateur with the largest collection of Higo camellias in Europe. He grows all the 109 cultivars which the Japanese authorities recognise. He has begun to propagate them, partly in an attempt to make them available to fellow enthusiasts and partly to encourage more people to grow them.

Il Giardino delle Rose
Via Palastra, 27, I–50020 Chiesanuova (FI)
☎ & Fax 00 39 55 8242388
English-speaking contact Dr Maria Giulia Cimarelli Nenna

Specialities Roses
Catalogue 19,000 lire (posted)
Mail order Italy only

This Italian nursery specialises in the classic roses of Peter Beales and Jean Pierre Guillot. Among the more recent novelties introduced from Guillot are 'Mozabito', 'Manuel Canova' and 'Sonia Rykel'. The display garden has about 450 varieties.

L'Antico Pomario (Vivai Dalmonte)
Via Casse, 9, I–48013 Brisighella
☎ 00 39 546 81037   Fax 00 39 546 80061
English-speaking contact Carlo Dalmonte
Specialities Fruit
Catalogue Free
Mail order Yes

Dalmonte is a large modern nursery with a wide choice of all fruit varieties. It has, for example, almost a complete collection of minor Italian wine grapes. L'Antico Pomario is a small undertaking within the whole company, devoted to ancient (pre-1850) and old (pre-1900) varieties, many with evocative names. The list has about 40 apples (e.g. 'Gambafina Piatta', 'Sasso' and 'Decio'), 20 pears (e.g. 'Brutti e Buoni' and 'Volpino') and 10 peaches (e.g. 'Poppa di Venere'). Their hardiness, disease resistance and ability to survive makes such varieties of special interest to bio-friendly growers.

L'oasi del Geranio di Giorgio Carlo
Via Aurelia, 312, I–17023 Ceriale (SV)
☎ 00 39 182 990280
Specialities *Pelargonium*
Catalogue Cost of postage
Mail order Italy only

This small nursery is founded on the enthusiasm for pelargoniums of a husband and wife who have a magnificent list of over 200 species and 700 cultivars for sale. They are keen to help people to understand the enormous diversity of the genus – not just the zonals and ivy-leaved hybrids but also the climbers, succulents and geophytes among them. Recently introduced species include *P. caledonicum*, *P. fissifolium* and *P. parvipetalum*: among the newer cultivars are 'Meriblu' and 'Gen. Rena'. Worth a visit for any visitor to the Riviera.

Mati Piante Az. Agr. di Cesare Mati
Via Bonellina, 49, I–51100 Pistoia
☎ 00 39 573 380051   Fax 00 39 573 382361
English-speaking contact Paolo, Andrea or Cristina Mati
Specialities Shrubs; trees
Catalogue 12,000 lire
Mail order Yes

One of the biggest and best of the Pistoia nurseries with a large range of trees and shrubs. They specialise in the supply and transplantation of outsize trees.

Mini-Arboretum di Guido Piacenza
I–13057 Pollone (BI)
☎ 00 39 15 61693   Fax 00 39 15 61498
English-speaking contact Guido Piacenza
Specialities Roses; shrubs; trees; unusual plants
Catalogue 7,000 lire
Mail order Yes

Modern plantsman's nursery which has been responsible for introducing many English plants to Italy, particularly shrubs and old-fashioned roses: Harold Hillier was Guido Piacenza's mentor. Recent introductions are *Prunus* × *yedoensis* 'Ivensii' and *Aucuba japonica* 'Rozannie'. Guido Piacenza owns Villa Boccanegra, Ellen Willmott's Riviera garden. His latest list includes some old Piedmontese apple varieties.

Montivivai dei F.lli Monti
Picciorana per Tempagnano, I–55010 Picciorana (LU)
☎ 00 39 583 998115   Fax 00 39 583 998117
English-speaking contact Signora Arianna Monti
Specialities Camellias; fruit
Catalogue Free
Mail order Yes

Garden designers and maintainers, with a good basic catalogue of every kind of plant but also an interest in old varieties of roses, camellias and fruit trees. They have set about rediscovering old varieties from the Lucca region and have made a success of finding, naming and propagating some 20 old camellias, including 'General Coletti', 'Prof. Giovanni Santarelli' and 'Rosa Risorta'. Their classic collection of roses offers nothing new to UK gardeners, but their fruit tree list has some unusual names.

Oscar Tintori Vivai
Via Tiro a Segno, 55, I–51012 Castellare di Pescia (PT)
☎ 00 39 572 429191   Fax 00 39 572 429605
English-speaking contact Alberto Tintori
Specialities Citrus fruit
Catalogue Free
Mail order Collection only

Oscar Tintori has the best citrus nursery in Italy. His extensive glasshouses are geared mainly to the wholesale trade, but direct retail sale is also available at the nursery. He publishes an extremely handsome catalogue in English and German. Among last year's novelties were *Citrus* 'Kucle', a cross between a kumquat and a clementine. All their plants are sold in pots: they have a good line in large specimens growing in traditional Tuscan terracotta vases.

Rose & Rose Emporium
Contrada Fossalto, 9, I–05015 Fabro (TR)
☎ 00 39 763 82812   Fax 00 39 763 82828
Specialities Roses
Mail order Yes

A comprehensive list of roses, stylishly designed and based on Peter Beales' collection, with a number of Italian oldies added. 'Clementina Carbonieri', 'Gartendirektor O. Linne' and 'Guglielmo Betto' are among the rarer items. The nursery is just off the main A1 motorway, one hour north of Rome, and has a very pretty demonstration garden.

Rose Barni
Via Autostrada, 5, I–51100 Pistoia
☎ 00 39 573 380464   Fax 00 39 573 382072
English-speaking contact Piero or Enrico Barni
Specialities Roses
Catalogue Free
Mail order Yes

This famous old firm of rose breeders, introducers and growers was founded in 1882 and is now the largest in Italy. Their catalogue is highly colourful and middle-market. They list every type of rose, from gallicas to David Austin's 'English' roses, but the heart of their business is the wonderful choice of traditional HTs and floribundas which Barni themselves have bred for the Italian climate. These open slowly and keep their colours in strong sunlight: worth trying in southern England.

Venzano
Loc. Venzano, Mazzolla, I–56048 Volterra (PI)
☎ & Fax 00 39 588 39095
English-speaking contact Don Leevers
Specialities Aromatic and scented plants; herbs; shrubs
Catalogue Free
Mail order Yes

This nursery in the heart of Tuscany is English-owned and English-run. Don Leevers has a plantsman's catalogue with an excellent mixture of English plants that do well in Italy and plants that he has acquired from his years in the Mediterranean. He has a particularly comprehensive list of herbs, old pinks and scented pelargoniums. He is more than happy to advise expats on making and planting a garden in Italy and he is also an acute observer of the Italian gardening scene.

Vivai Isola del Sole
Cda. San Biagio, I–95013 Fiumefreddo (CT)
☎ & Fax 00 39 95 641854
English-speaking contact Jan Petiet
Specialities *Hibiscus rosa-sinensis; Bougainvillea*
Catalogue Free
Mail order No

This Sicilian nursery lists over 400 varieties of *Hibiscus rosa-sinensis* and over 100 varieties of *Bougainvillea*. Both are available as standards. Jan Petiet is keen to grow his collections still further: no mail order, but definitely worth a journey.

Vivai Nord
Via Brianza, 1/A, I–22040 Lurago d'Erba (CO)
☎ 00 39 31 699749   Fax 00 39 31 699804

English-speaking contact Francis Milner
Specialities Herbaceous perennials; shrubs; trees
Catalogue Free
Mail order Yes

A consortium of four nurseries, one producing liners, another shrubs, the third trees and the fourth herbaceous plants. Among their exclusives are *Pinus cembra* 'Sartori' and a wonderful fastigiate oak *Quercus* 'Mauri' which is thought to be a cross between *Q. rubra* and either *Q. coccinea* or *Q. palustris*.

VIVAI PIERLUIGI PRIOLA
Via Acquette, 4, I–31100 Treviso (TV)
☎ 00 39 422 304096   Fax 00 39 422 301859
English-speaking contact Please write
Specialities Alpines; herbaceous perennials
Catalogue Free
Mail order Yes

An excellent herbaceous and alpine nursery whose main business is now wholesale. They have a stock of 4,000 plants, of which a selection is always available for purchase, while the rest may be ordered for later delivery. Many of their plants come originally from English, German, Dutch and east European nurseries, but they have also hybridised, selected and named plants themselves. Among their many recent introductions are *Delphinium* 'Dämmerung', *Sedum cauticola* 'Robustum' and *Myosotis palustris* 'Perle von Ronnenberg'. Strongly recommended.

VIVAI TORSANLORENZO S.R.L.
Via Campo di Carne, 51, I–00040 Ardea (Roma)
☎ 00 39 6 91019005   Fax 00 39 6 91011602
Specialities Shrubs

The biggest nursery in Italy, where you can buy almost anything you want, except herbaceous perennials. The scale is enormous: over 100 hectares – we were driven through their polytunnels in a Range Rover. Big trees are one of their many specialities, including 100-year-old olives and palms. But there are vast areas of camellias, citrus fruit, oleanders and hundreds of other desirable plants. Highly recommended to all landscapers, Brits abroad and visitors to Rome.

VIVAIBAMBÙ DI MARIO BRANDUZZI
Via Dosso di Mattina, 19, I–26010
Credera/Rubbiano
☎ & Fax 00 39 373 61009
English-speaking contact Dr Mario Brandazzi
Specialities Aquatic plants; bamboos
Catalogue 10,000 lire
Mail order Yes

This nursery offers a remarkable selection of 120+ bamboos, 100+ aquatics and many tropical plants. Among recent introductions are: *Bambusa ventricosa* 'Kimmei', *Bambusa balcooa*, *Phyllostachys bambusoides*, *Dendrocalamus asper*, *Tricosanthes kirilowii* var. *japonica* and *Rhus javanica*.

VIVAIO GUIDO DEGL'INNOCENTI
Via Colle Ramole, 7 – Loc. Bottai, I–50029
Tavarnuzze (FI)
☎ 00 39 237 45 47   Fax 00 39 202 06 76
English-speaking contact Mrs Elisabeth or Mrs Fiorella
Specialities *Iris*
Catalogue 10,000 lire
Mail order Yes

A large nursery with a distinguished history. Innocenti means irises, and they list 400+ varieties, most of them tall bearded, but there are some interesting *Iris* Oucocyclus hybrids too. Almost all are gloriously illustrated in their spectacular catalogue. Prices vary from Lit. 3,000 for popular lines to Lit. 35,000 for the latest American hybrids, but the most common prices are Lit. 4,000 and Lit. 5,000, so they are not expensive. They have a useful second line in *Hemerocallis* and herbaceous plants and have also begun to introduce aquatics.

VIVAIO LUCIANO NOARO
Via Vittorio Emanuele, 151, I–18033 Camporosso (IM)
☎ & Fax 00 39 184 288225
English-speaking contact Signora Linda Noaro
Specialities Mediterranean plants; exotic fruit; variegated plants
Catalogue 6,000 lire
Mail order Yes

This excellent list is widely spread among trees, shrubs, climbers and herbaceous plants, mainly Mediterranean or tropical. There are some interesting palms and large specimens of such exotic flowering plants as *Doryanthes palmeri*, as well as a fine selection of salvias, jasmines, tropical thunbergias, and edible species of *Eugenia*. The stock is always changing as Noaro winkles out new rarities from his frequent forays abroad. Recommended.

VIVAI-FATTORIA 'LA PARRINA'
Località La Parrina, I–58010 Albinia (GR)
☎ 00 39 564 865060   Fax 00 39 564 862636
English-speaking contact Fabio Fusari
Specialities Australian plants; Mediterranean plants; oleanders
Catalogue 3,500 lire
Mail order No

Among the many novelties recently introduced by this plantsman's nursery were *Coleonema album* and a pink-flowered form of *Westringia fruticosa* called 'Wynabbie Gem'.

WALTER BRANCHI
Le Rose, Corbara, 55, I–05019 Orvieto (TR)
English-speaking contact Prof Walter Branchi
Specialities Roses
Catalogue Free
Mail order Yes

A niche nursery with a very comprehensive list of Tea roses (c. 60), China roses (40+) and Noisettes (c. 25), both bush and climbing varieties. This is probably the most complete list in the world of these fashionable 19th-century roses: about a dozen more are added to it each year. Walter Branchi is a delightful retired Professor of Music and speaks fluent American.

THE NETHERLANDS

BELLE ÉPOQUE ROZENKWEKERIJ
Oosteinderweg 489, NL-1432 BJ Aalsmeer
☎ 00 31 297 342546   Fax 00 31 297 340597
Specialities Roses
Catalogue Hfl. 8
Mail order Yes

The best rose list in The Netherlands, handsomely illustrated and offering some 750 cultivars, from the oldest gallicas to the most modern English roses. Among a fair number which are not available in the UK, we noted 'White Dorothy', 'Orange Morsdag' and 'Royal Queen', which is a climbing sport of 'White Queen Elizabeth'. They also sell wholesale under the trading name 'J D Maarse & Zonen BV'. Worth investigating.

BOOMKWEKERIJ ANDRÉ VAN NIJNATTEN BV
Meirseweg 26a, NL-4881 DJ Zundert
☎ 00 31 76 597 2605   Fax 00 31 76 597 5360
Specialities Shrubs; trees
Catalogue Free to trade
Mail order Yes

This firm of wholesalers has an interesting list of ornamental trees. It specialises in new introductions. We particularly recommend *Acer campestre* 'Nanum' among three cultivars of the field maple not yet grown in this country. Other exciting novelties include *Carpinus betulus* 'Fastigiata Nana', *Malus* 'Pom Zai', *Ligustrum japonicum* 'Grace' and five new cultivars of *Tilia cordata*. Every adventurous nurseryman or garden centre owner should investigate further.

COEN JANSEN
Ankummer Es 15, NL-7722 RD Dalfsen
☎ 00 31 5294 34086
Specialities Herbaceous perennials
Catalogue Hfl. 7.50

This nursery offers a good list of herbaceous plants, and the catalogue (in Dutch) has particularly long and helpful plant descriptions. Coen Jansen are particularly good at tracking down and introducing new cultivars from other countries. Among many familiar plants are a good number of names that do not appear in *The Plant Finder* – four named cultivars of *Salvia nemorosa*, for example, half-a-dozen delphiniums, three cultivars of *Helenium*, several geraniums and many others. Worth investigating.

DE GENTIAAN
PO Box 51, NL-9620 AB Slochteren
☎ & Fax 00 31 59 8421380
English-speaking contact John – after 7 pm Dutch time
Specialities Bulbs
Catalogue Two international reply coupons
Mail order Yes

Bulb specialists, particularly rare species and bulk orders for naturalising. *Agapanthus*, *Allium* and cyclamen are their main lines: recent novelties include a long-leaved form of *Cyclamen hederifolium* with pale lilac flowers and an *Allium giganteum* × *schubertii* hybrid.

DE GRIENÊ HÂN
Weaze 29, NL-8495 HE Aldeboarn (Frl.)
☎ 00 31 566 631226
English-speaking contact Auke R. Kleefstra
Specialities Fruit
Catalogue Free
Mail order Yes

Specialists in old fruit tree varieties; about 60 apples, 50 pears, 20 plums, 10 cherries and some interesting nut cultivars. Some are familiar, but there is a good sprinkling of Dutch names and local varieties.

FA. C. ESVELD
Rijneveld 72, NL-2771 XS Boskoop
☎ 00 31 172 213289   Fax 00 31 172 215714
English-speaking contact All staff
Specialities Herbaceous perennials; shrubs; trees
Catalogue £5
Mail order Yes

One of the biggest nurseries in Europe – over 7,000 different varieties of trees, shrubs and hardy plants. This year's novelties alone number several hundreds. Their list is a fat handbook, like a spiral-bound version of Hillier's *Guide* without the detailed descriptions. The number of unusual varieties which are not grown in the UK is enormous – almost every genus seems to have at least one new name. Every keen plantsman needs this catalogue.

FA. JAC VERSCHUREN-PECHTOLD BV
Kalkhofsweg 6A, NL-5443 NA Haps
☎ 00 32 485 316258   Fax 00 32 485 322300
English-speaking contact Koen Verschuren
Specialities Roses

Long-established rose nursery (founded in 1875) that produces over one million bushes a year. Their current list contains over 700 varieties: 'White Dorothy' and 'Abbaye de Cluny' are among those that are not available in the UK. Collection only.

FUCHSIA-KWEKERIJ SPEK
1e Hoornerveensewg 7, NL-8181 LW Heerde
☎ 00 31 578 693604   Fax 00 31 578 696052
English-speaking contact Yes
Specialities Fuchsias; pelargoniums

Catalogue Hfl. 5
Mail order Yes
One of the great European fuchsia nurseries, with more than 2,000 varieties. These include about 60 species (and forms of species), 50 hardy forms (hardy in The Netherlands means hardy anywhere in the UK) and a long list of hybrids old and new. They also have a video on fuchsia growing.

JOS FRIJNS EN ZONEN BV
Groot-Welsden 30, NL–6269 EV Margraten
☎ 00 31 43 4581246   Fax 00 31 43 4582734
English-speaking contact Mr J M H Frints
Specialities Fruit
Catalogue Free

Fruit tree specialists with an excellent list of around 250 apples, 110 pears, 60 cherries and a very wide range of everything else. A good proportion of the names does not appear in *The Plant Finder*, especially varieties bred in Germany and the Netherlands. Very interesting.

KWEKERIJ OUDOLF
Broekstraat 17, NL–6999 DE Hummelo
☎ 00 31 314 38 11 20   Fax 00 31 314 38 11 99
English-speaking contact Piet Oudolf
Specialities Herbaceous perennials
Catalogue Free
Mail order No

Piet Oudolf is best known (and very highly regarded) as one of the pioneers of the new style of planting perennials. It comes as no surprise, therefore, to discover that his catalogue is stocked with plants both familiar and unfamiliar: all are chosen for their excellence in planting schemes. Cultivars unknown in England rub shoulders with the commonplace. Worth careful study.

KWEKERIJ TH. PLOEGER EN ZN. BV
Blauwkapelsenweg 73, NL–3731 EB De Bilt
☎ 00 31 30 2202602   Fax 00 31 30 2204494
Specialities Herbaceous perennials
Catalogue Yes
Mail order Yes

This long-established and first-rate herbaceous nursery has a steady stream of introductions. Recent introductions include *Salvia nemorosa* 'Schneehügel', *Sanguisorba tenuifolia* 'Pink Elephant' and *Aubrieta* 'Sauerland'.

M M BÖMER BOOMKWEKERIJ
Vagevuurstraat 6, NL–4882 NK Zundert
☎ 00 31 76 5972735   Fax 00 31 76 5974585
English-speaking contact J Bömer
Specialities Trees
Catalogue Free
Mail order Yes

This remarkable nursery has a niche market in rare oaks, beeches, horse chestnuts and hazels. There are some 65 cultivars of *Fagus sylvatica*, 130 *Quercus* and an amazing 99 cultivars of *Corylus*. It goes without saying that many are unknown in England. Essential reading for all dendrophiles.

MOERHEIM PLANTENWINKEL
Moerheimstraat 78, NL–7701 CG Dedemsvaart
☎ 00 31 523 612345   Fax 00 31 523 617140
English-speaking contact Most staff
Specialities Herbaceous perennials
Catalogue Hfl. 15
Mail order Yes

Famous old herbaceous nursery (*Helenium* 'Moerheim Beauty') with a sound all-round catalogue. Their range includes trees, shrubs, alpines, roses (from Meilland), aquatics and fruit and there are a number of unusual varieties among them.

PIETER ZWIJNENBURG
Halve Raak 18, NL–2771 AD Boskoop
☎ 00 31 172 216232   Fax 00 31 172 218474
English-speaking contact Pieter Zwijnenburg
Specialities Conifers; shrubs; trees
Catalogue £2
Mail order Yes

This is one of the best all-round nurseries in Europe. Its herbaceous list alone is better than most UK nurseries'. But it really scores with the sheer number of trees and shrubs it offers. There are, for example, more than 20 *Quercus robur* cultivars, over 50 *Fagus sylvatica* and 20 *Liquidambar styraciflua*. But page after page, genus after genus, Zwijnenburg shows that it is comprehensive and has an eye for new forms and cultivars. This is an essential source for anyone in search of the unusual.

Courses for Amateurs

ALL GARDENERS want to become better at gardening, to understand better, to learn more and to achieve more. Until comparatively recently there was really no provision for the fulfilment of this desire: you joined your local village gardening club and hoped that every so often there might be a really good lecture which you would learn something from. Now, however, we are spoilt for choice, and the only problem is knowing how to go about finding something that will prove interesting, instructive and rewarding.

Start with your county horticultural colleges. Almost all will have a programme for amateurs, with courses and study days run by members of the teaching staff, alongside the vocational courses for young professionals. Kingston Maurward College in Somerset is typical: last year it had courses on Botanical Illustration, The Conservation of Historic Gardens, Plant Propagation and several other interesting and useful topics as well as a series of courses run on Saturday mornings on such subjects as Plant Identification and How to Raise Plants from Seeds and Cuttings. Among the best are the courses at Capel Manor, Pershore College and Writtle College.

Many Further Education colleges also run recreational courses, seminars and lectures on aspects of gardening. Last year Probus, in Cornwall, ran a good programme of events in conjunction with three local colleges. Among the many subjects offered were: A History of Garden Design; Gardening in Dry Conditions; Seed Sowing; Plants for Flower Arranging; Orchids; Plant Hunting; Pruning. The length of courses can vary considerably: some may be a single all-day course while others consist of a two-hour evening lecture once a week for six weeks.

It is worth investigating summer schools. They are usually attached to public schools and universities who wish to make the fullest use of their accommodation by renting it out during the summer holiday or long vacation. Such courses usually take place in the dog days of July and August, when there is little to do at home except to mow the grass and water the greenhouse. So, if you live near Eton, Millfield or Cambridge, it is certainly worth ringing up to ask if you can be put in touch with the summer school organisers.

Many of the leading nurseries and garden centres arrange courses, talks and practical demonstrations for their customers: some even become the centre for a thriving horticultural club. Whitehall Garden Centre in Wiltshire, for example, lays on an interesting talk every Wednesday afternoon. Endsleigh Garden Centre in Devon offers a series of courses which meet once a week for several weeks: they include Botanical Painting, Garden Design and a course for the RHS General Examination in Horticulture. Other nurseries who run courses of which we have received favourable reports include Hilliers Nurseries at Ampfield in Hampshire, Hollington Nurseries in Berkshire, and Harry Tomlinson's Bonsai Nursery in Nottinghamshire.

More garden owners are now beginning to run courses for people and use their garden as a teaching resource. These can be very rewarding. We have heard good reports of the courses run by Mary-Anne Robb at Cothay in Somerset. Other sources for courses of which we know are: the Museum of Garden History, where Caroline Holmes is running a series of day courses with such titles as the Georgian Garden, and Clock House School of Garden Design, where John Brookes runs a four-week course on Garden Design (01243 542808). Many National Trust gardens offer demonstrations regularly throughout the season: Cotehele in Cornwall, for example. It is always worthwhile to contact the nearest Regional Centre of the National Trust to find out what is on offer.

The RHS is running many more regular talks and demonstrations for keen gardeners. Details of most of them appear in our calendar section. There are full programmes of events of every kind in every region.

COURSES FOR AMATEURS

The following organisations have a national profile and are experienced organisers of courses for amateurs:

BURFORD HOUSE GARDENS
Burford House, Tenbury Wells. Hereford & Worcester WR15 8HQ
☎ 01432 830083
Fax 01432 830110

Acorn Activities run courses on Garden Design and Flower Gardens at Burford throughout the season.

CABBAGES & KINGS
Wilderness Farm, Hadlow Down, East Sussex TN22 4HU
☎ 01825 830552

In recent years the Centre for Garden Design has run educational workshops from March to October. Garden walks and design surgeries draw on the experience of Ryl Nowell, Gay Search and Andrew Lawson.

CAMBRIDGE GARDEN COURSES
Dullingham House, Newmarket, Cambridgeshire CB8 9UP
☎ 01638 508186

A series of eight workshops, which can be attended individually, or as a course on consecutive Mondays. Gardeners are taught how to plan ahead, then offered practical sessions on such topics as: herbaceous perennials; pruning roses; seed collecting; lawn care; winter protection; planting bulbs; composts.

CATRIONA BOYLE'S GARDEN SCHOOL
Penpergwm Lodge, Abergavenny, Gwent NP7 9AS
☎ 01873 840208

This well-established school offers one-day courses by really top personalities: Rosemary Verey, Jekka McVicar and Roy Lancaster are among them. Highly recommended.

CLOCK HOUSE SCHOOL OF GARDEN DESIGN
Denmans, Fontwell, Arundel, West Sussex BN18 0SU
☎ 01243 542808

Four-week courses and day seminars all through the year from a top-on-the-range school. There is a wide choice of topics: definitely worth investigating.

COURSES AT ENGLEFIELD
Englefield Estate Office, Theale, Reading, Berkshire. RG7 5DU
☎ 0118 930 2221
Fax 0118 930 2226

An interesting programme of lectures, workshops and demonstrations concentrating upon conservation: this includes water conservation, preserving endangered plants, and establishing seed banks.

ENGLISH GARDENING SCHOOL
Chelsea Physic Garden, 66 Royal Hospital Road, London SW3 4HS
☎ 0171 352 4347
Fax 0171 376 3936

The English Gardening School at the Chelsea Physic Garden has short courses, seminars and demonstrations for amateurs on a wide choice of practical and creative topics. They may be all-day courses on such topics as Down to Earth Gardening, Planting Plans & How to Draw Them, Reliable Roses, and Interesting Irises, or longer courses such as the four-day course on Planting and Planning, personally run by the school's principal Rosemary Alexander and top garden-designer Anthony du Gard Pasley. They also offer a summer school on garden design for one week in July.

GARDENERS' BREAKS
Special Plants Nursery, Hill Farm Barn, Greenways Lane, Cold Ashton, Chippenham, Wiltshire SN14 8LA
☎ 01225 891868

Derry Watkins runs day-long courses in such topics as: Planting Up Containers; Taking Cuttings; Conservatory Gardening; Growing Plants for Sale. Most of the courses are in September, October and November.

HARLOW CARR BOTANICAL GARDENS
Crag Lane, Harrogate, North Yorkshire HG3 1QB
☎ 01423 565418

The Northern Horticultural Society offers a wide range of courses and lectures, up to the level of the RHS General Examination in Horticulture. They are so numerous that we can only list a sample: Garden Design (14 consecutive Fridays); Plant Appreciation (12 consecutive Fridays); Rare & Unusual Plants (10 consecutive Thursdays); Plants & Gardens of Yorkshire (12 Tuesday evenings at fortnightly intervals); Botanical Painting (9 consecutive Mondays); Flower Photography (one day); Traditional Hedges and their Maintenance (one day); Alpine Sinks & Troughs (half day); Raising Plants from Seed (one day); Constructing Rock-gardens (one day); Minimum Cultivation (one day); Drystone Walling (one day); Pruning (one day).

HENRY DOUBLEDAY RESEARCH ASSOCIATION
Ryton Organic Gardens, Ryton-on-Dunsmore, Coventry, Warwickshire CV8 3LG
☎ 01203 303517
Fax 01203 639229

HDRA runs day-long special events and workshops for people who wish to understand more about the organic approach to gardening. Titles include: Organic Garden

Design; The Management of Small Woodlands; An Introduction to Permaculture; Compost-making.

INSTITUTE OF ADVANCED ARCHITECTURAL STUDIES
The University of York, The King's Manor, York YO1 2EP
☎ 01904 433963

The IAAS is well-known in horticultural circles for the pioneering work of Dr Peter Goodbody on garden history. Every year, the Institute runs short courses (one to eight days) on such issues as Garden Maintenance, Public Parks, Management Plans and Garden Archaeology.

KINGCOMBE CENTRE
Toller Porcorum, Dorchester, Dorset DT2 0EQ
☎ 01300 320684

Residential courses include: Organic Gardening; Fungi. Some of the day courses may also be of interest.

OPEN COLLEGE OF THE ARTS
Houndhill, Worsborough, Barnsley, South Yorkshire S70 6TU
☎ 01226 730495
Fax 01226 730838

The College offers courses in garden design, one for beginners and one for more advanced students. Both can be taken as correspondence courses or with face-to-face tuition.

ROYAL BOTANIC GARDENS, KEW
Education and Marketing Department, Richmond, Surrey TW9 3AB
☎ 0181 332 5623 or 5626

Kew's Education and Marketing Department runs short courses (up to two weeks) and study days throughout the year. Examples of their courses are: Botanical Illustration; Plants in Focus; Plant Conservation Techniques; Water Gardening; Aspects of Gardening.

ROYAL HORTICULTURAL SOCIETY
Education Department, RHS Garden Wisley, Woking, Surrey GU23 6QB
☎ 01483 224234
Fax 01483 211750

The RHS has an extensive programme of educational events, courses, lectures and demonstrations. Most are listed in the Calendar section (q.v.). All such events receive good publicity in *The Garden*.

WEST DEAN COLLEGE
Chichester, West Sussex PO18 0QZ
☎ 01243 811301
Fax 01243 811343

West Dean College is set in one of the most beautiful and exciting gardens in the south of England. Its study days and residential courses (up to nine days) cover a wide range of topics including the following: Garden design; Sculptural plants; Ironwork for the garden; Towards an organic garden; Garden photography.

GETTING MORE SERIOUS

An increasing number of amateurs study for the RHS General Examination in Horticulture. This was originally instituted over a hundred years ago as a qualification for career horticulturists and it remains a good starting point for professionals, but it is also attractive to keen gardeners who would like to put their horticultural knowledge to the test. The syllabus is designed to cover fundamental horticultural practices and the application of scientific principles to the tasks of gardening. It does not require a detailed knowledge of plants.

The subjects covered in the course include: the social and legal context; plant taxonomy and nomenclature; plant structure and characteristics; plant processes such as pollination; plant physiology and environmental factors affecting plant growth and development; the principles of genetics and breeding for plant improvement; soils and other growing media; weeds, pests, diseases and disorders; practical husbandry in relation to the main horticultural activities, including cut flowers, soft fruit, aquatic plants, roses and vegetables; the selection and use of plants in relation to location; health, safety, regulations and codes of practice.

There follows a selection of horticultural and adult education colleges, listed in alphabetical order of county, which prepare candidates for the RHS General Examination in Horticulture. For a full list of centres offering courses which lead to the exam, contact the RHS Education Department, RHS Garden Wisley, Woking, Surrey GU23 6QB.

HIGHLANDS COLLEGE
P. O. Box 1000, St Saviour, Jersey JE4 9QA
☎ 01534 608608

BARNFIELD COLLEGE
New Bedford Road, Luton, Bedfordshire LU2 7BF
☎ 01582 569600

COURSES FOR AMATEURS

BERKSHIRE COLLEGE OF AGRICULTURE
Hall Place, Burchetts Green, Maidenhead,
Berkshire SL6 6QR
☎ 01628 824444

AYLESBURY COLLEGE
Hampden Hall, Stoke Mandeville,
Buckinghamshire HP22 5TB
☎ 01296 434111

CHESHAM ADULT C E CENTRE
Amersham School, Stanley Hill, Amersham,
Buckinghamshire HP7 9HH
☎ 01494 726224

REASEHEATH COLLEGE
(Cheshire College of Agriculture), Reaseheath,
Nantwich, Cheshire CW5 6DF
☎ 01270 613211

BUDE & LAUNCESTON ADULT EDUCATION
Gregson Centre, New Road, Stratton, Bude,
Cornwall EX23 9AP
☎ 01288 356629

DUCHY COLLEGE
Rosewarne, Camborne, Cornwall TR14 0AB
☎ 01209 710077

PROBUS GARDENS
Probus, Truro, Cornwall TR2 4HQ
☎ 01726 882597

NEWTON RIGG COLLEGE
Cumbria College of Agriculture and Forestry,
Newton Rigg, Penrith, Cumbria CA11 0AH
☎ 01768 863791

BROOMFIELD COLLEGE
Morley, Derby, Derbyshire DE7 6DN
☎ 01332 831245

BICTON SCHOOL OF HORTICULTURE
East Budleigh, Budleigh Salterton, Devon EX9 7BY
☎ 01395 68353

JOHN KITTO COMMUNITY CENTRE
Honicknowle Lane, Pennycross, Plymouth, Devon
PL5 3NE
☎ 01752 208230

PILTON COMMUNITY COLLEGE
Chaddiford Lane, Barnstaple, Devon EX31 1RF
☎ 01271 346710

ST LOYE'S COLLEGE
Topsham Road, Exeter, Devon EX2 6EP
☎ 01392 55428

KINGSTON MAURWARD COLLEGE
Kingston Maurward, Dorchester, Dorset DT2 8PY
☎ 01305 264738

HOUGHALL COLLEGE
Houghall, Durham, Durham DH1 3SG
☎ 0191 386 1351

BRIGHTON COLLEGE OF TECHNOLOGY
Pelham Street, Brighton, East Sussex BN1 4FA
☎ 01273 667788

PLUMPTON COLLEGE
Ditchling Road, Plumpton, Lewes, East Sussex
BN7 3AE
☎ 01273 890454

CHELTENHAM & GLOUCESTER COLLEGE OF HIGHER EDUCATION
Francis Close Hall Campus, Swindon Road,
Cheltenham, Gloucestershire GL50 4AZ
☎ 01242 532922

HARTPURY COLLEGE
Hartpury House, Gloucester, Gloucestershire
GL19 3BE
☎ 01452 700283

SOUTH GLOUCESTERSHIRE EDUCATION
244 Station Road, Yate, Bristol BS17 4AF
☎ 01454 315603

UNIVERSITY OF BRISTOL BOTANIC GARDEN
Bracken Hill, North Road, Leigh Woods,
Gloucestershire BS8 3PF
☎ 0117 973 3682

MANCHESTER CITY COLLEGE
Wythenshawe Park Centre, Moor Road,
Wythenshawe, Greater Manchester M23 9BQ
☎ 0161 957 1525

RIDGE DANYERS CENTRE
Cheadle Road, Cheadle Hulme, Greater
Manchester SK8 5HA
☎ 0161 485 4372

TAMESIDE COLLEGE OF TECHNOLOGY
Beaufort Road, Ashton-under-Lyne, Greater
Manchester OL6 6NX
☎ 0161 330 6911

COURSES FOR AMATEURS

WIGAN & LEIGHT COLLEGE
Parsons Walk, Wigan, Greater Manchester
WNI IRS
☎ 01942 761501

FARNBOROUGH COLLEGE OF TECHNOLOGY
Boundary Road, Farnborough, Hampshire
GU14 6SB
☎ 01252 391319

SPARSHOLT COLLEGE HAMPSHIRE
Sparsholt, Winchester, Hampshire SO21 2NF
☎ 01962 776441

NORTH EAST WORCESTERSHIRE COLLEGE
Blackwood Road, Bromsgrove, Hereford & Worcester B60 1PQ
☎ 01527 572838

PERSHORE COLLEGE OF HORTICULTURE
Avonbank, Pershore, Hereford & Worcester
WR10 3JP
☎ 01386 552443

OAKLANDS COLLEGE
Hatfield Road, St Albans, Hertfordshire AL4 0JA
☎ 01727 850651

WEST HERTS COLLEGE
Leggatts Way, Watford, Hertfordshire WD2 6BJ
☎ 01923 684848

ISLE OF WIGHT COLLEGE
Medina Way, Newport, Isle of Wight PO30 5TA
☎ 01983 526631

HADLOW COLLEGE
Hadlow, Tonbridge, Kent TN11 0AL
☎ 01732 850551

BLACKPOOL & THE FYLDE COLLEGE
Carr Head Lane, Poulton-le-Fylde, Lancashire
FY6 8JB
☎ 01253 894079

MYERSCOUGH COLLEGE
Myerscough Hall, Bilsborrow, Preston, Lancashire
PR3 0RY
☎ 01995 640611

NELSON & COLNE COLLEGE
Barrowford Road, Colne, Lancashire BB9 9QS
☎ 01282 440200

SKELMERSDALE COLLEGE
Northway, Skelmersdale, Lancashire WN8 6LU
☎ 01695 728744

BROOKSBY COLLEGE
Brooksby, Melton Mowbray, Leicestershire
LE14 2LJ
☎ 01664 434291

LOUGHBOROUGH COLLEGE
Radmoor, Loughborough, Leicestershire
LE11 3BT
☎ 01509 215831

GRIMSBY COLLEGE
Nins Corner, Grimsby, Lincolnshire DN34 5BQ
☎ 01472 311222

BRENTFORD ADULT EDUCATION
Boston Manor Road, Brentford, London
☎ 0181 569 7212

CAPEL MANOR COLLEGE
Bullsmoor Lane, Enfield, London EN1 4RQ
☎ 0181 366 4442

EALING TERTIARY COLLEGE
Norwood Green, Southall, London UB2 4LA
☎ 0181 231 6265

JOHN KELLY CENTRE
Crest Road, Dollis Hill, London NW2 7SN
☎ 0181 208 4654

LAMBETH COLLEGE
Clapham Centre, 45 Clapham Common Southside,
London SW4 9ESX
☎ 0171 501 5048

MERTON ADULT COLLEGE
Whatley Avenue, Wimbledon, London SW20 9NS
☎ 0181 543 9292

THE ENGLISH GARDENING SCHOOL
Chelsea Physic Garden, 66 Royal Hospital Road,
London SW3 4HS
☎ 0171 352 4347

THE INSTITUTE – HAMPSTEAD GARDEN SUBURB
Central Square, London NW11 7BN
☎ 0181 455 9951

COURSES FOR AMATEURS

KNOWSLEY COMMUNITY COLLEGE, LANDBASED INDUSTRIES
The Kennels, Knowsley Park, Prescot, Merseyside
L34 4AQ
☎ 0151 549 1500

SOUTHPORT COLLEGE OF ART AND TECHNOLOGY
Mornington Road, Southport, Merseyside
PR9 0TT
☎ 01704 500606

ST HELEN'S COLLEGE
Crow Lane East, Newton le Willows, Merseyside
WA12 9TT
☎ 01925 220451

WIRRAL METROPOLITAN COLLEGE
Carlett Park, Eastham, Merseyside L62 0AY
☎ 0151 551 7402

ASKHAM BRYAN COLLEGE
Askham Bryan, York, North Yorkshire YO2 3PR
☎ 01904 702121

BISHOP BURTON COLLEGE
Bishop Burton, Beverley, North Yorkshire
HU17 8QG
☎ 01964 550481

NORTHERN HORTICULTURAL SOCIETY
Harlow Carr, Harrogate, North Yorkshire
HG3 1QB
☎ 01423 565418

MOULTON COLLEGE
West Street, Moulton, Northamptonshire
NN3 1RR
☎ 01604 491131

KIRKLEY HALL COLLEGE
Ponteland, Newcastle-upon-Tyne, Northumberland
NE20 0AQ
☎ 01661 860808

BRACKENHURST COLLEGE
Southwell, Nottinghamshire NG25 0QF
☎ 01636 817000

FAIRHAM COMMUNITY COLLEGE
Farnborough Road, Clifton, Nottingham,
Nottinghamshire NG11 9AE
☎ 0115 974 4400

NORTH NOTTINGHAMSHIRE COLLEGE
Carlton Road, Worksop, Nottinghamshire
S81 7HP
☎ 01909 473561

NORTH OXFORDSHIRE COLLEGE & SCHOOL OF ART
Broughton Road, Banbury, Oxfordshire
OX16 9QA
☎ 01295 252221

WEST OXFORDSHIRE COLLEGE
Warren Farm Centre, Horton-cum-Studley,
Oxfordshire OX33 1BY
☎ 01865 351794

MARKET DRAYTON COMMUNITY EDUCATION
The Grove School, Markey Drayton, Shropshire
TF9 1HF
☎ 01630 652121

WALFORD COLLEGE OF AGRICULTURE
Baschurch, Shrewsbury, Shropshire SY4 2HL
☎ 01939 260461

CANNINGTON COLLEGE
Cannington, Bridgwater, Somerset TA5 2LS
☎ 01278 652226

NORTON RADSTOCK COLLEGE
South Hill Park, Radstock, Bath, Somerset BA3 3RW
☎ 01761 433161

ST LUKE'S CENTRE
Wellsway, Bath, Somerset BA2 2BD
☎ 01272 612646

BARNSLEY COLLEGE
Church Street, Barnsley, South Yorkshire S70 2AX
☎ 01226 730191

DONCASTER COLLEGE
Waterdale, Doncaster, South Yorkshire DN1 3EX
☎ 01302 553553

SHEFFIELD COLLEGE
Parson Cross Centre, Remington Road, Sheffield,
South Yorkshire S5 9PB
☎ 0114 260 2500

RODBASTON COLLEGE
Rodbaston, Penkridge, Staffordshire ST19 5PH
☎ 01785 712209

COURSES FOR AMATEURS

STOKE-ON-TRENT COLLEGE
Burslem Campus, Moorland Road, Burslem,
Staffordshire ST6 1JJ
☎ 01782 208208

CHESSINGTON ADULT EDUCATION
Crabtree Drive, Givons Grove, Leatherhead,
Surrey KT22 8LJ
☎ 01372 372515

KEW SCHOOL OF HORTICULTURE
Royal Botanic Gardens, Kew, Richmond, Surrey
TW9 3AB
☎ 0181 332 5545

MERRIST WOOD COLLEGE
Worplesdon, Guildford, Surrey GU3 3PE
☎ 01483 232424

NESCOT
Reigate Road, Ewell, Surrey KT17 3DS
☎ 0181 394 1731

WARWICKSHIRE COLLEGE
Moreton Centre, Moreton Morrell, Warwick,
Warwickshire CV11 6BH
☎ 01203 345435

BOURNVILLE COLLEGE OF FURTHER EDUCATION
Bristol Road South, Northfield, Birmingham, West
Midlands B31 2AJ
☎ 0121 411 1414

SOLIHULL COLLEGE
Blossomfield Road, Solihull, West Midlands
B91 1SB
☎ 0121 711 2111

SOUTH BIRMINGHAM COLLEGE
Cole Bank Road, Hall Green, Birmingham, West
Midlands B28 8ES
☎ 0121 694 5000

STOURBRIDGE COLLEGE
Horticulture and Conservation Unit, Leasowes
Park Nursery, Leasowes Lane, Stourbridge, West
Midlands B62 8QF
☎ 0121 550 0007

TILE HILL COLLEGE
Tile Hill, Coventry, West Midlands CV4 9SV
☎ 01203 694200

WOLVERHAMPTON ADULT EDUCATION
Old Hall Street, Wolverhampton, West Midlands
WV1 3AU
☎ 01902 558180

BRINSBURY COLLEGE
North Heath, Pulborough, West Sussex
RH20 1DL
☎ 01798 873832

AIREDALE & WHARFDALE COLLEGE
Calverley Lane, Horsforth, Leeds, West Yorkshire
LS18 4RQ
☎ 0113 239 5800

CALDERDALE COLLEGE
Francis Street, Halifax, West Yorkshire HX1 3UZ
☎ 01422 357 357

HUDDERSFIELD TECHNICAL COLLEGE
New North Road, Huddersfield, West Yorkshire
HD1 5NN
☎ 01484 536521

SHIPLEY COLLEGE
Exhibition Road, Saltaire, Shipley, West Yorkshire
BD18 3JW
☎ 01274 757222

WAKEFIELD DISTRICT COLLEGE
Station Road, Hemsworth, Pontefract, West
Yorkshire
☎ 01924 789628

LACKHAM COLLEGE
Lacock, Chippenham, Wiltshire SN15 2NY
☎ 01249 443111

EAST DOWN INSTITUTE
Donard Street, Newcastle, Co. Down BT33 0AP
☎ 01396 722451

SCOIL STOFÁIN NAOFA
Tramore Road, Cork, Co. Cork
☎ 00 353 51 643105

ST GOBAN'S COLLEGE
Sheskin, Bantry, Co. Cork
☎ 00 353 210 27 50989

KILDALTON AGRICULTURAL AND HORTICULTURAL COLLEGE
Piltown, Co. Kilkenny, Eire
☎ 00 353 51 643105

LANGSIDE COLLEGE
School of Horticulture, Woodburn House, 27 Buchanan Drive, Rutherglen, Strathclyde G73 3PF
☎ 0141 647 6300

ANGUS COLLEGE
Keptie Road, Arbroath, Tayside DD11 3EA
☎ 01241 432600

WELSH COLLEGE OF HORTICULTURE
Northop, Mold, Clwyd CH7 6AA
☎ 01352 840861

PENCOED COLLEGE
Pencoed, Bridgend, Mid Glamorgan CF35 5LG
☎ 01554 748259

RHS DIPLOMA IN HORTICULTURE

The RHS Diploma in Horticulture is the next step up from the RHS General Examination in Horticulture. It is primarily intended for professional horticulturists, but attracts entries from some dedicated and experienced amateur gardeners.

Candidates are examined in practical and applied horticultural knowledge and therefore a period of broad horticultural experience is essential. Success in the RHS Diploma is essential for those wishing to proceed to the Master of Horticulture (RHS) Award.

The examination comprises four three-hour written papers and, for those who achieve the necessary standard, a practical and oral examination.

THE MASTER OF HORTICULTURE (RHS)

The MHort (RHS) is said to be the premier qualification for horticultural professionals. Registration is open to those who have achieved the RHS Diploma in Horticulture and who have the necessary appropriate professional horticultural experience.

The examination comprises four three-hour written papers: two compulsory papers which test candidates' knowledge of the principles of management and their application to horticulture; and two horticultural technology papers, selected by candidates from a range of options, which test in-depth knowledge of their specialism, including current practice, trends, research and development. Candidates achieving the necessary standard proceed to the Managerial and Technical Competence Assessment which comprises technical skills assessment; management case study and associated oral examinations; and dissertation and associated oral examination.

Further details of each of the qualifications mentioned, including entry requirements, application forms and fees can be obtained from the RHS Examinations Office at Wisley.

The RHS also provides a range of training opportunities at Wisley for young people embarking on a vocational career and for people making a new career. The Wisley Diploma in Practical Horticulture is a two-year course of paid work experience and academic studies, validated by a practical examination at the end of the programme. Successful candidates will be entitled to use the designation 'Dip. Hort. (Wisley)' after their names, and will be able to sit the written part of the RHS Diploma in Horticulture examination (as an additional qualification) after the course finishes. The One Year Specialist Certificate is a twelve-month programme of paid work experience offered in five different disciplines: Ornamental Horticulture; Fruit Cultivation; Rock & Alpine Gardening; Orchid Culture & Glasshouse Technique; and Estate Management with Arboriculture. Schools-related work experience is offered to Year 10 & 11 students in blocks of one or two weeks. Training and career guidance is available on-site. Voluntary internships are available for periods in excess of four weeks to bona fide students of horticulture who require short term work experience.

Part Four

Useful Addresses

Societies: UK and Worldwide
Specialist Bookshops
Seed Merchants
Organisations

SOCIETIES

SPECIALIST SOCIETIES

ALPINE GARDEN SOCIETY
AGS Centre, Avon Bank, Pershore, Hereford & Worcester WR10 3JP
☎ 01386 554790
Fax 01386 554801

Contact Bill Simpson (Secretary)
Aims To encourage interest in all aspects of alpine and rock-garden plants
Membership 14,000
Subscriptions £15 single; £18 joint
Services Lectures; gardens; seed scheme; library; publications; advice; awards; shows; journal; special-interest and regional groups; outings; new rock garden at Pershore; travel awards to provide field experience for the serious study of alpine plants

Founded in 1929. The AGS caters for anyone interested in rock gardening or alpine plants. You join the national organisation which entitles you to numerous benefits including free entry to the 20 or so shows, the bulletin, the seed exchange scheme, and the advisory service. If you wish you can also join one of some 60 local groups: there is a small additional subscription which varies from group to group. You have to be a member of the national AGS in order to join. Local groups organise their own busy programmes of events, including lectures, shows and visits. The *Quarterly Bulletin of the Alpine Garden Society* is an authoritative illustrated magazine which covers alpines in cultivation and in the wild. The AGS organises guided expeditions to many countries for its members, and these are both popular and respected. It also publishes monographs and alpine titles (including the mammoth new alpine encyclopedia), and members can use the slide and postal book libraries. At local level, AGS groups are an excellent and informal way to learn and develop an interest in alpines. Some groups are more active than others: it depends on local demand. Many of the lecturers are acknowledged experts, as will be some of the group members. The dates for the national shows, and a number of group events, appear in our calendar. Most local groups allow members to bring guests and will usually admit visitors for a small charge, though if you expect to attend regularly then you should really sign up properly. AGS headquarters can put you in touch with your nearest group. The Society's newly made rock garden at the AGS Centre, Pershore, is well worth a visit.

BOTANICAL SOCIETY OF THE BRITISH ISLES
c/o Dept of Botany, The Natural History Museum, Cromwell Road, London SW7 5BD

Contact Hon. General Secretary
Aims The study of British and Irish flowering plants and ferns
Membership 2,500
Subscriptions £18; reduced rate for junior members
Services Lectures; publications; advice; journal; outings; exhibition meetings

This association of amateur and professional botanists traces its history back to 1836. Three regular publications (*Watsonia*, *BSBI Abstracts* and *BSBI News*) cover the society's activities, articles on the taxonomy and distribution of plants in the British Isles, and an annual bibliography. The society also arranges conferences, exhibitions and study trips, and undertakes research projects and surveys. Members have access to a panel of experts on the British flora and can buy various works on British botany at reduced prices. The *New Atlas of the British Flora* will be published in 2000.

BRITISH & EUROPEAN GERANIUM SOCIETY
4 Higher Meadow, Clayton-le-Woods, Chorley, Lancashire PR5 2RS
☎ 01772 453383

Contact Mrs Joan Hinchcliffe (Hon. Membership Secretary)
Aims To promote the geranium (*Pelargonium*)
Membership 975
Subscriptions £6 single; £8 double
Services Lectures; gardens; library; publications; advice; awards; shows; journal; special-interest and regional groups; outings; plant finder

The British & European Geranium Society is dedicated to growing, hybridising and exhibiting pelargoniums. The society is divided into regional groups which organise programmes of events including lectures and shows. There is an annual national show; every other year a conference is also staged. Members receive three *Gazettes* and a *Year Book*. The society has other publications too. A new service is a computerised plant finder which has details of sources for any pelargonium which is available in Europe.

BRITISH CACTUS & SUCCULENT SOCIETY
15 Brentwood Crescent, York, North Yorkshire YO1 5HU
☎ 01904 410512

Contact The Secretary

SOCIETIES / SPECIALIST 299

Membership 3,800
Subscriptions £12 in UK; £13 abroad
Services Lectures; seed scheme; library; advice; shows; journal; outings

Founded in 1983 by the amalgamation of two earlier cactus and succulent societies, the BCSS is the premier national society with associated branches in more than 100 towns throughout the British Isles. Members receive the quarterly *Journal*, a quality magazine with a wide range of good articles. The yearbook *Bradleya* is available for an extra payment. There is a good choice of activities, which cater for all interests.

BRITISH CLEMATIS SOCIETY
4 Springfield, Lightwater, Surrey GU18 5XP
☎ 01276 476387

Contact The Secretary
Aims To encourage and extend clematis cultivation, and to share knowledge with fellow members
Membership 1,200
Subscriptions £12.50 single; £18.50 joint; £15 Europe; £20 overseas; £17 overseas joint
Services Lectures; seed scheme; advice; shows; journal; outings; plant sales; demonstrations

A fast-growing society which organises meetings throughout the country and publishes a substantial illustrated journal, *The Clematis*, each year as well as supplements and newsletters. The society organises visits to gardens and nurseries. Members can obtain advice on clematis cultivation and join in the seed exchange programme. The society also produces a list of good clematis gardens and a list of clematis nurseries. It has established a fine clematis collection at the Gardens of the Rose.

BRITISH FUCHSIA SOCIETY
15 Summerfield Lane, Summerfield, Kidderminster, Hereford & Worcester DY11 7SA
☎ 01562 66688

Contact Hon. Secretary
Aims To further interest in the cultivation of fuchsias
Membership 5,700
Subscriptions £6 individual; £9 joint; £10 affiliated societies
Services Advice; shows; journal; special-interest and regional groups; rooted cuttings

The British Fuchsia Society organises eight regional shows and a London show. Members receive the *Fuchsia Annual* and a twice-yearly bulletin, as well as three rooted cuttings. They can also obtain advice from the society's experts, either by post or telephone. Special-interest groups are devoted to old cultivars and hybridising. Around 300 societies are affiliated to the national society, many of which organise programmes of events and festivals.

BRITISH GLADIOLUS SOCIETY
10 Greenway, Ashbourne, Derbyshire DE6 1EF
☎ 01335 346446

Contact Acting Secretary
Aims To stimulate interest in and improve gladiolus growing
Membership 400
Subscriptions £10 single; £11 family
Services Lectures; seed scheme; library; publications; advice; awards; shows; journal; special-interest and regional groups

Founded in 1926 the British Gladiolus Society stages four major shows each year: the National (please ring for details of date and place), the Southern at Capel Manor, the Midland at Bingley Hall in Staffordshire and the Northern at Belsay Hall. There are regional groups in Sussex and Buckinghamshire. Members keep in touch with society news through three bulletins and the yearbook, *The Gladiolus Annual*, which is published each spring. The society runs trials at three sites, and also has a book, slide and video library available for members and affiliated societies. Council members can advise on gladiolus cultivation, and the society raises money by distributing cormlets. A small range of booklets on showing and growing gladiolus is also available.

BRITISH HOSTA & HEMEROCALLIS SOCIETY
Toft Monks, The Hithe, Rodborough Common, Stroud, Gloucestershire GL5 5BN

Contact Mrs Lynda Hinton
Aims To foster interest in the cultivation of hostas and hemerocallis
Membership 300
Subscriptions £8 single; £10 joint; £12 overseas. £2 joining fee
Services Lectures; library; advice; awards; journal; outings; annual plant auction

Founded in 1981, the British Hosta & Hemerocallis Society has members spread throughout the world. It publishes an annual bulletin, and regular newsletters to keep members informed of news and events. Garden visits and lectures are arranged, and members can borrow by post from the society's specialist and comprehensive library. An annual award is presented for a hosta and a hemerocallis. Expert advice is provided via the secretary. There are some eight relevant NCCPG National Collections.

BRITISH IRIS SOCIETY
1 Sole Farm Close, Great Bookham, Surrey KT23 3ED
☎ 01372 454581

Contact Hon. Secretary
Aims To encourage and improve the cultivation of irises
Membership 740
Subscriptions £12 single
Services Lectures; seed scheme; library; publications; advice; awards; shows; journal; special-interest and regional groups; plant sales scheme; lectures for clubs and societies

The British Iris Society was founded in 1922 and caters for all levels of interest in this varied genus. The illustrated and authoritative *Iris Year Book* is supplemented by three newsletters. The society's programme includes three annual shows and occasional lectures. There are regional groups in Mercia

SOCIETIES / SPECIALIST

and Kent, and special-interest groups for species, Japanese, Siberian and Pacific Coast irises. Members can borrow from the reference library, and the society has an extensive slide collection. As well as a plant sales scheme there is also a seed distribution scheme, and expert advice is available on request. New hybrids are trialled at Wisley, and the Dykes Medal is awarded to the best British-bred hybrid in the trial.

BRITISH IVY SOCIETY
14 Holly Grove, Huyton, Merseyside L36 4JA
☎ 0151 489 1083

Contact Hon. Secretary

Unfortunately, the future of this society was said to be 'uncertain' as we went to press.

BRITISH NATIONAL CARNATION SOCIETY
Linfield, Duncote, Towcester, Northamptonshire NN12 8AH
☎ 01327 351594

Contact Mrs B M Linnell (Secretary)
Aims To improve the cultivation of the *Dianthus* family
Membership 450
Subscriptions £9 single; £10 joint
Services Lectures; publications; advice; shows; journal; discount coupon scheme

The British National Carnation Society was founded in 1949, so it is celebrating its 50th birthday this year. The society organises several shows annually: the principal ones are at RHS Westminster shows in June and October. Members receive the illustrated *Carnation Year Book* each year as well as two newsletters. New members can also choose one of the society's cultural booklets when they join. Medals and show cards are available for affiliated societies, and together the society and its affiliates hold area shows throughout the country. A coupon in the autumn newsletter gives a discount on plants from selected nurseries. A panel of carnation experts can be called on to answer questions. Other societies can hire lectures: a fee is charged to non-affiliated societies.

BRITISH ORCHID COUNCIL
PO Box 1072, Frome, Somerset BA11 5NY
☎ 01373 301501

Contact Peter Hunt (Secretary)
Membership 5,000
Services Judges training scheme; panel of speakers

The BOC is a coordinating forum for amateur and professional orchid growers. Its members include over 50 local and regional societies, the British Orchid Growers' Association, the RHS, RBG Kew and other botanical institutions. The Society publishes a useful *Grower's & Buyer's Guide to Orchids* which profiles all its members and what they offer.

BRITISH PELARGONIUM & GERANIUM SOCIETY
75 Pelham Road, Bexleyheath, Kent DA7 4LY
☎ 01322 525947

Contact Les Hodgkiss (Secretary)
Aims To promote interest in *Pelargonium*, *Geranium* and other Geraniaceae
Membership 1,000
Subscriptions £7 single; £9 joint
Services Seed scheme; advice; shows; journal; bi-annual conference; books on pelargoniums available by post

The British Pelargonium & Geranium Society was founded in 1951. It publishes a *Year Book* and three issues of *Pelargonium News* annually. The society's annual show, held in June, moves around the country, and includes classes for beginners and flower-arrangers. Every other year a conference is held. Members can take advantage of a postal advisory service, and free seeds. They stage publicity and information stands at Chelsea, Malvern and the RHS Westminster shows, and encourage other societies to join as affiliated members.

CARNIVOROUS PLANT SOCIETY
100 Lambley Lane, Burton Joyce, Nottingham, Nottinghamshire NG14 5BL

Contact Derek Petrie
Aims To bring together all those interested in carnivorous plants
Membership 650
Subscriptions £11 single; £12 Europe; £15 world
Services Seed scheme; advice; shows; journal; outings; plant search service

The Carnivorous Plant Society publishes an annual colour journal and four newsletters. It organises a number of events including visits to nurseries, field trips and open days. A plant search scheme is run, and members have free access to the seed bank. The information officer can provide advice on all topics.

COTTAGE GARDEN SOCIETY
Hurstfield House, 244 Edleston Road, Crewe, Cheshire CW2 7EJ
☎ 01270 250776
Fax 01270 250118

Contact Membership Secretary
Aims To promote and conserve cottage-garden plants and to encourage cottage-style gardens
Membership 8,000
Subscriptions £5 individual; £8 joint
Services Lectures; seed scheme; publications; shows; journal; special-interest and regional groups; list of members' gardens which can be visited

The Cottage Garden Society promotes and conserves worthwhile old-fashioned garden plants, and encourages owners of small gardens to garden in the cottage style. Members receive a quarterly bulletin and can take part in the annual seed distribution. The society has a growing number of active regional groups: each organises lectures, meetings, visits and other events. The society hires out slides to members.

Cyclamen Society
Tile Barn House, Standen Street, Iden Green, Benenden, Kent TN17 4LB
Contact Peter Moore
Aims To further interest in and scientific knowledge of cyclamen
Membership 1,700
Subscriptions £7 individual; £8 family
Services Lectures; gardens; seed scheme; library; advice; awards; shows; journal; annual weekend conference

The Cyclamen Society has an international membership but is based in Britain. Its work includes research and conservation, while members benefit from the twice-yearly journal, a seed distribution scheme and access to expert advice through the society's advisory panel. It exhibits and stages shows, organises meetings and lectures, and maintains a specialist library of literature and slides on cyclamen.

Daffodil Society
The Meadows, Puxton, Weston-super-Mare, Somerset BS24 6TF
☎ 01934 833641
Contact Jackie Petherbridge (Secretary)
Membership 700
Subscriptions £5 individual; £7.50 family
Services Seed scheme; publications; advice; shows; journal; special-interest and regional groups

Established in 1898, the Society caters for breeders, exhibitors and lovers of daffodils. It also has over 200 affiliated societies as members. It is closely involved in the competitions at RHS Westminster shows, and the Harrogate Spring show as well as running its own show at Solihull (17–18 April 1999). Members receive the annual *Journal* in February and the *Newsletter* in July. In addition to the seed scheme, there are good opportunities to acquire new cultivars in the annual Bulb Lottery.

Delphinium Society
Takakkaw, Ice House Wood, Oxted, Surrey RH8 9DW
☎ 01883 715049
Contact Membership Secretary
Aims To encourage and extend the culture of delphiniums
Membership 1,400
Subscriptions £5 single & joint; £6 overseas
Services Seed scheme; publications: *Simply Delphiniums*, £2.50; advice; awards; shows; journal

The Delphinium Society dates back to 1928. New members receive a mixed packet of seed when they join, and all members can buy the society's hand-pollinated seeds of garden hybrids and species. The illustrated *Year Book* is a unique source of information about the genus. Two shows, at which cups are awarded, are held each year. Members gain free entry to the shows, and can also take advantage of advice on cultivation and a number of social events.

Friends of Brogdale
The Brogdale Horticultural Trust, Brogdale Farm, Faversham, Kent ME13 8XZ
☎ 01795 535286
Fax 01795 531710
Contact The Director
Aims Fruit research and conservation
Membership 1,700
Subscriptions £15 ordinary; £25 family
Services Lectures; advice; journal; grafting service

The Brogdale Experimental Horticultural Station was bought from the government by the Brogdale Trust in 1991 to safeguard its work. It carries out commercial research and trialling, and maintains exceptional reference collections of fruit varieties, including over 2,300 different apples. Friends receive free entry to the site, priority booking for events, and access to a Friday afternoon information line. There is also a quarterly newsletter.

Fruit Group of the Royal Horticultural Society
80 Vincent Square, London SW1P 2PE
☎ 0171 630 7422
Fax 0171 233 9525
Contact Mavis Sweetingham
Aims To promote interest in the cultivation of fruit
Membership 400
Services Gardens; publications; shows; outings

Membership of the Fruit Group is open to all members of the RHS. The Group exhibits at the Chelsea Flower Show, the RHS Great Autumn Show, the Harrogate Autumn Show and the Malvern Autumn Show. Members have the opportunity to exhibit at RHS shows and join Group outings, but perhaps the best meetings are those at Wisley, where they can study the RHS's fruit collection at close quarters, in the company of knowledgeable members of staff and other experts. These meetings often have a practical aspect: the occasional 'gooseberry tastings' are not to be missed. The Group balances its activities between top fruit and soft fruit, so that all members' interests are accommodated within the annual programme. It has also begun to set up sub-groups, e.g. in the West Midlands (based at Pershore) and the south-west (run from Rosemoor).

Hardy Plant Society
Little Orchard, Great Comberton, Pershore, Hereford & Worcester WR10 3DP
☎ 01386 710317
Contact Mrs Pam Adams (Administrator)
Aims To stimulate interest in growing hardy herbaceous plants
Membership 12,000
Subscriptions £10 single; £12 joint (in 1998)
Services Lectures; gardens; seed scheme; publications; advice; shows; journal; special-interest and regional groups; outings; slide library

SOCIETIES / SPECIALIST

The Hardy Plant Society has its own garden at the Pershore College of Horticulture. Members join the national society and can then choose to join one of about 40 regional groups. In addition there six special-interest groups (Grasses; Hardy geraniums; Half-hardy plants; Pulmonarias; Peonies; and Variegated plants) and a Correspondents Group for those who cannot come to meetings. Two journals are sent to members each year, along with regular newsletters. The national society attends Chelsea and the RHS Westminster shows, while area groups patronise local shows and arrange their own programmes of events. An annual seed distribution list is circulated to all members. The society is also involved in conserving old cultivars and introducing new ones, and has produced a number of useful publications. It has grown fast in recent years and is going through a period of change. The local groups organise their own busy programmes of meetings, trips and garden visits: the additional cost of joining such a group is usually very small. Full details of the local and specialist groups are available from the national society: only HPS members can join a local or specialist group. Because all HPS events are for HPS members only they are not included in our calendar.

Hardy Orchid Society
54 Thorncliffe Road, Oxford, Oxfordshire OX2 7BA

Contact Richard Manuel
Membership 300
Subscriptions Single £6; family £9
Services Lectures; advice; shows; journal

The society is interested in all terrestrial orchids, British and foreign. There are two meetings a year, at Pershore, as well as field meetings in Europe.

Heather Society
Denbeigh, All Saints Road, Creeting St Mary, Ipswich, Suffolk IP6 8PJ

☎ & Fax 01449 711220

Contact Administrator
Aims To promote interest in heathers and provide a friendly meeting place for enthusiasts
Membership 650
Subscriptions £10 single; £12 joint
Services Publications; advice; shows; journal; special-interest and regional groups; slide library

The Heather Society was founded in 1963. Members receive the society's authoritative *Year Book*, which is edited by Dr Charles Nelson, and a twice-yearly bulletin of news and events. Competitions are held through the RHS at Westminster. A slide library is maintained, and expert advice on cultivation and other technical queries is available. Regional groups arrange a series of local events, and an annual weekend conference, linked to the AGM, is held at a different location each year (Falmouth, 10–13 September in 1999). There are national collections at Wisley, Surrey, and Cherrybank, Perth.

Hebe Society
Rosemergy, Hain Walk, St Ives, Cornwall TR26 2AF
☎ 01736 795225

Contact Hon. Secretary
Aims To encourage, conserve and extend the cultivation of hebe, parahebe and all New Zealand native plants
Membership 350
Subscriptions £7 single; £9 joint; £12 professional
Services Publications; advice; shows; journal; special-interest and regional groups

An international society, based in Britain. It was established in 1985, and has since expanded its brief to include other New Zealand plants. Quarterly issues of *Hebe News* keep members in touch with activities, and include botanical and horticultural articles. Local groups have been formed in the north-west of England, Cornwall and the Cotswolds. The society maintains a slide library, operates a cutting exchange service and produces booklets about hebes and parahebes. Society members can also obtain written advice on request. Five National Collections are held by members.

Henry Doubleday Research Association (HDRA)
Ryton Organic Gardens, Ryton on Dunsmore, Coventry, West Midlands CV8 3LG
☎ 01203 303517
Fax 01203 639229

Contact Jackie Gear
Aims To promote and advise on organic gardening, growing and food
Membership 24,000
Subscriptions £17 single; £20 joint
Services Gardens; seed scheme; library; publications; advice; journal; special-interest and regional groups; trials; product discounts

Europe's largest organic organisation, founded in 1958. At the Ryton headquarters there is a ten-acre garden, and a reference library which members can use. Members are kept up to date with HDRA events through a quarterly magazine. In addition there are over 50 local groups around the country. The society provides free advice on organic gardening to its members, and they receive discounts on HDRA products and books. They can also join the Heritage Seed programme for £8 (£16 for non-members): this scheme propagates and preserves vegetable varieties which have been squeezed out of commerce by current legislation. Since they are not allowed to be sold, the HDRA gives them away to subscribers. Hand in hand with this project is *The Vegetable Finder*. The HDRA also carries out scientific research, consultancy work for industry and public bodies, and worldwide research and agricultural aid projects. Members are entitled to free entry to Brogdale, Harlow Carr, West Dean in West Sussex, the three RHS gardens at Wisley, Hyde Hall and Rosemoor, and the Centre Terre Vivante near Grenoble. The association publishes a directory of organic gardens belonging to members and open to fellow members. Last year HDRA released

SOCIETIES / SPECIALIST 303

a disease-resistant rose called 'Natural Beauty'.

HERB SOCIETY
Deddington Hill Farm,
Warmington, Banbury,
Oxfordshire OX17 1XB
☎ 01295 692000
Contact Nicolette Westwood
Aims To bring together all who have an interest in herbs
Membership 2,400
Subscriptions Adults £20; OAPs £17.50; overseas £28
Services Lectures; gardens; journal

Founded in 1927 as the Society of Herbalists, the Society aims to bring together all with an interest in herbs. Members receive three copies of the Society's magazine *Herbs*, and four copies of the newsletter *Herbarium* each year. Seminars and workshops are arranged nationwide in appropriate settings. Information on suppliers, literature and all aspects of growing herbs is available to members. The Society's garden is part of the Henry Doubleday Research Association's new garden at Yalding in Kent.

JAPANESE GARDEN SOCIETY
Groves Mill, Shakers Lane, Long Itchington, Warwickshire CV23 8QB
☎ 01926 632746
Contact Mrs Kira Dalton
Aims To record, conserve and encourage Japanese-style gardens
Membership 500
Subscriptions £20 single; £30 couple
Services Lectures; library; shows; journal; special-interest and regional groups; outings

A new society which is devoted to gardens influenced by the Japanese tradition of design. It is compiling a register of Japanese gardens in the UK (some 200+ recorded so far), and works for the conservation of existing gardens and the creation of new ones. The Society organises tours to Japan and publishes a list of Japanese gardens open for the NGS. It has seven regional groups: members receive the quarterly journal *Shakkei*.

LILY GROUP OF THE ROYAL HORTICULTURAL SOCIETY
Wilton Cottage, Drakes Bridge Road, Eckington, Pershore, Hereford & Worcester WR10 3BN
☎ 01386 750794
Fax 01386 750524
Contact Michael Upward
Aims To encourage the cultivation of *Lilium* and related genera
Membership 600
Subscriptions £5
Services Lectures; seed scheme; publications; awards; shows; journal; outings; bulb auction

Membership of the Lily Group is open to all members of the RHS. It is the largest lily society in Europe and the only one in Britain. Members receive three newsletters a year. Lectures are associated with RHS shows at Westminster (at least two a year), and the Group also exhibits at Hampton Court. There is an annual bulb auction at the late-autumn show and the Group issues a Seed List early in the year: it offers a remarkable choice of lily and Liliaceae seed sent by donors at home and abroad. Advice on all aspects of growing these plants is available from the General Secretary, via the RHS.

NATIONAL ASSOCIATION OF FLOWER ARRANGEMENT SOCIETIES
21 Denbigh Street, London SW1V 2HF
☎ 0171 828 5145
Fax 0171 821 0587
Contact The Secretary
Aims To encourage of the love of flowers and demonstrate their decorative value
Membership 75,000
Subscriptions Payable to local clubs
Services Lectures; library; publications; awards; shows; journal; special-interest and regional groups; outings; book service

Founded in 1959. NAFAS is the umbrella organisation for nearly 1,500 flower-arrangement clubs. The Association is very active in training and teaching arrangers of all skill levels. Local clubs organise demonstrations and competitions, and area groups stage exhibits at NAFAS and local shows. Regular flower festivals are organised to raise money for charitable causes, and arrangements in hospitals are another important part of the NAFAS activity. Members coordinate the flowers at Westminster Abbey, and do the arrangements for major occasions including royal weddings. *The Flower Arranger* is circulated quarterly; members can use the book service, and there is a book and slide library at the London headquarters. Prospective members should write to headquarters in the first instance: they will put you in touch with a local club. Subscriptions to these clubs vary and are usually modest. All clubs are represented at area level: there are over 20 areas throughout Britain. The 6th International Show of the World Association of Flower Arrangement Societies takes place in Durban, South Africa, on 11–14 February. The next show, in 2002, will be in Scotland.

NATIONAL AURICULA AND PRIMULA SOCIETY (MIDLAND & WEST SECTION)
6 Lawson Close, Saltford, Somerset BS18 3LB
☎ 01225 872893
Contact Peter Ward (Hon. Secretary)
Aims To improve and encourage the cultivation of florists' auriculas
Membership 500+
Subscriptions £5 home; £6 abroad
Services Lectures; publications; advice; awards; shows; journal

Founded in 1900. Members receive the year book *Argus* and two newsletters every year. The society also publishes information sheets on cultivation, guides to varieties and a history of auriculas. Three shows are held a year, one at Saltford (between Bristol and Bath) and two in the Midlands at Knowle. Plant sales are held at the society's shows: some varieties are not available commercially.

SOCIETIES / SPECIALIST

NATIONAL AURICULA AND PRIMULA SOCIETY (SOUTHERN SECTION)
67 Warnham Court Road, Carshalton Beeches, Surrey SM5 3ND
Contact Hon. Secretary
Aims To improve and encourage the cultivation of auriculas and hardy primroses
Membership 400
Subscriptions £7 home; £8 overseas
Services Lectures; publications; advice; awards; shows; journal; special-interest and regional groups
Founded in 1876. Members receive a *Year Book* and an annual newsletter. Three shows will be held this year: the Early Primula Show at Wisley on 13 March, the Primula Show on 3 April at Datchet Village Hall and the Auricula show on 24 April, also at Datchet. Plants are for sale at all three shows. Members can seek advice on all aspects of primula cultivation and exhibition. The society has a third section serving the North (146 Queens Road, Cheadle Hulme, Cheshire SK8 5HY).

NATIONAL BEGONIA SOCIETY
33 Findern Lane, Willington, Derbyshire DE65 6DW
☎ 01283 702681
Contact Hon. Secretary
Aims To promote and encourage the cultivation of all begonias
Membership 800
Subscriptions £6 single; £6.50 joint; additional enrolment fee £1
Services Lectures; publications; advice; awards; shows; journal; special-interest and regional groups
Established in 1948, the society celebrated its 50th birthday last year. New members receive a cultural handbook, and the journal appears three times a year. Meetings are arranged through the regional groups, five of which also organise an annual area show. In addition there is a national show with many classes. New cultivars can be submitted for awards to the floral committee. An advisory service is available through the secretary. The Society is producing a register of all cultivars in cultivation.

NATIONAL CHRYSANTHEMUM SOCIETY
George Gray House, 8 Amber Business Village, Amber Close, Tamworth, Staffordshire B77 4RD
☎ & Fax 01827 310331
Contact Mrs Y Honnor
Aims To promote the chrysanthemum and offer advice
Membership 4,500
Subscriptions Single £13; joint £16
Services Publications; advice; awards; shows; journal; special-interest and regional groups; videos
The National Chrysanthemum Society holds two national shows each year in Bingley Hall, Stafford (September and November). The advisory bureau helps with queries about chrysanthemums and handles membership enquiries.

NATIONAL COUNCIL FOR THE CONSERVATION OF PLANTS AND GARDENS
The Pines, RHS Garden, Wisley, Woking, Surrey GU23 6QP
☎ 01483 211465
Fax 01483 211750
Contact Rodger Bain
Aims To encourage the conservation of plants and gardens
Membership 6,000
Subscriptions Apply to local group for details
Services Lectures; publications; shows; journal; special-interest and regional groups; outings
Founded in 1978. The NCCPG is divided into about 40 local and county groups who organise their own programmes of events. The national body works to preserve individual plants and endangered gardens. The society's most successful innovation has been the establishment of more than 600 National Collections of genera (and part genera). These gather together as many representatives of the genus as possible and form a unique resource. Many can be visited: full details appear in the *1999 National Plant Collections Directory*, which is available from the NCCPG (£6 to include p&p). The NCCPG has close relations with similar movements throughout the world.

NATIONAL DAHLIA SOCIETY
19 Sunnybank, Marlow, Buckinghamshire SL7 3BL
☎ 01628 473500
Contact General Secretary
Aims To promote the cultivation of dahlias
Membership 3,000
Subscriptions £10.50 single; £12 joint
Services Lectures; library; publications; advice; awards; shows; journal; special-interest and regional groups; judging examinations; classification of new varieties
The National Dahlia Society holds two main shows: at the National *Amateur Gardening* show at Shepton Mallet and at Harrogate during the Autumn Show. It runs trials at Leeds and Wisley, and gives an annual award for the best new British and new overseas seedlings. Members receive the society journal twice a year, and can take part in its annual conference and lecture programme. There are about 900 affiliated societies: they can use the society's medals and certificates for their own shows. A range of books and pamphlets is available for members at reduced prices.

NATIONAL POT LEEK SOCIETY
147 Sea Road, Fulwell, Sunderland SR6 9EB
☎ 0191 549 4274
Contact Hon. Secretary
Aims To improve and encourage leek growing
Membership 11,000
Subscriptions £10
Services Lectures; publications; advice; awards; shows; journal; items for sale
The society produces a *Year Book* and two newsletters for its members. Advice can be provided by letter or phone, and the society produces a growing guide *Sound All*

Round, and a video *Growing Leeks with the Experts*. Among the items on sale are measuring equipment and charts and a video. Most of the members live in the north-east of England.

NATIONAL SWEET PEA SOCIETY
3 Chalk Farm Road,
Stokenchurch, High Wycombe,
Buckinghamshire HP14 3TB
☎ 01494 482153

Contact Hon. Secretary
Aims To encourage the cultivation and improvement of the sweet pea
Membership 1,200
Subscriptions £12 single; £10 affiliated society; £15 overseas
Services Lectures; advice; awards; shows; journal; special-interest and regional groups; joint RHS/NSPS trials

The National Sweet Pea Society was founded in 1900, which means it will be celebrating its centenary next year. Meanwhile, it is celebrating 300 years since the sweet pea was first introduced into cultivation in 1699. The society's *Annual* appears every June, and further bulletins in February and September. The *Annual* is a substantial publication. Its three major shows are the National at Althorp Park, Northants (where the Spencer sweet peas were first bred at the turn of the century), the Provincial at Cambridge on 29 and 30 June, and a 'mini' Provincial at Wem in Shropshire on 24 and 25 July. Each county has an area representative who arranges programmes for local members. The society actively promotes new varieties, and members can send their own seedlings to the trials at Wisley each year.

NATIONAL VEGETABLE SOCIETY
33 Newmarket Road, Redcar,
Cleveland TS10 2HY
☎ 01642 484470

Contact L Cox (Hon. Secretary)
Aims To advance the culture, study and improvement of vegetables
Services Library; publications; advice; awards; shows; journal; special-interest and regional groups

The National Vegetable Society was founded in 1960 and caters for individual members and societies. The latter can use the NVS medals and award cards. Membership spans the expert and the novice vegetable grower. The new quarterly *National Bulletin* and the regional bulletins that members receive contain advice on all aspects of growing and showing vegetables. A *National Newsletter* gives details of all Society activities. The National Vegetable Championships are held at a different location each year and major awards are presented at it.

ORCHID SOCIETY OF GREAT BRITAIN
Athelney, 145 Binscombe
Village, Godalming, Surrey
GU7 3QL
☎ 01483 421423

Contact Hon. Secretary
Aims To encourage amateur growers of orchids
Membership 1,200
Subscriptions £13 single; £16 double; £5 joining fee
Services Lectures; library; publications; advice; awards; shows; journal; special-interest and regional groups; outings; plant exchanges and sales

The nationwide orchid society. It produces an informative journal four times a year and stages two major shows annually. In addition there is a monthly meeting in the Napier Hall, London, which may include a lecture and a show. The library lends books and slides, and members can obtain cultural advice in person or in writing from the Cultural Adviser. There is a plant exchange forum, and a sales table at most meetings. The society publishes a small booklet on orchid cultivation which is a useful introduction to the subject (£3).

RHODODENDRON, CAMELLIA & MAGNOLIA GROUP OF THE RHS
Netherton, Buckland
Monachorum, Yelverton, Devon
PL20 7NL
☎ & Fax 01822 854022

Contact Josephine Warren (Hon. Secretary)
Aims To bring together all who share an interest in rhododendrons, camellias and magnolias
Membership 700
Subscriptions £15 Europe; £17.50 outside Europe (airmail)
Services Lectures; gardens; publications; advice; awards; shows; journal; special-interest and regional groups; outings

Membership is open to all members of the RHS. New members are assigned to the nearest regional branch and advised of the garden visits and lectures programme. The Group organises a Spring Tour and an Autumn Weekend, and mounts a display at the main Rhododendron Show at Vincent Square (27 and 28 April in 1999). The *Bulletin* is published three times a year. The *Year Book* is issued in December for the following year.

ROYAL HORTICULTURAL SOCIETY
PO Box 313, 80 Vincent Square,
London SW1P 2PE
☎ 0171 834 4333
Membership hotline:
☎ 0171 821 3000 (9 am – 5.30 pm Monday to Friday) – Save £5 on RHS Membership – see page 5.
Shows: ☎ 0171 649 1885 (24-hour recorded information) – see also *The Garden* magazine.

Contact Switchboard
Aims The encouragement and improvement of the science, art and practice of horticulture in all its branches
Membership 261,000
Subscriptions £34 Individual (includes a £7 one-off enrolment fee)
Services Publications; gardens; shows; lectures; advice; library; seeds; awards; special-interest groups

For 200 years the RHS, Britain's Gardening Charity, has been providing inspirational shows, gardens and horticultural expertise for experts and amateurs alike.

Behind the scenes the RHS is involved in scientific and technical horticulture and it plays a vital role in educating and encouraging gardeners at all levels; its academic courses include the much-prized RHS Master of Horticulture. Through its extensive trials programme at RHS Garden Wisley, researchers also tackle the very real issues that affect gardeners and provide solutions and information on a variety of problems. The Society liaises with national and trade organisations in the interests of horticulture, and is increasingly active in the international arena. There are additional specialist sections covering fruit, lilies, and rhododendrons and camellias.

The cost of the work of the RHS is borne wholly by the Society and Membership subscriptions represent a vital element of its funding. With currently over 261,000 Members, Membership is growing all the time and the RHS offers an excellent benefits package for gardeners (Save £5 on RHS Membership, see page 5).

RHS Publications

The Garden magazine, packed with current horticultural news, is sent free to Members every month. The RHS also produces *The New Plantsman* – aimed at the specialist, and *The Orchid Review* – the definitive journal for Orchid enthusiasts; both journals require a separate subscription. A number of other publications are produced and the RHS promotes a collection of gardening titles in association with commercial publishers.

Free access to gardens

Members have free access for themselves plus one guest to the famous RHS Garden Wisley in Surrey, Rosemoor in Devon and Hyde Hall in Essex. Members are also entitled to free admission to a further 24 gardens in 1999: Trebah and Trewithen in Cornwall; The Garden House in Devon; Abbotsbury in Dorset; Forde Abbey in Somerset; Westonbirt and Hidcote Manor in Gloucestershire; Hillier in Hampshire; Nymans and Sheffield Park in Sussex; Bedgebury, Bogdale, Yalding and Broadview in Kent; Waddesdon in Buckinghamshire; Waterperry in Oxfordshire; East Ruston and Fairhaven in Norfolk; Ryton in Warwickshire; Ness in the Wirral; Harlow Carr in North Yorkshire; Bodnant in North Wales; Picton Castle in Pembrokeshire; and Arboretum Kalmthout in Belgium.

RHS Shows

RHS shows nurture talent and the development of new ideas. Chelsea and the Hampton Court Palace Flower Show foster the very highest standards in gardening, from plant cultivation to brilliant and innovative design. Members can buy tickets at reduced prices for these shows and both offer days reserved exclusively for Members. Members are also entitled to reduced price admission to BBC Gardeners' World Live, Scotland's National Gardening Shows, the Malvern Spring and Autumn Shows, and the new RHS Flower Show at Tatton Park. Members have free entry to the monthly Westminster Flower Shows, where the RHS and specialist societies hold plant competitions and Members can bring along plants for exhibition or cultural awards (see Calendar for dates).

The RHS around Britain

The RHS is working in partnership with leading Colleges of Horticulture to offer practical workshops and programmes of talks. The RHS also organises special events at nurseries and owner-led garden tours across Britain. Members are admitted to these events at concessionary rates, and free of charge to most lectures. (Apply for tickets in writing to the RHS Regional Development Department.)

Free gardening advice

Members are entitled to free gardening advice from RHS experts; this service is accessible by post, at RHS Shows and in person at RHS Garden Wisley.

Lindley Library

Members have access to the Lindley Library in London. The library is a precious and priceless historical resource which contains the most comprehensive collection of horticultural books in the world.

Free seeds

Seeds from RHS Garden Wisley are available for Members in December each year for a nominal charge.

ROYAL NATIONAL ROSE SOCIETY

The Gardens of the Rose, Chiswell Green, St Albans, Hertfordshire AL2 3NR
☎ 01727 850461
Fax 01727 850360

Contact Reception
Aims To promote the love of roses
Membership 13,700
Subscriptions £17 single; £24 joint; £9 student; £5 extra for Historic Roses Group
Services Lectures; gardens; library; publications; advice; awards; shows; journal; special-interest and regional groups; outings

Founded in 1876. The society has its headquarters near St Albans: the Gardens of the Rose display over 1,700 different roses. Members enter free. The society also maintains 12 regional rose gardens. An illustrated quarterly journal *The Rose* gives news of the society and the rose world, and there are regular shows including the British Rose Festival at the Hampton Court Palace Flower Show. The society always has hundreds of new roses on trial for awards at St Albans: the trial fields can be visited. There is a full advisory service for members and regular pruning demonstrations which anyone can attend. There are some regional groups, and special-interest sections for exhibitors and rose breeders (The Amateur Rose Breeders Association). For an additional £5 RNRS members can join the Historic Roses Group, which organises its own programme of events and visits. The RNRS Rose 2000 Development has enormously expanded the activities of the Society and its garden.

SAINTPAULIA & HOUSEPLANT SOCIETY

33 Church Road, Newbury Park, Ilford, Essex IG2 7ET
☎ 0181 590 3710

Contact Hon. Secretary
Aims To grow better and more beautiful houseplants, and to help the public to do the same
Membership 700
Subscriptions £4 single; £5 joint (£1.50 extra for overseas)
Services Lectures; library; publications; advice; shows; journal; special-interest and regional groups; outings; *Saintpaulia* leaf distribution

The society holds regular Tuesday evening meetings at the RHS, usually to coincide with the Westminster shows. There are competitions at the meetings, and an annual show in the New Hall at the August show. Members receive the bulletin four times a year. The society arranges visits and has several local groups with their own programmes. Members can borrow from the society's specialist library, and take part in the annual leaf distribution.

SAXIFRAGE SOCIETY

7 Alpha Court, Hockliffe Road, Leighton Buzzard, Bedfordshire LU7 8JW

Contact Adrian Young (Secretary)
Aims To encourage the cultivation and enjoyment of saxifrages
Subscriptions £6 UK; £10 overseas
Services Lectures; publications; journal; slide library

This newish society seeks to promote the cultivation of saxifrages in the garden. It also aims to maintain a collection of reference material.

TOMATO GROWERS CLUB

27 Meadowbrook, Old Oxted, Surrey RH8 9LT
☎ 01883 715242

Contact Colin Simpson
Aims To collect and maintain a seed library of open-pollinated tomatoes

Membership 10,000
Subscriptions Nil, a minimum purchase of £10 seed or plants in first year only
Services Seed scheme; journal

The club exists to preserve worthwhile strains of tomato varieties which are available to members for trialling; currently about 500 are on offer. There is an annual newsletter and seed catalogue in December. Members can get help with tomato disease problems.

WILD FLOWER SOCIETY

Woodpeckers, Hoe Lane, Abinger Hammer, Dorking, Surrey

Contact Mrs Pat Verrall (Hon. Gen. Secretary)
Membership 720
Subscriptions £8 single; £12 family
Services Lectures; publications; special-interest and regional groups

The society aims to promote a greater knowledge of field botany, especially among the young. Members receive three copies of *The Wild Flower* magazine and a copy of *The Wild Flower Diary*. This is a printed list of some 1,000 species which members are encouraged to use to record the plants they find each year.

REGIONAL SOCIETIES

AVON GARDENS TRUST

30 Hurle Crescent, Abbots Leigh, Bristol BS8 2SZ
☎ 0117 974 1033

Contact Malcolm Douglas
Membership 160
Subscriptions £7.50 single; £10 family
Services Lectures; publications; journal; outings

The trust works to conserve the gardens of the former county through monitoring planning applications and advising owners on surveys and restoration plans. The twice-yearly *Newsletter* is readable and informative. Garden visits and other interesting events are staged for members throughout the year. The Trust has published books on historic parks of Bath and Weston-super-Mare, parks and gardens of Avon, and the Goldney garden in Clifton. A book on Bristol gardens will follow shortly.

CORNWALL GARDENS SOCIETY

Poltisko, Silver Hill, Parranwell Station, Truro, Cornwall TR3 7LP
☎ 01872 863300

Contact Miss Pat Ward
Aims To foster a love and knowledge of plants and gardening
Membership 1,500
Subscriptions £15 single
Services Lectures; publications; advice; shows; journal; outings; garden openings

A scaled-down model of the RHS, with an excellent magazine, good bulletins and a famous show – this year 16–18 April at Carlyon Bay. The society also organises a garden scheme and publishes a splendid *Gardens Open* guide.

CORNWALL GARDENS TRUST

Tredarvah Vean, Penzance, Cornwall TR18 4SU
☎ 01736 63473

Contact Membership Secretary
Aims To preserve, enhance and recreate the gardens of Cornwall
Membership 220
Subscriptions £10
Services Lectures; gardens; publications; advice; awards; journal; outings

Formed in 1988, the Trust carries out conservation and preservation work, and organises special events and garden visits for its members. It is putting much of its efforts at the moment into assembling an archive of Cornwall garden records. The annual *Journal* is a quality publication. Last year the society published *Glorious Gardens of Cornwall* (£11.95), a gazetteer of all Cornish gardens open to the public, with a foreword by Roy Lancaster.

DERBYSHIRE HISTORIC GARDENS
Yokecliffe Cottage, West End, Wirksworth, Derbyshire DE4 4EG
☎ 01629 825964
Contact Melanie Morris

DEVON GARDENS TRUST
7 The Close, Exeter, Devon EX1 1EZ
☎ 01392 252404
Contact The Secretary
Aims To preserve the gardens of Devon
Membership 420
Subscriptions £10 single; £15 joint
Services Lectures; advice; journal; outings

A successful gardens trust, which surveys Devon gardens, and works to protect their future. Members benefit from lectures, special garden visits and seminars, and are kept informed of the trust's research and conservation work.

DORSET GARDENS TRUST
20 Holmead Road, Poundbury, Dorset DT1 3GE
Contact Val Hurlston-Gardiner

FRIENDS OF THE ROYAL BOTANIC GARDEN EDINBURGH
The Royal Botanic Garden, Inverleith Row, Edinburgh EH3 5LR
☎ 0131 552 5339
Contact The Secretary
Aims To support the garden and raise funds for its activities
Membership 1,600
Subscriptions £20 single; £25 family
Services Lectures; gardens; journal

The Friends raise funds for and promote the work of the Royal Botanic Garden Edinburgh. There is no admission charge to this great garden, but friends have free entry to the three regional gardens (Logan, Dawyck and Younger). There is a regular newsletter, and an excellent series of lectures and social events.

FRIENDS OF THE ROYAL BOTANIC GARDENS KEW
Cambridge Cottage, Kew Green, Kew, Richmond, Surrey TW9 3AB
☎ 0181 332 5922
Fax 0181 332 5901
Contact Dianne Owens
Aims Fund-raising for Royal Botanic Gardens, Kew
Membership 42,000
Subscriptions £34 single; £45.50 family; concessions for OAPs & students
Services Lectures; gardens; shows; journal; discounts in Kew and Wakehurst Place shops; guest passes

The Friends of the Royal Botanic Gardens Kew raises funds for Kew's scientific work, hence the relatively high subscription. After that has been paid, free entry to Kew, Wakehurst and 11 further gardens in Britain is a valuable benefit. The Friends' journal *Kew*, published three times a year, is colourful and outstandingly good. Lectures are given monthly throughout the year, and there is an annual plant auction in the autumn. Friends receive discounts on shop purchases, and complimentary day passes to the gardens for their guests.

GLOUCESTERSHIRE GARDENS & LANDSCAPE TRUST
Court Lodge, Avening, Tetbury, Gloucestershire GL8 8NX
☎ 01453 833660
Contact Peter Lindesay (Chief Executive)
Aims To conserve gardens and landscape
Membership 170
Subscriptions £12 single; £20 joint
Services Lectures; advice; journal; outings

The trust exists to protect valuable gardens and landscapes. As well as conservation work it has a programme of lectures, garden visits and other events for members. One of the most dynamic of the county garden trusts.

HAMPSHIRE GARDENS TRUST
Jermyns House, Jermyns Lane, Ampfield, Romsey, Hampshire SO51 0QA
☎ 01794 367752 (mornings)
Fax 01794 368520
Contact The Secretary
Aims To care for Hampshire's gardens and parks
Membership 450
Subscriptions £10 single; £15 joint
Services Lectures; library; advice; journal; outings; research into Hampshire's historic gardens and landscapes

The first of the county gardens trusts, formed with help from Hampshire County Council in 1984, and in every way the model still for all others. The trust is active in conservation and education work, and has an excellent programme of events for members.

ISLE OF WIGHT GARDENS TRUST
Cassies, Billingham, Newport, Isle of Wight PO30 3HD
☎ 01983 721344
Contact Membership Secretary
Aims To care for the island's outstanding gardens, parklands and landscapes
Membership 200
Subscriptions £5 individual; £7.50 joint
Services Lectures; journal; outings

The trust helps to record the island's parks and gardens and to assist in their conservation. Talks and garden visits are staged for members, and they can also get involved in conservation work.

LINCOLNSHIRE GARDENS TRUST
Wayside Cottage, 23 High Street, Caythorpe, Grantham, Lincolnshire NG32 3DR

☎ 01400 273650
Contact Amanda Townsend
Subscriptions £8.50 single; £15 family
Services Lectures; journal; outings

The LGT has widely drawn aims. They include: fostering interest in gardening; researching historic park and gardens; helping new gardeners; and encouraging gardening in schools.

LONDON HISTORIC PARKS & GARDENS TRUST
Duck Island Cottage, St James's Park, London SW1
☎ 0171 839 3969
Contact Elizabeth Fry (Secretary)
Membership 430
Subscriptions £12 adults; £6 concessions
Services Lectures; publications; advice; journal; outings

Founded in 1994, to encourage greater protection for the capital's parks and gardens, the society has already completed a survey of 1,200 sites throughout Greater London and embarked upon an educational programme. Members receive a quarterly newsletter. The upmarket journal *The London Gardener* follows an 18th-century format: its articles are scholarly and enjoyable. The series of excellent winter lectures at the Linnean Society has become a regular feature of London's intellectual life.

MARCHER APPLE NETWORK
Orchard Barn, Ocle Pychard, Hereford, Hereford & Worcester HR1 3RB
☎ 01432 820204
Contact John Aldridge
Aims To rescue and preserve old cultivars of apples
Membership 250
Subscriptions Adults £5
Services Lectures; gardens; advice; journal; outings

This society was formed by a group of people living in the Welsh Marches with the aim of rescuing old apple cultivars from extinction. They identify old trees, propagate them and establish new orchards to preserve them. They also organise events to celebrate and encourage the revival of interest in traditional fruit varieties.

NORTH OF ENGLAND ROSE, CARNATION AND SWEET PEA SOCIETY
10 Glendale Avenue, Whitley Bay, Tyne & Wear NE26 1RX
☎ 0191 252 7052
Contact The Acting Secretary
Aims To further interest in the three named flowers, and gardening in general
Membership 300
Subscriptions £3
Services Lectures; library; publications; advice; awards; shows; journal; special-interest and regional groups; outings

The society – Rosecarpe for short – was founded in 1938. Its interests extend beyond its three main flowers. Members can attend the regular meetings, usually on the first Monday of most months in the Civic Centre, Gateshead, for lectures or demonstrations. The four shows play an important part in the society's life, notably the Gateshead Spring and Summer Flower Shows organised in association with the Metropolitan Borough Council, and two Rosecarpe Flower Shows. Trophies are presented at all of the shows. A *Year Book* is produced, and members can also borrow the society's books and videos, and draw on the advice of the society's many experts. Rosecarpe attends other shows and horticultural college events, and is affiliated to the national Rose, Carnation, Sweet Pea and Daffodil societies.

NORTHERN HORTICULTURAL SOCIETY
Harlow Carr Botanical Gardens, Crag Lane, Harrogate, North Yorkshire HG3 1QB
☎ 01423 565418
Fax 01423 530663
Contact Barry Nuttall
Aims To promote the science and practice of horticulture
Membership 11,000
Subscriptions £24

Services Lectures; gardens; seed scheme; library; publications; advice; awards; journal; special-interest and regional groups

Founded in 1947, the Northern Horticultural Society is a focus for gardeners in the north of England. Members receive free entrance to the Harlow Carr Botanical Gardens which are the society's headquarters. The annual programme includes a series of day and longer courses throughout the year at the garden. The garden also trials vegetable and flower varieties specifically for their suitability to northerly climates, and visitors can assess the new and unreleased varieties which are undergoing trial. An illustrated journal, *The Northern Gardener*, appears four times a year. Members can also take advantage of the seed scheme, the reference and lending library, and an advisory service (in writing only). There are special-interest sections for alpines, bonsai, bulbs, delphiniums, ferns, rhododendrons and roses. A reciprocal arrangement with the Royal Horticultural Society allows free access to the three RHS gardens and another eight throughout England.

NORTHERN IRELAND DAFFODIL GROUP
77 Ballygowan Road, Hillsborough, Co Down, Northern Ireland BT26 6EQ
Contact Richard McCaw (Secretary)
Membership 120
Subscriptions £7.50 for 1 year; £18 for 3 years
Services Lectures; shows; journal; annual bulb auction

Daffodils are a major interest in Northern Ireland. The NIDG has many affiliated societies, who exhibit at the City of Belfast Spring Show. It also issues two newsletters a year to all members.

ROSE SOCIETY OF NORTHERN IRELAND
15 Carnduff Road, Larne, Co Antrim, Northern Ireland BT40 3NJ
☎ 01574 272658

Contact Mrs Elizabeth Moore (Hon. Secretary)
Membership 165
Subscriptions £5
Services Lectures; advice; shows; journal; outings

The society has a very active programme of events as well as publishing newsletters and an annual.

Royal Caledonian Horticultural Society
28 Silverknowes Southway, Edinburgh EH4 5PX
☎ 0131 336 5488
Fax 0131 336 1847

Contact Hon. Secretary
Aims The improvement of horticulture in all its branches
Membership 700
Services Lectures; library; publications; advice; awards; shows; journal; special-interest and regional groups; outings

The Royal Caledonian Horticultural Society was founded in 1809. It publishes an annual *Journal*, and a newsletter *Preview* three times a year. There is a regular lecture programme from October to April, while in the summer months a series of garden visits takes place. The society's president is the custodian of their library. There is an annual spring show and an AGM, at which the society presents three prestigious awards: the Queen Elizabeth the Queen Mother Medal, the biennial Neill Prize to a botanist, and the Scottish Horticultural Medal, the number of whose recipients is limited to 50. The 'Cally' has begun to establish a coordinating function among Scottish horticultural societies.

Royal Horticultural Society of Ireland
Swanbrook House, Bloomfield Avenue, Morehampton Road, Dublin 4
☎ 00 353 1 668 4358

Contact Mrs Monica Nolan (Secretary)
Aims To encourage a greater awareness of gardening and plants
Membership 1,200
Services Lectures; library; awards; shows; journal; outings

Founded in 1830, the society encourages people to make gardens and grow a wide variety of plants. Lectures, demonstrations, courses, garden visits and plant sales are held throughout the year. The newsletter (three a year) keeps members up to date with activities.

Scottish Rhododendron Society
Stron Ailne, Colintraive, Argyll, Strathclyde PA22 3AS
☎ 01700 841285

Contact Hon. Secretary
Aims To encourage the cultivation of rhododendrons
Membership 254
Subscriptions £22
Services Lectures; gardens; seed scheme; publications; advice; awards; shows; journal; special-interest and regional groups; outings; automatic membership of the American Rhododendron Society

The Scottish Rhododendron Society was founded just over ten years ago to provide a forum at which Scottish growers could meet and exhibit. Many of the best Scottish rhododendron gardens belong, but a fair proportion of the members live outside Scotland. An excellent newsletter is produced three times a year, and there are at least two meetings annually. Their national show, at a different venue each year, is probably the top show in Britain for rhododendrons. Members can purchase a range of books at reduced prices, seek specialist advice through the secretary, and gain free admission to Arduaine Gardens in Strathclyde. The society is also a chapter of the excellent American Rhododendron Society, which means that members automatically belong directly to the American society too. This gives them the scholarly quarterly journal, access to all the other ARS chapters (from Denmark and Holland to India), and the opportunity to raise seeds from the ARS seed bank.

Scottish Rock Garden Club
PO Box 14063, Edinburgh, Lothian EH10 4YE

Contact Sandy Leven (Publicity Manager)
Aims To promote the cultivation of alpine and peat-garden plants
Membership 3,750
Services Lectures; seed scheme; library; publications; advice; awards; shows: organised by ten of the local groups; journal: twice yearly; special-interest and regional groups; slide library; annual conference

Founded in 1933, this is now the largest horticultural society in Scotland, with overseas members in nearly 40 countries. There are regional groups throughout Scotland, each responsible for organising a programme of events including lectures. Some members also open their gardens. The society journal, *The Rock Garden*, appears twice a year: it is a well-produced and authoritative magazine which covers rock-garden plants both in cultivation and in the wild. The seed exchange scheme is among the best of its kind.

Shropshire Parks & Gardens Trust
The Grey House, Little Ryton, Dorrington, Shropshire SY5 7LS
☎ 01743 718237

Contact Belinda Cousens

Somerset Gardens Trust
St Peter's Vicarage, 62 Eastwick Road, Taunton, Somerset TA2 7HD

Contact Membership Secretary
Subscriptions £10 single; £15 joint
Services Lectures; journal; outings

Works to conserve and protect Somerset's parks and gardens. As well as conservation and education work, talks and garden visits are arranged.

Staffordshire Gardens & Parks Trust
c/o Planning Department, South Staffordshire District Council, Wolverhampton Road, Codsall, Wolverhampton WV8 1PX

Contact The Secretary
Aims To record and encourage the conservation of parks and gardens

Membership 100
Subscriptions £8.50 single; £11 joint
Services Lectures; advice; journal; outings; training; exhibitions

The trust aims to record the county's most valuable gardens and work for their conservation. Members can assist in this task, and take part in study visits. Meetings and lectures are held in Stafford.

SURREY GARDENS TRUST
c/o Planning Department, Surrey County Council, County Hall, Kingston on Thames KT1 2DT
☎ 0181 541 9419
Contact The Secretary
Aims To identify, enhance and re-create outstanding park and gardens in Surrey
Membership 220
Subscriptions £10 single; £15 joint
Services Lectures; advice; journal; outings; research; restoration work

Members receive a twice-yearly newsletter, and there is a programme of lectures and garden visits. Those wanting more active involvement may train as recorders, carry out archive research and assist on garden-improvement projects. The trust is making a study of Jekyll gardens in the county.

SUSSEX GARDENS TRUST
Bowling Alley Cottage, The Green, Horsted Keynes, West Sussex RH17 7AP
☎ 01825 790970
Contact Sally Walker

WAKEFIELD & NORTH OF ENGLAND TULIP SOCIETY
70 Wrenthorpe Lane, Wrenthorpe, Wakefield, West Yorkshire WF2 0PT
Contact Hon. Secretary
Aims The growing, breeding and showing of English florists' tulips
Membership 300
Services Seed scheme; publications; awards; shows; journal; outings

This long-established society, devoted to florists' tulips, publishes an annual journal and holds two shows each year. Other events include formal and informal meetings and garden visits. Surplus bulbs are distributed in October. *The English Tulip and its History* is available from the society, as are slide lectures.

WELSH HISTORIC GARDENS TRUST
Ty Leri, Talybont, Ceredigion SY24 5ER
☎ & Fax 01970 832268
Contact Ros Laidlaw (Secretary)
Aims To assist in and initiate conservation of gardens and designed landscapes in Wales
Membership 700
Subscriptions £10 single; £15 family
Services Lectures; advice; journal; special-interest and regional groups; outings

Through the trust office and local branches this organisation assists and initiates the conservation of important gardens, parks and landscapes. Members can become involved in research, surveying and other conservation work which is carried out at branch level: there are branches in Brecon and Radnor, Ceredigion, Clwyd, Gwynedd, Glamorgan, Gwent, and Pembrokeshire. The *Newsletter* is informed and informing, while the Trust itself has become a powerful force for conservation within the principality.

WILTSHIRE GARDENS TRUST
Treglisson, Crowe Lane, Freshford, Bath, Somerset BA3 6EB
Contact Hon. Secretary
Membership 600
Subscriptions £10 single; £15 joint
Services Lectures; seed scheme; library; publications; journal; special-interest and regional groups; outings

This group doubles as the county garden trust and (for an additional subscription) as the Wiltshire branch of the NCCPG. Its excellent programme of events includes lectures and garden visits.

YORKSHIRE GARDENS TRUST
The Manor House, Skeeby, Richmond, North Yorkshire DL10 5DX
Contact Mrs Valerie Hepworth
Subscriptions £10 single; £15 double
Services Lectures; publications; journal; outings

Yorkshire comprises three counties, which contain some of the country's finest historic landscapes. The Trust exists to raise awareness of this heritage and to encourage appreciation of gardening in Yorkshire.

WORLDWIDE SOCIETIES

AFRICAN VIOLET SOCIETY OF AMERICA INC
PO Box 3609, Beaumont, TX 77704, USA
☎ 00 1 409 839 4725
Fax 00 1 409 839 4329
Contact The Secretary
Membership 10,000
Subscriptions US$18; US$20.50 abroad
Services Lectures; library; publications; advice; shows; journal; special-interest and regional groups; plant sales

This thriving society opens the world of African violets to all home-owners and gardeners. It also acts as the International Registration Authority for *Saintpaulia* and publishes the *Master Variety List of African Violets* (available on paper or on disk) which lists all registered cultivars since 1949 – tens of thousands of them! Members receive the bi-monthly magazine *African Violet*: one of the advertisers offers more than 800 cultivars for sale.

AMERICAN BAMBOO SOCIETY
750 Krumkill Road, Albany, NY 12203-5976, USA
☎ 00 1 518 458 7618
Fax 00 1 518 458 7625
Contact Michael Bartholomew (Newsletter Editor)
Membership 900
Subscriptions US$35

Services Publications; advice; journal; special-interest and regional groups; outings; rare plant auction

The American Bamboo Society is for everyone who is interested in the cultivation, appreciation and use of 'woody grasses' – amateurs, aesthetes, horticulturists, botanists, conservationists and craftsmen. Members receive a bi-monthly newsletter and a scientific annual. There are twelve chapters, all in the USA.

AMERICAN CONIFER SOCIETY

PO Box 360, Keswick, VA 22947-0360, USA
☎ 00 1 804 984 3660
Contact Maud Henne
Aims To encourage the development, conservation and propagation of dwarf and unusual conifers
Membership 1,350
Subscriptions US$25 single/joint; US$32 overseas
Services Lectures; seed scheme; advice; shows; journal; special-interest and regional groups; outings; plant sales

A thriving international society – the best in its field – with an excellent bulletin and a long calendar of events and tours. Members may attend regional meetings throughout the USA and Canada. The emphasis is upon conifers that are dwarf or unusual. It also issues an annual US$500 grant to conserve and propagate dwarf or unusual cultivars.

AMERICAN DAFFODIL SOCIETY INC

4126 Winfield Road, Columbus, OH 43220-4606, USA
☎ 00 1 614 451 4747
Fax 00 1 614 451 2177
Contact Naomi J Liggett (Executive Director)
Membership 1,400
Subscriptions US$20
Services Publications; awards; shows; journal

The society runs about 30 shows throughout the USA. Membership includes a subscription to the quarterly *The Daffodil Journal*, a substantial publication with many good articles.

AMERICAN HEMEROCALLIS SOCIETY

PO Box 10, Dexter, GA 31019, USA
Contact Membership Secretary
Membership 9,600
Subscriptions US$18 USA; US$25 Canada & overseas
Services Gardens; seed scheme; publications; awards; shows; journal; special-interest and regional groups

The Society's quarterly publication *The Daylily Journal* is both colourful and informative: it has articles on cultivation, hybridisation, new cultivars and forthcoming events. There are dozens of advertisements by nurseries in the States, where *Hemerocallis* are a major horticultural interest.

AMERICAN HEPATICA ASSOCIATION

195 North Avenue, Westport, CT 06880, USA
Contact Paul Held
Membership 125
Subscriptions US$25
Services Seed scheme; advice; journal

A newish society for the many *Hepatica* enthusiasts around the world. The main benefits are the quarterly newsletter and a quick seed exchange in July (quick, because *Hepatica* seed quickly loses its viability).

AMERICAN HIBISCUS SOCIETY

PO Box 321540, Cocoa Beach, FL 32932-1540, USA
☎ 00 1 407 783 2576
Contact Executive Secretary
Membership 2,000
Subscriptions US$17.50. US$10 extra for non-USA airmail
Services Lectures; seed scheme; publications; advice; awards; shows; journal

The society was founded in 1950 and has members in about 45 countries. It now has some 20 chapters, almost all in Texas, Florida and the Virgin Islands. Hybridisation and the raising of new varieties are an important part of the society's activities: members have access to the society's seed bank and the quarterly magazine is called *The Seed Pod*.

AMERICAN HOSTA SOCIETY

338 East Forestwood Street, Morton, IL 61550, USA
Contact Cindy Nance
Membership 2,700
Subscriptions US$19 single; US$25 Canada; US$35 overseas
Services Lectures; gardens; publications; advice; shows; journal; special-interest and regional groups; outings; registration of new cultivars; sales

The society brings together the activities of *Hosta* enthusiasts throughout North America. Some 50 local and state *Hosta* societies are amalgamated into half-a-dozen US regions, with a seventh for Canada. *The Hosta Yearbook* has details of all the societies' activities and a complete membership list. The quarterly *Hosta Journal* carries good articles on botany, classification, cultivation and new varieties from correspondents in the USA and abroad. The society also publishes a source list of some 30 US nurseries offering quality *Hosta* plants and acts as the international registrar for new varieties: sometimes over 100 a year. The 1999 annual convention will be at Ann Arbor, Michigan, in June.

AMERICAN IRIS SOCIETY

8426 Vine Valley Drive, Sun Valley, CA 91352-3656, USA
☎ 00 1 408 722 1810
Contact Jeanne Clay Plank (Secretary)
Membership 7,000
Subscriptions US$18 USA; US$23 overseas
Services Lectures; gardens; seed scheme; library; publications; advice; awards; shows; journal; special-interest and regional groups

The society's main event is the National Convention, which will be

SOCIETIES / WORLDWIDE 313

held in Oklahoma city on 4–8 May 1999. There are several dedicated specialist iris societies in the USA, including the Spuria Iris Society, the Society for Japanese Iris and the Aril Society International: details on the website.

AMERICAN ORCHID SOCIETY
6000 South Olive Avenue, West Palm Beach, FL 33405-4199, USA
☎ 00 1 561 585 8666
Fax 00 1 561 585 0654
Web *http://orchidweb.org*
Contact Lee Coke (Executive Director)
Membership 30,000+
Subscriptions US$36 USA; US$42 abroad
Services Lectures; library; publications; advice; awards; shows; journal; special-interest and regional groups

A well-established, large (and growing) society with members all over the world and more than 500 affiliated societies. Members receive the monthly *AOS Bulletin*, a substantial publication with over 100 pages, many in full colour: the advertisements alone are an education. The *Awards Quarterly* and the society's scientific review *Lindleyana* are published separately. The 1999 World Orchid Conference takes place at Vancouver BC from 23 April to 2 May. Comprehensive website.

AMERICAN PENSTEMON SOCIETY
1569 South Holland Court, Lakewood, CO 80232, USA
Contact Ann Bartlett (Membership Secretary)
Membership 450
Subscriptions US$15
Services Seed scheme; library; journal

Members have access to the excellent seed exchange (15 free packets a year) as well as receiving the quarterly *Bulletin of the American Penstemon Society* which has articles on collecting, cultivation and hybridisation.

AMERICAN RHODODENDRON SOCIETY
11 Pinecrest Drive, Fortuna, CA 95540, USA
☎ 00 1 707 725 3043
Fax 00 1 707 725 1217
Contact Executive Director
Membership 6,000
Services Seed scheme; shows; journal; special-interest and regional groups
Represented in the UK by the Scottish Rhododendron Society, the American Rhododendron Society exists to encourage interest in and disseminate knowledge about rhododendrons and azaleas.

AMERICAN ROSE SOCIETY
PO Box 30,000, 8877 Jefferson Paige Road, Shreveport, LA 71130-0030, USA
☎ 00 1 318 938 5402
Fax 00 1 318 938 5405
Contact Membership Secretary
Membership 24,000
Subscriptions US$32 USA; US$47 overseas
Services Lectures; gardens; library; publications; advice; awards; shows; journal; special-interest and regional groups; outings

The world's largest rose society, founded in 1892 and based in the 118-acre Gardens of the American Rose Center. It has nearly 400 affiliated societies and a steady membership. Traditionally concerned with modern roses, it is increasingly involved in the heritage rose movement. The monthly *American Rose Magazine* and the yearly *American Rose Annual* are quality publications.

ARCHE NOAH
Obere Straße, A-3553 Schiltern, Austria
☎ 00 43 2734 8626
Fax 00 43 2734 8627
Contact Peter Scherenzel
Aims The conservation of old seeds and fruit cultivars
Membership 3,500
Subscriptions ÖS 350
Services Lectures; gardens; seed scheme; publications; advice; shows; journal; outings

The Austrian society for the conservation of old fruit and vegetable cultivars. Over 1,000 are grown at the society's garden at Schiltern. Their seed catalogue lists about 2,500.

ASSOCIATION OF AUSTRALIAN BEGONIA SOCIETIES
79 Chuter Street, Stafford, Queensland 4053, Australia
An umbrella organisation for the begonia societies of the individual states. UK begoniaphiles rate this and the American Begonia Society as the two foreign societies they enjoy belonging to most.

ASSOCIATION OF SOCIETIES FOR GROWING AUSTRALIAN PLANTS
PO Box 744 Place, Blacktown, NSW 2148, Australia
☎ 00 61 2 9621 3437
Web *www.silo.riv.com.au/SPAG*
Contact Maeve McCarthy, Administration Officer
Membership 4,400
Services Lectures; seed scheme; library; publications; advice; journal; special-interest and regional groups; outings

There are societies for growing native plants in every Australian state – this is the address of the New South Wales society – and many local societies within each state. The main benefits to members overseas are the excellent publications (a quarterly newsletter and an annual) and the comprehensive seed lists. Good website.

ASSOCIATION POUR LA SAUVEGARDE DU PATRIMOINE FRUITIER
4, avenue de la Résistance, F-30270 Saint Jean-du-Gard, France
☎ 00 33 4 66 85 33 37
Fax 00 33 4 66 86 19 66
Aims Preserving the heritage fruit of France
Membership 450
Subscriptions FF 150

Services Lectures; publications; advice; shows; journal; outings

A conservation group devoted to fruit – everything from apples and pears to olives and figs. The excellent quarterly bulletin *Fruits Oubliés* is subtitled *Revue de Pomologie Vivante* and *Sauve qui Pomme*.

AUSTRALASIAN PLANT SOCIETY

74 Brimstage Road, Heswall, Merseyside L60 1XQ
☎ 0151 342 1703

Contact Jeff Irons
Aims To encourage the cultivation of Australian & New Zealand plants
Membership 125
Subscriptions £6
Services Journal; outings

Members receive the twice-yearly newsletter *Pentachondra* and take part in an annual weekend visit. The society's excellent seed list has many species which are not listed elsewhere.

BONSAI CLUBS INTERNATIONAL

PO Box 1176, Brookfield, WI 53008-1176, USA
☎ 00 1 414 860 8807
Fax 00 1 414 641 0757

Contact Mary Turner (Business Manager)
Aims To foster an appreciation and knowledge of bonsai
Membership 20,000
Subscriptions US$34
Services Lectures; library; shows; journal; special-interest and regional groups

The top American organisation for bonsai clubs publishes the excellent bi-monthly magazine *Bonsai*.

BOTANICAL SOCIETY OF SOUTH AFRICA

Kirstenbosch, Claremont, Cape Town 7735, South Africa
☎ 00 27 797 2090

Aims Conservation, cultivation, study and use of native southern African plants
Membership 23,000
Services Lectures; gardens; seed scheme; publications; outings

Based at Kirstenbosch in Cape Province, the society has for many years been very successful in spreading information about the rich native flora of South Africa. Members have free entry to all the many regional gardens which it runs throughout the republic, as well as Kirstenbosch itself. The chief benefit to overseas members is the generous annual allocation of seed of native Cape species. The Society's exhibits have for many years been one of the sensations of the Chelsea Flower Show and, more recently, the Hampton Court show.

CACTUS & SUCCULENT SOCIETY OF AMERICA

PO Box 2615, Pahrump, NV 89041-2615, USA
Fax 00 1 702 751 1357

Contact Mindy Fusaro
Membership 3,700
Subscriptions US$35 USA; US$40 overseas
Services Lectures; seed scheme; library; advice; shows; journal; special-interest and regional groups; outings

The leading society in its field, with a good number of members from Europe and about 100 affiliated societies all over North America. All members receive the impressive bi-monthly *Cactus and Succulent Journal*. The society also publishes a scientific journal *Haseltonia*. The 1999 convention will be in Las Vegas on 11–16 April.

DEUTSCHE DAHLIEN- FUCHSIEN- UND GLADIOLEN- GESELLSCHAFT E V

Drachenfelsstraße 9a, D-53177 Bonn, Germany
☎ 00 49 228 35 58 35
Fax 00 49 228 35 58 37

Contact Elisabeth Göring
Membership 650
Subscriptions DM 60
Services Lectures; journal

This important European society was founded in 1897. Members receive three issues of the magazine *Rundbriefe* a year and the annual *Jahrbuch* which is a substantial publication (170 pages) with useful reports and articles. There is a panel of experts to advise on problems of cultivation.

DEUTSCHE KAKTEEN- GESELLSCHAFT E V

Betzenriedweg 44, D-72800 Eningen unter Achalm, Germany
Membership 7,000
Subscriptions DM 60 (Germany), DM 70 (abroad)
Services Lectures; seed scheme; library; publications; advice; awards; shows; journal; special-interest and regional groups; outings; plant sales

Founded in 1892, and one of the most distinguished horticultural associations in Europe. The Society has about 130 affiliated local groups, and specialist working groups for *Astrophytum*, *Echinopsis*, *Gymnocalycium*, *Rebutia* and *Tephrocactus*. There is a large lending library of specialist books for members' use. The society also publishes a list of about 40 specialist cactus nurseries in Germany. The illustrated monthly journal *Kakteen und andere Sukkulenten* is of high quality, with informative articles of botanical and horticultural interest.

DEUTSCHE ORCHIDEEN- GESELLSCHAFT

Fößweg 11, Schloß Stuckenbrock, D-33758, Germany
☎ 00 49 5207 920607
Membership 8,000
Subscriptions DM 85
Services Lectures; library; publications; advice; awards; shows; journal; special-interest and regional groups; outings

The German orchid society is one of the best and its bi-monthly *Die Orchidee* (over 100 pages per issue) is a journal of standing.

DEUTSCHE RHODODENDRON GESELLSCHAFT

Botanischer Garten u. Rhododendron-Park, Marcusallee 60, D-28359 Bremen, Germany
☎ 00 49 421 361 3025
Fax 00 49 421 361 3610
Contact Julia Westhoff

Aims To promote rhododendrons and other evergreen shrubs
Membership 1,100
Subscriptions DM 40 single; DM 50 double
Services Lectures; gardens; publications; awards; shows; journal; special-interest and regional groups; outings

This Bremen-based society is a fair match for the RHS Rhododendron Group. Its publications illustrate its botanical and horticultural qualities: the *Jahrbuch* is an authoritative scientific publication while the handsomely illustrated quarterly magazine *Immergrüner Blätte* is of more horticultural interest but of equally high standard. In addition to the seed exchange, members are entitled to take a number of cuttings and pollen from the Rhododendronpark in Bremen: the Rhododendronpark is Germany's answer to the Savill Gardens and Valley Gardens in Windsor Great Park. The society gives awards to new *Rhododendron* cultivars and mounts a big exhibition every four years (next in 2002). Its annual study tours are an important feature of its events programme.

EIBENFREUNDE
Dachauer Str. 52, D-82256
Fürstenfeldbruck, Germany
☎ 00 49 8141 9278
Contact Thomas Scheeder
Aims The study and promotion of *Taxus*
Subscriptions DM 15
Services Journal; outings

This is the only society in the world dedicated to the study of yews. Last year it ran a trip to the north-west Caucasus to see the tallest yew tree in the world, which is more than 30 m. high.

EUROPÄISCHE BAMBUSGESELLSCHAFT
John-Wesley-Str. 4, D-63584
Gründau/Rothenbergen,
Germany
☎ 00 49 6051 17451
Contact Frau Edeltraud Weber
Membership 700
Subscriptions DM 50

Services Lectures; seed scheme; journal; outings; slide library

This vigorous German bamboo society has members all over Europe. The authoritative quarterly *Bambusbrief* has articles on every aspect of bamboo botany, cultivation and use.

EUROPEAN BOXWOOD & TOPIARY SOCIETY
The Dower House, Crimp Hill,
Old Windsor, Berkshire
SL14 2HL
☎ 01753 854982
Contact Comtesse Véronique Goblet d'Alviella
Membership 350
Subscriptions £15
Services Lectures; journal

This new society has got off to a flying start with visits to famous topiary gardens in several European countries. This year they plan to spend three days on Lake Como in the autumn, and visit such gardens as West Green and Hatfield House. The magazine *Topiarius* is a high-quality publication.

FRUCTUS
Waisenhausstrasse 4, CH-8820
Wädenswil, Switzerland
Contact Dr Karl Stoll
Aims The conservation of traditional fruit cultivars
Subscriptions SFr 30
Services Lectures; advice; shows; journal; outings

This very active society has been particularly successful in preserving Swiss cultivars of tree fruits. The quarterly newsletter is a mine of information about everything from the history of diversification to the introduction of new cultivars.

GARDEN HISTORY SOCIETY
77 Cowcross Street, London
EC1M 6BP
☎ 0171 608 2409
Contact Linda Wigley
Aims To study garden history and preserve parks and gardens
Membership 2,200
Subscriptions £20

Services Lectures; advice; journal; special-interest and regional groups; outings

Founded in 1965. This learned society is concerned with the study of garden and landscape history. It is also actively involved in conservation and regularly advise local authorities on such issues. The twice-yearly journal *Garden History* publishes new research, while regular newsletters carry details of conservation matters and society events. These events include lectures and garden visits, at home and abroad. There is a regional group in Scotland. Events are limited to society members only but the public are admitted to the excellent winter lectures in London.

GARDENIA SOCIETY OF AMERICA
PO Box 879, Atwater, CA
95301, USA
Contact Lyman Duncan
Aims To promote interest in all phases of the culture of the gardenia
Services Journal

The society exists to promote interest in the genus *Gardenia*, scientific research into its culture, standardisation of its cultivar names, certification of new cultivars, and to promote the organisation and affiliation of local gardenia societies in the USA. But it also has members in Europe.

GESELLSCHAFT DER STAUDENFREUNDE
Meisenweg 1, D-65975
Hattersheim, Germany
☎ & **Fax** 00 49 6190 3642
Contact Geschäftsführer (Secretary)
Membership 4,000
Services Lectures; seed scheme; journal; special-interest and regional groups

The German Perennial Society developed from the Iris and Lily Society but now encompasses all hardy perennials. There are over 30 regional and five special-interest groups (alpines, *Hemerocallis*, lilies, peonies and wildflowers) which all organise their own lectures and outings. Members receive the excellent quarterly journal *Der*

Staudengarten, which is comparable to *The Hardy Plant*. The society's seed scheme centres on an annual list, not confined to perennials, which offers about 4,000 items. We strongly recommend all Hardy Planters to consider membership.

GESELLSCHAFT FÜR FLEISCHFRESSENDE PFLANZEN IM DEUTSCHSPRACHIGEN RAUM
Zweibrückenerstr. 31, D-40325 Düsseldorf, Germany
Web *www.gfp.org*
Contact Frank Gallep
Subscriptions DM 45
Services Seed scheme; journal

The German carnivorous plant society has a bi-annual newsletter called *Das Taublatt* and an exchange of plants as well as seeds.

HEMEROCALLIS EUROPA
Homburg 14, D-79761 Waldshut-Tiengen, Germany
☎ & Fax 00 49 7741 63068
Contact Matthias Thomsen-Stork
Services Lectures; seed scheme; shows; journal; trial gardens

Germany-based but bilingual (German and English) society that seeks to study, evaluate and popularise the best daylilies for Europe. It has members all over the continent. The society encourages the breeding of new varieties, and runs trials for their garden-worthiness in Germany and at Ventnor Botanic Gardens in the Isle of Wight. Members of the society receive three newsletters and a substantial *Year Book*.

HERITAGE ROSE FOUNDATION
1512 Gorman Street, Raleigh, NC 27606-2919, USA
☎ & Fax 00 1 919 834 2541
Contact Charles Walker (President)
Membership 600
Subscriptions US$10 USA; US$12 Bermuda, Canada & Mexico; US$15 elsewhere
Services Lectures; gardens; library; journal; outings

The Foundation is concerned to conserve old roses, especially those which are no longer available commercially. It also hopes to establish its own garden where rare and unnamed old varieties may be preserved, studied and propagated.

INTERNATIONAL BULB SOCIETY
PO Box 92136, Pasadena, CA 91109-2136, USA
Aims Disseminating knowledge of geophytic plants
Subscriptions US$30 USA; US$40 overseas
Services Journal

The society started in 1933 as the American Amaryllis Society and is still primarily concerned with such genera as *Amaryllis*, *Crinum*, *Hippeastrum* and *Lachenalia*. The society's annual *Hibbertia* is an important journal, supplemented by two newsletters per year.

INTERNATIONAL CAMELLIA SOCIETY
41 Galveston Road, East Putney, London SW15 2RZ
☎ 0181 870 6884
Fax 0181 874 4533
Contact UK Membership Representative
Aims To foster the love of camellias and maintain and increase their popularity throughout the world
Membership 1,700
Subscriptions £10.50 single; £13 double
Services Gardens; advice; shows; journal; special-interest and regional groups; outings

Founded in 1962. There are now some 1,600 members worldwide. The society has several trial grounds in the UK; the National Collection is at Mount Edgcumbe, Cornwall. Members receive the *International Camellia Journal* annually, and a UK newsletter twice a year. The society takes a stand at the main spring shows, and holds weekend meetings in spring and autumn. Informal advice on camellias is available to members, as is a worldwide network of fellow enthusiasts.

INTERNATIONAL CARNIVOROUS PLANT SOCIETY
c/o Fullerton Arboretum, California State University, Fullerton, CA 92634-6850, USA
Contact Leo C Song, Jr
Membership 828
Subscriptions US$20 USA; US$25 overseas
Services Seed scheme; publications; journal; special-interest and regional groups

The society is dedicated to understanding, preserving, growing, selecting, propagating, studying and appreciating the natural flora of the earth, with special-interest in carnivorous plants. International conferences are arranged every two years – next in 2000.

INTERNATIONAL CLEMATIS SOCIETY
3 Cuthberts Close, Cheshunt, Waltham Cross EN7 5RB
☎ 01992 636524
Contact Fiona Woolfenden
Membership 200
Subscriptions £18.50
Services Seed scheme; shows; journal; outings

The society is international in its membership and aspirations: it aims to provide a channel of communication for clematis growers across the world. Its main event is the annual tour, attended by international members, during which there are shows and meetings. Members receive an annual *Journal*. The excellent seed list contains up to 100 items.

INTERNATIONAL DENDROLOGY SOCIETY
Hergest Estate Office, Kington, Hereford & Worcester HR5 3EGF
Contact J A H Greenfield
Aims To promote the study and conservation of trees, woody plants and shrubs
Membership 1,500
Subscriptions £25 single; £350 life
Services Lectures; seed scheme; publications; journal; special-interest and regional groups;

outings; conservation and research; annual bursary

This prestigious international society has a worldwide membership. It encourages and helps fund conservation and research projects by registered charities, and has established a busary to allow a dendrology student from eastern Europe to study in the UK every year. The IDS holds a dendrological symposium every two years. Members also receive the *Year Book* and newsletters, and can take part in the seed exchange scheme and the excellent botanical tours. Membership of the society is restricted, at the invitation of existing members only, and is subject to the approval of the council.

INTERNATIONAL LILAC SOCIETY

c/o The Holden Arboretum, 9500 Sperry Road, Kirtland, OH 44094-5172, USA
☎ 00 1 216 256 1110
Fax 00 1 216 256 1655
Contact Dave Gressley
Membership 400
Subscriptions £10 single; £100 life membership
Services Lectures; library; publications; advice; journal

English members speak enthusiastically about this society. In addition to receiving the extremely informative *Quarterly Journal of the International Lilac Society*, members can purchase rare *Syringa* taxa and take part in the annual convention.

INTERNATIONAL OAK SOCIETY

PO Box 310, Pen Argyl, PA 18072-0310, USA
☎ 00 1 610 588 1037
Fax 00 1 610 252 7064
Aims To encourage the study and cultivation of the genus *Quercus*
Membership 300
Subscriptions US$15
Services Seed scheme; publications; journal

The society gives members all over the world an opportunity to acquire acorns of rare species.

INTERNATIONAL OLEANDER SOCIETY INC

PO Box 3431, Galveston, TX 77552-0431, USA
☎ 00 1 409 762 9334
Contact Elizabeth Head (Secretary)
Membership 200
Subscriptions US$10 single; US$15 double
Services Lectures; gardens; seed scheme; publications; journal; cuttings scheme

Galveston is the Oleander City and the society has its reference collection of varieties at the Moody gardens there. The main publication is the quarterly *Nerium News*, but the society has also issued videos on oleanders and their cultivation.

INTERNATIONAL VIOLET ASSOCIATION

Devon Violet Nursery, Rattery, South Brent, Devon TQ10 9LG
☎ 01364 643033
Contact Membership Secretary
Aims To bring together all those interested in the violet and its near relations
Membership 350
Subscriptions £10 or $15
Services Lectures; advice; journal

A new and growing international society which originated in the USA, though the president is British. Its aims include bringing the violet back into gardens, assisting in the preservation of its natural habitats, and recording and introducing new cultivars. Membership is not limited to growers and collectors. A newsletter is produced four times a year, and the president offers an advisory service to European members.

INTERNATIONAL WATER LILY SOCIETY

92 London Road, Stapeley, Nantwich, Cheshire CW5 7LH
☎ 01270 628628
Fax 01270 624188
Contact The Treasurer (IWLS Europe)

Aims To further interest in all aspects of water gardening
Membership 800
Subscriptions £15 single; £17.50 family
Services Lectures; library; awards; journal; special-interest and regional groups; outings

The International Water Lily Society is based in the USA but has members throughout the world. The membership spans amateurs and professionals, and the society carries out a range of research and educational work, including hybrid registration. Members receive the quarterly journal. There are National Collections of Water Lilies at Burnby Hall, Yorkshire, and Stapeley Water Gardens, Cheshire.

IRISH GARDEN PLANT SOCIETY

c/o National Botanic Gardens, Glasnevin, Dublin 9, Eire
Aims To conserve garden plants and gardens
Membership 500
Subscriptions I£15 single; I£22 family (in 1998)
Services Lectures; seed scheme; publications; journal; special-interest and regional groups; outings; plant sales

Formed in 1981 as the Irish equivalent to the NCCPG, the Society has a particular mission to locate and propagate plants raised in Ireland, whether by amateurs or nurserymen. The Society is the only group within Ireland that is registered with the NCCPG. There are branches in Munster and Northern Ireland, each with their own programme. Members receive a quarterly newsletter as well as the society's journal *Moorea*, which has articles of a historical nature about Irish plants, gardens and gardeners.

MAGNOLIA SOCIETY INC

6616 81st Street, Cabin John, MD 20818, USA
☎ & Fax 00 1 301 320 4296
Contact Hon. Secretary
Membership 600
Subscriptions US$20 USA; US$25 Canada & overseas

Services Lectures; gardens; seed scheme; library; publications; advice; awards; journal; outings

Founded in 1963 to promote the exchange of knowledge about magnolias, the Society is the major association devoted to this genus. Members receive the twice-yearly journal *Magnolia* as well as a newsletter. The journal has articles on such subjects as cultivation, propagation, breeding, and gardens. The society offers a seed exchange, library and registration service for new cultivars.

MEDITERRANEAN GARDEN SOCIETY

PO Box 14, Peania 190 02, Greece
☎ 00 30 1 664 3089

Contact The Secretary
Membership 1,000
Subscriptions £15
Services Seed scheme; publications; journal

An excellent young society, principally for people who live in the Mediterranean region and want to garden in the English manner, i.e. with plants!

NATIONALE BOOMGAARDEN STICHTING

Postbus 49, B-3500 Hasselt 1, Belgium
☎ & Fax 00 32 12 237001

Contact Ludo Royen
Membership 2,000
Subscriptions BEF 750; £15 for UK
Services Lectures; publications; shows; journal; special-interest and regional groups; outings; scion exchange

An active and enthusiastic Flemish society, dedicated to the conservation of fruit trees. It sustains the Belgian National Collections of apples, pears, plums, cherries, quinces and medlars. The quarterly journal *Pomologia* is an authoritative publication. The society is considerably involved with organising the International Fruit Show Europom in Limburg this year.

NEDERLANDS-BELGISCHE VERENIGING VAN LIEFHEBBERS VAN CACTUSSEN

Prins Willem Alexanderlaan 104, NL-6721 AE Bennekom, The Netherlands

Contact J M Smit-Reesink (Secretary)
Membership 2,500
Subscriptions HFl 50
Services Seed scheme; library; publications; shows; journal; special-interest and regional groups; outings

The Benelux Succulent society has many attractions, including a seed list of rare species and the attractive bi-monthly *Succulenta*. British members rate it highly. The 33 regional societies have their own programmes of events and shows.

NORTH AMERICAN ROCK GARDEN SOCIETY

PO Box 67, Millwood, NY 10546, USA
☎ 00 1 914 762 2948

Contact Executive secretary
Membership 4,500
Subscriptions US$25 USA; US$30 overseas
Services Lectures; gardens; seed scheme; library; publications; awards; journal; special-interest and regional groups

The society offers an excellent quarterly journal and the longest society seed list we know of (6,000 items): as a result, it has many members in the UK.

POMONA

Via Bramante, 29, I-20154 Milano, Italy
☎ 00 39 2 3494775
Fax 00 39 2 33105281

Contact Dr Paolo Belloni
Subscriptions Lit. 100,000
Services Lectures; gardens; advice; special-interest and regional groups; outings

An extremely active Italian society dedicated to the conservation of old fruit varieties, particularly of tree fruits. It has been extremely successful in raising public consciousness of the importance of protecting traditional cultivars of apples, pears, plums and peaches.

ROCK GARDEN CLUB PRAGUE

Marikova 5, 162 00 Praha 2, Czech Republic

Contact J U Dr. Ing. Josef Adanec
Membership 1,400
Subscriptions US$20, plus US$5 for seed exchange
Services Lectures; seed scheme; library; shows; journal

The Czechs have a long history of excellence with alpine plants. The Club's quarterly bulletin *Skalnicky* is published with English abstracts: more than 10% of its members live abroad. The annual seed list has about 1,500 items. Many of these items are collected in central or eastern Europe.

SINO-HIMALAYAN PLANT ASSOCIATION

81 Parlaunt Road, Slough, Berkshire SL3 8BE
☎ 01753 542823

Contact Chris Chadwell (Secretary)
Aims To bring together and spread information on Sino-Himalayan flora
Membership 150
Subscriptions £8 UK; £10 overseas
Services Lectures; gardens; seed scheme; library; journal; outings

Formed in 1990, this is an informal Association. Members receive a twice-yearly newsletter and meetings take place in varying venues around the country. There is a small display garden as well as a seed exchange.

SOCIÉTÉ DES AMATEURS DE JARDINS ALPINS

43, rue Buffon, F-75005 Paris, France

Contact G Dumont (Membership Secretary)
Aims To promote the cultivation of alpine and rock plants
Membership 600
Services Seed scheme; shows; journal; special-interest and regional groups; outings

SOCIETIES / WORLDWIDE   319

The French alpine society, though small, is a regular exhibitor at French flower shows. The society is concerned with the botany and conservation of alpine plants as well as their cultivation.

SOCIÉTÉ FRANÇAISE DES IRIS ET PLANTES BULBEUSES
19, rue du Docteur Kurzenne, F-78350 Jouy en Josas, France
☎ 00 33 2 39 56 12 24
Contact Mme Anne-Marie Chesnais
Membership 400
Subscriptions FF 180 France; FF 210 abroad
Services Lectures; seed scheme; advice; outings; registration of new hybrids

Irises are very popular in France, where many more varieties are grown than in the UK. Members of the French society receive the quarterly bulletin *Iris et Bulbeuses*, which has a mixture of articles about varieties, botany, breeding, new introductions and reports of events. The society is planning a big exhibit in Brittany next year to illustrate the development of irises throughout the 20th century.

SOCIÉTÉ FRANÇAISE DES ROSES 'LES AMIS DES ROSES'
Roseraie du Parc de la Tête d'Or, F-69006 Lyon, France
☎ 00 33 16 78 94 31 07

The French rose society gives a good focus on roses in France itself. The biennial conference of the International Heritage Rose Association will take place at Lyon in May.

SOCIÉTÉ NATIONAL D'HORTICULTURE DE FRANCE
84, rue de Grenelle, Paris F-75007, France
☎ 00 33 1 44 39 78 78
Fax 00 33 1 45 44 96 57

Contact Georges Soubeyrand
Aims The promotion of all aspects of horticulture in France
Services Lectures; library; publications; advice; awards; shows; journal; special-interest and regional groups; outings

The SNHF was founded in 1827 and operates through a dozen sub-societies for the promotion of particular plants, including orchids, cacti, fuchsias and roses. Members receive the excellent monthly magazine *Jardins de France*.

SUCCULENT SOCIETY OF SOUTH AFRICA
Private Bag X10, Brooklyn, 0011 Pretoria, South Africa
Fax 00 27 12 991 2988
Subscriptions £19 surface mail; £29.50 airmail
Services Seed scheme; journal

The society's quarterly journal *Aloe* concentrates upon the rich succulent flora of southern Africa.

SZO. CZS. MARTAGON (CZECH LILY SOCIETY)
Mochovská 33, 190 00 Praha 9, Czech Republic
Contact Dr Karel Veres (President)
Membership 250
Subscriptions CzK. 80
Services Lectures; seed scheme; shows; journal; outings; bulb exchange

The Czech lily society has been operating at a high level for many years and is very well regarded by liliophiles. Its quarterly bulletin (in Czech) runs regular reports on Czech-raised hybrids and there is an annual show.

VEREIN DEUTSCHER ROSENFREUNDE
Waldseestrasse 14, D-76530 Baden-Baden, Germany
☎ 00 49 7221 31302
Fax 00 49 7221 38337
Contact Frau H Bartetzko

Membership 8,500
Subscriptions DM 42 single; DM 50 double
Services Lectures; gardens; library; publications; advice; awards; shows; journal; special-interest and regional groups; outings

Lieben Sie Rosen? Dann sollten Sie VDR Mitglied werden – Do you love roses? Then you should become a member of the VDR. The German rose society is the best-run rose society in Europe and offers good value to members abroad through its informative quarterly *Rosenbogen* and its quality *Jahrbuch*. There are three great rose gardens in Germany: at Westfalen Park in Dortmund, at Sangerhausen and at Wilhelmshöhe in Kassel. Each has more than twice as many cultivars as any garden in the UK.

WORLD PUMPKIN CONFEDERATION
Gowanda State Road, Collins, NY 14034, USA
☎ 00 1 716 532 5995
Fax 00 1 716 532 5690
Contact Ray Waterman (President)
Aims Growing and studying pumpkins, melons & squashes
Membership 2,000
Subscriptions US$15 USA; US$20 Canada; US$25 other countries
Services Shows; journal; competitions

Largely devoted to competitions for the heaviest pumpkins, squashes and watermelons, the confederation has members, competitions and correspondents in over 30 countries, including the UK. A prize of $50,000 is available to the first person to raise a 1,500-lb pumpkin. Even a 1,000-lb pumpkin seemed a far cry when it was first offered in 1986 and the world record stood at 671 lb. But the current world record is 1,061 lb, so it is only a matter of time before someone claims the big one.

Specialist Bookshops

New gardening books appear each year in unrelenting numbers. Some are excellent, most more run-of-the-mill. Branches of nationwide chains such as Waterstones and Dillons, Foyles, and the university booksellers, including Heffers and Blackwells, all carry an impressive selection of new books and usually offer mail order or account facilities. Ordinary second-hand bookshops can prove fruitful hunting grounds for reasonably priced gardening books but much of their stock is out-of-date and best forgotten. The specialists are your most reliable source for older and more recent classics, floras and affordable but worthwhile titles from overlooked authors. They will also have highly illustrated and collectable books: since these appeal also to non-gardeners, you must expect to pay accordingly. The Provincial Booksellers Fairs Association (PBFA) (01763 249212) organises regular sales around the country. Many of the specialist bookshops which we list are regular exhibitors at RHS shows. It is always worth asking whether they could reserve books for you to collect at the show. We heartily recommend *www.abebooks.com* as a source of out-of-print books from all over the world.

Anna Buxton Books
Redcroft, 23 Murrayfield Road, Edinburgh, Lothian EH12 6EP
☎ 0131 337 1747
Fax 0131 337 8174

Contact Mrs Anna Buxton
Speciality New books; secondhand and antiquarian books; botany; general gardening; horticulture; illustrated books or prints; trees and forestry; Scottish gardening, plant-hunters, garden history
Catalogue On request. Christmas supplement
Mail Order Yes

An attractively produced and readable list, which includes general titles, collectable works and some new books. All books are described, and appear alphabetically by author.

Arnold Books
11 New Regent Street, Christchurch, New Zealand
☎ 00 64 3 365 7188
Fax 00 64 3 365 2630

Contact John Palmer
Speciality Botany; horticulture; natural history

The leading bookshop in New Zealand for second-hand gardening books. Readers should also ask for their Economic Botany list, for that is where books on fruit, vegetables and herbs are listed. e-mail them at *arnold@mac.co.nz*

Besleys Books
4 Blyburgate, Beccles, Suffolk NR34 9TA
☎ 01502 715762

Contact P Besley
Open 9.30 am – 5 pm. Closed Wednesdays and Sundays and sometimes for lunch. After hours contact 01502 675649
Speciality Secondhand and antiquarian books; botany; flower-arranging; general gardening; horti-culture; illustrated books or prints; natural history; trees and forestry
Catalogue On request. One a year
Mail Order Yes

An annotated sectional list: bibliographic details rather than descriptions. A wide selection from general gardening titles to specialist and illustrated books.

Bookmark, Books of the World
PO Box 728, Nowra, NSW 2541, Australia
☎ 00 61 44 217360
Fax 00 61 44 235195

Speciality New books; botany; horticulture
Catalogue Free
Mail Order Yes

This bookshop is a good source of English-language titles from non-UK publishers. Their list of Australian publications is particularly comprehensive.

Brooks Books
PO Box 21473, Concord, CA 94521, USA
☎ 00 1 510 672-4566
Fax 00 1 510 672-3338

Contact Philip Nesty
Speciality Botany; horticulture
Mail Order Yes

Probably the biggest second-hand bookshop in the world that specialises in botany and ornamental horticulture, with the emphasis on plants rather than design or history. Their general list is an excellent source of English-language books from every country. In addition, they publish regular lists devoted to cacti and succulents, and trees and shrubs. E-mail them at *brooksbk@interloc.com*

BSBI Publications; F & M Perring
Green Acre, Wood Lane, Oundle, Peterborough PE8 5TP
☎ 01832 273388
Fax 01832 274568

Contact Mrs Margaret Perring
Open By appointment only
Speciality New books; botany; natural history; county floras and checklists
Catalogue On request. Regular supplements
Mail Order Yes

Official agents for the Botanical Society of the British Isles. In addition to the society's publications, they stock local, British and overseas floras and other botanical, conservation and reference titles.

Capability's Books, Inc
2359 Highway 46, Deer Park, Wisconsin 54007, USA
☎ 00 1 715 269 5346

Contact Paulette Rickard
Speciality New and secondhand books
Catalogue Free
Mail Order Yes

This excellent American bookshop lists about 60% of all horticultural titles now in print and a large number that are no longer available. It is also worth remembering that what is out-of-print in the UK may still be available in the USA. The list is especially helpful: it gives longish descriptions of each title.

Cape Seed & Book Suppliers
PO Box 23709, Claremont 7735, Cape Town, South Africa
☎ 00 27 21 61 2005
Fax 00 27 21 683 3279

Speciality Botany; horticulture; natural history
Mail Order Yes

This company specialises in books about South African botany, horticulture and natural history. Their list is impressively comprehensive and should be the first point of reference for anyone who wants information about their country.

Carol Barnett Books
3562 NE Liberty St., Portland, OR 97211-7258, USA
☎ 00 1 503 282-7036

Speciality Horticulture; natural history

Carol Barnett produces regular catalogues on Botany and Gardening. She is an excellent source for secondhand books on every aspect of American gardening.

Chantrey Books
24 Cobnar Road, Sheffield, South Yorkshire S8 8QB
☎ 0114 2748958

Contact Clare Brightman
Open By appointment only
Speciality Secondhand and antiquarian books; botany; general gardening; horticulture; illustrated books or prints; natural history; rural life
Catalogue On request. Three a year
Mail Order Yes

A pleasing general list, divided into subheadings. Some interesting older books too, as well as natural history and rural titles. They generally attend some of the RHS shows.

Fa. C. Esveld
Rijneveld 72, 2771 XS Boskoop, The Netherlands
☎ 00 31 1727-13289
Fax 00 31 1727-15714

Speciality New books
Mail Order Yes

This bookshop is situated in the garden centre attached to one of Europe's biggest nurseries. It stocks new books in several languages.

Garden Books
11 Blenheim Crescent, London W11 2EE
☎ 0171 792 0777
Fax 0171 792 1991

Contact Valerie Scriven

Open 9 am – 6 pm, Monday to Saturday
Speciality New and secondhand books; horticulture
Mail Order Books sent worldwide

Bookshop in Notting Hill which stocks mostly new gardening titles. The range is extensive, balanced and focused, and they are happy to search for and post anything that is not in stock. A visit is recommended (specialist cookery and travel bookshops are nearby).

Herbaceous Books
15 Westville Avenue, Ilkley, West Yorkshire LS29 9AH
☎ 01943 602422

Contact Yvonne Luke
Speciality Secondhand and antiquarian books
Catalogue Free
Mail Order Yes

Despite its name, this firm offers a wide range of titles, not just confined to hardy plants. The books tend to be good practical guides and inexpensive classics, rather than antiquarian.

Honingklip Book Sales
402 CPOA, 231 Main Road, Rondebosch, 7700 Cape Town, South Africa
☎ 21 689 1940
Fax 21 689 1945

Contact W J & Mrs E R Middelmann
Speciality Secondhand and antiquarian books; botany; horticulture; flora & gardens of southern Africa
Catalogue Free
Mail Order Yes

Honingklip is an excellent source of botanical and horticultural books about every aspect of South African plants, gardens and wildflowers. The list has prices in US$, but cheques in sterling are accepted.

Ingrid Sophie Hörsch
Garten- und Pflanzenbücher International, Hagenwiesenstr. 3, D-73006 Ühingen, Germany
☎ 00 49 7163 4196
Fax 00 49 7163 4789

Contact Ingrid Sophie Hörsch

Open 2 – 10 pm daily
Speciality New and secondhand books
Catalogue Free
Mail Order Yes

This well-established dealer issues two lists a year (new and old) and special lists for roses, rhododendron and camellias, trees and shrubs, and climbers, among others. About half the titles are in German and half in English, from the USA, South Africa, Australia, New Zealand and Canada, as well as the UK. Mrs Hörsch speaks excellent English and her husband is secretary of the German group of the International Clematis Society. Her catalogues are carried on the European Plant Finder *PPP-Index* CD-Rom.

IVELET BOOKS LTD
18 Fairlawn Drive, Redhill, Surrey RH1 6JP
☎ 01737 764520
Fax 01737 760140

Contact Mr D J and Mrs E A Ahern
Speciality Secondhand and antiquarian books; general gardening; horticulture; illustrated books or prints; natural history; landscape and architecture, garden history
Catalogue On request. Three or four a year
Mail Order Yes

A good range for gardeners and collectors: the list is strongest on 20th-century classics such as Jekyll and Bowles, and is also a source for standard and historical works. They also specialise in Landscape and Architecture, and attend some of the RHS shows and summer festivals.

JOHN HENLY
Brooklands, Walderton, Chichester, W Sussex PO18 9EE
☎ 01705 631426
Fax 01205 631544

Contact John Henly
Open By appointment only
Speciality Secondhand and antiquarian books; botany; general gardening; horticulture; natural history; trees and forestry; geology, palaeontology
Catalogue On request. Four a year
Mail Order Yes

The catalogues are helpfully subdivided into subjects. Individual entries have full bibliographic notes, but descriptions are kept to a minimum. Good for standard works, especially from the mid-20th century. E-mail is *johnhenly1@compuserve.com*

KEW SHOP
Mail Order Section, Royal Botanic Gardens, Kew, Richmond, Surrey TW9 3AB
☎ 0181 332 5653

Open 9 am – 5 pm for telephone orders; Victoria Gate Shop normally open 9.30 am – 5.30 pm (Summer and Christmas period) or until last garden admissions
Speciality New books; botany; flower-arranging; horticulture; natural history; trees and forestry
Catalogue Scientific books; gifts
Mail Order Yes

An excellent choice of current horticultural and botanical books, including numerous scientific publications. A large section is devoted to children's books and attractive gift items. Entrance is normally through the garden, but you can get in directly if you give advance notice. The closing time changes with the season (info on 0181 940 1171).

LANDSMAN'S BOOKSHOP LTD
Buckenhill, Bromyard, Hereford & Worcester HR7 4PH
☎ 01885 483420
Fax 01885 483420

Contact K J Stewart
Open 9 am – 4.30 pm, Monday – Friday, Saturdays by appointment
Speciality New books; remaindered books; secondhand and antiquarian books; botany; flower-arranging; general gardening; horticulture; natural history; trees and forestry
Catalogue £1.25
Mail Order Yes

From their substantial catalogue Landsman's aims to supply all gardening books which are in print. Mainly mail order and through agricultural and horticultural shows. They also have remaindered and secondhand material (of interest to horticultural students). Agriculture is stocked in similar depth, and they publish a few titles of their own. Landsman's Bookshop attends some of the RHS shows. e-mail them at *landsmans@dialprop.com*

LLOYDS OF KEW
9 Mortlake Terrace, Kew, Richmond, Surrey TW9 3DT
☎ 0181 940 2512

Contact Lloyds of Kew
Open 10.30 am – 5.30 pm, Tuesday – Saturday
Speciality Secondhand and antiquarian books; botany; flower-arranging; general gardening; horticulture; illustrated books or prints; trees and forestry
Catalogue Annually, on request

Specialists for secondhand and antiquarian gardening books. Tucked away just off Kew Green, the shop also carries a general secondhand stock. They operate a free finding service (without obligation) and are regular exhibitors at Chelsea.

MARY BLAND
Augop, Evenjobb, Presteigne, Powys LD8 2PA
☎ 01547 560218

Contact Mary Bland
Open By appointment only
Speciality Secondhand and antiquarian books; botany; flower-arranging; general gardening; horticulture; illustrated books or prints; trees and forestry
Catalogue On request. About three a year
Mail Order Yes

Good general and collectors' stock, with many interesting and reasonably priced titles across the whole range of gardening books. The list is divided into sections, with bibliographic details and some descriptions. Prints available at RHS shows, which Mary Bland regularly attends. Will search for titles.

MIKE PARK
351 Sutton Common Road, Sutton, Surrey SM3 9HZ
☎ 0181 641 7796

Contact Mike Park or Ian Smith

Open Sales mainly mail order and shows; viewing occasionally possible by appointment
Speciality Remaindered books; secondhand and antiquarian books; botany; flower-arranging; general gardening; horticulture; illustrated books or prints; natural history; trees and forestry; foreign floras
Catalogue One or two a year

Mike Park has an excellent stock and is widely regarded as the brand leader. He goes to most of the gardening shows and is a welcome and familiar exhibitor at RHS shows in Vincent Square.

RHS Enterprises Ltd
RHS Garden, Wisley, Woking, Surrey GU23 6QB
☎ 01483 211113
Fax 01483 211003

Contact Barry Ambrose
Open 10 am – 5.30 pm, Monday – Saturday, closes at 6.30 pm in summer; 11.30 am – 5.30 pm Sundays, March to December, 10 am – 4 pm, January, February
Speciality New books; botany; flower-arranging; general gardening; horticulture; illustrated books or prints; natural history; trees and forestry; plant monographs, floras, academic
Catalogue On request. Two a year
Mail Order Yes (01483 211320)

The range of gardening and botanical books on sale at Wisley is the best in the country. Twice-yearly catalogues detail an extensive part of the stock, and allow for mail order purchase. We find the catalogues so comprehensive that we need to look no further for sourcing new books. The RHS bookshop is particularly good at offering overseas books from the English-speaking world. The shop also sells gift items.

St Ann's Books
Rectory House, 26 Priory Road, Great Malvern, Hereford & Worcester WR14 3DR
☎ 01684 562818
Fax 01684 566491

Contact Chris Johnson

Speciality Secondhand and antiquarian books; botany; horticulture; natural history
Catalogue Three a year
Mail Order Yes

This well-established dealer in secondhand books on ornithology has begun to publish an excellent catalogue of antiquarian and secondhand books on botany and gardening. Many are of interest to collectors, but it is also a good source for not-so-collectable books that are just hard to find nowadays. And they have new titles, too.

Summerfield Books
Summerfield House, High Street, Brough, Kirkby Stephen, Cumbria CA17 4BX
☎ 017683 41577
Fax 017683 41577

Contact Jon and Sue Atkins
Open By appointment
Speciality New books; remaindered books; secondhand and antiquarian books; botany; horticulture; illustrated books or prints; natural history; trees and forestry; country and foreign floras, cryptogams
Catalogue On request. Two a year
Mail Order Yes

A substantial list with an individual style. Very good for local and foreign floras (old and new), botany, plant hunting, cryptogams and forestry titles. Some interesting general titles also: everything from collectors' rarities to £2 bargains. Free finding service. They are opening a shop in Brough early this year. E-mail them on summerfield@iclweb.com

W C Cousens
The Leat, Lyme Road, Axminster, Devon EX13 5BL
☎ 01297 32921

Contact W C Cousens
Open By appointment only
Speciality Secondhand and antiquarian books; flower-arranging; general gardening; horticulture; trees and forestry
Catalogue SAE; Four a year

Book-search facility available.

Wells & Winter
Mere House Barn, Mereworth, Maidstone, Kent ME18 5NB
☎ 01622 813627

Contact Sir John Wells
Open Sell from shows only
Speciality New books; remaindered books; secondhand and antiquarian books; general gardening; horticulture; trees and forestry
Mail Order No

New and secondhand books: available at RHS shows only. The stand also sells botanical cards, labels and other garden products.

Whitestone Gardens Ltd
Sutton, Thirsk, North Yorkshire YO7 2PZ
☎ 01845 597467
Fax 01845 597035

Speciality Secondhand and antiquarian books; horticulture
Catalogue Four 2nd-class stamps

This excellent nursery for cacti and succulents also has the best list of secondhand and out-of-print books on the subject in the UK. It includes German, American and South African works.

Wyseby House Books
Kingsclere Old Bookshop, 2a George Street, Kingsclere, Newbury, Berkshire RG20 5NQ
☎ 01635 297995
Fax 01635 297995

Contact Dr Tim Oldham
Open 10 am – 5 pm, Tuesday – Saturday
Speciality Secondhand and antiquarian books; botany; general gardening; horticulture; natural history; trees and forestry; garden history, architecture
Catalogue On request. Up to five a year
Mail Order Yes

The horticultural titles run from affordable classics from the last 150 years to more recent works. Of interest to both gardeners and specialists. Other areas include zoology and the history of science.

Seed Merchants

England

B & T World Seeds
Whitnell House, Fiddington,
Bridgwater TA5 1JE
☎ & Fax 01278 733209

Specialists in exotic seeds supplied from (and to) most of the world. The system is based on a computerised master list of over 30,000 items, and 187 specialist lists (say Californian natives or salt-tolerant) derived from it. Seed lists don't come any longer than this one: the range is phenomenal. Be aware that many species will be ordered specially for you and that this may take time.

S & N Brackley
117 Winslow Road, Wingrave,
Aylesbury HP22 4QB
☎ 01296 681384

Sweet pea specialists, both as seeds and as young plants: garden and exhibition varieties. You can see their displays at the many – mainly southern – shows which they attend. They also produce exhibition vegetable seeds, with leek and onion plants available in April.

D T Brown & Co Ltd
Station Road, Poulton le Fylde
FY6 7HX
☎ 01253 882371
Fax 01253 890923

Flower and vegetable seed merchants, with some young plants, grass seed and horticultural sundries. A large range is sold from their clear and concise catalogue. They issue a separate seed catalogue for commercial growers and florists.

Carters Tested Seeds Ltd
Hele Road, Torquay TQ2 7QJ

☎ 01803 616156
Fax 01803 615747

Long-established seed company in the Suttons group. The flower and vegetable range is sold through garden centres and some supermarkets. Details of stockists from the company.

John Chambers' Wild Flower Seeds
15 Westleigh Road, Barton Seagrave, Kettering NN15 5AJ
☎ 01933 652562
Fax 01933 652576

Biggest and best-known of the wildflower merchants, with everything from British natives and butterfly plants to mixtures and ornamental grass seeds. There is also a good choice of books in the somewhat frenetic catalogue.

Chiltern Seeds
Bortree Stile, Ulverston LA12 7PB
☎ 01229 581137
Fax 01229 584549

The distinctive long, tall catalogue is uniquely comprehensive. Some 4,500 items are enthusiastically described in 300 pages of carefully written descriptions. A good proportion are novelties, 400–500 most years.

CN Seeds
Denmark House, Pymoor, Ely
CB6 2EG
☎ 01353 699413
Fax 01353 698806

Wholesale herb and flower seed merchants, but retail customers are welcome. Prices are quoted by weight and quantities given. There is a wide range, from British wildflowers to exotic trees but they are particularly good on herbaceous plants. Try them for *Fritillaria meleagris* to naturalise:

1 gram will cost you £3 plus VAT, and yield about 800 seeds.

Samuel Dobie & Son Ltd
Long Road, Paignton TQ4 7SX
☎ 01803 629444
Fax 01803 615150

General seed company with a catalogue of flower and vegetable varieties. They also specialise in young annual plants, and have a decent range of garden equipment.

Emorsgate Seeds
The Pea Mill, Market Lane,
Terrington St Clement, King's Lynn PE34 4HR
☎ 01553 829028
Fax 01553 829803

Wildflowers, wild grasses and mixtures for retail and wholesale customers. The seed stocks are based on native-collected seed which is then grown at the farm: the source county is given and stocks are regularly replenished. A good choice of wild and amenity grasses. Flower and grass mixtures are available for different soil types, and some are derived (with permission) from specified nature reserves.

Mr Fothergill's Seeds Ltd
Gazeley Road, Kentford,
Newmarket CB8 7QB
☎ 01638 751161
Fax 01638 751624

General seed company selling flowers, vegetables and some sundries from colourful catalogues. Three are devoted to seeds: the 1999 Main Seed Catalogue with some 71 new flower varieties and 88 new vegetable lines this year; the Enthusiasts' Catalogue for lovers of rare and old-world plants; and the Young Plants

Catalogue which catches the growing market for plugs.

PETER GRAYSON – SWEET PEA SEEDSMAN
34 Glenthorne Close, Brampton, Chesterfield S40 3AR
☎ 01246 278503
Fax 01246 566918

An enticing list which includes unrivalled collections of *Lathyrus* species, and pre-Spencer Grandifloras (or Heirlooms), and some of Mr Grayson's introductions. There will be hollyhocks this year. Seed is produced on site. Wholesale and retail.

KINGS
Monks Farm, Pantlings Lane, Coggeshall Road, Kelvedon CO5 9PG
☎ 01376 570000
Fax 01376 571189

Good value retail seed list. All the seed is untreated, so suitable for organic gardeners too. Strong on herbs and sweet peas. They also have a large wholesale flower and vegetable seed business aimed at growers.

MARSHALLS
S E Marshall & Co Ltd, Wisbech PE13 2RF
☎ 01945 583407
Fax 01945 588235

This fenland seed company specialises in vegetables and seed potatoes, but also has a range of popular flowers. Like the other major seed firms they place great emphasis on looking after their customers: there are free seeds for larger orders and even some opportunities to trial (and report) on varieties before they are properly introduced.

MONOCOT NURSERY
Jacklands, Jacklands Bridge, Tickenham, Clevedon BS21 6SG
☎ 01275 810394

Specialist nursery with an amazing collection of bulbous plants (including tubers, rhizomes and corms). The stock is mostly of species, and subspecies, grown from seed, frequently from named collectors and sources. The seed list appears in October. Very strongly recommended indeed.

ANDREW NORFIELD SEEDS
Lower Meend, St Briavels GL15 6RW
☎ 01594 530134
Fax 01594 530113

Pre-germinated seed, mainly of trees and shrubs, with some rare items among them. You pay a premium on the ordinary seed price, but do not have to wait for lengthy or difficult germination conditions to be fulfilled. We have been happy customers for several years.

NORTH GREEN SEEDS
16 Witton Lane, Little Plumstead, Norwich NR13 5DL

A pleasantly eclectic range of good things from around the world. Order in summer for autumn sowing.

PLANT WORLD BOTANIC GARDENS
St Marychurch Road, Newton Abbot TQ12 4SE
☎ & Fax 01803 872939

The nursery sells a selection of alpines, perennials and shrubs. There is an illustrated seed list with fresh material from the gardens and some interesting collected species. The four-acre gardens are planted out as special habitat zones: worth a long journey to visit in their own right.

W ROBINSON & SONS LTD
Sunny Bank, Forton, Preston PR3 0BN
☎ 01524 791210
Fax 01524 791933

Home of the 'Mammoth' seed strain: exhibition and garden vegetable seeds, including the 'Mammoth Improved Onion' and their new climbing French bean 'Kingston Gold'. Seedlings and small plants are also available. Their show exhibits are superb.

SEEDS-BY-SIZE
45 Crouchfield, Boxmoor, Hemel Hempstead HP1 1PA
☎ 01442 251458

Over 1,400 vegetable strains, and around 4,200 flower varieties. Seeds are sold by weight in any quantity from 0.5 gram up: the pricing system looks more daunting than it really is. Mr Size is a good source for many old and hard-to-obtain varieties. Take your pick from 64 carrots, 57 lettuces, 222 sweet peas or 52 asters, for example.

SIMPSON'S SEEDS
27 Meadowbrook, Old Oxted RH8 9LT
☎ & Fax 01883 715242

Quite the most unusual seedsman in the world. Colin Simpson runs his operation as a society (see the Tomato Growers' Club) which enables him to import and export seeds much more easily than he would as a nurseryman. His specialities are tomatoes, peppers and seed potatoes: his descriptive list has a fascinating number of these and other vegetables from all over the world. His own garden is open in early autumn for fellow fans of unusual varieties to see them growing.

SUTTONS SEEDS
Hele Road, Torquay TQ2 7QJ
☎ 01803 614455
Fax 01803 615747

Famous old seed house with a strong catalogue of flowers and vegetable varieties as well as a highly useful range of garden sundries, young plants and bulbs.

THE SEED HOUSE
9a Widley Road, Cosham, Portsmouth PO6 2DS
☎ 01705 325639

Interesting list of Australian native plants, including *Callistemon* and *Eucalyptus* as well as less common genera. The species are specially chosen for their suitability for a European climate.

THE VAN HAGE GARDEN COMPANY
Great Amwell, Ware SG12 9RP
☎ 01920 870811
Fax 01920 871861

Long-established and award-winning garden centre and seed merchants. The seed catalogue covers flowers and vegetables, and includes the record-breaking carrot 'Flak' as well as some untreated seed which is suitable for organic gardeners.

THOMPSON & MORGAN
Poplar Lane, Ipswich IP8 3BU
☎ 01473 688588
Fax 01473 680199

Established in 1855. The T & M list is the world's largest illustrated seed catalogue and perhaps the most famous. It combines a tradition of good new introductions with a wide choice of less easily attainable plants. Among many new strains for 1999 are a pale yellow foxglove called 'Primrose Carousel', *Zinnia* 'Desert Sun' and a mixture of six different cultivars of basil.

EDWIN TUCKER & SONS
Brewery Meadow, Stonepark, Ashburton TQ13 7DG
☎ 01364 652403
Fax 01364 654300

Long-established seed merchants, with a retail and agricultural catalogue. They have over 80 seed potatoes, including continental varieties, as well as a splendid range of vegetable, garden flower and grass seed. Some garden products are also available by mail order. Their working malthouse (near Newton Abbot railway station) can be visited daily, except Saturdays, from Easter to October (01626 334734).

UNWINS SEEDS LTD
Histon, Cambridge CB4 4LE
☎ 01223 236236
Fax 01223 237437

Long-famous as breeders of sweet peas, Unwins are actually the market leader for seeds of annuals and bedding plants, as well as offering a full choice of vegetable seeds. Good value, innovative and always extremely reputable.

ROY YOUNG SEEDS
23 Westland Chase, West Winch, King's Lynn PE33 0QH
☎ & Fax 01553 840867

A vast range of cactus and succulent seeds by post, for retail and wholesale customers. Much of the seed is harvested from their own plants. The *Lithops* range is especially notable, with a great number of different forms listed under collectors' numbers. Many items are in short supply, and so telephone orders are not accepted.

YSJ SEEDS
Kingsfield Conservation Nursery, Broadenham Lane, Winsham, Chard TA20 4JF
☎ & Fax 01460 30070

The nursery specialises in British native trees and shrubs (of British provenance), either open-ground or container-grown. Wildflowers are sold as plugs or as seed. Advice or consultations are available.

WALES

JIM & JENNY ARCHIBALD
Bryn Collen, Ffostrasol, Llandysul SA44 5SB

Serious alpine seed list for serious alpine enthusiasts. The Archibalds are professional collectors, and the list is based on their extensive trips. It includes detailed collection, cultivation and historical notes.

REPUBLIC OF IRELAND

MACKEY'S GARDEN CENTRE
Castlepark Road, Sandycove
☎ 00 353 1 280 7385
Fax 00 353 284 1922

The garden centre outlet of a famous old seed merchants (founded in 1777). There are many interesting plants in the all-round range, most notably the Australian collection. Mackey's Seed Ltd is at 22 St Mary Street, Dublin.

AUSTRALIA

D ORRIELL – SEED EXPORTERS
45 Frape Avenue, Mt Yokine, Perth, WA 6060
☎ 00 61 9 344 2290
Fax 00 61 9 344 8982

One of the leading Australian native seed merchants but primarily wholesale, since their minimum quantity is 25 grams. As well as a general list, they offer several special lists: hardy eucalypts; Australian everlastings for dried flowers; Australian conifers; Proteaceae; palms, cycads, pandanus and palm-like species. The scope is impressive: 75 *Banksia* species, nearly 50 *Grevillea* and 75 *Hakea*. Small test packets of most items are available.

HARVEST SEEDS CO
325 McCarrs Creek Road, Terrey Hills, NSW 2084
☎ 00 61 29 450 2699
Fax 00 61 29 450 2750

Strictly wholesale – but what a list! – and they do have some gift-pack sizes available too. The company majors on Australian native seeds, many from specific provenances: over 200 *Eucalyptus* and 30 *Melaleuca*, for example. Native grass seed is another speciality. Minimum quantities are 25 grams: the 22 *Callistemon* species cost between A$4 and A$15 – and 25 grams goes a very long way.

M L FARRAR PTY LTD
PO Box 1046, Bomaderry, NSW 2541
☎ 00 61 44 217966
Fax 00 61 44 210051
Web *www.farrar.com.au/*

A good list for trees and shrubs, most of them Australian, but not all. There are, for example, about 40 *Pinus* species alongside the 150 species of *Acacia* and endless *Eucalyptus*. Strictly wholesale, but in practice (like most Australian wholesalers) they offer trial packets of seeds at A$3.50. Recommended.

NINDETHANA SEED SERVICE PTY LTD
PO Box 2121, Albany 6330 WA
☎ 00 61 98 44 3533
Fax 00 61 98 44 3573

This well-known supplier of native Australian seed has a splendid list of trees, shrubs and wildflowers. *Acacia* (over 400 species) and *Eucalyptus* (c. 550 species) feature strongly, but so do such lesser-known genera as *Hakea* (c. 90 species) and *Drosera* (c. 60 species). But there are many smaller and monospecific genera too. Thoroughly recommended.

CZECH REPUBLIC

EUROSEEDS
PO Box 95, 741 01 Novy Jicin

This excellent alpine and herbaceous list is written in English and payment may be made in any major currency: the catalogue itself costs US$2. The owner, Mojmr Pavelka, collects every year in a different mountain region and receives wild seed from correspondents elsewhere, notably the USA. The list therefore changes: strongly recommended to plantsmen.

FRANCE

CATROS GÉRAND
1, avenue de la Gardette,
F-33560 Carbon Blanc
☎ 00 33 5 57 80 90 90
Fax 00 33 5 56 06 80 11

A good middle-range French catalogue, handsomely printed with helpful descriptions. The list of vegetable seeds will be of particular interest to UK readers: most of the items offered are traditional French strains. The lists of peas and beans are particularly long and varied.

GRAINES BAUMAUX
BP 100, F-54000 Nancy
☎ 00 33 3 83 15 86 86
Fax 00 33 3 83 15 86 80

One of the best French mail-order catalogues for seeds and bulbs. The choice of vegetable seeds, in particular, is excellent: nearly 100 different types of beans, 25 of carrots and a huge number of gastronomic rarities – different colour forms of *Chenopordium*, *Campanula rapunculus* (you eat the roots) and *Oxalis crenata* from Peru (potato-like tubers). Absolutely fascinating to anyone who is interested in experiencing variety.

VILMORIN
B P 37, F-38291 St Quentin F. Cedex
☎ 00 33 4 74 82 10 10
Fax 00 33 4 74 82 11 11

Vilmorin is the most famous seed house in France, with a reputation that goes back 250 years. They offer some interesting bedding plants – strains not grown in the UK – but the joy of Vilmorin's list is that it opens the door to the world of French vegetables – *c*. 30 varieties of lettuce, *c*. 25 haricot beans, 10 types of turnip and even five strains of mâche.

GERMANY

ALBERT SCHENKEL GMBH
Postfach 1304, D-22872 Wedel
☎ 00 49 4103 601088
Fax 00 49 4103 601089

Albert Schenkel was founded in Tenerife in 1862 and specialises to this day in seeds of exotic plants from warm climates. Its list is a good source of seeds for plants for the conservatory or for homes abroad. It has a fair selection of Australian and South African plants, including a separate list for *Protea*, but it is also worth looking at for *Drosera*, *Sarracenia* and *Musa*. Their cacti and succulents list is good all-round, but particularly strong on *Gymnocalycium*, *Mamillaria*, *Opuntia* and *Lithops*.

EXOTISCHE SÄMEREIEN
Postfach 1348, D-72074 Tübingen
☎ & Fax 00 49 7071 73541

An excellent list, in the best tradition of German glasshouse horticulture. Most of the seeds it offers are of subtropical and Mediterranean plants, with a good proportion of rarities. It is particularly good for palms, cycads and Australian plants, most of them unknown in the UK. Recommended.

JELITTO STAUDENSAMEN GMBH
Postfach 1264, D-29685 Schwarmstedt
☎ 00 49 5071 4085
Fax 00 49 5071 4088

Jelitto is one of the greatest seed houses in Europe and a good source of unusual herbaceous material for keen plantsmen, gardening clubs and small nurserymen. Strictly speaking, Jelitto deal only with the trade, in wholesale quantities, but they also offer seeds in packets, subject to a minimum order. The list includes more than 50 campanulas, 20 gentians and 20 silenes, as well as a number of species which have been pre-treated to break seed dormancy. Thoroughly recommended.

SAMEN & TÖPFE
Peter & Monika Klock, Postfach 520604, D-22596 Hamburg
☎ 00 49 40 8991698
Fax 00 49 40 8901170

This German nursery is particularly good for houseplants and conservatory plants: 30+ *Passiflora*, for example. Seeds come in three packets sizes, containing 12, 50 and 100 seeds respectively.

ITALY

FRATELLI INGEGNOLI
Corso Buenos Aires, 54, I-20124 Milano
☎ 00 39 2 29513167
Fax 00 39 2 29529759

This famous old firm was founded in 1817 and is still one of the leading Italian seed houses and growers. Theirs is the best list we know for Italian vegetable seeds – chicory, radicchio, red onions, yellow beans, aubergines and tomatoes – and very good for melons, zucchini and squashes too.

NEW ZEALAND

KINGS SEEDS
1660 Great North Road – PO Box 19.084, Avondale, Auckland
☎ & Fax 00 64 9 828 7588

A good general seed catalogue of the English type: lots of annuals and perennials, plus vegetables, herbs and dried flower seeds. What makes it so interesting is the number of un-English varieties, many from Australia, south-east Asia and the USA. The Heirloom tomatoes (black, pink and purple as well as red and yellow) are particularly fascinating.

SOUTHERN SEEDS
The Vicarage, Sheffield, Canterbury
☎ & Fax 00 64 3 318 3814

This catalogue consists almost entirely of New Zealand alpine species, hardy in the UK. The contents differ according to the season but are always impressive for their range – comprehensive lists of *Aciphylla*, *Coprosma*, *Myosotis* and *Ranunculus* among many other genera. Highly recommended.

SOUTH AFRICA

RUST-EN-VREDE NURSERY
PO Box 753, Brackenfell, 7560
☎ 00 27 21 9814515
Fax 00 27 21 9810050

Specialist in native South African bulb seeds, with a good list of *Gladiolus*, *Moraea* and *Lachenalia* among others.

SILVERHILL SEEDS
PO Box 53108, Kenilworth 7745
☎ 00 27 21 762 4245
Fax 00 27 21 797 6609

An excellent list of South African native seeds, most of them collected in the wild. Annuals, perennials, bulbs, shrubs and trees: the list extends to about 2,000 names, including long lists of *Aloe*, *Erica*, *Leucadendron* and *Pelargonium*. Highly recommended.

USA

ALPLAINS
PO Box 489, Kiowa, CO 80117-0489
☎ 00 1 303 621 2247
Fax 00 1 303 621 2864

Allplains specialise in species native to the North American West, though the list does include a good range of taxa from other parts of the world. That said, many of the items they list are uncommon in cultivation because they have not received much horticultural exposure. Allplains actively seeks out wildflowers with good potential and the results are impressive: 15 *Eriogonum* species, 25 *Astragalus* and over 60 *Penstemon*. The helpful catalogue has good descriptions of the plants and the growing conditions they require. Strongly recommended.

NORTHWEST NATIVE SEED
4441 S. Meridian St, #363, Puyallup, WA 98373

Seeds of native plants of the western United States, much of it collected in the wild. The catalogue is impressive, and contains over 600 items. There is an emphasis on bulbs and herbaceous species and, as you would expect, there are long lists of *Allium*, *Astragalus*, *Calochortus*, *Eriogonum* and *Penstemon*.

SOUTHERN EXPOSURE SEED EXCHANGE
PO Box 170, Earlysville, VA 22936
☎ 00 1 804 973 4703
Fax 00 1 804 973 8717

This is a fascinating list with long historical descriptions: it makes for compulsive reading. Heritage varieties are the main line, most of them edible plants. Varieties come from all over the world. Take tomatoes, for example. There are over 70 listed. They include original species from South America; a hybrid developed for the Siberian summer; a pickling tomato; tiny wild ones like redcurrants; strains from Italy, Germany, Hungary, the Czech Republic, Bulgaria and every part of the USA; tomatoes in red, pink, purple, yellow, white and stripes. Highly recommended.

SOUTHWESTERN NATIVE SEEDS
Box 50503, Tucson, AZ 85703

Long-established plant-hunters and native seed suppliers with over 400 species, most of them collected in the wild. About half come from Arizona and New Mexico and most of the rest from California, Utah, Mexico and Montana. They are divided according to habitat and type: desert or mountain and trees, shrubs, wildflowers and succulents. Most are wildflowers, meaning herbaceous, and the list is very impressive, but we like it (and have bought from it for 20 years) because there is no better source for American trees and shrubs. But there are endless species of *Agastache*, *Aquilegia*, *Calochortus* and so on down to *Yucca*. Highly recommended.

ORGANISATIONS

ADAS
ADAS Headquarters, Oxford Spires Business Park, The Boulevard, Kidlington, Oxfordshire OX5 1NZ
☎ 01865 842742
Fax 01865 845055
Web *www.adas.co.uk*

ADAS is the leading business and technical consultancy serving the horticultural industry in the UK, with 70 qualified horticultural consultants and a total staff of 1,300.

ALL YEAR ROUND CHRYSANTHEMUM GROWERS ASSOCIATION
30 Pern Drive, Botley, Hampshire SO30 2GW
☎ 01489 786638

Formed to represent the industry and distribute information to growers. Acts as a liaison between the growers, the government and other bodies. In the past their work has included pest control and the new plant passport scheme. They have recently become involved in publicity, and are active in promoting British chrysanthemums.

ARBORICULTURAL ASSOCIATION
Ampfield House, Romsey, Hampshire SO51 9PA
☎ 01794 368717
Web *http://dspace.dial.pipex.com/treehouse/*

A registered charity and the professional body for some 2,000 arboriculturists. The AA publishes a useful directory of consultants and contractors who have met the organisation's stringent standards for training, work and insurance: contact the Secretariat for details. A range of other publications is also available. There is a local group structure, and keen amateurs can join as part of the Tree Club.

ARCHITECTURAL ASSOCIATION
34–36 Bedford Square, London WC1B 3ES
☎ 0171 636 0974
Fax 0171 414 0782
Web *www.arch-assoc.org.uk*

This school of architecture – the oldest in England – has an excellent collection of prints, drawings and photographs. It is an essential resource for anyone concerned with historic gardens.

ASSOCIATION OF GARDEN TRUSTS
8 Glasshouse Lane, Kenilworth, Warwickshire CV8 2AJ
☎ 01926 852976

The association is a national organisation representing county garden trusts. It provides support for the trusts and encourages the sharing of information, resources, training and experience. It aims to promote a proper understanding of the importance of parks and gardens at local and national level.

ASSOCIATION OF NATIONAL PARK OFFICERS
c/o The Old Vicarage, Bondgate, Helmsley, North Yorkshire YO6 3BP
☎ 01439 770657
Fax 01439 770691

ASSOCIATION OF PROFESSIONAL LANDSCAPERS
Creighton Lodge, Hollington Lane, Stramshall, Uttoxeter, Staffordshire ST14 5ES
☎ 01889 507256
Fax 01889 507391
Web *www.martex.co.uk/hta*

Launched in 1995, the APL is a specialist group within the Horticultural Trades Association and seeks to raise the profile of the Landscape Contracting sector. It has about 60 members, all professional gardeners working as, for example, metal workers, motor mechanics, plantspersons, groundsworkers and aquatics workers.

BIO-DYNAMIC AGRICULTURE ASSOCIATION
Woodman Lane, Clent, Stourbridge, West Midlands DY9 9PX
☎ 01562 884933

Offers help to bio-dynamic growers: bio-dynamics are based on the anthroposophical theories of Rudolph Steiner and combine organic principles with celestial ones. The phase of the moon is believed to influence planting times.

BIOTECHNOLOGY & BIOLOGICAL SCIENCES RESEARCH COUNCIL
Polaris House, North Star Avenue, Swindon, Wiltshire SN2 1UH
☎ 01793 413200
Fax 01793 413201
Web *www.bbsrc.ac.uk*

BBSRC took over the work of the Agriculture and Food Research Council in 1994, along with parts of the programme of the former Science and Engineering Research Council. It supports and funds research into all biological fields. This includes work at HRI Wellesbourne and the John Innes Centre and by many graduate students at universities.

ORGANISATIONS

BOTANIC GARDENS CONSERVATION INTERNATIONAL
Descanso House, 199 Kew Road, Richmond, Surrey TW9 3BW
☎ 0181 332 5953
Fax 0181 332 5956
Web *www.rbgkew.org.uk/*

Based at Kew, this organisation supports botanic gardens all over the world to use their resources for wild plant research, conservation, education and the promotion of environmental awareness. It has a good website.

BRITAIN IN BLOOM
Tidy Britain Group, The Pier, Wigan, Lancashire WN3 4EX
☎ 01942 824620
Fax 01942 8247778
Web *www.tidybritain.org.uk*

Split into about 15 regions throughout the UK. Entry forms and advice are available from the regional organisers.

BRITISH AGRICULTURAL & GARDEN MACHINERY ASSOCIATION
14–16 Church Street, Rickmansworth WD3 1RQ
☎ 01923 720241
Fax 01923 896063
Web *www.bagma.com*

BRITISH AGROCHEMICALS ASSOCIATION
4 Lincoln Court, Lincoln Road, Peterborough PE1 2RP
☎ 01733 349225
Fax 01733 562523
Web *www.baa.org.uk*

Trade association for manufacturers, distributors and retailers of pesticides. It publishes a useful handbook and a list of its own many helpful publications – among them, a guide to the products available for amateur gardeners.

BRITISH ASSOCIATION OF LANDSCAPE INDUSTRIES (BALI)
Landscape House, Henry Street, Keighley, W Yorkshire BD21 3DR

☎ 01535 606139
Fax 01535 610269
Web *www.bali.co.uk*

The national body representing Landscape Contractors, founded in 1972. BALI promotes the interests of its members at national and regional level, and works to maintain high standards in the industry. Member firms cover the full spectrum of landscaping, both interior and exterior, design, construction and maintenance. They are required to carry adequate insurance, to abide by the code of conduct, and to maintain a certain standard in their work (which is subject to inspection). Probationary membership is available for companies which have been trading for less than two years.

BRITISH ASSOCIATION OF LEISURE PARKS, PIERS & ATTRACTIONS
25 Kings Terrace, London NW1 0JP
☎ 0171 383 7942
Fax 0171 383 7925

Founded in 1936 as the trade association for most of the UK's private-sector leisure parks, piers and attractions, its members now include managers of theme parks and wildlife attractions.

BRITISH ASSOCIATION OF SEED ANALYSTS
3 Whitehall Court, London SW1A 2EQ
☎ 0171 930 3611
Fax 0171 930 3952

This organisation represents about 130 individual seed analysts, including those working with vegetable and ornamental stocks.

BRITISH ASSOCIATION REPRESENTING BREEDERS (BARB)
9 Portland Street, King's Lynn, Norfolk PE30 1PB

Formerly the British Association of Rose Breeders. Collects payments due under Plant Breeders' Rights, and promotes protected varieties.

BRITISH BEDDING & POT PLANT ASSOCIATION
164 Shaftesbury Avenue, London WC2H 8HL
☎ 0171 331 7281
Fax 0171 331 7410

Now funded in part by a Horticultural Development Council levy, the association is actively concerned with establishing standards and practice codes for the industry, as well as marketing and publicity.

BRITISH BEE-KEEPERS' ASSOCIATION
National Agricultural Association, Stoneleigh, Warwickshire CV8 2LZ
☎ 01203 696679
Fax 01203 690682
Web *www.bbka.demon.co.uk/index.htm*

The BBA represents about 13,000 bee-keepers, mainly in England. It produces leaflets, runs seminars and conventions, supports local groups of bee-keepers and supervises examinations. It also represents the industry at UK and European government levels. There are membership associations throughout the country.

BRITISH CHRISTMAS TREE GROWERS ASSOCIATION
18 Cluny Place, Edinburgh, Lothian EH10 4RL
☎ 0131 447 0099
Fax 0131 447 6443
Web *www.bctga.co.uk*

Mainly to represent the growers and wholesalers, but the association does publish a list of retailers selling Christmas trees.

BRITISH COMMERCIAL GLASSHOUSE MANUFACTURERS ASSOCIATION
c/o Cambridge Glasshouse Co Ltd, Barton Road, Comberton, Cambridge CB3 7BY
☎ 01223 262395
Fax 01223 262713

The association was set up to provide a common forum for

commercial glasshouse manufacturers, research authorities, government controlling bodies and customers. Its members have a common purpose in maintaining consistently high standards of manufacture, customer service, training and safety.

BRITISH DRAGONFLY SOCIETY

The Haywain, Hollywater Road, Bordon, Hampshire GU35 0AD
☎ 01420 472329

The society aims to promote and encourage the study and conservation of dragonflies and their natural habitats, especially in the UK. It has about 1,300 members and 30 local groups. Members may attend the society's meetings and field days, and receive a newsletter and journal.

BRITISH ECOLOGICAL SOCIETY

26 Blades Court, Deodar Road, Putney, London SW15 2NU
☎ 0181 871 9797
Fax 0181 871 9779
Web www.demon.co.uk/bes

Founded in 1913 to promote the science of ecology through research, the society is the oldest of its kind in the world. It seeks to use its research to educate the public and to influence policy decisions which involve ecological matters. It has some 5,000 members.

BRITISH HERB TRADE ASSOCIATION

c/o NFU, Agriculture House, 162 Shaftesbury Avenue, London WC2E PLY
☎ 0171 331 7415
Fax 0171 331 7410

The trade organisation for commercial herb growers.

BRITISH HERBAL MEDICINE ASSOCIATION

Sun House, Church Street, Stroud, Gloucestershire GL5 1JL
☎ 01453 751389
Fax 01453 751402

BHMA was founded in 1964 to advance the science and practice of herbal medicine. It aims to defend the right to choose herbal remedies, to encourage wider knowledge and recognition of the value of herbal medicine, and to foster research into phytotherapy. BHMA is a member of the European Scientific Co-operative for Phytotherapy.

BRITISH INDEPENDENT FRUIT GROWERS' ASSOCIATION

'Aylsham', Broad Oak, Brenchley, Tonbridge, Kent TN12 7NN
☎ 01892 722080
Fax 01892 724540

A marketing and advisory organisation for some of the independent fruit growers in Great Britain. The association has about 40 members.

BRITISH LANDSCAPE INDUSTRY TRAINING ORGANISATION

11a North Queen Street, Keighley, West Yorkshire BD21 3DL
☎ 01535 691179
Fax 01535 691182
Web www.blito.org.uk

Part of BALI, established in 1993 to coordinate training for the landscape sector.

BRITISH LIBRARY

96 Euston Road, London NW1 2DB
☎ 0171 636 1544
Web www.bl.uk

The British Library is the UK's national library, at the centre of the library and information network. Its services are based on the largest collections in the UK: over 18 million volumes. In addition to the British Library, there are five further legal deposit libraries which are entitled under the provisions of the Copyright Act, 1911 to receive a free copy of any book published in the United Kingdom: Bodleian Library, Broad Street, Oxford OX1 3BG (01865 277000); Cambridge University Library, West Road, Cambridge CB3 9DR (01223 333030); National Library of Scotland, George IV Bridge, Edinburgh EH1 1EW (0131 226 4531); The National Library of Wales, Aberystwyth, Dyfed SY23 3BU (01970 623816); Trinity College Library, College Street, Dublin 2 (00 353 1 6772941).

BRITISH MYCOLOGICAL SOCIETY

PO Box 30, Stourbridge, West Midlands DY9 9PZ

This learned society was founded in 1896 and promotes the study of all types of fungi, from mushrooms to moulds. It has about 30 local groups.

BRITISH NATURALISTS' ASSOCIATION

48 Russell Way, Higham Ferrers, Wellingborough, NN10 8EJ
☎ & Fax 01933 314672

The Association exists to encourage education, study and research in all branches of natural history and wildlife conservation. David Bellamy is the President.

BRITISH ORCHID GROWERS ASSOCIATION

38 Florence Road, College Town, Camberley, Surrey GU15 4QD
☎ 01276 32947

A trade association for orchid nurserymen and sundry traders to promote and maintain standards.

BRITISH PEST CONTROL ASSOCIATION

3 St James' Court, Friar Gate, Derby, Derbyshire DE1 1ZU
☎ 01332 294288
Fax 01332 295904

Trade association for everyone concerned with pest control.

BRITISH RETAIL & PROFESSIONAL FLORISTS ASSOCIATION

49 Meadway, Enfield, London EN3 6NX
☎ 01992 767645

BRITISH ROSE GROWERS ASSOCIATION
4 Peewit Road, Hampton, Evesham, Hereford & Worcester WR11 6NH
☎ & Fax 01386 442307

A vigorous trade association which works for the well-being of the rose-growing industry and for the promotion of the rose itself. Roses sold under the BRGA logo have a guarantee of quality.

BRITISH SOCIETY OF PLANT BREEDERS
Woolpack Chambers, Market Street, Ely, Cambridgeshire CB7 4ND
☎ 01353 664211
Fax 01353 661156

Represents the interests of commercial and state sector plan breeders covering farm crops, vegetables and ornamentals. The Society issues sub-licences and collects royalties from sub-licensees on behalf of plant breeders. It is an officially recognised body for conducting trials that are a legal requisite for National Listing of new varieties.

BRITISH TOURIST AUTHORITY
Thames Tower, Black's Road, Hammersmith, London W6 9EL
☎ 0181 846 9000
Web *www.visit-britain.org.uk*

A list of British tourist information centres is available. Local centres can often provide information on gardens and events in their area. The website is excellent.

BRITISH TRUST FOR CONSERVATION VOLUNTEERS (BTCV)
36 St Mary's Street, Wallingford, Oxfordshire OX10 0EU
☎ 01491 839766
Fax 01491 839646
Web *www.btcv.org.uk/*

Carries out practical conservation projects, including tree-planting. They run training courses and offer working conservation holidays, including some involving garden restoration.

BULB DISTRIBUTORS ASSOCIATION
Springfield Gardens, Camelgate, Spalding, Lincolnshire PE12 6ET
☎ 01775 724843
Fax 01775 711209

A trade organisation, founded in 1945, which now has 30 corporate members. It aims to organise and protect the interests of distributors of bulbs, and to cooperate in and deal collectively with all matters concerning the industry.

BUTTERFLY CONSERVATION
Box 222, Dedham, Colchester, Essex CO7 6EH
☎ & Fax 01206 322342
Web *www.butterfly conservation.org.uk*

This thriving society (8,500 members) works to safeguard the future of butterflies and moths. One way of doing so is to promote butterfly-friendly gardening.

CADW: WELSH HISTORIC MONUMENTS
Brunel House, 2 Fitzalan Road, Cardiff CF2 1UY
☎ 01222 500200
Fax 01222 826375
Web *www.wales.gov.uk*

CADW has begun to publish a register of Parks and Gardens of Special Historic Interest in Wales. The registers for Gwent and Clwyd have already been published: Gwynedd and Dyfed are imminent. The standard modern work on the subject is *The Historic Gardens of Wales* by Elizabeth Whittle (HMSO, 1992).

CENTRE FOR ALTERNATIVE TECHNOLOGY
Machynlleth, Powys SY20 9AZ
☎ 01654 702400
Web *www.cat.org.uk*

The centre demonstrates a range of sustainable technologies, including organic food production. It also runs courses, sells books and publishes various information leaflets on the environmental approaches to gardening.

CITES
15, chemin des Anémones, CP 456, 1219 Châtelaine, Geneva Switzerland

This is the address of the international secretariat. Further information is also available from the Department of the Environment, which is the management authority for the UK, and from RBG Kew, which is the scientific authority.

CIVIC TRUST
17 Carlton House Terrace, London SW1Y 5AW
☎ 0171 930 0914
Fax 0171 321 0180
Web *www.civictrust.org.uk*

This pressure group is concerned to improve the built environment, which includes the regeneration of public parks and gardens. Its members include some 1,000 local civic societies.

COMMERCIAL HORTICULTURAL ASSOCIATION
National Agricultural Association, Stoneleigh, Warwickshire CV8 2LZ
☎ 01203 690330
Fax 01203 690334

A trade organisation for manufacturers and suppliers of goods and services to the commercial horticultural industry. The CHA Suppliers Guide is available to professional horticulturists and the trade.

COMMON GROUND
Seven Dials Warehouse, 44 Earlham Street, London WC2H 9LA
☎ 0171 379 3109

Rather an unusual environmental group, which encourages people to appreciate local diversity. Common Ground is the moving force behind National Apple Day (21 October) and the movement towards community orchards.

ORGANISATIONS 333

CONSERVATION FOUNDATION
1 Kensington Gore, London SW7 2AR
☎ 0171 591 3111
Fax 0171 591 3110
Web *www.newsnet-21.org.uk*

Manages, creates and funds environmental programmes with business sponsorship, and assists conservation groups with publicity and financing. Among its larger co-workers are Ford Motors, Wessex Water and Lloyds Bank.

COUNCIL FOR ENVIRONMENTAL EDUCATION
94 London Street, Reading, Berkshire RG1 4SJ
☎ 0118 950 2550
Fax 0118 950 2550
Web *www.cee.org.uk*

The national body for the coordination and promotion of environmental education in England, Wales and Northern Ireland. Formed in 1968, it represents and works with the 80+ national organisations and 250 associates which are its members.

COUNCIL FOR NATIONAL PARKS
246 Lavender Hill, London SW11 1LJ
☎ 0171 924 4077
Fax 0171 924 5761
Web *http://members.aol.com/cnphq/homepage.html*

An independent charity which promotes the conservation, quiet enjoyment and general understanding of the National Parks in England and Wales.

COUNCIL FOR THE PROTECTION OF RURAL ENGLAND
Warwick House, 25 Buckingham Palace Road, London SW1W 0PP
☎ 0171 976 6433
Fax 0171 976 6373
Web *www.greenchannel.com/cpre*

COUNTRY HOUSES ASSOCIATION
Suite 10, Aynhoe Park, Aynho, Northamptonshire OX17 3BQ
☎ 01869 812800
Fax 01869 812819
Web *www.cha.org.uk*

Founded in 1955 to save buildings (including their grounds and gardens) of historic and architectural merit for the public benefit, the association now has about 2,400 members. It owns some of the most beautiful historic houses in southern England, all of which offer residential accommodation for active retired people from all walks of life.

COUNTRY LANDOWNERS ASSOCIATION
16 Belgrave Square, London SW1X 8PQ
☎ 0171 235 0511
Fax 0171 235 4696
Web *www.cla.org.uk*

An influential body: the CLA's 50,000 members own and manage 60% of the countryside.

COUNTRYSIDE COMMISSION
John Dower House, Crescent Place, Cheltenham GL50 3RA
☎ 01242 521381
Web *www.countryside.gov.uk*

The Countryside Commission is the agency charged with advising the government on matters relating to the countryside and landscape of England. It aims to ensure that the English countryside is protected and that it can be used and enjoyed now and for the future. It will merge with the Rural Development Commission in April.

COUNTRYSIDE COUNCIL FOR WALES
Plas Penrhos, Ffordd Penrhos, Bangor, Gwynedd LL57 2LQ
☎ 01248 370444
Fax 01248 385506
Web *www.ccw.gov.uk*

The Council is the statutory advisor on wildlife and conservation in Wales and the executive authority for the preservation of its landscape.

CUT FLOWER GROWERS' GROUP
Druimsallie, Peewit Road, Hampton, Evesham, Hereford & Worcester WR11 6NH
☎ & Fax 01386 442307

A new trade organisation to represent the interests of members of the cut flower producers.

DEPARTMENT OF AGRICULTURE FOR NORTHERN IRELAND
Dundonald House, Upper Newtonards Road, Belfast, Co Down BT4 3SG
☎ 01232 520100

The government department for horticulture in the province.

DRY STONE WALLING ASSOCIATION OF GREAT BRITAIN
YFC Centre, National Agricultural Centre, Kenilworth, Warwickshire CV8 2LG
☎ 0121 378 0493

The association was founded in 1968 and has about 1,200 members. It works to promote all aspects of the craft of dry stone walling throughout Great Britain.

ENGLISH HERITAGE
Fortress House, 23 Savile Row, London W1X 1AB
☎ 0171 973 3000
Fax 0171 973 3146
Web *www.english-heritage.org.uk*

English Heritage is responsible for the national register of parks and gardens of special historic interest. Dr Harriet Jordan is currently overseeing a comprehensive upgrade of the register, with the aim of publishing a fully revised edition in 2000. Excellent website.

ENGLISH NATURE
Northminster House, Peterborough PE1 1UA
☎ 01733 455000
Fax 01733 568834
Web *www.english-nature.org.uk*

English Nature was set up in 1990 as the statutory service responsible for England's wild plants and animals, biodiversity and its geological interest. English Nature is funded by the government but usually works in partnership with other organisations.

FAUNA & FLORA INTERNATIONAL
Great Eastern House, Tenison Road, Cambridge, Cambridgeshire CB1 2DT
☎ 01223 571000
Fax 01223 461481
Web *www.ffi.org.uk*

The society was founded in 1903, which makes it the world's oldest conservation society: it now has over 4,000 individual members. Much of its energy is currently directed at the trade in wild-collected bulbs and creating indigenous plant areas in such countries as Turkey.

FEDERATION TO PROMOTE HORTICULTURE FOR THE DISABLED
Thorngrove, Common Mead Lane, Gillingham, Dorset SP8 4RE
☎ 01747 822242

The federation liaises with people working in horticulture and with people suffering from disabilities.

FERTILISER MANUFACTURERS ASSOCIATION
Greenhill House, Thorpe Road, Peterborough PE3 6GF
☎ 01733 331303
Fax 01733 332909
Web *www.fma.org.uk*

Trade organisation for manufacturers: it advises on storage, handling, transport, health and safety, as well as producing market information and educational material and representing the industry to governments in the UK and Europe.

FLEUROSELECT
Parallel Boulevard 214d, 2202 HT Noordwijk, The Netherlands
☎ 00 31 7136 49101
Fax 00 31 7136 49102
Web *www.fleuroselect.com*

Represents and promotes ornamental flower breeders and distributors worldwide. Best known for its international trials and awards to new bedding-plant strains.

FLORA FOR FAUNA
c/o The Linnean Society, Burlington House, Piccadilly, London W1V 0LQ
☎ 0171 434 4479
Fax 0171 287 9364

A conservation group which encourages people to garden with native plants and seeks to 'bring biodiversity into everyone's backyard'. They publish a CD-ROM called *Postcode Plants Database* which matches people's postcodes to the 10km-squares used by the Botanical Society of the British Isles to map the UK's flora. You can then see what plants are not only suitable to your garden, but actually indigenous.

FLOWER COUNCIL OF HOLLAND
Catherine Chambers, 6–8 Catherine Street, Salisbury, Wiltshire SP1 2DA
☎ 01722 337505
Fax 01722 336898
Web *www.bbh.nl* and *www.flowerweb.nl*

Established in 1980 to promote Dutch cut flowers and pot plants worldwide, the Council has offices in Paris, Milan and Düsseldorf, as well as its head office in Leiden. The UK is a prime market: we buy less *per capita* than most EU nations, and the Council is keen to encourage us to spend more.

FLOWERS & PLANTS ASSOCIATION
Covent House, New Covent Garden Market, London SW8 5NX
☎ 0171 738 8044
Fax 0171 622 5307
Web *www.flowers.org.uk*

Formed in 1984 to promote the sale of flowers and plants, the Association now has 160 members in the cut flowers and indoor pot plants industry, including such chains as Interflora. Funded by the EU.

FOREST ENTERPRISE
Forest Research Station, Alice Holt Lodge, Wrecclesham, Farnham, Surrey GU10 4LS
☎ 01420 23666
Fax 01420 22082

This part of the Forestry Commission is concerned with the management of publicly owned woodlands.

FORESTRY AUTHORITY
Alice Holt Lodge, Wreccelsham, Farnham, Surrey GU10 4LF
☎ 01420 23337
Fax 01420 22988

This part of the old Forestry Commission advises on matters relating to private woodlands, including the payment of grants and the issue of licences for felling.

FORESTRY COMMISSION
231 Corstorphine Road, Edinburgh, Lothian EH12 7AT
☎ 0131 334 0303
Fax 0131 334 4473
Web *www.forestry.gov.uk*

The Commission's objectives are to protect Britain's forests and woodlands, expand Britain's forest area, enhance the economic value of our forest resources, conserve and improve the biodiversity of woodlands, develop recreational opportunities and increase public participation and understanding. It publishes an extremely useful telephone and address directory which outlines the work of every British organisation concerned with forestry. It has three divisions: Forestry Authority, Forest Enterprise (q.v.), and Forest Research.

FORESTRY TRUST
The Old Estate Office, Englefield Road, Theale, Reading, Berkshire RG7 5DZ
☎ 0118 932 3523

Education and conservation trust dedicated to sustainable forestry. They produce a series of regional guides, *Exploring Woodlands*.

Friends of the Earth
26 Underwood Street, London
N1 7JQ
☎ 0171 490 1555
Web *www.foe.co.uk*

Friends of the Earth claims to campaign on more issues than any other environmental group in the country. Its website is extremely active and informative.

Garden Centre Association
38 Carey Street, Reading, Berkshire RG1 7JS
☎ 0118 939 3900
Web *www.gca.org.uk*

This industry body has about 260 members, representing the smaller owners and a total of about 160 of the best garden centres. Members are independently inspected.

Garden Industry Manufacturers Association
225 Bristol Road, Birmingham, West Midlands B5 7VB
☎ 0121 446 6688
Fax 0121 446 5215

The association's 65 members include the largest players in most major sections of the market, with an annual retail worth of billions of pounds.

Garden Writers' Guild
14–15 Belgrave Square, London
SW1X 8PS
☎ & Fax 0171 245 6943

Membership is open to anyone who earns a significant part of their income from writing, broadcasting or photographing related to horticultural matters. The Guild aims to improve the standing of its members and to raise the quality of their work.

Gardenex – Federation of Garden & Leisure Manufacturers
60 Claremont Road, Surbiton, Surrey KT6 4RH
☎ 01959 565995

The Federation's function is to promote and expand exports of British garden and leisure products to the EU and overseas markets. It has about 170 corporate members.

Geologists Association
Burlington House, Piccadilly, London WIV 9AG
☎ 0171 434 9298
Web *www.nhm.ac.uk/ hosted_sites/GA/*

Georgian Group
6 Fitzroy Square, London
W1P 6DX
☎ 0171 387 1720
Fax 0171 387 1721
Web *www.heritage.co.uk/ heritage/georgian*

The Georgian group is a statutory national amenity body and exists to save Georgian buildings, monuments, parks and gardens from destruction or disfiguration. It runs an imaginative and lively programme of activities for its members.

Good Gardeners Association
Pinetum Lodge, Churcham, Gloucestershire GL2 8AD
☎ & Fax 01452 750402

This organic association believes that the earth does not belong to man, but man to the earth. It promotes the practice of companion planting: for example, beetroot associates well with onions and kohlrabi, but not with beans.

Health & Safety Executive (HSE)
Information Centre, Broad Lane, Sheffield S3 7HQ
☎ 0541 545500
Fax 0114 289 2333
Web *www.open.gov.uk/hse/ hsehome.htm*

The HSE should be the first point of reference on any matter whatsoever relating to gardening health and safety, particularly as it affects the workplace.

Historic Gardens Foundation
34 River Court, London
SE1 9PE
☎ 0171 633 9165
Fax 0171 401 7072

This new conservation charity with international objectives is particularly strong in France and the UK.

Historic Houses Association (HHA)
2 Chester Street, London
SW1X 7BB
☎ 0171 259 5688
Fax 0171 259 5590
Web *www.historic-houses-assn.org*

A representative association of private owners which campaigns on their behalf. Many members have houses which are open to the public. Membership of the Friends of the HHA gives free admission to many of these properties. The association's brief includes gardens and designed landscapes.

Historic Scotland
Longmore House, Salisbury Place, Edinburgh, Lothian EH9 1SH
☎ 0131 668 8600
Web *www.historic-scotland. gov.uk*

Historic Scotland is responsible for the maintenance of historic houses and gardens in the care of the Secretary of State for Scotland. Carol Kernan is working on an extension to the *Inventory of Gardens & Designed Landscapes in Scotland*.

Horticultural Development Council
Bradbourne House, Stable Block, East Malling ME19 6DZ
☎ 01732 848383
Fax 01732 848498

HDC commissions research on behalf of the horticultural industry. It is funded by an annual levy on growers. There are many projects currently under way relating to bulbs, field vegetables, hardy nursery stock, glasshouse crops and fruit.

HORTICULTURAL RESEARCH INTERNATIONAL
Wellesbourne, Warwickshire CV35 9EF
☎ 01789 470382
Fax 01789 470552
Web *www.hri.ac.uk*

The main English organisation for scientific research and development in all aspects of horticulture, with several stations around the country. Legally, it is a non-departmental government body, sponsored by MAFF, as well as a charity and a registered company.

HORTICULTURAL THERAPY
The Geoffrey Udall Building, Trunkwell Park, Beech Hill, Reading, Berkshire RG7 2AT
☎ 0118 988 5688
Web *http://ourworld.compuserve.com/homepages/hort_therapy*

This charity is dedicated to helping people with special needs gain independence, new skills and quality of life through gardening. Its has set standards through its pioneering work in the community, helping projects and groups, and assisting individuals with information and educational opportunities.

HORTICULTURAL TRADES ASSOCIATION (HTA)
Horticulture House, 19 High Street, Theale, Reading, Berkshire RG7 5AH
☎ 0118 930 3132
Fax 0118 932 3453
Web *www.martex.co.uk/hta*

The trade association for amenity and leisure horticulture, with around 1,700 members. They publish a magazine, *Nurseryman and Garden Centre*, and a useful reference *Year Book*: both are also available to non-members. Business advice and negotiated discounts are provided to members. They promote horticulture generally, including the HTA National Garden Gift Tokens. Good website.

INSTITUTE OF GRASSLAND AND ENVIRONMENTAL RESEARCH (IGER)
Aberystwyth, Dyfed SY23 3EB
☎ 01970 823000
Fax 01970 828357
Web *www.iger.bbsrc.ac.uk/igerweb*

IGER incorporates the Welsh Plant Breeding Station, founded in 1919, and best known for breeding new grasses and disease-resistant cereals.

INSTITUTE OF GROUNDSMANSHIP
19–23 Church Street, The Agora, Wolverton, Milton Keynes, Buckinghamshire MK12 5LG
☎ 01908 312511
Fax 01908 311140
Web *www.iog.org*

Founded in 1934 to improve the status of groundsmen and the standards of groundsmanship, the Institute is a respected professional organisation which publishes its own journal *The Groundsman* and supervises the training and education of groundsmen. In 1998 it absorbed the Association of Landscape Managers.

INSTITUTE OF HORTICULTURE (IoH)
14–15 Belgrave Square, London SW1X 8PS
☎ 0171 245 6943
Web *www.horticulture.demon.co.uk*

The professional body for horticulturists of all descriptions. The strict membership requirements demand a combination of education and experience, so membership confers recognised professional status. Student membership is also available. The IoH acts as a forum for the collection and dissemination of horticultural information to its members and the public. It also promotes and represents the horticultural industry. Its website is one of the best we know, and brilliant for those contemplating horticulture as a career.

INSTITUTE OF LEISURE AND AMENITY MANAGEMENT (ILAM)
Lower Basildon, Reading, Berkshire RG8 9NE
☎ 01491 874800
Fax 01491 874801
Web *www.Ilam.co.uk*

The professional body for leisure professionals. ILAM represents every aspect of leisure, cultural and recreational management and seeks to improvement management standards throughout the industry.

INTERNATIONAL ASSOCIATION OF HORTICULTURAL PRODUCERS
Postbus 93099, NL-2509 AB 's-Gravenhage, The Netherlands
☎ 00 31 70 381 4631
Fax 00 31 70 347 7176

An international association for horticultural producers, including cut flowers, nursery stock and bulbs.

INTERNATIONAL GARDEN CENTRE ASSOCIATION
Pompmolenlaan 18, NL-3447 GK Woerden, The Netherlands
☎ 00 31 348 430676
Fax 00 31 348 431038

This association has more than 2,000 members in about 30 countries.

INTERNATIONAL INSTITUTE OF BIOLOGICAL CONTROL
Silwood Park, Buckhurst Road, Ascot, Berkshire SL5 7TA
☎ 01344 872999
Fax 01344 875007
Web *www.cabi.org*

A research centre which publishes advice and information on biological control of insect pests and weeds.

INTERNATIONAL INSTITUTE OF ENTOMOLOGY
56 Queen's Gate, London SW7 5JR
☎ 0171 584 0067

INTERNATIONAL INSTITUTE OF PARASITOLOGY
395A Hatfield Road, St Albans, Hertfordshire AL4 0XU
☎ 01727 833151

INTERNATIONAL PLANT PROPAGATORS SOCIETY
Wegg's Farm, Common Road, Dickleburgh, Diss, Norfolk IP21 4PJ
☎ & Fax 01379 741999
Web www.accessone.com/~ipps

The Great Britain and Ireland region of an international society. The IPPS is aimed at practical and academic horticulturists. Its motto 'Seek and Share' reflects its aim of bringing together and distributing information about propagation and production techniques.

INTERNATIONAL TREE FOUNDATION
Sandy Lane, Crawley Down, Crawley, W Sussex RH10 4HS
☎ 01342 712536
Fax 01342 718282

Formerly Men of the Trees, this is an international tree planting and conservation organisation. Membership costs £12.50 (1999).

JOHN INNES MANUFACTURERS ASSOCIATION
Links View House, 8 Fulwith Avenue, Harrogate, North Yorkshire HG2 8HR
☎ 01423 879208
Fax 01423 870025

The trade organisation for manufacturers of John Innes seed and potting composts. Members have to meet the quality standards: they can then display the seal of approval. JIMA actively promotes the use of loam-based composts by amateur gardeners. The John Innes Centre, the oldest UK centre for studying plant breeding, is a separate organisation: its address is Norwich Research Park, Colney, Norwich NR4 7UH.
Tel: 01603 452571.

LANDSCAPE FOUNDATION
14 Doughty Street, London WC1
☎ 0171 490 4877
Fax 0171 608 3409

The Landscape Foundation was formed to encourage and promote sensitive design and best practice in relation to all matters affecting the landscape. 'Best practice' means combining the best of design with the best planning and business practices.

LANDSCAPE INSTITUTE
6-7 Barnard Mews, London SW11 1QU
☎ 0171 738 9166

The professional body for landscape architects, landscape managers and landscape scientists. The LI sets and maintains standards and accredits educational courses. It represents the profession's interests and disseminates information to its members. Members hold the qualification ALI: a directory of firms where at least one of the principals is a registered member is available from RIBA Publications (0171 251 0791). The Landscape Institute can advise potential clients free of charge about suitable firms for large or specialised projects.

LANTRA
NAC, Kenilworth, Warwickshire CV8 2LGY
☎ 0345 078007

Founded in 1998 as the National Training Organisation for the horticultural industry.

LEARNING THROUGH LANDSCAPES
3rd Floor, Southside Offices, The Law Courts, Winchester, Hampshire SO23 9DL
☎ 01962 846258
Fax 01962 869099
Web www.ltl.org.uk

This charity exists to encourage schools to make improvements to the use and quality of school grounds for the benefit of children. Its main method is to teach children about plants and gardens.

LEISURE AND OUTDOOR FURNITURE ASSOCIATION LTD (LOFA)
PO Box 233, Redhill, Surrey RH1 4YU
☎ 01737 644016
Fax 01737 644988

LOFA is a trade association to represent and promote companies in the garden furniture and barbecue market.

LINNEAN SOCIETY OF LONDON
Burlington House, Piccadilly, London W1V 0LQ
☎ 0171 434 4479
Fax 0171 287 9364
Web www.linnean.org.uk

The Linnean Society was founded in 1788, which makes it the world's oldest active biological society. It is named after Carl Linnaeus (1707–1778), the founder of the modern system of binomial classification, and owns Linnaeus's collection of plants, animals, papers and books. The aim of the Society is 'the cultivation of the Science of Natural History in all its branches'.

MERLIN TRUST
The Dower House, Boughton House, Kettering, Northamptonshire NN14 1BJ
☎ 01536 482279
Fax 01536 482294

The leading UK charity dedicated to helping young horticulturists to extend their knowledge. Applicants must be aged between 18 and 30 and show how their project would help their present work. All ideas are considered: travel, work experience, photography, seed collection, conservation work, travel to study plants. The trustees say that personal enthusiasm counts for more than qualifications.

METROPOLITAN PUBLIC GARDENS ASSOCIATION
3 Mayfield Road, Croydon, Surrey CR4 6DN
☎ 0181 689 4197

MINISTRY OF AGRICULTURE, FISHERIES AND FOOD
3 Whitehall Place, London SW1A 2HH
☎ 0171 270 8080
Fax 0171 270 8443
Web *www.maff.gov.uk/maffhome.htm*

General enquiries on the above number. See your local telephone directory (under 'Agriculture') for the addresses of MAFF's regional centres. There is an Information Division Helpline on 0645 335577.

MUSEUM OF GARDEN HISTORY
Lambeth Palace Road, London SE1 7LB
☎ 0171 261 1891
Web *www.compulink.co.uk/~museumgh/*

The only museum of its kind, housed in the (now disused) church where the two John Tradescants, father and son, were buried.

NATIONAL ASSOCIATION OF DECORATIVE & FINE ART SOCIETIES (NADFAS)
8 Guilford Street, London WC1N 1DT
☎ 0171 430 0730

An arts educational charity with 300 branches and over 70,000 members. The branches organise programmes of lectures, outings and study days: some are of interest to garden-owners and garden historians.

NATIONAL FARMERS UNION
Agriculture House, 164 Shaftesbury Avenue WC2H 8HL
☎ 0171 331 7200
Fax 0171 331 7313
Web *www.nfu.org.uk*

The farmers' trade association has a horticulture section which represents growers. Associated organisations include BGLA Ltd (organisers of two trade exhibitions), British Bedding and Pot Plant Association (q.v.), British Herb Trade Association (q.v.), and Farm Shop and PYO Association. Specialist advisers can help members with law, taxation, employment and plant health.

NATIONAL GARDENS SCHEME
Hatchlands Park, East Clandon, Guildford, Surrey GU4 7RT
☎ 01483 211535
Web *www.ngs.org.uk*

The National Gardens Scheme was founded in 1927. 90% of its income comes from the 3,500 or so gardens which are open to the public and from sales of the Yellow Book. In 1997 it donated nearly £1.5m to gardening and nursing charities.

NATIONAL INSTITUTE FOR AGRICULTURAL BOTANY
Huntingdon Road, Cambridge CB3 0LE
☎ 01223 276381
Fax 01223 277602

NIAB carries out testing of seeds and other laboratory and environmental research on behalf of the government and commercial customers. The Wisley Handbook, *Vegetable Varieties for the Gardener*, by J Chowings and M J Day, passes on the results of NIAB tests.

NATIONAL INSTITUTE OF MEDICAL HERBALISTS
56 Longbrook Street, Exeter, Devon EX4 6AH
☎ 01392 426022
Fax 01392 498963

A professional group of about 380 practitioners of herbal medicine (phytotherapy). Entry is by examination following a four-year training course.

NATIONAL PLAYING FIELDS ASSOCIATION
25 Ovington Square, London SW3 1LQ
☎ 0171 584 6445
Fax 0171 581 2402
Web *www.npfa.co.uk*

Founded in 1925, the association is the only privately financed organisation which is concerned with the protection and maintenance of playing fields.

NATIONAL TRUST
36 Queen Anne's Gate, London SW1H 9AS
☎ 0171 222 9251
Web *www.nationaltrust.org.uk*

Conservation body with many outstanding gardens and landscapes under its care. Membership gives admission to all the Trust's properties and is strongly recommended to anyone who is interested in gardens. Numerous events are organised throughout the year. Excellent website, full of information about the Trust, including all its gardens.

NATIONAL TRUST FOR SCOTLAND
5 Charlotte Square, Edinburgh EH2 4DU
☎ 0131 226 5922
Fax 0131 243 9501
Web *www.nts.org.uk*

This Scottish conservation body has a number of excellent gardens in its care; members also receive free entry to National Trust properties under a reciprocal arrangement. Self-catering and working holidays are available. Good website, which also carries the SGS homepage.

NATURAL HISTORY MUSEUM
Cromwell Road, London SW7 5VD
☎ 0171 938 9123
Web *www.nhm.ac.uk*

Gardeners will be interested in the Insect Information Service which is offered by the Entomological Department on 0171 938 9462. Chirpy website.

NORTHERN IRELAND HORTICULTURE AND PLANT BREEDING STATION
Department of Agriculture, Manor House, Loughgall, Co. Armagh BT61 8JB

ORGANISATIONS   339

☎ 01762 892300
Fax 01762 892320

Famous for the breeding of new amenity grasses with tolerance to herbicides, but most of the research work at Loughgall is directed at supporting local growers like top fruit nurserymen and hardy ornamental stock producers.

NORTHERN IRELAND TOURIST BOARD
St Anne's Court, 59 North Street, Belfast BT1 1NB
☎ 01232 231221
Fax 01232 240960

This very helpful organisation publishes *The Gardens of Northern Ireland*, available from its tourist information offices.

PEAT PRODUCERS ASSOCIATION
PO Box 15s Street, Stowmarket, Suffolk IP14 3RD
☎ 07071 7802730
Fax 01449 614614

A trade association which sets out the 'other' side of the argument. It points out that there are 400 million hectares of peatland worldwide and 1.6 million hectares in the UK, of which no more than 6,000 hectares is used by the UK industry.

PESTICIDES TRUST
Eurolink Business Centre, 49 Effra Road, London SW2 1BZ
☎ 0171 274 8895
Fax 0171 274 9084
Web *www.gn.apc.org/pesticidestrust*

This environmental pressure group advises on the health effects of pesticides. Among its aims is a reduction in their use. Its activities include research, policy analysis, advisory consultancy and publishing.

PLANT BREEDING INTERNATIONAL
Maris Lane, Trumpington, Cambridge CB2 2LQ
☎ 01223 840411
Fax 01223 845514
Web *www.pbi-camb.co.uk*

Britain's major plant breeder, bought up by Monsanto last year. It is principally concerned with agricultural crops (2,000 crosses of winter wheat are made every year) but also with such horticultural crops as potatoes, peas, apples and soft fruit.

PLANT VARIETY RIGHTS OFFICE AND SEEDS DIVISION
White House Lane, Huntingdon Road, Cambridge CB3 0LF
☎ 01223 277151
Fax 01223 342386

The main function of this division of MAFF is to receive, consider and reach decisions on applications for the grant of rights in new varieties of plants – in short, to implement the Plant Varieties and Seeds Act, 1964. It also acts as a postbox for the European Union Community Plant Variety Office. The office issues a very useful *Guide to Plant Breeders' Rights*.

PLANTLIFE
The Natural History Museum, Cromwell Road, London SW7 5BD
☎ 0171 938 9111
Fax 0171 938 9112

The only conservation charity in Britain solely devoted to saving wild plants. It has over 10,000 members and the individual subscription is £19. Projects include rescuing individual species, protecting peat bogs, and the Great Hedge Project.

RAMBLERS ASSOCIATION
1–5 Wandsworth Road, London SW8 2XX
☎ 0171 339 8500
Fax 0171 339 8501
Web *www.ramblers.org.uk*

The Ramblers' Association was founded in 1935 and now has members in over 400 groups.

ROYAL ENTOMOLOGICAL SOCIETY
41 Queens Gate, London SW7 5HU
☎ 0171 584 8361

A learned society, whose fellows are for the main part academics. They provide expert witnesses and publish scientific reports but are not the people to ask for advice on insects in your garden: members of the RHS should write to Wisley instead.

ROYAL FORESTRY SOCIETY OF ENGLAND, WALES & NORTHERN IRELAND
102 High Street, Tring, Hertfordshire HP23 4AF
☎ 01442 822028
Fax 01442 893095
Web *www/rfs.org.uk/*

An active society which seeks to encourage the conservation, improvement and expansion of Britain's woodlands by positive management. It has over 4,500 members in 21 divisions, each with its own programme of events. The *Quarterly Journal of Forestry* is the industry leader.

ROYAL GARDENERS' ORPHAN FUND
48 St Alban's Road, Codicote, Hertfordshire ST4 8UT
☎ 01438 8207783

Founded in 1887 to help the orphans of gardeners 'by giving them regular allowances and grants for special purposes'. The fund also offers assistance to needy children whose parents are employed full-time in horticulture. It has an annual budget of c.£50,000.

ROYAL INSTITUTE OF BRITISH ARCHITECTS (RIBA)
66 Portland Place, London W1N 4AD
☎ 0171 580 5533
Fax 0171 255 1541

ROYAL METEOROLOGICAL SOCIETY
104 Oxford Road, Reading, Berkshire RG1 7LJ
☎ 0118 956 8500
Fax 0118 956 8571
Web *http://itu.rdg.ac.uk/rms/rms.html*

Essential membership for scientists, professional weathermen and enthusiastic amateurs who want to know more about the British gardener's greatest obsession. The website is excellent.

ROYAL SCOTTISH FORESTRY SOCIETY
62 Queen Street, Edinburgh, Lothian EH2 4NA
☎ & Fax 0131 225 8142

ROYAL SOCIETY FOR THE PROTECTION OF BIRDS
The Lodge, Sandy, Bedfordshire SG19 2DL
☎ 01767 680551
Fax 01767 692365
Web *www.rspb.org.uk*

This charity takes action for wild birds and the environment. The RSPB is the largest wildlife conservation charity in Europe and enrolled its one- millionth member in September 1997.

RURAL DEVELOPMENT COMMISSION
141 Castle Street, Salisbury, Wiltshire SP1 3TP
☎ 01722 336255
Fax 01722 824410
Web *www.argonet.co.uk/rdc*

A government agency concerned with the economic and social well-being of England's rural communities. It does *not* concern itself with agriculture or horticulture but does offer discretionary grants for redundant buildings in rural areas. It will merge early this year with the Countryside Commission.

SCOTLAND'S GARDEN SCHEME
31 Castle Terrace, Edinburgh EH1 2EL
☎ 0131 229 1870
Fax 0131 229 0443

Over 300 gardens open for the SGS, which is closely modelled on the English National Gardens Scheme. Owners are encouraged to open their gardens to the public and the proceeds are then distributed among various charities. The SGS is proud to be able to show a higher return per gardens than the NGS. The Scottish Tourist Board carries further information on its website (*www.travelscotland.co.uk*).

SCOTTISH CROP RESEARCH INSTITUTE
Invergowrie, Dundee, Tayside DD2 5DA
☎ 01382 562731
Fax 01382 562426
Web *www.scri.sari.ac.uk*

This agency receives about 65% of its income from the Scottish Office. It employs about 400 staff and undertakes research on horticultural crops, their pests and diseases, and on processes common to all plants which improve the quality of life and the environment.

SCOTTISH NATURAL HERITAGE
12 Hope Terrace, Edinburgh EH9 2AS
☎ 0131 447 4784
Web *www.snh.org.uk*

SNH's mission is 'to work with Scotland's people to care for our natural heritage'. This includes safeguarding Scotland's natural, genetic and scenic diversity, and encouraging considerable environmental sustainability.

SCOTTISH TOURIST BOARD
23 Ravelston Terrace, Edinburgh EH4 3EU
☎ 0131 332 2433
Fax 0131 315 2906
Web *www.holiday.scotland.net/*

The source of all useful information about travel in Scotland.

SOCIETY OF BOTANICAL ARTISTS
1 Knapp Cottages, Wyke, Gillingham, Dorset SP8 4NQ
☎ 01747 825718

Founded in 1985 to 'honour and strive to continue in the great tradition of talent, beauty and infinite care apparent in the art of botanical painting through the ages'. The society has an expanding membership, holds regular open exhibitions and can act as a channel for commissions.

SOCIETY OF FLORISTRY
59 Tree Tops, Portskewett, Gwent NP6 4RT
☎ 01291 424039

The society, which was started in 1951, works to maintain standards in professional floristry. Part of this work includes professional awards at intermediate level and above. The National Diploma of the Society of Floristry is the highest floristry qualification. Members are drawn from all sectors of the industry. The society stages displays and demonstrations, including some of the RHS's shows.

SOCIETY OF GARDEN DESIGNERS
14–15 Belgrave Square, London SW1X 8PS
☎ 0171 838 9311

The leading professional body for full-time garden designers. Only about 80 of its 1,000 members are recognised as Full Members or Fellows. Membership depends upon a combination of training and experience, and work is inspected. The Society distributes information about its members to enquirers free of charge: contact the Secretary. Full members use the initials FSGD and MSGD.

SOIL ASSOCIATION
86–88 Colston Street, Bristol, Gloucestershire BS1 5BB
☎ 0117 929 0661

Founded in 1949, the association exists to promote and develop alternatives to intensive agriculture. It calls its headquarters the Organic Food & Farming Centre. The British Organic Farmers and Organic Growers Association are also based here.

SPORTS TURF RESEARCH INSTITUTE
Bingley, W Yorkshire BD16 1AU
☎ 01274 565131
Fax 01274 561891
Web *www.stri.org.uk*

ORGANISATIONS 341

Founded in 1929 to carry out research into grasses and turf management. The institute advises the National Trust and private owners, at home and overseas, as well as sports associations and golf course managers.

STANLEY SMITH HORTICULTURAL TRUST
Cory Lodge, PO Box 365, Cambridge CB2 1HR

This trust makes grants every year totalling some £50,000 and welcomes applications from individuals, organisations and institutions. The trustees try to maintain a balance across the whole spectrum of amenity horticulture and between small (up to £1,500) and larger grants. Recent projects supported include plant-collecting, books on horticultural subjects, garden restoration and the breeding of new hybrids. Grants are awarded twice a year, in April and October.

SWIMMING POOL & ALLIED TRADES ASSOCIATION LTD (SPATA)
1a Junction Road, Andover, Hampshire SP10 3QT
☎ 01264 356210

The national organisation for trading and consumer standards in the swimming pool industry. Members must observe the Association's standards. Publications include *The Swimming Pool Guide*, *The Pool Owner's Handbook* and a list of members for owners and would-be owners to approach for advice.

TREE COUNCIL
51 Catherine Place, London SW1E 6DY
☎ 0171 828 9928
Fax 0171 828 9060

The RHS is a member of the Tree Council, which promotes the planting and conservation of trees and woods throughout the UK. Send an A4 SAE for a free copy of their excellent magazine *Tree News*.

TREE REGISTER OF THE BRITISH ISLES
77a Hall End, Wootton, Bedfordshire MK43 9HP
☎ 01234 768884

The Register aims to aims to identify and record full details of exceptional trees. Its *Newsletter* is a fascinating read for anyone who enjoys the sheer variety and size of old trees.

VICTORIAN SOCIETY
1 Priory Gardens, London W4 1TT
☎ 0181 994 1019
Fax 0181 995 4895

Formed in 1958 to protect Victorian buildings, the society has now widened its remit to include Victorian and Edwardian gardens. There is an extremely active and varied programme of events.

WALES TOURIST BOARD
Brunel House, 2 Fitzalan Road, Cardiff CF2 1UY
☎ 01222 499909
Fax 01222 485031
Web *www.visitwales.com*

Information on places to visit and holidays in Wales.

WILDFOWL & WETLANDS TRUST
Slimbridge, Gloucester, Gloucestershire GL2 7BT
☎ 01453 890333
Fax 01453 890527
Web *www.greenchannel.com/wwt*

WWT's mission is to save wetlands for both wildlife and people.

WILDLIFE TRUSTS
The Green, Witham Park, Waterside South, Lincoln LN5 7JR
☎ 01522 544400
Fax 01522 511616
Web *www.wildlifetrust.org.uk*

The Wildlife Trusts is made up of the local wildlife trusts and some 50 urban groups with a total of 220,000 members. They manage some 2,000 nature reserves, campaign on conservation issues,

and encourage people to become involved in conservation.

WOMEN'S FARM & GARDEN ASSOCIATION
175 Gloucester Street, Cirencester, Gloucestershire GL7 2DP
☎ 01285 658339

A useful voluntary organisation for women whose livelihood is connected with the land. Among its activities is the Women's Returners to Amenity Gardening Scheme which arranges placements in private gardens for women wishing to return to work.

WOODLAND TRUST
Autumn Park, Dysart Road, Grantham, Lincolnshire NG31 6LL
☎ 01476 581111
Fax 01476 590808

This charity is concerned solely with the conservation of Britain's woodland heritage of broadleaved trees. It now owns and manages over 900 woods across Britain.

WORLD CONIFER DATA POOL
Little Reach, Venlake Edge, Uplyme, Lyme Regis, Dorset DT7 3SF

Acts as a collecting agency for data on new conifer introductions from around the world. They published *The World Checklist of Conifers* through Landsman's Bookshop.

WORSHIPFUL COMPANY OF GARDENERS
25 Luke Street, London EC2A 4AR
☎ 0171 739 8200
Fax 0171 739 8470

A City Guild, incorporated in 1605. It has always played an active part in horticultural affairs. Its charity fund makes grants to deserving projects, including horticultural therapy schemes and garden designs for special schools.

INDEX

Abbey Brook Cactus Nursery, 155
Abbey Dore Court Garden, 175
Abbots Ripton Hall, 142
Abbotsbury Subtropical Gardens, 160
Abbotsford, 231
Abbotswood, 170
Abriachan Garden Nursery, 237
ACE Study Tours, 260
Achamore Gardens, 238
Achiltibuie Hydroponicum, 237
Achnacloich, 242
Acorn Bank Garden, 151
ADAS, 329
Adlington Hall, 145
African Violet Centre, 194
African Violet Society of America Inc, 311
Airedale & Wharfdale College, 295
Albert Schenkel GMBH, 327
Allangrange, 237
All Year Round Chrysanthemum Growers Association, 329
Alpengarten Pforzheim, 277
Alpengarten Zenz, 270
Alpine Garden Society, 298
Alpine Staudengärtnerei Siegfried Geißler, 277
Alplains, 328
Altamont Garden, 252
Althorp House, 196
Alton Towers, 207
American Bamboo Society, 311
American Conifer Society, 312
American Daffodil Society Inc, 312
American Hemerocallis Society, 312
American Hepatica Association, 312
American Hibiscus Society, 312
American Hosta Society, 312
American Iris Society, 312
American Museum, 203
American Orchid Society, 313
American Penstemon Society, 313
American Rhododendron Society, 313
American Rose Society, 313
Ammerdown Park, 206
An Cala, 238
Andrew Norfield Seeds, 323
Anglesey Abbey, 140
Angus College, 296
Angus Garden, 239
Animal Aunts, 267
Anna Buxton Books, 320
Annes Grove Gardens, 252
Antico Pomario (Vivai Dalmonte), 284
Antony House, 146
Arbigland, 232
Arboretum Altdorf, 277
Arboretum National des Barres, 272
Arboretum Waasland, 271
Arboricultural Association, 329
Arbury Hall, 219
Arche Noah, 313
Archibald, Jim & Jenny, 326
Architectural Association, 329
Architectural Plants, 218
Ardanaiseig Hotel Garden, 239
Ardchattan Priory, 239
Ardfearn Nursery, 237
Ardgillan Park, 253
Ardkinglas Woodland Garden, 239
Ardnamona, 253
Ardtornish Garden, 239
Arduaine Garden, 239
Arley Hall & Gardens, 142
Arlington Court, 156
Arne Herbs, 206
Arnold Books, 320
Arrow Cottage, 175
Ascott House & Gardens, 138
Ashwood Nurseries Ltd, 222
Askham Bryan College, 294
Assens Planteskole, 271
Association of Australian Begonia Societies, 313
Association of Garden Trusts, 329
Association of National Park Officers, 329
Association of Professional Landscapers, 329
Association of Societies for Growing Australian Plants, 313
Association pour la Sauvegarde du Patrimoine Fruitier, 313
Athelhampton House & Gardens, 160
Attingham Hall, 201
Audley End, 164
Austin Roses, David, 202
Australasian Plant Society, 314
Avebury Manor, 222
Avon Bulbs, 206
Avon Gardens Trust, 307
Aylesbury College, 292
Aylett Nurseries Ltd, 179
Ayr Flower Show, 40

B & T World Seeds, 323
Bailey Ltd, Steven, 175
Ballymaloe Cookery School Garden, 252
Ballynacourty, 255
Ballyrogan Nurseries, 250
Bambous de Planbuisson, 272
Bambouseraie de Prafrance, 273
Bambuschulen Janssen, 278
Bank House, 186
Barnett Books, Carol, 321
Barnfield College, 291
Barnsdale Plants and Gardens, 187
Barnsley College, 294
Barnsley House, 166
Barrington Court, 203
Bassi Vivai, 283
Bateman's, 214
Bates Green Farm, 214
Bath Botanic Gardens, 203
Batsford Arboretum, 166
Baumschule Böhlje, 278
Baumschule Franz Praskac, 270

INDEX 343

Baumschule H. Hachmann, 278
Baumschule Röhler, 278
Baytree Nurseries & Garden Centre, 188
BBC Gardeners' World Live, 40
Beale Arboretum, 178
Beales, Peter, Roses, 194
Bede's World Herb Garden, 219
Bedgebury National Pinetum, 181
Beeches Hotel & Plantation Garden, 263
Bell's Cherrybank Gardens, 244
Belle Époque Rozenkwekerij, 287
Belmont Park, 181
Belsay Hall, 196
Belton House, 187
Belvoir Castle, 186
Beningbrough Hall, 225
Benington Lordship, 179
Bennetts Water Gardens, 163
Benthall Hall, 202
Berkeley Castle, 166
Berkshire College of Agriculture, 292
Berrington Hall, 175
Besleys Books, 320
Beth Chatto Gardens, 164
Bicton Park Gardens, 159
Bicton School of Horticulture, 292
Biddulph Grange Garden, 207
Bide-a-Wee Cottage, 196
Biggar Park, 242
Bio-Dynamic Agriculture Association, 329
Biotechnology & Biological Sciences Research Council, 329
Birmingham Botanical Gardens & Glasshouses, 221
Birr Castle Demesne, 256
Bishop Burton College, 294
Blackmore & Langdon, 206
Blackpool & The Fylde College, 293
Blackthorn Nursery, 174
Bland, Mary 322
Blattgrün, 278
Blenheim Palace, 199
Blickling Hall & Garden, 192
Blossoms, 140
Bluebell Nursery & Arboretum, 154
Bodenham Arboretum, 178
Bodnant Gardens, 245
Bodysgallen Hall, 247
Bolehyde Manor, 225
Bömer Boomkwekerij, M M, 288

Bonsai Centrum, 278
Bonsai Clubs International, 314
Bonsaï Rémy Samson, 272
Bookmark, Books of the World, 320
Boomkwekerij André van Nijnatten BV, 287
Boomkwekerij De Linde, 271
Borde Hill Garden, 216
Bosvigo, 146
Botanic Gardens Conservation International, 330
Botanic Nursery, 225
Botanical Society of South Africa, 314
Botanical Society of the British Isles, 298
Botanische Raritäten, 278
Botanischer Alpengarten F. Sündermann, 278
Boughton House, 194
Boureau, Bernard, 272
Bournville College of Further Education, 295
Bourton House, 166
Bowden, Ann & Roger, 159
Bowes Museum Garden & Park, 163
Bowood House, 222
Boxwood Tours: Quality Garden Holidays, 260
Brackenhurst College, 294
Brackley, S & N, 324
Bradshaw & Son, J, 185
Bramdean House, 171
Bramham Park, 229
Brandy Mount House, 174
Branklyn Garden, 242
Brantwood, 151
Brentford Adult Education, 293
Bressingham Gardens & Steam Museum, 192
Bressingham Plant Centre, 138
Brickwall House & Gardens, 216
Bridgemere Garden World, 143
Brighton College of Technology, 292
Brightwater Holidays, 260
Brinsbury College, 295
Britain in Bloom, 330
British & European Geranium Society, 298
British Agricultural & Garden Machinery Association, 330
British Agrochemicals Association, 330

British Association of Landscape Industries (BALI), 330
British Association of Leisure Parks, Piers & Attractions, 330
British Association of Seed Analysts, 330
British Association Representing Breeders (BARB), 330
British Bedding & Pot Plant Association, 330
British Bee-Keepers' Association, 330
British Cactus & Succulent Society, 298
British Christmas Tree Growers Association, 330
British Clematis Society, 299
British Commercial Glasshouse Manufacturers Association, 330
British Dragonfly Society, 331
British Ecological Society, 331
British Fuchsia Society, 299
British Gladiolus Society, 299
British Herb Trade Association, 331
British Herbal Medicine Association, 331
British Hosta & Hemerocallis Society, 299
British Independent Fruit Growers' Association, 331
British Iris Society, 299
British Ivy Society, 300
British Landscape Industry Training Organisation, 331
British Library, 331
British Mycological Society, 331
British National Carnation Society, 300
British Naturalists' Association, 331
British Orchid Council, 300
British Orchid Growers Association, 331
British Pelargonium & Geranium Society, 300
British Pest Control Association, 331
British Retail & Professional Florists Association, 331
British Rose Growers Association, 332
British Society of Plant Breeders, 332
British Tourist Authority, 332
British Trust for Conservation Volunteers (BTCV), 332
Broadlands, 171

INDEX

Broadleas, 222
Broadleigh Gardens, 206
Brodick Castle, 239
Brodie Castle, 235
Brodsworth Hall, 228
Brogdale, 181
Brook Cottage, 199
Brook Lodge Farm Cottage, 213
Brooks Books, 320
Brooksby College, 293
Broomfield College, 292
Broughton Castle, 199
Broughton House & Gardens, 233
Brown & Co Ltd, D T, 324
Bryan's Ground, 176
Bryn Bras Castle, 248
BSBI Publications; F & M Perring, 321
Buckingham Nurseries and Garden Centre, 140
Buckland Abbey, 156
Bude & Launceston Adult Education, 292
Bulb Distributors Association, 332
Bulbes d'Opale, 272
Burford Garden Centre, 201
Burford House Gardens, 176, 290
Burnby Hall Gardens, 226
Burncoose Nurseries & Gardens, 146
Burton Agnes Hall Gardens, 228
Burton Constable Hall, 226
Buscot Park, 199
Butterfields Nursery, 140
Butterfly Conservation, 332
Butterstream, 256

Cabbages & Kings, 214, 290
Cactus & Succulent Society of America, 314
Cactus Esterel, 273
CADW: Welsh Historic Monuments, 332
Cae Hir, 245
Caerhays Castle Gardens, 146
Cailloux Vivants, E.A.R.L. des, 273
Calderdale College, 295
Calke Abbey, 154
Cally Gardens, 234
Calvisi Manlio, 283
Cambo Gardens, 235
Cambridge Garden Courses, 290
Cambridge University Botanic Garden, 141

Camelie Borrini SNC, 283
Canal Gardens, 229
Cannington College, 294
Cannington College Heritage Garden, 203
Cannizaro House, 263
Cannizaro Park, 189
Canons Ashby House, 194
Capability's Books Inc, 321
Cape Seed & Book Suppliers, 321
Capel Manor, 189
Capel Manor College, 293
Capesthorne Hall, 143
Capitanio Stefano, 283
Carclew Gardens, 151
Carnivorous Plant Society, 300
Carters Tested Seeds Ltd, 323
Carwinion, 151
Castle Ashby Gardens, 195
Castle Bromwich Hall, 221
Castle Drogo, 156
Castle Howard, 226
Castle Kennedy Garden, 233
Castle Ward, 251
Castlewellan National Arboretum, 250
Catforth Gardens, 186
Catriona Boyle's Garden School, 290
Catros Gérand, 327
Cawdor Castle, 236
Cayeux SA, 273
Cefn Bere, 248
Cellarina di Maria Luisa Sotti, 283
Celyn Vale Nurseries, 245
Centre for Alternative Technology, 332
Chantrey Books, 321
Charlecote Park, 219
Chartwell, 182
Chatsworth, 154
Chatsworth Garden Centre, 155
Chelsea Flower Show, 40
Chelsea Physic Garden, 189
Cheltenham & Gloucester College of Higher Education, 292
Chenies Manor, 139
Chesham Adult C E Centre, 292
Chessington Adult Education, 295
Chiffchaffs, 160
Chillingham Castle, 196
Chiltern Seeds, 323
Chilworth Manor, 210
Chirk Castle, 245

Chiswick House, 189
Cholmondeley Castle Gardens, 143
Chyverton, 151
CITES, 332
Civic Trust, 332
Clandon Park, 210
Clare College Fellows' Garden, 141
Claremont Landscape Garden, 210
Clifton Nurseries, 191
Clinton Lodge, 216
Cliveden, 139
Cliveden House Hotel, 263
Clock House, 199
Clock House School of Garden Design, 290
Clumber Park, 197
Cluny House, 242
Clyne Gardens, 246
CN Seeds, 324
Coates Manor, 218
Cobblers, 216
Coen Janssen, 287
Colby Woodland Garden, 246
Coleton Fishacre Garden, 156
Coltivazione Riviera del Conero di Oste Lucio, 283
Colzium Walled Garden, 240
Commercial Horticultural Association, 332
Common Ground, 332
Compton Acres Gardens, 160
Congham Hall Hotel, 263
Conock Manor, 225
Conservation Foundation, 333
Cooke's House, 218
Coolcarrigan Gardens, 255
Cornwall Gardens' Society, 307
Cornwall Gardens Trust, 307
Corsham Court, 222
Cotehele, 147
Cothay Manor, 203
Coton Manor, 195
Cottage Garden Society, 300
Cottesbrooke Hall, 195
Coughton Court, 219
Council for Environmental Education, 333
Council for National Parks, 333
Council for the Protection of Rural England, 333
Country Cousins, 267
Country Houses Association, 333

INDEX   345

Country Landowners Association, 333
Countryside Commission, 333
Countryside Council for Wales, 333
County Park Nursery, 165
Courses at Englefield, 290
Courts, The, 222
Cousens, W C, 323
Cowdray Park, 218
Cowley Manor, 170
Cox & Kings Travel, 260
Cragside, 196
Craigieburn Garden, 234
Cranborne Manor, 161
Crarae Gardens, 240
Crathes Castle, 235
Creagh Gardens, 252
Croftway Nursery, 218
Crossing House Garden, 141
Crowe Hall, 206
Crowther Nurseries and Landscapes, 165
Croxteth Hall & Country Park, 191
Crûg Farm Plants, 248
Cruickshank Botanic Garden, 235
Culzean Castle & Country Park, 240
Curraghmore, 256
Cut Flower Growers' Group, 333
Cyclamen Society, 301

Daffodil Society, 301
Dalemain, 152
Dalmeny House, 237
Dam Farm House, 156
Darley House, 156
Dartington Hall, 156
Dawyck Botanic Garden, 231
De Gentiaan, 287
De Grienê Hân, 287
Deacon's Nursery, 181
Dean's Court, 163
Delbard, 273
Delphinium Society, 301
Denmans, 216
Department of Agriculture for Northern Ireland, 333
Derbyshire Historic Gardens, 307
Derreen, 254
Deutsche Dahlien- Fuchsien- und Gladiolen-Gesellschaft E V, 314
Deutsche Kakteen-Gesellschaft E V, 314

Deutsche Orchideen-Gesellschaft, 314
Deutsche Rhododendron Gesellschaft, 314
Devon Gardens Trust, 307
Dibleys, 245
Dillon Garden, 253
Dingle, The, 246
Dingle Nurseries & Garden, 249
Dinmore Manor, 176
Dino Pellizzaro, 273
Dobie, Samuel & Son Ltd, 324
Dochfour Gardens, 236
Docton Mill, 157
Docwra's Manor, 141
Doddington Hall, 188
Dolwen, 249
Doncaster College, 294
Dorfold Hall, 143
Dorothy Clive Garden, 207
Dorset Gardens Trust, 307
Dower House, The, 202
Downderry Nursery, 185
Drake, Jack, 237
Drum Castle, 235
Drummond Castle Gardens, 242
Dry Stone Walling Association of Great Britain, 333
Duchy College, 292
Duncombe Park, 226
Dunham Massey, 171
Dunrobin Castle Gardens, 236
Dunster Castle, 204
Dyffryn Botanic Garden, 246
Dyrham Park, 166
Ealing Tertiary College, 293
East Bergholt Place, 209
East Down Institute, 295
East Lambrook Manor Garden, 204
East Ruston Old Vicarage, 192
Eastgrove Cottage Garden & Nursery, 176
Eastnor Castle, 176
Easton Lodge, 165
Edmondsham House, 163
Edrom Nurseries, 232
Edzell Castle, 243
Eibenfreunde, 315
Elsing Hall, 192
Elton Hall, 141
Elvaston Castle County Park, 154
Emmetts Garden, 182
Emorsgate Seeds, 324

Englefield House, 137
English Gardening School, 290, 293
English Heritage, 333
English Nature, 333
Enterprise Travel, 261
Erddig, 245
Ernest Wilson Memorial Garden, 170
Escot, 157
Esveld, Fa. C., 287, 321
Éts. Hort. Hodnik, 273
Éts. Kuentz: Le Monde des Cactus, 273
European Boxwood & Topiary Society, 315
Europäische Bambusgesellschaft, 315
Euroseeds, 327
Euston Hall, 208
Exbury Gardens, 171
Exeter University Gardens, 159
Exotische Sämereien, 327

Fairfield House, 174
Fairfield Lodge, 253
Fairham Community College, 294
Fairhaven Gardens Trust, 192
Falkland Palace, 234
Family Trees, 174
Farnborough College of Technology, 293
Farnborough Hall, 220
Farrar Pty Ltd, M L, 326
Fauna & Flora International, 334
Federation to Promote Horticulture for the Disabled, 334
Felbrigg Hall, 192
Felley Priory, 198
Fenton House, 189
Fernhill, 253
Fertiliser Manufacturers Association, 334
Fibrex Nurseries Ltd, 221
Fine Art Travel Ltd, 261
Finlaystone, 240
Fisk's Clematis Nursery, 209
Five Arrows Hotel, 263
Fletcher Moss Botanical Gardens, 171
Fleuroselect, 334
Floors Castle, 231
Flora 2000, 284
Flora for Fauna, 334
Flora Mediterranea, 279
Florence Court, 251

Floricultura Hillebrand, 284
Flower Council of Holland, 334
Flowers & Plants Association, 334
Folly Farm, 138
Forde Abbey, 161
Forest Enterprise, 334
Forestry Authority, 334
Forestry Commission, 334
Forestry Trust, 334
Fota, 252
Foxgrove, 138
Foxhill Arboretum, 146
Frampton Court, 170
Fratelli Ingegnoli, 327
Friends of Brogdale, 301
Friends of the Earth, 335
Friends of the Royal Botanic Garden Edinburgh, 307
Friends of the Royal Botanic Gardens Kew, 307
Friesland Staudengarten (Uwe Knöpnadel), 279
Fructus, 315
Fruit Group of the Royal Horticultural Society, 301
Fuchsia's Michiels-De Smedt, 271
Fuchsia-Kwekerij Spek, 287
Fuchsien Kulturen Lakonig, 270
Furzey Gardens, 172

Galloway House Gardens, 233
Garden Books, 321
Garden Centre Association, 335
Garden History Society, 315
Garden House, The, 157
Garden Industry Manufacturers Association, 335
Garden Writers' Guild, 335
Gardeners' Delight Holidays, 261
Gardeners' Break, 290
Gardenex – Federation of Garden & Leisure Manufacturers, 335
Gardenia Society of America, 315
Gardens of the Rose, 179
Gartenbau F. Westphal, 279
Gartenbaubetrieb Engelhardt, 279
Gash Gardens, 255
Gaulden Manor, 204
Geologists Association, 335
Georg Arends, 279
Georgian Group, 335
Gesellschaft der Heidefreunde, 315

Gesellschaft für Fleischfressende Pflanzen, 316
Getting more serious, 291
Gidleigh Park Hotel, 159
Glansevern Gardens, 249
Glasgow Botanic Garden, 240
Glen Chantry, 165
Glenarn, 241
Glendoick Gardens, 244
Glendurgan Gardens, 147
Glenveagh Castle, 253
Glenwhan Garden, 233
Gliffaes Country House Hotel, 263
Glin Castle, 255
Gloucestershire Gardens & Landscape Trust, 307
Gnome Reserve & Wild Flower Garden, 159
Godington Park, 182
Goldbrook Plants, 209
Golden Acre Park, 230
Goldney Hall, 170
Good Gardeners Association, 335
Goodnestone Park, 182
Goscote Nurseries Ltd, 187
Gowranes, 244
Graines Baumaux, 327
Granada Arboretum, 143
Gravetye Manor, 263
Gravetye Manor Hotel, 218
Grayson, Peter – Sweet Pea Seedsman, 325
Graythwaite Hall, 152
Great Barfield, 140
Great Comp, 182
Great Dixter, 214
Great Garden and Countryside Festival, 40
Green Farm Plants, 213
Greenbank Garden, 241
Greencombe Gardens, 204
Greentours Natural History Holidays, 261
Greenways, 201
Greywalls, 263
Grimsby College, 293
Grimsthorpe Castle, 188
Groombridge Place Gardens, 182
Grosvenor Garden Centre, 146
Groves & Son, C W, 163
Grow '99, 40
Grübele Baumschulen, 279
Gunby Hall, 188

Guy Wilson Daffodil Garden, 250
Gärtnerei Hermann Ermel, 279

Haddon Hall, 154
Hadlow College, 293
Hadspen Garden, 204
Ham House, 190
Hampshire Gardens Trust, 307
Hampton Court Palace, 190
Hampton Court Palace Flower Show, 41
Hanbury Manor Hotel, 263
Hannays of Bath, 206
Hardwick Hall, 155
Hardwicke House, 142
Hardy Orchid Society, 302
Hardy Plant Society, 302
Hardy's Cottage Garden Plants, 174
Hare Hill Garden, 143
Harewood House, 230
Harlow Carr Botanical Gardens, 226, 290
Harrogate Great Autumn Flower Show, 41
Harrogate Spring Flower Show, 41
Hartpury College, 292
Hartside Nursery Garden, 153
Hartwell Manor, 264
Harvest Seeds Co, 326
Hatchlands, 211
Hatfield House, 179
Haughley Park, 210
Hawkstone Park Hotel, 264
Headland, 151
Heale House, 223
Health & Safety Executive (HSE), 335
Heather Society, 302
Hebe Society, 302
Helmingham Hall, 208
Hemerocallis Europa, 316
Henry Doubleday Research Association, 290
Henry Doubleday Research Association (HDRA), 302
Henly, John, 322
Herb Nursery, The, 187
Herb Society, 303
Herbaceous Books, 321
Hergest Croft Gardens, 176
Heritage Rose Foundation, 316
Herterton House Gardens & Nursery, 197

Hestercombe House, 204
Hever Castle, 183
Hexham Herbs, 197
Heywood Gardens, 255
Hidcote Manor Garden, 167
High Beeches, The, 216
Highclere Castle, 172
Highdown, 217
Highlands College, 291
Hiley, Brian & Heather, 213
Hill House, 180
Hill House Nursery & Garden, 157
Hill of Tarvit, 234
Hillbarn House, 225
Hiller Garden Centre, 221
Hillside, 253
Hinton Ampner House, 172
Hippopottering Nursery, 188
Historic Gardens Foundation, 335
Historic Houses Association (HHA), 335
Historic Scotland, 335
Hodges Barn, 167
Hodnet Hall Gardens, 202
Hodsock Priory, 198
Hoecroft Plants, 194
Hoghton Tower, 186
Holden Clough Nursery, 186
Holdenby House Gardens, 195
Hole Park, 185
Holehird Gardens, 152
Holiday Homewatch, 267
Holidays for Gardeners, 260
Holker Hall, 152
Holkham Hall, 193
Hollies Park, The, 230
Hollington Nurseries, 138
Holly Gate Cactus Garden, 219
Holme Pierrepont Hall, 198
Home & Pet Care, 267
Home Covert, 225
Homesitters Ltd, 267
Honingklip Book Sales, 321
Hope End Hotel, 264
Hopleys Plants Ltd, 180
Horn Park, 163
Horning Fuchsiari: V/H. Og B. Hojer, 272
Hörsch, Ingrid Sophie, 321
Horticultural Development Council, 335
Horticultural Research International, 336

Horticultural Therapy, 336
Horticultural Trades Association (HTA), 336
Hotels with good Gardens, 263
Houghall College Gardens, 163
Houghton Lodge Garden & Hydroponicum, 172
House of Dun, 243
House of Pitmuies, 243
Housewatch Ltd, 267
How Caple Court Gardens, 177
Howick Hall Gardens, 197
Huddersfield Technical College, 295
Hughenden Manor, 140
Hunts Court, 167
Hutton-in-the-Forest, 152

Ickworth, 209
Iden Croft Herbs, 185
Iford Manor, 223
Ightham Moat, 185
Il Giardino delle Higo, 284
Il Giardino delle Rose, 284
Ingwersen Ltd, W E Th, 219
Institute, The – Hampstead Garden Suburb, 293
Institute of Advanced Architectural Studies, 291
Institute of Grassland and Environmental Research (IGER), 336
Institute of Groundsmanship, 336
Institute of Horticulture (IoH), 336
Institute of Leisure and Amenity Management (ILAM), 336
International Association of Horticultural Producers, 336
International Bulb Society, 316
International Camellia Society, 316
International Carnivorous Plant Society, 316
International Clematis Society, 316
International Dendrology Society, 316
International Garden Centre Association, 336
International Institute of Biological Control, 336
International Institute of Entomology, 337
International Institute of Parasitology, 337
International Lilac Society, 317

International Oak Society, 317
International Oleander Society Inc, 317
International Plant Propagators Society, 337
International Tree Foundation, 337
International Violet Association, 317
International Water Lily Society, 317
Inveresk Lodge Garden, 237
Inverewe, 236
Iris en Provence, 273
Irish Garden Plant Society, 317
Isabella Plantation, 190
Isle of Wight College, 293
Isle of Wight Gardens Trust, 307
Ivelet Books Ltd, 322
Ivy Cottage, 161

Jac Verschuren-Pechtold BV, Fa., 287
Japanese Garden Society, 303
Japanese Gardens, 255
Jardin Aquatique, 273
Jelitto Staudensamen GMBH, 327
Jensen GMBH, Ingwer J., 280
John Chambers' Wild Flower Seeds, 324
John F Kennedy Arboretum, 257
John Innes Manufacturers Association, 337
John Kelly Centre, 293
John Kitto Community Centre, 292
Johnstown Castle Gardens, 257
Jorgensen, Arne Kr., 271
Jos Frijns en Zonen BV, 288
Journées des Plantes de Courson, 41

Kailzie Gardens, 231
Kakteen Haage, 280
Kakteengärtnerei Max Schleipfer, 280
Karl Foerster-Stauden GMBH, 280
Kawana, 271
Kaye Ltd, Reginald, 186
Kedleston Hall, 155
Keepers Nursery, 185
Kellie Castle, 234
Kelmscott Manor, 201
Kelways Ltd, 206
Ken Caro, 147
Kenchester Water Gardens, 178
Kenwith Nursery, 159
Kenwood, 191
Kew School of Horticulture, 295

Kew Shop, 322
Kiftsgate Court, 167
Kildalton Agricultural and
  Horticultural College, 295
Kildrummy Castle Gardens, 235
Kilfane Glen & Waterfall, 255
Killerton, 157
Kingcombe Centre, 291
Kings, 325
Kings Seeds, 328
Kingston Lacy, 161
Kingston Maurward College, 292
Kingston Maurward Gardens, 163
Kinross House, 243
Kirkley Hall College, 294
Klaus Oetjen, 280
Knap Hill Nursery Ltd, 213
Knebworth House, 179
Knightshayes Garden, 158
Knoll Gardens, 161
Knowsley Community College,
  Landbased Industries, 294
Kordes' Söhne, W, 282
Kwekerij Oudolf, 288
Kwekerij Th. Ploeger en Zn. BV, 288

Lackham College, 295
Lackham Country Attractions, 223
Ladham House, 183
Lainston House Hotel & Restaurant, 264
Lambeth College, 293
Lamorran House, 147
Land Farm Gardens, 230
Landscape Foundation, 337
Landscape Institute, 337
Landsman's Bookshop Ltd, 322
Langside College, 296
Langthorns Plantery, 165
Lanhydrock, 148
Lanterns, 151
Lantra, 337
Latour Marliac SA, 273
Lea Gardens, 155
Learning Through Landscapes, 337
Leeds Castle, 183
Leeming House Hotel, 264
Leighton Hall, 185
Leisure and Outdoor Furniture
  Association Ltd (LOFA), 337
Leith Hall, 236
Lens Roses, 271
Leonardslee Gardens, 217

Levens Hall, 153
Lily Group of the Royal
  Horticultural Society, 303
Lime Close, 201
Lincolnshire Gardens Trust, 307
Linnean Society of London, 337
Linnemann Strauchpäonien, W, 282
Lismore Castle, 256
Little Moreton Hall, 144
Little Thakenham Hotel, 264
Lloyds of Kew, 322
Lochalsh Woodland Garden, 237
Lodge Park Walled Garden, 255
Logan Botanic Gardens, 233
London Historic Parks & Gardens
  Trust, 308
Long Barn, 185
Long Close, 186
Long Cross Hotel, 264
Longleat House, 223
Longstock Water Gardens, 172
Longthatch, 173
Lost Gardens of Heligan, 147
Lotherton Hall, 230
Loughborough College, 293
Lower Hall, 202
Lower House Farm, 247
Lower Severalls Herb Nursery, 206
Loyalty Garden, The, 174
Lumen, 273
Lydney Park Gardens, 167
Lygon Arms, The, 265
Lyme Park, 144
Lynge Staudegartneri, 272
Lytes Cary Manor, 205

MacGregor, Elizabeth, 234
Mackey's Garden Centre, 326
Macpennys Nurseries, 163
Madrona Nursery, 185
Magnolia Society Inc, 317
Malleny House Garden, 238
Mallet Court Nursery, 206
Malvern Autumn Show, 41
Malvern Spring Gardening Show, 41
Manchester City College, 292
Manderston, 231
Mannington Gardens, 193
Manoir aux Quat' Saisons, 264
Manor House, Birlingham, 177
Manor House, Bledlow, 140
Manor House, Stanton Harcourt, 199

Manor House, Upton Grey, 174
Manor House, Walton-in-Gordano, 207
Mapperton Gardens, 162
Marcel Lecoufle, 273
Marcher Apple Network, 308
Margam Park, 247
Market Drayton Community
  Education, 294
Marshalls, 325
Marston Exotics, 178
Marwood Hill Gardens, 158
Mati Piante Az. Agr. di Cesare Mati, 284
Mattocks Roses, 201
Mediterranean Garden Society, 318
Megginch Castle, 244
Meilland Richardier, 275
Melbourne Hall, 155
Mellerstain, 232
Merlin Trust, 337
Merriments Gardens, 215
Merrist Wood College, 295
Merton Adult College, 293
Mertoun Gardens, 232
Metropolitan Public Gardens
  Association, 338
Meudon Hotel, 264
Michelham Priory, 215
Middlethorpe Hall, 264
Mill Garden, Warwick, 220
Mill Hill Plants, 198
Millais Nurseries, 213
Mills Farm Plants and Gardens, 210
Milton Lodge, 205
Mini-Arboretum di Guido Piacenza, 285
Ministry of Agriculture, Fisheries and
  Food, 338
Minterne, 162
Miserden Park, 168
Moerheim Plantenwinkel, 288
Monksilver Nursery, 142
Monocot Nursery, 325
Montacute House, 205
Monteviot House Gardens, 232
Montivivai dei F.lli Monti, 285
Moseley Old Hall, 207
Mottisfont Abbey, 173
Mottistone Manor, 180
Motts Leisure Ltd, 261
Moulton College, 294
Mount Edgcumbe Gardens, 148

INDEX 349

Mount Grace Priory, 226
Mount Stewart, 250
Mount Stuart, 241
Mount Usher Gardens, 257
Mr Fothergill's Seeds Ltd, 324
Muckross House & Gardens, 254
Muncaster Castle, 153
Munstead Wood, 214
Museum of Garden History, 191, 338
Myddelton House Gardens, 190
Myerscough College, 293

National Association of Decorative & Fine Art Societies (NAD, 338
National Association of Flower Arrangement Societies, 303
National Auricula and Primula Society (Midland & West Section), 303
National Auricula and Primula Society (Southern Section), 304
National Begonia Society, 304
National Botanic Gardens, Dublin, 253
National Chrysanthemum Society, 304
National Collection of Passiflora, 206
National Council for the Conservation of Plants and Gardens, 304
National Dahlia Society, 304
National Farmers Union, 338
National Garden Exhibition Centre, 258
National Gardens Scheme, 338
National Institute for Agricultural Botany, 338
National Institute of Medical Herbalists, 338
National Playing Fields Association, 338
National Pot Leek Society, 304
National Sweet Pea Society, 305
National Trust, 338
National Trust for Scotland, 338
National Vegetable Society, 305
Nationale Boomgaarden Stichting, 318
Natural History Museum, 338
Nature et Paysages, 275
Naturescape, 198
Naturetrek, 261

Naturwuchs, 280
Nederlands-Belgische Vereniging van Liefhebbers van Cactusse, 318
Nelson & Colne College, 293
Nescot, 295
Ness Botanic Gardens, 144
Newby Hall, 227
Newstead Abbey, 198
Newton Rigg College, 292
Nindethana Seed Service Pty Ltd, 327
Norfolk Lavender Ltd, 194
North American Rock Garden Society, 318
North Court, 181
North East Worcestershire College, 293
North Green Seeds, 325
North Nottinghamshire College, 294
North of England Rose, Carnation and Sweet Pea Society, 308
North Oxfordshire College & School of Art, 294
Northern Horticultural Society, 308
Northern Horticulutral Society, 294
Northern Ireland Daffodil Group, 308
Northern Ireland Horticulture and Plant Breeding Station, 338
Northern Ireland Tourist Board, 339
Northwest Native seed, 328
Norton Priory Museum & Gardens, 144
Norton Radstock College, 294
Notcutts Nurseries, 210
Nuneham Courtenay Arboretum, 200
Nunwell House, 180
Nymans Garden, 217

Oaklands College, 293
Oare House, 225
Oasi del Geranio di Giorgio Carlo, 284
Old Court Nurseries, 178
Old Manor, The, 170
Old Rectory Cottage, 138
Old Rectory, Burghfield, 138
Old Rectory, Farnborough, 201
Old Rectory, Sudborough, 196
Old Vicarage, The, 225
Olivers, 165
Open College of the Arts, 291

Orchid Society of Great Britain, 305
Orriell, D – Seed Exporters, 326
Osborne House Garden, 180
Oscar Tintori Vivai, 285
Osnabrücker Staudenkulturen P. und B. zur Linden, 280
Osterley Park, 190
Other Accommodation, 265
Oulton House, 208
Overbecks Museum & Garden, 158
Overbury Court, 178
Owlpen Manor, 168
Oxburgh Hall, 193
Oxford Botanic Garden, 200

P W Plants, 194
Packwood House, 220
Padlock Croft, 142
Page & Moy, 261
Paignton Zoo & Botanical Gardens, 158
Painshill Park, 211
Painswick Rococo Garden, 168
Pantiles Plant & Garden Centre, 214
Paradise Centre, 210
Paradise Park, 216
Parcevall Hall Gardens, 227
Parham, 217
Park, Mike, 322
Park Farm, 165
Park Green Nurseries, 210
Parnham House, 162
Pashley Manor Garden, 215
Pearl Sulman, 210
Peat Producers Association, 339
Peckover House, 142
Pen-y-Banc Nursery, 246
Pencarrow, 148
Pencoed College, 296
Penjerrick, 148
Penpergwm Lodge, 247
Penrhyn Castle, 247
Penshurst Place, 183
Pép. Botanique Jean Thoby, 275
Pép. Charentaises, 275
Pép. Christophe Delay, 275
Pép. Claude Thoby, 275
Pép. Côte Sud des Landes, 275
Pép. de l'Arboretum de Balaine, 275
Pép. de la Foux, 276
Pép. de la Vallée de l'Huveaune, 276
Pép. Eric Dumont, 276
Pép. Filippi, 276

Pép. Jean Rey, 276
Pép. Marie-Pierre Fournier, 276
Pép. Rhône-Alpes A. Gayraud, 276
Pépinières Travers, 276
Peover Hall, 146
Pershore College of Horticulture, 293
Pesticides Trust, 339
Petersfield Physic Garden, 175
Petworth House, 217
Picton Castle Trust, 246
Pilton Community College, 292
Pine Lodge Gardens, 149
Pinewood House, 214
Pitmedden, 236
Pivoines Michel Rivière, 277
Plant Breeding International, 339
Plant Variety Rights Office and Seeds Division, 339
Plantasia, 247
Plantlife, 339
Plas Brondanw Gardens, 247
Plas Newydd, 248
Plas Penhelig Country House Hotel, 248
Plas-yn-Rhiw, 248
Pleasant View Nursery & Garden, 159
Plumpton College, 292
Polesden Lacey, 211
Pommiers du Pays d'Auge, 277
Pomona, 318
Portmeirion, 249
Potterton and Martin, 188
Pound Hill House, 224
Powderham Castle, 160
Powerscourt Gardens, 257
Powis Castle, 249
Preen Manor, 202
Primrose Hill, 254
Prior Park, 205
Priorswood Clematis, 180
Priorwood Garden, 232
Priory, The, 168
Probus Gardens, 151, 292

Queen's Wood Arboretum & Country Park, 177

Ram House Garden, 257
Ramblers Association, 339
Ramster, 211
Reads Nursery, 194

Reaseheath College, 145, 292
Red House Museum & Gardens, 163
Renishaw Hall, 155
Rhinefield House Hotel, 264
Rhodes & Rockliffe, 165
Rhododendron, Camellia & Magnolia Group of the RHS, 305
Rhododendron-Haven Planteskole, 272
RHS Enterprises Ltd, 323
RHS Flower Show at Tatton Park, 41
RHS Garden Hyde Hall, 164
RHS Garden Rosemoor, 158
RHS Garden Wisley, 211
Ribanjou, E.A.R.L., 273
Riber Hall Hotel, 264
Rickards Hardy Ferns Ltd, 178
Ridge Danyers Centre, 292
Ripley Castle, 227
Riseholme Hall, 188
Riverhill House Gardens, 185
Robinson & Sons Ltd, W, 325
Roche Court, 225
Rock Garden Club Prague, 318
Rockingham Castle, 195
Rodbaston College, 294
Rode Hall, 145
Rodmarton Manor, 168
Roger Ltd, R V, 228
Röllke Orchideenzucht, 281
Romantic Garden Nursery, 194
Rose & Rose Meporium, 285
Rose Barni, 285
Rose Society of Northern Ireland, 308
Rosen von Schultheis, 281
Rosenplanteskolen I Love, 272
Rosenschule Martin Weingart, 281
Roseraies Pierre Guillot, 277
Roses Anciennes de André Eve, 273
Roses Anciennes du Lot, 277
Rougham Hall Nurseries, 210
Rousham House, 200
Rowallane Garden, 250
Royal Botanic Garden, Edinburgh, 238
Royal Botanic Gardens, Kew, 190, 291
Royal Caledonian Horticultural Society, 310
Royal Entomological Society, 339

Royal Forestry Society of England, Wales & Northern Ireland, 339
Royal Gardeners' Orphan Fund, 339
Royal Horticultural Society, 291, 305
Royal Horticultural Society of Ireland, 310
Royal Institute of British Architects (RIBA), 339
Royal Meteorological Society, 339
Royal National Rose Society, 306
Royal Scottish Forestry Society, 340
Royal Society for the Protection of Birds, 340
Rudolf u. Klara Baum (Fuchsienkulturen), 281
Rufford Old Hall, 186
Rural Development Commission, 340
Rushfields of Ledbury, 178
Rust-en-Vrede Nursery, 328
Ruthall Manor, 202
Rydal Mount, 153
Ryton Organic Gardens, 220

Saga Holidays Ltd, 261
St Andrews Botanic Garden, 234
St Ann's Books, 323
St Anne's Park, 254
St Goban's College, 295
St Helen's College, 294
St Loye's College, 292
St Luke's Centre, 294
St Michael's Mount, 149
St Paul's Walden Bury, 180
Saintpaulia & Houseplant Society, 307
Saling Hall, 165
Saltram, 159
Samen & Töpfe, 327
Sandringham House, 193
Santonine, 277
Sarastro, 270
Savill Garden, The, 212
Saxifrage Society, 307
Sayers Travel, David, 260
Schimana Staudenkulturen und Wassergärten, 281
Schryve Jardin, 277
Schöppinger Irisgarten (Werner Reinermann), 281
Scoil Stofáin Naofa, 295
Scone Palace, 243

INDEX 351

Scotland's National Gardening Show, 42
Scotland's Garden Scheme, 340
Scotney Castle Garden, 183
Scottish Crop Research Institute, 340
Scottish Natural Heritage, 340
Scottish Rhododendron Society, 310
Scottish Rock Garden Club, 310
Scottish Tourist Board, 340
Scotts Nurseries Ltd, 207
Seaforde Gardens, 251
Seed House, The, 325
Seeds-by-Size, 325
Sezincote, 169
Sharcott Manor, 224
Sheffield Botanical Gardens, 229
Sheffield College, 294
Sheffield Park Garden, 215
Sherborne Garden, 205
Sherbourne Park, 221
Sheringham Park, 193
Sherston Parva Nursery Ltd, 225
Shipley College, 295
Shrewsbury Flower Show, 42
Shrewsbury Quest, The, 202
Shropshire Parks & Gardens Trust, 310
Shrubland Hall, 209
Shugborough Hall, 208
Silver Dale Nurseries, 160
Silverhill Seeds, 328
Simpson's Seeds, 325
Sino-Himalayan Plant Association, 318
Sir Harold Hillier Gardens & Arboretum, 173
Sissinghurst Castle Garden, 184
Sizergh Castle, 153
Skippet, The, 201
Sklemersdale College, 293
Sledmere House, 227
Sleightholmedale Lodge, 228
Smith, Alan C, 185
Snowshill Manor, 169
Society of Botanical Artists, 340
Society of Floristry, 340
Society of Garden Designers, 340
Société des Amateurs de Jardins Alpins, 318
Société Française des Iris et Plantes Bulbeuses, 319
Société Française des Roses 'Les Amis des Roses', 319

Société National d'Horticulture de France, 319
Soil Association, 340
Solihull College, 295
Somerleyton Hall & Gardens, 209
Somerset Gardens Trust, 310
Sonderborg Planteskole, 272
South Birmingham College, 295
South Gloucestershire Education, 292
South Lodge Hotel, 264
Southcombe Gardens, 160
Southern Exposure Seed Exchange, 328
Southern Seeds, 328
Southport College of Art and Technology, 294
Southport Flower Show, 42
Southview Nurseries, 175
Southwestern Native Seeds, 328
Sparsholt College Hampshire, 293
Specialtours, 261
Spetchley Park, 177
Spinners, 173
Sports Turf Research Institute, 340
Spring Plant Fair Day, 42
Springfields Show Gardens, 188
Squerryes Court, 184
Staffordshire Gardens & Parks Trust, 310
Stancombe Park, 170
Standen, 215
Stanley Smith Horticultural Trust, 341
Stansfield, 200
Stanway House, 170
Stapehill Abbey, 162
Stapeley Water Gardens Ltd, 145
Starborough Nursery, 185
Stauden Feldweber, 270
Staudengärtner Klose, 281
Staudengärtnerei Dieter Gaissmayer, 281
Staudengärtnerei Gräfin von Zeppelin, 282
Staudengärtnerei Wolfgang Sprich, 282
Staudengärtnerei Zinser, 282
Staudenkulturen Stade, 282
Sticky Wicket, 162
Stillingfleet Lodge Nurseries, 228
Stoke-on-Trent College, 295
Ston Easton Park, 207, 265

Stone House Cottage Garden, 177
Stoneacre, 184
Stonehurst, 219
Stonor Park, 200
Stourbridge College, 295
Stourhead, 224
Stourton House, 224
Stowe Landscape Gardens, 139
Stowell Park, 170
Stratfield Saye House, 174
Studley Royal, 227
Succulent Society of South Africa, 319
Sudeley Castle & Gardens, 169
Südflora Baumschulen, 282
Sulgrave Manor, 195
Summer Lodge Hotel, 265
Summerfield Books, 323
Suntrap Garden, 238
Surrey Gardens Trust, 311
Sussex Gardens Trust, 311
Sutton Park, 228
Suttons Seeds, 325
Swallow Hayes, 202
Swimming Pool & Allied Trades Association Ltd (SPATA), 341
Swiss Garden, The, 137
Syon Park, 191
Szo. Czs. Martagon (Czech Lily Society), 319

Talbot Botanic Gardens, 254
Tameside College of Technology, 292
Tapeley Park, 159
Tatton Park, 145
Temple Newsam Park, 230
Thompson & Morgan, 326
Thompson's Hill, 225
Thornbury Castle Hotel, 265
Thornhayes Nursery, 160
Thorp Perrow Arboretum, 228
Threave Garden, 233
Tile Hill College, 295
Tintinhull House, 205
Tirley Garth Trust, 146
Tivey & Son, Philip, 187
Toddington Manor, 137
Tomato Growers Club, 307
Toobees Exotics, 214
Torosay Castle & Gardens, 241
Traquair House, 232
Travelsceene Ltd, 261
Trebah Garden Trust, 149

Tree Council, 341
Tree Register of the British Isles, 341
Treffinger-Hofmann, Fa., 278
Tregrehan, 149
Trehane, 149
Trehane Nursery & Camellia Centre, 163
Trelissick Garden, 150
Trengwainton Gardens, 150
Trentham Park Gardens, 208
Trerice, 150
Tresco Abbey, 150
Trewithen, 151
Trinity College Botanic Garden, 254
Tropen Express, 282
Trossachs Garden Tours, 262
Tucker, Edwin & Sons, 326
Tudor House Garden, 175
Tullynally Castle Gardens, 256
Tunkl, Silvia, 270
Turn End, 139
Tweedie Fruit Trees, J, 234
Tylney Hall Hotel, 265

University of Bristol Botanic Garden, 169, 292
University of Dundee Botanic Garden, 243
University of Durham Botanic Garden, 164
University of Leicester Botanic Garden, 187
Unwins Seeds Ltd, 326
Upton House, 220

Valclusa Gardens & Nursery, 258
Vale End, 214
Valley Gardens, Harrogate, 228
Valley Gardens, Windsor, 212
Van Hage Garden Company, 180, 325
Vann, 213
Ventnor Botanic Garden, 180
Venzano, 285
Verein Deutscher Rosenfreunde, 319
Vernon Geranium Nursery, 214
Victoria Travel, 262
Victorian Society, 341
Vilmorin, 327

Vivai Isola del Sole, 285
Vivai Pierluigi Priola, 286
Vivai Torsanlorenzo S.R.L., 286
Vivai-Fattoria 'La Parrina', 286
Vivaibambù di Mario Branduzzi, 286
Vivaio Guido Degl'Innocenti, 286
Vivaio Luciano Noaro, 286
Vivia Nord, 285
Volpaia, 165
von Allesch, Michael, 280
Voyages Jules Verne, 262

Waddesdon Manor, 139
Wakefield & North of England Tulip Society, 311
Wakefield District College, 295
Wakehurst Place, 218
Wales Tourist Board, 341
Walford College of Agricutlure, 294
Wallington, 197
Walmer Castle Gardens, 184
Walpole House, 191
Walter Branchi, 286
Wartnaby Gardens, 187
Warwick Castle, 220
Warwickshire College, 295
Waterperry Gardens, 201
Wayford Manor, 205
Webbs of Wychbold, 178
Wells & Winter, 323
Welsh College of Horticulture, 296
Welsh Historic Gardens Trust, 311
Wentworth Castle Gardens, 229
West Dean College, 291
West Dean Gardens, 218
West Green House, 174
West Herts College, 293
West Oxfordshire College, 294
West Wycombe Park, 140
Westbury Court, 169
Westdale Nurseries, 225
Westholme Hall, 164
Weston Park, 208
Westonbirt Arboretum, 170
Westwell Manor, 201
Whatton House, 187
White Windows, 175
Whitestone Gardens Ltd, 323

Whitfield, 178
Wigan & Leight College, 293
Wightwick Manor, 221
Wilcote House, 201
Wild Flower Society, 307
Wildfowl & Wetlands Trust, 341
Wildlife Travel, 262
Wildlife Trusts, 341
Willapark Manor Hotel, 265
Wilton House, 224
Wiltshire Gardens Trust, 311
Wimpole Hall, 142
Winderwath, 153
Winkworth Arboretum, 213
Wirral Metropolitan College, 294
Wirth Dahlien, 270
Wisley Flower Show, 42
Witley Court, 178
Woburn Abbey, 137
Wolff's Pflanzen, 283
Wolverhampton Adult Education, 295
Women's Farm & Garden Association, 341
Woodfield Bros, 221
Woodland Trust, 341
World Conifer Data Pool, 341
World Pumpkin Confederation, 319
Worshipful Company of Gardeners, 341
Wrest Park, 137
Wyke House, 194
Wyken Hall, 209
Wyld Court Rainforest, 138
Wylmington Hayes Gardens, 160
Wyseby House Books, 323

Yalding Organic Gardens, 184
Yew Tree Cottage, 219
Ynyshir Hall, 265
York Gate, 230
Yorkshire Gardens Trust, 311
Young Seeds, Roy, 326
Younger Botanic Garden, Benmore, 241
YSJ Seeds, 326

Zwijnenburg, Pieter 288